The Seventies in America

The Seventies in America

Volume II
Football—Roller skating

Editor
John C. Super
West Virginia University

Managing Editor
Tracy Irons-Georges

SALEM PRESS, INC.
Pasadena, California
Hackensack, New Jersey

Editorial Director: Christina J. Moose
Managing Editor: Tracy Irons-Georges   *Production Editor:* Joyce I. Buchea
Copy Editor: Sarah M. Hilbert   *Acquisitions Editor:* Mark Rehn
Assistant Editor: Andrea E. Miller   *Graphics and Design:* James Hutson
Photo Editor: Cynthia Beres   *Layout:* William Zimmerman

Title page photo: *South Vietnamese people desperately try to enter the U.S. embassy during the fall of Saigon.*
(AP/Wide World Photos)

Cover images: *Saturday Night Fever* (Hulton Archive/Getty Images)
"Sorry no gas until the 1st" (Hulton Archive/Getty Images)
President Richard Nixon (Hulton Archive/Getty Images)

Library of Congress Cataloging-in-Publication Data

The seventies in America / editor, John C. Super ; managing editor, Tracy Irons-Georges.
     p. cm.
Includes bibliographical references and index.
ISBN-10: 1-58765-228-5 (set : alk. paper)
ISBN-13: 978-1-58765-228-8 (set : alk. paper)
ISBN-10: 1-58765-230-7 (vol. 2 : alk. paper)
ISBN-13: 978-1-58765-230-1 (vol. 2 : alk. paper)
   1. United States—Civilization—1970—Encyclopedias.   2. Nineteen seventies—Encyclopedias.
I. Super, John C., 1944-   II. Irons-Georges, Tracy.
E169.12.S447 2006
973.924—dc22
                                                                2005023549

First Printing

■ Table of Contents

■ Complete List of Contents

Volume I

Volume II

Volume III

The Seventies
in America

■ Football

Definition   Team sport

During the 1970's, professional football solidified its place as the leading American spectator sport. Meanwhile, college football saw a falling-off in its popularity as a fissure developed between large schools with dominant football programs and the vast majority of smaller National Collegiate Athletic Association (NCAA) schools. In both cases, the prime factor was television.

The year 1970 marked a turning point for professional football. The old age was ushered out with the death of Vince Lombardi, the embodiment of the old-school coach and general manager who, like George Halas of the Chicago Bears, was able to browbeat young, physically dominant athletes both financially and emotionally with a combination of psychology and personality.

The year also marked the official end of the war between the National Football League (NFL) and the American Football League (AFL). In Super Bowl IV, the AFL Kansas City Chiefs beat the NFL Minnesota Vikings convincingly, 23-7, proving that the AFL New York Jets' victory over the NFL Baltimore Colts in the previous Super Bowl was no fluke. In 1970, the NFL and AFL completed their merger, creating two divisions within the NFL: the National Football Conference (NFC) and the American Football Conference (AFC).

Television   The most important introduction of 1970 was the debut of *Monday Night Football*. Professional football was already becoming wildly popular on television—Super Bowl IV had higher ratings than the 1969 moon landing. *Monday Night Football*, the brainchild of American Broadcasting Company (ABC) sports chief Roone Arledge, applied to professional football the improvements that he had made over the previous decade in televising college football. Arledge's credo was to mix show business into the coverage of sports, mainly by humanizing it—depicting "the agony of defeat," as the introduction to his series *Wide World of Sports* put it. In the production of *Monday Night Football*, ABC used many of the devices perfected by Ed and Steve Sabol in their company NFL Films: miking of the sound on the field; close-up reaction shots of players, fans, and coaches; and slow motion and instant replay.

The brilliance of ABC's technical achievements was overshadowed, however, by the verbal antics emanating from the press box. The inspired pairing of Howard Cosell, with his self-declared unique journalistic integrity, and Don Meredith, former Dallas Cowboys quarterback and all-around "good old boy," ensured that viewers would return to find out what these two would say next. The addition of Frank Gifford as play-by-play announcer, but by talent a more natural color commentator, lent an added fillip of excitement; Gifford could make such egregious mistakes as declaring that a play had been made by Thurman Munson, the recently deceased New York Yankee catcher. Even with the loss of Meredith mid-decade to pursue an acting career, *Monday Night Football* secured a place for professional football as a part of the prime-time television schedule.

Another factor in increasing professional football's television popularity, which the NFL did nothing to encourage, was the 1973 federal law lifting the television blackout of home games if they were sold out seventy-two hours in advance. Although NFL commissioner Pete Rozelle testified several times before Congress against the legislation, the antiblackout law caused no significant immediate harm to the league. Indeed, eleven new stadiums were built in the period from 1970 to 1976.

In areas more under its control, the NFL tried to increase its appeal throughout the decade by changing the rules to make it easier to score. The most successful teams of the earlier part of the decade all featured an effective running game and controlling defense: the Miami Dolphins' "no-name" defense, the Dallas Cowboys' "flex" defense, and the Pittsburgh Steelers' "steel curtain" defense. However, successful offenses and big-play capability are what fuel audience popularity, and a series of rule changes implicitly recognized that fact: the moving inward of the hash marks in 1972, an overtime period in regular-season games in 1974, kickoffs moved back to the 35-yard line in 1974, the ball placed at the spot of the attempt if a field goal was missed from outside the 20-yard line in 1974, a single bump or "chuck" allowed defenders on wide receivers in 1977, and pass defenders given greater physical latitude in 1978. The result of the rule changes was apparent in the number of points scored by the Steelers in their Super Bowl victories: an average of 18.5 in 1975 and 1976, compared to an average of 33 in 1979 and 1980.

Several scheduling changes also made the game more appealing. In 1977, the league went to a sixteen-game regular-season schedule. It also introduced a form of "stacked" scheduling, in which teams with similar records faced each other the next season, thus keeping more teams in contention longer in the season. The 1977 television contracts reflected the NFL's increased popularity, as each team's share of revenues rose from $2 million to $5.2 million.

Problems Perhaps as a result of the sport's increased visibility, a number of problems associated with professional football arose during the decade. The nation's most politically prominent football fan was President Richard Nixon, who made the presidential phone call to Super Bowl victors de rigueur and suggested plays for the Washington Redskins. Some of his political actions carried an overt football

connotation, such as the renewed bombing of North Vietnam being called Operation Linebacker. Mistrust of Nixon seeped into football. Critics noted that Nixon's advice to the Redskins involved a deceptive play. Although much of this connection was due to guilt by association, other aspects of criticism were associated with social problems of the decade.

Football's violent nature has always been admitted, and much of its history involves efforts to contain and minimize the effects of this violence. However, previous eras of professional football had gloried in its opportunities to display a fierce form of masculinity: players playing both ways, the lack of protective equipment, and the ability to deal out punishments, such as the clothesline tackle, that were later made illegal. The sheer ferocity and level of injuries came to be questioned in works such as Peter Gent's novel *North Dallas Forty* (1973), and two bookend events served to spotlight this concern: the

Tom Landry, head coach of the Dallas Cowboys, is given a victory ride following his team's defeat of the Denver Broncos at Super Bowl XII in 1978. (AP/Wide World Photos)

on-field death of Detroit Lions wide receiver Chuck Hughes from a heart attack in 1971, and the paralysis of New England Patriots wide receiver Darryl Stingley after a fierce hit from Oakland Raiders cornerback Jack Tatum in a 1978 exhibition game. Critics wondered if the male human body had become too large and swift to engage safely in such testosterone-driven contests.

Another contemporary problem becoming connected with football in the 1970's was the use of drugs. Professional football players had been self-medicating with alcohol for years. Now there were broad hints at the widespread use of amphetamines to jump-start, marijuana to relax, and painkillers to narcotize.

Other societal problems also emerged, such as the place of African Americans in U.S. society. With an ever-increasing number of African American athletes entering the NFL, many questioned why they were relegated to certain positions, or why so few of them were not coaches or front-office personnel. Steelers quarterback Joe Gilliam ran a deliberately slow forty-yard dash so that he would not be changed into a wide receiver or cornerback.

With the NFL-AFL bidding war over, questions over players' rights came to the forefront. The so-called Rozelle rule, in which the commissioner assessed the compensation due to a team who lost a player to another team, inhibited the signing of free agents. Changing the rule to a complicated formula did not decrease player dissatisfaction, nor did a brief players' strike in 1974. A futile attempt to launch another league, the World Football League, lasted only two seasons (1974-1975), and its most lasting result was the dismantling of the Miami Dolphins' dynasty.

America's Team   Perhaps no professional team epitomizes the perception of the NFL during the 1970's more than does the Dallas Cowboys. Originally thought of as a regional team, with quaint personalities such as Meredith and Coach Tom Landry, the reality of the team was much more modern, as Landry and general manager Tex Schramm perfected the use of computers in grading players and scouting prospects. The criticism of such methodology was most famously voiced by running back Duane Thomas, who declared Landry "a plastic man" and Schramm a faithless negotiator.

Meanwhile, Schramm ensured that male audiences would be more enthralled than enraged with the introduction of the Dallas Cowboy cheerleaders in 1972; soon teams all over the league were aping their wholesomely packaged sex appeal. Schramm's shrewd publicity moves during the decade ensured that criticisms such as those made in *North Dallas Forty* did not stick. In 1978, an NFL Films publicist first called Dallas "America's team," and the initial controversy over the term's accuracy soon faded into general acquiescence.

College Football   During the 1970's, college football split into various constituencies as professional football's popularity became ever more apparent. In 1970, the NFL's television revenue was $45.6 million, while the NCAA received $12 million. The passing of Title IX in 1972, which ensured gender equality in collegiate athletics, put more pressure on major football programs to support sports that did not produce revenue. Although a team could earn almost a half a million dollars for a nationally televised appearance by mid-decade, major programs were frustrated by the NCAA's appearance rule, which allowed a team to appear only five times nationally within two years. Major colleges were also alarmed by a proposal in 1975 for a form of revenue sharing. These concerns led to the formation of the College Football Association (CFA) in 1976 by sixty-three major schools, with the exception of the Big Ten and Pac-8. This organization became much more important in the next decade, when a federal antitrust case led to deregulation of the televising of college football.

The decade also saw the rise of the bowl game. Although the College All-Star Game was stopped in 1976, the introduction of major postseason bowls such as the Fiesta in 1971 led to more television revenue. In fact, television income passed that from ticket sales; the Rose Bowl's $2 million in 1974 became $4.3 million in 1981. Interest in bowl games grew when Notre Dame dropped its no-bowl policy in 1970 and the Big Ten and Pac-8 allowed other conference teams besides their champions to participate in bowl games in 1974.

The most successful coaches and football programs of the decade included Darrell Royal's Texas, Bo Schembechler's Michigan, and Woody Hayes's Ohio State, although Hayes's career came to an ignominious conclusion in the 1978 Gator Bowl when he punched a Clemson defensive back in the helmet for intercepting a pass. Bear Bryant's Alabama won three national championships in 1973, 1978, and 1979, while Barry Switzer's Oklahoma won back-to-back championships in 1974 and 1975. Individual player accomplishments include Tony Dorsett's 177 yards per game rushing average during the University of Pittsburgh's undefeated season in 1976 and Archie Griffin's two Heisman trophies with Ohio State in 1974 and 1975.

Impact As football became more popular in the 1970's, the problems associated with it on both professional and college levels became more apparent. Some wondered whether the ideals associated with a winning football program were those of a free, democratic society. Others questioned whether college football players were student athletes or preprofessionals. These issues would continue to be debated in the decades to come.

Further Reading

Blount, Roy, Jr. *About Three Bricks Shy of a Load.* Boston: Little, Brown, 1974. An account of the Pittsburgh Steelers during the 1973 season. Depicts not only the characters on the team but also growing concerns such as violence, racial issues, and players' rights.

Corcoran, Michael. *The Game of the Century: Nebraska vs. Oklahoma in College Football's Ultimate Battle.* New York: Simon & Schuster, 2004. A retrospective account of a game that fulfilled its hype: first-ranked Nebraska's 35-31 defeat of second-ranked Oklahoma on Thanksgiving Day, 1971.

Dunnavant, Keith. *The Fifty-Year Seduction: How Television Manipulated College Football, from the Birth of the Modern NCAA to the Creation of the BCS.* New York: Thomas Dunne Books, 2004. Traces the ever-complicated synergy among television, college football, and the college bowl games.

Gent, Peter. *North Dallas Forty.* New York: William Morrow, 1973. A thinly disguised portrait of the Dallas Cowboys and their problems. The plot is overly melodramatic, but the overall portrayal is devastating.

MacCambridge, Michael. *America's Game: The Epic Story of How Pro Football Captured a Nation.* New York: Random House, 2004. Shows how professional football, under the astute leadership of Pete Rozelle, became America's most popular sport. Too uncritical at times of Rozelle and such movers and shakers as Tex Schramm and Art Modell.

Plimpton, George. *Mad Ducks and Bears.* New York: Random House, 1973. Account of Plimpton's experience as a Baltimore Colts exhibition-game quarterback in 1971, but also an extended portrait of former Detroit Lions teammates John Gordy and Alex Karras.

Zimmerman, Paul. *The Last Season of Weeb Ewbank.* New York: Farrar, Straus and Giroux, 1974. Portrait of the coach who made John Unitas and Joe Namath stars. Shows how the stress of being general manager in an era of increasing players' dissatisfaction took its toll.

William Laskowski

See also Cosell, Howard; *Monday Night Football;* Payton, Walter; Simpson, O. J.; Sports; Television in the United States; Title IX of the Education Amendments of 1972.

■ Ford, Gerald R.

Identification U.S. congressman, 1948-1973; U.S. vice president, 1973-1974; U.S. president, 1974-1977

Born July 4, 1913; Omaha, Nebraska

In 1974, Ford became the first president to hold the office without having been elected either president or vice president. He generated controversy by pardoning former president Richard Nixon of any crimes pertaining to the Watergate investigation.

Gerald R. Ford, a U.S. representative from Michigan and minority leader of the U.S. House, became vice president under the Twenty-fifth Amendment on December 6, 1973, and was sworn as the thirty-eighth president on August 9, 1974, upon the resignation of President Richard Nixon. He served until January 20, 1977, when he was succeeded by Jimmy Carter, who had defeated Ford in the previous year's presidential election.

Early Life and Congressional Career Ford was an all-star football player at the University of Michigan and then earned a degree from Yale Law School in 1944, graduating in the top fourth of his class. He passed the Michigan bar and set up a partnership with his fraternity brother Philip A. Buchen, who would later serve as counsel to the president. Ford became active in reform Republican Party politics and served in the U.S. Navy during World War II. His wartime service matured him politically. Always popular among his peers, he exchanged his prewar isolationism for a broader internationalist view of the world. In 1948, he defeated incumbent Congressman Bartel Jonkman and married department store fashion consultant Elizabeth Ann "Betty" Bloomer Warren, who would be a lifelong political asset. The couple would have three sons, Michael, John, and Steven, and a daughter, Susan.

For twelve terms, Ford built a reputation as a party loyalist and advocate of an activist foreign policy. Succinctly, he labeled his views as "a moderate in domestic affairs, an internationalist in foreign affairs, and a conservative in fiscal policy." During the 1950's, Ford rejected efforts by his party seeking his candidacy for the U.S. Senate and the Michigan governorship. His goal, never realized, was to become Speaker of the House.

Presidential candidate Richard Nixon considered Ford as a running mate in the 1960 campaign. It was in Congress, however, that Ford made his reputation. Always strong in his own party, he dealt cordially with Democrats. President Lyndon Johnson selected Ford for the Warren Commission to investigate the November 22, 1963, assassination of President John F. Kennedy, which gave Ford national visibility.

Ford and Nixon   Ford's association with Nixon was a long one. Both men were World War II Navy veterans. They had served in the postwar Congress, Nixon representing California and Ford representing Michigan. During the 1950's, Ford built a solid reputation for himself in Congress, conciliatory to foes while also advocating his mixture of Republican internationalism and fiscal frugality. In 1965, Ford and his "Young Turks" successfully challenged House Minority Leader Charles A. Halleck. Thus, Ford found himself only a few steps away from the speakership.

Nixon, in turn, served from 1953 to 1961 as Dwight Eisenhower's vice president. Nixon suffered a narrow loss of the presidency to John F. Kennedy in 1960, followed by a shocking 1962 defeat at the hands of Pat Brown in the California gubernatorial race. In 1968, Nixon fought for his party's presidential nomination. Ford campaigned for Nixon that year but resisted Nixon's efforts to lure him onto the ticket as vice president, and Ford helped Nixon narrowly defeat the fractured Democratic Party's Hubert Humphrey and independent George Wallace.

As minority leader, Ford demonstrated his party loyalty. He had allies in all sectors of the GOP and used these friends to support Nixon's domestic and foreign policies. By 1969, the Vietnam War had generated serious opposition, especially among America's youth. Ford supported Nixon's "secret plan" of gradual disengagement from the increasingly unpopular conflict, called Vietnamization. Additionally, the minority leader criticized the remnants of former President Johnson's Great Society, an array of social programs that Ford considered ineffective and costly.

Watergate and the Vice Presidency   The nation in the 1970's was split over the war. Violence on college campuses—for example, the massacre of five protesting students in May, 1970, by the National Guard at Ohio's Kent State University—shook the country. Nixon's gradual Vietnamization, to some, was too slow. Young people urged immediate withdrawal from Southeast Asia, while the administration promoted "peace with honor." Ford was a Nixon loyalist and shared the commander in chief's dismay at the

Gerald R. Ford. (Library of Congress)

Excerpt of Gerald R. Ford's remarks on taking the oath of office as president, delivered on August 9, 1974:

"I believe that truth is the glue that holds government together, not only our Government but civilization itself. That bond, though strained, is unbroken at home and abroad.

In all my public and private acts as your President, I expect to follow my instincts of openness and candor with full confidence that honesty is always the best policy in the end.

My fellow Americans, our long national nightmare is over.

Our Constitution works; our great Republic is a government of laws and not of men. Here the people rule. But there is a higher Power, by whatever name we honor Him, who ordains not only righteousness but love, not only justice but mercy.

As we bind up the internal wounds of Watergate, more painful and more poisonous than those of foreign wars, let us restore the golden rule to our political process, and let brotherly love purge our hearts of suspicion and of hate."

1971 publication of the Pentagon Papers, a damning indictment of duplicitous foreign policy in Vietnam.

Nixon allowed the creation of the Committee to Re-elect the President (CRP), its sole mission to prevent electoral defeat in 1972. The president then directed his attention to historic diplomatic missions to Communist China and the Soviet Union. Ford applauded both of these endeavors as Nixon, in what would be called détente, reached out to communist adversaries while simultaneously trying to complete Vietnamization. In November, 1972, the electorate gave Nixon an overwhelming victory over Democratic Senator George McGovern of South Dakota.

In June of that year, however, burglars with ties to CRP had been apprehended in the offices of the Democratic Party in Washington, D.C.'s Watergate Complex. Earlier, operatives had pilfered the psychiatric files of the man who had leaked the Pentagon Papers to *The New York Times*. The Internal Revenue Service (IRS) had been allowed to persecute administration critics. An Enemies List had been compiled. Campaign contributions had been illegally squeezed from businesspeople for use by CRP. These actions, collectively, would come to be called Watergate, or the "White House Horrors."

Still, Minority Leader Ford remained steadfast in his support of Nixon. Congress in 1973 began investigating the Watergate break-in and the other actions deemed inappropriate. A frequent question would be asked, "What did the president know and when did he know it?" Whispers of "cover-up" and "hush money" swept through Washington, D.C. By early 1973, several Nixon aides were implicated in the widening scandal, among them Nixon's chief of staff H. R. Haldeman and domestic adviser John Ehrlichman. Televised hearings, led by North Carolina Senator Sam Ervin, exposed extensive wrongdoing that went far beyond a late-night burglary at Democratic Party headquarters.

Compounding Nixon's problems was war in the autumn of 1973 in the Middle East. Punished for its support of Israel, the United States suffered gas shortages and an embargo of oil by Arab nations. In late 1973, Nixon's vice president, Spiro T. Agnew, pled "no contest" to bribe-taking and kickbacks that had occurred when he governed Maryland. Agnew's admission led to his resignation and Ford's subsequent appointment as vice president on December 6, 1973, through provisions of the Twenty-fifth Amendment to the Constitution.

While Ford was respected on both sides of the congressional aisle and had escaped the stain of Watergate, Nixon remained under siege. Ford's allies in Congress, while not questioning Ford's integrity, moved swiftly toward the impeachment of Nixon. The House Judiciary Committee built upon what the Ervin Committee had unearthed. By the summer of 1974, Nixon, exposed on tape recordings of Oval Office conversations to be an active conspirator in the Watergate scandal, resigned the presidency.

President Ford   Gerald Ford took the oath of office as the United States' only unelected president on August 9, 1974, remarking that "our long national nightmare is over. Our Constitution works." Swiftly, he nominated Nelson Rockefeller to succeed him in the vice presidency. Nevertheless, the taint of Watergate affected Ford. Although he pledged not to pardon Nixon for Watergate-related misdeeds, within a month he had done just that. Many Americans suspected that Nixon had secured this pardon before leaving office.

Ford's presidency was crippled by the Nixon pardon and by a sputtering economy. Inflation was surging, and Ford's simplistic Whip Inflation Now slogan was woefully inadequate. A new television show, *Saturday Night Live*, ridiculed Ford weekly as an inept klutz, which was remarkable because of his proven athletic prowess. Images of Ford tripping on airplane steps and bouncing golf balls off the bodies of spectators created an impression of a chief executive prone to accidents, a man not ready to lead the nation on the road to political and economic recovery.

Furthermore, Ford presided over the final act in the Vietnam tragedy. American combat troops had been withdrawn in early 1973, but the communists refused to honor their pledge to allow South Vietnam to continue its existence. In the spring of 1975, Ford ordered Operation Frequent Wind, a massive evacuation of Americans and allies from Saigon. The world watched as helicopters lifted off Saigon rooftops with human cargo fleeing the approaching communists. By April 30, Southeast Asia was in the hands of the enemy. As Ford explained to Nixon's former chief of staff Alexander Haig, "America doesn't have the stomach for Vietnam anymore." Prophetically, Haig, who had argued for last-minute American support for beleaguered South Vietnam, commented, "Well, Mr. President, you'll be a one-term president."

The following month, Cambodian communists, the Khmer Rouge, seized the SS *Mayaguez*, an American merchant vessel. Ford ordered a rescue attempt, which secured the release of the crew, but forty-one military personnel were killed by hostile fire.

In September, 1975, female assassins Lynette "Squeaky" Fromme and Sara Jane Moore tried to kill Ford during two separate California trips. While unsuccessful, these troubling attempts illustrated the chaos of the Ford presidency, an era characterized by the debris of Vietnam, the ghost of Nixon, and a weak economy. Ford's position was further eroded when Ronald Reagan battled him for the GOP nomination during his 1976 quest to remain in the White House.

The Democratic Party, sensing Ford's weakness, nominated former Georgia governor Jimmy Carter, a Washington outsider who pledged, "I'll never lie to you." The two candidates sparred in a series of televised debates, one of which found Ford erroneously asserting that "Eastern Europe is not now under So-

viet domination." The country, weary of Watergate, war, and a sluggish economy, chose Carter over a man who was, in the voters' minds, too much of a Washington insider.

Impact   Squeezed by the horrors of the United States' longest war, his pardon of a disgraced former president, and an anemic economy, Gerald Ford was a prisoner of his time, and his tenure in the White House was unsuccessful. While Ford was likable and decent, he could not escape the problems that he inherited from Richard Nixon.

Further Reading

Cannon, James. *Time and Chance: Gerald Ford's Appointment with History.* New York: HarperCollins, 1994. Cannon had unrestricted access to Ford's papers. In telling the story of Ford's rise and Nixon's ruin, he offers new insights into this period of U.S. history.

Firestone, Bernard J., and Alexej Ugrinsky, eds. *Gerald R. Ford and the Politics of Post-Watergate America.* 2 vols. Westport, Conn.: Greenwood Press, 1993. This two-volume collection draws together essays commissioned for the Hofstra University Presidential Conference on Gerald R. Ford.

Ford, Gerald R. *A Time To Heal: The Autobiography of Gerald R. Ford.* New York: Harper & Row, 1979. Ford examines his life and career shortly after leaving office.

Greene, John Robert. *The Limits of Power: The Nixon and Ford Administrations.* Bloomington: Indiana University Press, 1992. An examination of the effects of Watergate and Nixon's resignation and pardon on the office of president.

_____. *The Presidency of Gerald R. Ford.* Lawrence: University Press of Kansas, 1995. A comprehensive study based on interviews with Ford and more than sixty prominent individuals from his administration.

Lee, J. Edward, and H. C. "Toby" Haynsworth. *Nixon, Ford, and the Abandonment of South Vietnam.* Jefferson, N.C.: McFarland, 2002. Argues that political, social, and economic factors distracted both Nixon and Ford and led to the abandonment of South Vietnam.

Reeves, Richard. *A Ford, Not a Lincoln.* New York: Harcourt Brace Jovanovich, 1975. A journalist describes Ford's first hundred days as president. Portrays Ford as a well-meaning fool who succeeded through naïveté and party loyalty.

TerHorst, Jerald F. *Gerald Ford and the Future of the Presidency.* New York: Third Press, 1974. A biography covering Ford's early life through the first month of his presidency. TerHorst was Ford's press secretary but resigned as a result of the Nixon pardon.

Joseph Edward Lee

See also　Agnew, Spiro T.; Business and the economy in the United States; Carter, Jimmy; Cold War; Elections in the United States, 1972; Elections in the United States, 1976; Fall of Saigon; Ford assassination attempts; Middle East and North America; Nixon, Richard M.; Nixon's resignation and pardon; Reagan, Ronald; Rockefeller, Nelson; Vietnam War; Watergate.

■ Ford assassination attempts

The Event　Two attempts in the same month to kill U.S. president Gerald R. Ford
Date　September, 1975

The assassination attempts disrupted the already faltering momentum of the Ford reelection campaign and revived public fears of political violence in the United States.

Gerald R. Ford assumed the presidency of the United States on August 9, 1974, in the midst of a national crisis. A former congressman who served eight years as minority leader of the House of Representatives, Ford was chosen to succeed Spiro T. Agnew as vice president after Agnew resigned rather than face bribery and tax evasion charges. Ford then became president under the provisions of the Twenty-fifth Amendment to the U.S. Constitution after President Richard M. Nixon was forced to step down as a result of the Watergate affair.

After Ford took the presidential oath, becoming the first person to serve as both vice president and president of the United States without having been elected to either office, he declared that "our long national nightmare is over." However, the scandal and its aftermath had shaken the confidence of

Lynette "Squeaky" Fromme (left), President Gerald R. Ford's first would-be assassin, arrives at a pretrial hearing for other members of the Manson Family cult in 1970. (AP/Wide World Photos)

President Ford is hurried into his limousine after a shot is fired on September 22, 1975, the second assassination attempt against him in three weeks. (AP/Wide World Photos)

Americans in their government, presidency, and political process.

In addition to scandal and disruption at the highest levels of the U.S. government, the threat of political violence continued to loom over American politics in the mid-1970's. The country had borne witness to a rash of politically motivated murders in the 1960's, including the assassinations of President John F. Kennedy in 1963 and the shootings of presidential candidate Robert Kennedy and civil rights leader Martin Luther King, Jr., in 1968. The attempted assassination of Alabama governor George Wallace in 1972 reminded Americans that presidential candidates and prominent political figures were still potential targets for would-be assassins.

Ford began campaigning for his first presidential election in late 1975 under criticism both from the public for his unconditional pardon of Nixon and from conservatives within the Republican Party for his choice of moderate Nelson Rockefeller as his vice president. Facing formidable opposition in the Republican primaries from former California gover-

nor Ronald Reagan, Ford had planned several campaign stops in California in September, 1975. Ford and his staff were expecting to meet with hostile reactions in the state, which was not only the home state of his chief rival but also a hotbed of ultraconservative and leftist political activity. Two of his stops, however, would be marred by unexpected violence.

The Attempts   On September 5, 1975, Ford, scheduled to deliver a speech at the state capitol in Sacramento, chose to walk the short distance between his hotel and the capitol building. When a small redhaired women stepped into his path, Ford moved toward her to shake her hand. The woman produced a revolver and attempted to shoot the president at close range, but as she pulled the trigger, a Secret Service agent lunged at the gun, placing his hand between the hammer and the firing pin. The woman was quickly apprehended and identified as Lynette "Squeaky" Fromme, a member of the infamous Manson Family, who told authorities that she had planned to assassinate President Ford in retaliation for the imprisonment of Charles Manson and several other "family" members for a series of grisly murders in 1969.

Ford continued to campaign in California, wearing a bulletproof vest to public appearances. Shots rang out again on September 22 outside the St. Francis Hotel in San Francisco as the president walked from his hotel to his limousine. The Secret Service, distracted by a group of protesters across the street, did not immediately notice a middle-aged woman less than forty feet away from the president pulling a .38-caliber revolver from her raincoat. However, a bystander—former Marine Oliver Sipple—knocked the shooter off balance as she fired and grabbed the revolver before she could pull the trigger a second time. The woman was identified as Sara Jane Moore, a forty-five-year-old housewife and civil rights activist with a history of mental instability.

Impact Although Ford escaped the assassination attempts unharmed, his campaign for a first full term as president, already losing momentum, suffered from the disruption. His campaign team had hoped that Ford would receive sympathy from the public as a result of the attacks; instead, he was criticized for his handling of the incidents after he refused to invite Sipple, who had been revealed as a homosexual, to the White House. Meanwhile Ford, facing a vigorous challenge from within his party from Reagan, was forced to maintain a grueling campaign schedule despite the disruptions. He narrowly defeated Reagan for the Republican nomination but alienated party moderates by choosing Bob Dole instead of Rockefeller as his running mate. The weary president went on to lose the 1976 election to former Georgia governor Jimmy Carter after a disastrous stretch run, during which he claimed in a debate with Carter that Eastern Europe was not under the control of the Soviet Union.

Subsequent Events Reagan considered Ford as his vice presidential running mate in 1980, but Ford remained in private life after leaving the presidency, occasionally resurfacing in the role of elder statesman. Both Fromme and Moore received life sentences for their attempts to assassinate Ford under a 1965 federal law that made attempted assassination of a president punishable by life imprisonment. Moore pleaded guilty to the crime, but Fromme fought the charges and was convicted in a trial that featured the videotaped testimony of President

Ford. Both women were repeatedly denied parole and remained incarcerated at the outset of the twenty-first century. However, the threat of political assassinations remained in the national consciousness for the remainder of the 1970's and was revived in 1981 by the shooting of President Reagan.

Further Reading

Cannon, James M. *Time and Chance: Gerald Ford's Appointment with History.* Ann Arbor: University of Michigan Press, 1998. This biography of Ford makes extensive use of his personal papers as well as interviews with close friends, family, and administration personnel.

Ford, Gerald R. *A Time to Heal: The Autobiography of Gerald R. Ford.* New York: Harper & Row, 1979. In his memoir, Ford provides a personal perspective on key events of his presidency.

Greene, John Robert. *The Presidency of Gerald R. Ford.* Lawrence: University of Kansas Press, 1995. This balanced analysis of the Ford presidency focuses on his administrative style and agenda.

Schulman, Bruce J. *The Seventies: The Great Shift in American Culture, Society, and Politics.* New York: DeCapo Press, 2002. Discusses the Ford presidency and assassination attempts in the broader context of the United States in the 1970's.

Michael H. Burchett

See also Elections in the United States, 1976; Ford, Gerald R.; Manson Family; Nixon's resignation and pardon; Rockefeller, Nelson.

■ Ford Pinto

Identification Subcompact car developed by Ford Motor Company
Date Produced from 1971 to 1980

The Pinto was Ford's answer to the subcompact car craze of the 1970's, but it wound up being criticized because of structural defects.

The Ford Pinto was an automobile created in 1971 to compete with foreign and domestic subcompact cars. It was designed to be a simple car that Ford could produce with little time and money. In the early 1970's, Lee Iacocca was the executive vice president of Ford Car and Trucks. Iacocca wanted to make an "econocar" that would weigh less than two thousand pounds and cost less than two thousand dollars. The Pinto came with a standard 98-cubic

The owner of a 1975 Ford Pinto warns other motorists about the danger of tailgating her. A design flaw made the model vulnerable to explosion following a rear-end collision. (AP/Wide World Photos)

inch, or 1.6-liter, engine. It was an inline, overhead valve 4-cylinder engine. The buyer could also upgrade to a 122-cubic-inch, or 2.0-liter, inline single overhead cam 4-cylinder. Standard equipment included ventless door windows, bucket seats, and vinyl upholstery.

Ford intended to change aspects of the Pinto from year to year because of new rules and regulations for improved safety and to meet growing consumer demand for better fuel economy. Ford also implemented changes in order to appeal to the younger generation. The Pinto was introduced as a two-door vehicle, but a third door was added with the introduction of the Runabout Pinto. In 1972, the Runabout also received a larger rear window, and the two-door Pinto wagon was introduced. In 1976, the 2.3-liter engine became the standard, and the Pinto was available with a V6, 2.8-liter engine, an option only available in the station wagon model

By the mid-1970's, research revealed defects in the Pinto's design. The cars tended to catch fire in rear-end collisions because the gas tank was just six inches from the nonsturdy bumpers. Doors also tended to jam shut, and the fuel filler tube was prone to separation and spillage in accidents. The solutions would have added weight to the car, and the entire vehicle would have to be transformed, including the brakes, engine, and transmission. The necessary changes were too costly for Ford and would have ruined Iacocca's concept of a small, cheap subcompact car. Ford knew about the rear-end dangers because of its own testing, but the company figured that the cost of the repairs would far exceed the cost of lawsuits, and the defects were allowed to stand.

Ford apologists and lobbyists in Washington, D.C., argued that there was not a car on the road without a safety hazard known to its manufacturer. Before these safety issues came to light, Ford had the reputation of being a pioneer in safety with its introduction of seat belts. Further, Ford had not been the only company that placed a price tag and cost-value on human life. After a government investigation, however, Ford was forced to recall 1.4 million Pintos manufactured between 1971 and 1976 for safety issues. It was the most expensive recall in automotive history as Ford had to pay more than one hundred lawsuits amounting to millions of dollars in damages. To address the safety issues, Ford installed two high-density polyethylene shields around the fuel tank. The Pinto's last year of production was 1980.

Impact The Pinto began Ford's quest to succeed in the subcompact car market. However, because of safety negligence, the Pinto gave Ford a bad name because of its alleged safety defects, and the Ford Escort replaced it on the production line.

Further Reading

Consumer Guide. *One Hundred Years of the American Auto.* Lincolnwood, Ill.: Publications International, 2003.

Flammang, James M. *Cars of the Sensational Seventies: A Decade of Changing Tastes and New Directions.* Lincolnwood, Ill.: Publications International, 2000.

David Treviño

See also Air bags; Automobiles; Gas shortages.

■ Foreign policy of Canada

Definition The interactions of the Canadian government and its representatives and diplomats with other countries of the world

Canada's foreign policy during the 1970's reflected international trends in the Cold War and the global economy, domestic political concerns, and the country's relationship to the United States.

During the 1970's, many aspects of Canada's foreign policy decisions were tied in some form to its most important relationship, that with the United States. Efforts to demonstrate its independence in relation to its friend and ally across the border were combined with a particular emphasis on multilateralism in international relations.

Seeking Independence After the 1960's, many Canadians expressed concern about the country's continued dominance by its southern neighbor, the United States. The government of Prime Minister Pierre Trudeau shared this sentiment. The fact that a lessening of tensions between the Soviet Union and the United States in the form of détente was underway provided Canada with the opportunity to assert a degree of its own independence from the United States. In 1971, Trudeau, while on a visit to the Soviet Union, went so far as to say that the United States represented a threat to Canada's identity. Privately, his government had held serious discussions about withdrawing Canada from the North Atlantic Treaty Organization (NATO). In the end, Canada decided to stay in the alliance but with a reduced military presence in Europe.

Canada asserted its independence from the United States in its foreign policy toward two communist nations: the People's Republic of China and Cuba. Canada had sold wheat to China in the early 1960's and recognized the country diplomatically in 1969. Negotiations occurred behind the scenes in 1970, leading to an exchange of ambassadors. In 1973, Trudeau visited China on an official visit, gaining an audience with Chairman Mao Zedong. In the case of Cuba, Canada maintained full diplomatic relations and trade ties with the island nation, and Trudeau enjoyed a warm relationship with Fidel Castro.

Relations with the United States Canada's relationship with the United States remained the centerpiece of its foreign policy. Nevertheless, tensions existed between the two countries when, in August, 1971, the United States introduced radical economic measures to shore up a slumping economy but, in the process, threatened the stability of the Canadian economy with duties that affected Canadian exports. Trudeau traveled to Washington, D.C., in December, 1971, to plead his country's case and, in the end, convinced the Nixon administration to drop the economic policy in question.

The message from Washington, D.C., however, was clear: The United States would look after its own interests first, even at the expense of those of Canada. A 1973 motion that passed in the Canadian parliament condemning an American bombing campaign against North Vietnam fueled the growing division between the two governments. Collectively, these trends—plus growing nationalism at home—encouraged the Trudeau government to pursue what became known as the "third option." This involved reducing Canada's economic reliance on the United States by seeking trade opportunities elsewhere, specifically with the European Community and Japan. Structurally, however, making such a shift proved virtually impossible since Canada could not overcome the reality of the geographic, cultural, and linguistic closeness of the American market.

The Commonwealth and La Francophonie   One way for Canada to pursue multilateralism and demonstrate its independence from the United States was to play a more prominent role in the British Commonwealth, the worldwide association of nations that were once part of the British Empire. This move also allowed Trudeau to pursue his interest in fostering relations with the wealthy industrialized world as well as poor developing nations, many of which once belonged to the Commonwealth.

In the second half of the 1970's, domestic politics increasingly impinged on and dominated the focus of Canadian foreign policy. The Province of Quebec became a key priority for the Trudeau administration in December, 1976, when a separatist party was elected to power. Canada soon found itself involved in diplomacy to undermine efforts by the separatist government to achieve international support and recognition for its cause of independence for Quebec. In this policy, the Canadian government was only partially successful. It received support from the new presidential administration of Jimmy Carter in the United States, which made clear its desire for a united Canada. However, France actively encouraged Quebec on the international stage, arranging for it to be invited along with other French-speaking nations to meetings of La Francophonie, the French equivalent of the Commonwealth.

Political Change   The Trudeau government faced an election in 1979 and found itself defeated by the Progressive Conservative Party under Joe Clark, who won a minority government. That government would last for only nine months with little impact on Canadian foreign policy save for a promise by the Clark government to move the Canadian embassy in Israel from Tel Aviv to Jerusalem; Arab opposition forced the Clark government to renege on its promise. Clark's administration also dealt with a crisis of refugees from Southeast Asia. Canada led the world by accepting thousands of Vietnamese refugees, labeled "boat people" because of their method of transportation from Vietnam.

Impact   Canadian foreign policy in the 1970's, particularly in its relationship to the United States, reflected a growing sense of nationalism and rejection of American dominance. However, in pursuing these policies, the Trudeau government had to work within the reality of the continuing Canadian dependence on the United States. It also had to pursue policies that took into consideration the economic and domestic political realities of the decade.

Further Reading

Blanchette, Arthur E., ed. *Canadian Foreign Policy, 1945-2000: Major Documents and Speeches.* Toronto: Golden Dog Press, 2000. A collection of primary documents related to the foreign policy of Canada.

Clarkson, Stephen, and Christina McCall. *The Magnificent Obsession.* Vol. 1 in *Trudeau and Our Times.* Toronto: McClelland and Stewart, 1990. Biography of Trudeau covering his political career.

Hillmer, Norman, and J. L. Granatstein. *Empire to Umpire: Canada and the World to the 1990's.* Toronto: Irwin, 1994. A history of Canada's foreign policy.

Morton, Desmond. *A Short History of Canada.* Toronto: McClelland and Stewart, 2001. Accessible historical examination that includes the 1970's.

Steve Hewitt

See also   Business and the economy in Canada; Canada and the British Commonwealth; Canada and the United States; Clark, Joe; Cold War; Europe and North America; International trade of Canada; International trade of the United States; Japan and North America; Middle East and North America; Soviet Union and North America; Trudeau, Pierre; United Nations.

■ Foreign policy of the United States

Definition   The interactions of the United States government and its representatives and diplomats with other countries of the world

As the relative power of rivals abroad grew during the 1970's, divisions within the United States undermined American efforts to counteract these trends.

Three presidents guided U.S. foreign policy during the turbulent decade of the 1970's: Richard M. Nixon (1969-1974), Gerald R. Ford (1974-1977), and Jimmy Carter (1977-1981). Maximizing U.S. national interests while dealing with growing congressional limitations on presidential authority proved difficult for each president.

Many new legal strictures grew directly from congressional and public skepticism about the manner in which the Cold War appeared to have been waged. Over strong objection from the Nixon administration, on June 13, 1971, *The New York Times* first published excerpts from a secret, multivolume Department of Defense study of U.S. involvement in Vietnam. These so-called Pentagon Papers documented how several earlier administrations had misled Congress and the public in order to secure support and authorization for the Vietnam War. Emboldened further by revelations of unauthorized bombing in Cambodia and questionable Central Intelligence Agency (CIA) covert actions between 1973 and 1975, Congress passed a series of laws designed to trim traditional powers of the presidency. Each enactment presumed the U.S. defeat in Vietnam and other setbacks to be caused by curable flaws in the republic. Eminent historian Arthur Schlesinger summed up this situation in the best-seller *The Imperial Presidency* (1973): "The checks and balances of the U.S. Constitution had been set aside by the imperial presidency."

Under control of the Democratic Party, Congress set a new course. The 1973 War Powers Resolution demanded that future decisions to use troops should gain the formal consent of the legislature. Since Congress, much of the public, and the leaders of U.S. armed forces were reluctant to use American troops again after Vietnam, foreign aid and military exports

As national security adviser and later secretary of state, Henry Kissinger (left), walking with President Richard M. Nixon, influenced U.S. foreign policy during the 1970's through his use of "shuttle diplomacy." (Library of Congress)

became the important tools by which the United States could continue to exercise influence. For example, an emergency airlift of U.S. equipment to Israel during the October, 1973, Yom Kippur War helped turn the tide of battle and contributed to the defeat of Egypt and Syria. Arab League states then reacted with a policy of withholding shipments of oil to the United States. Combined with a quadrupling of oil prices by the Organization of Petroleum Exporting Countries (OPEC), these "oil shocks" caused American gasoline prices to skyrocket.

Congress Shapes Ties to U.S. Allies Under all three presidents during the 1970's, the United States attempted to win favor with nearly all sides in the Middle East region through inducements such as the

sale of weapons. Iran, under pro-U.S. ruler Mohammad Reza Shah Pahlavi, and Saudi Arabia became the largest customers in the 1970's. Small groups of U.S. military advisers also trained the armed services of friendly countries in the region and worldwide; other American officials trained civilian police forces through a public safety program.

However, Congress was troubled by the impact that these policies often had on the growing influence of nondemocratic political institutions in the underdeveloped parts of the world. A series of amendments to existing foreign assistance laws were passed in 1973 and 1974. These laws required that military security assistance be reduced substantially if a country that the United States president sought to aid persisted in violating the human rights of its citizens. Military aid in support of particularly problematic allies, such as the military government of General Augusto Pinochet Ugarte that ruled Chile after September 11, 1973, proved so difficult to end fully that Congress enacted a new general law, the Arms Export Control Act of 1976. Under its terms, presidents were required formally to notify Congress of plans to sell major military equipment systems to any country, and Congress assigned to itself thirty days to act to stop the sale from going forward. When allegations of training in torture surfaced, the public safety program was ended entirely by Congress in 1975.

Some U.S. allies sharply rebuffed attempts by the United States to dictate the manner of response to internal threats that they declared arose from communist subversion. However, in 1977, at Notre Dame University, President Carter declared that the time had come to transcend excessive fear of communism. Military rulers of Argentina, El Salvador, and Guatemala spurned further U.S. security assistance when President Carter energetically embraced the human rights concerns that Congress had articulated earlier. Other allies, notably Iran and Nicaragua, continued to buy U.S. weapons and declared their willingness to meet U.S. human rights conditions, only to find that the United States ultimately would not come decisively to their aid when revolutionary forces were on the verge of seizing power.

Revolutions and Détente   In 1975, when the United States withdrew from Southeast Asia, leaders of both Republican and Democratic Parties viewed it as a necessary adjustment, one that did not necessarily have broad significance for the rest of the Cold War. Four years later, in 1979, the rise to power of the revolutionary anti-American governments both of the Sandinistas in Nicaragua and of Islamic militants led by Ayatollah Khomeini in Iran more clearly demonstrated that a broad, global decline in the influence of the United States had occurred during the decade. Militant Sandinistas—Marxist-Leninists who soon would ally with Cuba and the Soviet Union—controlled territory in North America. Islamic extremists seized the U.S. embassy in Tehran, Iran, on November 4, 1979, foreshadowing the consolidation of a radically anti-American Iranian regime that sat virtually atop the world's key source of oil, the Persian Gulf region. The forward movement of the Soviet Red Army into neighboring, neutral Afghanistan in

December, 1979, for the first time brought hostile MIG aircraft into a position to menace oil tankers exiting the Persian Gulf through the Strait of Hormuz. The crises of this era were furthered by the fact that the Nixon Doctrine—a strategy of relying on allies, not U.S. troops, to protect vital interests—was in shambles; Vital energy supplies for key allies in East Asia and Western Europe were at risk by the end of the 1970's, and gas lines and soaring prices greeted Americans for the second time in the decade.

The Afghanistan invasion also brought an end to a decade of U.S. efforts to engage the communist Soviet Union in dialogue, trade relationships, and arms-control negotiations. Begun under Nixon and continued by Ford and Carter, this policy of détente had sought to reduce tensions through persuasion. Direct summit conversations by top leaders reinforced ongoing formal consultations by negotiators throughout the 1970's. In an atmosphere of mutual desire to avoid misunderstandings that might lead to general, even nuclear, war, some dangerous crises were managed successfully.

Détente was predicated on acceptance by both sides that fundamental differences in ideology, national interest, and economic systems were likely to continue into the indefinite future. Nevertheless, the chief architect of the policy, Nixon cabinet member Henry Kissinger, believed that a higher order of cooperation was necessitated by each state's rational interest in avoiding nuclear catastrophe. Ultimately, the policy assumed that the graying leadership of the Soviet Union could be induced to play a role in global politics that more closely would resemble that of an ordinary state, rather than be guided by the revolutionary doctrines of world domination associated with its founders.

The Short Dividends of Détente   Under the policy of détente, good behavior by the Soviet Union was rewarded, and in 1972, a long-term agreement to permit the export of U.S. grain to the communist superpower was the diplomatic hand that was extended first. However, efforts by Congress to condition such trade on improvements in Soviet adherence to human rights standards tied presidential hands. Though these Jackson-Vanik trade amendments ultimately led the Soviets grudgingly to permit increased numbers of their Jewish citizens to emigrate to the West, their immediate effect was to induce the Soviets to cancel the trade deal in 1975. A

1975 Helsinki treaty on security in Europe signed by the Soviets pledged them again to respect human rights, but little genuine reform occurred for more than a decade.

Important steps toward controlling the form that the continuing Soviet-U.S. nuclear arms race would take also seemed to emerge under détente: The Strategic Arms Limitation Treaty (SALT I), signed in May, 1972, limited the number of Soviet missiles to 1,600 and U.S. missiles to 1,054. This pact pledged each nation to limit sharply further development of defensive antiballistic missiles (ABMs), but it also spurred each toward further utilization of advanced technologies that would permit deployment of multiple independently targeted reentry vehicles (MIRVs) on the missiles. In this technological area of the arms race, the United States held a significant advantage, one that widened throughout the decade of the 1970's and beyond.

Détente was part of a set of diplomatic maneuvers designed by Kissinger to maximize U.S. influence in the light of two factors: public reticence to support the use of force to achieve U.S. goals and the increasing power of the Soviet Union and its allies relative to that of the United States and its allies. To create further incentives for the Soviets to cooperate with the United States, the Nixon-Kissinger team secretly negotiated with rivals of the Soviet Union within the communist camp. The opening of a U.S. dialogue with the radical communist leader Mao Zedong of the People's Republic of China, symbolized by Nixon's visit to Beijing in 1972, greatly concerned Soviet leader Leonid Brezhnev, whose armed forces had skirmishes with the Chinese in 1969. Carter formalized diplomatic relations with China in 1979.

However, despite the appearance of an emerging U.S.-Soviet understanding, the Soviet Union never desisted from fomenting revolutions, training terrorists, and in other ways continuing the Cold War, especially in the Third World. After victory in Vietnam by its allies, the Soviet Union provided equipment and financial support that was instrumental to Vietnam's conquest of Cambodia in 1978. Swift Soviet diplomatic recognition and military aid buttressed an armed group that seized power in 1974 in Ethiopia, a former U.S. ally. Soviet aid and Cuban advisers fueled communist victories in civil wars in Angola and Mozambique in 1975, creating safe havens for other communist activists seeking revolutionary change in neighboring Namibia and South Africa.

Only in the Middle East did the decline in American worldwide influence during the 1970's not lead to large new gains for the Soviets, as Syria and Iraq never yielded to complete Soviet domination. After 1973, American influence in Egypt eclipsed that of the Soviet Union, as President Anwar Sadat concluded that to regain national territories lost to Israel in the 1967 war, the path passed through Washington, not Moscow. At the end of the decade, the 1979 Soviet conquest of Afghanistan so enraged the Islamic peoples and governments of the Middle East and South Asia that a basis for reversing the slide in American status was created.

Impact   The foreign policy changes of the 1970's reinforced perceptions abroad that the United States was unable or unwilling to act decisively to protect its national interests in foreign affairs. Legal restraints on presidential leadership created during this era continued to slow the reversal of this trend until a new consensus favoring presidential leadership emerged in the wake of the terrorist attacks on the World Trade Center and the U.S. Pentagon on September 11, 2001.

Further Reading

Brzezinski, Zbigniew. *Power and Principle: Memoirs of the National Security Advisor, 1977-1981.* New York: Smithmark, 1983. Anti-Soviet American official explains the geopolitical thinking that guided foreign policy decisions during the Carter years. Circumspect about rivalries and office politics.

Garthoff, Raymond. *Détente and Confrontation.* Washington, D.C.: Brookings Institution, 1985. Nearly 1,200 pages carefully explain diplomatic negotiations and various crises of the 1970's through the lens of U.S.-Soviet relations.

Hook, Steven W., and John Spanier. *American Foreign Policy Since World War II.* 16th ed. Washington, D.C.: CQ Press, 2004. Puts these years of decline into broader perspective. Organized chronologically to make a thematic case that throughout history, Americans have been saved from themselves by the recklessness of their enemies.

Kissinger, Henry. *Ending the Vietnam War.* New York: Simon & Schuster, 2003. Expanding on his earlier memoirs, Kissinger explains the human element in national statecraft. Brings the impact of domestic detractors and single-minded communist negotiators into sharp focus.

_____. *White House Years.* Boston: Little, Brown,

1979. The Nobel Peace Prize-winning architect of U.S. policy portrays his central role. Covers administrative intrigue within Nixon and Ford periods, seminal interactions with leaders in China and the Soviets, and other issues.

LaFeber, Walter. *America, Russia, and the Cold War, 1945-2002.* New York: McGraw-Hill, 2002. After a standard retelling of the Vietnam debacle, highlights the confusion and rivalries that produced further American decline during the Carter years.

Rubin, Barry. *Paved with Good Intentions: The American Experience and Iran.* New York: Oxford University Press, 1980. Detailed account of the U.S. relationship with the shah of Iran in the 1970's and of the various actors in the 1979 Islamic Revolution.

Strong, Robert A. *Working in the World: Jimmy Carter and the Making of American Foreign Policy.* Baton Rouge: Louisiana State University Press, 2000. In eight sharply focused case studies, the author finds coherence and some success in the often criticized Carter era.

Gordon L. Bowen

See also Africa and the United States; Cambodia invasion and bombing; Camp David Accords; Carter, Jimmy; Central Intelligence Agency (CIA); China and the United States; Cold War; Europe and North America; Fall of Saigon; Ford, Gerald R.; Foreign policy of Canada; Iranian hostage crisis; Israel and the United States; Japan and North America; Kissinger, Henry; Latin America; Mexico and the United States; Middle East and North America; Nixon, Richard M.; Nixon's visit to China; Oil embargo of 1973-1974; Panama Canal treaties; Paris Peace Accords; Pentagon Papers; POWs and MIAs; Soviet invasion of Afghanistan; Soviet Union and North America; United Nations; Vietnam War; War Powers Resolution of 1973.

■ Francophonie, La

Identification Consortium of states and governments that use French as a common language, of which Quebec is a part

Date Began in 1970

During the 1970's, Quebec asserted the primacy of French in the province and engendered a Canadian national policy of tolerance for minority languages and rights. Reforms favoring the dominance of the French language were advanced by the Quebec Party after it took power in the province in 1976.

First colonized by France, Canada was transferred to Britain in the eighteenth century. The original French-speaking, Roman Catholic population became a minority primarily concentrated in the eastern province of Quebec while British Canada expanded westward as an English-speaking, Protestant country. French speakers made up approximately one-fourth of the national population. They were overwhelming dominant in Quebec, yet they were marginalized culturally, economically, and politically in the rest of the country. Nevertheless, French-speaking Canadians formed part of the worldwide community of French-speaking countries known as La Francophonie.

During the 1960's, growth of the English-speaking population of Canada outpaced that of the French-speaking population of Quebec, which underwent a Quiet Revolution, changing from a rural and agricultural society to a more urban one. To redress this imbalance politically, the Parti Québécois (or Quebec Party) was founded in 1968 under the leadership of René Lévesque and was committed to the independence of Quebec as a sovereign nation in an associated status with Canada. Buoyed by Francophonie support, the legislative assembly of Quebec passed an Official Language Act in 1974, sponsored by the Liberal Party, to make French the sole official language of the province.

The Quebec Party, however, found this legislation too tame. In 1976, it swept into power, and the following year, it passed the Charter of the French Language (Bill 101). It made French the language of public business, applied strict French-language testing standards for admission to the professions, and required businesses with more than fifty workers to operate in French.

Impact Alarmed by the actions of the Quebec Party, large numbers of English-speaking professionals left the province. In 1979, the Canadian Supreme Court struck down provisions of Bill 101 that impinged on the rights of expression and conduct by non-French speakers, and the Canadian government rejected the incorporation of language rights in the national constitution.

Subsequent Events In a 1980 referendum, Quebec itself rejected a declaration of the province's independence. By 1982, however, the Quebec Party succeeded in the Canadian Parliament in passing legislation that recognized French and English as official languages at the federal level. Moreover, Canada began an extensive program to protect the rights of all minorities through their languages and cultures.

Further Reading

Guindon, René, and Pierre Poulin. *Francophones in Canada: A Community of Interests.* Ottawa: Canadian Heritage, 1996.

"Je parle français": A Portrait of La Francophonie in Canada. Ottawa: Canadian Heritage, 1999.

Laroussi, Farid, and Christopher L. Miller, eds. *French and Francophone: The Challenge of Expanding Horizons.* New Haven, Conn.: Yale University Press, 2003.

Lévesque, René. "For an Independent Quebec." *Foreign Affairs* 54, no. 4 (July, 1976).

Sanders, Carol, ed. *French Today: Language in Its Social Context.* Cambridge, England: Cambridge University Press, 1993.

Edward A. Riedinger

See also Canada and the British Commonwealth; Charter of the French Language; Elections in Canada; Lévesque, René; October Crisis; Quebec Charter of Human Rights and Freedoms.

■ Free agency

Definition The right of a professional baseball player to sell his services to the highest bidder

Date Instituted in 1976

The change to a system of "free agents" created the modern era of high-salary players who change teams several times in a career.

Before the mid-1970's, through the so-called reserve clause, a baseball team could indefinitely renew a player's contract or prevent him from signing with another team. Thus, a baseball player had to play his entire career for the same team unless that team traded him or chose to get rid of him. This prohibited a player from switching teams and destroyed a player's ability to negotiate a higher salary from his current team.

Then, in 1975, Andy Messersmith, a successful pitcher with the Los Angeles Dodgers, refused to sign the contract given to him by the team. The Dodgers automatically renewed his contract for the next year using the reserve clause. Messersmith argued in an arbitration case against the team that his contract was over and that he was free to sign with any team. The arbitrator assigned to the case agreed with Messersmith and decided that the standard baseball contract did not create a perpetual contract between the team and the player.

The decision was revolutionary. Messersmith and many other players took advantage of their newfound freedom to negotiate higher salaries with new teams or signed new contracts with their old teams for equally high salaries. The owners attempted to restrict free agency in later labor agreements with the players union, but they were largely unsuccessful, and a series of strikes by the players and lockouts by the owners ensued.

Impact Free agency forever changed the game of baseball on the field and in terms of the business of the game. Before the 1970's, most star players were relatively underpaid and tended to play their entire careers with a single team. After the advent of free agency, players had greater bargaining power and used that power to obtain the best deals for themselves. Although beneficial for the players, free agency later contributed to the loss of a stable team identity and a growing disparity between the ability of richer and poorer teams to sign free agents and consistently put together winning teams.

Subsequent Events The owners continued to fight unsuccessfully the effects that the new free agency system forced on them. During the 1980's, the owners illegally conspired to refuse to sign free agents and were forced to pay millions of dollars of damages to the affected players. From that time forward, player salaries have continued to rise.

Further Reading

Abrams, Roger I. *The Money Pitch: Baseball Free Agency and Salary Arbitration.* Philadelphia: Temple University Press, 2000.

Waller, Spencer Weber, Neil B. Cohen, and Paul Finkelman. *Baseball and the American Legal Mind.* New York: Garland, 1995.

Spencer Weber Waller

See also Baseball; Sports.

■ *Free to Be . . . You and Me*

Identification   Children's record album, television special, and book

Date   Recording released in 1972; program and book created in 1974

In an era when the women's liberation and Civil Rights movements were gaining momentum, Free to Be . . . You and Me *helped children learn to challenge gender and racial stereotypes and encouraged the development of positive self-esteem.*

The 1970's is often called the "Me Decade" in reference to the preponderance of inward self-absorption and a cultural preoccupation with the individual. Self-help books emerged, the fitness movement gained popularity, and segments of the population were beginning to demand, and oftentimes receive, new rights and roles within society.

Actor, social activist, and feminist Marlo Thomas conceived an idea that brought this focus on self-esteem and individual empowerment to children. After reading to her young niece, Thomas realized that storybooks and children's programming seemed limited for children and dictated specific roles for them—usually defined strictly along gender lines. She asked friends in the entertainment industry to help her produce a record album that would open youngsters' minds to the world around them and the myriad directions that their lives could take.

The result, *Free to Be . . . You and Me*, was released as an album in 1972 and was written with the help of actor-director Carl Reiner and author-poet Shel Silverstein. It was presented in short vignettes and used well-known personalities such as Alan Alda, Mel Brooks, Harry Belafonte, Kris Kristofferson, Carol Channing, Rosie Grier, Cicely Tyson, and Diana Ross. Some of the vignettes were sung—"Parents Are People," "Sisters and Brothers," and "When We Grow Up" among them—and many more were spoken in poem or story format, including "Don't Dress Your Cat in an Apron," "Boy Meets Girl," and "Ladies First." Humor was evident in several segments, while diversity and the disruption of traditional gender roles emerged repeatedly as themes. Several vignettes explored the range of human emotions, such as "Glad to Have a Friend Like You" or "It's Alright to Cry," sung by husky football player Grier, who assured children that "big boys cry too."

With the unexpected success of the album,

Thomas set to work on a television special, which aired in 1974. The program used most of the material from the album, with live action and animated segments. Mainstream networks were routinely criticized during this era for showing children's programming that contained violence or that held little quality content. *Free to Be . . . You and Me* was embraced by parents and educators as model television. The book was released in the same year.

Impact   *Free to Be . . . You and Me* was groundbreaking in its ability to translate a number of the tenets of the women's and Civil Rights movements to an audience made up primarily of children. It also brought the era's focus on self-improvement and self-esteem to its young audience. The television program won an Emmy Award for Outstanding Children's Special, and it made a formative impression on an entire generation of children.

Further Reading

Fisch, Shalom M. *Children's Learning from Educational Television: "Sesame Street" and Beyond.* Mahwah, N.J.: Lawrence Erlbaum, 2004.

Hart, Carole, et al., eds. *Free to Be . . . You and Me.* Conceived by Marlo Thomas. New York: Bantam Books, 1974.

Sarah M. Hilbert

See also   Children's literature; Children's television; Feminism; Literature in the United States; Television in the United States; Women in the workforce.

■ *French Connection, The*

Identification   Motion picture

Director   William Friedkin (1935-   )

Date   Released in 1971

The French Connection, *which chronicles a famous 1962 narcotics bust in New York City, made a star out of its forty-one-year-old leading actor, Gene Hackman, and set the standard by which subsequent suspense films would be judged.*

In 1962, two New York City narcotics detectives stationed in Harlem, Eddie Egan and Sonny Grosso, made history with the largest heroin seizure by U.S. law enforcement officials up until that time. A few years later, author Robin Moore, with uncredited help from Edward M. Keyes, chronicled the story in

The French Connection: The World's Most Crucial Narcotics Investigation (1969).

Following the success of his influential 1968 film *Bullitt*, Hollywood producer Phillip D'Antoni turned his efforts to the screen adaptation of Moore's book. Propelled by Ernest Tidyman's screenplay and William Friedkin's direction, the film succeeded in capturing the nature of police work, as well as the complexity of the story's characters.

With *Bullitt*, D'Antoni had defined the genre of suspense drama in which the main character is a police officer who bucks authority, often skirts the law himself, and, in the end, gets the bad guys. In Egan, D'Antoni had the real-life equivalent: a fast-talking, tough, and streetwise police officer whose disregard for suspects' rights produced results. *Bullitt*, moreover, featured a prominent car chase that electrified audiences and revolutionized the film industry. D'Antoni recognized that his next film would have to build on his success and not repeat what was fast becoming a cliché. Friedkin thus turned to filming on New York's streets and adopted a semi-documentary style for much of the film with the use of handheld cameras and with an emphasis on the seedier aspects of life in the city. D'Antoni avoided a repeat of his earlier film's car chase by substituting a subway train for one of the cars and filming underneath the city's elevated tracks. The result was a gripping, tense sequence that included a real crash when a car backed onto the street. Throughout production, Friedkin and the crew benefited from the presence of Egan himself, who ensured police cooperation and lent authenticity to the film.

Initially, D'Antoni and Friedkin contemplated other actors for the role of Egan, who was renamed Jimmy "Popeye" Doyle for the film, before deciding on Gene Hackman. Even Hackman expressed doubts about his portrayal of Egan, whose abusive behavior he found disturbing. However, when filming the opening sequence in which Popeye and the Grosso character, renamed Buddy "Cloudy" Russo, chase down a suspect, Hackman seemed to become Egan.

Impact   Although Egan and Grosso had cameo appearances in the film, Gene Hackman and Roy Scheider, who played Russo, became linked inextricably to their characters. At the 1972 Academy Awards, they were rewarded with Best Actor and Best Supporting Actor nominations. Hackman won one of the five Academy Awards won by the film, which enjoyed critical and popular success. In 1975, Hackman would reprise the Popeye role for John Frankenheimer's *French Connection II*, which saw him travel to France to track down his nemesis who had eluded the police in the earlier film.

Further Reading

Leuci, Robert. *All the Centurions: A New York City Cop Remembers His Years on the Street, 1961-1981.* New York: HarperCollins, 2004.

Moore, Robin, and Milt Machlin. *The Set Up: The Shocking Aftermath to "The French Connection."* Guilford, Conn.: Lyons Press, 2004.

Whalen, John, and Jonathan Vankin. *Based on a True Story: Fact and Fantasy in One Hundred Favorite Movies.* Chicago: Chicago Review Press, 2005.

Paul D. Gelpi, Jr.

See also   Academy Awards; Blockbusters; Film in the United States.

G

■ Gas shortages

Definition Insufficient supplies of gas in 1973 because of oil price increases and subsequent inflation, as well as the shortages of natural gas between 1976 and 1978

U.S. gas shortages demonstrated the country's reliance on Middle Eastern oil and caused a national crisis as many Americans voiced their anger at the high prices of natural gas and oil. The price hikes spurred Americans to look for alternative energies and caused the U.S. government to explore the possibility of domestic energy production.

The 1973 price spikes of oil in the United States were caused by two issues. First, throughout the period from 1950 to 1970, the United States had become increasingly dependent on foreign oil. Domestic oil production could not keep up with demand, and the United States started to import oil from other countries, including those in the Middle East. Second, the Arab Middle Eastern countries were angry with the United States. The Arab neighbors of Israel did not recognize Israel's right to exist and were unhappy with the way that the United States supported Israel. In 1973, war once again erupted in the Middle East with the Yom Kippur War, and the United States played a vital role in backing Israel. The Arab Middle Eastern countries, angered over their inability to defeat Israel, decided to cut off the supply of oil to the United States and Europe.

This embargo lasted for five months and quadrupled the price of crude oil. The price of a gallon of gas rose from forty cents a gallon to nearly sixty cents, and in turn, this rise sparked inflation, which hit 9 percent in 1973 and 12 percent in 1974. After Jimmy Carter's election to the American presidency in 1976, the economic situation stabilized for a time.

Natural Gas Between 1976 and 1978, however, there were shortages of natural gas. The price of natural gas had been kept artificially low, which encouraged people to use it instead of petroleum for electricity production. Those using natural gas between 1958 to 1978 enjoyed the low prices, but the prices compromised substantial profits for the producers of natural gas. This fact subsequently discouraged companies from moving to the use of natural gas, and it discouraged current producers from finding new fields or processes for energy production. Therefore, demand far outstripped supply, and many schools and factories had to close. This was particularly evident in 1977, which had one of the coldest winters on record. The situation corrected itself somewhat by the end of 1978, with the help of legislation that called for stricter regulation of pricing.

Another Gas Shortage The Organization of Petroleum Exporting Countries (OPEC) wanted to raise oil prices in 1979 and successfully did so. Gas prices passed one dollar a gallon in 1979, and there were long lines at gas stations and widespread fears of gas shortages. Gas prices remained high through 1980, and price increases in gasoline were passed along to the consumer. The high price of gasoline was $1.27 in 1979, which, in 2004 prices, would be $3.27.

The high prices caused inflation of more than 10 percent in 1979 and 1980. People began to buy more-fuel-efficient cars, often foreign produced, which, in turn, hurt American car companies. Moreover, the policies undertaken in order to limit inflation had negative effects. The Federal Reserve Board increased interest rates starting in 1979, and this move caused Americans to be less able to start businesses and buy homes, which further dampened the economic outlook. Interest rates on mortgages rose from 9 percent in 1978 to 18 percent in 1981.

Impact The U.S. economy was hurt badly by the gas shortages and subsequent price increases during this era, but the relatively temporary nature of the increases precluded most Americans from turning to long-term changes in their use of energy—although many consumers did buy more fuel-efficient cars—or, for example, to long-term developments in mass transit by state and local governments.

Long lines formed at gas stations in 1973 as a result of shortages. (AP/Wide World Photos)

Subsequent Events After 1980, prices of oil began to drop again. Many members of OPEC were more interested in making money for themselves than in keeping OPEC strong. Therefore, many of the member countries pumped more than OPEC told them to, which drove down the price of oil. Furthermore, other short-term oil sources were found. With these developments, prices dropped from $1.27 in 1979 to under a dollar a gallon by 1986, and the trend continued generally downward until 1998. Interest in alternative fuels, which were difficult to develop, decreased as gas prices dropped.

Further Reading

Knopman, Debra S. *Assessing Natural Gas and Oil Resources.* Santa Monica, Calif.: Rand, 2003. This short treatise examines the amount of oil and natural gas left in the United States.

Skeet, Ian. *OPEC: Twenty-five Years of Prices and Politics.* Cambridge, England: Cambridge University Press, 1988. This short history of OPEC examines its interaction with world politics and the oil situation.

Tsai, Hui-Liang. *Energy Shocks and the World Economy: Adjustment Policies and Problems.* Westport, Conn.:

Greenwood, 1989. Examines the way in which national economies adjust to external developments and discusses the energy crises of the 1970's in depth.

Yergin, Daniel. *The Prize: The Epic Quest for Oil, Money, and Power.* New York: Simon & Schuster, 1991. Examines the race all over the world for oil production and its interaction with world politics, including the Gulf War of the early 1990's.

Scott A. Merriman

See also Alaska Pipeline; Automobiles; Energy crisis; Environmental movement; Inflation in the United States; Mopeds; Oil embargo of 1973-1974; Transportation.

■ Gaye, Marvin

Identification African American singer, songwriter, and producer

Born April 2, 1939; Washington, D.C.

Died April 1, 1984; Los Angeles, California

Gaye was a versatile musician and producer who helped make Motown Records a more progressive label during the

1970's. He took soul music in numerous directions, mirroring the stylistic diversity of the decade itself.

Marvin Gaye emerged from the 1960's as one of Motown's most successful solo artists, known for the smooth soul sound that also was the label's signature. He had been paired with such singers as Mary Wells, Kim Weston, and, most important, Tammi Terrell, whose death in March, 1970, sent Gaye into several months of seclusion. Resuming his career in 1971, he convinced Motown to allow him more artistic control over his recordings. The result was the brilliant concept album *What's Going On?* (1971), whose strong percussive beat and sensuous, often edgy vocals marked a departure from the usual Motown style. The songs also addressed issues that were new to the label: "What's Going On?" criticized the Vietnam War, "Mercy, Mercy Me (The Ecology)" confronted environmental problems, and "Inner City Blues (Make Me Want to Holler)" addressed civil rights, drugs, poverty, and the breakup of the family.

In 1972, Gaye turned in other directions. He composed the soundtrack for the blaxploitation film *Trouble Man*, a primarily instrumental score with jazz, soul, and funk elements, and the following year, he collaborated with Diana Ross on an album of sensuous duets. His next album, the overtly sexual *Let's Get It On* (1973), began a pattern that would last for the rest of the decade: the shift in songs among social, religious, and sexual topics, mirroring conflicts in Gaye's own life.

When his first marriage ended in 1975, Gaye's personal problems, including depression and drug use, escalated. The following year, he released the critically acclaimed *I Want You*, written by Leon Ware, and in 1977, he ventured successfully into disco with "Got to Give It Up, Part 1," recorded on his album *Live at the London Palladium*. In 1978, he issued a bitter commentary on his divorce on the album *Here, My Dear*. Gaye's last album of the decade, *In Our Lifetime*, a soul-funk-disco fusion with philosophical and religious overtones, was recorded in Europe, where he had gone to escape tax problems. Its lack of success led Gaye to accuse Motown of remixing and editing the album without his consent and to his eventual parting with the label.

Impact   Gaye's stylistic breadth made him one of the most important and commercially successful soul artists of the decade. His ability to fuse soul with other styles and to communicate intensely personal feelings influenced many other musicians, including Stevie Wonder and George Clinton.

Further Reading

Dyson, Michael Eric. *Mercy, Mercy Me: The Art, Love, and Demons of Marvin Gaye.* New York: Basic Civitas Books, 2004.

Gordy, Berry. *To Be Loved: The Music, the Magic, the Memories of Motown.* New York: Warner Books, 1994.

Werner, Craig. *A Change Is Gonna Come: Music, Race, and the Soul of America.* New York: Plume, 1999.

Mary A. Wischusen

See also   African Americans; Blaxploitation films; Music; Racial discrimination; Soul music; Wonder, Stevie.

Marvin Gaye. (DPA/Landov)

■ Genetics research

Definition Scientific investigations on the origin and consequences of variations between and within species of biological organisms

Advances in genetics research during the 1970's served as the foundation for the emergence of biotechnology and genetic engineering in the following decades.

The publication of the essay "Experiments in Plant Hybridization" by Gregor Johann Mendel in 1866 is credited with the founding of the scientific field of experimental genetics, which is distinguishable from the field of evolution that is attributed to Charles Darwin's 1859 publication of *On the Origin of Species by Means of Natural Selection*. The identification of deoxyribonucleic acid (DNA) as the primary substance responsible for the heritability of traits from parents to offspring occurred in the early part of the twentieth century. The discovery of DNA's chemical structure by James D. Watson and Francis Crick in 1953 effectively merged genetics research with evolution science, thereby combining genetics research into the discipline of molecular biology.

The magnificence of the convergence of two scientific fields was not fully realized until the 1970's, when powerful techniques became available to manipulate DNA by splicing and recombining segments of this molecule from different organisms and, by consequence, to determine the evolutionary fate of organisms. The 1970's also brought the realization that the new scientific discipline of genetic engineering held potentially great influence on social and cultural issues.

Biotechnology Enzymology is the subdiscipline of molecular biology that provided the tools for the revolutionary emergence of biotechnology. Several scientists contributed to the discovery of enzymes that made the precise manipulation of DNA molecules possible. In 1970, Hamilton O. Smith and his collaborator Kent W. Wilcox published a report on the discovery of a restriction enzyme that could "cut" DNA molecules at specific sequences from the bacterium *Haemophilus influenza*. This fundamental discovery of a naturally occurring enzyme was soon followed by the announcement in 1972 by Har Gobind Khorana and his collaborator Vittorio Sgaramella that they had discovered a ligase enzyme that could "paste" together two different DNA segments. The restriction and ligase enzymes together therefore provided the necessary tools for "cut-and-paste" genetic engineering.

Furthermore, in 1972, Paul Berg and colleagues David A. Jackson and Robert H. Symons reported the use of both restriction and ligase enzymes to create a "recombinant" DNA hybrid molecule. The commercial biotechnological application of this technique became apparent when Herbert W. Boyer's research team reported in 1977 that it had created a bacterium capable of producing the mammalian hormone somatostatin. In 1978, Stanley Cohen and colleagues created a bacterium that produced the mouse enzyme dihydrofolate reductase. These methodological advances led directly to the creation of the first biotechnology corporation devoted to commercial exploitation of genetic engineering. In 1976, Boyer and venture capitalist Robert A. Swanson established Genentech, the premier biotechnology company.

Other remarkable advances in enzymology and molecular genetics during the 1970's included the discovery in 1970 of ribonucleic acid (RNA)-dependent DNA polymerase by David Baltimore and Howard M. Temin and his collaborator Satoshi Mizutani. This enzyme, later known as reverse transcriptase, was crucial for the inclusion of an important group of human pathogens, RNA viruses, in the genetic engineering revolution and applications of biotechnology for the improvement of human health. Later in the 1970's, methods were developed to improve the precision and speed of determining the sequence of nucleotides in DNA molecules. These improvements were published in 1977 by Walter Gilbert and his colleague Allan M. Maxam in the United States and Fred Sanger and colleagues in Great Britain.

The Asilomar Conference The rapid expansion of creativity and invention in genetics research that occurred during the 1970's was accompanied by the necessity of inventing new rules for interactions among scientists engaged in genetic engineering research and between these scientists' results and society at large. For example, new questions were raised about the ethical issues involved in "playing God" both by creating new organisms and by patenting "chimeric" organisms produced via recombinant DNA research. Much controversy surrounded the application filed by Ananda Chakrabarty in 1972 to patent a microorganism created through genetic engineering methods. In 1979, Cohen and Boyer also applied for a patent to cover the process for producing biologically functional molecular chimeras.

In 1975, active molecular biologists convened a historic conference in Asilomar, California, to explore the ethical, safety, and scientific challenges confronting the rapidly developing field. The conference itself did not produce a consensus on how to proceed, but it did represent a watershed in the history of scientific introspection. The outcome of the Asilomar Conference served as a template for future regulations and guiding policies regarding the social and cultural ramifications of advanced genetics research.

Impact The invention of powerful new experimental techniques in the 1970's effectively transformed genetics research and molecular biology into the field of biotechnology. Genetics research, through biotechnology, became one of the most powerful branches of empirical and applied science, influencing human food resources, health, environment, and nearly all domestic and industrial materials. Moreover, the principles of scientific engagement with genetic engineering that were established in the 1970's profoundly influenced in subsequent decades the political and ethical debates surrounding cloning, genetically engineered foods, and genetic profiling of individuals.

Commercial applications of these new fields of science profoundly influenced human societies, particularly regarding human health, food production, environmental management, and source tracking of human remains in legal matters.

Further Reading

Aldridge, Susan. *The Thread of Life: The Story of Genes and Genetic Engineering.* Cambridge, England: Cambridge University Press, 1998. A comprehensive and accessible account of the revolutionary discovery of DNA's structure and the emergence of molecular biology and genetic engineering during the 1970's.

Beckwith, Jon. "A Historical View of Social

Responsibility in Genetics." *Bioscience* 43, no. 5 (May, 1993): 327-334. An introduction to the science and controversies surrounding genetics research by one of the foremost thinkers on the social role of genetic knowledge from both historical and contemporary perspectives.

Davies, Julian, and William Reznikoff, eds. *Milestones in Biotechnology: Classic Papers on Genetic Engineering.* Boston: Butterworth-Heinemann, 1992. An excellent compilation of groundbreaking publications that framed genetic engineering and biotechnology.

Oladele A. Ogunseitan

See also Health care in Canada; Health care in the United States; Inventions; Medicine; Nobel Prizes; Science and technology; Test-tube babies.

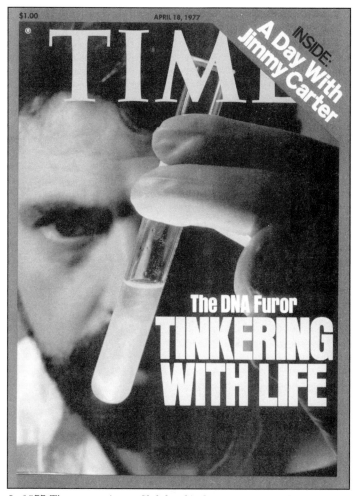

In 1977, Time *magazine profiled the ethical concerns surrounding genetic research.* (Hulton Archive/Getty Images)

■ *Get Christie Love*

Identification   Television detective series
Date   Aired from September, 1974, to July, 1975

Get Christie Love was a milestone in television's inclusion of women and minorities in its depiction of American life: It was the first hour-long drama series starring an African American woman in the central role.

Black women first starred in television series as early as 1950, when first Ethel Waters and then Louise Beavers played the title role in *Beulah*. In 1963, Cicely Tyson appeared as an important, though not primary, character in *East Side/West Side* with George C. Scott. However, it was not until the appearance of *Get Christie Love* on the American Broadcasting Company (ABC) network in 1974 that American viewers saw an African American woman cast as protagonist in a drama or action show. Teresa Graves starred as Christie Love, a detective in the Los Angeles Police Department. The series was much in the mode of ABC's other crime dramas of the 1970's, such as *Baretta* and *Starsky and Hutch*: a great deal of gunplay and chases, with a risk-taking, wisecracking protagonist who often clashed with colleagues and superiors. To bolster the series' sense of realism, producers based the series on a novel by best-selling former police officer Dorothy Uhnak and hired Detective Olga Ford of the New York Police Department to offer technical advice. Nevertheless, the series drew only mediocre ratings and was not renewed for a second season.

Industry pundits and social critics pondered the possibility that the series failed because American audiences were not ready for action series with women, especially minority women, in key roles. However, *Police Woman* and *Charlie's Angels* were successful in the 1970's, and both were television action series starring women. Moreover, both Pam Grier and Tamara Dobson became cult figures during the decade by starring in central roles in blaxploitation films that were popular at the time with young people of all races. It is possible that *Get Christie Love* failed in large part because of a trend in the entertainment industry that originated long before the 1970's: public resistance to an artist trying to "cross over" from one genre to another. Graves, like Goldie Hawn, had risen to fame as a dancer and comedian on *Rowan and Martin's Laugh-In*, one of the most popular shows of the 1960's. Viewers might have

been reluctant to accept her as a hard-hitting action heroine. A more serious and substantive problem with the series, however, was the quality of writing, which was often mediocre and uninspired.

Impact   Although it ran for only one year and was quickly forgotten both by viewers and by industry insiders, *Get Christie Love* remains unique in the annals of American television history—a prime-time action series starring an African American woman in the title role.

Further Reading

Brooks, Tim, and Earle Marsh. *The Complete Directory to Prime Time Network and Cable TV Shows: 1946-Present.* 8th ed. New York: Ballantine, 2003.

MacDonald, J. Fred. *Black and White TV: African Americans in Television Since 1948.* 2d ed. Chicago: Nelson-Hall, 1992.

Thomas Du Bose

See also   African Americans; Blaxploitation films; *Charlie's Angels*; Police and detective shows; Television in the United States.

■ Gilmore, Gary

Identification   American murderer
Born   December 4, 1940; McCamey, Texas
Died   January 17, 1977; Salt Lake City, Utah

Gilmore's execution in 1977, the first in the United States since the 1976 reinstatement of the death penalty after a ten-year ban, caused a sensation throughout the country, as Gilmore turned the system inside out by refusing to appeal the sentence and campaigning for his own death.

Gary Gilmore was raised in a highly dysfunctional family by an alcoholic father and a cold, emotionally distant mother. By the age of thirty-five, he had spent nearly half his life in prison. He embarked upon his final crime spree in July of 1976, motivated by the need for money to pay for his new truck and anger over a breakup with his girlfriend, Nicole Baker. In Orem, Utah, he demanded that gas station attendant and newlywed Max Jensen empty his pockets, then ordered him to lie down on the floor and shot him in the head twice—once, he later said, for himself and once for Baker. The next day, Gilmore entered the City Center Motel in Provo, Utah, took the cash box from the manager, new father Ben Bushnell, and also ordered him to lie on the floor and shot him in the head. Gilmore was captured easily and soon confessed to his crimes. His trial lasted only two days in October, 1976, and he was sentenced to death.

Gilmore brought the attention of the world upon himself and Utah when he refused the appeal process and requested that his death sentence be carried out immediately. He did not want to spend the rest of his life in prison and believed that it was his karma to die. When he was not immediately executed, he attempted suicide, as did his girlfriend. After her suicide attempt, Baker was institutionalized and was not allowed to see Gilmore again. The execution was stayed three times, but on January 17, 1977, the sentence was finally carried out. Gilmore was shot by a firing squad, his last words reportedly being "Let's do it."

Impact Gary Gilmore's execution brought enormous attention to the ongoing death penalty debate during the 1970's. Admittedly guilty of two random, senseless murders and demanding to be put to death for his crimes, Gilmore was a sensational test of the newly reinstated death penalty. He became an international celebrity, attracting press interest from all over the world. In 1979, Norman Mailer published the Pulitzer Prize-winning *The Executioner's Song*, dealing with Gilmore's life and death.

Further Reading

Gilmore, Mikal. *Shot in the Heart.* New York: Doubleday, 1994.

Mailer, Norman. *The Executioner's Song.* Little, Brown, 1979.

Mary Virginia Davis

See also Berkowitz, David; Bundy, Ted; Death penalty; Mailer, Norman; Manson Family; Zodiac killer.

■ Giovanni, Nikki

Identification African American poet and activist
Born June 7, 1943; Knoxville, Tennessee

Giovanni rose to prominence as a poet who lent her voice to the Civil Rights and the Black Arts movements in the 1960's, but during the 1970's, she also became recognized for her private and personal poems, which often dealt with the paradoxical human need both for freedom and for community.

Regarded by some readers as the "princess of black poetry," Nikki Giovanni enjoyed widespread popularity during the 1970's, lecturing on college campuses as well as on television and in prisons. In 1970, she established Niktom Limited, a publishing cooperative, took part in the collecting and editing of poems for *Night Comes Softly: An Anthology of Black Female Voices,* and published her third poetry collection, *Re:Creation,* which revealed a new poetic lyricism. For her 1971 recording *Truth Is on Its Way,* she read her poems against a gospel music background. Further recordings included *Like a Ripple on a Pond* (1973), *The Way I Feel* (1975), *Legacies* (1976), and *The Reason I Like Chocolate* (1976).

Two poetry volumes in 1971 suggested her flexible range of tone and style—*Gemini: An Extended Autobiographical Statement on My First Twenty-five Years of Being a Black Poet,* a poetic exploration of attitudes and reforms required to bring about a moral revolution, and *Spin a Soft Black Song: Poems for Children,* an affirming collection in which her dreams for her own child connect with dreams for all children.

In December, 1971, Giovanni joined African American writer James Baldwin for a conversation between writers of different generations on a Public Broadcasting Service (PBS) program. Enthusiasm for the program led the two authors to issue the transcribed conversations as *A Dialogue* (1973). A subsequent conversation between Giovanni and African American writer Margaret Walker resulted in the 1974 publication of *A Poetic Equation.*

Shifting from her typical political tone in the 1972 poetry collection *My House,* Giovanni emphasized love, home, and family, indicating that political activity is futile. In 1973, she published a volume especially for adolescents, *Ego-Tripping, and Other Poems for Young Readers.* During the second half of the 1970's, she published two poetry collections for adults, *The Women and the Men* (1975) and *Cotton Candy on a Rainy Day* (1978). As the decade ended, she began to broaden her literary vision to include the individual in modern society.

Giovanni won a variety of awards during this decade, including, in 1971, the *Mademoiselle* magazine award for outstanding achievement and the Omega Psi Phi fraternity award for Outstanding Contributions to Arts and Letters. In 1972, she won a life membership and scroll from the National Council of Negro Women, the *Ladies Home Journal* Woman of the Year award, the Youth Leadership Award, and keys to the cities of Dallas, Texas, and Gary, Indiana.

Impact Nikki Giovanni gained fame as she wrote boldly yet lyrically about the need for reform in the United States and about the importance of family, emphasizing in both matters a need to focus on shared humanity. While her role as a poetic voice in the Civil Rights movement led to her eminent position as an African American poet, her poems about family and community during the 1970's gained for her a lasting place as an American poet of lyrical power.

Further Reading

Bain, Robert, and Joseph Flora, eds. *Contemporary Poets, Dramatists, Essayists, and Novelists of the South: A Bio-Bibliographical Sourcebook.* Westport, Conn.: Greenwood Press, 1994.

Giovanni, Nikki. *Conversations with Nikki Giovanni.* Edited by Virginia C. Fowler. Jackson: University Press of Mississippi, 1992.

Bes Stark Spangler

See also Black Arts movement; Literature in the United States; Poetry; Racial discrimination.

■ *Godfather* films

Identification Motion pictures
Director Francis Ford Coppola (1939-   )
Date Released in 1972 and 1974

The Godfather and The Godfather, Part II were two of the most popular and influential films of the 1970's. They launched the careers of many actors and of writer-director Francis Ford Coppola.

Two of the most popular and critically acclaimed films of the 1970's were a three-generation saga of the Corleone family, an Italian American Mafia group. Both films won an Academy Award for Best Picture and were box-office successes. The films, directed by Francis Ford Coppola, influenced many other directors and actors.

The first film, *The Godfather,* starred Marlon Brando as the aging patriarch Don Vito Corleone—known as the Godfather—and three young actors as his sons: Sonny (played by James Caan), Freddy (John Cazale), and Michael (Al Pacino). The film was based on a best-selling 1969 novel by Mario Puzo, who coauthored the screenplay with Coppola.

The film follows the trials of and threats to the Corleone family as their power is challenged by the new generation of gangsters who wish to deal in drugs. After rival gangsters attempt to kill Don Corleone, the family becomes involved in a violent gang war. Each of the three sons show his true personality during this crisis: Sonny is violent and emotional, Freddy is weak, and Michael is most like his father. Don Corleone's adopted son, Tom Hagen (Robert Duvall), is the family lawyer, and his daughter Connie (Talia Shire) disappoints him by her choice of a husband.

Don Corleone is a sly but generally nonviolent leader who argues for "reasonableness" in all things. His most famous line—"I'll make him an offer he can't refuse"—is a signal of both his businesslike sensibilities and his veiled ruthlessness. In the film's most famous scene, the head of a race horse is cut off and placed in the bed of a film producer who refuses to bend to Don Corleone's wishes.

The film also shows how the youngest son, Michael, wishes to escape the family's history and marry a non-Italian. However, he is brought into the business little by little. After Sonny is killed and Michael kills the family's main enemy (and his police chief bodyguard), Don Corleone returns to settle the war and to bring his son home from exile. By the end of the film, the aged Vito Corleone has died, and Michael has become head of the family when he takes bloody revenge on the family's enemies.

The Godfather was named Best Picture in 1972 and also won Academy Awards for Best Actor for Brando and Best Screenplay. The film was a box office champion that earned millions of dollars for Paramount Studios. Brando, who had gotten the part against the studio's wishes, refused the Academy Award as a protest against racist depictions of American Indians in films and the recent incident at Wounded Knee, South Dakota.

A Sequel In 1974, Coppola made a sequel of sorts to *The Godfather. The Godfather, Part II* follows two story lines. One depicts a young Vito Corleone (played by Robert De Niro) as he leaves Sicily and goes to New York City to escape the vengeance of a local Mafia don. This track shows his rise in the United States to become Don Corleone. The second track shows the modern don Michael Corleone trying to move the family out of illegal operations and into legal gambling in Nevada and Cuba. The film goes back and forth between the two stories and the two generations.

In the course of the two stories, the audience sees

how young Vito Corleone rises to become a "man of respect" in the Italian American culture and how he eventually returns to his native Sicily to exact revenge on the people who murdered his family and forced him to move to the United States. We also see how Michael's efforts to gain respectability are frustrated by the treachery of others. Michael's life and family are threatened by a conspiracy between Jewish mobster Hyman Roth (Lee Strasberg) and his own brother, Freddy.

As Michael's extended Mafia family thrives, his immediate family disintegrates. His wife (Diane Keaton) becomes estranged enough to abort their third child, his sister Connie loses all family connections, and his brother betrays him. By the end of *Godfather, Part II*, both Michael and Vito's enemies have been murdered, and their fates as Mafia overlords have been sealed. Michael is alone, having disowned his wife and ordered the murder of his brother.

The Godfather, Part II also won the Academy Award for Best Picture, Best Supporting Actor for De Niro, Best Adapted Screenplay, and Best Director. The film was another box office success and garnered acclaim as one of the best films of the decade.

Al Pacino (left) and Marlon Brando in a scene from The Godfather. (Museum of Modern Art/Film Stills Archive)

Impact The success of the *Godfather* films launched the careers of many young actors. Additionally, the films allowed Coppola the freedom to become one of the most important directors of the 1970's and of subsequent decades, who in turn influenced other directors, such as Martin Scorsese. Many aspects of *The Godfather* can be seen throughout American popular culture, including lines such as, "Do me this favor," and "I'll make him an offer he can't refuse." In 1998, the American Film Institute named *The Godfather* number three on its list of the one hundred greatest films. *The Godfather, Part II* was ranked number thirty-two on the same list. A third film, *The Godfather, Part III*, was released in 1990.

Further Reading

Elsaesser, Thomas, and Noel King, eds. *The Last Great American Picture Show: New Hollywood Cinema in the 1970's*. Amsterdam: Amsterdam University Press, 2004. Recognizes the decade as a crucial turning point in American filmmaking and discusses how pivotal films of the 1970's influenced motion pictures of subsequent decades.

Lebo, Harlan. *"The Godfather" Legacy*. New York: Simon & Schuster, 1997. A behind-the-scenes look at the filming and personalities of the Godfather trilogy. Includes filming details, photographs, and discussion of how Coppola secured the help of the real Mafia in planning the film.

Puzo, Mario. *The Godfather*. Rev. ed. New York: New American Library, 2002. Puzo's original story with the addition of a new introduction by Robert J. Thompson and an afterword by Peter Bart.

Sigoloff, Marc. *Films of the Seventies: A Filmography of American, British, and Canadian Films, 1970-1979*. Jefferson, N.C.: McFarland, 2000. An encyclopedic reference book that lists one thousand films from the decade and provides listings of cast and credits, awards won, and a summary of the plot, among other details.

Charles C. Howard

See also Academy Awards; Blockbusters; Brando, Marlon; De Niro, Robert; Film in the United States; Pacino, Al.

■ Golf

Definition Individual sport

During the 1970's, golf continued to rise in popularity both as public recreation and as a professional sport played by men and women.

Interest in the game of golf continued to grow throughout the 1970's. The number of golfers in the United States had doubled in the previous ten years, and estimates indicated more than ten million people participated in the sport. Interest in professional golf would also expand, thanks to high-profile stars such as Jack Nicklaus.

Men's Professional Golf During the 1970's, Nicklaus reigned as the best golfer in the world and became the first golfer to win each of the four professional majors twice. In 1976, Nicklaus led the Professional Golfers' Association (PGA) tour in earnings for the eighth time. The decade also experienced a shifting of the guard in professional golf. In 1970, in one of their final head-to-head battles on the PGA tour, Nicklaus and Arnold Palmer played the final thirty-six holes of regulation together at the Byron Nelson Classic before Nicklaus won the title in a playoff. Although in 1973 Palmer would win the Bob Hope Chrysler Classic, his sixty-second on the PGA tour, this victory would be his last.

In 1971, Bobby Jones, winner of thirteen professional and amateur major tournaments and founder of Augusta National, passed away. However, new faces emerged on the golf scene. Among the fan favorites were the likes of Ben Crenshaw, Tom Watson, and Hale Irwin, who won the U.S. Open at a very difficult course at Winged Foot in 1979. Most notable was the rise of a young star named Johnny Miller, who in 1974 won eight events on the PGA tour and, in one of golf's greatest final round performances, shot a 63 at Oakmont Country Club to win the U.S. Open. In 1977, Al Geiberger became the first player to break 60 in a PGA tour event, shooting 59 in the Danny Thomas Memphis Classic.

This period also witnessed the emergence of several successful minority golfers. Lee Trevino, the first Mexican American on the tour, overcame extreme poverty to win numerous professional golf titles and was the recipient of the prestigious Hickok Professional Athlete of the Year and the Associated Press Athlete of the Year awards. Lee Elder emerged as one of the first African American golfers to play on the PGA tour. In 1973, Elder finished in the top five in four tournaments and in April of the following year won the Monsanto Open in Pensacola, Florida. His PGA tour victory qualified him for the 1975 Masters tournament in Augusta, Georgia, making Elder the first African American to qualify since the Masters began in 1934.

Women's Professional Golf The Ladies Professional Golf Association (LPGA) also also expanded during the decade. Kathy Whitworth, who won her first LPGA tournament in 1962, became the most successful female professional golfer with her eighty-third official title in 1972. Sandra Haynie also impressed the golf world, particularly by winning two majors in one year, the U.S. Women's Open and LPGA Championship in 1974. Perhaps the biggest boost to women's professional golf was Nancy Lopez,

Lee Trevino (left) and Jack Nicklaus, who battled each other in an eighteen-hole playoff for the 1971 U.S. Open championship, were two of the most dominant players of the decade. (AP/Wide World Photos)

who burst onto the scene in 1978 with five consecutive wins on the LPGA tour, and nine wins overall. Lopez followed her rookie season with eight additional wins, the Vare Trophy, and the Player of the Year award.

New and more lucrative golf tournaments were also added to the women's circuit. The Colgate Dinah Shore Winners Circle event became the first women's golf tournament with a purse of more than $100,000. Players collected bigger paychecks. Judy Rankin earned $150,734 in 1976 and became the first LPGA tour player to earn more than $100,000 in a season.

Title IX legislation, initially passed by Congress in 1972, would soon force colleges to provide more opportunities for female athletes. The expansion of women's college golf increased the talent pool of the LPGA tour.

Innovations and Rule Changes Astronaut Alan Shepard's golf shot on the moon in 1971 symbolized a new era for golf, as technological innovations had a significant impact on the game. In 1971, Titleist introduced the icosahedron dimple pattern, an aerodynamically superior golf ball design. It was followed the next year by the two-piece Top Flight ball, constructed with a solid core inside a durable synthetic cover.

In 1972, Aldila began manufacturing graphite shafts, and in 1979 TaylorMade introduced its first metal wood at the PGA merchandise show. Taylor-Made's metal wood started the growth of the product and eventually replaced persimmon-made golf clubs. The changes in ball and club design would allow both amateur and professional golfers to add yards to their distances.

The continued growth of television contributed to the sport's popularity thanks to the earlier duels between Palmer and Nicklaus and later memorable battles, such as when Tom Watson defeated Nicklaus at the British Open at Turnberry in 1977. Golf rules were modified to fit television schedules. Most notable was the introduction of a sudden death system. Soon afterward, Lanny Wadkins defeated Gene Littler at the PGA Championship in an exciting sudden death playoff that was caught on television in its entirety.

Impact During the 1970's, golf—played by men, women, young, old, professional and amateur alike— truly became one of America's greatest pastimes.

The popularity of the game was at an all-time high.

International golf also had an impact on the American golf scene. International players such as South Africa's Gary Player experienced success in the United States. In 1979, Ryder Cup matches, traditionally played between the United States, Great Britain, and Ireland, were opened to players from all of Europe, although the U.S. team still maintained its dominance. The Legends of Golf, a team event pairing senior golfers for a tournament in Austin, Texas, premiered in 1978 and led to the formation of the senior golf tour in 1980.

Further Reading

Dawkins, Marvin, and Graham Kinloch. *African-American Golfers During the Jim Crow Era.* Westport, Conn.: Praeger, 2000. An interesting account of the rich history of African American golfers.

Hobbs, Michael, and Peter Alliss. *Golf to Remember.* New York: Doubleday, 1978. Descriptions of some of the most memorable golf duels, including Jack Nicklaus and Tom Watson at Turnberry in 1977.

Moss, Richard. *Golf and the American Country Club.* Urbana: University of Illinois Press, 2001. An interesting analysis of the rise of the country club and its impact on the growth of the game of golf. Scholarly but easy to read.

Nickerson, Elinor. *Golf: A Women's History.* Jefferson, N.C.: McFarland, 1987. A concise but detailed history of women's participation in golf. Special attention is given to the later decades of the twentieth century.

Mary McElroy

See also Hobbies and recreation; Lopez, Nancy; Nicklaus, Jack; Sports.

■ Graffiti

Definition Inscriptions or designs commonly made with spray paint on public surfaces, such as subway cars, signs, and building walls

As an art movement, graffiti manifested itself in many forms, but the unique styles arising in New York City and Los Angeles were most influential during the 1970's. Later considered the visual element of hip-hop culture in New York City, "spray can art" creatively depicted the cultural symbols of inner-city youth. In Los Angeles, artists marked gang territories and created murals of Mexican tradition to achieve notoriety among peers and gain recognition in the city.

In the late 1960's and early 1970's, graffiti writers in Philadelphia began "bombing" or "tagging" public property by using spray paint. By 1971, the illegal art form had migrated to New York City, where artists began tagging signs and buildings with their nicknames in an effort to earn recognition. A distinct youth culture arose around this unique form of expression, and a spirit of competitive camaraderie characterized the participants.

What began as hastily scrawled nicknames evolved into a highly stylized art form that included large-scale murals and lettering. Graffiti artists began targeting subway cars because they were decidedly visible throughout New York City. "Crews," consisting of five or more youths often from varied ethnic backgrounds, entered the subway yards at night to create huge multicar works that attracted the attention of tourists and the chagrin of city officials. These painters called themselves "aerosol artists" or "graffiti writers" and considered the subways to be their canvases. However, they were not appreciated as artists by city officials, who tried to control the proliferation of graffiti by passing ordinances against the sale of spray paint to minors and launching expensive removal campaigns.

The art form took a different turn in Los Angeles. In contrast to the multicultural crews of New York City, Los Angeles artists were associated with ethnically homogeneous gangs. While New York's graffiti traversed neighborhood borders and did not promote violence, Los Angeles gang writers marked their territories and sent messages to rival groups. The focus was not the moving canvas of a subway car but rather stationary and enduring buildings and signs. Many of the large-scale murals exhibited a Mexican American identity. The Los Angeles police department organized task forces that were determined to remove the visual proof of gang activity.

The products of both styles were ephemeral, perhaps lasting only days before they were removed, which in turn gave rise to a certain legendary status for the artists and their creations. Artists from both locales took a great deal of pride in their work, and many possessed genuine talent.

Impact Graffiti's distinctive style had an impact on commercial logos, music videos, set designs in film and television, gallery shows, fashion design, and skateboard graphics. The visual impact of graffiti became ubiquitous to urban settings, and although

New York City and Los Angeles were the original sites for the unique 1970's styles of "writing," graffiti quickly moved throughout the United States, infiltrating nearly every metropolitan area in the country in subsequent decades.

Further Reading

Chalfant, Henry, and James Prigoff. *Spraycan Art.* New York: Thames and Hudson, 1987.

Cooper, Martha, and Henry Chalfant. *Subway Art.* New York: Holt, Rinehart, and Winston, 1984.

Miller, Ivor. *Aerosol Kingdom: Subway Painters of New York City.* Jackson: University Press of Mississippi, 2002.

Valerie Brown

See also   Art movements; Hip-hop; Latinos; Music; Pop art.

■ Grasso, Ella

Identification   U.S. representative, 1970-1974; governor of Connecticut, 1975-1980
Born   May 10, 1919; Windsor Locks, Connecticut
Died   February 5, 1981; Hartford, Connecticut

Grasso was the first woman to be elected governor of a state in her own right and not because of the death of her husband or father. She was also the first Italian American to be elected governor of Connecticut.

Ella Grasso was active in politics at the local level beginning in 1943, gaining her first official position in the Connecticut House of Representatives in 1952. In 1970, she was elected to the U.S. Congress, and she was reelected in 1972. However, her first concern was always Connecticut, which she disliked leaving for Washington, D.C. She felt unable to address her home state's needs adequately while in Congress. Therefore, in 1974, when the incumbent Republican governor of Connecticut, Thomas Meskill, decided not to seek reelection, she campaigned for and won the Democratic nomination for that post.

Grasso won the election for governor by more than 200,000 votes. Governor Meskill left office with a deficit of seventy million dollars, which Grasso, a fiscal conservative, changed into a surplus through the use of a state lottery and an increase in the state's gasoline tax. She was also judicious in the use of state funds by, for example, laying off some state workers and holding back on the implementation of some of the social programs that she had promised. For a while this approach caused her popularity to drop drastically, but as her tactics improved the budgetary situation, she was able to rehire workers, balance the budget, reduce business taxes, and increase aid to cities and towns.

Grasso's popularity increased dramatically during the blizzard of February, 1978, when she took a hands-on approach to helping citizens recover from the killer storm. She easily won reelection that year. With a large surplus and a reputation as a socially liberal politician, she was able to increase social spending. For instance, she created the Urban Action Program, which sent funds to impoverished areas of the state in order to improve housing, day care, mass transit, and the situation of the elderly.

Impact   Ella Grasso opened the way for other women to achieve the highest position in state government. In March, 1980, she was diagnosed with cancer, forcing her to resign her position as governor, much to the sorrow of the people of her state. Her popularity was so great that upon her death in 1981, many cars in Connecticut sported bumper stickers reading "Thank You, Ella."

Further Reading

Bysiewicz, Susan. *Ella: A Biography of Governor Ella Grasso.* Old Saybrook, Conn.: Peregrine Press, 1984.

Glashan, Roy R. *American Governors and Gubernatorial Elections, 1775-1975.* Stillwater, Minn.: Croixside Press, 1975.

Lieberman, Joseph I. *The Legacy: Connecticut Politics, 1930-1980.* Hartford, Conn.: Spoonwood Press, 1981.

Mary LeDonne Cassidy

See also   Elections in the United States, 1972; Liberalism in U.S. politics; Women's rights.

■ *Gravity's Rainbow*

Identification   Controversial novel commenting on the troubled nature of humankind
Author   Thomas Pynchon (1937-   )
Date   Published in 1973

In Gravity's Rainbow, *Pynchon probes the tangled nature of truth and ethics in light of the horrors of twentieth century history, the banality of the century's culture, and the unsettling change unleashed by its science and technology.*

The reclusive Thomas Pynchon earned a reputation for shunning media attention but launching intellectual salvos into the public arena in the form of puzzling and controversial books. *Gravity's Rainbow* became one of the most admired and most reviled books of the 1970's. To the extent that this lengthy novel with more than four hundred characters has a central hero, it is the fictional Lieutenant Tyrone Slothrop. However, additional historical figures abound, ranging from British prime minister Winston Churchill and Nazi scientist Wernher von Braun to the Rolling Stones and President Richard Nixon, as well as a rich stew of mythical and folk characters drawn from the dawn of human history down to Walt Disney's animated elephant, Dumbo. Although Pynchon shatters narrow chronological and geographical bounds, the novel is mainly set in war-torn and occupied Europe from December, 1944, to September, 1945. One end of gravity's rainbow shimmers over London, while the parabola of V-2 rockets trace their way back to the other end of the rainbow, to their launch sites in German-occupied territory.

The nebulous plot surrounds the quest for mastery of the V-2 rocket, especially the Rocket 00000, with mysterious figures bent on using such technology to establish total human control of the natural world. Subplots abound, as characters struggle to understand the forces that control the world around them and that lock humanity into a headlong rush toward self-annihilation. The multitude of characters and plots allows Pynchon to explore his main concern: the nature of twentieth century culture and the future of humanity.

Impact   Readers who were prepared for Thomas Pynchon's writing style and intellectual concerns by his previous books—*V.* (1963) and *The Crying of Lot 49* (1966)—greeted *Gravity's Rainbow* with enthusiasm. The book received the National Book Award, as well as awards from the National Institute of Arts and Letters and the American Academy of Arts and Letters. However, an uproar ensued when the press learned that the Pulitzer Prize judges had unanimously voted to give the prize to *Gravity's Rainbow* but had been overruled by the Pulitzer trustees, who, in an unprecedented action, made no award that year. Despite this controversy, Pynchon's daring and erudite probing of twentieth century culture and history inspired a generation of writers and readers.

Further Reading

Bloom, Harold, ed. *Thomas Pynchon's "Gravity's Rainbow."* New York: Chelsea House, 1986.

Hume, Kathryn. *Pynchon's Mythography: An Approach to "Gravity's Rainbow."* Carbondale: Southern Illinois University Press, 1987.

Weisenburger, Steven. *A "Gravity's Rainbow" Companion: Sources and Contexts for Pynchon's Novel.* Athens: University of Georgia Press, 1988.

William E. Pemberton

See also Literature in the United States.

■ Gray Panthers

Identification Civil rights organization for older and retired Americans
Date Formed in l970

The Gray Panthers gained widespread support for its ability to tie its concerns with that of other civil rights groups and brought attention to the problems faced by aging Americans.

The drive for equality for all Americans that had begun in the 1960's continued during the 1970's, as more groups began to organize and take action to secure respect from society and fair treatment under the law. The Gray Panthers began in order to fight discrimination against older people, especially those nearing or past retirement age. The organization grew out of a circle of recently retired friends in Philadelphia, Pennsylvania, who began meeting informally to discuss both the problems and the sense of freedom that their new status had brought them. Maggie Kuhn, retired from a long career of social work, most of it associated with the Young Women's Christian Association (YWCA) and the Presbyterian Church, emerged as the group's leader.

Kuhn, who had been forced to retire at sixty-five, along with her friends sought to end mandatory retirement, ensure health care for elderly Americans, and address other issues pertaining to aging and the aged. Kuhn is credited with having coined the term "ageism," which refers to prejudice against older people. Kuhn and her friends were eager to combine their cause with those of other activist groups and soon joined forces with a local antiwar students' group, calling themselves the Consultation of Older and Younger Adults for Social Change. The name Gray Panthers, patterned after the name of the militant African American rights group the Black Pan-

thers, began as a media joke made at one of the coalition's talk-show appearances in 1972, but the phrase proved popular and was ultimately adopted officially, even though the organization was never formed solely of older people.

In only a few years, the Gray Panthers grew from one chapter to eleven, which were called "networks" within the organization. The networks began to meet in annual conventions in 1975. The Gray Panthers used many of the tactics of other civil rights groups of the 1960's and 1970's: marches, rallies, speeches, street theater, mailings, and media appearances.

Impact Because the Gray Panthers always sought to ally their quest for fair treatment for the elderly with other related causes, it was never a single-issue group. This fact, along with the increasing percentage of elderly people in the United States, helped the group remain active and viable long past the 1970's.

Subsequent Events By the early years of the twenty-first century, the organization was made up of some fifty networks with a membership of about twenty thousand. Kuhn maintained her leadership role within the organization until her death at the age of ninety in 1995.

Further Reading

DiCanio, Margaret B. *Encyclopedia of American Activism: 1960 to the Present.* Santa Barbara, Calif.: ABC-Clio, 1998.

Kuhn, Maggie, Christina Long, and Laura Quinn. *No Stone Unturned: The Life and Times of Maggie Kuhn.* New York: Ballantine, 1991.

Thomas Du Bose

See also Age Discrimination Act of 1975; Antiwar demonstrations; Black Panthers; Social Security Amendments of 1972.

■ *Grease*

Identification Motion picture
Director Randal Kleiser (1946-   )
Date Released in 1978

Grease, one of the last of the big-production film musicals, was a tribute to the 1950's musical genre and romanticized that era for Americans yearning for simpler times.

Olivia Newton-John and John Travolta rehearse a scene for the 1978 film version of the musical Grease. *(AP/Wide World Photos)*

The film adaptation of the 1972 Broadway musical *Grease* opened to some lackluster reviews but went on to become the top-grossing musical and one of the highest-grossing films ever. The story line, set in the 1950's, involved Danny (played by John Travolta), a "greaser" who is in love with "good girl" Sandy (Olivia Newton-John). Their on-again, off-again relationship is resolved when Sandy decides to change her image and shows up at the annual high school carnival smoking and wearing a black leather outfit. Sandy's transformation occurs just as Danny has attempted to transform his image by lettering in track in order to impress Sandy. *Grease* also starred Stockard Channing as Rizzo and Didi Conn as Frenchy—two of the members of the girl gang, the Pink Ladies—and Jeff Conaway as Danny's friend Kenickie.

Although the setting is the 1950's, some themes in the film are timeless and easily allowed a 1970's audience to relate: Rizzo's pregnancy scare, Frenchy's embarrassment after dropping out of beauty school, Sandy's infatuation with a "bad boy," the boys' desire to fix up an old jalopy in order to race it, and all of the characters' preoccupation with image.

The music for the film version of *Grease* was updated with a dicso edge in order to appeal to the audiences of the late 1970's. The title song, although sung by 1950's icon Frankie Valli, was written by Barry Gibb of the Bee Gees. The Bee Gees were on the top of the music charts at the time with the soundtrack to *Saturday Night Fever* (1977), which also starred Travolta. Several of the songs from the *Grease* soundtrack made it to the Top 10 of the *Billboard* charts, including two that went to number one: "Grease" and "You're the One That I Want," sung by Newton-John and Travolta. The soundtrack sold more than eight million copies.

Impact   Nostalgia for the 1950's was an important part of the popular culture of the 1970's. *Happy Days*, a popular television show about the 1950's, was at the top of the Nielsen ratings when Grease was in production, and *American Graffiti* (1973)—another film about the 1950's—gained unexpected success among U.S. audiences. To those Americans who were experiencing a peak in the nation's homicide rate, a dramatic increase in inflation rates, and government scandal, the 1950's represented a simpler time with lower crime rates, a robust, post-World War II economy, and a presidency that was perceived as stable and fair.

Further Reading

Hischak, Thomas. *Film It with Music: An Encyclopedic Guide to the American Movie Musical.* Westport, Conn.: Greenwood Press, 2001.

Sigoloff, Marc. *Films of the Seventies: A Filmography of American, British, and Canadian Films, 1970-1979.* Jefferson, N.C.: McFarland, 2000.

Pamela Hayes-Bohanan

See also   *American Graffiti*; Bee Gees, The; Blockbusters; Broadway musicals; *Happy Days*; *Saturday Night Fever*; Travolta, John.

■ Great Lakes Water Quality Agreement of 1972

Identification International environmental agreement

Date Signed in 1972; renewed in 1978

The Great Lakes Water Quality Agreement expressed a commitment between the United States and Canada to restore and maintain the chemical, physical, and biological integrity of the Great Lakes Basin ecosystem.

The Great Lakes Water Quality Agreement was first signed by representatives of the United States and Canada in 1972 and renewed in 1978. The agreement stated specific objectives and guidelines as a means to attain these goals and also reaffirmed the sovereign rights and obligations of the United States and Canada under the Boundary Waters Treaty of 1909. In signing the agreement, both parties agreed to make a maximum effort to develop programs, practices, and technologies necessary for a better understanding of the Great Lakes Basin ecosystem. They also agreed to eliminate or reduce the discharge of pollutants into the Great Lakes system, including streams, rivers, lakes, and other bodies of water that are within the drainage basin on the St. Lawrence River at, or upstream from, the point that the river becomes the international boundary between Canada and the United States.

The general objectives of the agreement clearly stated that Great Lakes waters should be free from substances that directly or indirectly enter the waters as a result of human activity and adversely affect aquatic life and waterfowl. Moreover, it stated that the Great Lake waters should be free from floating materials and chemicals; free from materials and heat-producing color, odor, taste, or other conditions that interfere with beneficial water uses, or produce toxic or harmful conditions to human, animal, or aquatic life; and be free from nutrients directly or indirectly entering the waters in amounts creating growths of aquatic life that interfere with beneficial water uses. All aspects of the agreement are monitored by the Great Lakes Science Advisory Board of the International Joint Commission of the Boundary Waters Treaty. While the agreement adopted minimum levels of water quality desired in the Great Lakes system, it did not preclude the establishment of more stringent standards.

Impact Having entered into the Great Lakes Water Quality Agreements of 1972 and 1978, Canada and the United States soon recognized that restoration and enhancement of the boundary waters could not be achieved independently of other parts of the Great Lakes Basin aquatic ecosystem. In addition, during the 1970's, several of the general and specific objectives of the agreement were not being met because of certain human activities in specific locations within the basin. These locations needed to be identified and a concentrated effort was needed to work toward elimination of certain human activities as point-source polluters.

After a decade, it became clear that the best means to preserve the aquatic ecosystem and achieve improved water quality throughout the Great Lakes Basin was by adopting common objectives, developing and implementing specific programs and other measures, and assigning special responsibilities and functions to the International Joint Commission. In 1983, a protocol outlining these objectives was added to the 1978 agreement.

Further Reading

Elfont, C. J., and E. A. Elfont. *Sand Dunes of the Great Lakes.* Chelsea, Mich.: Sleeping Bear Press, 1997.

National Research Council of the United States and The Royal Society of Canada, eds. *The Great Lakes Water Quality Agreement: An Evolving Instrument for Ecosystem Management.* Washington, D.C.: National Academy Press, 1985.

Randall L. Milstein

See also Canada and the United States; Environmental movement; Environmental Protection Agency (EPA); Safe Drinking Water Act of 1974; Water pollution.

■ Green Revolution

Definition Program designed to increase agricultural yields in developing countries through technological means

Sponsored by U.S. foundations and government agencies, the Green Revolution achieved extraordinary successes during the 1970's in increasing the food supply of developing countries. At the same time, however, the ecological and demographic consequences of the revolution came under increasing critical scrutiny.

In 1970, Dr. Norman Borlaug, an American agronomist, received the Nobel Peace Prize for his exceptional achievements in improving agricultural output and the food supply of developing countries, thereby helping to alleviate world hunger. His first success had been in Mexico as a member of the team of research scientists at the International Maize and Wheat Improvement Center, sponsored by the Rockefeller Foundation.

Through genetic manipulation of seed grains that resulted in more productive and resistant strains, the center aided Mexico to become self-sufficient in food production. From the mid-1940's to the late 1960's, Mexico tripled its production of corn and quintupled that of wheat. In 1968, the head of the U.S. Agency for International Development (USAID) used the term "Green Revolution" to describe the phenomenon whereby high-yield-variety (HYV) seeds radically increased the food supply of developing nations.

Progress in Asia   During the 1970's, the Green Revolution engendered a wave of successes in Asia, most notably India. One of the most populous countries in the world and infamous for mass famines, India spectacularly augmented its food supply during the decade. India, like other developing nations, began to employ the use of HYV seeds, enlarged the area of land under cultivation, expanded irrigation, mechanized farming, and intensively applied chemical fertilizers and pesticides. These were methods that the United States had been developing and applying for more than a century, thereby achieving its historic abundance of food.

By the late 1970's, India became one of the world's major producers of grains, principally rice, wheat, corn, and millet, with more than 100 million tons. Particularly noteworthy in this regard was the development of the K68 strain of wheat by Dr. M. P. Singh, a central figure in the advance of the Green Revolution in India. Pakistan, Indonesia, and the Philippines also obtained spectacular increases in grain foods by using similar methods.

Critiques   By the 1970's, however, a disturbing consequence of the Green Revolution, along with global improvements in sanitation and public health, emerged ever more ominously: rapid population growth. The population of Earth first reached one billion people during the nineteenth century. By the middle of the following century, it had more than doubled to over two billion. By the 1970's, in little more than one generation, it doubled again, mounting to more than four billion people.

Critics argued that although the Green Revolution had increased the world's food supply and drastically reduced hunger, it was also contributing to a growth of population that could exhaust Earth's natural resources and jeopardize other species. The 1970's witnessed growing critical analysis of a revolution that had initially been viewed as miraculous but now appeared as a Pandora's box of unexpected consequences. It chemically increased the fertility of soils rather than naturally renewing them, thereby requiring ever more intensive and costly fertilizers. While the agricultural techniques increased production through scientific improvements, the Green Revolution did not address, and actually ignored, economic and political issues that could achieve a more equitable social distribution of food.

Impact   In terms of socioeconomic impact, the Green Revolution acted as a stimulant to other sectors, serving as an engine for development. Insofar as it required more water for irrigation, it stimulated construction of dams and thereby the expansion of a hydroelectric industry. Further growth occurred in petrochemical industries as the demand rose for fertilizers and pest control. By improving the production capacity of a country, the revolution allowed an increase in national income and revenue to pay down loans for agricultural investments. The initial stages of the Green Revolution were primarily effective in expanding grain production but not all types of agricultural produce. By considerably augmenting the food supply, it served purposes of social and political pacification.

Subsequent Events   From India, the American techniques of the Green Revolution spread to China. By the end of the twentieth century, these countries each had populations of more than one billion people. Earth itself had six billion human inhabitants, an unprecedented triple increase since the 1970's. Over the same period, the rate of species extinction accelerated at a rate that had not been seen since the end of the age of the dinosaurs more than 70 million years ago. Moreover, many of the earth's resources, such as fresh water, minerals, and petroleum, were being depleted at a rate whereby they could not be replenished by nature. Approximately one billion people in the world continued to suffer from hunger and malnutrition. To address this situation, many called for a second Green Revolution but one based on high yields from organic farming and with adequate sociopolitical guarantees for the equitable distribution of its benefits.

Further Reading

Brown, Lester R. *Seeds of Change: The Green Revolution and Development in the 1970's*. New York: Praeger, 1970. Analyses of the world's food supply in terms of agronomy and agricultural economics and business.

Conway, Gordon. *The Double Green Revolution: Food for All in the Twenty-first Century*. Ithaca, N.Y.: Comstock, 1997. Collection of articles on intense agriculture in terms of ecological consequences and rural development.

Dahlberg, Kenneth A. *Beyond the Green Revolution: The Ecology and Politics of Global Agricultural Development*. New York: Plenum Press, 1979. Focuses on the agricultural ecology of the Green Revolution and role of the public sector.

Karim, M. Bazlul. *The Green Revolution: An International Bibliography*. New York: Greenwood Press, 1986. Synopsis of literature from the early 1960's to the mid-1980's.

Pearse, Andrew Chernocke. *Seeds of Plenty, Seeds of Want: Social and Economic Implications of the Green Revolution*. Oxford, England: Clarendon Press, 1980. Critical review of the socioeconomic consequences of the Green Revolution.

Wharton, Clifton R., Jr. "The Green Revolution: Cornucopia or Pandora's Box?" *Foreign Affairs* 47 (April, 1969): 464-476. Evaluates the expected positive and unanticipated negative results of the Green Revolution.

Wu, Felicia, and William P. Butz. *The Future of Genetically Modified Crops: Lessons from the Green Revolution*. Santa Monica, Calif.: Rand Science and Technology, 2004. Builds on criticism of consequences of the initial Green Revolution to address key issues of transgenic plants and genetic engineering.

Edward A. Riedinger

See also Agriculture in the United States; Genetics research; *Population Bomb, The*; Science and technology.

■ Greening of America, The

Identification   A best-selling book that explained the generation gap
Author   Charles A. Reich (1928-2004)
Date   Published in 1970

The Greening of America: How the Youth Revolution Is Trying to Make America Livable *set the terms for the debate in the United States over the new and, at times, controversial values of many young people. It predicted revolutions based on "people power," not armed confrontations.*

In one of the most widely discussed books of its kind during the 1970's, Yale law professor Charles A. Reich championed the new consciousness of rebellious youth. He attacked the military-industrial complex and advocated rock music, sexual liberation, civil rights, war protests, psychedelic drugs, and environmentalism.

In his book, Reich argues that one's consciousness is the overall configuration of one's attitude toward and perception of experience. American history has seen three kinds of consciousness. Consciousness I, as Reich calls it, refers to the rugged individualism found among early pioneers, entrepreneurs, and family farmers, all of whom engaged in relatively unfettered competition under conditions of economic scarcity before the twentieth century. Consciousness II grew as a reaction against robber barons of the Gilded Age, some of whom amassed personal fortunes greater than the national treasury. The public good was valued above individual freedom. Personal income was taxed for the first time, businesses were regulated by government, and corporations gained enormous economic and political power. Since constitutional restraints on government's interference with individual freedom do not apply to private employers, citizens can be manipulated as workers to make low-cost products, which they as consumers then buy at a price high enough to give corporations more profits and power. With an ethic based on materialistic success, the worker-consumer thus lives a "schizophrenic" life, working under repressive regimentation, then seeking satisfaction in pricey pleasures. In the name of growth and progress, this corporate state depersonalizes life, marginalizes spirituality, and ruins environments to extract natural resources.

Reich found among youth alienated from this

materialism a superior Consciousness III, which rejects subordinating self to system and places a higher value on individual freedom, self-direction, the pursuit of happiness through free forms of intellectual and sexual expression, the enjoyment of music and art, and contemplation, sometimes facilitated by drugs.

Impact   Charles Reich believed that Consciousness III would produce a new kind of revolution, based not on violent uprisings but on empowering people to adopt unconventional lifestyles. As he explained, the era's fascination with free love, drugs, and rock music led to a broad transformation of political and social sensibilities, most notably in developments such as no-fault divorce, the antiwar movement, clemency for draft dodgers, the rise of consumerism and the environmental movement, and the augmented role of entertainment in American life. Reich's kind of people power influenced world politics during the 1970's and in ensuing decades.

Further Reading

Braunstein, Peter, and Michael William Doyle, eds. *Imagine Nation: The American Counterculture of the 1960's and '70's.* New York: Routledge, 2001.

Nobile, Philip, ed. *The Con III Controversy: The Critics Look at "The Greening of America."* New York: Pocket Books, 1971.

Reich, Charles A. *The Sorcerer of Bolinas Reef.* New York: Random House, 1976.

John L. McLean

See also   Antiwar demonstrations; Clemency for Vietnam draft evaders and deserters; Drug use; Earth art movement; Earth Day; Environmental movement; Hard rock and heavy metal; Hippies; Marriage and divorce; "Me Decade"; Music; Open marriage; Sexual revolution; Swingers.

■ Greenpeace

Identification   International pro-ecology environmental organization

Date   Began in 1971

Greenpeace emerged in the 1970's as a leading organization in North America and Europe in an increasingly global movement to protect the environment and be sensitive to the needs of species beyond humankind. It was particularly notable for its media-grabbing demonstrations of di- *rect action and its use of nonviolent tactics to raise public consciousness and effect positive change.*

Greenpeace originated in 1971 after Sierra Club activists Jim Bohlen, Paul Cote, and Irving Stowe formed the Don't Make a Wave Committee in Vancouver, British Columbia, to rally against a nuclear test that the U.S. government planned to hold in the Aleutian Islands. The committee decided to take its antinuclear demonstration to a new level by defying U.S. authorities in chartering a vessel and sailing it directly into the vicinity of the planned blast to draw attention to its disapproval and to stop the bomb test. That vessel, the *Phyllis Cormack*, was rechristened *Greenpeace*, and the committee became the Greenpeace Foundation. The crew of twelve Canadians brought along for inspiration a book of Native American legends titled *Warriors of the Rainbow: Strange and Prophetic Dreams* (1962) and sailed out on their mission. Their strategy failed, they returned to port, and the test proceeded. However, this provocative approach won support across Canada, garnered more attention in the United States, and ultimately prompted the U.S. Atomic Energy Commission, under public pressure, to announce an end to all nuclear testing in the Aleutian Islands. Greenpeace had won its first victory.

Going Global, New Focus   Quaker activism, Sierra Club conservation concerns, and the hippie counterculture as it evolved in Vancouver proved to be direct influences on the emergence of Greenpeace in Canada. In 1972, the group convinced Canadian David McTaggart, then living in New Zealand, to sail the *Vega* to international waters close to the little atoll of Moruroa in the South Pacific in order to disrupt a nuclear test planned by the French government. In international waters, French commandos intervened, boarded the *Vega*, seized McTaggart, and beat him severely. Again the nuclear test took place, but the subsequent media attention over photographs depicting the attack on McTaggart forced France to bow to international pressures and to announce in 1974 that any future French nuclear testing would take place underground.

In 1974, Greenpeace experienced the death of influential founding member Stowe, who had been committed to an antinuclear focus for the group, and a faction eager to save whales from commercial killing gained ascendancy. The new strategy called for activists to find whaling fleets, then place them-

Greenpeace uses an inflatable whale as a part of a 1979 protest march. (Hulton Archive/Getty Images)

selves in inflatable dinghies between hunters and the sea mammals. On April 27, 1975, the *Phyllis Cormack* and *Vega* set sail from Vancouver to disrupt the Russian whaling fleet off the coast of California. Film documentarian Fred Easton joined the crew for this venture, and international wire services carried exciting close-up images of successful disruptions of the whaling hunts captured by photographer Rex Weyler. As a result of this excursion, Greenpeace gained free publicity, and more supporters began calling for limitations or bans on international whaling. A second antiwhaling campaign by Greenpeace the next year claimed to save one hundred whales by direct action and at least thirteen hundred more by keeping whalers from their regular hunting grounds.

In 1976, Greenpeace expanded its efforts by taking direct action to save seal pups from Norwegian sealers harvesting the animals in Newfoundland. By then, active membership in the organization had risen to eight thousand, and the photogenic cuteness of the seal pups juxtaposed with photographs of their clubbing deaths alarmed animal lovers

throughout the world. In 1977, French actor Brigitte Bardot joined the Greenpeace demonstrators in trying to block such clubbings through direct action, and the international publicity not only successfully decreased the number of seals taken that year but also made the direct action an annual event for the organization.

On April 29, 1978, the Greenpeace vessel *Rainbow Warrior,* a converted 145-foot trawler, sailed out of London to obstruct the paths of North Atlantic whaling fleets. The vessel later also tailed a British vessel trying to dump radioactive waste in international waters, and its crew was arrested several times for civil disobedience. In June, 1979, Greenpeace skydivers, calling themselves the Splat Squad successfully parachuted into the largest nuclear power plant site in the world in Ontario, Canada, while dozens of fellow demonstrators below simultaneously vaulted its fences. The antinuclear focus that created the group was still present at the decade's end, but the organization had moved into several animal rights and deep ecology areas as well.

Acclaim had come to Greenpeace faster than organizational skills, and as the 1970's drew to a close, serious and sometimes legal tensions developed between Vancouver-based leaders and Greenpeace advocates in San Francisco, Ontario, and Europe. Luckily for the group, the original skipper of the *Vega*, McTaggart, devised a new structure to be called Greenpeace International, based in the Netherlands. Under this plan, national groups would maintain considerable autonomy and develop their own major campaigns, but major solidarity decisions would be made by the international council that encompassed representatives from a mix of the participating nations: Canada, Great Britain, the Netherlands, Australia, New Zealand, France, and the United States.

Impact   Greenpeace was founded in the same year that the first Earth Day celebration was held and was part of a growing concern for environmental awareness throughout North America during the 1970's. What made Greenpeace distinct among the range of environmental organizations and groups that arose during this time period was its success in capturing media attention through its strategies of direct action and civil disobedience, strategies that it appropriated from Quaker activism and the Civil Rights movement.

Further Reading

Brown, Michael, and John May. *The Greenpeace Story.* New York: Dorling Kindersley, 1991. Twentieth anniversary retrospective history of the organization as told by insiders.

Hunter, Robert. *Warriors of the Rainbow: A Chronicle of the Greenpeace Movement.* New York: Henry Holt, 1979. A memoir from a Vancouver journalist who participated in the formation and subsequent growth of the group.

Weyler, Rex. *Greenpeace: How a Group of Ecologists, Journalists, and Visionaries Changed the World.* Emmaus, Pa.: Rodale, 2004. Emphasizes the philosophy and practice of direct action, elucidating influences and repercussions.

Scot M. Guenter

See also   Antinuclear movement; Canada and the United States; Earth Day; Endangered Species Act of 1973; Environmental movement; Environmental Protection Agency (EPA); Europe and North America; Hippies.

H

■ Hairstyles

Definition   Styles or manners of arranging the hair

Hairstyles in the 1970's often reflected American society's preference for natural and organic styles and products. Men and women of all races also cut, straightened, or let their hair grow into certain styles as public indications of their political and social philosophies.

Straight, long, center-parted hair was the ideal for white women for most of the decade. To straighten their hair, some women rolled it on empty soup or orange juice cans or ironed it. The women's liberation movement encouraged women to rid themselves of feminine symbols such as makeup, hair bands, long hair, and other "oppressive" emblems of beauty. Further, while many women adopted the natural look, which translated into less time cutting, styling, and setting hair, others made radical changes by wearing very short, layered hair. The first trend of the decade, the shag cut, emerged in 1971 when Jane Fonda sported the short, layered-toward-the-face style in the film *Klute.*

Men's hairstyles varied as much as those of women during this period: long, Afro, and shaggy. By the 1970's, very short hair on men was nearly impossible to find. White men abandoned the crew cut and grew their hair long. As men's hair grew longer, it needed more care than barbers could offer. Statistics indicate that between 1972 and 1982, barber shops declined by 28 percent. Men instead flocked to beauty shops, where hairdressers could care properly for their more elaborate hair. Once inside the beauty salon, long-haired male customers were also open to perms, coloring, and other styling advances.

Controversy over the length of men's hair was significant, and the issue played out in schools, courtrooms, and at sporting events. Anger from conservatives and the older generation was aimed at long-haired men or anyone who failed to conform to the traditional standards of male identity. To those from older generations, long hair worn by men was a sign of the things that had gone wrong in the country. Those opposed to long hair for men argued that the style made it difficult to tell men and women apart.

Several organizations, such as the Federal Bureau of Investigation (FBI) and police departments, preserved strict guidelines for men's hairstyles. The civilian workplace was another arena for conflict about hairstyles. Employers were concerned that hairstyles would offend their customers and other employees or blemish the company's professional image. Extreme hairstyles such as Afros, cornrows, and dreadlocks were discouraged or prohibited.

Racial Identity   Many African American women rebelled against straightening combs, which they felt upheld oppressive white standards that equated beauty with straightened hair. African American women also tended to abandon chemical processes and celebrated texture by letting their hair grow into Afros, or naturals. Prior to the 1970's, they pulled their hair back into "puffs" or kept it braided close to the scalp in cornrows. Some African American women felt that they were rejected or accepted by social groups depending upon how they wore their hair. Straightened hair indicated a refusal to identify with African heritage. In fact, this issue transcended race and sex, as white men and women, as well as African Americans, were defined by their choice of hairstyle.

African American men and women celebrated their heritage by adopting the Afro. As a popular style that often transcended race, the Afro signified black nationalism, and some prominent wearers of the hairstyle, such as Angela Davis, were noted for their militancy and disdain for authority and conservative politics. To achieve the Afro, the hair was picked, raked, and fluffed into the form and then oiled or sprayed to hold its shape. Some white women, such as Barbra Streisand, also experimented with adding texture similar to Afros to their own hair when the crimping iron was created in

1972. Beauty schools and women's magazines incorporated black hairstyling techniques and products in their repertoire.

African Americans were concerned with preserving their freedom of expression via the Afro or cornrows. However, the styles soon crossed racial barriers and were adopted by white Americans. The media focused on ethnic styles, and mainstream beauty manufacturers sought to capture the growing ethnic market, which previously was served by ethnic manufacturers. Even wigs started crossing racial lines: White women donned Afro-like wigs, and African American women wore blonde wigs. Another ethnic crossover occurred in 1979. Bo Derek popularized cornrows for white women when her character wore them in the film *10.*

Stories appeared in *Time, Life,* and *Newsweek* when African American soldiers who refused to cut their Afros went on trial. The military's opposition to the Afro was twofold. First, wearing military headgear atop the Afro was sometimes impossible or appeared comical. Second, military barbers were unskilled in African American hair care. The military eventually sent barbers to complete a special Afro styling course at the San Diego Naval Station and allowed African American soldiers to maintain their Afros.

Unisex Styles   After men entered the beauty shop, the trend of nationwide unisex salons transpired. Unisex hairstyles were popular especially for women who worked outside the home and did not have time to style elaborate hairstyles like those that had characterized the preceding decades. Women grew weary of the time, money, and rituals associated with a trip to the beauty shop. Traditional men's haircuts at the barber shop cost less than women's styles and took about ten minutes to execute. Women and men sought inexpensive generic cuts at unisex salons, and the "wash and wear" styles offered by Vidal Sassoon and other stylists liberated them from the constant maintenance of their hair. Prior to Sassoon's innovative cuts that required only monthly upkeep, women visited the beauty shop weekly. His trademark short haircuts became iconic of the decade and were considered classics. Women's lives changed, and his approach to cutting and styling reflected their time needs.

Celebrities and Popular Culture   Many hairstyle trends in the 1970's originated from popular culture. In 1976, two hairstyles synonymous with the de-

cade captured the nation's attention. Sassoon's ideal of freedom of movement for hair was best illustrated by Olympic athlete Dorothy Hamill, whose wedge haircut was inspired by a 1974 style of Sassoon's. The wedge was a bob underpinned by steeply graduated layers. The top layers were brushed back into the nape, thus forming a wedge. Allen Edwards cut *Charlie's Angels* star Farrah Fawcett-Majors's famous feathery shag the same year. Layered around the face, the hair was feathered with a comb and sprayed into shape. Feathering had unisex appeal, and the style was easily adapted to short layered hair. Furthermore, men used products and sprays and often carried a comb in their back pocket to diligently maintain the delicate style that John Travolta popularized in the film *Saturday Night Fever* (1977).

Rock star David Bowie's ambiguous sexuality and hairstyle symbolized the unisex trend, and the mullet he modeled as his alternate persona, Ziggy Stardust, in 1972 started a fad for men and women that incorporated short hair in the front and long hair in the back, a style eventually popular with sports figures.

As early as 1974, spikes and mohawks appeared on the London punk scene, and punk styles emerged in the United States by the end of the decade. Punk hairstyles were bleached and styled into spiky points. Punks demonstrated their youthful ideals in their confrontational and unnaturally colored hairstyles. For some youth, natural products were swept aside by 1976 when punk styles emerged. Hair was stripped of its pigment and colored brilliant hues of green, red, or magenta. While punk trends were not adopted by everyone, elements of the style were incorporated into the mainstream. Punk rockers shaved their heads into mohawks and experimented by applying multiple colors to the ends and roots of their hair. Singer Debbie Harry's two-tone hair color and hard-core glamour set the standard for progressive women. The shaping of spikes was achieved by using glue and later by colored gelatin.

Manufacturers responded to punk innovation by developing gels and other hair products that molded and held hair into extreme shapes. Throughout the decade, manufacturers responded to cultural trends by expanding their products. By the late 1970's, styles moved away from straight to curly, and the perm emerged as a popular choice for white men and women. In fact, the root perm was essential for achieving punk-inspired styles.

Impact Hairstyles during the 1970's encouraged ethnic diversity and self-acceptance. Early in the decade, the focus on natural styling and natural products echoed the nation's ecological concerns. Later, Americans became more experimental and looked to celebrities and pop culture for inspiration.

Further Reading

Braunstein, Peter. *Imagine Nation: The American Counterculture of the 1960's and 1970's.* New York: Routledge, 2001. Racial identity and the hippie culture are just two of the broad themes covered in this book, both of which proved important in influencing hairstyles.

Fishman, Diane, and Marcia Powell. *Vidal Sassoon: Fifty Years Ahead.* New York: Rizzoli International, 1993. Serves as a biography of sorts for Vassoon, discussing his innovative hairstyling techniques and the influence of the punk movement, among other topics.

Waldrep, Sheldon, ed. *Seventies: Age of Glitter in Popular Culture.* New York: Routledge, 2000. Among other topics, this book covers pop music, blax-ploitation films, and American vogue during the decade, all of which influenced hairstyles.

Willett, Julie A. *Permanent Waves: The Making of the American Beauty Shop.* New York: New York University Press, 2000. Examines the hairstyling industry during the twentieth century.

Rebecca Tolley-Stokes

See also African Americans; Afros; Bowie, David; *Charlie's Angels*; Davis, Angela; Fads; Fashions and clothing; Fonda, Jane; Hamill, Dorothy; Punk rock; *Saturday Night Fever*, *10*; Travolta, John.

■ Haldeman, H. R.

Identification Chief of White House staff under Richard M. Nixon

Born October 27, 1926; Los Angeles, California

Died November 12, 1993; Santa Barbara, California

As Nixon's chief of staff and top political adviser, Haldeman actively participated in the Watergate cover-up. He was forced to resign in 1973 and later went to prison.

H. R. Haldeman leaves after testifying in front of the Senate Watergate Committee in June, 1973. (Dennis Brack/Landov)

Harold Robbins "Bob" Haldeman, an advertising agency executive, was an early political supporter of President Richard M. Nixon. He worked on Nixon's behalf in five political campaigns, first as an advance man and ultimately as campaign chief of staff in Nixon's successful race for the presidency in 1968. Shortly after election day, Nixon selected Haldeman to be his chief of staff in the White House.

By 1970, under Haldeman's direction, the administrative structure of the White House staff had assumed the pattern that it was to follow for the remainder of Nixon's presidency. As chief of staff, Haldeman directed a small staff of his own, substantially controlled the president's scheduling for trips and appointments, and met almost daily with the president's chief policy advisers—John Ehrlichman on domestic policy and Henry Kissinger on foreign policy. As decisions were made, Haldeman attempted to coordinate them with the federal bureaucracy in the departments outside the White House.

Soon after the Watergate burglary occurred in 1972, Haldeman was drawn into the cover-up. In part, this was because Nixon himself had compartmented access to information about the burglary and its genesis. The basic scheme of the cover-up was to buy silence from the burglars by funneling campaign funds to them while simultaneously trying to divert the Federal Bureau of Investigation (FBI) from from the matter: The administration used the Central Intelligence Agency (CIA) to claim that an FBI investigation would disclose foreign intelligence secrets. By concealing his role in these plans, Haldeman obstructed justice, and he, Ehrlichman, and White House counsel John Dean, the architect of the cover-up, were forced to resign from their positions in 1973. Haldeman was later convicted of conspiracy and perjury for his testimony to the Watergate investigating committee and served an eighteen-month prison term.

Impact   Haldeman's resignation crippled the Nixon administration: Nixon was forced to endure the remainder of the Watergate struggle with a less coordinated staff unfamiliar with the details of Watergate and the cover-up. However, the organizational structure for the White House staff that emerged during Haldeman's tenure became the starting point for subsequent presidents, although few chiefs of staff have wielded as much power as Haldeman did. Furthermore, Haldeman's fate in the Watergate affair served as a warning to later administrations that the people who occupy the position of chief of staff have to be selected for their familiarity with the usual legal and political constraints that operate in American government.

Further Reading

Haldeman, H. R. *The Ends of Power.* New York: Times Books, 1978.

Safire, William. *Before the Fall: An Inside View of the Pre-Watergate White House.* Garden City, N.Y.: Doubleday, 1975.

White, Theodore H. *Breach of Faith: The Fall of Richard Nixon.* New York: Atheneum, 1975.

Robert Jacobs

See also   Agnew, Spiro T.; Dean, John; Ehrlichman, John; Enemies List; Ervin, Sam; Houston Plan; Mitchell, John; Nixon, Richard M.; Nixon tapes; Scandals; Watergate.

■ Hamill, Dorothy

Identification   American figure skater
Born   July 26, 1956; Chicago, Illinois

Hamill won the gold medal in ladies' figure skating at the 1976 Winter Olympics; she was as famous for her sleek wedge hairstyle as for her athletic ability.

In 1970, fourteen-year-old Dorothy Hamill won the silver medal at the U.S. Junior Figure Skating Championships, where she introduced a unique skating maneuver that she had developed with the help of her coach, Gustave Lussi. The new move, a combination of a flying camel and a sit-spin, became known as the "Hamill camel."

In 1971, Hamill qualified as a senior-level skater. Working with new coach Carlo Fassi, Hamill came in third at the Eastern Sectional Figure Skating Championships, then fifth at the U.S. National Figure Skating Championships (also known as Nationals). In 1972, Hamill placed fourth in Nationals, too low to qualify for the U.S. Olympic team. However, after the Olympics, American bronze medalist Janet Lynn withdrew from the team, and Hamill's fourth-place win at Nationals qualified her to take Lynn's place at the World Figure Skating Championships (also known as World's). Hamill placed seventh at World's but first in two other competitions the same year, winning the International Grand Prix and the Nebelhorn Trophy.

In 1973, Hamill placed fourth at World's and won the Richmond International Trophy; she won silver medals at World's in 1974 and 1975. After placing second in Nationals in 1973, Hamill was Senior Ladies' National Champion three years running from 1974 through 1976.

At the 1976 Winter Olympics in Innsbruck, Austria, nineteen-year-old Hamill won the gold medal in ladies' figure skating. Hamill's friends, family, and coaches believed that her Olympic victory was the ultimate accomplishment for a figure skater and that there was no need for Hamill to skate in World's only a month later. However, Hamill insisted on competing and won her first World Figure Skating Championship.

Hamill's gold medal at World's was the first in eight years for an American woman. At the time, she was one of only four American women figure skaters to have won gold medals at Nationals, World's, and the Olympics. Although Hamill was able to perform triple jumps, she never attempted triples in competition; she was the last woman to win an Olympic gold medal in figure skating without landing any triple jumps.

Later in 1976, Hamill left amateur competition. For the next several years, she was a star attraction in the Ice Capades, a touring professional skating show.

Impact After her Olympic win, Hamill's youthful, girl-next-door image made her a popular media personality. She was featured in several television specials and appeared in advertisements for products including Clairol's Short and Sassy hair conditioner. Many American women copied Hamill's smooth wedge hairstyle, which had been designed for her especially to stay in place while she skated.

Further Reading

Dolan, Edward F., Jr., and Richard B. Lyttle. *Dorothy Hamill, Olympic Skating Champion.* New York: Doubleday, 1979.

Hamill, Dorothy, with Elva Clairmont. *Dorothy Hamill*

Dorothy Hamill displays her gold medal in figure skating from the 1976 Winter Olympics. (AP/Wide World Photos)

On and Off the Ice. New York: Alfred A. Knopf, 1983.

Van Steenwyk, Elizabeth. *Dorothy Hamill, Olympic Champion.* New York: Harvey House, 1976.

Maureen Puffer-Rothenberg

See also Fads; Hairstyles; Olympic Games of 1976; Sports.

■ *Happy Days*

Identification Television situation comedy
Producer Garry Marshall (1934-   )
Date Aired from 1974 to 1984

In the aftermath of the disastrous Vietnam War and its ensuing psychological and economic ramifications, a wave of nostalgia for the "simpler" times of the Eisenhower era swept the country. Capitalizing on the success of the 1950's-themed Broadway musical Grease *(1972) and the film* American Graffiti *(1973),* Happy Days *became the first television series to address this growing preoccupation with 1950's nostalgia.*

Set in 1950's Milwaukee, Wisconsin, *Happy Days* began as the story of a suburban middle-class family, the Cunninghams—father Howard (played by Tom Bosley), mother Marion (Marion Ross), son Richie (Ron Howard), and daughter Joanie (Erin Moran).

The early episodes centered on the adolescent misadventures of shy, naïve Richie and his two friends, worldly Potsie Webber (Anson Williams) and jokester Ralph Malph (Donny Most)—all students at Jefferson High School and frequenters of Arnold's Drive-in, a local malt shop.

To differentiate the show from its stereotypical family-oriented counterparts, producers added a motorcycle-riding high-school dropout—the streetwise but benevolent Arthur Fonzarelli (Henry Winkler), affectionately known as "Fonzie" or "the Fonz." At first, Fonzie played a minor role, but as his popularity grew among the youthful baby-boomer audience, the series began to focus on his character. A hood with a code of ethics, Fonzie had the ability to make grown men cower, to activate a jukebox with a pound of his fist, and to captivate female admirers with the snap of his fingers, but he could also don eyeglasses unabashedly and carry a library card with pride. His pseudo-delinquent style made him a rather unorthodox role model for youthful viewers. With Winkler's expanded role as Fonzie, success grew for *Happy Days* until, in 1976, it was ranked number one in the Nielson ratings and continued to be one of the most popular television programs throughout the late 1970's.

Impact   Over the decades, many actors had become superstars via television, but few series had ever revised story lines or altered cast billing to exploit the popularity of a supporting actor as was done with Henry Winkler. Fonzie's trademark thumbs-up gesture, as well as his signature expressions, including "aayyy," "whoa," and "sit on it," made their way into the vernacular and psyche of the 1970's boomer generation. Fonzie mania, which inundated Winkler with crazed fans, marriage proposals, and a plethora of products sporting his likeness, is best exemplified by the inclusion of the Fonz's leather jacket in the Smithsonian Museum of American History, a testament to his cult-figure status and to the role of *Happy Days* in 1970's pop culture. Nostalgia generated by *Happy Days* also spawned several spin-off series, including the highly rated *Laverne and Shirley* and *Mork and Mindy*, which helped extend its legacy as a television icon among later generations.

Further Reading

Brooks, Tim, and Earle Marsh. *The Complete Directory to Prime Time Network and Cable TV Shows, 1946-Present.* 7th ed. New York: Ballantine Books, 1999.

Marc, David. *Comic Visions: Television Comedy and American Culture.* 2d ed. Malden, Mass.: Blackwell, 1997.

Papazian, Ed. *Medium Rare: The Evolution, Workings, and Impact of Commercial Television.* New York: Media Dynamics, 1991.

Karen L. Gennari

See also   *All in the Family*; *American Graffiti*; *Brady Bunch, The*; Fads; *Grease*; *Jeffersons, The*; *Partridge Family, The*; *Sanford and Son*; Sitcoms; Television in the United States.

■ Hard Hat Riot of 1970

The Event   Violence erupts in New York City's financial district when helmeted construction workers attacked anti-Vietnam War protesters

Date   May 8, 1970

Along with highlighting the class divisions in Americans' attitudes toward the Vietnam War, the riot also called into question police coverage in New York City and the role of unions in encouraging construction workers to participate.

Campus unrest and antiwar sentiment was on the increase during the summer of 1970. News had recently surfaced about President Richard M. Nixon's secret bombing campaign in Cambodia, and on May 4, four student deaths at the hands of the National Guard at Kent State University made headlines. In memoriam for the Kent State students, administrators at New York's City Hall had lowered the American flag to half staff. Peaceful demonstrators amassed the morning of May 8 in the streets outside the New York Stock Exchange urging a withdrawal of troops from Vietnam. However, at noon, an estimated two hundred construction workers suddenly stormed the scene and attacked them. The construction workers continued their rampage and forced their way into City Hall, demanding that the flag be raised to full staff. By the time the ensuing melee was halted by police, seventy people had been injured.

Criticisms arose regarding the police and their inability to control the situation. Witnesses to the event contended that the police did little or nothing to stop the violence, and Mayor John Lindsay requested an investigation of the police's failure to handle the situation. A later report stated that police forces were spread too thin throughout the city and that there was a lack in communication to effectively

Construction workers in New York City march in 1970 in support of the Vietnam War one week after antiwar demonstrators were attacked in what became known as the Hard Hat Riot. (AP/Wide World Photos)

quell the mob. However, the Knapp Commission, formed by Lindsay to delve into police corruption in June, 1970, asserted that clashes between protesters and workers had taken place earlier in the same vicinity. *The New York Times* and police had also received phone calls warning them that such fighting would escalate in the days prior to the attack. Despite claims from union leaders that workers acted on their own accord, speculation also began that union organizers may have provoked the riot by offering cash bonuses to those who participated in it.

Impact Media coverage of the event reinforced perceptions of social class distinctions in attitudes toward America's involvement in the war. The incident was used by the press to illustrate that such conflicts were dividing Americans. Blue-collar workers became viewed as political "hawks" who were supportive of Nixon's Vietnam policies. Moreover, the anger and violence inflicted upon the protesters by construction workers reflected a deep resentment among lower classes throughout the country that their sons were being sent to Vietnam while student protesters from the middle- to upper-income strata received deferments.

Further Reading

Foner, Philip S. *U.S. Labor and the Vietnam War.* New York: International, 1989.

Freeman, Joshua B. "Hardhats: Construction Workers, Manliness, and the 1970 Pro-War Demonstrations." *Journal of Social History* 26 (Summer, 1993): 725-744.

Levy, Peter B. *The New Left and Labor.* Chicago: University of Illinois Press, 1994.

Gayla Koerting

See also Antiwar demonstrations; Kent State massacre; Vietnam War.

■ Hard rock and heavy metal

Definition   Heavily amplified rock-and-roll genre based loosely on the blues

Until the arrival of disco music in the mid-1970's, hard rock and heavy metal were the decade's most popular rock styles and the ones most responsible for turning rock concerts into high-tech, large-scale forms of mass catharsis.

Hard rock and heavy metal are forms of rock-and-roll music characterized by distorted electric guitars, pounding drums, and strident vocals. Few groups of the 1970's were exclusively hard rock or heavy metal, but many used these forms some of the time. For example, such pop and soft-rock luminaries as Elton John, Neil Young, Paul McCartney, and the Eagles recorded songs characterized by bursts of mad guitar and frenzied drumming. Similarly, performers such as David Bowie, Lou Reed, and Iggy Pop, generally classified as art rock or punk rock musicians, each recorded several albums or songs emblematic of the hard-rock ethos. Conversely, hard rockers such as Led Zeppelin, KISS, Alice Cooper, and Boston released songs in slower, gentler styles as well.

Sex and Drugs   Although Jimi Hendrix, the musician generally regarded as the greatest electric guitarist of all time, is usually associated with the 1960's, three of the seven albums that he authorized during his lifetime were released in 1970 or 1971, thus guaranteeing that, along with Led Zeppelin, he would have the greatest influence in the decade's first half. Rooted in the blues, Hendrix and Led Zeppelin represented not only hard rock's cultural dichotomy—Hendrix was a black American, the members of Led Zeppelin were white Englishmen—but also the degree to which drugs, sex, and the grimness resulting from an obsession with both would become inextricable from the music. Indeed, it became commonplace to refer to the guitar as a phallic symbol, even during those rare instances when it was wielded by a woman—for example, Heart's Nancy Wilson. As for drugs, their effect was twofold: They enabled the musicians to lose themselves in their music more easily, thus facilitating the creation of longer and more loosely structured compositions such as Led Zeppelin's "Stairway to Heaven," and they enabled music fans to go along more willingly for the ride.

Despite the popularity of at least two hard-rock, drug-abjuring teetotalers—Randy Bachman of the Guess Who and Bachman-Turner Overdrive and Ted Nugent—the music's landscape was dominated by an increasingly overt fascination with heightened sensual stimulation. The androgynous "glam" or "glitter rock" acts that emerged in the early to mid-1970's, such as Sweet and Slade in Great Britain and Alice Cooper and KISS in the United States, while generally less serious in their exaltation of dissolute living, added an element of calculated outrageousness that ultimately only underscored hard rock's appeal to its audience's baser instincts. The heavily drug-influenced apocalyptic necromancy of Black Sabbath, while never a force on the singles chart, remained steadfastly popular despite mainstream trends.

Blurred Distinctions   The difficulty of defining the precise moment at which hard rock gave birth to heavy metal (or vice versa) has led to the terms often being used interchangeably. The distinctions that did develop were largely cultural. Acts identified closely with the United States, such as Aerosmith, Lynyrd Skynyrd, Grand Funk, and Cheap Trick, tended to receive the "hard rock" label, whereas their stylistically similar non-American counter-

Notable Hard Rock and Heavy Metal Songs of the 1970's

Song	Artist
"Dream On"	Aerosmith
"Runnin' with the Devil"	Van Halen
"School's Out"	Alice Cooper
"Iron Man"	Black Sabbath
"Rock and Roll All Night"	KISS
"Cat Scratch Fever"	Ted Nugent
"Smoke on the Water"	Deep Purple
"Exciter"	Judas Priest
"Stairway to Heaven"	Led Zeppelin
"Highway to Hell"	AC/DC
"Magic Man"	Heart
"(Don't Fear) The Reaper"	Blue Oyster Cult

parts, such as Deep Purple or AC/DC, tended to be labeled "heavy metal."

However, even these categories proved fluid, as the American group Van Halen, due in large part to its Led Zeppelin-like configuration, was initially considered more "heavy" than "hard," while British bands such as Foghat and Bad Company, primarily because of the good-time "boogie" element of their music, were considered more "hard" than "heavy." Confounding the situation even more were groups that emerged in the late 1970's such as Foreigner and Heart, the nationality of whose members was mixed, and the power-trio Rush, which was Canadian. With the arrival in the summers of 1977 and 1978 of the "hard-rock Woodstock" known as the California Jam, the importance of categories appeared to disappear altogether, when acts as tenuously connected as Nugent, Aerosmith, and Heart shared the bill with the likes of Santana, Dave Mason, and Bob Welch, none of whom had ever been, or would ever be, considered heavy metal or hard rock.

Impact The greatest effect of the 1970's hard-rock and heavy metal pioneers was their establishment of the electric guitar as the ultimate totem of rock expression. Despite competition from genres that deemphasized the guitar, such as disco and rap, guitar-heavy rock persisted, in permutation after permutation, as the music of choice for listeners reared on the belief that power chords and flashy solos represent the height of emotional release.

Further Reading

Bangs, Lester. *Psychotic Reactions and Carburetor Dung.* New York: Anchor Books, 1988. A posthumous collection of seminal rock criticism.

Christgau, Robert. *Rock Albums of the '70's: A Critical Guide.* New York: Da Capo Press, 1990. Along with presenting reviews of music from all genres, Christgau insightfully and tersely analyzes the cultural or aesthetic significance of many hard-rock and heavy metal recordings.

Eddy, Chuck. *Stairway to Hell: The Five Hundred Best Heavy Metal Albums in the Universe.* New York: Da Capo Press, 1998. An opinionated guide to seminal heavy metal albums that focuses especially on the 1970's.

Marsh, Dave. *The Heart of Rock and Soul: The 1001 Greatest Singles Ever Made.* New York: Da Capo Press, 1999. A self-professed lover of rhythm and blues and rock's pre-metal days, Marsh nevertheless appreciates and discusses many hard-rock artists.

Strong, M. C. *The Great Metal Discography.* 2d ed. Edinburgh, Scotland: Mojo, 2002. Provides complete discographies for many heavy metal bands and claims to list "every track recorded by more than 1,200 groups."

Arsenio Orteza

See also Aerosmith; Cooper, Alice; Drug use; Heart; KISS; Led Zeppelin; Music; Progressive rock; Punk rock; Queen; Ramones, The; Rush; Van Halen; Who, The.

■ Harold and Maude

Identification Motion picture
Director Hal Ashby (1929-1988)
Date Released in 1971

This dark comedy and social satire exploring antiestablishment themes became an instant cult classic by commenting on the stifling conformity of materialist culture in modern society.

In *Harold and Maude*, Harold (played by Bud Cort) is a depressed teenager alienated from his mother's rich, materialistic, and intellectually shallow world. He stages suicide attempts at their opulent mansion to try to get her attention, but the gestures never work. She ignores him, buys him expensive cars, and sets him up with women from a dating service. She decides that the solution to his problems is for him to join the military and sends him to visit his uncle, who is an army colonel with only one arm. Their meeting becomes a commentary on the absurdity of war and represents a protest against the conflict in Vietnam.

Harold attends funerals of people whom he does not know, and at one of them, he meets Maude (Ruth Gordon), a full-of-life free spirit who is about to turn eighty. Maude and Harold become friends, and she shows him how life is meant to be embraced fully and to be lived on one's own terms. The film intersperses scenes of Harold and Maude together in beautiful settings with scenes of Harold at home, where he continues to stage suicides.

Harold falls in love with Maude, and they become lovers. He comes to understand the wonders that life can hold, but thinks meaning and beauty come only from being with Maude. When she ends her own life on her eightieth birthday, Harold is devastated and drives off a cliff. For a moment, it seems that he is also dead, but then the camera pans to the top of the cliff and Harold is seen playing a banjo and dancing through a field. He has embraced life on his own.

Colin Higgins's screenplay of the film originally was written to be thirty minutes long and intended to be his master's thesis at the University of California at Los Angeles (UCLA), but he expanded it to a full-length script and sold it to Paramount executives. Paramount chose Hal Ashby as the film's director because they felt Higgins did not have the experience to direct a feature film. Shot in thirteen weeks and entirely on location in the San Francisco Bay area, *Harold and Maude* opened to mixed reviews in 1971.

Impact   *Harold and Maude* represented something around which people alienated from a society based on materialist values could rally. Among some people who had seen the film, there was an instant bonding, an acknowledgment of common values, and a connection to something vital. *Harold and Maude* offered hope during a time of turmoil and confusion in American society.

Further Reading

Elsaesser, Thomas, and Noel King, eds. *The Last Great American Picture Show: New Hollywood Cinema in the 1970's*. Amsterdam: Amsterdam University Press, 2004.

Higgins, Colin. *Harold and Maude*. Philadelphia: Lippincott, 1971.

Sigoloff, Marc. *Films of the Seventies: A Filmography of American, British, and Canadian Films, 1970-1979*. Jefferson, N.C.: McFarland, 2000.

Jerry Shuttle

See also   Film in the United States; Hippies; *Jonathan Livingston Seagull*; *One Flew over the Cuckoo's Nest*.

■ *Hawaii Five-0*

Identification   Television detective series
Date   Aired from September, 1968, to April, 1980

Hawaii Five-0 combined realistic action with the beauty of the fiftieth American state to become the most successful series of its genre during the 1970's.

Filmed almost entirely on location, *Hawaii Five-0* opened Americans' eyes to the tropical paradise of

Jack Lord, the star of the television series Hawaii Five-0. (CBS/ Landov)

the fiftieth state to enter into the Union. The show centered upon an elite investigative team that was a special unit of the state police. Led by hard-nosed Steve McGarrett (played by Jack Lord), the original detective team included Danny Williams (James MacArthur), Chin Ho Kelley (Kam Fong), and Kono Kalakaua (Zulu). Later additions included Ben Kokua (Al Harrington) and Duke Lukela (Herman Wedemeyer). The team worked with local police on cases, though they reported directly to the governor (Richard Denning). McGarrett would line up the work and bark orders to his subordinates.

Cases ranged from individual acts of wrongdoing to organized crime. However, there was a recurring plot revolving around the effort of the "Red Chinese" to infiltrate the Hawaiian islands, which pitted McGarrett against nemesis Wo Fat (Khigh Dhiegh). Though their periodic encounters would always end with Wo Fat escaping justice, McGarrett finally got his man in the last episode of the series.

Several of the issues covered in episodes mirrored those in society during the decade: military service, the drug culture, terrorism, prison overcrowding, environmental challenges, and lack of gun control. Moreover, the show depicted improvements in law enforcement techniques wrought by forensic science and computers.

During its long run on the Columbia Broadcasting System (CBS) network, *Hawaii Five-0* boasted a veritable who's-who list of guests, including Oscar winners Helen Hayes, George Chakiris, Patty Duke, Eileen Heckart, Christopher Walken, and Geraldine Page. The show itself won only two Emmy Awards, both for music score. However, the popularity of the series was evident, as it remained among the top twenty-five in television ratings for eight of its twelve years, climbing as high as number three in its fifth season in 1972-1973.

Impact   During the run of *Hawaii Five-0*, fans loved to repeat the usual last words of McGarrett at the end of each episode: "Book 'em Dano, murder one." The series was also parodied by several comedy shows. An important influence of the show occurred within Hawaii itself, where tourism soared. Perhaps one of the enduring legacies of the show is its use of native Hawaiians in lead roles, which helped change stereotypes of Asian Americans.

Subsequent Events   After *Hawaii Five-0* ended, it was immediately followed by another detective show set in Hawaii, *Magnum P.I.* (1980-1988). Not only did the characters in this series refer to Detective Steve McGarrett and his Five-0 unit from time to time, but the show utilized many of the same production facilities as its predecessor as well. Furthermore, the realism of *Hawaii Five-0* gave impetus to shows such as *Law and Order*, which in the early twenty-first century overtook it as the longest-running crime drama on television. *Hawaii Five-0* continued to be seen in dozens of countries around the world through syndication, increasing its popularity substantially.

Further Reading

Jacobs, Ron. *"Five-0* Forever." *Hawaii Magazine*, February 1993.

Rhodes, Karen. *Booking "Hawaii Five-0": An Episode Guide and Critical History of the 1968-1980 Television Detective Series.* Jefferson, N.C.: McFarland, 1997.

Samuel B. Hoff

See also   Police and detective shows; Television in the United States.

■ Health care in Canada

Definition   The delivery of medical services to the Canadian public

Social democratic reforms in the 1930's laid the foundation for Canada's national health insurance system. Additional reforms first instituted in the 1960's were continued through the 1970's. As a result, Canada offers a government-funded and guaranteed primary health care by physicians and hospitals and supplementary health benefits such as prescription drugs.

The Cooperative Commonwealth Federation (later the New Democratic Party), a social democratic movement and party, led massive reforms in Canada in the 1930's calling for a planned, socialized economy and nationalized welfare programs. Saskatchewan was the first province to adopt a modern welfare system; noting the popularity of that system, the federal government implemented a national health insurance scheme in the 1960's. Similar programs in each of the provinces and territories soon supplemented the federal program.

Waiting times, cost controls, streamlining, and public versus private systems were the major health care issues of the 1970's. Escalating health care costs prompted serious scrutiny by government officials and debates on reform, culminating in the Canada Health Act passed by the Canadian Parliament in 1984. This act improved efficiency with a publicly administered, single-payer system based on the belief that health care is a right, not a privilege, and that access should be guaranteed without regard to personal income and medical history. By the Canadian Constitution, responsibility for health care rests with the provinces, where it is overseen by health ministers and deputy ministers. The systems vary somewhat by province and territory in pay scales and care priorities, but in essence, the same cradle-to-grave philosophy underlies them all.

Persons excluded from coverage include tourists, visitors, transients, and federal prisoners. Patients are permitted to choose their doctors, seek multiple diagnoses, and change doctors at any time. Access to medical care is guaranteed and can be carried from one province or territory to another. Doctors are paid according to a fee-for-service plan, and these fee schedules are normally negotiated between medical associations and provincial governments.

Impact Today, the Canadian health care system consists of ten provincial and three territorial health insurance plans that interlock with one another. In order to ensure comprehensive coverage, the federal, provincial, and territorial governments work collaboratively and federal transfer dollars supplement provincial and territorial revenues. Federal assistance is provided to the provinces through transfer payments, but as social democracy has declined since the 1970's, the share of federal revenue has dwindled steadily from 50 percent to less than 20 percent. The system is financed largely by taxation of personal and corporate income, with far lesser amounts provided by businesses and insurance companies.

In 1988, 95 percent of Canadians polled indicated that they preferred the Canadian health care system over that of the United States.

Further Reading

Bennett, Arnold, and Orvill Adams, eds. *Looking North for Health: What We Can Learn from Canada's Health Care System.* San Francisco: Jossey-Bass, 1993.

Fulton, Jane. *Canada's Health Care System: Bordering on the Possible.* New York: Faulkner and Gray, 1993.

Reinhardt, Uwe E. *National Health Insurance in Australia, Canada, France, West Germany, and the Netherlands: A Synopsis.* Rockville, Md.: National Center for Health Care Research, 1977.

Ann M. Legreid

See also Health care in the United States; Medicine.

■ Health care in the United States

Definition The delivery of medical services to the U.S. public

The 1970's were marked by the transition from a willingness to spend large sums of money for health care to a realization that the U.S. health care system was in financial chaos. By the middle of the decade, the cost of health care was increasing at a much faster rate than that of general inflation.

Medicare, a federal program providing health benefits to the elderly, and Medicaid, a federal-state sharing program providing benefits to the poor, set the stage for the federal government's significant involvement in the health care system during the 1970's. The passage of these two major government-sponsored health initiatives in 1965 would pave the way for the introduction of the concept of "fiscal intermediary," a system by which the government purchases health services for eligible persons and pays for them via a financial agent. Blue Cross of America was selected as the first prime contractor during the early 1970's.

The federal government continued to expand health and health-related programs during the 1970's. In addition to significant increases in the Medicare and Medicaid programs, Congress passed numerous health-related amendments to its Social Security program. Government-sponsored rural health initiatives, such as the Hospital Survey and Construction Act, provided funds to deal with the urban-rural geographic imbalances in the availability of hospital beds. New community mental health centers and neighborhood health centers provided access to health care that would close the gap between the rich and the poor.

The federal government also supported several programs that addressed the shortage of well-trained health professionals. In 1971, the Comprehensive Health Manpower Training Act authorized $2.9 billion for constructing and operating medical schools and to provide loans and scholarships for medical students. The Nurse Training Act authorized more than $855 million to aid schools and students of nursing. Federal funding also supported the expansion of emergency medical systems, including the development of trauma centers in each hospital.

Rising Costs The federal government's desire to make its federal health initiatives work proved financially disastrous as there was little or no attention paid to containing costs. In order to reduce the inequities in health care for the poor and elderly, physicians and hospitals were encouraged to do more and more for their patients' benefit. Fees were paid on a retrospective or after-the-fact basis. By the end of the 1970's, annual spending for health care grew dramatically with no signs of slowing down. In 1965, when Medicare and Medicaid were first introduced, $41.7 billion or 6.0 percent of the gross national product (GNP) was spent on health care. Expenditures for health care in 1976 totaled more than $139 billion. By 1980, health care costs had risen to more than $249 billion, or 9.5 percent of the GNP. By the end of the decade, the calls were no longer for equity in health care delivery but for containing escalating costs.

As health care costs continued to soar, numerous efforts to bring health care spending under control were tried, most of them with little success. Many of these efforts were driven by Congress, whose role to regulate health care was now considered legitimate since it directly provided health care funding via Medicare and Medicaid. From 1973 to 1975, ninety health care bills were introduced into Congress although none went beyond the hearing stage.

After his election in 1976, President Jimmy Carter made several attempts to assert control over rising health care costs, but he met with the same lack of success as his predecessors. During 1977, the Carter administration introduced to Congress an ambitious hospital cost containment proposal designed to temporarily limit both revenues and expenditures of nonfederal hospitals. His plan required more careful regional planning for expensive medical facilities and a closer scrutiny of the payment practices of physicians. Although the legislation was not adopted, largely because of strong opposition from the American Medical Association (AMA), it did initiate a voluntary nationwide program to address spiraling health care costs. Organizations such as the AMA, American Heart Association, Blue Cross & Blue Shield, Federation of American Hospitals, Health Industry Manufacturers Association, and the Health Insurance Association of America began to work together to help address the problems of rising health care costs.

The Rise of Health Maintenance Organizations In an effort to slow the rapid rise in health care costs, new ways of delivering health care services were considered, most noteworthy of which was the emergence of managed health care. Managed health care systems include health maintenance organizations (HMOs), preferred provider organizations, or networks of doctors and hospitals that adhere to given guidelines and fees in return for receiving a certain number of patients. The managed health care system tried to control costs by stipulating set fees for services, restricting payment for tests and surgical procedures, and highlighting preventive care.

The newly formed prepaid group practice that slowly would take the place of the fee-for-visit structure was the health maintenance organization.

Medicare and Medicaid beneficiaries benefited from membership in an HMO as they were viewed as low-cost alternatives to hospitals and private doctors. During the 1970's, Kaiser Permanente and similar health organizations provided health care to larger populations at reasonable costs. Health care services, many of which were part of employee benefits packages, provided comprehensive services, including hospital, surgical, and medical benefits. Throughout the decade, enrollments surged in these managed care plans.

The federal government believed that a nationwide system of prepaid group practice would be cost efficient and would help alleviate the escalating costs of Americans' health care. In 1973, the Nixon administration supported and Congress passed the Health Maintenance Organizations Act designed to increase the number of comprehensive prepaid health care programs. The act, which provided grants to employers who set up HMOs for their employees, spent more than $375 million in federal subsidies for more than five years to prepaid group practices with twenty-five or more employees. Thus, health insurance became a popular fringe benefit for many working Americans.

The increased availability of health insurance coverage and other health benefits created a need for comprehensive data on employee benefits. In 1979, the Bureau of Labor Statistics began the Employee Benefits Survey, which provided information on the incidence and characteristics of employee benefit plans, including health, life, and disability insurance retirement plans and paid leave. The survey included data on the percentage of employees participating in health insurance plans and of participants who have coverage available for selected types of care. According to the survey, in 1979, health insurance was provided by the employer for 97 percent of full-time employees.

Attention to Women's Health Issues The concern for women's health during the 1970's became part of the larger Civil Rights movement. The health movement would urge women to take control of their bodies and health care decisions. Participants in a women's conference held in Boston in 1971 first raised the issue of women and their bodies. The gathering, known as the Boston Women's Health Collective, published a series of articles relating to women's health, which was later turned into the groundbreaking book *Our Bodies, Ourselves* (1973).

Feminist health efforts focused primarily on reproductive issues, such as childbirth, birth control, and abortion rights. As part of their health education efforts, feminists published books and articles, gathered and analyzed information, sponsored workshops, designed and taught courses, and supported consciousness raising groups. The women's liberation movement also influenced women's experiences by providing a political framework for women's relationships with the medical profession. Women were empowered to examine their relationship with their health care providers, particularly their own physicians. The Civil Rights Amendment was also modified to prohibit sex discrimination on the basis of pregnancy for all job-related programs, including health insurance and sick leave. The Pregnancy Discrimination Act was signed into law in 1978.

The dangers of the Dalkon Shield, an intrauterine device (IUD) used for birth control, also caught the attention of the women's health movement. The IUD was a popular form of contraception among women. Manufacturers of IUDs, however, were not required to test their products for safety or effectiveness. In 1976 alone, it was reported that 36 women died and 3,500 were hospitalized because of complications with the device. During the same year, the Food and Drug Administration (FDA) added medical devices to its list of products that must be proven safe and effective before being put on the market.

A major debate concerning abortion rights took center stage during the 1970's. The Supreme Court decision in 1973, *Roe v. Wade*, made abortion legally available during the first two trimesters of pregnancy. Prior to the Supreme Court decision, a number of states had already adopted less restrictive laws indicating a shift in a more permissive direction. At the same time, Congress passed laws to limit federal Medicaid benefits for elective abortions. The court ruling, known as *Maher v. Doe*, found that a state participating in the Medicaid program was not required to pay for nonlife-threatening abortions. In June, 1977, the House of Representatives voted to prohibit the use of federal funds to pay for abortions or to promote or encourage abortions. The Senate voted to bar the use of federal money for abortions except in cases of rape, incest, and medical necessity. Prolife and pro-choice groups formed and continued to debate the abortion issues decades later.

Impact The government's role in health care became increasingly complex during the 1970's. Federal involvement in health care resulted in major changes in the quality and quantity of medical care. The federal government funded hospital construction and the expansion of biomedical research. Its role in subsidizing medical care for the poor and elderly, as well as the development of innovative programs in professional training and delivery of health care, provided greater access to health care. The United States, however, did not develop a health insurance plan that would cover all Americans.

The escalating costs of health care during the 1970's contributed to the gathering sense of crisis that overtook the American health care system. As a result of cost containment strategies and a growing belief by policy analysts that health care must be viewed as a business, the health care landscape was radically altered. By the end of the decade, the health care system in the United States was at a critical juncture in its history.

Further Reading

Callahan, Daniel. "Abortion and Medical Ethics." *Annals of the American Academy of Political and Social Science* 437 (1978): 116-127. A detailed analysis of the medical ethics issues surrounding the abortion issue that emerged during the 1970's.

Cooter, Roger, and Pickstone, John, eds. *Medicine in the Twentieth Century.* Singapore: Harwood Academic, 2000. Covers many issues related to health and medicine in the twentieth century with a particularly strong discussion regarding the U.S. government's role in health care.

Duffin, Jacalyn. *History of Medicine.* Toronto: University of Toronto Press, 1999. A detailed analysis of the major social issues in medicine with particular attention given to women's health issues.

Wagenfeld, M. O., and William Riley. "Health Care in the United States: From Lancets to Lasers—The Evolution of the United States Health Care System. Part I." *Radiology Management*, Summer, 1986, 12-15. Traces the evolution of the U.S. health care system with particular attention given to the role of expanding government during the 1960's and 1970's.

Mary McElroy

See also Abortion rights; Feminism; Health care in Canada; Medicine; *Our Bodies, Ourselves*; Pregnancy Discrimination Act of 1978; *Roe v. Wade.*

■ Hearst, Patty

Identification   American newspaper heir,
   kidnapping victim, and convicted criminal
Born   February 20, 1954; Los Angeles, California

Hearst, a newspaper heir, became famous in the 1970's when she was kidnapped by the Symbionese Liberation Army (SLA) and later, either willingly or unwillingly, joined the group and participated in a bank robbery. For that crime, she served three years in prison.

One of three daughters of newspaper magnate Randolph Hearst and granddaughter of the famous William Randolph Hearst, Patricia (Patty) Hearst led a privileged but largely anonymous life, attending private schools and then the University of California, Berkeley. However, her life changed dramatically on February 4, 1974, when, at the age of nineteen, she was kidnapped from her university apartment.

Hearst had been spending the evening with her fiancé when she was taken by members of the SLA, a small and radical left-wing group that sought the overthrow of the American government. Targeted because of her family's wealth, she was held hostage, and eventually the SLA extorted more than two million dollars from her family without releasing Hearst. It directed some of the money toward the poor of Southern California.

The SLA members kept Hearst blindfolded and locked in a closet in its safe house. They subjected her to physical and psychological torture, and eventually she agreed to make statements on behalf of the SLA. Assuming the name Tania, she announced that she had become a member of the group that had kidnapped her. Her participation in the SLA was confirmed when, more than two months after her kidnapping, she joined the group in robbing a bank. Pictures from the bank's surveillance camera, widely played in the media, showed her carrying a weapon during the robbery. The mood of the public began to turn against Hearst, and the attorney general of the United States suggested that she willingly had joined the group. The Federal Bureau of Investigation (FBI) included her in a wanted poster as a "material witness" to the bank holdup.

The police found the SLA but not Hearst on May 17, 1974, when six SLA members were killed in a siege. Hearst, on the run with other group members, fled to the eastern United States before returning to California. On September 18, 1975, some nineteen months after her abduction, the police arrested her. In March, 1976, in a highly publicized trial, she was convicted of bank robbery and a firearms felony and sentenced to seven years in prison. She eventually served three years before being paroled in 1979.

Impact   The coverage of Patty Hearst's kidnapping, crime, and arrest highlighted the American public's fascination with celebrity and crime that would increasingly grip the United States in the decades following the 1970's. Her case received widespread media attention and was subjected to considerable public discussion. She subsequently married one of her bodyguards, became a mother, and wrote a book about her ordeal. In January, 2001, she was officially pardoned by President Bill Clinton.

Newspaper heir Patty Hearst arrives for her bank robbery trial in 1976, accused of aiding her kidnappers. (AP/Wide World Photos)

Further Reading

Alexander, Shana. *Anyone's Daughter: The Times and Trials of Patricia Hearst.* New York: Viking Press, 1979.

Hearst, Patricia. *Every Secret Thing.* New York: Bantam Dell, 1981.

Steve Hewitt

See also   Federal Bureau of Investigation (FBI); Munich Olympics terrorism; Symbionese Liberation Army (SLA); Terrorism.

■ Heart

Identification   American rock group
Date   Formed in 1963

The performances and chart success of Heart—a band fronted by women—helped to open the world of hard rock to female performers.

Heart began as a band named the Army, formed in Seattle, Washington, in 1963 by Steve Fossen, Roger Fisher, and Mike Fisher. Later renamed White Heart and then simply Heart, the band was joined in 1971 by Ann Wilson as lead vocalist and moved to Vancouver, British Columbia, when Mike Fisher was about to be drafted into the U.S. Army. Originally playing covers of hard-rock numbers, especially Led Zeppelin songs, Heart began adding original material to its performances. Wilson's younger sister Nancy joined the group in 1974 as guitar player and vocalist.

Heart built a fan base playing in Canadian clubs and signed a contract with a small Canadian record label, Mushroom, in 1975. The group's first album, *Dreamboat Annie* (1976), yielded the singles "Magic Man" and "Crazy on You," which rose high on the charts in Canada and the United States. This success led to a record contract with a larger American label, Portrait/CBS. Heart moved back to Seattle after the U.S. government granted amnesty to Vietnam draft dodgers in 1977 and released the albums *Little Queen* (1977) and *Dog and Butterfly* (1978), with the singles "Barracuda" and "Straight On" achieving chart success.

Ann Wilson's powerful lead vocals and Nancy Wilson's fierce guitar playing established their credentials as hard-rock musicians. Their creative contribution to the band also included writing or cowriting most of its songs, recorded on albums that intermingled hard-rock numbers with power ballads and folk-rock music. The Wilson sisters presented themselves as women fully integrated into a mixed-gender band, which allowed them to avoid some of the harsh critiques that media and critics had made of previous female hard-rock musicians. The novelty of a mixed-gender band, however, did gain the band much attention, and both the media and the publicity strategies employed by Mushroom and Portrait focused on Ann and Nancy Wilson.

Impact   While previous women rock musicians had suffered from stereotyping as either being intensely macho or being overly sexual, the Wilson sisters, as members of a mixed-gender band, were able to project a more realistic female persona. Their skill in performing and songwriting enabled Heart to carve a niche for female performers in the masculine world of hard rock.

Subsequent Events   The 1980's saw the Wilson sisters lead Heart to even higher chart success, as the band shifted to a synthetic pop musical style and a music-video friendly look. Amid changes in personnel and occasional hiatuses, Heart later returned to the hard-rock style of its early years and, with the Wilson sisters still at its core, continued to perform and record.

Further Reading

Garr, Gillian G. *She's a Rebel: The History of Women in Rock and Roll.* 2d ed. New York: Seal Press, 2002.

O'Brien, Lucy. *She Bop II: The Definitive History of Women in Rock, Pop, and Soul.* New York: Continuum, 2002.

Bethany Andreasen

See also   Hard rock and heavy metal; Music; Led Zeppelin.

■ Hip-hop

Definition   Cultural movement

Hip-hop culture of the 1970's encompassed disc jockey-driven rap music, break dancing, graffiti, and casual fashion, all associated with a street ethos in direct opposition to black and white middle-class values.

Early rap music was defined largely by the disc jockeys (DJs)—known as MCs, a term derived from "emcee," "master of ceremonies," or "mic controller"—as opposed to the rappers. In the early 1970's, house party DJs were adapting and refining the pioneering methods of DJ Kool Herc, a Jamaican immigrant generally recognized as the founder of rap. The first rap record was "King Tim III (Personality Jock)" by the Brooklyn funk band, Fatback. The second, "Rapper's Delight," by the Sugar Hill Gang, became a major international hit.

Along with rap music, break dancing, graffiti, and casual fashion defined hip-hop culture. Break dancing derived from the Brazilian dance caporeia, a form of competition between opponents. Break dancing initially had a similar function: Gang members would compete against one another in the streets of the South Bronx. At the same time, graffiti morphed into an art form in New York City when graffiti artists began "tagging" subway trains, buses, barriers, walls, and the sides of buildings. Some individual graffiti artists became so popular that their work began appearing in New York City art galleries. Finally, sports jerseys, sweatsuits, and hiking boots were worn by hip-hop artists because they were comfortable and relatively cheap. The casual wear also signaled to fans that, however successful the artists might become, they retained their street smarts and relevance.

Impact Hip-hop's emphasis on working-class and street credibility in its fashion and language made it both a logical successor to the counterculture dreams of popular music from the 1960's and a rival to the emerging punk rock movement for the passions of the up-and-coming generation. New Wave rock artists—deriving from the punk movement—were heavily influenced by hip-hop fashion and, to a lesser extent, rap music. Even punk rock artists such as the Clash incorporated raps and disco into some of their music.

Further Reading

George, Nelson, Sally Banes, Susan Flinker, and Patty Romanowski. *Fresh: Hip Hop Don't Stop.* New York: Random House/Sarah Lazin Books, 1985.

Hebdige, Dick. *Cut 'n' Mix: Culture, Identity, and Caribbean Music.* New York: Methuen, 1987.

Rose, Tricia. *Black Noise: Rap Music and Black Culture in Contemporary America.* Hanover, N.H.: Wesleyan University Press, 1994.

Tyrone Williams

See also African Americans; Disco; Fads; Fashions and clothing; Films in the United States; Graffiti; Music; Punk rock; Soul music.

■ Hippies

Definition Youth subculture that embraced alternative art, fashion, politics, and lifestyles

Hippies fostered artistic creativity, alternative lifestyles, and political change. Their emphasis on freedom, peace, and love contributed to important social changes, including opposition to the Vietnam War, support for human rights, environmentalism, holistic health, and consciousness exploration.

Hippie culture reached it widest influence in the 1970's, after emerging during the 1960's. Following the privations of the Great Depression and World War II, Americans sought to return to normalcy on the wave of postwar economic growth that offered the middle class a chance for material affluence. Hippies perceived the price paid for such status seeking as an alienating pressure to "fit in" with corporate values by "running the rat race" to "keep up with the Joneses." Opting out of what they saw as a narrow and spiritually empty life defined by material possessions, hippies sought a more authentic fulfillment. Rather than striving to be well adjusted to stereotypical norms of hierarchical power structures, they prized self-expression and an antiauthoritarian ethos of "do your own thing." Furthermore, rather than endlessly deferring intrinsic pleasure for the grim pursuit of materialistic goals, they sought happiness in the present.

A Confluence of Movements This hippie renunciation of social norms involved a "deconditioning" of prevailing assumptions. Five contexts converged to support this process. First, growing political activism, such as the Civil Rights movement, the free speech movement, and the antiwar movement against U.S. policy in Vietnam profoundly highlighted the limitations of old assumptions. The massacre of protesting students at Kent State University by the National Guard in 1970 galvanized such change. Second, popular music increasingly reflected these new attitudes. Folk, soul, and rock musicians offered powerful anthems of the times. The Woodstock Music Festival in 1969 instantiated a loose-knit "Woodstock Nation" as an alternative community.

Third, the sexual revolution influenced the hippie movement. In contrast to previous inhibited or repressive attitudes, or "hang-ups," hippies experimented with new possibilities of sexual activity and nonbinding relationships. Fourth, psychedelic drugs, especially marijuana and LSD, fostered awareness of the social construction of much of reality. Fifth, the importation of nondual spiritual philosophies from Asia, especially yoga, meditation, Hinduism, and Buddhism, promoted visions of a trans-egoic human identity and the meaning of life.

The Emergence of a Counterculture   In 1967, hippie subculture established in the Haight-Ashbury district of San Francisco attracted enormous media attention and pilgrimages by young people, culminating in the famous Summer of Love. That year inaugurated a turning point, as the hippie phenomenon shifted from the deeply lived alternative lifestyle of a few to a worldwide phenomenon enacted more superficially by many. It spread quickly based on the timely appeal of its three central values: freedom, peace, and love.

During the 1970's, communes were popular among many hippies, such as this member of The Farm in Tennessee. (AP/Wide World Photos)

Hippies believed that freedom was what everyone wanted, but most surrendered to conform to what one was "supposed" to be. To reclaim freedom, hippies disengaged from society's presuppositions by questioning authority, taking risks, and pushing boundaries. Hippies often lived this emphasis on freedom by self-expression through alternative fashion—long hair, no bras, flowing clothes, ankle bracelets—by living outside the dominant economy on little money, often in communal arrangements, and through consciousness; that is, disengaging society's alienating assumptions by "consciousness raising," a "mind-blowing" change often enabled by psychedelic drugs.

Peace was another central value. To seek peace for the world, hippies cultivated peace from within. They practiced balance, harmony, sharing, tolerance, nonviolence, and unity in place of greed, competitiveness, and self-righteousness. They sought, beyond the oppression of prejudice, a common ground of kinship, compassion, and kindness.

Finally, hippies believed in the power of love to change the world—Make Love, Not War! was a familiar motto during this era. They emulated such Beatles' lyrics as "All you need is love" and "And in the end, the love you take is equal to the love you make." Hippies embraced free love, the idea that love was meant to be given without conditions, not as a means to an end but as an end in itself. They experimented with a wide range of novel living arrangements and open relationships. Exploring varieties of sexualized love, some found a transcendent web of interdependence in a larger whole. Within hippie culture, a great degree of nonjudgmental acceptance, trust, and support was given to one another.

Impact   By the late-1970's, the countercultural edge shifted from hippies to punks, their gentle innocence replaced with jagged cynicism. What remained of intact hippie culture moved to rural areas, where aging hippies sought to live with nature out of the media's limelight. Others blended back into the mainstream and quietly carried on hippie values.

Though the mass movement ended, an enduring impact remained. Politically, African Americans, Native Americans, and women gained civil rights, and gays and lesbians made some inroads on homophobia. Aspects of everyday life also changed, from the use of natural fabrics and organic foods to socially responsible investing. New age spirituality, holistic health, and environmentalism reflected hippie values in subsequent decades.

Further Reading

Braunstein, Peter, and Michael Doyle, eds. *Imagine Nation: The American Counterculture of the 1960's and 1970's.* New York: Routledge, 2001. An anthology about the popular culture, media, drugs, politics, sex, and communal issues of the era.

Coyote, Peter. *Sleeping Where I Fall.* New York: Counterpoint, 1999. A personal memoir by one of the leading San Francisco hippies.

Echt, David. *Messenger from the Summer of Love.* Bandon, Oreg.: Reed, 2001. An engaging description of what it was like to be twenty in the midst of the flowering of hippie culture.

Miller, Timothy. *The Hippies and American Values.* Knoxville: University of Tennessee Press, 1991. Reviews hippie culture in four major categories: drugs, sex, rock music, and the sense of community.

Reich, Charles. *The Greening of America.* New York: Random House, 1970. A lively analysis of the late 1960's as a cultural revolution and a description of the new consciousness of those who adopted it.

Roszak, Theodore. *The Making of a Counter Culture.* Garden City, N.Y.: Doubleday, 1969. An overview of the sociological, philosophical, historical, and spiritual influences on the counterculture.

Christopher M. Aanstoos

See also Antiwar demonstrations; Bell-bottoms; Cohabitation; Drug use; Earth Day; Environmental movement; Fads; Fashions and clothing; *Greening of America, The*; Hairstyles; Human potential movement; New Age movement; Religion and spirituality in Canada; Religion and spirituality in the United States; Sexual revolution; Slogans and slang; Vietnam War.

■ *Hite Report, The*

Identification Controversial book on female sexuality
Author Shere Hite (1942-   )
Date Published in 1976

The Hite Report was the first book to discuss women's self-perceptions of sexuality from a feminist perspective.

As the influences of the sexual revolution and the feminist movement increased during the 1970's, more attention was given to the study of female sexual pleasure. *The Hite Report: A Nationwide Study of Female Sexuality* was based on the author's analysis and interpretation of lengthy open-ended questionnaires received from 3,019 women—100,000 had requested questionnaires—who were largely from the United States, although thirty-six were from Canada. Supported by the New York chapter of the National Organization for Women (NOW), it was a controversial book that received both positive and critical reviews on its methodology and ideology.

The report's subtitle suggested that the book was a representative national study. However, the methodology of collecting responses skewed toward young, single, and liberal women. For example, more than two-thirds of the respondents were thirty-three or younger, and two-thirds were not married. Moreover, although New York accounted for 9 percent of the U.S. population at that time, that locale represented 27.5 percent of the report's respondents; ten southern states accounted for 17.4 percent of the population but totaled only 5.7 percent of the respondents. Finally, most respondents were recruited from feminist or liberal groups. Shere Hite was criticized for including tables that made the book look scientific but were, in fact, simplistic. The open-ended answers allowed tremendous flexibility in interpretation by the author, another major criticism.

The results did, however, give an in-depth understanding of new sexual attitudes and new sexual demands for a selected part of the population. Hite included lengthy discussions on orgasm, intercourse, masturbation, lesbianism, and other aspects of sexuality. Her major themes were that penis-vagina intercourse was male-oriented and a result of male domination, that most women did not receive enjoyable orgasms from vaginal sex, that most women who masturbated regularly had orgasms, and that clitoral sex was preferred by women. Other studies, including *The Redbook Report on Female Sexuality* (1975), which was also written by a feminist researcher, concluded that many women did enjoy intercourse with men, that sex was an act of love rather than an act of political liberation, that "a liberated orgasm is any orgasm a woman likes," and that many of Hite's claims were overstated.

Impact *The Hite Report*, which reached number nine on the best-seller list for 1976-1977, was successful in giving increased attention to types of sexual practices that some women enjoyed, although some female and male critics viewed it as emphasizing female pleasure to the exclusion of male pleasure, instead of encouraging pleasure for both partners. Nevertheless, the book did have a major impact on feminist perspectives of sexuality and on women's rights and power.

Further Reading

Hite, Shere. *The Hite Report on Shere Hite: Voice of a Daughter in Exile.* London: Arcadia Books, 2000.

Petersen, James R. *The Century of Sex: Playboy's History of the Sexual Revolution, 1900-1999.* New York: Grove Press, 1999.

Tavris, Carole, and Susan Sadd. *The Redbook Report on Female Sexuality.* New York: Delacorte Press, 1975.

Abraham D. Lavender

See also *Everything You Always Wanted to Know About Sex but Were Afraid to Ask*; Feminism; Homosexuality and gay rights; *Joy of Sex, The*; National Organization for Women (NOW); Sexual revolution; Women's rights.

■ Hobbies and recreation

Definition Pastimes of Americans

Americans sought healthier lifestyles during the decade, which influenced their hobby and recreation choices. Meanwhile, changing interests and priorities, coupled with technological innovations, resulted in new pastimes and diversions.

After a decade of turbulence, Americans during the 1970's experienced calm after a storm of war, protests, and civil unrest. People no longer focused on fixing the world's problems but rather on improving themselves through diet, exercise, and therapy. This inward examination, along with extra leisure time and income, created a generation of Americans whose goals were self-improvement and gratification. New products, recreations, and activities, as well as a resurgence of updated classic hobbies, were embraced by a society seeking amusement along with self-actualization. Although Americans strived to achieve healthy lifestyles and personal development from activities in which they participated, above all, they wanted to have fun with their free time, and the decade offered them many new leisure pursuits.

Health and Recreation Author Tom Wolfe dubbed the 1970's the "Me Decade," claiming that affluent postwar America created a society possessing leisure time, money, and personal freedom. This society's focus was the individual, resulting in new self-awareness trends and recreations. Parks, beaches, and neighborhood streets were overrun with joggers, while enrollment in fledgling aerobics classes skyrocketed across the country. Awareness of diet and nutrition launched new health food products and diet drinks, as titles such as Jim Fixx's *The Complete Book of Running* and George Sheehan's *Running and Being* topped the best-seller lists of 1978.

Americans seeking self-actualization also began practicing yoga and meditation, joining therapy groups, and reading numerous self-help books. People experimented with alternative remedies such as crystal therapy, hypnosis, and acupuncture, as well as purchased astrological charts and read daily horoscopes, which appeared in 1,200 of the nations 1,750 newspapers by 1972.

Outdoor Recreation Elements of popular culture, combined with technological improvements, reintroduced classic sports and activities into the mainstream. Roller skating reappeared, this time in combination with a pop culture phenomenon—disco. By 1978, roller skating was the sixth-most popular sport in the country, with the United States housing more than three thousand roller rinks, many transforming into discotheques nightly.

This resurgence was also due to a new urethane wheel invented by Frank Nasworthy in 1973 for skateboards. These wheels, along with fiberglass boards and advanced axels, allowed skateboarders to hold tight corners and make sharper turns and pivots, boosting skateboarding's popularity. By 1976, people were spending up to two hundred dollars on skateboards, making it a $250 million industry, with another half million dollars spent on safety equipment. The sport became so widespread and the injuries so plentiful that many towns banned it as a public safety hazard.

An equally popular (and dangerous) recreation was mini-biking. Children and adults commandeered dirt roads and subdivisions at speeds reaching thirty-five miles per hour on bikes that averaged four feet tall and sixty-five pounds and contained a lawn mower's engine with up to five horsepower. As with skateboarding, the injuries with mini-biking were abundant, which caused them to be banned quickly from public roads.

Although Wham-O introduced the Frisbee in the 1950's, the toy soared to superstar status during the 1970's with millions of Americans buying them. Frisbee throwing became a beloved recreation, resulting in Frisbee parks and national and international competitions that showcased distance, accuracy, and even catching of Frisbees by dogs.

Hobbies and Games During the 1970's, Americans enjoyed new games and hobbies, as well as a revival of the classics. For many belonging to the "Me Decade," these diversions went beyond hobbies and often became obsessions.

In 1972, amid the Cold War, American chess player Bobby Fischer defeated Russian Boris Spassky, sparking patriotism and renewing interest in chess. By 1974, Fischer abdicated the championship, and the country lost interest in the game. That same year, Hungarian architecture professor, Erno Rubik, created a new hobby, the Rubik's cube. The object of the task was to shuffle fifty-four multicolored squares, then rearrange them into six solid sides of color. With trillions of possible combinations, the cube became a compulsion for millions of Americans.

Unable to find a distributor for the game Dungeons and Dragons, Gary Gygax founded Tactical Studies Rules (TSR) in 1974, and his game quickly became an obsession for many. The open-ended fantasy role-playing game required imagination, multi-sided dice, and four basic books: *Player's Handbook, Dungeon Master's Guide, Monster Manual,* and *Deities and Demigods.* Dungeons and Dragons attracted as much criticism as converts, with community and church groups claiming that it encouraged Satanism and violence.

When the National Maximum Speed Limit of fifty-five miles per hour passed in 1973, truck drivers relied upon citizens band (CB) radios as warning systems for highway patrol, also called "smokies" in CB lingo. CB radio rapidly became a popular hobby for many Americans, with more than one billion licenses granted by 1976 and 650,000 new applications per month. Enthusiasts were clambering to use the small band width that the Federal Communications Commission (FCC) reserved in the 1940's for use in areas without telephone service. By the late 1970's, these airwaves were cluttered with people using CB jargon dictionaries to communicate with one another, including First Lady Betty Ford, with her handle "First Mama."

Impact A shift in focus from changing the world to changing one's self occurred in the American psyche during the 1970's. Craving emotional fulfillment as well as physical health, Americans took an interest in diet, exercise, and "self help," seeking activities that helped them achieve these goals. As people adopted healthier lifestyles, outdoor recreation increased in popularity. Running, jogging, and aerobics filled people's free time, while technological innovations to sports such as roller skating and skate boarding packed the streets with skating kids and adults alike.

The 1970's focus on the individual allowed Americans to obsess over new hobbies like Dungeons and Dragons and Rubik's cube. This focus transformed into patriotism for some, with chess experiencing a rebirth after Fischer's defeat of Spassky during the Cold War. While for others, the focus became a sense of American rebellion through a resurgence of CB radios and open airwaves.

Further Reading

Hoffman, Frank W., and William G. Bailey. *Sports and Recreation Fads.* Binghamton, N.Y.: Harrington Park Press, 1991. A thorough discussion of sports-related pastimes.

Johnson, Richard A. *American Fads.* New York: Beech Tree Books, 1985. Examines how American fads have changed throughout the course of the twentieth century.

Sann, Paul. *American Panorama.* New York: Crown, 1980. Offers a review of national hobbies during the twentieth century.

Skolnik, Peter L., L. Torbet, and N. Smith. *Fads: America's Crazes, Fevers, and Fancies.* New York: Thomas Y. Crowell, 1978. Provides good insight into the popular culture of the 1970's and the fads and pastimes that drove it.

Sara Vidar

See also Arts and crafts; Astrology; CB radio; Disco; Dungeons and Dragons; Fads; Fitness movement; Food trends; "Me Decade"; Roller skating; Rubik's cube; Self-help books; Skateboards; Slogans and slang; Sports; Streaking; Toys and games; Video games.

■ Hockey

Definition   Team sport

The fan base for hockey increased with the expansion of the National Hockey League, the emergence of the World Hockey Association, and the victories of Team Canada and Team USA over the Soviet Union during two Winter Olympics.

In the 1970's, the world of professional hockey was punctuated by seminal events near both ends of the decade. Team Canada's 1972 victory over the Soviet Union's national team to win the Winter Olympics gold medal was momentous; it was not, however, as world-shattering as the so-called Miracle on Ice: Team USA's stunning upset victory over the Soviet Union to win the gold medal during the 1980 Winter Olympics.

These two victories for North American hockey teams over the long-dominant Soviet national team reverberated politically during the Cold War and stimulated public interest in professional hockey in the United States. As a result, two Californians, Dennis Murphy and Gary Davidson, decided to take advantage of this interest in 1972 by forming a professional hockey league to rival the old and, according to some, staid National Hockey League (NHL).

The World Hockey Association   The World Hockey Association (WHA) was formed in 1972 with twelve teams and eventually expanded to twenty-seven franchises in all. The league got off to a rousing start when the Winnipeg Jets drafted and signed left wing Bobby Hull, the future Hall-of-Fame star of the Chicago Black Hawks. The league scored another coup when the legendary right-winger Gordie Howe came out of retirement to play with his sons, Mark and Marty, for the Houston Aeros.

The WHA was characterized by several innovations designed to broadened hockey's appeal in the United States. For example, the league used red-and-blue pucks in its first two seasons and, eventually, turned to electronic chips implanted in standard black pucks, which allowed television cameras to follow the puck's "signal" during play. Player and referee uniforms were brightly colored to appeal to the television audience. The WHA also altered several long-standing rules of the NHL in order to create a more offensive-minded, exciting game. Restrictions on stick curvatures were lifted, resulting in

high-scoring games. Rough play was winked at; fighting was a minor (not major) penalty. Finally, and perhaps most important, the league offered players a limited form of free agency.

Despite its innovations, the WHA was not able to sustain its initial marketing successes. Its teams and players were as good as, and often better than, its NHL rivals; the WHA actually had a winning record during the seasons that it played NHL teams in exhibition games. However, the huge salaries that it lavished upon players, coupled with a failure to rouse public interest in traditionally resistant markets of the United States (such as California and Texas), caused several teams to move or, worse, fold. Eventually, in 1979, the WHA struck a deal with the NHL, allowing four of its teams—the Edmonton Oilers, Winnipeg Jets, Quebec Nordiques, and Hartford Whalers—to enter the older league.

The National Hockey League   The late 1960's and 1970's saw tremendous expansion of the National Hockey League. Between 1967 and 1979 the so-called original six saw an almost 300 percent increase in size as sixteen new franchises (not counting the ones that moved) were added to the league. Despite the tremendous acceleration in growth, several stars emerged that demonstrated that the NHL could sustain growth without compromising the quality of performance that it offered to its fans. Ironically, one of them would do for hockey what the WHA had sought to do with its innovations: increase offensive firepower and the entertainment value of professional hockey.

Boston Bruin defenseman Bobby Orr became the most important defenseman in NHL history. Prior to Orr, defensemen focused on defense, supporting the offense when necessary. Orr changed all that, turning defensive play into an offensive tool, often carrying the puck the length of the ice to set up plays. Orr led Boston to the Stanley Cup in 1970 and twice won the Art Ross scoring championship, the only defenseman ever to do so. Young stars such as Mike Bossy and Wayne Gretzky loomed on the horizon, but Orr was the most dominant player of the first half of the decade.

Still, the two most dominant teams of the 1970's were the Philadelphia Flyers and Montreal Canadiens. Led by the brash, young, rough-housing Bobby Clarke, the Flyers became the first expansion team (having joined the league in 1967) to win the Stanley

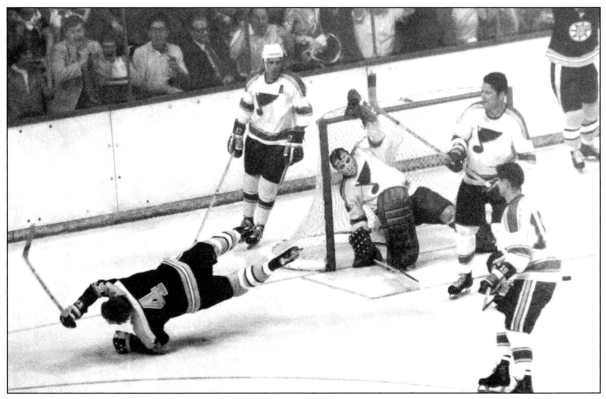

Bobby Orr is tripped after scoring the winning goal for the Boston Bruins over the St. Louis Blues for the 1970 Stanley Cup. (AP/Wide World Photos)

Cup. The Flyers' 1974 coup was repeated when the team won the cup for a second consecutive year. Yet if the "Broadway Bullies," as they were known, reflected the new emphasis on entertainment in professional sports in general, then their counterparts were the Montreal Canadiens, led by Hall-of-Famers Guy Lafleur and Ken Dryden. Winners of four straight Stanley Cups at the end of the decade, the Canadiens embodied the best of traditional hockey: unmatched skating grace and sleight-of-hand puck-handling skills.

Impact The 1970's saw the expansion of the National Hockey League from its original six teams to twenty-four by the end of the 1970's, the emergence and collapse of the World Hockey Association, and the victories over the Soviet Union during the Olympics. As a result, the popularity of professional hockey rose across North America. The NHL would go through unprecedented growth in terms of popularity during the following decade, but growth would also bring player dissatisfaction and a crip-

pling strike in 1987 would destroy whatever momentum the league had accumulated in the 1970's.

Further Reading

Dryden, Ken. *The Game: A Thoughtful and Provocative Look at a Life in Hockey.* New York: Times Books, 1983. The former Montreal Canadien goalie chronicles his career with an honest, unflinching eye. Dryden is not afraid to criticize himself and his teammates. One of the best autobiographies in professional hockey.

Goyens, Chris, and Frank Orr. *Blades on Ice: A Century of Professional Hockey.* Harrisburg, Pa.: Hushion House, 2000. Goyens and Orr have compiled a comprehensive compendium of hockey lore, focusing on the major and minor players, teams, and events that shaped the rise of professional hockey from 1901 to 1999. The book features hundreds of photographs, dozens of interviews, and plenty of anecdotes to satisfy any fan, novice or veteran.

Quarrington, Peter, ed. *Original Six: True Stories from*

Hockey's Classic Era. Toronto: Reed Books, 1996. Six writers offer their takes on the early days of the National Hockey League. As a whole, the book celebrates the romance and drama of the league in its infancy up to the 1967 expansion that doubled its size. Extremely valuable for hockey historians.

Willes, Ed. *The Rebel League: The Short and Unruly Life of the World Hockey Association.* Toronto: McClelland & Stewart, 2004. This humorous, gossip-filled chronicle charts the highs and lows of the WHA. Most important, Willes demonstrates that, for all the shenanigans, the league had positive effects on the NHL, forcing it to modernize, expand, and protect players at a faster rate than it might have done otherwise.

Tyrone Williams

See also   Cold War; Lafleur, Guy; Olympic Games of 1972; Orr, Bobby; Soviet Union and North America; Sports.

■ Hockney, David

Identification   British visual artist
Born   July 9, 1937; Bradford, Yorkshire, England

Hockney was one of the leading representational artists of the 1970's. In a period dominated by abstraction and popular culture images, Hockney explored the questions of form raised by the cubists and other early twentieth century artists and examined formal concerns of conveying emotion in representative painting.

In 1970, a retrospective of David Hockney's work demonstrated that his reputation was established as perhaps the most significant representative painter of the 1960's. A retrospective for an artist in his early thirties was unusual, and the popularity of the exhibit showed that his work was admired widely. Many of his fans were drawn by his paintings of California swimming pools. The clean, bright colors and appealing designs attracted many viewers who found the prevailing movements of minimalism and pop art difficult to comprehend or enjoy.

In the early 1970's, Hockney took photographs to capture his subjects before painting them. Some of his paintings were based on single photographs, but for many, Hockney took a series of photographs as a way to study his subject matter. He believed that paint was more expressive than photography because, while a photograph captured only one moment in time, a painting could capture the experience hinted at in a series of photographs.

Hockney, who had a long-standing interest in cubist painter Pablo Picasso, began working with cubist elements in his own paintings. He also experimented with perspective to add impact or better approximate a viewer's vision of a subject. However, much of his work continued to be naturalistic portraits. Many were of gay friends and lovers, and Hockney sought to portray the emotions of homosexual attraction in his painting.

In 1974, Hockney was asked to design a production of the Igor Stravinsky opera *The Rake's Progress* (1951). This project began a series of set and costume designs that included a backdrop for the ballet *Septentrion* (1975) and designs for the Wolfgang Amadeus Mozart opera *Die Zauberflöte* (1791; *The Magic Flute,* 1911).

From August to October, 1978, Hockney worked on a series of "Paper Pools." The works were made from paper pulp poured into metal frames on the surface of the paper and then pressed. These works, more abstract than Hockney's earlier swimming pool paintings, allowed him to continue exploring ways to represent water.

After almost a decade in Europe and New York, Hockney returned to California in the late 1970's. There he began painting with acrylic paint, creating brighter and less natural colors in his works. Overall, his work of the 1970's shows a gradual move away from naturalism, as he began incorporating more abstract elements and more formal experimentation.

Impact   David Hockney influenced a generation of artists who were interested in the classical concerns of art—conveying emotion in figurative painting, the interplay of the depth of subject and the flat surface of the canvas, and the interplay of light and dark in painting. He also influenced artists who explored homoeroticism in their work.

Further Reading

Hockney, David. *David Hockney.* New York: H. N. Abrams, 1977.

Livingston, Marco. *David Hockney.* Rev. ed. New York: Thames and Hudson, 1996.

Joan Hope

See also   Art movements; Homosexuality and gay rights; Pop art.

■ Hoffa disappearance

The Event Jimmy Hoffa, labor leader and former International Brotherhood of Teamsters president, vanishes after a luncheon meeting with known Mob figures

Date July 30, 1975

Hoffa's disappearance created an American legend out of the former union boss and ex-convict.

Jimmy Hoffa is presumed dead as the result of a Mafia hit, his disappearance becoming one of the United States' biggest crime mysteries. His body has never been found, although there seems to be consensus as to who killed Hoffa and why. A Federal Bureau of Investigation (FBI) memo in 1975 stated that Hoffa's disappearance probably was connected to his attempts to regain the powerful position of Teamsters president that he once held.

The day of his mysterious disappearance, Hoffa was to meet with known mobster Anthony "Tony Jack" Giacalone as well as Anthony "Tony Pro" Provenzano, who was a member of the Genovese crime family. Hoffa went to the meeting believing it was to discuss his intentions to return to power as president of the Teamsters. Hoffa led the union from 1957 to 1967, until his conviction for jury tampering, conspiracy, and mail fraud in 1964 brought an end to his reign. President Richard Nixon granted Hoffa clemency just before Christmas in 1971, releasing him from the Lewisburg, Pennsylvania, penitentiary, where Provenzano was also an inmate. However, things had changed during the years Hoffa spent behind bars. The Mafia, who had worked with Hoffa in the past, found his handpicked successor, Frank Fitzsimmons, easier to manipulate. Therefore, the mob was not quite ready to acquiesce to Hoffa's desire to recapture control.

On July 30, 1975, Hoffa arrived at the scheduled meeting at the Machus Red Fox Restaurant in Bloomfield Township, Michigan. It long has been assumed that Hoffa's friend and the man he took in as a child, Charles (Chuckie) O'Brien, persuaded Hoffa to get into a 1975 maroon Mercury Marquis Brougham, seen in the area by a truck driver who claimed to have seen Hoffa in the backseat. O'Brien borrowed the car from Joe Giacalone, the son of Anthony Giacalone, and O'Brien maintained at the time of the disappearance that he was cutting a forty-pound salmon into steaks, later taking the vehicle to a car wash to clean some of the salmon blood that had leaked onto the backseat. Shortly after the disappearance, trained police dogs were used. They sniffed some articles of clothing that Hoffa wore the day before his disappearance and indicated that Hoffa's scent was in the rear of the Mercury. After his ride in the Mercury Marquis Brougham that day, Hoffa was never seen again.

Former Teamsters boss Jimmy Hoffa leaves the penitentiary in Lewisberg, Pennsylvania, in 1971 after being granted clemency by President Richard M. Nixon. He would disappear four years later, the assumed victim of a Mafia hit. (AP/Wide World Photos)

Impact Hoffa's disappearance put intense scrutiny on union ties to the mob and came to be the identifying factor of his life, overshadowing most of his labor efforts.

Further Reading

Brandt, Charles. *I Heard You Paint Houses: Frank "The Irishman" Sheeran and the Inside Story of the Mafia, the Teamsters, and the Final Ride of Jimmy Hoffa.* Royalton, Vt.: Steerforth, 2004.

Sloane, Arthur A. *Hoffa.* Cambridge, Mass.: MIT Press, 1991.

Kimberly A. Manning

See also   Business and the economy in the United States; Federal Bureau of Investigation (FBI); Racketeer Influenced and Corrupt Organizations (RICO) Act; Unions in the United States.

■ Hoffman, Dustin

Identification   American actor
Born   August 8, 1937; Los Angeles, California

Short and ordinary looking, Hoffman was the most unlikely film superstar of the decade, appearing in the greatest variety of roles of any actor.

As a struggling young New York actor, Dustin Hoffman lived for periods with his fellow unknowns Robert Duvall and Gene Hackman, little suspecting that all would be major stars by the 1970's. Hoffman was an Off-Broadway veteran by the time that he won the lead in the film *The Graduate* (1967) and became an overnight star.

In *Little Big Man* (1970), Hoffman is transformed by Dick Smith's makeup and ages from a teenager to a 121-year-old; he plays the only white survivor of the Battle of the Little Bighorn. His character, Jack Crabb, alternates between living in white American and Native American cultures. Much like Crabb's different identities, Hoffman adopted completely different personas in each of his eleven films during the 1970's.

Hoffman became notable for the way in which he became a character actor in his leading roles, often totally reinventing himself with each film. Hoffman's characters are almost always neurotic. In *Who Is Harry Kellerman and Why Is He Saying Those Terrible Things About Me?* (1971), he is a guilt-ridden songwriter who persecutes himself. In Sam Peckinpah's controversial *Straw Dogs* (1971), he is a mild-mannered mathematician who resorts to violence to protect his sexy young wife in a small British village. As a bank clerk frustrated by his marriage in the Italian comedy *Alfredo, Alfredo* (1972), Hoffman took the unusual step of surrendering his voice, since his performance was dubbed into Italian by another actor. This role and that in *Little Big Man* underscores Hoffman's debt to such silent-film stars as Buster Keaton and Charlie Chaplin, evidenced by his desire to accent the physical sides of his performances.

After playing a French convict in *Papillon* (1973), Hoffman played controversial comedian Lenny Bruce in *Lenny* (1974). With perhaps Hoffman's darkest role, the film presents Bruce both as a victim of the censorship of the 1960's and as a ruthless manipulator of others. In *All the President's Men* (1976), Hoffman emphasizes the often difficult personality of *Washington Post* reporter Carl Bernstein. He is a graduate student pursued by a Nazi war criminal in *Marathon Man* (1976), an unrepentant criminal in *Straight Time* (1978), and another reporter in *Agatha* (1979). Hoffman ended the decade by winning his first Academy Award, following three previous nominations, as a father battling for the custody of his son in *Kramer vs. Kramer* (1979). Because his character had initially neglected the boy in favor of his career, the film can be seen as an indictment of the "Me Decade."

Impact   Dustin Hoffman proved that someone who looks nothing like a film star could, in fact, become one and remain at the top of the acting profession through a devotion to the craft and a refusal to be typecast. Furthermore, audiences often identified with his characters' insecurities, increasing his popularity even more.

Further Reading

Brode, Douglas. *The Films of Dustin Hoffman.* Secaucus, N.J.: Citadel, 1988.

Lenburg, Jeff. *Dustin Hoffman: Hollywood's Anti-Hero.* New York: St. Martin's Press, 1983.

Michael Adams

See also   Academy Awards; *All the President's Men*; Film in the United States; *Kramer vs. Kramer.*

■ Home Box Office (HBO)

Identification   The first premium service to offer cable television subscribers access to unedited, uncensored, commercial-free theatrical motion pictures in their homes
Date   Introduced nationwide in 1976

HBO allowed viewers to watch motion pictures in the privacy of their own homes. It also made films accessible to peo-

ple in underserviced areas who previously had to rely on heavily censored films, sometimes of dubious print quality, interrupted by commercials, and scheduled at inconvenient times by networks and local stations.

HBO was founded in 1972 as a sports and film cable service available only in New York. Its success led to expansion, but the company was not truly successful until 1975, when it used satellite technology to showcase the famous heavyweight boxing match between Muhammad Ali and Joe Frazier, called the "Thrilla in Manila." As cable television expanded and technology developed, HBO began offering a regular subscription film service nationwide by 1976.

During its beginnings, the number of motion pictures was limited for contractual reasons, and long segments of footage of people riding bikes through picturesque scenery filled the gaps between films. Little time passed, though, until the films became more frequent and diverse, and the filler footage disappeared completely. As the company expanded, it diversified further. However, its most innovative developments—videocassette releases, partnership in Tri-Star Productions, and eventually, original programming available to all subscribers—did not occur until the 1980's and 1990's.

During the 1970's, the majority of HBO's fare was unedited, commercial-free motion pictures, which it could show because it was not subject to the same regulations as regular broadcast television. In its early years, the cable service did not have access to many recent films; thus, older or more obscure motion pictures were its mainstay. Gradually HBO began showing more recent theatrical releases, thus increasing its popularity.

Impact   Culturally, HBO did what cable television in general did: It expanded home-viewing choices with complete privacy. While avoiding pornography, HBO offered serious films such as *Going Places* (1973) and *A Clockwork Orange* (1971) that went far beyond what broadcast television could show in terms of sexuality, violence, and language. Objections to such programming, which continued to be prohibited by networks and local stations, were countered by the fact that HBO was a subscription service and, as such, brought stronger material only into homes that specifically requested and paid for it. It acted more like a film theater in the home than a television network. Therefore, it foreshadowed the later development of pay-per-view television and pornography

available in the privacy of the home, while gradually making more explicit material available.

Further Reading
Adler, Richard, ed. *The Electronic Box Office: Humanities and Arts on the Cable.* New York: Praeger, 1974.

Mair, George. *Inside HBO: The Billion Dollar War Between HBO, Hollywood, and the Home Video Revolution.* New York: Mead, 1988.

Charles Lewis Avinger

See also   Advertising; Censorship in the United States; Communications in Canada; Communications in the United States; Film in Canada; Film in the United States; Inventions; Pornography; Science and technology; Television in Canada; Television in the United States; Videocassette recorders (VCRs).

■ Home furnishings

Definition   Items used to decorate and outfit a place of residence for utility and aesthetics

The decoration of homes in the 1970's made a statement about the attitudes and beliefs of the inhabitants. Very often, these attitudes were reactions against the traditionalism and conventionalism of the 1950's and resulted in decor that was antiestablishment and, in some instances, outlandish and downright ugly.

Homes in the 1970's ranged from traditional detached structures and apartments to communes, ashrams (religious retreats), gated communities, geodesic domes, and tent structures. The way in which they were decorated often reflected the lifestyles of the inhabitants, be they "flower children" (hippies), mainstream Americans, or those whose professions or customs required that they present a traditional facade but whose inclinations dictated an avant-garde decor.

Simple Domiciles   The living quarters of those referred to as hippies or flower children were usually an eclectic assemblage of offbeat styles. *The Whole Earth Catalog*, which was published twice a year between 1968 and 1972 and sporadically thereafter, advertised pre-modern furnishings that appealed to antiestablishment occupants who wanted not only to do away with what they saw as the conventionally modern but also to harken back to earlier, simpler times, when humans lived close to the land. Wood stoves, candle light, and wind generators were often used to supply the energy for communes, replacing gas and electric utilities. Instead of sleekly manufactured furnishings bought at department stores, hippies chose bean bag chairs filled with polyurethane granules and rush matting for their floors, and they covered their walls with posters and "op art" for an unencumbered living space. Earth tones dominated, a tribute to hippies' desire to return to the simple life. They deliberately used only a minimal amount of furniture, which was often made of salvaged parts.

Part of this impulse to simplicity was based on the prevailing custom of nomadism and the need to quickly mobilize from one habitat to another. Whatever the reason, an element of American society in the 1970's preferred to travel light and accrue only the bare necessities so that they were ever ready to move on.

Mainstream Homes The more traditional Americans, often those who had grown up under the influence of the 1950's culture, lived in cluster housing, communities with as many as three thousand condominiums on a thousand rural acres; in gated communities close to metropolitan areas; or in individual structures similar to those in which they grew up in the earlier part of the twentieth century. Some were do-it-yourself practitioners who tried to follow the hands-on decorating trends depicted in the home decoration magazines of the time; for example, they covered their walls with vinyl wallpapers or emulsion paints and installed window, portable, or central air conditioning units to cool their homes. The more affluent and trendy of them insisted upon having a hot tub. Mist curlers, electric combs, and shoe polishers were part of their bathroom equipment.

In their living rooms, one might find a parson's-style table, leather and chrome chairs, and Lucite coffee tables. Many pieces of furniture were made of molded plastic, aluminum, or wood. Some chairs were even made of paper or cardboard, making them easily disposable when they had outlived their usefulness. The walls might be covered in wallpaper that very often matched the upholstery of the sofa and chairs as well as the draperies. The effect was sometimes disorienting because many of the items in the room blended together to the point of seeming to disappear. Some bedrooms had mattresses made of foam rubber instead of springs and fiber. Depending on how affluent the homeowner was,

there might even be an adjust-a-bed in the master bedroom.

Among the gadgets contributing to the family's enjoyment of the home were the telephone (available in colors to match that of the walls or furniture), reel-to-reel tape machines, and the ubiquitous television set. Videocassette recorders (VCRs) were still expensive, costing as much as two thousand dollars in 1975, and they were both cumbersome and complicated to use. However, because the recorders allowed people to choose when and where they could watch a film (rental movies on videotape were becoming readily available), increasingly more people were acquiring them. The stereo record player of the 1950's and 1960's was starting to give way to compact disc (CD) players, although the hi-fi system—composed of turntable, amplifier, and sets of speakers—was still popular with those who claimed an aficionado's taste for superb sound for their music. Those homeowners who were more vigilant and cautious were likely to have smoke detectors hanging on the ceilings of many of their rooms.

In the kitchen, microwave ovens that cost nearly five hundred dollars began to appear. There might also be a fifty-dollar coffeemaker and a food processor. The refrigerator, larger than the old-fashioned ice box and most likely frost free, would be decorated with magnets holding lists, announcements, reminders, and, if there were small children in the house, colorful original drawings. Kitchen magnets had been introduced during the 1960's and were made in the shapes of pots, pans, and flowers, By the 1970's, they appeared in other forms as well, such as brand name logos, and gradually they became something of an art form. Automatic or electric dishwashers were still expensive but gradually became a necessity for many households.

By the late 1970's a personal computer (PC) had a place in some homes. Video game players, electronic typewriters, and electronic sewing machines also began to be more prevalent.

Trendsetters Americans with money or who saw themselves as arbiters of "mod" taste and style, as well as those whose professions compelled them to be more contemporary than their mainstream neighbors, often chose eclectic, even garish furnishings and styles for their homes. Some embraced the "high-tech" movement, which celebrated the aesthetic of industrial production and reflected their at-

Feminist Gloria Steinem relaxes in her New York City apartment in 1970. Home decorating during the decade often involved the use of bold prints and patterns. (AP/Wide World Photos)

titude toward work and home: One New York designer furnished an apartment in surgeons' stainless steel sinks and hospital doors and used metal fencing to partition some room spaces and make closets. Others appreciated the soft sculptures of Claes Oldenburg, which served as furniture and were made in the shapes of gloves, food, hands, and other unusual objects.

Waterbeds were popular; they were mattresses filled with water fitted into a lined frame that was supposed to prevent or at least retard leaks. An installed heater helped maintain a level of warmth in the beds. Those who slept on waterbeds had to add bleach to the water from time to time to prevent a buildup of algae. Moreover, to prevent the sound of water sloshing about, air pockets periodically had to be eliminated from the mattress.

The walls might be covered with wallpaper of sometimes outlandish patterns that were repeated in the upholstery of the sofas, the curtains or drapery, and the carpeting, giving an almost claustrophobic effect. Bright plaids, amoebic shapes, paisley prints, stripes, and geometric patterns were sometimes randomly mixed for a bright, garish, psychedelic effect—an indirect influence from the era's drug culture. Super graphics adorned walls, especially huge arrows and large-scale lettering, often in bold whites or primary colors. Surreal effects were achieved on walls with huge and often bizarre murals that were painted in varying shades of the same color. Another popular way to cover a wall was with floor-to-ceiling "cubbyholes," in which small curios and bric-a-brac could be displayed.

Popular furnishings included wicker chairs and

sofas and decoupaged bedroom chests of drawers, dining room sideboards, kitchen cabinets, and various chests. Using "found" items such as huge cable spools for table tops or bed headboards was part of the trend toward being less wasteful and more conservationist, a reflection of the hippie concern to be in harmony with the earth. The old-fashioned footed bathtub from the early twentieth century was brought back, often painted a bright color. Shag rugs covered floors in bright, eye-stunning colors.

Impact   The two decades before the 1970's had been periods of both conservatism and upheaval. The 1970's produced a generation that reacted to both. It had experienced the traditionalism of the 1950's and the rebellion of the 1960's, and people from this generation seemed to want to take something from each era in order to express their own views of what they wanted their lives to be. As a consequence, they recast the hippie lifestyle, retaining some of its more environmentally friendly concepts but adopting enough of the traditional in order to divorce themselves from what they seem to think was the hippies' negative vogue. They aimed for a "hip" lifestyle without embracing an actual "hippie" one.

The home decor of the decade produced such styles as the conversation pit, which tried to create a cozier milieu for family gatherings. The shag rug with all its faults encouraged people to sit on the floor although it soon proved difficult to keep clean. The bright colors of the walls and furnishings lightened up rooms, which had for generations been dim and even gloomy. These new illuminated interiors certainly encouraged a brighter psychological outlook for those who lived in those places. Rather than follow the trends of a few, the 1970's home owners gradually learned to let their instincts and personal preferences dictate the atmosphere in which they would spend many hours. As the decade came to an end, the garish colors and patterns lost their appeal, and people's taste began to become less outrageous and more in tune with the drug-free sensibilities of the householder of the next decade.

Further Reading

Lileks, James. *Interior Desecrations: Hideous Homes from the Horrible '70's.* New York: Crown, 2004. A humorous look at the interior styles of the decade's homes.

Massey, Anne. *Interior Design of the Twentieth Century.* New York: Thames & Hudson, 1990. The interior design of the 1970's is discussed briefly, especially as it relates to that of the two preceding decades, giving the impression that little worthwhile decoration evolved during the era.

Schulman, Bruce J. *The Seventies.* New York: Free Press, 2001. This well-written source provides contextual discussions of 1970's politics, society, and culture, all of which had some bearing on the furnishings and considerations of "home" during the decade.

Jane L. Ball

See also   Architecture; Arcology; Computers; 8-track tapes; Fads; Fashions and clothing; Food processors; Food trends; Hippies; Hot tubs; Housing in Canada; Housing in the United States; Inventions; Lava lamps; LED and LCD screens; Pet rocks; Quadraphonic sound; Video games; Videocassette recorders (VCRs).

■ Homosexuality and gay rights

Definition   Same-sex relationships and the struggle for legal and cultural acceptance of gay men and lesbians

In the early 1970's, gay rights activists accomplished tremendous social gains in the United States. However, internal fighting brought a slump in the movement, and backlash against gay rights in the latter part of the decade brought political goals into sharper focus.

Rioting at the Stonewall Inn in Greenwich Village, New York, when police raided the bar in June, 1969, marked the formal beginning of the gay rights movement. Following the riots, increasingly more gay men and lesbians took activist roles. Many members of the gay community also began to be more open about their sexuality, and the subject of homosexuality began making headlines. For example, in 1970, a gay couple applied for a marriage license in Minneapolis, while in 1975, Elaine Nobel in Massachusetts became the first openly gay elected state representative.

Social Activism and Revolution   In 1971, lesbian activists Del Martin and Phyllis Lyon pushed the National Organization for Women (NOW) to to vote that lesbian concerns were also part of feminism. In 1973, activists also caused the American Psychiatric Association to reclassify homosexuality, deleting it from its manual's long list of mental diseases. Homosexuals also pushed for equal rights under the law and wanted communities to remove discriminatory legislation. Equal rights legislation was passed in more than forty cities across the nation.

Gay activists often took a militant stand against repression. Though short lived, the Gay Liberation Front (GLF) in New York helped many gay men and lesbians see the connections between militancy and homosexuality. The Gay Activists Alliance (GAA), which was launched by former GLF members, was much longer lived and had a strong impact on gay rights. However, by the conclusion of the decade, infighting between gay and lesbian groups with differing goals for the movement began to cause stagnation that would not begin to lift until the 1980's, when the acquired immunodeficiency syndrome (AIDS) crisis brought a new need for unified organization.

Backlash The gay rights movement saw a shift toward the end of the 1970's from a social revolution to a political one. Though political goals were always important to gay rights activists, backlash against the movement late in the decade demonstrated the need for concentrated political activism. Dade County, Florida, home of Miami, passed legislation guaranteeing nondiscriminatory housing and employment. However, this legislation soon came under attack. Spearheading the attack was Anita Bryant, a singer famous for promoting Florida oranges. She pushed through a vote on a referendum repealing the legislation by appealing to stereotypes and voters' fears about homosexuality. Bryant charged that gays were attempting to "recruit" school-age children. Not all attempted referendums were successful, however. In California, conservatives attempted to pass the Briggs Initiative, which would have forbidden homosexuals from teaching in the public schools. The referendum failed by more than one million votes.

There was also a distinctly violent element to some of the antigay backlash. Harvey Milk, San Francisco's first openly gay city supervisor, and Mayor

Demonstrators in Hollywood, California, call for an end to discrimination against homosexuals in 1970. (AP/Wide World Photos)

George Moscone were murdered by former city supervisor Dan White, who universally opposed anything that he saw as pro-gay. His resulting light sentence led to widespread rioting in San Francisco, called the White Night Riots, which reenergized the gay rights movement. The 1979 National Lesbian and Gay Rights March on Washington, D.C., demonstrated that committed activists continued to exist, even in the midst of the movement's decline in potency.

Impact The gay and lesbian rights movement of the 1970's demonstrated that social activism was necessary and effective in improving the status of gays and lesbians across the United States. Backlash against the movement, beginning with Bryant's crusade in Dade County and including the tragic deaths of Milk and Moscone, showed that continued organization would be necessary to avoid splintering the movement and decreasing its effectiveness.

Subsequent Events The gay rights movement was galvanized in the early 1980's by the AIDS crisis but was initially unable to provide a consistent response. AIDS victims were attacked by the Religious Right, who saw AIDS as God's curse on homosexuals. However, in time, activists energized and unified to fight the disease and the prejudice surrounding it. By the end of the 1980's, activists had pushed Congress to fund AIDS research. Gay marriage in the 1990's and early twenty-first century also helped solidify the gay community in its fight for equal rights.

Further Reading

Bull, Chris, ed. *Witness to Revolution: "The Advocate" Reports on Gay and Lesbian Politics, 1967-1999*. Los Angeles: Alyson Books, 1999. Reprints articles from *The Advocate* over a thirty-two-year period. Topics covered in the 1970's section include Senator Ted Kennedy's support for gay rights, early attempts to legalize gay marriage, and Harvey Milk.

Cruikshank, Margaret. *The Gay and Lesbian Liberation Movement*. New York: Routledge, 1992. With a particular focus on lesbian concerns, Cruikshank examines the efforts of men and women to liberate gay men and lesbians from oppression.

Duberman, Martin. *Stonewall*. New York: Dutton, 1993. Examines the gay and lesbian revolution through the eyes of six gay men and lesbians, examining both the movement's militancy and the social currents that were such important shaping forces in the 1970's.

Rutledge, Leigh W. *The Gay Decades: From Stonewall to the Present—The People and Events That Shaped Gay Lives*. New York: Penguin, 1992. Examines the two decades following the Stonewall Inn riots, focusing on gay culture. Also depicts many activists from the straight community who have had an influence on gay culture.

Jessie Bishop Powell

See also Acquired immunodeficiency syndrome (AIDS); Bryant, Anita; Feinstein, Dianne; Milk, Harvey; Moscone, George; National Lesbian and Gay Rights March of 1979; Sexual revolution; *Torch Song Trilogy*; White Night Riots.

■ Horror films

Definition Films dealing with suspense, the supernatural, and violence

Horror films proved to be a popular and important cinematic genre during the 1970's, when a number of superb films—most notably William Friedkin's The Exorcist *(1973)—not only increased the respect accorded the once-disdained horror genre but also drew attention to young directors such as Steven Spielberg, David Cronenberg, Ridley Scott, and Tobe Hooper.*

During the 1970's, long-established trends within the horror film genre faltered while a vital new trend established itself, one that focused on the new decade's preoccupations with the proliferation of senseless violence and Americans' growing concerns about sexuality and reproductive rights. The long, profitable franchise of Frankenstein and Dracula films failed at last, resulting in romantic revisionism, such as the 1979 film version of the Broadway revival of *Dracula*, starring Frank Langella, or campy, sexed-up spoofs such as the Paul Morrisey and Andy Warhol films *Flesh for Frankenstein* (1973) and *Blood for Dracula* (1974). The series of imports from the British studio Hammer, popular in the United States during the 1960's, played out as well, resulting in missteps such as an attempt to revive the vampire film in an action-hero vein with *Captain Kronos: Vampire Hunter* (1974).

Gratuitous Violence and the Nature of Humanity As the Vietnam War ended, American filmmakers tended to produce works that reflected a disenchantment with the optimistic worldview of the anti-war movement of the 1960's. They introduced instead a cinematic cosmology in which horror derives from the inherent, inexplicable, and frequent recurrence of pointless cruelty and grotesque violence. Whereas in films of past decades, horror proceeded from the violation of nature—including undead vampires eking out their unnatural lives or Dr. Frankenstein and countless other mad scientists playing God in a laboratory—in the best and most popular genre exercises of the 1970's, violence and rapaciousness are depicted as natural or inevitable. The pathos evoked by the protagonists who struggle against these forces stems primarily from their naïveté in ever thinking that the world might be anything other than brutal and predatory. The painfully smug tourists who stumble into murder, madness, and cannibalism in the backwoods in such films as Tobe Hooper's *The Texas Chainsaw Massacre* (1974) and Wes Craven's *The Hills Have Eyes* (1977) learn this lesson. Likewise, much of the horror and pathos in *Jaws* (1975) derives from Steven Spielberg's constant stressing of the vulnerability of the naïve tourists who complacently splash in the sea, blissfully unaware of the danger threatening them in the form of a shark—a wholly "natural" predator.

In William Friedkin's horrific tale of demoniac possession, *The Exorcist*, Regan (played by Linda Blair), the possessed girl, has done nothing to invite the monster that comes for her, and her mother (Ellen Burstyn) and authority figures are nearly powerless to aid her. Her eventual salvation comes from a rash act on the part of the priest performing the exorcism, rather than from the rite itself. In *The Exorcist*, the depiction of a cosmos in which humankind is a helpless and all-but-hopeless prey to inimical and powerful forces is neatly contrasted by the film-within-a-film starring Regan's mother, which is clearly an upbeat 1960's-style motion picture about social justice and student protest.

The fact that the defenseless protagonists of the era's horror films are menaced as much by human greed, violence, and incompetence as by anything preternatural makes the worldview of the films even bleaker. In *Jaws*, the "monster" is simply a hungry fish: It is the greed and intransigence of the mayor and the local merchants that put the tourists into prolonged peril. In *The Hills Have Eyes* and *The Texas Chainsaw Massacre*, the "monstrous" antagonists are altogether human—however deranged—and in George A. Romero's *Dawn of the Dead* (1978), a vicious motorcycle gang presents a threat as great as that of the film's voracious ghouls.

Second-Guessing Sex A second theme that threads its way through many horror films of the 1970's reflects questions both about the traditional pre-1960's stereotype of family and about the post-1960's openness about sexuality. While the 1960's glorified sex and idealized childhood, horror films of the 1970's undertook dark investigations of the seamy, dangerous dimensions of these issues. In *The Exorcist*, the demoniac Regan spews obscene blasphemies, vomits on priests, abuses herself with a crucifix, and causes the death of three people. The heroine of David Cronenberg's *The Brood* (1979), played by Samantha Eggar, is a woman whose rage over past abuses at the hands of men causes her to produce parthenogenically a hoard of monstrous, miniature offspring who threaten her own daughter, among others. Ridley Scott's *Alien* (1979), a masterful amalgam of horror film, monster movie, and science-fiction spectacle, abounds in brutal and graphic images of sexual violation, both vaginal and oral, and bloody, stomach-churning parodies of procreation and childbirth, the most infamous being the scene in which an alien infant bursts forth from the chest of a character played by John Hurt.

Impact Varying factors probably led to the emergence in the 1970's of the horror film as a commercially viable, artistically valid cinematic genre. Perhaps the free-thinking attitudes of the 1960's created a greater tolerance among moviegoers for previously marginalized types of films. More certainly, technological advances in the 1970's spared directors interested in horror the laughable special effects and ludicrous set designs of previous decades. In any case, the 1970's produced numerous excellent horror films that, while addressing concerns of the era, established the genre as an important one in North American cinema for decades to come.

Further Reading

McCarty, John. *The Modern Horror Film*. New York: Citadel Press, 1990. Contains separate articles on most of the important horror films of the decade, including *Jaws*, *Alien*, and *The Exorcist*.

Muir, John Kenneth. *Horror Films of the 1970's*. New York: McFarland, 2002. An excellent, exhaustive study of the subject.

Skal, David J. *The Monster Show.* New York: Penguin, 1993. One of the best books ever written about horror films, with excellent observations about films of the 1970's.

Thomas Du Bose

See also *Alien*; Blaxploitation films; Blockbusters; Disaster films; *Exorcist, The*; Film in Canada; Film in the United States; *Jaws*; Science-fiction films; Special effects.

■ Horse racing

Definition Contests of speed between horses often held for the purpose of betting

The unifying effect of sports in troubled times was magnified in horse racing by the unprecedented performances of a handful of superb thoroughbreds, which drew new audiences to a sport long stereotyped as one followed only by rich dilettantes and gritty gamblers.

The 1970's were memorable in horse racing for producing three Triple Crown winners, as well as several other magnificent thoroughbreds. First in the decade by birth and achievement was Secretariat, born at Meadow Farm Stables in Virginia in March, 1970. Although he had a distinguished bloodline and was a large, well-muscled colt, he underperformed in his early workouts. Once he started to race, however, it was clear that he was an extraordinary horse who, even with a slow start, would outrun most competitors. In 1973, Secretariat swept the Kentucky Derby, the Preakness, and the Belmont Stakes to become the first Triple Crown winner in twenty-five years. His Derby win shaved three-fifths of a second off the previous record, all the more remarkable because he was still recovering from an abscess in the mouth. The Belmont win was even more spectacular. As the grandson of Bold Ruler, Secretariat had to fight the expectation that he would flag on this longest race in the triad, yet he won thirty-one lengths ahead of the nearest competitors. Called the "horse of the century" by some sportswriters, he finished the 1973 season with a lifetime sixteen wins out of twenty-one races before retiring. By any measure, he was among the best racing thoroughbreds of all time.

Another unique champion was Seattle Slew, who was so uncoordinated after his birth in 1975 that he was nicknamed "Baby Huey." By the time he was a two-year-old, however, he had undergone a transformation into a hard-driving and tightly wound run-ner. In 1977, he was the first horse to win the Triple Crown as an undefeated champion. Afterward, he set an all-time speed record at Belmont for the fastest one-and-a-quarter-mile run ever recorded, and in the only race featuring two Triple Crown champions, he defeated 1978 Triple Crown winner Affirmed in the Marlboro Stakes. Seattle Slew's other lasting legacy came after retiring. He sired more than one hundred stakes winners and other descendants.

The 1978 Triple Crown competition was marked by an intense rivalry between Affirmed and Alydar, who were so closely matched in accomplishments that they had alternated in winning earlier stakes contests. Although Affirmed came through to win all three Triple Crown races, Alydar was right behind him, and his Belmont win was by less than the proverbial nose. This year was the only time that the same two horses finished in one-two order in all three races.

Among the many other great horses of the 1970's were Forego, famous as a "weight horse," who continued running and winning until his eighth year; Spectacular Bid, the 1979 Derby winner whose ownership was syndicated the next year for an unprecedented $22 million; and Secretariat's stablemate and early competitor Riva Ridge, winner of the 1972 Derby. Ruffian, an almost-black filly born in 1972, was often called the world's fastest horse. She set new records in all ten races that she won, only to tragically shatter an ankle and break down in a 1975 match race against Foolish Pleasure.

Gambling Horse racing was almost unique on the American sports scene in being so closely tied to legal gambling. As more states loosened their opposition to all gambling, new possibilities for revenue emerged, including racing wagers from remote locations. New York introduced off-track betting parlors in 1971, and in 1975, Connecticut, which had no in-state track, opened a large Teletrack, where New York races were carried live via satellite. In 1977, the money wagered legally at off-track sites was larger than total on-site wagers for the first time. This trend accelerated, as a result of large-scale simulcasting, in future years.

Impact The 1970's was the decade when the United States became preeminent in international racing circles. Both American and foreign investors paid

Secretariat runs away with the Belmont Stakes, winning by thirty-one lengths, on his way to the 1973 Triple Crown. Horse racing claimed two other Triple Crown winners during the decade. (AP/Wide World Photos)

record amounts at auctions for promising yearlings. Total amounts won by horses also broke some records; both Affirmed and Spectacular Bid topped the two-million-dollar mark for lifetime earnings. With the influx of so much money and frequent television coverage, the sport became one in which millions of Americans had at least a surface interest.

At the same time, average attendance figures at racetracks went down. There were probably several reasons, including the investment in time that fans needed to follow racing closely and the increasing accessibility of all sports on home television.

Further Reading

Devaney, John, and Howard Liss. *Right from the Horse's Mouth! The Lives and Races of America's Great Thoroughbreds.* New York: Crown, 1987. Despite its gimmick of first-person accounts as told by the horses themselves, this book contains a wealth of information on five champions of the 1970's. Good background especially on trainers and owners and the physical condition of the horses.

Reeves, Richard Stone, and Patrick Robinson. *Decade of Champions: The Greatest Years in the History of Thoroughbred Racing, 1970-1980.* New York: Fine Arts, 1980. Lavish coffee-table book with paintings by Reeves along with the text.

Shoop, Robert. *Down to the Wire: The Lives of the Triple Crown Champions.* New York: Dean, Russell, 2003. Gives basic facts, background, and a wealth of quotations from sportscasters and racing industry insiders.

Simon, Mary. *Racing Through the Century: The Story of Thoroughbred Racing in America.* Irvine, Calif.: Bowtie Press, 2002. Gives a historical perspective, along with tables of top runners for each decade and a wealth of photographs. Author is an editor at *Thoroughbred Times.*

Emily Alward

See also Secretariat; Sports.

■ Hot tubs

Definition   Large tubs made of wood, fiberglass, or other materials and filled with heated water

Date   Introduced in 1968

Once used for medical treatments, hot tubs began appearing in private homes in the late 1960's and became a social fixture in homes during the 1970's.

Hot tubs, or "spas" as they are sometimes known, have been around for centuries. The ancient Romans, Greeks, and Nordic cultures enjoyed many variations of communal bathing in heated tubs or pools. In the late 1800's and early 1900's, resorts offered their wealthy patients hot water bathing and spa treatments called hydrotherapy.

In 1954, Joseph Jacuzzi invented and patented a portable whirlpool pump. The original version was a freestanding unit designed to be placed in the bathtub and was intended solely for medical applications. Later variations incorporated air jets, which increased the water agitation and improved the therapeutic effects.

While the Jacuzzi family continued to improve the design of the whirlpool bath, primitive versions of what would come to be called "hot tubs" began appearing in private homes, first in California, then in other areas of the United States. Some of the earliest models were created from recycled wine barrels. These homemade tubs were often unheated and lacked the agitation features of the Jacuzzi. It was not until 1968 that Roy Jacuzzi, a grandson of the original inventor, began marketing the first self-contained, fully integrated whirlpool with the air jets embedded in the sides of the tub.

Throughout the 1970's, the whirlpool baths became larger, so that more people could fit inside and enjoy the fun. Heating and filtration systems were added, and hot tubs became as much a part of the affluent backyard landscape as pools and barbecue grills. However, hot tubs offered more than just the opportunity to relax and massage tired muscles. "Hot tub parties" became a decadent addition to the late 1970's hedonistic lifestyle. By the end of the decade, more than 300,000 hot tubs and in-ground spas were in use in homes across the United States.

Impact   Once the novelty wore off, the popularity of hot tubs began to decline in the 1980's. For many, concerns about cleanliness and the possible health risks overshadowed the social and relaxation aspects. In the years that followed, improved filtration systems, water treatment options, and construction materials allowed hot tubs and spas to remain a fixture in many suburban homes and backyards.

Further Reading

Edelstein, Andrew J., and Kevin McDonough. *The Seventies: From Hot Pants to Hot Tubs.* New York City: E. P. Dutton, 1990.

Schulman, Bruce. *The Seventies: The Great Shift in American Culture, Society, and Politics.* Cambridge, Mass.: Da Capo Press, 2002.

Silversmith, John. *Tubbing: How to Plan, Build, and Use Your Hot Tub.* New York: Crown, 1979.

P. S. Ramsey

See also   Fads; Home furnishings.

■ Housing in Canada

Definition   Home ownership, rental opportunities, and public housing to shelter the Canadian population

During the 1970's, Canadians faced housing issues related to home ownership, rental construction, public housing, cooperative housing, and suburbanization.

In the mid-twentieth century, the National Housing Act of 1938 and Canadian Mortgage Housing Corporation of 1949 built an effective mortgage finance system with fixed-rate government mortgage guarantees to promote home ownership, construction of rental units, and rent subsidies for Canadians. Public housing was secondary.

Rental construction dropped off during the early 1970's as a result of rent controls, tax changes, inflation, and greater profits from commercial real estate and private single-family housing. Low-income renters suffered, but Canadian officials responded with more public and cooperative housing. In 1973, Prime Minister Pierre Trudeau declared that good housing at a reasonable cost was the social right of every citizen.

As in the United States, Canadian public housing during the 1960's focused on low-income households, which typically paid from 25 to 30 percent of their incomes to live in public housing. When household income improved, the household was forced out and was replaced by another low-income family. Housing projects suffered physical and social decline. The National Housing Act was amended in 1972 to improve the social mix in public housing by reducing evictions as income rose. This led to criticisms that middle-income households were benefiting from the expansion in public housing. Income mixing was discontinued in the 1980's.

By the 1970's, Canadians were disillusioned with American-style urban renewal and public housing projects. The Canadian alternative was small-scale, mixed-income cooperative housing, which was federally and provincially funded and was sponsored, built, owned, and managed by community-based, not-for-profit groups.

Canadians had experimented in the past with cooperative retail stores, student housing, and membership housing. A 1973 National Housing Act Amendment authorized government funding of cooperative housing units in Toronto; twenty-one other regional housing associations quickly developed.

Suburbanization occurred in every Canadian city during the 1970's. In the United States, Levittown was the model for suburban development. In Canada, the equivalent model was the Don Mills community. During the 1950's, financier E. P. Taylor and landscape architect Macklin Hancock purchased farmlands northeast of Toronto and developed the community. The plan featured compact neighborhoods with an elementary school as the focal point. Curving, looped, discontinuous road systems passed through green spaces with mature trees and preserved natural geologic features. New types of housing structures were positioned randomly on angular building lots and provided a mix of single, semi-detached, and row houses, as well as apartments.

Impact A rapid response to housing needs during the 1970's allowed Canada to house foreign immigrants, maturing baby boomers, and migrants from the rural areas but did not fully meet the home-owning aspirations of Canadians or the demand for quality affordable housing. The election of the Brian Mulroney government in 1984 brought cutbacks in government funding and involvement in housing.

Further Reading

Dreier, Peter, and J. David Hulchanski. "The Role of Nonprofit Housing in Canada and the United States: Some Comparisons." *Housing Policy Debate* 4, no. 1 (January, 1993): 43-80.

Fallick, Arthur L., and H. Peter Oberlander. *Housing a Nation: The Evolution of Canadian Housing Policy.* Ottawa, Ont.: Canadian Mortgage and Housing Cooperation, 1992.

Van Dyk, Nick. "Financing Social Housing in Canada." *Housing Policy Debate* 6, no. 4 (October, 1995): 815-848.

Gordon Neal Diem

See also Architecture; Business and the economy in Canada; Demographics of Canada; Home furnishings; Housing in the United States; Immigration to Canada.

■ Housing in the United States

Definition Home ownership, rental opportunities, and public housing to shelter the U.S. population

The 1970's brought an unprecedented housing boom in the United States as a result of an oil boom, legislation, government assistance, and new technology.

During the 1970's, a number of factors came together to create rapid growth in the housing industry. An oil boom in the southwestern United States caused enormous increases in demand for new and pre-existing larger homes. The new housing legislation passed in the late 1960's permitted more families than ever before to move from rented housing into homes of their own. Further, the formation of the United States government department of Housing and Urban Development (HUD) provided many new assistance programs to first-time home buyers, low-income families, and those with disabilities. Finally, new methods and technologies meant that builders were constructing much more energy-efficient homes than had been built previously.

During the first few years of the 1970's, approximately 1.5 million new homes were built per year. Most of these new homes were built for middle- and upper-class families. The median price for a new home in 1971 was approximately $25,000. In 1979, approximately 1.8 million new homes were constructed and sold for an average price of $63,700. This rapid increase in property values during the 1970's allowed many Americans to upgrade to bigger and newer homes.

The geodesic dome as a home had a sizable group of enthusiasts, mainly coming from the environmentally conscious segment of the population, and many were built during the 1970's. Traditional and early

American styles of architecture were very popular among new home buyers, and floor plans ranging from 1,200 to 2,000 square feet of living space were the typical sizes of new homes. During 1974, mobile homes became prefabricated structures to differentiate between travel trailers and homes that were meant to serve as a nearly permanent base. The prefabricated housing industry experienced steady growth throughout the 1970's with many new manufacturers starting production. New technologies as well as more stringent government-mandated standards brought quality and efficiency to new levels.

Subsidized Housing By 1972, approximately one million reduced-rent residential units existed in the United States. The construction and maintenance for these units was subsidized 90 percent by the federal government and 10 percent by state and local government. The United States government estimated that nearly 700,000 subsidized units per year needed to be built to meet the needs of the low income and elderly. However, early in the 1970's, an average of only 30,000 units per year were constructed, thereby creating a severe under supply of homes. This fact was largely due to middle-class and suburban homeowners, many of whom fought against having any public housing in their immediate vicinity. Instead, inner cities became the primary construction site for subsidized housing, which led to charges by the lower class that the government was participating in the encouragement of segregation.

Weary of being criticized, the federal government placed a moratorium on any new projects and any new legislation in 1973. The Housing and Community Development Act, passed in 1974, provided a program called Section 8. Section 8 allowed for individuals to select housing virtually anywhere they desired, and the government then paid the subsidy to the landlord directly. The Section 8 program was a huge success as it effectively ended segregation in public housing.

Impact The Housing and Community Development Act of 1974, with its Section 8 program, was a major turning point in U.S. social history and policy. Millions of low-income families as well as low-income elderly and disabled persons were pulled from the inner-city slums and got the chance to live in more desirable areas. For many, the endless circle of living hand-to-mouth on government handouts was broken. Moreover, the oil booms in the southwestern United States created a housing boom that lasted through the end of the 1970's and created a large upper-middle class. The rapid increases in real estate values made many Americans sizable profits when they sold their homes. Most of these people put the money right back into a new home, thus expanding the market further.

Further Reading

Bingham, Richard D. *Public Housing and Urban Renewal: An Analysis of Federal-Local Relations.* New York: Praeger, 1975. A technical examination of the federal programs and their impact upon the localities where they were utilized for projects.

Fried, Joseph P. *Housing Crisis U.S.A.* New York: Praeger, 1972. This book covers extensively the social issues that the United States faced concerning housing in the 1970's.

Fuerst, J. S. *Public Housing in Europe and America.* New York: John Wiley and Sons, 1974. This work contains extensive information and statistics on public housing as it existed in the United States in the early 1970's.

Mitchell, J. Paul. *Federal Housing Policy and Programs: Past and Present.* New Brunswick, N.J.: Rutgers University Press, 1985. This is an extensive study of the United Stated federal government's policies and available programs for subsidized housing units for low-income, disabled, and elderly populations.

Wedin, Carol S., and L. Gertrude Nygren. *Housing Perspectives: Individuals and Families.* Minneapolis: Burgess, 1976. This book offers a broad survey on housing as it relates to architecture, technology, environment, floor plan design, and much more.

Glenn S. Hamilton

See also Architecture; Business and the economy in the United States; Demographics of the United States; Home furnishings; Housing in Canada; Real estate boom.

■ Human potential movement

Definition Cultural phenomenon involving practices that facilitate personal growth

The human potential movement redefined psychological growth. In contrast to the prevailing view of change from "deficiency" to "normality," this movement promoted growth beyond the norm to the fulfillment of one's potential.

The human potential movement was never a formal organization. It never had a central office, leaders, by-laws, or membership criteria. Nevertheless, it provided a powerful new vision of psychological health and growth, and it helped millions to enhance their own. It emerged in the 1960's, blossomed rapidly, reached its peak influence between 1964 and 1984, and is ongoing. The movement paralleled the general renaissance of humanistic thought during that time, with which it mutually intertwined. It reflects the perennial vision of the greatness of human possibility and the human birthright to fulfill that destiny.

Emergence of the Movement This ancient intuition of untapped human potential was echoed in the 1950's by neuroscience speculation that people used only a small portion of their brains. The curiosity of fascinated lay audiences was further piqued by the synthesis of psychotropic chemicals, such as lysergic acid diethylamide (LSD). Writer Aldous Huxley published an engaging description of his experience of opening "the doors of perception" with such chemicals. He termed these largely untapped capabilities "human potentiality" and identified rationality, kindness, affection, and creativity as examples of capacities awaiting fuller development.

This message was particularly timely. In the 1950's, many Americans felt pressured to conform to rigidly narrow, stereotypical social norms. Some believed that they had untapped potential and hungered for greater self-fulfillment. As a movement emerged in the 1960's to access those potentialities, it found a ready audience.

A formative precursor was small group interpersonal relations training. Psychologist Kurt Lewin, at the Massachusetts Institute of Technology (MIT), recognized that human relations was an important but neglected skill. In 1947, his associates began the first T-group (T for training). The National Training Laboratories formed and trained clients to become aware of group process and their own interactions. It was found that communication could be enhanced and that group participants formed deeply trusting and caring relationships. At about the same time, psychologist Carl Rogers, at the University of Chicago, began small group training with counselors to enhance their expertise. Rogers found that when they felt safe, participants expressed themselves honestly, fostered mutual trust, exchanged helpful feedback, and learned how each appeared to the

others. The improved self-understanding and communication skills were experienced as deeply transformative, enhanced their counseling effectiveness, and were practiced effectively with significant others in their lives.

Role of Esalen Institute A major development occurred in 1962 when Michael Murphy and Dick Price decided to offer programs at a coastal resort that Murphy owned near Big Sur, California. As they considered what to present, they recalled Huxley's lectures on "human potentiality" and chose that title for their first program. They named their center the Esalen Institute and identified its mission as "the exploration of the human potential . . . to promote the harmonious development of the whole person." They specified that its programs were not psychotherapy but alternative education for healthy persons to grow beyond the norm, deeply trusting "the miracle of self-aware consciousness."

Esalen quickly became the successful crossroads for a burgeoning human potential movement, whose name was inspired by Esalen's orientation. Its early programs, presented in lecture format, drew from psychology, spirituality, arts, and Asian and Western philosophy. Presenters included Huxley, Rogers, philosopher Alan Watts, psychologist Abraham Maslow, anthropologist Gregory Bateson, writer George Leonard, mythologist Joseph Campbell, and author and inventor R. Buckminster Fuller.

A shift occurred to more experiential programs, of two types: body work and group work. Body work included massage, Rolfing, yoga, martial arts, sensory awareness, and bioenergetics. Prominent leaders included Moshe Feldenkrais and Ida Rolf. Among the group leaders were Will Schutz, Fritz Perls, and Virginia Satir. Schutz developed encounter groups combining the T-group with body work and psychodrama, Perls innovated Gestalt work, and Satir designed groups for families. When asked what they do in group, Schutz famously replied, "We tell the truth." The work is based upon a profound trust that each person can do that and can hear others do so. In describing his own group work, Price identified three keys: "trust process, stay with process, and get out of the way."

While encounter groups tended for a time to predominate, Esalen always provided diverse programming; no single approach ever set its focus. Instead, its range afforded everyone the opportunity to find whatever they needed in a safe and accepting environment.

Impact During the 1970's, there were hundreds of growth centers throughout the United States offering a wide variety of practices for millions of people. As programs evolved, the harder-edged Gestalt encounter group orientation softened, and a subsequent generation sought more intellectual experiences. In response to criticisms about their absence, more workshops with social themes appeared, including emphases on racism, holistic health, and ecology.

Subsequent Events In the 1980's, many growth centers closed as a result of the economic recession and the national shift to more conservative, materialistic interests. Newer movements tended to be more entrepreneurial, such as Werner Erhard's est seminars, or more cultlike, such as the group led by Bhagwan Shree Rajneesh. As the New Age orientation grew, it added its spiritual metaphysics to the stew. In the 1990's, "life coaching" became a new form for facilitating growth. Esalen Institute continued to thrive.

Further Reading

Anderson, Walter. *The Upstart Spring: Esalen and the American Awakening.* Reading, Mass.: Addison-Wesley, 1984. A readable insider's history of Esalen Institute, from its founding through 1983.

Perls, Fritz. *The Gestalt Approach and Eyewitness to Therapy.* Palo Alto, Calif.: Science and Behavior Books, 1973. Perls's final book, revising Gestalt therapy to take into account what he developed at Esalen Institute.

Peterson, Severin. *A Catalog of the Ways People Grow.* New York: Ballantine, 1971. Presents excerpts about dozens of growth-oriented practices, from ancient Asian to contemporary western.

Rogers, Carl. *Carl Rogers on Encounter Groups.* New York: Harper & Row, 1970. An historical overview and analysis of various practices of "planned, intensive, group experiences."

Roszak, Theodore. *Person/Planet.* New York: Doubleday, 1978. Relates the social, political, and ecological movements with the human potential movement, seeing each as affirming the value of the person.

Christopher M. Aanstoos

See also Buddhism; *Culture of Narcissism, The*; Hippies; *I'm OK, You're OK*; New Age movement; *Passages*; Psychology; Pyramid power; Religion and spirituality in the United States; Scientology; Self-help books.

■ Huston Plan

Identification Short-lived government scheme to unify intelligence agencies in order to spy on Americans illegally

Date 1970

The Huston Plan proposed coordinated, unconstitutional activities and formed one of the articles of impeachment against President Richard M. Nixon.

When President Richard M. Nixon approved the Huston Plan in 1970, it was the first time in U.S. history that a president authorized a political police structure with powers that violated the law and the Constitution. The plan was a covert, domestic-intelligence effort recommending illegal wiretaps, electronic surveillance, mail intercepts, and burglaries. It also suggested increasing informants and infiltrators on U.S. college campuses and setting up a working group made up of representatives from the Federal Bureau of Investigation (FBI), the Central Intelligence Agency (CIA), the White House, the National Security Agency (NSA), the Defense Intelligence Agency, and the three military intelligence services, all freed from judicial warrants. Nixon later said that the intelligence community already had engaged in such unorthodox activities in secret.

Proposed and coordinated by Thomas Charles Huston, a young White House aide for whom it was named, the Huston Plan was influenced by FBI administrator William Sullivan. For his part, Sullivan, head of the FBI's intelligence division, sought to reinstate the extreme intelligence-gathering practices that FBI director J. Edgar Hoover had banned in 1966 and to heal a rift between the FBI and CIA.

The rationale for the Huston Plan was that anti-Vietnam War protests, campus unrest, minority and countercultural demonstrations—a few of them violent—could be considered "domestic terrorism." Further, the relationships between intelligence agencies were strained, a situation formalized by Hoover in early 1970, when he cut off all ties to U.S. intelligence interests except the White House.

On June 5, 1970, Nixon convened an Oval Office meeting with the newly formed Interagency Committee on Intelligence (ICI) to assess the threat posed by political radicals and to present options to fill gaps in intelligence about them. By June 25, the committee sent a forty-three-page report accompanied by Huston's memo recommending lifting restraints on intelligence and conducting espionage on Americans. On July 14, Haldeman told Huston that Nixon approved the plan, and Huston notified the agencies on July 23 that the measures would go into effect on August 1, weeks before the new school year. Four days later, however, Hoover complained about the plan's risks directly to his superior, U.S. attorney general John Mitchell, who got Nixon to kill the scheme within twenty-four hours.

In August, Huston's domestic-intelligence responsibilities were given to new White House counsel John Dean, who then discussed with Mitchell a plan to revive an Intelligence Evaluation Committee (IEC) as a less-volatile alternative to the Huston Plan. In December, a new IEC was formed, made up of representatives of the FBI, CIA, NSA, and White House, plus the Secret Service and Departments of Justice and Defense.

Impact Officially killed, the Huston Plan became the framework around which its recommendations continued, albeit in a decentralized way, throughout the 1970's and without formal White House approval. The CIA stepped up domestic intelligence through its Operation CHAOS program, the FBI used its Counterintelligence Program (COINTELPRO) against dissident groups, various militants reported increased incidents of burglaries, and the White House formed its Special Investigations Unit ("the Plumbers") in order to stop information leaks and engage in more partisan missions, including bugging the Democratic National Committee's offices at the Watergate Hotel.

After the 1972 Watergate break-in and subsequent investigations, Dean revealed in 1973 the Huston Plan to federal Judge John J. Sirica, who turned it over to the U.S. Senate investigating committee. Nixon's Huston Plan approval, however temporary, made up much of the second of 1974's Articles of Impeachment, alleging his abuse of presidential power. Huston later extensively testified about the plan to the U.S. Senate's Select Committee studying government operations and intelligence activities.

Further Reading

Donner, Frank J. *The Age of Surveillance: The Aims and Methods of America's Political Intelligence System.* New York: Vintage Books, 1981.

Lukas, J. Anthony. *Nightmare: The Underside of the Nixon Years.* New York: Viking Press, 1973.

Riebling, Mark. *Wedge: The Secret War Between the FBI and the CIA.* New York: Knopf, 1994.

White, Theodore H. *Breach of Faith: The Fall of Richard Nixon.* New York: Atheneum, 1975.

Bill Knight

See also *All the President's Men*; Antiwar demonstrations; Central Intelligence Agency (CIA); Dean, John; Enemies List; Federal Bureau of Investigation (FBI); Mitchell, John; Nixon, Richard M.; Nixon's resignation and pardon; Sirica, John J.; Watergate.

■ I'm OK, You're OK

Identification Self-help psychology book
Author Thomas A. Harris (1913-   )
Date Published in 1967

A best-seller highly regarded by its readership, I'm OK, You're OK *helped many people live and work more effectively and helped their relationships.*

I'm OK, You're OK: A Practical Guide to Transactional Analysis sold more than fifteen million copies, had an enormous impact throughout the 1970's, and was subsequently appropriated in fields such as marketing, education, and religion. It skillfully presented three major themes: Unconscious psychological issues can distort ordinary interactions with others, these dynamics are formed by dysfunctional experiences earlier in life, and these unhealthy patterns can be changed to achieve a more fulfilling life.

This book was an extension of Dr. Eric Berne's theory of transactional analysis. Berne was Thomas A. Harris's own mentor, and his best-seller *Games People Play: The Psychology of Human Relationships* (1964) appeared before Harris's book. Berne introduced the concept that in addition to the "adult" state of realistically engaging others, people also interact from "child" and "parent" states, the former derived from their child perspective when they were younger and the latter from their own parents' perspective. For example, an interaction might involve one person addressing the other's adult state, while the other replies from his or her child state. Within such "transactions," a variety of unconscious dynamics, or "games," are possible, as Berne illustrated. In *I'm OK, You're OK,* Harris specified the various types of same-state and cross-state communications and exemplified them cleverly.

Harris identified four "life positions" that underlie interpersonal relations. These positions are formed by core beliefs that each person adopts early in life: that oneself and others are either "OK" or "not OK." Thus the four possible life positions that people bring to every encounter are "I'm OK, you're OK"; "I'm OK, you're not OK"; "I'm not OK, you're OK"; and "I'm not OK, you're not OK."

While the "I'm OK, you're OK" position is the psychologically healthy one, Harris claimed that it is not the one with which people start. His view was that the newborn's perception of the birth process leads to the early assumption of an "I'm not OK, you're OK" position. For many people, this position remains the fundamental belief from which they interact with others. However, in early childhood, this belief can shift in two ways. If the parental caregiving is deficient, then the child might come to the conclusion that "I'm not OK, you're not OK." If the child is able to make up for that deficiency with self-caring, then the shift might be to a position of "I'm OK, you're not OK." These three positions are unconscious; however the fourth position of "I'm OK, you're OK" is a conscious decision. If it is not attained in childhood, then it can be achieved in adulthood, but only by an understanding of the impact of the previously embedded beliefs.

Impact During the 1970's, Thomas A. Harris's theory of self and interpersonal relations reached a wide audience, which continued to appreciate the book's insights for many years. The book had an impact both on the development of transactional analysis and on other writers of self-help books.

Further Reading
Berne, Eric. *Games People Play: The Psychology of Human Relationships.* New York: Grove Press, 1964.
James, Muriel, and Dorothy Jongeward. *Born to Win.* Reading, Mass.: Addison-Wesley, 1971.
                                    Christopher M. Aanstoos

See also Human potential movement; Marriage and divorce; New Age movement; Psychology; Religion and spirituality in the United States; Self-help books; Slogans and slang.

■ Immigration Act of 1976

Identification National legislation that established new ground rules for migration into Canada
Date Passed on August 5, 1977

The act facilitated the immigration into Canada of minorities from Asia, Africa, and Latin America; helped address labor market needs; and fostered multicultural understanding.

Immigration into Canada before 1967 was based primarily on national preferences, with the British, French, American, and assorted West European groups given priority. The 1967 Immigration Act introduced the points system, which was used to base admission on education, occupation, age, and language facility, all factors considered important for success in an urban, industrialized society. Immigration policy in Canada is written and administered at the federal level while the provinces provide mostly immigrant support services.

The change in Canadian policy during the 1970's was largely a product of the country's labor market needs, although Canada's image around the world was also of growing concern. In the middle of the decade, slightly more than 70 percent of Canada's immigrants were French and British, with large numbers coming also from the United States, Hong Kong, Jamaica, Lebanon, India, the Philippines, Portugal, Italy, and Guyana. The proportion of immigrants of European origin declined through the decade, while Asians made the greatest gains.

The Immigration Act included a nondiscrimination clause that made it illegal to use ethnicity, race, religion, gender, and nationality as the basis for admission. A 1975 Green Paper identified labor force needs in the remote areas of the country and called for government action. Labor shortages, especially of professional and technical personnel, prompted the country to open its doors to an ever-widening swath of skilled immigrants from around the world. While sending countries bore the training costs and lost the brain power, Canada reaped the benefits of an immediate and trained labor force.

The act also facilitated the reunification of family members, provided safe haven for refugees, revised the points system, and introduced a business immigrant program. Under the business program, immigrants with money could "buy" points by investing in employment for themselves and other Canadians.

The points system itself was modified and made more responsive to labor market needs, particularly in areas beyond the southern core. The 1976 legislation was also intended to foster international understanding, cultural and scientific exchange, and international travel and tourism into Canada.

Impact The Immigration Act of 1976 ushered in sweeping changes in Canada's ethnic and racial mosaic. Ethnoracial diversity increased markedly in the country's metropolitan centers, especially in Toronto, Vancouver, and Montreal. Smaller cities were less affected and immigration into rural areas was notable by its absence.

Subsequent Events Following the initial passage of the Immigration Act of 1976, the act was amended more than thirty times. The intent was to aid family reunification, protect refugees, and to grow the Canadian economy through business investments. The business program has been effective and expanded multiple times.

Further Reading

Adelman, Howard, et al. *Immigration and Refugee Policy: Australia and Canada Compared.* Toronto: University of Toronto Press, 1994.

Hawkins, Freda. *Canada and Immigration.* 2d ed. Montreal: McGill-Queen's University Press, 1988.

Migus, Paul M., ed. *Sounds Canadian: Languages and Cultures in Multi-ethnic Society.* Toronto: Peter Martin, 1975.

Ann M. Legreid

See also Canadian Citizenship Act of 1977; Demographics of Canada; Immigration to Canada; Minorities in Canada.

■ Immigration to Canada

Definition Migration to Canada from other countries

During the 1970's, the influx of non-European minorities changed the face of Canada and added fuel to the debates about immigration and multiculturalism.

The 1970's witnessed a dramatic shift in the composition of immigrant streams into Canada and resulted in noticeable changes to Canada's ethnic fabric, especially in the country's major metropolitan centers.

Immigration policies before 1967 gave preference to migrants from Great Britain, the United States, France, Belgium, the Netherlands, and other western European countries. As late as the 1990's, the British and French made up about 70 percent of Canada's immigration. The 1960's were a time of far-reaching change for Canada, however, a time when citizens and politicians laid the groundwork for the country's multicultural policy. World Refugee Year in 1960, a white paper calling attention to labor needs in 1966, the Geneva Convention Protocol in 1969, and hoards of world refugees through the decade helped change the tone and scope of Canada's immigration policy. The Immigration Act of 1967 introduced a point system that based admission on age, education, language ability, and technical or professional training. The new emphasis on labor market needs led to a broadening of admissible classes to include migrants from Asia, Latin America, and Africa. British and French dominance eroded, while Asians made the greatest gains in the decades that followed.

The Immigration Act of 1976 was the decade's major immigration legislation. The act effectively ended discrimination on the basis of race, ethnicity, religion, gender, and national origins. It also facilitated the protection of refugees, family reunification, and investment in the Canadian economy through a special business immigrant program. For the first time, immigrants could earn points toward entrance into the country based on personal finances. They were required to invest a portion of their money into the Canadian economy in order to create jobs for themselves and others.

Canada has modified its immigration policy more than thirty times since 1978, most notably strengthening sections that assist family members and refugees. Immigration policy is established and administered at the federal level, while the country's provinces provide basic services to immigrants such as job and language training.

Demographic Shifts The removal of ethnic and racial criteria in Canada's immigration policy resulted in dramatic changes to the country's ethnic mosaic. Between 1971 and 1981, the population increased about 16 percent, most of which was attributable to immigration. In 1976, the leading immigrant groups into Canada hailed from Great Britain, the United States, Hong Kong, Jamaica, Lebanon, India, the Philippines, Portugal, Italy, and Guyana. Sizable refugee flows came from Tibet, Uganda, and Vietnam.

Nearly 90 percent of the decade's immigrants settled in Canadian cities, mainly Toronto, Vancouver, and Montreal, creating new ethnic neighborhoods and adding to urban ethnic diversity, such as Chinatowns in Toronto and Vancouver. The population of Toronto increased by 400,000 through the decade, while Vancouver increased by 200,000 and Montreal by 100,000. Smaller cities were less affected, and relatively few migrants settled in rural areas. Immigrants congregated in areas where economic opportunity was perceived to be the greatest. Ontario and British Columbia received the largest immigrant streams, while Newfoundland, Prince Edward Island, and Quebec remained the most ethnically homogenous.

Owing to the strict "one language policy" in Quebec Province in the 1970's, more immigrants left the province than entered it. Quebec did, however, receive significant numbers of Chileans, Haitians, and Vietnamese refugees during the decade. The Immigration Act of 1976 facilitated the absorption of immigrants into remote areas of the country where labor needs had been especially acute, although the overall impact in these areas was not significant.

Ethnic language newspapers, books, and other media emerged in the major urban centers, primarily Toronto and Vancouver. Immigrants were inclined to support the Liberal Party, although immigrant preferences have shifted as more and more middle-class immigrants have taken residence in suburbs rather than inner-city enclaves. Immigrant groups displayed varying degrees of residential segregation, with Jews, Portuguese, and Pacific Islanders generally the most highly segregated. Studies have shown Jews, Asians, and Italians to be the most dissimilar from the rest of the Canadian labor force, suggesting somewhat different ethnic goals and profiles from their host societies.

Ethnic origin continues to have an impact on occupational preferences, although the relationship is weakening, and gender-based occupational differences are now more prevalent. Immigrants have been absorbed into a bilingual society. Most immigrants know at least one of the official languages upon entry, although female immigrants are less likely than males to have this language facility.

Impact In the 1970's, Canada had no political party or organization that was openly anti-immigrant, yet the immigration issue remained a contentious one. The decade saw occasional backlashes against the newcomers, mostly nonviolent and linked to economic downswings when unemployment rose. Concerns over unemployment, cultural identity, and the provision of social services remained at the forefront in national conversations during the decade, sometimes in an atmosphere of media-driven xenophobia. Immigrants were required to be law-abiding and economically self-sufficient upon entry.

Today, immigrants live in a spirit of mutual accommodation with their hosts, a condition reinforced by a national ideology of multiculturalism. They have not yet appeared prominently on the political scene, but they have made advances in the workplace and play a significant role in Canada's rich cultural and economic life.

Further Reading

Burnet, Jean, and Howard Palmer. *Coming Canadians: An Introduction to the History of Canada's Peoples.* Toronto: McClelland and Stewart, 1988. Examines indigenous patterns as well as the settlement of European and non-European immigrants.

Driedger, Leo, ed. *The Canadian Ethnic Mosaic: A Quest for Identity.* Toronto: McClelland and Stewart, 1978. Looks at the Canadian and ethnic identities of new groups.

Hawkins, Freda. *Canada and Immigration: Public Policy and Public Concern.* 2d ed. Montreal: McGill-Queen's University Press, 1988. An overview of immigration, with an emphasis on the adaptations of minority immigrants.

James, Carl E. *Seeing Ourselves: Exploring Race, Ethnicity, and Culture.* 2d ed. Toronto: Thompson Educational, 1999. An intimate look at diversity, racism, and cultural identity.

Li, Peter S. *Race and Ethnic Relations in Canada.* 2d ed. New York: Oxford University Press, 1999. An overview of ethnic origins and immigration policies in Canada.

Ann M. Legreid

See also Canadian Citizenship Act of 1977; Demographics of Canada; Immigration Act of 1976; Immigration to the United States; Minorities in Canada; Multiculturalism in Canada.

■ Immigration to the United States

Definition Migration to the United States from other countries

The 1970's marked the beginning of a new era in American immigration, with a rapid rise in the numbers of immigrants and a shift in their places of origin.

A new wave of immigration to the United States began in the 1970's. The country had gone through an earlier great wave of immigration at the end of the nineteenth century and in the early years of the twentieth century until the United States entered World War I. Immigration laws passed in 1921 and 1924 restricted immigration by establishing the national quota system as the basis of American immigration policy. Quotas of immigrants were admitted from each country, and the largest quotas were given to the nations of Western Europe. In 1965, Congress reversed this restrictive approach to immigration when it passed the Immigration and Nationality Act. This act did away with the European bias of the national quota system, and it made family reunification, rather than national origin, the primary qualification for admission. At first, it was thought that the 1965 act would not expand immigration greatly or change its character. However, the numbers of immigrants and their places of origin did change substantially in the years that followed.

Growth in Immigration Following the 1965 change in immigration law, the immigrant population of the United States began to increase rapidly. From 1971 to 1980, nearly five million immigrants were admitted into the country, an increase of 1,171,000 people from the decade 1961 to 1970. Throughout the decade, an average of 397,000 legal immigrants arrived in the United States each year. The largest number came in 1978, when slightly more than 600,000 people from other countries immigrated.

In 1970, U.S. Census statistics showed that 9,619,000 foreign-born people lived in the country, with the foreign-born making up 4.7 percent of the national population. Ten years later, there were more than fourteen million foreign-born residents, or 6.2 percent of the U.S. population. As the 1980's began, well over one-fourth of all the immigrants living in the United States had arrived during the previous decade.

The 1970's were also a time of rapid increase in immigration from Asia and Latin America, a trend that continued throughout the twentieth century and into the twenty-first. Before the 1970's, the overwhelming majority of immigrants had come from Europe. In 1970, 5,741,000 European immigrants lived in the United States—2.8 percent of the whole U.S. population and about 60 percent of all foreign-born people. By 1980, the number of European immigrants living in the United States had decreased to 5,150,000, or 2.3 percent of U.S. inhabitants and only 37 percent of foreign-born people. Asian Americans numbered only 825,000 in 1970, a number that increased to 2,540,000 in 1980. Asian Americans tri-

pled in numbers in that single decade. They went from 0.4 percent of the country's population to 1.1 percent and from only 9 percent of all foreign-born people to more than 18 percent of the foreign-born. The numbers of Latin Americans immigrating to the United States also showed dramatic increases, from 1,804,000 in 1970 to 4,372,000 in 1980. The Latin American population grew from less than 1 percent of all Americans to about 2 percent, and it increased from 19 percent of all foreign-born people to 31 percent.

Refugees from Southeast Asia   Refugees from the Southeast Asian nations of Vietnam, Cambodia, and

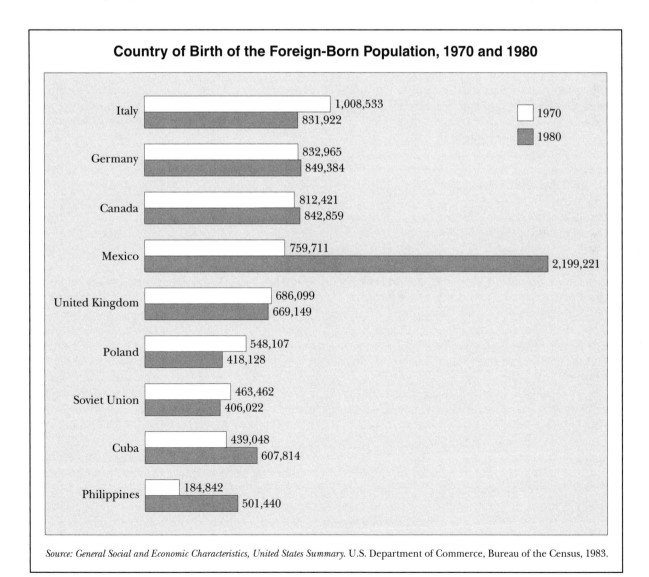

Country of Birth of the Foreign-Born Population, 1970 and 1980

Country	1970	1980
Italy	1,008,533	831,922
Germany	832,965	849,384
Canada	812,421	842,859
Mexico	759,711	2,199,221
United Kingdom	686,099	669,149
Poland	548,107	418,128
Soviet Union	463,462	406,022
Cuba	439,048	607,814
Philippines	184,842	501,440

Source: General Social and Economic Characteristics, United States Summary. U.S. Department of Commerce, Bureau of the Census, 1983.

Laos made up one of the most notable groups of new immigrants to the United States during the 1970's. People from this region had been only a tiny portion of the U.S. foreign-born population before 1975. During the two decades from 1951 to 1970, just under 5,000 people from this region, known as Indochina, migrated to the United States. In the four years between 1971 and 1974, 166 people from Cambodia, 166 people from Laos, and 13,211 people Vietnam entered the United States as immigrants. Immigration statistics do not record any people from Indochina before 1975 coming as refugees, a special category for those allowed into the United States who are fleeing from persecution.

However, in April, 1975, after years of American involvement in warfare in Vietnam and in the neighboring countries of Laos and Cambodia, the capital of Vietnam fell to invading North Vietnamese forces, and the radical Khmer Rouge marched into the capital of Cambodia. In Laos, the royal government had entered into a coalition with Laotian leftists. After the victories of communist forces in Vietnam and Cambodia, the leftists in Laos established control over that country. By the end of the year, the royal government of Laos crumbled, the king abdicated, and the Lao People's Democratic Republic was proclaimed.

American forces had fought against the factions that created these new governments in all three countries. Supporters of the former governments, who had been allies of the Americans, feared persecution. On April 18, 1975, President Gerald Ford authorized the entry of 130,400 refugees from the three Indochinese countries. Most of the immigrants in this first wave of refugees were Vietnamese (125,000). Only 4,600 refugees from Cambodia and 800 refugees from Laos came into the United States in 1975.

President Ford and the U.S. Congress saw the action as a one-time response to the victory of communist forces in Southeast Asia, and they did not believe that the refugee flow would continue. The flow did temporarily become a trickle after the 1975 wave. Only 14,500 refugees entered in 1976, and 2,600 in 1977. Most of those who came in 1976 were Laotians, who fled into neighboring Thailand and then were accepted by the United States as a result of an agreement with the Thai government. There were also 4,519 people in 1976 and 4,992 people in 1977 from these three countries admitted as regular immi-

grants, a rate that would roughly continue until the middle of the 1980's.

However, refugee admissions began to rise again in 1978, when 20,400 Indochinese refugees came into the United States. They included 8,000 people from Laos who had fled into Thailand and 11,100 people from Vietnam. In 1979, 80,700 refugees from Indochina came into the United States. This number doubled in 1980. The sudden increase was a result of events in Southeast Asia. On December 22, 1978, Vietnam responded to Cambodian attacks on Vietnamese villages along their border with an invasion of Cambodia. In February, 1979, China, wary of Vietnamese expansion, formed an alliance with the Khmer Rouge and launched raids on the northern provinces of Vietnam.

The warfare resulted in an outpouring of people from Vietnam and Cambodia and the beginning of a second wave of Indochinese refugees settling in the United States. By 1980, the United States was home to 262,125 people of Vietnamese origin, 52,887 people from Laos, and 16,044 Cambodians. In just half a decade, people from these three countries increased to about 300,000.

Changing Locations and Characteristics Immigrants in the 1970's were especially likely to live on the East and West Coasts of the United States. Over the course of the decade, their numbers decreased somewhat in the Northeast, and they became more concentrated in the West. When the decade began, nearly one out of every three foreign-born people in the United States lived in the Middle Atlantic region, made up of New York State, New Jersey, and Pennsylvania. For comparison, the Middle Atlantic states contained only 17 percent of the nation's native-born population. One out of every five immigrants lived in New York, particularly in New York City, which had been the site of the greatest concentration of immigrants since the great immigration wave of the late nineteenth and early twentieth centuries. A year after the decade ended, the 1980 U.S. Census showed that fewer than one out of every four immigrants were living in the Middle Atlantic region, and the proportion in New York State had decreased to 16 percent.

While the Northeast declined as a center of immigrant settlement, the West Coast, especially California, expanded. By 1980, 29 percent of the country's foreign-born population lived in the West, and one out of every four immigrants were in California. Among those who had arrived in the United States during the 1970's, 32 percent lived in the West, and 29 percent lived in California alone. This was a decisive decade in immigrant settlement, because it was the time when destinations shifted from the Northeast to the West Coast.

The immigrants who arrived during the 1970's were younger and lived in larger families than other Americans. By 1980, the average age of people who had come to the United States during the 1970's was 29.6, compared to just under 33 for Americans in general. Family sizes of immigrants who came during this decade averaged 4.1 people, compared to under 3.5 for other people in the United States.

As a result of the changing origins of immigrants, the new arrivals of the 1970's were of racial and ethnic backgrounds that differed from those of the population in general and from those of earlier immigrants. In 1980, 64 percent of the immigrant newcomers were classified as white; more than 86 percent of native-born Americans and 91 percent of earlier immigrants were categorized as white. The 1970's saw more black immigrants than had earlier decades, but there were fewer black people among the immigrants of this period than there were in the native-born population. A little more than 8 percent of immigrants during the 1970's were black; under 3 percent of those who had come earlier were classified in this way. Native black Americans, whose ancestors had come to America much earlier, made up a little more than 12 percent of the population.

Impact   The 1970's began a new wave of immigration. Immigrants arrived in larger numbers than they had since the early twentieth century. With new sources of immigration, the ethnic and racial makeup of the American population began to change and exposed native-born Americans to a rapidly growing array of cultures and traditions.

Subsequent Events   The flow of immigration that began immediately before and during the 1970's grew even greater over the next two decades. At the beginning of the twenty-first century, one out of every ten people in the United States was an immigrant, and immigration had become the major source of growth in the American population. The shift in immigration from Europe to Asia and Latin America also continued. By 2000, people from Asia

made up more than one out of every four foreign-born Americans, or 3 percent of the nation's population, and the majority of the foreign-born (51 percent) were from Latin America, constituting just under 6 percent of the people in the nation.

The events of the 1970's had established a Southeast Asian American population that would continue to grow. Throughout the 1980's and into the early 1990's, refugees continued to arrive from this part of the world, so that by 2000, there were about a million and a half people of Vietnamese, Cambodian, and Laotian origin in the United States.

Further Reading

Brimelow, Peter. *Alien Nation: Common Sense About America's Immigration Disaster.* New York: Random House, 1995. A controversial book that criticizes America's post-1965 immigration policy for changing the ethnic makeup of the United States.

Daniels, Roger. *Coming to America: A History of Immigration and Ethnicity in American Life.* 2d ed. New York: Perennial, 2002. A general overview of American immigration.

Suro, Roberto. *Strangers Among Us: Latinos' Lives in a Changing America.* New York: Vintage, 1998. A discussion of the critical issues surrounding a group that began to become the United States' largest immigrant group during the 1970's.

Zhou, Min, and Carl L. Bankston III. *Growing Up American: How Vietnamese Children Adapt to Life in the United States.* New York: Russell Sage Foundation, 1998. An examination of the lives of young people in the largest of the Southeast Asian refugee groups. Contains a brief history of Southeast Asian resettlement in the United States from 1975 onward.

Carl L. Bankston III

See also   Asian Americans; Demographics of the United States; Immigration Act of 1976; Immigration to Canada; Latin America; Latinos; Vietnam War.

■ Income and wages in Canada

Definition   Earning and payment of money deriving from capital or labor in Canada

The Canadian economy started the 1970's with significant structural differences from the U.S. economy but reacted to global changes in many of the same ways.

Canada began the 1970's with high expectations of continued economic growth. As in the United States, unemployment in Canada in the years after World War II had rarely exceeded 5 percent, with inflation averaging 2 percent per year. Growth in real (inflation-adjusted) income had risen at 4 to 5 percent per year as Canada worked to help supply the products demanded by a war-ravaged Europe. As Canada prospered in the years after 1945, its network of social service programs expanded exponentially. Federally funded health care, expanded unemployment insurance, and vastly increased old-age pensions and aid to higher education were instituted by the government of Lester Bowles Pearson during the 1960's and were continued by the government of Pierre Trudeau in the 1970's.

The 1970's were not to be an uninterrupted continuation of postwar prosperity, however. Canada's favorable trade relationship with Great Britain declined as a result of the latter's entry into the European Economic Community (EEC) in 1973. Most of Europe had regained its industrial capacity by 1970, and Canadian manufacturers had difficulty finding replacement markets for their goods. Canada had entered the transitional decade along with its neighbor to the south.

Many of the same demographic forces that affected wages and incomes in the United States had similar effects on Canada. The entry of the postwar baby boomers into the labor force during the 1970's was joined by an increase in the number of women working in paid employment. By 1970, married women made up just over one-third of the Canadian labor force, up from 25 percent in 1951. As in the United States, this influx in the labor force was blamed for unemployment rates rarely below 7 percent during the 1970's.

The nature of work had changed in Canada as well. Demand for manufacturing and agricultural workers declined (as did the real wages paid in these sectors) while service employment steadily gained ground. Average real wages for men stagnated, and greater income inequality was evident and growing during the 1970's as more highly educated workers increased the gap between themselves and manufacturing workers. The 1970's were a time of increased trade union membership and strike activity in Canada, but as in the United States, the pattern of greater income inequality continued unabated.

Impact The 1970's marked the end of the postwar economy in Canada. A period of seemingly endless growth and prosperity had ended, and with it the ability to afford a growing array of new social services. The 1970's marked the start of a new, more competitive economic arena in which the returns to education were substantially higher and the gap between rich and poor was increasing.

Further Reading

Bothwell, Robert. *A Traveller's History of Canada.* London: Cassell, 2001.

Riendeau, Roger. *A Brief History of Canada.* New York: Facts On File, 2000.

Betsy A. Murphy

See also Business and the economy in Canada; Business and the economy in the United States; Demographics of Canada; Education in Canada; Income and wages in the United States; Inflation in Canada; International trade of Canada; Unemployment in Canada; Unions in Canada.

■ Income and wages in the United States

Definition Earning and payment of money deriving from capital or labor in the United States

During the 1970's, high inflation rates and unemployment problems flattened the growth of real income and decreased real wages.

The 1970's represented a decade of considerable economic discomfort for workers and businesses in the United States. The trends in income and wages, as with other economic indicators, reflected a national economy that was struggling. The post-World War II economic expansion that characterized the 1950's and early 1960's was replaced by the inflation-prone Vietnam War economy, and the country entered the decade with a fragile economy.

The federal government's economic policies in 1969 were aimed at slowing down the economy to reduce inflation. This contractionary government policy helped bring about a recession in 1969-1970. In spite of the government's efforts, both inflation and unemployment were significant problems throughout the 1970's. After a modestly successful recovery from the 1969-1970 recession, the middle years of the decade were marked by difficult economic

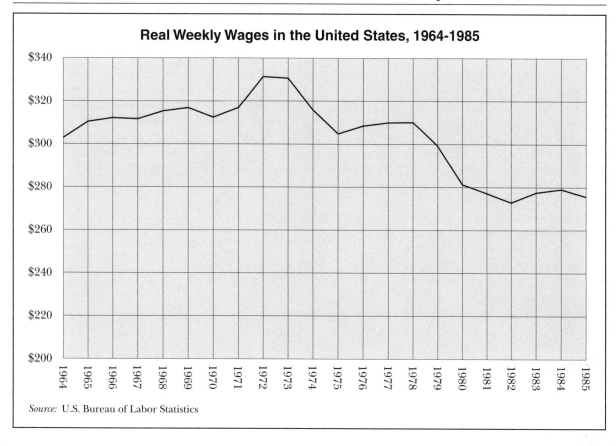

Real Weekly Wages in the United States, 1964-1985

Source: U.S. Bureau of Labor Statistics

times. The first oil-price shock in 1973 hit the economy hard, sending the country into a sharp recession in 1974-1975. The economy began to improve in 1976, but the second oil-price shock in 1979 once again set off a recession. Thus, the 1970's began and ended with recession.

The Money Illusion   Income trends in the 1970's illustrate a pattern known by economists as the "money illusion." Nominal income, or dollars not adjusted for changes in prices, showed a considerable increase during the decade. A common way of looking at the trend is to examine income for each person, referred to as per-capita income. Per-capita nominal income more than doubled during the 1970's, rising from $3,177 in 1970 to $7,168 in 1979. However, once adjustments were made to compensate for inflation, the actual increase in real income was much smaller. Per-capita income, adjusted to reflect 2001 dollars, rose only from $12,543 to $16,196.

Nominal income increased every year during the 1970's. The smallest gain, 7.34 percent, came in the

recession year of 1974; the largest gain, 11.58 percent, came in 1978. Inflation-adjusted income actually fell by 2.33 percent in 1974 and grew only by a miniscule one-tenth of a percent in 1975. For the entire decade, the average gain in nominal income was nearly 9.5 percent; for inflation-adjusted income, it was less than 3 percent.

The money illusion is significant because it fools people into thinking that they are wealthier than they really are. Feeling wealthy, people increase spending in the short term beyond sustainable levels. The gain in nonadjusted income over the decade was 125 percent, while the inflation-adjusted gain was slightly less than 30 percent. People spending money as if they had doubled their income eventually realized that they had overextended themselves and responded by cutting back on consumption in order to restore their economic stability. However, cutting back on consumption helped created unemployment. The unanticipated inflation that began in the late 1960's and early 1970's thus helped create the unemployment problems of the mid-1970's.

Declining Real Wages Income, even after adjusting for inflation, fared better than wages in the 1970's. As with income, the true picture for wages across multiple years is best portrayed by adjusting for changes in prices. Real wages reached an all-time peak in 1972 and then fell throughout the rest of the decade. Economists think about real wages in two ways. First, the average real wage per hour of employment indicates whether wages are generally rising or falling. However, a family's standard of living is determined both by the average wage and by the hours worked each week. The average real wage per hour multiplied by the average number of hours worked each week gives the real weekly wage. In thinking about overall economic performance, the weekly view is generally a better indicator. If workers receive a higher wage but are working fewer hours each week, then their income may not rise.

Using either average real wages or weekly real wages gives a similar picture of economic discomfort in the 1970's. Both reached all-time peaks in 1972 and then fell lower and lower through the remainder of the decade. In 1970, average real wages were $8.45 per hour, adjusted to 1982 dollars. This figure climbed to $8.99 in 1972 but fell to only $8.41 by 1979. The weekly real wage in 1970 was $312.38. It rose to $331.34 in 1972 but then fell to $299.20 in 1979. The weekly real wage fell faster than the hourly wage because the average number of hours worked also declined through the decade. Workers had a lower average real hourly wage and were working fewer hours.

If real wages were falling and if the number of hours worked each week was declining, then how could real per-capita income increase? Economists explained that more people went to work or that the labor force participation rate increased. In particular, the economic stress on families during this decade pushed millions of women into the labor force. The declining real wages and pronounced inflation of the 1970's eventually prompted many unions to negotiate cost-of-living-allowance (COLA) clauses in labor contracts. The COLAs automatically adjusted wages to inflation; they were also added to Social Security payments.

Impact The link between real income, real wages, and quality of life in the United States has been complicated to sort out historically. Material needs are socially determined, so the quantity of material goods considered "normal" changes over time. Where one car was once a luxury, American families routinely began to own two. Moreover, people tend to expect economic progress over time. The relatively slow growth of real income and declining real wages of the 1970's created a growing gap between expectations and economic reality for many working Americans. Increasing the labor force participation rate helped increase income, but it had secondary effects on family life and gender roles.

Further Reading

Economic Report of the President. Washington, D.C.: Government Printing Office, published annually. The annual reports from the 1970's explain the economic policies that each administration was following and give a wealth of information on income and wages.

Heilbroner, Robert, and Lester Thurow. *Five Economic Challenges.* Englewood Cliffs, N.J.: Prentice Hall, 1981. Two economics textbook authors give an accessible overview of the income and wage problems besetting the economy in the 1970's.

Heller, Walter W. *The Economy: Old Myths and New Realities.* New York: W. W. Norton, 1976. A prominent economist examines the economic difficulties of the 1970's.

Johnson, Arthur M. *The American Economy: An Historical Introduction to the Problems of the 1970s.* New York: Free Press, 1974. A collection of essays giving background information useful for understanding the 1970's.

Allan Jenkins

See also Business and economy in the United States; Earned Income Tax Credit program; Employee Retirement Income Security Act (ERISA) of 1974; Gas shortages; Income and wages in Canada; Inflation in the United States; Ninety-day freeze on wages and prices; Unemployment in the United States; Women in the workforce.

■ Indian Self-Determination and Education Assistance Act of 1975

Identification U.S. federal civil rights legislation
Date Passed on January 4, 1975

The act's provisions allow tribes to contract with federal agencies to operate services that were formerly federally oper-

ated, giving Native Americans more input into the delivery of such services as health and education.

In the 1970's, political leaders were beginning to realize the need for Indian self-determination. Native Americans were dissatisfied with federal control and the ways that they were receiving services. Several strongly worded reports in the late 1960's pointed out problems with Indian education, and public activism by Native Americans was beginning to bring this issue to the forefront. Presidents Lyndon B. Johnson and Richard M. Nixon had begun to solicit input from tribal leaders and encouraged the Bureau of Indian Affairs (BIA) to contract for services with the tribes rather than deliver what the bureau thought was best for them. The Indian Self-Determination and Education Assistance Act of 1975 made legal the procedures for such "contracting out." Through this act, tribes could have much greater control over services provided to and for them.

The act described an approach or process to handling funding for Native American services such as health and education. It included rules and procedures for using funds already existing in the BIA and other federal agencies. Thus, it was, more or less, a block grant program, in which funds could be passed from the federal government to state agencies, thereby giving more decision-making power to the levels closer to the sources of funding; for example, state, regional, and tribal levels. The intent of the legislation was to make services such as health and education more accountable to the local tribal communities in which services were provided.

Impact The Indian Self-Determination and Education Assistance Act of 1975 was called one of the most important pieces of legislation that influences federal policy toward Native Americans. It was the beginning of a movement to help Native Americans become more influential in deciding the types and content of services that they received.

Subsequent Events Many later critiques of this legislation pointed to evidence that the objectives were not met and, in terms of education, that the Bureau of Indian Affairs continued to control the educational content taught in schools. The act may not have achieved its purposes, but it was later amended and its goal reasserted several times following the 1970's. The act was amended in 1988 to correct some difficulties that had been noted with imple-

mentation since 1975. The spirit of the original act was kept intact. With each iteration, the movement seemed to be toward more autonomy and control for Native Americans in terms of federally funded education and health services.

Further Reading

Castile, George Pierre. *To Show Heart: Native American Self-Determination and Federal Indian Policy, 1960-1975.* Tucson: University of Arizona Press, 1998.

Reyhner, Jon. *Effective Language Education Practices and Native Language Survival.* Choctaw, Okla.: Native American Language, 1990.

Mary C. Ware

See also American Indian Movement (AIM); American Indian Religious Freedom Act of 1978; Education in the United States; Native Americans; Trail of Broken Treaties; Wounded Knee occupation.

■ Inflation in Canada

Definition An increase in consumer and producer prices in Canada

Inflation was an intractable problem in both Canada and the United States during the 1970's. Defying conventional solutions, unchecked price inflation was at the root of many social and economic changes during this decade.

Inflation is commonly summarized as "too much money chasing too few goods and services." During the 1970's, the bill for Canada's expansion of social services and efforts at uniting its provinces came due at a time when its production of goods and services was slowing down. Canada, like the United States, had been one of the prime beneficiaries of a recovering Europe after World War II. By the late 1960's, however, demand for its products had slowed just as its government spending had accelerated, creating all the ingredients necessary for rapid price inflation.

Before the 1970's, economists had assumed a static trade-off between inflation and unemployment: Policies that alleviated one would exacerbate the other. By the mid-1970's, this assumption had been tested and found wanting, as both Canada and the United States were experiencing rapid price inflation coupled with high unemployment rates, a situation termed "stagflation." During the 1960's, inflation in Canada had averaged 2 percent per year and unemployment had averaged 3 to 5 percent per year. During the 1970's, inflation was running 9 to 12 percent per year, while unemployment hovered around 7 percent of the workforce for most of the decade.

The Liberal government of Pierre Trudeau sought to reduce inflation through regulation, and in 1975 the Anti-Inflation Board (AIB) was established to review prices and wages in business and industry. The AIB was given significant powers to curtail increases in prices or wages that would accelerate inflation, and its rulings resulted in widespread labor unrest and strikes by labor unions. For a three-year labor union contract, wage increases were limited to 8 percent in the first year, 6 percent in the second year, and 4 percent in the third year at a time when increases of 15 percent and 20 percent per year were not unusual.

Adding to the AIB's difficulties, energy shortages caused by the 1973 Organization of Petroleum Exporting Countries (OPEC) embargo resulted in higher prices for petroleum and its derivatives. The Trudeau government, in its drive for Canadian energy self-sufficiency by 1990, temporarily increased inflation by providing subsidies to Canadian energy companies for oil exploration.

Unpopular with the public and unsuccessful at reining in inflation, the AIB was unceremoniously dismantled in 1978. Inflation increased even more rapidly for a short time, as labor agreements that had been overruled by the AIB took effect, but by then confidence that inflation could be regulated in this manner was seriously eroded. Inflation would not be tamed in Canada (or in the United States) until the next decade, when central bankers (monetary authorities) in both nations sharply reduced the amount of money in circulation.

Impact The 1970's were a time of great social and economic changes, with rapid price inflation casting its shadow on most of them. The failure of the Trudeau government to solve the inflation problem successfully left its policies on other fronts vulnerable to criticism.

Further Reading

"Canada: Election Promises Meet Reality." *The Economist,* December 15, 1979, 73.

"Wages and Prices." *Business Week,* March 15, 1976, 28.

Betsy A. Murphy

See also Business and the economy in Canada; Business and the economy in the United States; Energy crisis; Income and wages in Canada; Inflation in the United States; Oil embargo of 1973-1974; Unemployment in Canada; Unions in Canada.

■ Inflation in the United States

Definition An increase in consumer and producer prices in the United States

The price level doubled over the 1970's, leading to anxiety and social tension, record high interest rates, significant changes in economic theory, and contributing to Jimmy Carter's defeat in the election of 1980.

The index of consumer prices, which stood at 109.8 in 1969 (100 in 1967), rose to 217.4 by 1979. Year-to-year changes in the price level from 1965 to 1983 are shown in the table. The inflationary process displayed three distinct spikes. The inflation rate had been rising steadily from 1965 to 1970 and reached

President Gerald R. Ford asks citizens to sign up as inflation fighters as part of his campaign to Whip Inflation Now (WIN). (AP/Wide World Photos)

an initial peak in 1969-1970 near 6 percent. This phase reflected the war in Vietnam. As military spending increased, the government incurred increasing deficits. In response, the Federal Reserve Board bought government securities, and the supply of money increased rapidly. The episode reflected classic demand-pull inflation. Demand for goods rose more rapidly than production could expand. In response to production increases, unemployment declined to a very low 3.5 percent of the labor force in 1969.

By 1970, however, the government was beginning to withdraw from Vietnam, and the monetary and fiscal stimulus arising from the war was being reduced. This threw the economy into a business-cycle recession. Unemployment rose to 5.9 percent in 1971, partly in response to sizeable reduction in the armed forces. The inflation rate declined, reaching 3.4 percent in 1971 and 1972, partly because of the slowdown in demand, and partly because President Richard Nixon imposed direct controls on wages and prices in 1971.

The second inflation spike was set off in October, 1973, when members of the Organization of Petroleum Exporting Countries (OPEC) imposed an embargo on shipments of petroleum to the United States. Prices of crude oil, heating oil, and gasoline all rose substantially. The wholesale price of crude oil rose 27 percent over the year 1973. The embargo was lifted in March, 1974. Largely by coincidence, most wage-price controls were removed the following month—but not those on petroleum products. While this was going on, the Federal Reserve was generating a rapid increase in the money supply in an effort to reduce unemployment. The combination of restricted petroleum supply, higher business costs, and expanding demand drove the inflation to more than 12 percent in 1974.

As oil supplies improved, prices of gas and oil peaked in the summer of 1974 and then inched down. The inflation rate receded to less than 5 percent in 1976. Distressed by rising unemployment, Federal Reserve officials accelerated monetary expansion. This in turn raised the demand for goods and services. In January, 1979, Islamic militants drove Mohammad Reza Shah Pahlavi, the shah of Iran, from power and a new government stopped oil exports. In two months, Iranian oil prices rose 30 percent. The shock was quickly transmitted to the U.S. economy. By September, 1979, gasoline prices

December-to-December Change in Consumer Price Index, 1965-1983
(1967 = 100)

1966	3.4%
1967	3.0%
1968	4.7%
1969	6.1%
1970	5.5%
1971	3.4%
1972	3.4%
1973	8.8%
1974	12.2%
1975	7.0%
1976	4.8%
1977	6.8%
1978	9.0%
1979	13.3%
1980	12.4%
1981	8.9%
1982	3.9%
1983	3.8%

Source: Economic Report of the President, 1984.

were 52 percent above a year earlier, and heating oil prices 73 percent. The general inflation rate exceeded 13 percent per year in 1979, then started down in 1980.

A Gallup poll in 1973 reported that 89 percent of respondents believed the high cost of living was the nation's most critical economic problem. In May, 1978, *Business Week* commented that, "Anyone who is not at least mildly panicked about the inflation outlook for the U.S. does not recognize the seriousness of the situation." The magazine went on to describe "how inflation threatens the fabric of U.S. society." Much of this concern arose from public anxiety. People did not understand the inflationary process. They felt victimized by sellers, and even those whose incomes kept pace with inflation feared falling behind. The inflation generated animosity toward labor unions and business firms and eroded confidence in the government.

Effects The inflation of the 1970's raised money wage rates as well as product prices. An index of real hourly wage rates (money wage deflated by price index) stood at 95.7 in 1970 and 97.4 in 1979, indicating a close match between wage and price increases. Normally, however, real wages would increase in response to rising productivity, and that did not occur.

A response to inflation was Congress's decision in 1972 to index Social Security benefits. After 1974, benefits increased automatically in step with rising prices, thus sheltering older people from some of the inflation bite.

Because price increases made people eager to borrow and reluctant to lend, the inflation drove interest rates to high levels not previously experienced in the twentieth century. Already in the 1960's, rates on high-grade corporate bonds had risen sharply, reaching 8 percent in 1970. They fluctuated around this level, then rose to 9.6 percent in 1979 and 12 percent in 1980.

Higher costs and higher tax liabilities prevented a rapid rise in corporate profits, which dampened the stock market. Standard and Poor's stock-price index, which stood at 97.8 in 1969, fluctuated around this level and reached 103 in 1979. Thus stock prices did not share in the rise in product prices and wage rates.

Impact Economists struggled to interpret the experience of the 1970's. The unemployment rate, which had averaged less than 4 percent in 1966-1969, hovered around 7 percent in 1975-1979. The term "stagflation" came into common use. The inflation was blamed by some on wage demands of labor unions and by others on the monopoly power of big business. The chief cause, however, was rapid monetary growth. Under Arthur Burns and William Miller, the Federal Reserve chose to stimulate rising demand for goods by monetary expansion, hoping to reduce unemployment and interest rates but certainly aggravating the price increases. The appointment of Paul Volcker as Federal Reserve chairperson in 1979 signaled a shift toward monetary restriction.

Public discontent with inflation, high interest rates, and high unemployment all contributed to the victory of Ronald Reagan over Jimmy Carter in the presidential election of 1980.

Further Reading

Case, John. *Understanding Inflation.* New York: William Morrow, 1981. Concise, readable, and sensible overview, with a particular emphasis on the 1970's.

"The Great Government Inflation Machine." *Business Week*, May 22, 1978, 106-150. This "report from the battlefield" conveys a sense of the social tension and political unrest of the times.

Schmukler, Nathan, and Edward Marcus, eds. *Inflation Through the Ages: Economic, Social, Psychological and Historical Aspects.* New York: Brooklyn College Press, 1983. The fifty-three articles in this collection cover a breath-taking range of topics, including several on the causes and impact of the U.S. inflation of the 1970's.

Walton, Clarence C., ed. *Inflation and National Survival.* New York: Academy of Political Science, 1979. Sponsored by the life insurance industry, this study is clearly written for nonspecialists and covers a wide range of topics.

Paul B. Trescott

See also Business and the economy in the United States; Energy crisis; Gas shortages; Income and wages in the United States; Inflation in Canada; Ninety-day freeze on wages and prices; Oil embargo of 1973-1974; Unemployment in the United States.

■ International trade of Canada

Definition Canada's international exports and foreign trade imports

During the 1970's, Canada's trade flowed southward while the share of U.S. foreign investment and trade continued to eclipse that of Canada's other traditional trading partners. This increasing dependence fanned unease during a time of rising Canadian nationalism and exacerbated fears of U.S. economic dominance. This situation led to measures designed to lessen Canada's dependence on U.S. markets and direct investment in Canada.

Canada's dependence on the U.S. market was an irreversible trend. The post-World War II years continued to see the diminishing value of the once important trade and investment links with Great Britain and the Commonwealth. Great Britain's membership in the European Economic Community (EEC) in 1973 accelerated Canada's reliance on U.S. trade. The protectionist trade policies, particularly agricultural, of the EEC meant that the British market became less open to Canadian exports, which were primarily agricultural products such as grains, foodstuffs, or other resource-based commodities.

The gradual erosion of this market was somewhat offset by increases in lucrative wheat sales to China and the Soviet Union. Moreover, the growing resource demands of the Japanese economy and the insatiable appetite of U.S. consumers for Canadian resources such as forest products, oil, natural gas, aluminum, and motor cars, the latter assisted by the Auto Pact, produced the two fastest-growing and dominant markets for Canadian goods in the 1970's. The U.S. government, however, was often oblivious to the sheer enormity of its trade with Canada. On one occasion, President Richard M. Nixon mistakenly identified Japan as America's largest trading partner, when in fact it was clearly Canada.

The Nixon Shocks   The Canadian economy's reliance on the United States was plainly expressed through the shock and alarm that struck Canadian officials in August, 1971. President Nixon had announced a series of protectionist measures designed to address a balance of payments crisis and to protect domestic gold reserves. These measures threatened U.S. trade and investment with Canada and, subsequently, countless Canadian jobs.

This period was also marked by the distinct personalities of Canadian prime minister Pierre Trudeau and President Nixon, who did not share a common worldview. Although the two leaders disagreed on a number of issues, including East-West relations, U.S. secretary of state Henry Kissinger was successful in preventing the proposed U.S. measures from affecting Canada because of the potential impact on the country's primary trading partner.

The Third Option   It was clear to Canadian officials that the once special relationship between the two nations had changed and that it was necessary to reconsider Canada's foreign policy and trade options. In 1972, the Canadian secretary of state for external affairs, Mitchell Sharp, published a policy paper that concluded there were three separate foreign policy choices: Canada could maintain the status quo, which few supported; integrate more closely with the United States, which was already a prevailing concern; or reduce Canada's economic vulnerability by enhancing established or cultivating new relationships elsewhere.

The Canadian government endorsed what became known as the "third option" and began to show increased interest in expanding and diversifying economic and trade ties with Europe and Japan. Trade with the EEC had declined since the late 1950's, and although Japan was now Canada's second-largest trading partner, Canadian exports were one-sided and comprised mainly of resource materials.

The Status Quo   Between 1973 and 1976, the Canadian government energetically pursued increased trade with the EEC and Japan and successfully negotiated contractual links with each nation. These agreements were designed to promote trade and foster awareness of business opportunities between the respective signatories. The Canadian government also wished to export more finished products and technological goods and fewer resources.

Despite these initiatives, it proved difficult for Canadian officials to obtain the desired results. Many government trade officials and businesspeople were skeptical as geographical proximity, similar cultural norms, and common language made trade with the United States simpler than pursuing new foreign markets. In addition, Canadians continued to have difficulty penetrating the protectionist economies of the EEC and Japan. Conversely, European exporters did not show much enthusiasm in expanding their trade with Canada. Trade with Japan continued to grow impressively, but the Japanese remained focused on obtaining Canadian resources, shunning higher-end manufactured products. Thus, the postwar trend of mushrooming trade between Canada and the United States continued.

The Federal Investment Review Agency   The "third option" initiatives were not the only manifestation of nationalist economic and trade policy during the 1970's. In 1973, the Foreign Investment Review Agency (FIRA) was created by the Trudeau government. FIRA was designed to monitor foreign investment in Canada and appease nationalist fears of foreign ownership, especially by the United States. Nearly all takeovers and transfers of domestic ownership to foreign companies would be subject to government screening.

The creation of FIRA succeeded in doing little more than irritating the United States and sent an incongruent message to foreign investors at a time when the federal government wished to expand Canadian overseas markets. Despite the screening delays that occurred during the review process, most foreign investment cases were approved. The agency was eliminated in 1985.

Impact The fears of Canadian nationalists were not allayed as the 1970's ended. Canada's trade remained increasingly tied to the U.S. market, despite new protectionist initiatives aimed at monitoring U.S. investment and expanding trade links with Japan, Europe, and the Communist bloc. Canada's international trade continued to expand, but by 1985 approximately 80 percent of exports went to the United States. For better or worse, Canadian trade and, along with it, Canadian prosperity were linked with the United States. The decade set the stage for the eventual signing of a free trade agreement in the 1980's and closer economic integration.

Further Reading

Bothwell, Robert. *Canada and the United States: The Politics of Partnership.* Toronto: University of Toronto Press, 1992. A history of Canadian-American relations. Charts the development of the political, defense, and economic history behind the largest bilateral trading partnership in the world.

Granatstein, J. L., and Robert Bothwell. *Pirouette: Pierre Trudeau and Canadian Foreign Policy.* Toronto: University of Toronto Press, 1990. Remains the standard study of Trudeau's foreign policy, with a detailed treatment of foreign trade and national defense issues.

Granatstein, J. L., and Norman Hillmer. *Empire to Umpire: Canada and the World to the 1990's.* Toronto: Irwin, 2000. Provides a broad, engaging, and insightful overview of the history of Canadian foreign policy, from confederation to the uncertain years of the post-Cold War world.

Head, Ivan, and Pierre Trudeau. *The Canadian Way: Shaping Canada's Foreign Policy, 1968-1984.* Toronto: McClelland & Stewart, 1995. This study provides a practitioner's perspective of the development and reasoning behind Canadian foreign and trade policy during the 1970's by two people who directly shaped the policy and implementation.

Ryan M. Touhey

See also Agriculture in Canada; Agriculture in the United States; Business and the economy in Canada; Business and the economy in the United States; Canada and the British Commonwealth; Canada and the United States; Europe and North America; Foreign policy of Canada; Foreign policy of the United States; International trade of the United States; Japan and North America; Trudeau, Pierre.

■ International trade of the United States

Identification The United States' international exports and foreign trade imports

Important trade issues faced by the United States during the 1970's included trade imbalances, presidential power over international trade agreements, an oil embargo, and domestic inflation.

The international trade of the United States was affected extensively by the adoption by most countries of a flexible exchange rate system during the early 1970's. The change to a flexible rate of exchange was the result of the collapse of the gold-based system of exchange. The international trade of the United States, in monetary terms, grew at a rapid rate after the flexible exchange rate was adopted. At the same time, many other countries greatly increased their exports to the United States at a rate greater than the United States could match with any one of the individual countries. Thus began the trade imbalance, or trade deficit, that has existed in the United States since the early years of the 1970's.

There were many beneficial effects of the adoption of the flexible exchange rate system. The U.S. agricultural trade vastly expanded during the 1970's, which caused rapid increases in the productivity rate of providers of agricultural exports. This rapid expansion also brought about a corresponding increase in investment in capital agricultural equipment and capital improvements, creating many new jobs. Investment in agricultural land also increased, driving up the value of land substantially. Other sectors such as forestry, fisheries, and mining enjoyed a rapid increase in exports due to the adoption of the flexible exchange rate system in the early 1970's.

Derogatory effects were also produced by the trade imbalances created during the early 1970's. The devaluation of the U.S. dollar in the late 1970's in an attempt to remedy the increasing inflation throughout the middle of the decade brought about a recession, the full impact of which was not realized until the early 1980's.

The Trade Act of 1974   The Trade Act of 1974 was designed mainly to reduce import barriers to U.S. trade. The act gave the president of the United States broad authority to enter into international trade agreements. It also provided for protection to domestic producers that might be injured by competition with imported goods. The United States International Trade Commission was charged with identifying any injury or threats of injury to domestic sector providers, formulating a recommended course of action to correct the situation, and presenting these recommendations to the president.

The president could either follow the recommendations of the commission or propose his own course of action. In any case, the president was given the ultimate authority to act upon such injuries. Congress, however, did have the right to veto a president's formulated cure and force the use of the recommendations of the International Trade Commission. Other goals of the legislation were stimulating the U.S. economy and enlarging foreign markets for the products of U.S. producers in the agricultural, manufacturing, and mining sectors.

The Trade Act of 1974 did have some negative effects on the U.S. economy and some domestic manufacturers. The president was given the broad authority to negotiate and enter into trade agreements with other countries. Concessions were sometimes given in the name of foreign policy that actually widened the trade imbalance that began in the early 1970's. These concessions would sometimes take their form as unfair competition against domestically produced items, causing the loss of jobs. The United States, for the most part, helped to retrain and reclassify these dislocated workers; however, much resentment and discontent were created on a local level.

Trade Partners and Domestic Sectors   During the 1970's, the major trade partners of the United States were Canada, Japan, Germany, the United Kingdom, and Mexico. Although the United States traded with many other countries, the major trade partners accounted for more than 50 percent, in value, of U.S. exports and imports during the decade.

While most U.S. exports came from the manufacturing sector, the agricultural, fisheries, forestry, and mining sectors experienced a period of rapid and widespread growth in exports during the 1970's.

Many new jobs were created to produce these exports, which increased the average worker's salary and, in turn, increased Americans' demand for imported goods. These increases were for the most part beneficial, but they did create far-reaching negative effects, such as inflation, which produced consequences that were not experienced fully until the following decade.

Japanese imports had a greater influence on the U.S. economy than goods from any other trade partner. The early 1970's found Japan as one of the top five members of the International Monetary Fund (IMF). As the United States was declining in its status as a creditor nation, Japan was increasing its presence as a creditor. The largest impact upon the United States, in the early 1970's, came in the form of the sizable share of the textile market held by Japan. During the 1970's, Japan dominated the clothing, apparel, and accessories market in the United States. Starting in the mid-1970's and lasting into the twenty-first century, Japan also began its considerable influence in the American automobile market with its fuel-efficient imports. Japan began the 1970's with a sizable trade surplus that increased substantially through the decade. A huge percentage of the U.S. trade market share was taken over by the Japanese, causing many Americans to blame their economic problems on them.

The Energy Crisis   During the 1970's, the domestic consumption of oil increased considerably while domestic production decreased. American dependence on imported oil grew substantially during the decade. The largest external suppliers of oil to the United States were the Arab nations that made up the Organization of Petroleum Exporting Countries (OPEC). A series of conflicts between the Arab nations and Israel and U.S. involvement in them on the Israelis' side, brought about a retaliatory oil embargo against the United States by the OPEC countries in the fall of 1973.

An internal panic followed, which increased oil prices considerably and caused severe fuel shortages across the country. Long lines formed at filling stations across the United States, and many stations exhausted their supply before the daily demand was satisfied. Fear and discontent spread among American consumers that would have a dramatic and long-lasting effect on trade practices as well as the domestic automobile industry.

Workers at a Sony electronics factory in Tokyo in 1970. The 1970's saw the rise of Japanese imports as a threat to the U.S. economy. (AP/
Wide World Photos)

Although the oil embargo lasted only six months, its impact upon U.S. trade policies was far-reaching. The U.S. government mandated the creation of the Strategic Petroleum Reserve in order to build a domestic supply of petroleum that could be released to the U.S. economy in the event of another oil embargo. The government also tried to shore up trade agreements with other non-OPEC countries to supply some of the imported oil.

Inflation and Devaluation In the middle of the decade, in part because of the increasing trade imbalances, the U.S. dollar experienced a period of inflation. In the eleven years following 1971, prices in the United States rose 157 percent, marking the greatest inflation ever experienced in so short a period of time.

Those in control of monetary policy in the United States prescribed a series of devaluations in order to remedy the out-of-control inflation. The series of devaluations increased the trade deficit further and helped to create the economic recession of the early 1980's.

Impact Perhaps the greatest single impact of the trade issues of the 1970's was produced by the oil embargo of the OPEC nations against the United States. The fear created in the American people by the oil shortages and the increasing prices caused them to seek out and demand a more stable, cheaper, and more efficient fuel. Many Americans purchased energy-efficient automobiles imported from Japan. The trade imbalance widened even further when the quality of the Japanese automobiles surpassed that of domestic manufacturers. The effects of the energy crisis were still experienced in the twenty-first century. The American public continued to demand a continuous development of alternative fuels, one of the greatest motivations being the commonly held opinion that the United States is overly dependent upon imported oil.

The impact of Japanese automobile imports upon the domestic manufacturers was double-sided. On one side, the Japanese imports began to take on an ever-increasing share of the automobile market, costing the domestic manufacturers sales volume. Domestic manufacturers tried to combat this situation by appealing to the loyalty of American buyers, but that approach had a limited effect upon consumers faced with increasing fuel costs. The appeal of Japanese imports came from their fuel efficiency, and with the oil embargo and price increases, this appeal was considerable. The other side, the one that won in the end, was that domestic manufacturers had to compete with Japanese imports by building fuel-efficient automobiles. This realization, however, came late in the 1970's, and the American automobile industry would take many years to adapt and recover from the economic impact of the Japanese import market share.

Further Reading

Ashdown, Neil H. *The Impact of Banking Policy on Trade and Global Stability.* Westport, Conn.: Quorum Books, 2002. An extensive discussion on trade, including the global impact of U.S. international trade.

Burdekin, Richard C. K., and Pierre L. Siklos. *Deflation: Current and Historical Perspectives.* Cambridge, England: Cambridge University Press, 2004. Offers a section concerning the inflation, devaluation, and recession of the 1970's.

Kalt, Joseph P. *The Economics and Politics of Oil Price Regulation: Federal Policy in the Post Embargo Era.* Cambridge, Mass.: MIT Press, 1981. U.S. trade policy following the OPEC oil embargo is the main topic of this book.

Liker, Jeffery K. *Becoming Lean: Inside Stories of U.S. Manufacturers.* Portland, Oreg.: Productivity Press, 1998. An in-depth examination of the realization by U.S. automobile manufacturers that they would have to compete with Japanese imports by producing fuel-efficient automobiles.

Saxonhouse, Gary R. *Economic Statistics and Information Concerning the Japanese Auto Industry Final Report.* Washington, D.C.: Government Printing Office, 1980. A government report covering the impact upon the domestic economy caused by the increase in importation of Japanese automobiles during the 1970's.

U.S. Office of International Energy Affairs. *U.S. Oil Companies and the Arab Oil Embargo: The International Allocation of Constricted Supplies: Prepared for the Use of Subcommittee on Multinational Corporations of the Committee on Foreign Relations, United States Senate.* Washington, D.C.: Government Printing Office, 1975. A government report that discusses possible remedies to the effects of the OPEC oil embargo of 1973.

Wells, Donald R. *The Federal Reserve System: A History.* Jefferson, N.C.: McFarland, 2004. Includes an extensive examination of the inflation and devaluation in the U.S. economy caused, in part, by the trade imbalance of the 1970's.

Glenn S. Hamilton

See also Agriculture in the United States; Automobiles; Business and the economy in the United States; Canada and the United States; Energy crisis; Foreign policy of the United States; Gas shortages; Income and wages in the United States; Inflation in the United States; Israel and the United States; Japan and North America; Middle East and North America; Oil embargo of 1973-1974.

■ International Year of the Woman

Identification The commemoration of the international progress of women in achieving full human rights

Date 1975

The United Nations officially dedicated this year to promoting three main objectives: equality between men and women, integration of women into international economic and social development, and increased participation of women in achievement of world peace.

Also known as International Women's Year (IWY), 1975 marked the beginning of the Decade of the Woman as sponsored by the United Nations Educational, Scientific, and Cultural Organization (UNESCO). Pat Hutar, an American member of the U.N. Commission on the Status of Women (CSW), proposed holding a world conference as the focal point of IWY, emphasizing the importance of evaluating the effectiveness of CSW programs that had been implemented during the prior twenty-five years.

Held in Mexico City in June, the Conference on IWY attracted more than five thousand participants, including 133 national delegations. With forty-three members, the U.S. delegation stood as the largest in attendance. Rosalind Harris and Mildred Persinger, leaders of nongovernmental organizations (NGOs) based in New York, worked with the Mexican government in setting up an unofficial parallel conference in the same city at the same time. Known as the IWY Tribune, this conference drew more than six thousand participants—many from national women's organizations, including well-known feminists such as Betty Friedan, Bella Abzug, Gloria Steinem, and Angela Davis.

The Conference on IWY was the first world conference of governments regarding the status and rights of women, and it produced the World Plan of Action, the first international public policy document specifically aimed at improving women's conditions and opportunities across crucial areas of their development—economic, educational, legal, political, and social. By linking CSW commitments with the larger political agenda of the United Nations, the Conference on IWY achieved a monumental breakthrough in effectively advancing women's progress toward full citizenship.

Impact In the United States, IWY inspired the convocation of the 1977 National Women's Conference, commonly referred to as the Constitutional Convention for American Women, in Houston, Texas, with two thousand members and twenty thousand guests. As the conference's *Declaration of American Women* asserted, the power of federal, state, public, and private institutions had to be harnessed so that "everything possible under the law will (be) done to provide American women with full equality." Acting on that goal, the National Commission on the Observance of IWY (appointed by President Gerald Ford) assembled the National Plan of Action—covering a wide range of concerns, including child care, the Equal Rights Amendment (ERA), and the status of minority women—and presented it to President Jimmy Carter in 1978.

Further Reading

Allan, Virginia R., Margaret E. Galey, and Mildred E. Persinger. "World Conference of International Women's Year." In *Women, Politics, and the United Nations*, edited by Anne Winslow. Westport, Conn.: Greenwood Press, 1995.

Bird, Caroline, and members and staff of National Commission on the Observance of International Women's Year. *What Women Want: From the Official Report to the President, the Congress and the People of the United States.* New York: Simon & Schuster, 1979.

Radin, Beryl A., and Hoyt H. Purvis, eds. *Women in Public Life.* Austin, Tex.: Lyndon Baines Johnson Library and Lyndon B. Johnson School of Public Affairs, 1976.

Mary Louise Buley-Meissner

See also Davis, Angela; Equal Rights Amendment (ERA); Feminism; National Organization for Women (NOW); Steinem, Gloria; United Nations; Women's rights.

■ Inventions

Definition Newly created machines, processes, instruments, material, or other objects

The vast majority of inventions in the 1970's came from industrial research and development laboratories. The decade's most noteworthy inventions clustered around chemicals and electronics, which in turn made possible numerous innovations in space exploration.

Dissatisfaction with existing artifacts is at the core of all inventions and hence all changes in existing things. First, some new knowledge prompts an idea of doing or building something. When someone gains the experience to put the idea into practice, to make the idea work, an invention is created. One invention may lead to another. For instance, in the 1970's, were it not for the earlier invention of the integrated circuit by Robert Noyce in 1959, the modern computer would not have been possible.

The line among invention, innovation, and discovery is not clearly drawn. Generally, innovation is the application of invention—the realization of a device, gadget, or gizmo based on an invention, the bringing of a product to market. Discovery implies the previous existence of something now known or determined. Thus, it is not always easy, even for a patent office, to determine when an invention is unique or merely an adaptation of an earlier one, as an invention often represents a combination of dozens of separate technological advances.

Individuals may invent for economic gain or prestige, to satisfy curiosity, or to fulfill an urge to create. However, often a group need is in evidence. This need may be economic, such as the desire to speed up production; social, such as a medical breakthrough to address a dysfunction; or military, such as the warding off of a threat or the winning of a war.

Invention and innovation are recognized as underlying economic productivity and growth. Science, technology, and invention, linked as they are, all equate with human progress. At the level of individual enterprise, invention and innovation are often tantamount to survival if not success. To stay economically viable, a firm must remain at the cutting edge of invention. Consequently, most 1970's inventions were the products of industrial research and development laboratories.

The 1970's saw major inventions in the fields of transportation, medicine, communications, industry, entertainment, and military technology, with such highlights as the Boeing 747, CAT scans, MRI scans, ultrasonography, lasers, microprocessors, computers, fiber optics, Kevlar, video games, and the neutron bomb.

Transportation The Boeing 747, a four-engine wide-body jumbo jet, was brought into service in 1970. It could fly at around 600 miles per hour, with an initial range exceeding 5,500 miles without refueling and with a capacity of more than four hundred passengers. The 747 was planned to be more cost-effective than its predecessor, the Boeing 707, unveiled in 1958. It was also meant to counter flight congestion in the air lanes and at airports since, with its greater capabilities, fewer such planes would have to take to the air. The Boeing 747 dominated the high end of the civilian jet aircraft market for three decades, with frequent expansion of its range and even its payload.

Initially, fear of an air disaster was great, but the public nevertheless took to the aircraft, and many millions had flown on it safely by the end of the decade. However, the worst aviation disaster in history occurred in 1977 when two 747's crashed into each other on a runway in the Canary Islands, killing 570.

Medicine The computed axial tomography (CAT) scanner exemplified how, by the early 1970's, bioengineering blending medicine and electronic technology—especially computers—helped produce a better understanding and thus treatment of human dysfunctions. The CAT scanner, invented in 1972 by Godfrey N. Hounsfield, is an imaging device that combines multiple X rays to provide a complete cross-sectional picture, or tomogram, of a patient's organ.

A CAT scan is noninvasive, limiting trauma or disruption at the site examined. It provides a three-dimensional portrait enabling medical practitioners to peer into a body without incisions. The patient is placed on a gantry and moved into a hatch in a cylinder. Beams of X rays rotate and change angles, and the data are collected and stored. They are read and interpreted by a radiologist from a computer console.

Magnetic resonance imaging (MRI), also invented in 1972, is used primarily in the examination of soft tissue (such as the brain) and viscous areas (such as the lymphatic system or spinal fluid). It is less commonly known by its original designation, nuclear magnetic resonance (NMR). Radio waves are administered to the patient, who is placed in a cylinder surrounded by a strong magnet. The atoms in the subject's body resonate with these waves, identifying unhealthy cells, which respond differently than normal cells when they are magnetically stimulated. Those cells that take the longest to return to normal are the most malignant. It was only in 1977, through the efforts of Dr. Richard Damadian, that the first image of an actual person's chest (his assistant's) was obtained by MRI. The pictures using the process are several times more detailed than those from X rays. Unlike CAT scans, MRI scans do not involve the hazard of radiation.

By the mid-1970's, ultrasound became an effective and inexpensive diagnostic tool. It has long been known that different tissues possess different textures and that the latter reflect sound waves at different rates and intensities. With ultrasonography, high-frequency sound waves, or echograms, can be used in evaluating body textures and fluids, in detecting abnormalities in the brain, heart, or lungs, and in monitoring fetal development. As with CAT and MRI scans, ultrasound is noninvasive. It, too, makes a three-dimensional portrait possible, enabling medical practitioners to see inside a patient's body. In all three of these diagnostic instruments, computers are essential to the recombination of the textures, atoms, points, or planes detected by the procedure.

A laser, an acronym for "light amplification by the stimulated emission of radiation," is a light-emitting medium that produces an intense unidirectional monochrome beam of light. It is not the energy in-

Time Line of Select 1970's Inventions

1970
Automatic teller machine (ATM)
Boeing 747 wide-body jumbo jet aircraft
Fiber optics
Gene synthesis
Microprocessor
Polyurethane wheels for skateboards
Post-it note adhesive
Recombinant deoxyribonucleic acid (rDNA)
Scanning electron microscope
Smartcard

1971
Digital watch
Floppy disk
Home video game system
Liquid crystal display (LCD)
Mariner 9 Mars probe
Pocket calculator
Salyut 1 space station
Videocassette recorder (VCR)

1972
Anik A1 communication satellite
Computed axial tomography (CAT) scanner
Landsat I earth resources satellite
Laser (compact) disk
Magnetic resonance imaging (MRI) scanner
Video game (*Pong*)
Word processor

1973
Bar code (Universal Product Code, or UPC)
Food processor (Cuisinart)
Genetic engineering

Pioneer 10 Jupiter probe
Skylab space station
Snowboard

1975
Laser printer
Microchip
Music synthesizer
Stay-on can tab
Ultrasonography

1976
Disposable diaper
Gene splicing
Ink-jet printer
Kevlar fiber
Plastic pencil

1977
Artificial heart
Balloon angioplasty
Cartridge-based home video machine
Telephone fiber optics

1978
Home automation and remote control system
Pioneer Venus orbit

1979
Mobile cellular telephone (cell phone)
Personal stereo (Walkman)
Recumbent bicycle
Spreadsheet
Voyager 1 and 2 Jupiter probes

volved that is crucial but its intensity, By the 1970's, lasers were being used in medicine to spot-weld retinas in eye surgery and in other bloodless operations.

Communications Microprocessors are microchips made of silicon wafers, with each one containing hundreds of processors. A large number of circuits, semiconductors, can be crammed into each silicon wafer. These units are the operative parts of comput-

ers as well as of nearly every consumer electronic product.

Earlier computers had required entire rooms to house their cathode-ray-tube-activated hardware. For instance, the Electronic Numerical Integrator and Computer (ENIAC), which entered operation in 1946, was more than one hundred feet long, had eighteen thousand vacuum tubes, and required operators to trip thousands of switches to program even rudimentary calculations that had to flow through many of its one million parts over six hundred miles of wire.

In 1971, Intel's first 4004 microprocessor had 2,300 transistors and measured a mere one-eighth by one-sixteenth of an inch. It had the computational power of the gigantic ENIAC. Later models incorporated transistors, resistors, and capacitors, allowing more mathematical and logical functions.

The microprocessor found uses in many other fields beyond communications. It came to control the programmable equipment of automobiles, microwave ovens, washing machines, clothes dryers, thermostats, digital watches, cash registers, telephones, gas pumps, video recording devices, automatic teller machines (ATMs), and many others.

Computers are little more than a number of switches that use the binary language of ones and zeros to register electrical impulses. The discovery of semiconductors used in tiny transistors created in 1947 led to a revolution that made possible the building of faster, smaller, and cheaper computers beginning in the 1970's.

The original memory of a computer, the memory disk, was invented in 1971 by a team at International Business Machines (IBM) under the direction of engineer Alan Shugart. These flexible 8-inch plastic disks coated with magnetic iron oxide, dubbed "floppies," were eventually reduced to 5.25 inches by 1976 and 3.5 inches by 1981. Disk drives gripped and spun the floppy, while a head read or recorded information. Floppy disks provided a convenient and portable method of storing and transferring data and programs when compared with tapes.

In 1970, electrical engineer Douglas Engelbart patented what came to be known as the mouse—officially "an X-Y position indicator for a display system." Pointing and clicking activated whatever was being targeted on the visual display unit (VDU), or screen. The keyboard became the most common way of inputting information in a computer because it was already familiar to users from typewriters, telegraphs, teletypes, and keypunch machines. The keyboard retained its similarly commonplace QWERTY letter arrangement despite later complaints that this outdated design, originally devised to avoid keys sticking together in a typewriter, helped produce repetitive strain injuries to the wrists and fingers. The first desk computer for personal use became available in 1974.

During the 1970's, fiber optics, the use of glass fiber serving as a conduit for light, became widespread in communications, as well as in medicine, photoelectronics, night vision devices, photography, and elsewhere. Fiber made of glass or clear plastics can transmit light over a straight or curved path by reflection.

The first optical fiber suitable for long-range communications was produced by the Corning Glass Works in 1970. Glass fiber is made of silica and titanium in a fiber-optic line. The line is then heated and stretched into a minutely thin strand, a fraction of the thickness of a human hair. These glass-carrying fibers were discovered to have the capacity to transmit data more consistently than microwaves and thus replaced cables for the long-distance transmission of digitalized data. Indeed, by the early 1970's, a hair-thin optical fiber could carry as many messages as a copper cable containing 512 wires. Signals transmitted through fiber optics are more impervious to water and much less compromised by electric motors and generators, power lines, electromagnetic interferences, and lightning-caused static. Finally, fiber glass, being much lighter than copper wire, recommends its use in aircraft and spacecraft.

Industry The invention of the synthetic fabric Kevlar in the 1970's was the outcome of industry's attempt to find replacements for fast-depleting organic materials. Kevlar joined other synthetics such as nylon, rayon, vinyl, and polyethylene.

In 1976, Stephanie Kwolek and Herbert Blades of the DuPont Corporation invented a new process for spinning a polymer plastic into fiber. The molecular structure of this polymer gave it greater strength than steel of corresponding weight. Kevlar is also extremely resistant to heat and ultraviolet light, making its use ideal in automobile tires, fabrics, tapes, lines and ropes, and sports equipment and as a shield against X rays. It is also used in space shuttle components and spacesuits, in bullet-proof vests for police and army personnel, and in the protective gear worn by firefighters and hunters.

In industry, ultrasound can help detect flaws in solids, such as stress fissures in aircraft wings. Ultrasonic vibrations cleanse metals to facilitate soldering and welding. Ultrasound is employed in sonar devices to detect the presence of enemy ships and also in navigation, observation, and communication.

The applications of lasers in industry in the

1970's included reading bar codes at store checkouts, welding materials, and cutting, drilling, and heating. Lasers were also used to store data on disks with the development of the compact disk in 1972. The data can then be read back by another laser.

Entertainment In the field of entertainment, the 1970's brought video games, which changed the way in which the world plays. By the 1960's, Ralph Baer had built a small computer and hooked it up to a television set in order to view two electronic dots chase each other across the screen.

In short order, Baer, William Rusch, and William Harrison had turned this original idea into a system that could play Ping-Pong, football, and shooting games. It was released in 1972 as the Magnavox *Odyssey*, the first home video game system. It was really Nolan Bushnell, however, who achieved video game history by making video games commonplace in arcades and homes through Atari, which he founded in the mid-1970's.

Military Technology The 1970's witnessed the development of not only the Minuteman III intercontinental ballistic missile (ICBM) but also a new weapon with the potential to revolutionize warfare. The neutron bomb, also known as the enhanced radiation warhead, is a fusion explosive designed to produce blast and heat effects limited to a relatively small area. In its relatively confined space, however, the neutron bomb releases massive amounts of gamma and neutron radiation. The latter is able to penetrate most ordinary protective shields made of steel, concrete, or earth.

Because of this short-range rather than long-range destructive effect, this device can be used highly effectively against enemy units. It can be delivered by conventional ordnance such as howitzers, by missiles, or by attack aircraft without endangering friendly forces, the civilian population, or property outside the immediate vicinity. Because of public opposition, production of the neutron bomb was halted in 1978 by the Carter administration but tentatively resumed in 1981 by the Reagan administration.

Impact Inventions have always had economic, social, and intellectual impacts. There is no question that inventions have enabled individuals and entire societies to control their environment and to live healthier, longer, and often easier lives. They can also raise important ethical questions for society. For example, with the development in the 1970's of new electronics technology and the surveillance methods made possible by its use, concerns arose about restrictions to liberty and privacy, especially at a time when government agencies were bent on keeping track of real or imagined subversives.

Some people hold that much of the technology underlying inventions has or will come back to haunt humankind. They note the low-level radiation from computers or cell phones and the negative consequences of some chemicals used as drugs or food additives, in cosmetics, in industry, or even in war—such as the infamous defoliant Agent Orange sprayed by American forces in the Vietnam War during the 1970's, with allegedly ill effects on its users. They point to the near-meltdown of Unit 2 of the Three-Mile Island nuclear power plant outside Harrisburg, Pennsylvania, in March, 1979.

Therefore, while inventions are beneficial in many instances, they can be harmful in others. As always, the costs and benefits must be traded off.

Further Reading

Brockman, John. *Greatest Inventions of the Past Two Thousand Years: Today's Leading Thinkers Choose the Creations That Shaped the World.* New York: Simon & Schuster, 2000. Some of the most creative thinkers identify not only familiar material inventions, such as the computer, but also such nonmaterial innovations as democracy and social justice, the scientific method, and other discoveries beyond the physical.

Brown, David E. *Inventing Modern America: From the Microwave to the Mouse.* Cambridge, Mass.: MIT Press, 2002. An attractive, illustrated compendium organized functionally into five sections and by inventor.

Carlisle, Rodney. *Inventions and Discoveries.* New York: John Wiley & Sons, 2004. Part VI, entitled "The Atomic and Electronic Age, 1935 into the 21st Century," includes the major inventions of the 1970's briefly described. A text sponsored by *Scientific American* magazine.

Carlson, W. Bernard, ed. *Technology in World History,* Vol. 6. New York: Oxford University Press, 2005. Chapter 3, "The World Since 1970," includes a time line highlighting the historical and technological context for inventions of the 1970's.

Irving, Clive. *The Triumph of the 747*. New York: William Morrow, 1992. How the Boeing Company revolutionized the world's transportation patterns with its jumbo wide-body jet.

Petroski, Henry. *Invention by Design: How Engineers Get from Thought to Thing*. Cambridge, Mass.: Harvard University Press, 1998. Petroski, a widely published civil engineer and historian, explores the context of the inventive process—for instance, how economics, ecology, and ethics underlie the invention of stay-on can tabs in the 1970's.

Tenner, Edward. *Why Things Bite Back: Technology and the Revenge of Unintended Consequences*. New York: Random House, 1997. A critic's often negative view of some perverse effects of high-tech inventions, including those of the 1970's, such as the "disappointing outcomes" of computers.

Van Dulken, Stephen. *Inventing the Twentieth Century: One Hundred Inventions That Shaped the World*. New York: New York University Press, 2000. Inventions are discussed by decades. Thus, "1970-1979" covers the artificial heart, the dual cyclone vacuum cleaner, magnetic resonance imaging (MRI), the personal stereo, Post-it notes, the recumbent bicycle, the Rubik's cube, the smartcard, the snowboard, and wave energy.

Williams, Trevor I., et al., eds. *The History of Invention: From Stone Axes to Silicon Chips*. Rev. ed. New York: Facts On File, 1999. Factual information about major inventions, including artificial hearts, computers, and information technology. Also provides biographical highlights about the people who made these advances a reality.

Peter B. Heller

See also   Air bags; Aircraft; Anik communication satellites; Apple Computer; Atari; Automatic teller machines (ATMs); Automobiles; Bar codes; CAT scans; Closed captioning; Communications in Canada; Communications in the United States; Computer networks; Computers; Dolby sound; 8-track tapes; Genetics research; Hot tubs; Jumbo jets; LED and LCD screens; Medicine; Microprocessors; Microsoft; Mopeds; Neutron bomb; Polyester; Quadraphonic sound; RVs; Sanitary napkins with adhesive strips; Science and technology; Skateboards; Skylab; Toys and games; Transportation; Ultrasonography; Video games; Videocassette recorders (VCRs); Walkman.

■ Iranian hostage crisis

The Event   American employees are taken hostage in Iran and held for 444 days

Date   Began on November 4, 1979; ended January 20, 1981

Place   U.S. embassy in Tehran, Iran

This event was viewed as one of the major foreign policy crises of the Carter administration, as the United States was widely seen as helpless in freeing the hostages.

The roots of the Iranian hostage crisis lie, in many ways, in the 1950's, when the United States' support of the leader of Iran, Mohammad Reza shah Pahlavi, began. In 1953, the United States supported the overthrow of Muhammad Mussadegh, the popular leader of Iran, and helped the shah gain power. The United States opposed Mussadegh because of his communist ties and because he had nationalized the oil industry. The shah remained close to the United States over the next two decades. Iran was adjacent geographically to the the Soviet Union, the United States' main enemy in the Cold War, and Iran served as a good "listening post" for the United States to conduct electronic espionage on the Soviets. The United States rewarded the shah's allegiance with large amounts of military aid and training by the Central Intelligence Agency (CIA) of the shah's secret police. This secret police force was able to control the majority Shiite population, which generally opposed the shah because of his modern ways and the lack of emphasis on Islam in his government.

By the middle of the 1970's, cracks were beginning to show in Iran. The shah needed to transfer power to his son as he was suffering from non-Hodgkin's lymphoma (a type of cancer) and did not know how long he had to live. He thought that this power transfer would be difficult if the country was still run as a firm dictatorship. Therefore, the government eased repression of religious objectors, who in turn began to protest—a situation that eventually led to the government's overthrow. The shah left the country, winding up in Mexico. Needing better medical treatment, he then came to the United States. Radical Iranian students objected to the United States accepting the shah, and—urged by the top religious leader in Iran, the Ayatollah Khomeini—they took over the U.S. embassy and captured ninety of the embassy staff as hostages.

Negotiations and Rescue Attempt The United States tried to force Iran to release the hostages, but Iran made many demands on the United States in turn. One of these was that the United States had to release the shah and allow him to return to Iran to face trial on charges of war crimes against his own people. Because the shah had been a loyal ally of the United States, the American government would not allow this. Iran also wanted its funds in the West released or "unfrozen," as the United States and other nations had frozen Iran's bank accounts after the overthrow of the shah.

The Iranian government released some women and older prisoners early in the ordeal, but fifty-two hostages remained in Iran for the duration. U.S. president Jimmy Carter seemed to be somewhat paralyzed by this crisis, and his public opinion ratings plummeted. The United States and many Western nations had troubled histories with many non-Western nations, so many Americans felt insulted by the Iranian action. Some called for military action. However, the United States' allies were not going to support a military strike, and Iran was right next to the Soviet Union. Thus, the United States had to negotiate with Iran for the hostages' release, a move that put the United States, at best, on par with Iran and thereby proved the power both of the radical students and of the new Iranian government.

President Carter considered various options, but the only one really feasible, besides negotiation, was a military rescue. Carter tried this option using military helicopters in April, 1980, but the mission failed miserably, with one helicopter crashing and killing eight U.S. servicemen and injuring four more. Carter's approval ratings dropped even further.

Political Maneuvering Complicating the situation was the fact that a presidential election was approaching, and the Republicans used the hostage situation as political fodder. The Republicans, it

later was argued, also used the hostages for their political advantage, telling the Iranians that if the release was delayed until after the election, the Iranians would get a better deal. If true, the tactic worked, as Carter lost the election in a landslide.

The shah died in July, 1980, removing the issue of his extradition from the negotiations. The Iranians did not get all of the money that they wanted, receiving only eight billion dollars, but that was more than the United States initially wanted to give them. In addition to forcing the United States to deal with the terrorists, Iran had forced the United States to deal with a Muslim-based government as an equal, and the hostages were finally released on January 20, 1981, the same day Ronald Reagan took office as president of the United States.

Impact The Iranian hostage crisis furthered the perception, among Americans and abroad, that the United States was weak and had lost the superpower status that it enjoyed in the post-World War II period. The popular anger surrounding this crisis led to the election of Reagan and, some argue, the reignition of the Cold War. The hostage crisis, along with the general economic problems in the United States, are blamed by many to have led to the failure of the Carter administration.

Iranian demonstrators outside the U.S. embassy where American hostages are being kept mock the United States and show their reverence for Ayatollah Khomeini. (AP/Wide World Photos)

Further Reading

Bill, James A. *The Shah, the Ayatollah, and the United States*. New York: Foreign Policy Association, 1988. This book, by one of the leading historians of foreign policy, provides a good overview of the relationship between the United States and the two leading figures in Iran up to, and during, the crisis.

Houghton, David Patrick. *U.S. Foreign Policy and the Iran Hostage Crisis*. Cambridge, England: Cambridge University Press, 2001. This account looks at both the reasons for the hostage crisis and the reasons for the failure of the rescue mission, along with a summary of the other books written about the crisis.

Sick, Gary. *All Fall Down: America's Tragic Encounter with Iran*. New York: Random House, 1985. A good history of the Iranian hostage crisis and its origins.

_____. *October Surprise: America's Hostages in Iran and the Election of Ronald Reagan*. New York: Times Books, 1991. A discussion of the behind-the-scenes political maneuvering of the Republicans during the Iranian hostage crisis.

Scott A. Merriman

See also Carter, Jimmy; Central Intelligence Agency (CIA); Cold War; Foreign policy of the United States; Middle East and North America; Reagan, Ronald.

■ Israel and the United States

Definition   The diplomatic, supportive, and
strategic relationship between the United States
and Israel

*Events in the Middle East during the 1970's changed the
nature of American Jews' support for Israel and resulted in
the United States increasing its long-term aid to Israel and
committing itself to help Israel maintain its military edge
over its neighbors.*

The United States was the first country to recognize
Israel after it was created in 1948, consistent with a
1922 congressional resolution backing the League
of Nations mandate for a Jewish homeland in Palestine. Following 1948, the two countries developed a
solid bond, largely because Israel was the only country in the Middle East that resembled the United
States in its advanced democracy. The countries historically had mutual interests in deterring war, promoting stability, and eventually achieving peace. In
the United Nations, the United States did not cast its
first veto until 1972, which was on a Syrian-Lebanese
complaint against Israel. The United Nations has
been criticized by some as being hostile to Israel, and
often the United States was its sole defender in this
arena. Israel returned the friendship by voting with
the United States on virtually all issues.

American military involvement with Israel remained sporadic until the 1973 Yom Kippur War. In
1972, Palestine Liberation Organization (PLO) terrorists murdered eleven Israeli athletes at the Olympic Games in Munich, Germany. As a result, Israeli-
Arab relations deteriorated. Egypt attacked Israel in
1973 on Yom Kippur, the most solemn religious occasion on the Jewish calendar. Following an Egyptian refusal to accept a cease-fire and a successful Soviet military airlift to the Arab states, the Nixon
administration sent a U.S. airlift of weapons and supplies to Israel, enabling the country to recover from
the surprise attack. As a direct result of the Yom Kippur War, the United States quadrupled its foreign
aid to Israel and replaced France as Israel's largest
arms supplier.

Israeli Immigration   In the last decades of the communist regime in the Soviet Union, attempts were
made by Israel and Jews in the West to make clandes-
tine contacts with Soviet Jews. Visits were arranged,
books and Jewish artifacts were smuggled in, and

connections were established with groups of local
Jews, especially in the larger cities. In the 1970's, the
years of détente between the Soviet Union and the
United States, large numbers of Jews were allowed to
leave the Soviet Union for the first time in fifty years.
The rule was that Jews could leave only if they had an
official invitation and entry visa to another country.
Any Russian Jew who wanted to leave was assured of
an automatic entry visa to Israel, which was trying to
increase its Jewish population. Many of them, however, were looking for a way to the United States, particularly after the Yom Kippur War, when Israel was
portrayed negatively in the Soviet press.

Several organizations were willing to help Jews
come to the United States from the mid-1970's onward. The major American welfare agency for them
was the United Hebrew Immigrant Aid Service
(HIAS), which lobbied Congress to give Soviet Jews
special preference as refugees, which it did. With the
help of the American Jewish organizations that
opened an office in Rome, Russian Jews flooded to
the United States. By May, 1978, out of 1,169 Jews
who left the Soviet Union on Israeli visas, only 109
actually went to Israel. The emigration from the Soviet Union to the United States continued, and although it angered Israel, it created large Russian
Jewish populations in the United States, primarily in
Boston, Los Angeles, and other major cities. Later,
when the Iron Curtain fell, some 700,000 Russian
Jews did emigrate from the former Soviet Union to
Israel, creating a conservative voting block.

Impact   The United States, acting in accord with its
own interests, became Israel's partner in peace as
well as in war. Both countries shared the view that the
United States has a predominant role and responsibility in Middle East peacemaking, but Israel often
disagreed with the U.S. view of its role as an even-
handed peace broker among the parties to the Arab-
Israeli dispute.

The Carter administration was characterized by
active U.S. involvement in the peace process, which
led to some friction in U.S.-Israeli relations. Some
leaders in Israel felt that the peace process at Camp
David in Maryland placed pressure on Israel to take
risks for peace with Egypt. President Jimmy Carter's
support for a Palestinian homeland and for Palestinian rights created additional tensions. However,
President Carter guided Israeli prime minister
Menachem Begin and Egyptian president Anwar

Sadat to agree to two framework accords in 1978 that were officially signed in March, 1979. Known as the Camp David Accords, these cover an Egypt-Israel peace treaty and phased withdrawal of Israel from the Sinai Peninsula, a process that was completed three years later. It was the first peace treaty with an Arab state, but it contributed to the assassination of President Sadat in 1981 by Islamic terrorists during a military parade in Cairo.

Further Reading

Goldschmidt, Arthur, Jr. *A Concise History of the Middle East.* 5th ed. Boulder, Colo.: Westview Press, 1999. Written by a professor of Middle Eastern history, this edition is distinguished for its clear style, broad scope, and balanced treatment of the subject.

Hertzberg, Arthur. *The Jews in America.* New York: Columbia University Press. Covers the shifting relationships between American Jews and Israel.

Tessler, Mark. *A History of the Israeli-Palestinian Conflict.* Bloomington: Indiana University Press, 1994. Part of the Indiana Series in Arab and Islamic Studies, Tessler's work provides a useful overview of the numerous failed U.S. diplomatic solutions over the years.

Sheila Golburgh Johnson

See also   Camp David Accords; Carter, Jimmy; Foreign policy of the United States; Jewish Americans; Munich Olympics terrorism.

J

■ Jackson, Maynard, Jr.

Identification   Vice mayor of Atlanta, Georgia,
     1970-1974; Atlanta mayor, 1974-1982, 1989-1993
Born   March 23, 1938; Dallas, Texas
Died   June 23, 2003; Arlington, Virginia

*Jackson was the first African American mayor of Atlanta,
Georgia, and the youngest mayor of any major American
city.*

When he became vice mayor of Atlanta in 1970,
Maynard Jackson had recently lost his bid for election to the U.S. Senate by a small margin to long-
term senator Herman Talmadge. During his term as
vice mayor, Jackson continued to serve as a senior
partner in the noted Atlanta law firm of Jackson,
Patterson, and Parks.

In 1974, at age thirty-six, Jackson became Atlanta's outspoken and energetic mayor. In the same
year, African Americans Tom Bradley and Coleman
Young became mayors in Los Angeles and Detroit,
respectively. Jackson believed that local government
should respond promptly and effectively to the legitimate needs of citizens. As mayor, he acted accordingly. Taking full advantage of affirmative action
programs, Jackson expanded and improved public
housing throughout Atlanta and enhanced social
services to minorities as well as to his broader consti-
uency.

During Jackson's administration, Atlanta's convention facilities were greatly expanded, making the
city a major center for national and international
conventions. He gained public support to create a
mass transit system in Atlanta superior to any in the
United States. Moreover, Jackson's initiatives transformed Atlanta into a financial center and, because
of the excellence and efficiency of its transportation
facilities, a distribution hub for the nation.

Jackson quickly gained recognition as a rising star
among Democrats. In 1975, he was included among
Time magazine's two hundred most promising
young American leaders. The following year, he was
among those on *Ebony* magazine's roster of the one

hundred most influential black Americans. Near the
end of Jackson's second term as mayor, the *Almanac
of Places Rated* called Atlanta the best large American
city in which to live and work. Much credit for this
coveted distinction is attributable to Jackson's effectiveness as mayor over the years.

Impact   Aside from implementing important building programs and transforming Atlanta into a national and international convention and transportation center, Jackson deserves considerable credit for
his ability, as the city's first African American mayor,
to unite a racially diverse city when racial unrest
plagued much of the nation. His incumbency
marked the beginning of a crucial period of political
entitlement for African Americans. Furthermore,
that this transformation occurred in a South still
plagued by racial discrimination was quite remarkable. Jackson's leadership during the 1970's provided the bridge between solid white political rule
and the rise of black empowerment in Atlanta's politics. The consequences had a national impact.

Further Reading
Mabunda, L. Mpho. *The African American Almanac.*
     7th ed. Detroit: Gale, 1997.
Rutheiser, Charles. *Imagineering Atlanta: The Politics
     of Place in the City of Dreams.* New York: Verso, 1996.
Williams, Michael W., ed. *The African American Ency-
     clopedia.* New York: Marshall Cavendish, 1993.
                                        R. Baird Shuman
See also   Affirmative action; African Americans;
Byrne, Jane; Chisholm, Shirley; Daley, Richard J.;
Feinstein, Dianne; Jordan, Barbara; Koch, Ed; Mos-
cone, George; Racial discrimination; Young, Andrew.

■ Jackson, Reggie

Identification   African American baseball player
Born   May 18, 1946; Wyncote, Pennsylvania

*Jackson was one of the preeminent athletes of the 1970's
and an icon of the decade's popular culture.*

Reggie Jackson made his major league baseball debut with the Kansas City Athletics in 1967, followed the franchise to Oakland in 1968, and emerged as a power-hitting All-Star in 1969. Jackson's defining achievements, however, came during the 1970's. During that decade, Jackson, muscular and with a mustache and an Afro, was arguably baseball's most dominant offensive player and the game's most celebrated African American star.

Throughout the 1970's, the left-handed Jackson, playing for the Oakland Athletics (1970-1975), Baltimore Orioles (1976), and the New York Yankees (1977-1979), never hit less than twenty-three home runs in a season. He won two of his four American League (AL) home run titles in the 1970's, with thirty-two in 1973 and thirty-six in 1975. In 1973, the six-foot, two-hundred-pound right fielder also topped the AL in runs scored with 99, runs batted in (RBIs) with 117, and slugging percentage with .531, garnering the league's Most Valuable Player (MVP) award. More than half of the regular season RBIs (922 out of 1,702) and home runs (292 out of 563) of Hall of Famer Jackson's twenty-one-year major league career, which lasted from 1967 to 1987, came during the 1970's.

Although Jackson's inconsistent fielding, frequent strikeouts, modest batting average, and vocal self-regard found critics, his towering home runs, propensity for playing his best when it mattered the most, and centrality to championship teams rendered him one of baseball's best and best-known players of the 1970's. During the decade, Jackson's Oakland and New York teams won seven divisional titles (1971-1975, 1977-1978), five AL pennants (1972-1975, 1977-1978), and five World Series championships (1972-1975, 1977-1978). Called "Mr. October" for his dramatic postseason play, Jackson in the 1977 World Series slugged a record five home runs, three of them coming on first pitches in the decisive sixth game, bringing the Yankees a triumph over the Los Angeles Dodgers. For millions of television viewers, in addition to the 56,406 spectators at Yankee Stadium, Jackson's exploits in that game constituted one of the enduring memories of the 1970's.

Impact   Reggie Jackson's significance to the 1970's transcends sports. By leading the Yankees to victory in the 1977 World Series, the team's first since 1962, Jackson symbolically announced the resurgence of New York City, which had just endured near bank-

Reggie Jackson.(National Baseball Library, Cooperstown, N.Y.)

ruptcy, David Berkowitz's Son of Sam serial killings, and a major blackout.

Jackson's bravado and bombast mirrored the "Me Decade," as writer Tom Wolfe termed the 1970's. Jackson boasted that he was the straw that stirred the cocktail and feuded with other members of the Yankee organization, including catcher Thurman Munson, manager Billy Martin, and owner George Steinbrenner, leading pitcher Sparky Lyle to title his 1979 memoir *The Bronx Zoo.* Talented, controversial on and off the field, high salaried, egotistical, famous enough to be recognizable by his first name, and with a candy bar named after him, Jackson reflected the decade's "culture of narcissism."

Further Reading

Jackson, Reggie, with Mike Lupica. *Reggie: The Autobiography.* New York: Villard Books, 1984.

Kahn, Roger. *October Men: Reggie Jackson, George Steinbrenner, Billy Martin, and the Yankees' Miraculous Finish in 1978.* Orlando, Fla.: Harcourt, 2003.

William M. Simons

See also   African Americans; Baseball; Sports; Television in the United States.

■ James Bay and Northern Quebec Agreement of 1975

Definition Land claim agreement between federal and provincial governments, corporations, and the aboriginal peoples of northern Quebec Province

Date Signed on November 11, 1975; took effect on October 31, 1977

Following years of neglect of treaty agreements with Indians, or First Nations, in Canada, land claims were settled, compensation was paid, and the rights of aboriginal peoples were recognized by provincial and national governments. The James Bay and Northern Quebec Agreement was the first Canadian land claims settlement in modern history.

In the early 1970's the Quebec provincial government established the James Bay Development Corporation for the purposes of developing the region's water, mineral, forest, and recreational resources. The Quebec Association of Indians responded by applying to the Supreme Court for an injunction against the development on their lands. The injunction was granted but later overturned, and after lengthy and heated exchanges, a land claim agreement was signed on November 11, 1975. It became effective on October 31, 1977. The signatories were the Government of Quebec, the James Bay Energy Corporation, the James Bay Development Corporation, the Quebec Hydro-Electric Commission, the Grand Council of the Crees of Quebec, the Northern Quebec Inuit Association, and the Government of Canada.

In the agreement, the native peoples relinquished all claim to lands within the James Bay project area in exchange for $225 million in financial compensation from the Canadian and Quebec governments. The money was paid to the Cree Regional Authority and the Makivik Corporation of the Inuit and was exempt from taxation. Natives were also given exclusive use rights to 5,000 square miles of land and hunting, fishing, and trapping rights to an additional 60,000 square miles. The land was divided into categories of usage. Category I lands were for the exclusive use by native peoples, Category II lands were managed by both provincial and tribal governments, and Category III lands could be developed by both native and nonnative groups. All claims to land were settled and mechanisms set in place for future relations between native peoples and governments at all levels.

The Northeastern Quebec Agreement, signed in 1978 as a supplement to the James Bay document, gave rights and compensation to the Naskapi tribe near Schefferville. In 1993, the beneficiaries numbered 11,458 Cree, 7,066 Inuit, and 610 Naskapi.

Impact The indigenous peoples of Canada asserted their rights to land and resources. They asked for the administration of their lands, opposed major development schemes, and attracted the attention of politicians in Ottawa by demands of compensation and political independence. The James Bay and Northern Quebec Agreement of 1975 is testimony to the perseverance of the Cree (and some Inuit) in their battle against hydroelectric development on the James River.

Further Reading

Hornig, James F. *Social and Environmental Impacts of the James Bay Hydroelectric Project.* Ithaca, N.Y.: McGill-Queen's University Press, 1999.

Niezen, Ronald. *Defending the Land: Sovereignty and Forest Life in James Bay Cree Society.* Bacon: Allyn & Bacon, 1998.

Ann M. Legreid

See also Minorities in Canada; Native Americans; Quebec Charter of Human Rights and Freedoms.

■ Japan and North America

Definition Diplomatic and economic relations between the United States, Canada, and Japan

Japan's emergence as a global economic power during the 1970's allowed it to assert its independence in world politics, opening a new era of rivalry and friction with North America.

Japan's economy experienced astonishing growth after the end of U.S. occupation in April, 1952, resulting in a steady expansion of exports to the United States and Canada by 1970. The United States indirectly perpetuated a postwar pattern of funding Japanese prosperity with its military intervention in Vietnam, as U.S. spending in Japan by 1970 exceeded $450 million. Japanese exports of televisions, automobile parts, chemicals, and machinery to North America grew sharply during the decade, contributing to a widening U.S. trade deficit that caused intense bilateral friction. Japan's foreign exchange reserve already had jumped from two billion dollars in 1968 to more than seven billion dollars in 1971. President Richard M. Nixon acted to restore trilateral economic balance when he imposed a 10 percent surcharge on Japanese imports and abandoned fixed exchange rates. He lifted the surcharge only after Tokyo revalued the yen upward and agreed to voluntary reduction of Japanese textile and apparel exports to the United States. In February, 1972, Prime Minister Satō Eisaku also signed an agreement promising greater access for American imports to Japan.

During the decade, Japan abandoned a postoccupation foreign policy of unqualified support for U.S. economic, political, and military goals in Asia, including isolation of the People's Republic of China. In July, 1971, Nixon announced his impending visit to China just hours after notifying Satō. This "Nixon Shock" and rising mass opposition in Japan to the U.S. war in Vietnam combined to increase existing pressure for termination of the U.S.-Japan security alliance. The Japanese organization Beheiren (Citizens' Federation for Peace in Vietnam) organized demonstrations from 1968 to 1971 that involved nearly nineteen million people. Protesters also demanded restoration of Japanese control over Okinawa, which the U.S. military used as a staging base for operations in Vietnam. Satō's visit to Washington, D.C., in November, 1969, ignited demonstrations for immediate reversion resulting in 1,700 arrests and many injuries. Nixon agreed to restore Japan's administrative control on the condition that the provisions of the security treaties still would apply. The Okinawa Reversion Treaty took effect in May, 1972.

Strained Relationship Despite public protests, Japan renewed its security treaties with the United States in June, 1970. In response to U.S. disengagement from Vietnam, Tokyo began to assume more responsibility for its own defense, dramatically increasing military spending. Tanaka Kakuei, Satō's successor in 1972, was the first prime minister to separate Japan from U.S. foreign policy. He resisted U.S. pressure on Japan to accept new security commitments abroad, especially after the Yom Kippur War in 1973 led Arab states to threaten Japan, Canada, and other oil importing countries with the same embargo it imposed on the United States for its pro-Israel stance unless it showed support for their cause. Prime Minister Pierre Trudeau encouraged Japan's independence, urging participation in his "third option" for increased trade and investment. Tanaka agreed to "broaden and deepen" bilateral relations, but Japan still viewed Canada as a weaker twin brother of the United States.

Japanese-American relations remained frosty after Gerald R. Ford replaced Nixon, even though in November, 1974, he became the first U.S. president to visit Japan. A major reason derived from the Japanese government's decision to focus on raising productivity in knowledge-intensive and energy-efficient industries with export potential as the primary means to resume economic growth. Fear of U.S. tariff retaliation to halt its growing trade surplus caused Japan to impose voluntary quotas on exports to the United States of specialty steel and color televisions. However, American leaders remained dissatisfied with an elaborate system restricting access to Japan's domestic market. Adding to U.S. irritation, Prime Minister Miki Takeo announced that Japan would spend no more than 1 percent of its gross national product on defense. Later in 1976, Jimmy Carter's election as U.S. president alarmed the Japanese because he proposed the withdrawal of U.S. troops from Korea. This motivated Tokyo to expand its naval power. It extended its territorial limit to two hundred miles, allegedly for security reasons, but more likely to protect its fishing rights against U.S. pressure to limit catch totals.

Canada tried to exploit the strains in U.S.-Japan relations by negotiating several joint ventures to process raw materials. In 1976, Trudeau and Miki signed a Framework for Economic Cooperation, but little changed in Canadian-Japanese trade and investment patterns because Tokyo viewed Canada as a U.S. surrogate. As North America's trade deficit with Japan steadily expanded, U.S. politicians complained about continued funding for the U.S. military in Japan. American anger peaked after a revolution in Iran led to a second oil crisis in 1979. Tokyo, defying U.S. pressure, refused to unite with industrialized nations in reducing oil imports after the oil-producing nations raised prices. The United States then voiced displeasure with Japan during the Iran hostage crisis for refusing to join an oil embargo and even providing loans to the Iranian government. To placate Washington, Prime Minister Ohira Masayoshi agreed to open Japan's domestic market to more North American products. He also cooperated with

U.S. actions during 1980 to punish the Soviet Union for invading Afghanistan, as Japan joined in imposing economic sanctions and boycotting the Moscow Summer Olympics.

Impact During the 1970's, contention replaced cooperation as the essential ingredient in relations between Japan and North America. Japan's emergence as an economic competitor of the United States and Canada was the primary source of friction, but the American government was dissatisfied with Japan's refusal to contribute much to preserving global peace and stability. During subsequent decades, Japan would continue to resist pressure to open its markets, boost defense spending, and expand its global role.

Further Reading

Destler, M., Haruhiro Fukui, and Hideo Sato. *The Textile Wrangle: Conflict in Japanese-American Relations*. Ithaca, N.Y.: Cornell University Press, 1979. The authors describe how the internal politics of the United States and Japan worked to prevent easy resolution of economic disputes, often igniting major political crises in either country that damaged relations.

Langdon, Frank. *The Politics of Canadian-Japanese Economic Relations, 1952-1983*. Vancouver: University of British Columbia Press, 1983. Complex political considerations receive thorough and objective analysis in a series of case studies examining trade and investment patterns that the author uses to explain how Japan became Canada's most important overseas economic partner.

Matray, James I. *Japan's Emergence as a Global Power*. Westport, Conn.: Greenwood Press, 2000. This account of Japan's involvement in world affairs after 1945 has chapters focusing on relations with China and the Soviet Union, Korea and Southeast Asia, and the United States. It also contains a series of biographical sketches and reprints a selection of primary source documents.

Olsen, Edward A. *U.S.-Japan Strategic Reciprocity: A Neo-Isolationist View*. Stanford, Calif.: Hoover Institution Press, 1985. A summary history of postwar U.S.-Japanese security relations, this study stresses the coexistence of cooperation and conflict between the two nations in seeking preservation of mutual security interests.

Schaller, Michael. *Altered States: The United States and Japan Since the Occupation*. New York: Oxford University Press, 1997. An account that details U.S. relations with Japan from the end of the U.S. occupation in 1952 to the Nixon Shocks in 1972, the author portrays the partnership as tortured because of the assymetry in power and the rising friction over economic affairs.

James I. Matray

See also Automobiles; Business and the economy in Canada; Business and the economy in the United States; Foreign policy of Canada; Foreign policy of the United States; International trade of Canada; International trade of the United States; Nixon's visit to China; Videocassette recorders (VCRs); Vietnam War; Walkman.

■ *Jaws*

Identification Motion picture
Director Steven Spielberg (1946-   )
Date Released in 1975

Jaws, which became the most successful motion picture of its time by earning more than $100 million, was a Hollywood disaster film that exploited the era's hunger for sensational thrills, shocking images, and masculine American heroism in the face of unprecedented danger and terror.

Based on a pulp novel about a human-eating great white shark written by Peter Benchley, who also collaborated on the screenplay, *Jaws* was Steven Spielberg's second feature film. It was his first big commercial hit, arguably because it was able to exploit widespread fears about killer sharks. Like Spielberg's television film *Duel* (1971), which pitted an ordinary traveling salesperson against an anonymous driver of a menacing truck, the plot line of *Jaws* centered on a similar menace—a shark—that stalked unsuspecting characters. Perverse and even absurd in its plot, characters, and situations, Jaws nonetheless had a strong visceral appeal, and its visual style set a different course for disaster films.

Set in the small coastal resort community of Amity—the name means "friendship"—in New England, the film has three main protagonists, each with distinct personalities: Police Chief Martin Brody (played by Roy Scheider), ichthyologist Matt Hooper (Richard Dreyfuss), and tough old salt Quint (Robert Shaw). The three men set out on a small boat—slyly named *Orca*—to track down the great white shark that has been terrorizing the community with its savage attacks on swimmers. Brody

Time *magazine heralds the release of* Jaws *in 1975.* (Hulton Archive/ Getty Images)

point of view—with light filtering into the deep from above the surface. John Williams's chilling soundtrack to signal the shark's approach and Verna Fields's superb editing delivered shocks, and Spielberg, in a virtuoso decision, did not show the actual shark until past the halfway mark of the film, thus building the suspense masterfully. In this way, the horror of the shark's presence was expanded by the audience's imagination. The sheer pace of the storytelling and the uncomplicated nature of the tale helped to make the film immensely popular.

Impact   An experiment in film terror, *Jaws* was considered especially American for its ability to combine Freudian horror and suspense with themes of small-town politics and an Everyman-versus-nature struggle. The film made it acceptable for the public to express its private fears openly while appreciating a suspense film's flashes of black humor.

Further Reading

Crawley, Tony. *The Steven Spielberg Story.* London: Zomba Books, 1983.

Mott, Donald R., and Cheryl McAllister Saunders. *Steven Spielberg.* Boston: Twayne, 1986.

Taylor, Philip M. *Steven Spielberg—The Man, His Movies, and Their Meaning.* New York: Continuum, 1992.

Keith Garebian

See also   Disaster films; Dreyfuss, Richard; Film in the United States; Horror films; Science-fiction films; Spielberg, Steven.

discovers that primal horror cannot be escaped even in an otherwise idyllic setting, while Hooper finds that pure science is inadequate to deal with one of nature's unparalleled monsters. Quint, however, becomes the agent of madness or stupidity in opposition to the other characters' reason and science. Quint clearly represents Ahab, the protagonist in Herman Melville's novel *Moby Dick* (1851), and the 4,550-pound shark off Long Island becomes the equivalent of Melville's whale. Quint's obsession with the creature begins a descent into foolhardy bravado that ends with his gory death within the jaws of the shark.

Spielberg used the camera in bold ways, not limiting himself to conventional framing. He also made use of shadows against light, shooting swimmers from underwater—as if from the stalking shark's

∎ Jazz

Definition   Genre of American music

By taking inspiration from such musical forms as rock, funk, rhythm and blues, and world music, the jazz musicians of the 1970's broadened their commercial appeal while angering so-called jazz purists.

As a genre, jazz evolved out of ragtime and blues and emphasizes the importance of improvisation within the established continuity of a musical ensemble. During the late 1960's, the efforts of such jazz visionaries as guitarist Larry Coryell, vibraphonist Gary Burton, and the legendary trumpeter Miles Davis brought together a blending of jazz with rock. This style of music became known during the 1970's as fusion or jazz-rock. Around this same period, established rock groups such as Santana, Chicago, and Blood, Sweat, and Tears had incorporated jazz elements into their recordings.

In 1969, Davis produced two seminal fusion albums that changed the jazz landscape forever. Davis had been listening to Jimi Hendrix, Sly and the Family Stone, and other vibrant rock acts. While *In a Silent Way* gave listeners a taste of the new direction that Davis had decided to take, his double-album *Bitches Brew* truly merged jazz and rock and inspired much of what jazz musicians produced during the 1970's.

Fusion Forges Its Own Identity *Bitches Brew* took the jazz world by storm. For this album, Davis employed rock rhythms and electronic instruments. The band that he had assembled for this 1969 re-

cording included guitarist John McLaughlin, saxophonist Wayne Shorter, and keyboardists Joe Zawinul and Chick Corea. While critics argued about the virtues of *Bitches Brew*, the public made this jazz album a commercial success.

Because of rock and soul music, record buyers already were comfortable with listening to electronic instruments and the power of what studio recording equipment could produce. Fusion musicians of the 1970's refused to forgo all the new electronic gadgets of the time merely because jazz purists believed that what they were attempting to do constituted a form of heresy. In 1973, keyboardist Herbie Hancock, who had performed with Davis during the early 1960's, released the groundbreaking fusion album *Head Hunters*. *Head Hunters* incorporated jazz, funk, and electronics and became the best-selling jazz album of its time.

The jazz musicians who worked with Davis on *Bitches Brew* went on to form their own influential fusion groups. Shorter and Zawinul cofounded the band Weather Report in 1970. Although there

Jazz great Miles Davis in 1970. (Hulton Archive/Getty Images)

would be personnel changes over the years, Weather Report continued recording until the late 1980's. In 1976, the group released the commercially successful album *Heavy Weather*, which included the joyous song "Birdland." McLaughlin formed the Mahavishnu Orchestra in 1971. The group caused a sensation with its mixture of jazz-rock and Indian ragas. Meanwhile, Corea and bassist Stanley Clarke formed the group Return to Forever. While Corea had played free-jazz and Latin-jazz during the 1960's, he proved to be an extraordinary fusion innovator with Return to Forever. This electrified band produced five albums during the 1970's and was very popular at rock venues. The exciting and innovative nature of fusion, with its melding of various musical influences, including world music, lost a great deal of its momentum by the end of the 1970's, partly because of the rise of contemporary jazz.

Crossover Jazz Breeds Pop   By the mid-1970's, the terms "crossover," "contemporary," and "jazz-pop" had been added to the music lexicon and involved the blending of jazz and popular music. For jazz purists, this blending led to a watering down of the creative fire that is at the heart of jazz. Crossover jazz was considered less aggressive than jazz-rock or fusion, and many viewed it as being on the "easy-listening" end of the jazz spectrum. Such artists as David Sanborn, Tom Scott, Al Jarreau, Grover Washington, Jr., Chuck Mangione, Bob James, George Benson, Manhattan Transfer, and Spyro Gyra became very popular during the late 1970's. These acts produced accessible music that was very radio-friendly. The popularity of crossover jazz continued into the 1980's and beyond with the commercial success of artists such as Kenny G.

Impact   The jazz of the early 1970's was heavily influenced by the efforts of the legendary Miles Davis. Because of both his incorporation of electronic instrumentation and his inspiration from rock, soul, and world music, the direction of jazz was dramatically altered. Out of this integration of various genres, fusion was born. Fusion remained a vital force until the late 1970's, when a more easy-listening form of jazz gained prominence. The jazz of the 1970's must be considered as transitional. By the 1980's, jazz-pop or contemporary jazz had become popular with the listening public, while a return to the roots of jazz was being fostered by the talented and forceful presence of Wynton Marsalis.

Further Reading

Bogdanov, Vladimir, Chris Woodstra, and Stephen Thomas Erlewine, eds. *All Music Guide to Jazz: The Definitive Guide.* 4th ed. San Francisco: Backbeat Books, 2002. Considered the bible for all lovers of jazz music. Provides essential recordings of any jazz artist.

Collier, James Lincoln. *Jazz: The American Theme Song.* New York: Oxford University Press, 1993. A provocative history of jazz that focuses on the social aspects that have been at the core of the genre's evolution.

Coryell, Julie, and Laura Friedman. *Jazz-Rock Fusion: The People, the Music.* Milwaukee, Wis.: Hal Leonard, 2000. Includes a biography and interview of many of the most important fusion players of the 1970's, including Miles Davis, Michael Brecker, Herbie Hancock, and Chick Corea.

Feather, Leonard, and Ira Gitler. *The Encyclopedia of Jazz in the Seventies.* New York: Horizon Press, 1976. An important bio-bibliography of the period.

Gridley, Mark C. *Jazz Styles: History and Analysis.* 8th ed. Upper Saddle River, N.J.: Prentice Hall, 2003. An excellent overview of the history of jazz. It takes the time to detail each of the major styles of jazz, including jazz-rock.

Nicholson, Stuart. *Jazz-Rock: A History.* New York: Schirmer Books, 1998. A definitive study of jazz-rock to date.

Jeffry Jensen

See also   Music.

■ *Jeffersons, The*

Identification   Television situation comedy
Producer   Norman Lear (1922-   ) and Bud Yorkin (1926-   )
Date   Aired from 1975 to 1985

The Jeffersons was one of the first television programs to depict an affluent African American family that enjoyed the rewards of hard work and coexisted in white and African American cultures. Successful and long-running, the show evolved during its ten years on television.

A precursor of influential programs such as *The Cosby Show, The Jeffersons* was a groundbreaking concept during the mid-1970's. A spin-off from *All in the Family,* the show depicted a successful African American couple, George and Louise Jefferson, who "move on up" to a deluxe apartment in a prestigious New York

Marla Gibbs and Sherman Hemsley in a scene from the television series The Jeffersons. *(CBS/Landov)*

City neighborhood. *The Jeffersons* was created by Norman Lear, who developed numerous sitcoms during the 1960's and 1970's.

To some extent, George Jefferson was the African American counterpart of *All in the Family*'s Archie Bunker. Portrayed by Sherman Hemsley, he was brilliant in business but less skillful in dealing with people. George had moved up socioeconomically but did not change his basic attitudes. Louise ("Weezy"), played by Isabel Sanford, was loyal and supportive, while the couple's African American maid, Florence (Marla Gibbs), was a thorn in George's side. George's character was controversial, especially among African Americans. Although it was a positive development to present a show about a successful African American businessman, George's narrow-mindedness limited the character's potential. Weezy's natural charm compensated for George's boorishness, but he was often an embarrassment. One could argue that an African American Archie Bunker naturally grew out of *All in the Family*, but African Americans were more likely to see George's mannerisms and actions as stereotypical.

The Jeffersons also featured a wealthy interracial couple living in the same apartment building. Helen Willis (Roxie Roker), a smart and witty African American heir who was married to publisher Tom Willis (Franklin Cover), a genial giant, who liked George despite his cracks about "honkies." The Jefferson's son and the Willis's daughter eventually were married during the show's tenure.

A few other characters also contributed to the show: Harry Bentley (Paul Benedict), the English neighbor, and Ralph (Ned Wertimer), the greedy doorman, who would do almost anything for a tip. Mother Jefferson (Zara Cully) was featured prominently in the early years as a mother who believed her son could do no wrong.

Impact *The Jeffersons* was an early attempt to depict the emerging African American nouveau riche. Although one could argue that the portrayals both of George and of the interracial Willises were unrealistic at times, the show was a pioneering effort. By demonstrating that a comedy series about a upper-middle-class African American family could have a broad audience, it helped pave the way for later shows such as *The Cosby Show*.

Further Reading

Garner, Joe. *Stay Tuned: Television's Unforgettable Moments.* New York: McMeel, 2003.

Gray, Herman. *Watching Race: Television and the Struggle for "Blackness."* Minneapolis: University of Minnesota Press, 1995.

Means, Robert R. *African-American Viewers and the Black Situation Comedy.* New York: Routledge, 2000.

Norma C. Noonan

See also African Americans; *All in the Family*; *Maude*; Racial discrimination; Sitcoms; Television in the United States.

■ Jenner, Bruce

Identification   American track-and-field athlete
Born   October 28, 1949; Mount Kisco, New York

By winning the gold medal in the decathlon during the 1976 Summer Olympics, Jenner became a household name in the United States.

Bruce Jenner lettered in football, basketball, and track and field at Newtown High School in Connecticut and won the Eastern States water ski championship three times. He attended Graceland College in Iowa on a football scholarship, but a knee injury sidelined him from that sport after his freshman year. He competed in basketball and track and field, breaking a school record in his first decathlon in 1970 and finishing sixth at the Drake Relays.

Jenner trained in the decathlon for the next year and tried out for the 1972 U.S. Olympic team. At the Olympic trials in Eugene, Oregon, he ranked in eleventh place after the first five decathlon events. Jenner moved up to fifth place after nine events and

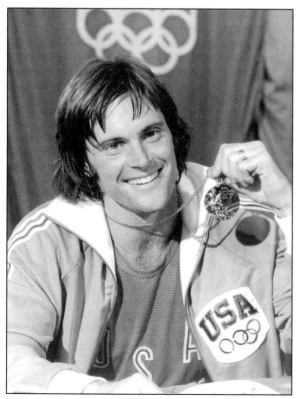

Bruce Jenner shows his decathlon gold medal from the 1976 Summer Olympics. (DPA/Landov)

needed to defeat the third-place athlete by eighteen points in the final event in order to make the Olympic team. He won the 1,500-meter race by twenty-one seconds, clinching the final decathlon spot on the Olympic team. Jenner finished a disappointing tenth place in the decathlon at the 1972 Summer Olympics in Munich, West Germany, with 7,722 points, far behind Russian gold medalist Nikolai Avilov's world record of 8,454 points.

After graduating in 1973 from Graceland, Jenner moved to San Jose, California, in order to train in the decathlon for the 1976 Olympics. He won the decathlon at the 1974 and 1976 Amateur Athletic Union Championships and at the 1975 Pan American Games in Mexico City. In a triangular meet with the Soviet Union and Poland at Eugene, Oregon, in 1975, he broke Avilov's world decathlon record with 8,524 points.

Riding on this success, Jenner was favored to win the decathlon at the 1976 Olympics in Montreal, Canada. During competition in the 100-meter dash, long jump, shot put, high jump, and 400-meter dash on the first day, he amassed 4,298 points and trailed Guido Kratschmer of West Germany by 35 points and Avilov by 17 points. On the second day, Jenner competed in the 110-meter hurdles, discus, pole vault, javelin, and 1,500 meters. He held a virtually insurmountable lead after the pole vault and ran a career best in the 1,500 meters to win the gold medal, breaking his world decathlon record with 8,618 points. Kratschmer won the silver medal with 8,411 points, and Avilov took the bronze medal with 8,369 points.

Jenner, who retired from decathlon competition that day, won the Associated Press Athlete of the Year, the Sullivan Award, and the *Sport* Performer of the Year Award as the outstanding amateur athlete of 1976. He wrote the autobiography *Decathlon Challenge: Bruce Jenner's Story* (1977), served as a motivational speaker for business corporations, worked for National Broadcasting Company (NBC) Sports and American Broadcasting Company (ABC) Sports, acted in films, and endorsed commercial products.

Impact   Bruce Jenner gained celebrity status as one of the world's greatest athletes, winning an Olympic gold medal while setting a world record in the most grueling track-and-field competition. He was elected to the National Track and Field Hall of Fame in 1980 and the U.S. Olympic Hall of Fame in 1986.

Further Reading

Aaseng, Nathan. *Bruce Jenner: Decathlon Winner.* Minneapolis: Lerner, 1979.

Holst, Don, and Marcia S. Popp. *American Men of Olympic Track and Field: Interviews with Athletes and Coaches.* Jefferson, N.C.: McFarland, 2004.

Jenner, Bruce, with Phillip Finch. *Decathlon Challenge: Bruce Jenner's Story.* Englewood Cliffs, N.J.: Prentice-Hall, 1977.

David L. Porter

See also Munich Olympics terrorism; Olympic Games of 1972; Olympic Games of 1976; Sports.

■ *Jesus Christ Superstar*

Identification Broadway musical drama
Authors Music by Andrew Lloyd Webber (1948-); book by Tim Rice (1944-)
Date Opened on Broadway on October 12, 1971

Conceived as a "rock opera," this staging of the events of Christian Holy Week was initially denounced by many as sacrilege but soon gained tremendous popularity both for its religious message and for its theatrical appeal.

Andrew Lloyd Webber and Tim Rice had already collaborated on a biblical subject, *Joseph and the Amazing Technicolor Dreamcoat* (1968), when they decided to tackle the Passion drama. Passion plays have a long and somewhat controversial history. In some cases, they were closed down because they made a raucous spectacle of the suffering of Jesus Christ. In other cases, they were criticized for perpetuating anti-Semitism by melodramatically blaming "evil" Jews for the killing of Christ.

The British creative team of Lloyd Webber and Rice based their opera on their reading of the New Testament Gospels from the King James (Protestant) Bible and from Bishop Fulton J. Sheen's Roman Catholic-oriented *Life of Christ* (1954). The opera unfolds in a series of dramatic confrontations between Jesus and his disciple Judas, between Jesus and the Jewish High Priests, and between Jesus and the Roman governor, Pilate. The confrontation with King Herod is played for comic relief. The drama ends with the crucifixion of Jesus. The resurrection, a key point in Christian belief, is not presented on stage.

Before the stage version was ever produced, the rock opera was recorded in London. In spite of some criticism on religious grounds, the recording was a major commercial and critical success. Based on this positive reaction, plans were laid for a stage version in New York, produced by Tom O'Horgan, and, a year later, a separate stage version in London. A motion picture version was made in 1973, filmed in the Holy Land.

Impact The impact of *Jesus Christ Superstar* during the 1970's was twofold. First, Andrew Lloyd Webber and Tim Rice became major stars. They followed up with *Evita* (1978), another—albeit very different—musical drama based on the life of Argentine icon

Tim Rice (left) and Andrew Lloyd Webber, the creators of Jesus Christ Superstar. *(AP/Wide World Photos)*

Eva Perón. Other musical theater collaborations followed, most meeting success on Broadway. Lloyd Webber became a Lord in 1997.

More important, influential elements of the American religious community adopted the popular approach of *Jesus Christ Superstar.* So many local productions sprang up all over the United States that guarding the copyright became a major legal task. Countless other "Christian pop" composers and performers followed in the play's footsteps, seeing opportunities for both for spreading a religious message in an increasingly secular-rock world and making lucrative careers for themselves.

Further Reading

Richards, Stanley, ed. *Great Rock Musicals.* New York: Stein and Day, 1979.

Swain, Joseph P. *The Broadway Musical: A Critical and Musical Survey.* New York: Oxford University Press, 1990.

Gordon R. Mork

See also Broadway musicals; *Chorus Line, A*; *Grease*; Music; Religion and spirituality in the United States; Sondheim, Stephen; Theater in the United States.

■ Jesus People Movement

Definition American religious fellowship

The rise of the Jesus People Movement, which came about in reaction to the 1960's counterculture, resulted in many American youth turning toward evangelical Christianity.

By the beginning of the 1970's, the countercultural "hippie" movement that dominated the media in the previous decade had reached its peak, and many disenchanted young adults who were caught up in the free-love culture turned instead to Christianity. Often referred to as Jesus freaks or Jesus People, they avowed fundamental Christian principles, and many found in this new fellowship a substitute for their drug-saturated, runaway lifestyles.

The focus of the Jesus People Movement centered on salvation through an "experience of faith in Jesus Christ." Like the Great Awakening of the eighteenth century, this youthful group believed in Pentecostalism, assumed the "end times" were near, and often spoke in tongues.

Beginnings Made up initially of many disparate Christian groups, the Jesus People Movement had its start in Southern California before rapidly dispersing throughout counterculture-oriented missionary groups. In 1971, the National Institutes of Health listed more than three thousand like-minded Christian groups within the United States. Out of this conglomeration of communal groups was born Jesus People USA in 1971.

The founders of the Seattle-based Jesus People Army, Jim and Sue Palosaari and Linda Meissner, migrated to Milwaukee, where they soon attracted twenty-five members and named themselves Jesus People Milwaukee. This initial seed group, which fully embraced the primary principle of dedicating their "entire life, every aspect, to following Jesus Christ," soon attracted a preponderance of young people, many of them drug addicts and runaways, who had over time become disenchanted with the hippie counterculture.

One of the Jesus People Movement's guiding forces, John Wiley Herrin, a pastor from the southern United States, joined with his family in October, 1971, and the group's numbers quickly escalated. By November of that year, the Jesus People Movement counted only one hundred members. However, just three months later, thanks in part to "street witnessing," whereby members went into the streets to attract new recruits, the Jesus People Movement had doubled in size and shortly doubled again.

Before long, the Jesus People Movement's addition of music into its rallies helped increase its numbers greatly. Two long-haired groups in particular, Resurrection and Jesus Rock, focused on a musical form of evangelism. As a result, the Jesus People Movement's popularity spread quickly across the Midwest before centering itself in Chicago, where it began a communal residence in Faith Tabernacle Church.

Scandal and Change By 1974, the Jesus People Movement showed signs of instability when its leader Herrin became involved in a scandal involving a young woman. Glenn Kaiser and Richard Murphy took control. Also, in the same year, the group came to be aligned with charismatic leader Jack Winters of Daystar, a group that practiced a form of corporal discipline "by the rod," whereby beatings were administered to recalcitrant youth. This association shed continued negative light on the Jesus People Movement.

By the middle of the decade, the Jesus People Movement realized it needed a permanent habita-

Members of Children of God, a part of the Jesus People Movement, sing before eating lunch in 1971. (AP/Wide World Photos)

tion for its followers and built a residence on Chicago's Paulina Street. Here it established the *Cornerstone* magazine, which over time became an influential national religious periodical. Further, in an effort to maintain a more stable income base, the Jesus People Movement established small home repair companies. By the end of the 1970's, the Jesus People Movement merged with a similar black urban Christian group and moved into a hotel near Chicago's Lake Shore Drive.

Impact The young followers of the Jesus People Movement, still defiant of the older generation despite a turn to religion, did not return to their parent's traditional Christian churches but looked instead to the new Jesus Revolution spreading throughout North America. Thus, by embracing the countercultural phenomena of communal Christian living, they were able to maintain the tenets of antiestablishment by still defying governmental and social authority while also adhering to Christian traditions.

The Jesus People Movement phenomenon only later became recognized for its widespread impact upon evangelical Christianity. The Reverend Billy Graham argues that the 1970's Jesus People Movement heralded a new spiritual awakening that caused people to pour into churches across the United States. In addition, the music that sprang out of the Jesus People Movement helped give rise to the subsequently prominent Christian youth culture and the multimillion-dollar Christian contemporary music industry.

Further Reading

Di Sabatino, David. *Jesus People Movement: An Annotated Bibliography and General Resource.* Portsmouth, N.H.: Greenwood-Heinemann, 1999. Explores the impact of evangelical Christianity in North America during the last half of the twentieth century.

Graham, Billy. *The Jesus Generation.* Grand Rapids, Mich.: Zondervan, 1971. The Reverend Billy Graham maintains that the Jesus People Movement heralded in a new spiritual awakening for America.

Schulmanm Bruce J. *The Seventies: The Great Shift in American Culture, Society, and Politics.* New York: Da Capo Press, 2002. Astute, thought-provoking historical analysis of the shifts in the 1970's popular and political culture, which helps explain the rise of the Jesus People Movement.

Ward, Hiley H. *The Far-Out Saints of the Jesus Communes: A Firsthand Report and Interpretation of the Jesus People Movement.* New York: Association Press, 1972. Firsthand account of the Jesus People Movement and its spread throughout North America.

M. Casey Diana

See also Christian Fundamentalism; Hippies; Jews for Jesus; Religion and spirituality in the United States.

■ Jewish Americans

Identification Americans of Jewish descent from many countries of origin

By the end of the 1970's, the population of Jews in the United States had risen to nearly five and a half million, and many in the community were moving to new locales in the American South and West. Within American society, they influenced politics, literature, science, and education.

The 1970's were marked by an increasing emphasis on, and pride in, ethnic identity. American Jews were freer and more powerful than any community of Jews had been in the Diaspora. The United States itself was changing ethnically, with the arrival of large numbers of Asians and Muslims. Jews were a striking and accepted part of the political landscape, and the pro-Israel lobby conducted business in Washington, D.C., as did the lobbies of other interest groups.

In Congress, Jewish members were consistent and almost unanimous in voting for aid packages for Israel. The large majority of Jews were committed to the Democratic Party, partly because of their historic commitment to social justice. Jews began to feel that they had achieved their dreams of equality and influence.

However, many in the community were troubled by certain trends. Intermarriage rates between Jews and non-Jews rose during this decade: In Boston intermarriage had reached 13 percent of all Jewish marriages by 1975, and in Rhode Island it rose to 27 percent. Meanwhile, the birth rate of Jews continued to fall. Religious observance was becoming perfunctory, diminishing in many cases to observance of Passover, Hanukkah, and Yom Kippur. As tensions rose in the Middle East, Jews also felt the need to support Israel under the rallying cry, in reference to the Holocaust, "Never again!" When Egypt attacked Israel on Yom Kippur day in 1973, the commitment to Israel among Jewish Americans was not as strong as it had been during the Six-Day War in 1967. Many felt that Jews in the United States were becoming more of an ethnic group and less of a religious one.

Cultural Influences Tremendous interest in Jewish life and culture arose among the general American public during the 1970's. The cover article of *Newsweek* on March 1, 1971, was titled "The American Jew Today," which listed Jewish achievements in the United States in glowing terms. The following year, the April 10 issue of *Time* featured a cover story titled "What It Means to Be Jewish" and quoted many prominent Jews such as author and humanitarian Elie Wiesel and Abraham Joshua Heschel, professor at the Conservative's Jewish Theological Seminary. A multidenomination group of theologians promoted the idea that Jews are unique, "a group joined together in relation to God."

Jewish writers who had been prolific for decades achieved wide recognition. Saul Bellow, a writer of general and Jewish culture, was an important American novelist of the period who presented in his work alienated heroes seeking salvation. In 1976, he won the Nobel Prize in Literature. Isaac Bashevis Singer, a Yiddish writer born in Poland and writing in New York, became a favorite of the American reading public. He seldom wrote of American subjects but of East European family life saturated with strong passions and visions of the supernatural. He won the Nobel Prize in Literature in 1978.

Jewish Feminism In the early 1970's, a feminism with a specifically Jewish focus developed along with the general feminist movement of the times. Jewish women explored feminism in the context of inequalities and oppression and began to study Judaism from a feminist perspective. The goals of Jewish feminism, as distinct from general feminism, were divided roughly into "communal" and "spiritual" areas. Communal areas were concerned with gaining access to seats of power, while the spiritualists were occupied with law, liturgy, and religious education.

Jewish family values were denounced by some feminists. The Jewish feminist movement also attacked the institution of female voluntarism, claiming that Jewish women were systematically shut out of decision-making positions. In 1972, only 13 percent of the combined Jewish federation boards of directors and 16 percent of the people serving on committees were women. However, under the assault of the Jewish feminist critique, these figures improved to 40 percent by the following decade.

The specifically religious issues on which Jewish feminists focused included Jewish divorce law and women's role in worship services. By late 1971, Jewish women's prayer and study groups were being formed, and the one in New York City grew in numbers until it formed the Ezrat Nashim, an influential organization committed to equality for women within Judaism. Many feminists attended the Conservative Rabbinical Assembly in 1972, the same year that the Reform Movement ordained the first female rabbi, Sally Priesand.

During the late 1970's, there was strong pressure within the conservative Jewish movement to change the seminary's policy and ordain women as conservative rabbis. In 1979, a report to the Rabbinical Assembly found that it would be morally wrong for the conservative movement to deny ordination to qualified women. It found that a majority of conservative congregations were ready to accept female rabbis, as were 75 percent of current rabbinical students. However, in December of that year, the faculty senate of the Jewish Theological Seminary voted 25-18 to table the question of female ordination. It was not until 1983 that the seminary faculty voted 34-8 to admit female rabbis. Amy Eilberg, already an advanced student, was the first woman to receive conservative ordination.

Impact While some trends began to occur that diluted the cohesiveness of the American Jewish identity, the decade overall proved to be one of visibility and growing influence for Jews in American culture and politics. The events in the Middle East had an impact on Jewish members of Congress, and feminist Jews found that their voices were increasingly heard.

Further Reading

Gurock, Jeffrey S. *American Jewish Life, 1920-1990.* Vol. 4. New York: Routledge, 1998. A collection of essays on diverse subjects such as "The Sephardim of the United States" and "Jewish Gender Stereotypes in American Culture." The essays are well-researched and supported by statistics and tables.

Hertzberg, Arthur. *The Jews in America.* New York: Simon & Schuster, 1989. Strong on political and social trends and written by one of the most prominent rabbis in the United States.

Karp, Abraham J. *Haven and Home.* New York: Schocken Books, 1985. This is an outstanding history of the American Jewish community from colonial times to the early years of the 1980's. It focusses on the social, religious, and cultural aspects of the American Jewish historical experience.

Sheila Golburgh Johnson

See also Allen, Woody; Brooks, Mel; Cosell, Howard; Dreyfuss, Richard; Feinstein, Dianne; Hoffman, Dustin; Israel and the United States; Jews for Jesus; Kaufman, Andy; Kissinger, Henry; Koch, Ed; Middle East and North America; Religion and spirituality in Canada; Religion and spirituality in the United States; Richler, Mordecai; Simon, Neil; Spielberg, Steven; Spitz, Mark; Steinem, Gloria; Walters, Barbara; Wilder, Gene.

■ Jews for Jesus

Identification Evangelical group of Christian Jews
Date Founded in 1973

Jews for Jesus began as a small countercultural evangelical movement in the early 1970's and underwent tremendous growth during the decade.

Spawned as an offshoot of the Jesus movement of the 1960's, Jews for Jesus was the brainchild of Martin Rosen, a convert to Christianity from Judaism. Rosen—who, after his conversion in 1953, called himself Moishe Rosen—had been ordained a Baptist minister in 1957. Rosen worked as a missionary for years and in 1967 was appointed to the American Board of Mission to the Jews. In 1970, he moved to San Francisco to become more involved in the countercultural Jesus movement, organizing a group of young people who had converted from Judaism and commissioning them as street evangelists. The organization was incorporated under the name Hineni Ministries (Jews for Jesus) in 1973. By that time, it included a traveling singing group, a drama company, and volunteer witnesses.

Dissatisfied with traditional methods of evangelization, Rosen advocated that his followers approach fellow Jews in a more direct manner, which included distributing humorous and informal religious tracts called broadsides. Citing the tradition of the first Jewish converts to Christianity, who were not encouraged to discard their Jewish heritage and customs, Jews for Jesus advocates retaining Jewish traditions and keeping Jewish holy days, although altering prayers and hymns to include references to Jesus. Since Jews for Jesus was designed as a ministry of Jewish Christians to proselytize to other Jews, only Jewish-born converts or those married to Jews could engage in evangelization. This was accomplished predominantly by one-to-one witnessing and by an outreach to Jewish "seekers" who contacted the organization. Volunteers signed on as itinerant missionaries who had to pledge to be "available, vulnerable, and mobile." The organization claimed to have no authoritarian hierarchical structure but instead encouraged mutual accountability within the framework of the missionary community.

Jews for Jesus was classified as Messianic Judaism. It recognized Jesus (referred to as "Yeshua") as the Messiah who fulfills the Hebrew Law. Relying on a fundamentalist interpretation of Scripture, Jews for Jesus regarded the First and Second Testaments of Scripture as divinely inspired and verbally inerrant. Only those traditional Jewish texts that conform to the literal texts of Scripture were recognized as worthy of study.

Impact   The Jews for Jesus organization became so successful in the United States that it soon spread outside its borders. After the establishment of a branch in Toronto, Canada, in 1981, branches began to sprout up all over the world. Its methods have evoked the ire of many orthodox Jewish leaders who label them offensive and insensitive.

Further Reading

Lipson, Juliene G. *Jews for Jesus: An Anthropological Study.* Rev. ed. Brooklyn, N.Y.: AMS Press, 1990.

Tucker, Ruth. *Not Ashamed: The Story of Jews for Jesus.* Sisters, Oreg.: Multnomah, 1999.

Mara Kelly-Zukowski

See also   Jesus People movement; Jewish Americans; Religion and spirituality in the United States.

■ Joel, Billy

Identification   Pop singer, pianist, and songwriter
Born   May 9, 1949; Bronx, New York

Joel released six albums and won four Grammy Awards between 1970 and 1979. His music, ranging from easy-listening ballads to hard-rock anthems, spoke to mainstream audiences and reflected the difficult life of a struggling performer.

Billy Joel launched his solo career in 1971 with the release of *Cold Spring Harbor.* Despite being his first recording of all original songs, the album received little attention critically or commercially because the sound quality was poor. At the time, the skilled musician and classically trained pianist supplemented his income by performing in piano bars. Meanwhile, "Captain Jack," a song that had been taped during a live concert broadcast in Philadelphia, was garnering the attention of important recording companies, including industry giant Columbia Records.

In 1973, Joel released his first album under the Columbia Records label, *Piano Man.* The songwriter composed the title track as a reflection of his time as a lounge pianist, and the song boosted the record to a Top 40 position.

Joel was touring as an opening act for groups such as the J. Geils Band and the Doobie Brothers when he released his third solo album, *Streetlife Serenade,* in 1974. The hit single "The Entertainer" confirmed that Joel had evolved from an opening act to a headlining performer.

Turnstiles, released in 1976, contained the hits "Say Goodbye to Hollywood" and "New York State of Mind." The album's moderate sales caused Joel to embark on his first major American concert tour. It was during this period that he hired his wife, Elizabeth, as his manager.

Following the very successful *Turnstiles* tour, Joel went on the road again in 1977, this time to promote his latest record *The Stranger.* This album enjoyed phenomenal commercial success and contained the hits "Only the Good Die Young," "Movin' Out (Anthony's Song)," "Just the Way You Are," and "The Stranger (She's Always a Woman)." "Just the Way You Are" earned Record of the Year and Song of the Year at the Grammy Awards in 1978.

In 1978, Columbia Records released *52nd Street,* which became Joel's first number-one album.

Buoyed by the singles "My Life," "Big Shot," and "Honesty," the album sold more than two million copies within one month of its release. The record also garnered the singer-songwriter Grammy Awards for Album of the Year and Best Pop Vocal Performance in 1979.

Impact   Billy Joel was considered one of the most versatile and musically talented songwriters of the decade. He was also a popular solo performer. His career demonstrated longevity as he continued to release top-selling records in the ensuing decades.

Further Reading

Gambaccini, Peter. *Billy Joel: A Personal File*. New York: Quick Fox, 1979.

McKenzie, Michael. *Billy Joel*. New York: Ballantine Books, 1985.

Valerie Brown

See also   Music; Singer-songwriters.

■ John, Elton

Identification   British rock musician
Born   March 25, 1947; Pinner, Middlesex, England

Thanks to his elaborate stage shows, prolific songwriting and dynamic piano playing, John was one of the most popular and top-grossing rock musicians of the 1970's.

Throughout the 1970's, a person could have heard an Elton John song almost every time the radio was on: John cowrote and sang some of the decade's most memorable pop songs. Like his contemporaries Billy Joel and James Taylor, John was a singer-songwriter who rarely recorded or sang a tune he had not written himself.

John began playing the piano by ear when he was three. He quit school as a teenager to take a job at a music store. At night, he played piano in pubs, primarily with the bands Bluesology and Long John Baldry. He met his lyricist, Bernie Taupin, through a 1967 record company ad for talent. He changed his name from Reginald Kenneth Dwight to "Elton" after a Baldry bandmate and "John" after Baldry.

John first performed in the United States in the summer of 1970 at the West Holly-

wood club, the Troubadour. Critics raved about the newcomer's exciting stage show. Two decades later, *Rolling Stone* magazine rated the show among the twenty concerts that changed rock and roll. For John, it was the beginning of decades of successful touring to millions of fans.

Between 1972 and 1976, John charted seven consecutive number-one albums in the United States. Two of them, *Captain Fantastic and the Brown Dirt Cowboy* (1975) and *Rock of the Westies* (1975), entered the charts at number one. His subsequent number-one singles in the United States included "Crocodile Rock," "Bennie and the Jets," "Lucy in the Sky with Diamonds," "Philadelphia Freedom," "Island Girl," and "Don't Go Breaking My Heart."

John's stage shows drew comparisons to Jerry Lee Lewis and Little Richard, two of John's idols. He quickly became a popular live act. He wore wigs, sequined outfits, ostrich feathers, big hats, and high-heeled boots. He was known for his dozens of pairs of wild, decorative (although prescriptive) eyeglasses. During his concerts, he often changed costumes. He would jump on top of his grand piano and could play the keyboard from every imaginable angle.

Elton John. (CBS/Landov)

John set attendance records just about everywhere that he performed during the decade. On October 25, 1975, he became the first rock star to play Dodger Stadium in Los Angeles since the Beatles in 1966. On November 28, 1974, former Beatle John Lennon joined John on stage at Madison Square Garden for what would be Lennon's last stage appearance.

Impact In terms of Elton John's impact on a decade's music and pop culture, many critics place him in the same category as Elvis Presley and the Beatles.

Further Reading

Bernardin, Claude, and Tom Stanton. *Rocket Man: The Encyclopedia of Elton John.* Westport, Conn.: Greenwood Press, 1995.

Norman, Philip. *Elton John: The Biography.* New York: Harmony Books, 1991.

Rosenthal, Elizabeth. *His Song: The Musical Journey of Elton John.* New York: Watson-Guptill, 2001.

Sherri Ward Massey

See also Music; Singer-songwriters.

John Paul II in 1978. (Mal Langsdon/Reuters/Landov)

■ John Paul II

Identification Roman Catholic Church cardinal, 1967-1978; Bishop of Rome and pope of the Roman Catholic Church, 1978-2005
Born May 18, 1920; Wadowice, Poland
Died April 2, 2005; Vatican City

John Paul II was the first pope of Slavic origin, the first pope from a communist country, and the youngest pope in modern times. His early papacy was marked by political involvement and an awareness of global problems.

The youngest of three children, Karol Jósef Wojtyła grew up in Nazi-occupied Poland, worked in an underground theater group in World War II, and later was ordained and gradually advanced up the Catholic hierarchy, first as auxiliary bishop of Kraków and, in 1967, as a Polish cardinal.

During the 1960's and 1970's, Wojtyła was active as a poet, mystic, and intellectual. He spoke to Vatican II, influenced Pope Paul VI on *Humanae Vitae*

(*On the Regulation of Birth,* 1968), and wrote papers and books on theology and philosophy in addition to his work with the Synod of Bishops in Poland and his extensive travels around the world. Throughout the 1970's, Cardinal Wojtyła developed the themes that later characterized his papacy, such as the value of suffering, devotion to Mary, the dangers of a secular world, and his pessimism about humankind's future. Working with the Polish people, he continually tried to get the Polish government to respect human rights and allow religious freedom. On October 16, 1978, his efforts attained a higher level when he was elected pope.

Between 1978 and 1980, Pope John Paul II traveled to nearly one hundred countries, supported the labor movement in his home country, and in 1979, wrote *Redemptor Hominis* (*The Redeemer of Man*), which criticized the nuclear arms race and communism and capitalism as well as called for an end to poverty.

Impact Pope John Paul II's papacy had an impact on global politics, helped promote mass democratic movements in Eastern Europe, and strengthened and expanded the Catholic Church's role in the world.

Subsequent Events On May 13, 1981, the pope was shot by a would-be assassin. He survived and continued even more intensely to promote his vision of Catholicism to the world for the next twenty-four years.

Further Reading

Formicola, Jo Renee. _Pope John Paul II: Prophetic Politician._ Washington, D.C.: Georgetown University Press, 2002.

Nachef, Antoine. _Mary's Pope: John Paul II, Mary, and the Church Since Vatican II._ Landham, Md.: Sheed and Ward, 2000.

Weigel, George. _Witness to Hope: The Biography of Pope John Paul II._ New York: Cliff Street Books, 1999.

Michael V. Namorato

See also Religion and spirituality in the United States.

■ Johnson, Sonia

Identification American feminist and the cofounder and first president of Mormons for ERA

Born February 27, 1936; Malad City, Idaho

Johnson's testimony before the Senate's Constitutional Rights Subcommittee on the Equal Rights Amendment (ERA) led to her excommunication from the Mormon Church.

Sonia Johnson was born and raised in the Church of Jesus Christ of Latter-Day Saints, also known as the Mormon Church. She helped organize and was active in Mormons for ERA, criticized the church for its anti-ERA activities, and was asked by Senator Birch Bayh of Indiana to testify before the U.S. Senate's Constitutional Rights Subcommittee, which was considering the request to extend the deadline for the ERA's ratification by the states.

Johnson was one of four Mormon women who organized Mormons for ERA during the winter of 1978, two years after she discovered the concept of patriarchy and a year after she discovered feminism. In 1976, the Mormon Church was actively opposing the amendment, having issued a statement that described the ERA as "a moral issue with many disturbing ramifications for women and for the family as individual members and as a whole."

In August, 1978, Bayh wanted a member of Mormons for ERA for a religious panel to testify for the extension before his committee, and Johnson was the only founder available to do so. She had less than a week to prepare her testimony. Others asked to speak included a black Presbyterian minister from New York representing the National Council of Churches and the Religious Committee for the ERA, a Catholic priest, and a woman representing the National Federation of Temple Sisterhoods.

Senator Orrin Hatch of Utah, a member of the subcommittee, took issue with Johnson during the hearing and the exchange alerted reporters, who magnified the controversy into a national news event. After the three-year extension was passed by Congress, Mormons for ERA continued to campaign for it.

A year later, in 1979, the church held a Bishop's Court on Johnson and excommunicated her on December 5. Proceedings of such actions are not reported by the church, but Johnson and Mormons for ERA distributed press releases on the night of her excommunication, claiming that it was because her actions undermined the authority of church leaders, rather than directly for her opposition to the ERA. At about the same time, she and her husband, Rick, divorced.

Impact Sonia Johnson served as the first president of Mormons for ERA and continued to promote the amendment as a speaker at numerous functions throughout the country as well as on television talk shows. In 1984, she became a candidate for the national presidency. She continued to produce feminist books and articles, became a lesbian separatist, and founded Wildfire, a commune for women that disbanded in 1993.

Further Reading

Johnson, Sonia. _From Housewife to Heretic: One Woman's Struggle for Equal Rights and Her Excommunication from the Mormon Church._ Garden City, N.Y.: Anchor Press/Doubleday, 1983.

Pottmyer, Alice Allred. "Sonia Johnson: Mormonism's Feminist Heretic." In _Differing Visions: Dissenters in Mormon History,_ edited by Roger Launius and Linda Thatcher. Urbana: University of Illinois Press, 1998.

Erika E. Pilver

See also Equal Rights Amendment (ERA); Feminism; Mormon Church lifting of priesthood ban for African Americans; Religion and spirituality in the United States; Women's rights.

■ *Jonathan Livingston Seagull*

Identification   Inspirational novel
Author   Richard Bach (1936-   )
Date   Published in 1970

Bach's novel was influenced by the American self-help movement and encouraged individuals not to heed the voices of traditionalists but to listen instead to their own inner voice that prompts them toward greatness.

Jonathan Livingston Seagull details the journey of a young seagull that, in spite of great difficulties, persists and becomes the greatest seagull flyer of all time. As a young gull, Jon finds himself dissatisfied with merely scavaging food. He desires to glide over the ocean as no gull has done before. His family and friends feel threatened, attempt to keep him in his place, and even banish him from the flock when he persists. Ultimately, through diligent practice, he comes to glide like the wind and ultimately experiences transcendence.

On the surface, Richard Bach's enormously popular novel appears to be a simple fable. However, as with all traditional fables like those, for instance, of Aesop, the true meaning lies beneath the surface. While the book appealed to some children, adults also found satisfaction in uncovering and interpreting Bach's metaphysical message: "Every problem has a gift for you in its hands." Ultimately, the book is an allegory about the value of seeking a higher purpose in life and never compromising. Readers claimed that everyone could find something in the novel, whether it be elements of Christianity, Buddhism, Islam, Christian Science, or myriad other philosophies. Bach's premise was that there is no one true meaning to life.

Bach's novel first took hold on college campuses, and its popularity grew quickly until, by the end of 1972, one million copies were in print. The novel remained on *The New York Times* best-seller list for thirty-eight weeks. In all, it sold millions of copies. The novel deeply touched the American "can-do," Puritan individualist psyche.

Impact   Critics interpreted the success of *Jonathan Livingston Seagull* in many ways. Some argued that the novel gave rise to a number of different movements that became popular across the United States, including the self-help, positive thinking, human potential, and New Age movements. Some called it a

parable of the time. It was undeniably influential in opening up the American populace to the idea of ethnic tolerance and multiculturalism, holding that all the world's voices deserve to be heard equally and that there is no single way to look at life. In the early twenty-first century, the novel remained in print, appealing primarily to adolescents and young people searching for life's answers.

Further Reading

Bach, Richard. *Illusions: The Adventures of a Reluctant Messiah.* New York: Delacorte Press, 1977.
Gardner, Richard M. "Stereotypes and Sentimentality: The Coarser Sieve." *Midwest Quarterly: A Journal of Contemporary Thought.* 29, no. 2 (Winter, 1988): 232-248.

M. Casey Diana

See also   Human potential movement; *I'm OK, You're OK*; Literature in the United States; "Me Decade"; New Age movement; Religion and spirituality in the United States; Self-help books.

■ Jonestown and the People's Temple

Identification   Community established in Guyana by an American religious cult founded by Jim Jones

In November, 1978, an estimated nine hundred followers of the People's Temple cult committed mass suicide by drinking cyanide-laced punch. The American public reacted with shock, horror, and a multitude of questions about fringe religious groups and the fate of these people.

In 1969, approximately one hundred members of the People's Temple Full Gospel Church, a congregation affiliated with the Disciples of Christ Church and led by its charismatic founder, Jim Jones, built a church called Happy Acres in Redwood Valley, California. Consisting largely of African Americans who had relocated to California from Indianapolis in 1965, the church also welcomed newer members, who tended to be white and relatively well educated. First organized by Jones in the racially heated mid-1950's, the People's Temple was dedicated to the pursuit of social justice along Marxist lines. Jones called his mission "apostolic socialism."

In 1970 and 1972, Jones opened branch churches in largely black communities in San Francisco and Los Angeles. The cultlike quality of the congregation's dedication to Jones and the presence of armed guards at services drew complaints and criticisms from members and the public at large. Partly as a result of this criticism, a few members were sent to Guyana in 1974 to establish a colony for the congregation. By 1975, fifty people occupied a 3,824-acre site.

Migration from the Bay Area and Los Angeles churches soon swelled the Jonestown population to more than one thousand. By most accounts, life in the community was thriving and healthy. About three-quarters of the population were African American, and members represented thirty-nine U.S. states. Reacting to the publication of scandalous reports about his behavior with congregants, Jones himself moved to Guyana in July, 1977.

Investigations and "Revolutionary Suicide" Meanwhile, Concerned Relatives, a group of congregants' friends and relatives, began organizing opposition to a church that they labeled a dangerous cult. De-spite their move away from the United States, members were not beyond the reach of authorities bent on examining Jones and those supporting his authority. Defectors from the church provided negative information about the group's activities, and Concerned Relatives convinced Congressman Leo Ryan of California to organize a more formal investigation. On November 1, 1978, Ryan sent a letter to Jones in which he requested permission to visit and inspect Jonestown. On November 9, Jones sent back a petition signed by the congregation that was meant to dissuade the congressman. Ryan, accompanied by journalists, a film crew, staff members, and members of Concerned Relatives, arrived in Georgetown, Guyana, on November 15. Despite Jones's misgivings, the party was invited to visit and did so late on November 17. Jones's wife, Marceline, met them and provided a guided tour.

As the inspection and interviews with members drew to a close on November 18, several People's Temple members asked to leave with the congressman. Ryan was injured in a scuffle, and armed men chased the delegation back to the airport, firing on them as the defectors began to board the airplane. Ryan, one the defectors, and three journalists died of the gunfire. Back in Jonestown, Jones set in motion a grisly ritual that the cult's leadership had planned for half a decade—"revolutionary suicide." More than 900 people, including 260 children, drank a poisoned beverage, while Jones and several others died of gunshot wounds. Some may have had the cyanide injected. Because only 7 of the nearly 917 dead cult members were given autopsies, no one is certain of the exact causes of death of each member. All told, 922 people, including the U.S. congressman, lay dead in the Guyana jungle. Many members fled into the jungle, and eighty-five of them survived the massacre; Jones's two sons and others were away playing basketball in Georgetown.

Impact Before the mass suicide of November, 1978, the notion that a religious cult could be inherently dangerous to its members or others was not a part of mainstream public consciousness. After the event, however, many Americans began to distrust fringe religious movements and to view those that developed around cults of personality in an especially bad light. Sociologists,

Jim Jones, the leader of the People's Temple cult. (DPA/Landov)

psychologists, and experts on American religion researched why seemingly normal people joined such a cult, relocated to a jungle, and apparently killed themselves. In some ways, religious pluralism and tolerance in the United States suffered a palpable setback following this tragedy.

Further Reading

Eden, Karl. *The Jonestown Massacre: The Transcript of Reverend Jim Jones' Last Speech, Guyana, 1978.* Philadelphia: Temple Press, 1993. Provides an important primary source to any study of the mass suicide event.

Layton, Deborah. *Seductive Poison: A Jonestown Survivor's Story of Life and Death in the People's Temple.* New York: Doubleday, 1999. Personalized view of the cult and its end.

Maaga, Mary M. *Hearing the Voices of Jonestown.* Syracuse, N.Y.: Syracuse University Press, 1998. A pastor's examination of the victims of the cult and how the search for social justice led them to their deaths.

Moore, Rebecca, et al. *People's Temple and Black Religion in America.* Bloomington: Indiana University Press, 2004. Readable academic account of the place of Jonestown in African American Christianity.

Reiterman, Tom, and John Jacobs. *Raven: The Untold Story of Reverend Jim Jones and His People.* New York: Penguin Books, 1982. Heavily detailed account by investigative journalists.

Weightman, Judith Mary. *Making Sense of the Jonestown Suicides: A Sociological History of People's Temple.* Lewiston, N.Y.: Edwin Mellen Press, 1983. Academic study of the attraction and membership of the cult.

Joseph P. Byrne

See also   African Americans; Cults; Religion and spirituality in the United States.

■ Jordan, Barbara

Identification   African American congresswoman, 1972-1978
Born   February 21, 1936; Houston, Texas
Died   January 16, 1996; Austin, Texas

Jordan was the first African American woman to represent a southern state in the U.S. Congress and the first to deliver the keynote address at a presidential nominating conven-

---

Excerpt from Congresswoman Barbara Jordan's keynote address at the Democratic National Convention, delivered on July 12, 1976:

"One hundred and forty-four years ago, members of the Democratic Party first met in convention to select a presidential candidate. Since that time, Democrats have continued to convene once every four years and draft a party platform and nominate a presidential candidate. And our meeting this week is a continuation of that tradition.

But there is something different about tonight. There is something special about tonight. What is different? What is special? I, Barbara Jordan, am a keynote speaker.

A lot of years passed since 1832, and during that time it would have been most unusual for any national political party to ask that a Barbara Jordan deliver a keynote address . . . but tonight here I am. And I feel that notwithstanding the past that my presence here is one additional bit of evidence that the American Dream need not forever be deferred."

---

tion. Her political success made Jordan a role model for minorities and women in public life during the 1970's.

With support from President Lyndon B. Johnson, Barbara Jordan entered politics in the 1960's and was elected to the Texas state senate in 1967. Not since Reconstruction had an African American held such an office. In 1972, Jordan was elected president pro tempore of the Texas state senate and also served as Texas "Governor for a Day." The second honor made Jordan the first African American woman to exercise a governor's authority.

Jordan made history again in 1972 with her election to the U.S. Congress, representing the Eighteenth District of Texas. During her tenure, Jordan helped expand the Voting Rights Act in 1975. She also supported Social Security benefits for women who work at home, the Equal Rights Amendment (ERA), and abortion rights.

In 1974, Jordan served on the House Judiciary Committee that voted to impeach President Richard M. Nixon for his involvement in the Watergate scandal. When she made a speech to explain her vote in favor of impeachment, Jordan affirmed the values of the U.S. Constitution and won respect from a national television audience.

Jordan's keynote speech at the Democratic National Convention in 1976 was her most celebrated moment of the decade. Her riveting oratory nearly upstaged nominee Jimmy Carter and made Jordan a leader in a party with increasing numbers of minorities and women. Also in 1976, Jordan was selected for *Time* magazine's list of the "Ten Women of the Year." When Carter became president in 1977, Jordan was interested in serving as attorney general but was not offered a cabinet post.

In 1978, Jordan left Congress for an academic career at the Lyndon B. Johnson School of Public Affairs in Austin, Texas, where she taught courses in politics and ethics. By this time, Jordan's health was increasingly poor as a result of multiple sclerosis (MS). She was diagnosed with the disease in the early 1970's but chose not to draw public attention to it. Eventually, her MS symptoms required Jordan to use a wheelchair and contributed to her death in 1996 at age fifty-nine.

Impact   Barbara Jordan's time in national politics was brief, but her reputation transcended gender, race, and party lines. She achieved progressive goals by using a bipartisan, pragmatic approach, finding support among those who were prepared to reject her on the basis of prejudice. Eloquent and erudite, Jordan helped create more opportunities for African American women in politics.

Further Reading

Fenno, Richard F. *Going Home: Black Representatives and Their Constituents.* Chicago: University of Chicago Press, 2003.

Jordan, Barbara, and Shelby Hearon. *Barbara Jordan: A Self-Portrait.* Garden City, N.Y.: Doubleday, 1979.

Rogers, Mary Beth. *Barbara Jordan: American Hero.* New York: Bantam, 1998.

Ray Pence

See also   Abortion rights; African Americans; Chisholm, Shirley; Congress, U.S.; Elections in the United States, 1972; Elections in the United States, 1976; Equal Rights Amendment (ERA); Feminism; Jackson, Maynard, Jr.; Nixon's resignation and pardon; Racial discrimination; Voting Rights Act of 1975; Women's rights; Young, Andrew.

■ Journalism in Canada

Definition   Distribution of significant information and news in Canada via print and electronic media

During the 1970's, Canadian journalists sought improved, professionalized standards despite corporate control of many newspapers and broadcasting channels.

Canadian journalism included English- and French-language newspapers, magazines, and radio and television stations. Some journalists reported in other languages for Canadians who belonged to ethnicities not represented by mainstream journalism. As Canada became urbanized, readers' demand for dailies increased, with some large metropolitan areas having two or more dailies. By 1974, 117 Canadian dailies totaled a circulation of approximately five million. Several chains, such as F.P. Publications (Free Press), and wealthy entrepreneurs, including Roy Thomson and Paul Desmarais, owned most Canadian newspapers and often controlled radio and television stations as well. Critics denounced these magnates for monopolizing journalism. Although some journalists wrote for alternative papers, covering issues that chain papers ignored, expenses limited circulation.

In 1970, journalism experienced scrutiny because of the Front de Libération du Québec (FLQ) abductions of two government officials. FLQ members provided Quebec radio stations CKLM and CKAC and Radio-Canada with a manifesto of the abductors' demands. The FLQ wanted quick, uncensored broadcasts and altered traditional Canadian journalism roles by prioritizing radio over television and newspapers. Journalists unintentionally became intermediaries between the terrorists and police. FLQ demands included journalists traveling with liberated political prisoners to safe places.

The abductions instigated debates about journalistic responsibility and ethics. Quebec journalists held conferences discussing media during crises and wrote articles examining how to report emergencies. They determined that journalistic accountability included media owners and editors. Those executives were often concerned primarily with advertising profits and the promotion of political allies, not editorial quality. Editors followed their investors' policies in determining whether to include or omit topics. After the crisis, some owners censored or fired any journalists, including employees at CKAC, who refused to be controlled. Many reporters resigned. In October, 1971, fifteen thousand people protested and burned an effigy of Desmarais during a newspaper strike.

Reporters met in Ottawa for Canada's first national journalism conference in 1971 in order to discuss professional concerns. Universities expanded journalism curricula. In 1973, 40 percent of urban Canadian journalists were university graduates. Journalists acquired technological skills, especially computing, transforming newsrooms with electronic text and image transmissions and typesetting. By 1978, the *Globe* used a satellite to distribute newspapers to all Canadian time zones, boosting circulation.

In 1970, the new Federation of Press Clubs of Canada (renamed the National Press Club of Canada mid-decade) presented the first Michener Awards for journalism. Honorees included journalists who superbly reported about public service topics having an impact on Canadians. By 1978, journalists established the Centre for Investigative Journalism, which became the Canadian Association of Journalists.

Impact   By the late 1970's, many Canadians chose television news broadcasts instead of newspapers because newspaper costs had increased. In autumn, 1979, the afternoon *Montreal Star* stopped circulation after 111 years as a result of limited finances. Throughout Canada, the number of afternoon papers declined. Many readers were dissatisfied by chain newspapers and aware of management biases. However, when newspapers printed poll results favoring preferred candidates prior to elections, that information often swayed voters. Reporters attempted to provide audiences impartial newsworthy content despite managerial interference.

Further Reading

Fetherling, Douglas. *The Rise of the Canadian Newspaper.* Toronto: Oxford University Press, 1990.

Rutherford, Paul. *The Making of the Canadian Media.* Toronto: McGraw-Hill Ryerson, 1978.

Elizabeth D. Schafer

See also   Censorship in Canada; Communications in Canada; Journalism in the United States; New Journalism; October Crisis; Photography; Radio; Science and technology; Television in Canada.

■ Journalism in the United States

Definition   Distribution of significant information and news in the United States via print and electronic media

U.S. journalists often refer to themselves as the "fourth estate," placing themselves next to national political leaders in terms of importance in the maintenance of a strong democratic society. As members of this fourth estate, journalists used their role as gathers and disseminators of news to influence U.S. political, economic, and social life during the 1970's.

The Vietnam War and the Civil Rights and women's movements of the 1960's continued to make headlines and lead broadcast newscasts during the 1970's. Other important news events during the 1970's included the information explosion, the space race, increasing urban problems, changing cultural patterns among young people, high inflation, and an energy crisis. Food and fuel shortages in 1973 prompted U.S. journalists to focus their attention on the ecology and the need to use the planet's human, land, water, and other resources more intelligently. Politics, including the Watergate scandal, the resignations of Vice President Spiro T. Agnew and President Richard M. Nixon, and the 1979 Iranian hostage crisis during President Jimmy Carter's administration also dominated the news during the 1970's.

The Presidency and the Press   Mutual distrust and dislike between President Nixon and many of the journalists assigned to cover the White House existed. This mistrust may have been a factor in Nixon's limited use of press conferences and extensive use of network television to speak directly to the public. Nixon's repeated verbal assaults on the media, his use of subpoenas against reporters, and his efforts to prevent the publication of the Pentagon Papers resulted in accusations that he was trying to intimidate the news media.

President Gerald R. Ford earned the praise of the press corps that were tired of the daily battles with the administration, and journalists applauded his intention to be open and candid with the news media and his regular news conferences. However, his honeymoon with the news media ended a month after it began when he appeared on national television on September 8, 1974, in order to announce his plans to grant Nixon a full presidential pardon for any offenses that he may have committed related to Watergate.

President Jimmy Carter in 1976 publicly dedicated himself to total honesty with the public. Carter lost no time trying to continue where Ford left off in improving the relationship between the presidency and the press by holding regular news conferences. Carter's public image suffered, however, whenever the antics of his brother Billy became news. Later, Billy Carter's financial dealings were categorized by the news media as "Billygate." Media coverage of the 1979 Iranian hostage crisis played a major role in Carter losing his reelection bid to Ronald Reagan in 1980.

Television Journalism Television played a dominant role in the mass communication of ideas and events in the United States during the 1970's. By 1975, almost every U.S. home had a television set— 112 million television sets in 68.5 million households. A 1970 survey revealed that 54 percent of the U.S. public believed that television brought people

the latest news more rapidly compared with the other types of news media, and television received the highest marks for providing the fairest and least biased news coverage—33 percent compared with 23 percent for newspapers and 19 percent for radio. A 1971 poll revealed that Americans preferred television to newspapers as the source for most of their news and that 40 percent of Americans found television the most believable medium for news compared to 20 percent for newspapers.

While newspapers carried early reports of the Watergate scandal in 1972, network television did not play a major role in covering the Watergate scandal until early the next year. By 1973, television news media, through their use of video and live coverage, delivered the latest details of Watergate during evening newscasts, special reports, and weekend interview programs. Live television coverage of congressional committee hearings investigating Watergate in the summer of 1973 revealed the seriousness of the accusations against President Nixon and his cohorts. The following summer, live telecasts of impeach-

At the beginning of the 1970's, journalism in the United States was still dominated by veteran news commentators such as Walter Cronkite (left), appearing with New York City mayor John Lindsay on his television show in 1970. (AP/Wide World Photos)

ment hearings conducted by the House Judiciary Committee uncovered Nixon's involvement not only in the Watergate break-in but also in an extensive campaign of illegal domestic spying conducted against those considered "enemies" of the White House. Nixon himself tried to use television to persuade the public of his innocence by holding press conferences, staging photo opportunities, and making speeches. However, the instantaneous coverage of the Watergate investigation via television damaged Nixon's public image and made his subsequent resignation inevitable.

Newspapers and New Technology   By the middle of the 1970's, an electronic revolution was well underway in the U.S. newspaper industry, which included the development and evolution of computers and their adaptation to newspaper typesetting. During the decade, newspaper reporters and editors abandoned their typewriters for the video display terminal. It had a keyboard similar to that of a typewriter. Instead of using paper, reporters typed on a visual display screen similar to a television screen. Video display terminals were used to generate and edit copy and lay out advertisements and whole pages, eliminating the need for the Linotype typesetter. Reporters were in effect setting type from their desks; fewer persons meant fewer mistakes, and fewer hands were cost saving. By late 1973, electronic editing enabled wire services to file more news, provide clearer and cleaner copy, and permitted the faster filing of important stories, thus helping newspapers become better able to compete with the television news media.

Journalism and Minorities   The U.S. news media made little effort to recruit minority journalists until the 1968 Kerner Commission Report—written after outbreaks of racial violence in various American cities in 1967—criticized the mass media for ignoring African Americans. The Kerner Commission charged the mass media with failing to communicate to their majority white audience the sense of "degradation, misery, and hopelessness" of being an African American living in the United States. The commission concluded that there had been no serious reporting on the African American community. As a result, it expressed concern about the effect, on white Americans as well as on black Americans, of a television world that was almost entirely white in

"both appearance and attitude." The commission also concluded that the token hiring of one or two African American reporters was not good enough and that news organizations needed to hire more African American reporters, editors, and commentators.

Affirmative action efforts in the journalism industry did occur after the Kerner Report, but progress was slow. By the end of the 1970's, minority newsroom employment had reached 6.6 percent, but 56 percent of the daily newspapers still had all-white editorial staffs. Newspapers under ten thousand in circulation reported the greatest gains in hiring minorities, up from 17 percent to 24 percent. Of the 54,700 newspaper journalists, 3,589 were African American, Hispanic, Asian American, and Native American. Statistics indicated that minorities held about 14 percent of jobs in television news and 10 percent in radio news but that these figures included many low-level jobs that did not lead to advancement into decision-making positions. The National Association of Black Journalists was formed in 1975 in an attempt to expand and balance media coverage of the African American community and to recruit more African American youth to pursue journalism careers. Hispanic journalists and Native American journalists would form their own associations in the early 1980's.

Journalism and Women   Women's rights activists insisted that women, like minorities, should be depicted more positively by the news media. Most daily newspapers in the early 1970's had a women's department that produced one or more pages of news intended primarily for women readers. A 1973 survey reported that 90 percent of the women readers and 80 percent of the men readers looked at the women's pages. Many of the changes in the women's pages during the 1970's were in response to readers' complaints that the women's pages printed too much trivial information and ignored public affairs and career-oriented stories. One of the most noticeable changes in the women's pages was the gradual deemphasis of society news such as engagement and wedding announcements, parties, and club news. Women's sections during the decade were expanded to include more public affairs and investigative stories. Articles on abortion, alcoholism, consumer needs, crime, hunger, and human rights, especially women's rights, started appearing in in-

By the middle of the decade, new faces began to emerge in U.S. journalism—often women, such as Jane Pauley of The Today Show, *or minorities.* (AP/Wide World Photos)

creasing numbers. Later, these women's pages would be transformed into lifestyle sections.

Alternative feminist publications grew from one newsletter in 1968 to more than 560 periodicals by 1973, including the mass circulation *Ms.* magazine. Written by women who often did not have formal training in journalism, these publications provided material on woman's health and other issues not normally offered in the mainstream media. However, the news content of the mainstream media did begin to broaden somewhat during the 1970's to include more stories about women as news organizations began to hire more female journalists.

Overt prejudice against female journalists in hiring and promotion did not end until the Civil Rights and women's movements of the 1960's and 1970's, when passage of federal legislation outlawed discrimination. Help for women in broadcast news

came from a Federal Communications Commission (FCC) ruling in 1971 that required women, like minorities, to be given equal opportunities in hiring. Women reporters slowly moved into areas formerly barred to them, such as government, police, business, war coverage, and sports news. However, women journalists in television, more than men, continued to be judged on their looks and appearance. Many of the gains of women in mainstream journalism came only after legal battles for equality. Sex discrimination complaints and lawsuits were brought forth in the 1970's against numerous news organizations and broadcasters. These lawsuits often ended after years of litigation with settlements calling for more opportunities for women.

In a 1979 report, *Window Dressing on the Set: An Update,* the U.S. Commission on Civil Rights found that despite increases in the numbers of minority and female employees at television stations during the 1970's, they were almost completely absent from decision-making positions. This study also found that during the decade, more than 82 percent of U.S. news correspondents were white men, and the newsmakers covered by television news reporters were predominantly white male government officials as well.

Impact   During the 1970's, as in the 1960's, journalists continued to be viewed as the conveyors of information and opinion vital to the operation of government and the maintenance of freedom. In the euphoric days following *The Washington Post's* Watergate revelations, 68 percent of the American public polled expressed trust and confidence in the U.S. news media. The human rights struggle continued to be a major topic of coverage in the 1970's as African Americans and women sought the same equal opportunities as white men, including jobs as reporters, editors, and producers in U.S. newsrooms.

Further Reading

Barrett, Marvin, ed. *Moments of Truth.* New York: Thomas Y. Crowell, 1975. This fifth duPont-Columbia University survey of broadcast journalism focuses on the 1973-1975 confrontation between the president and the press.

_____. *The Politics of Broadcasting.* New York: Thomas Y. Crowell, 1973. This fourth duPont-Columbia University survey discusses ways that Richard Nixon intimidated the press.

Blanchard, Margaret A., ed. *History of the Mass Media in the United States: An Encyclopedia*. Chicago: Fitzroy Dearborn, 1998. Covering three hundred years of U.S. mass media history, the book provides extensive background on how American media reached their positions of authority, influence, and controversy in U.S. society.

Crouse, Timothy. *The Boys on the Bus: Riding with the Campaign Press Corps*. New York: Random House, 1973. Description of the media coverage of 1972 presidential campaign in which journalists traveled together and tended to report basically the same things, giving rise to the terms "pack" and "herd" journalism.

Emry, Michael, and Edwin Emry. *The Press and America: An Interpretive History of the Mass Media*. 6th ed. Englewood Cliffs, N.J.: Prentice Hall, 1988. Extensive examination of the history of all media, the landmark events in communications history, and the effect that media coverage of major events in American history had on American life.

New York Times, editors of the. *The Pentagon Papers*. New York: Bantam, 1971. The publication of the decisions and documents leading up to the U.S. Supreme Court landmark decision on prior restraint, *New York Times v. United States*.

U.S. Commission on Civil Rights. *Window Dressing on the Set: An Update*. Washington, D.C.: Government Printing Office, 1979. A U.S. government report updating its 1977 report on the portrayal of women and minorities in television entertainment programming as well as the number of women and minority journalists in network television news.

Woodward, Bob, and Carl Bernstein. *All the President's Men*. New York: Simon & Schuster, 1974. *The Washington Post*'s reporters tell how they laid the groundwork for toppling Nixon.

Eddith A. Dashiell

See also *All the President's Men*; Censorship in the United States; Communications in the United States; Deep Throat; Feminism; Journalism in Canada; Mailer, Norman; "Me Decade"; Miss Manners column; *Ms.* magazine; National Public Radio (NPR); New Journalism; Pentagon Papers; Photography; "Radical Chic"; Radio; Scandals; *60 Minutes*; Steinem, Gloria; Television in the United States; Thompson, Hunter S.; Vietnam War; Walters, Barbara; Watergate; Wolfe, Tom; Woodward, Bob, and Carl Bernstein.

■ Joy of Sex, The

Identification Self-help sexuality book
Editor Alex Comfort (1920-2000)
Date Published in 1972

The Joy of Sex *quickly became a milestone in the literature of sex and love with its use of wit and its uninhibited combination of words and illustrations.*

During the 1970's, people were exhausted from the moral and political turmoil of the 1960's. However, that era introduced some liberating changes in American culture. Moreover, many Americans, looking for inspiration and happiness in troubled times, turned to self-help books, including those on the topic of sexuality. Alex Comfort subtitled his book *A Cordon Bleu Guide to Lovemaking*, using the name of the prestigious international culinary school—Le Cordon Bleu—centered in France. The institution forced him to remove the two words "Cordon Bleu," but he kept the rest of the subtitle as well as his approach of using references to gourmet food as analogies for enjoyable "gourmet" sex. Section titles included "Starters," "Main Courses," and "Sauces and Pickles"; this was gourmet sex that couples could "cook up."

Comfort viewed his book as a long overdue, sophisticated, and unhesitant account of the full repertoire of human heterosexuality. The writing was generally viewed as witty, open-minded, and frank, but unlike some other authors of popular sexuality books, Comfort also relied on knowledge gleaned from objective sexual researchers. Comfort's purpose in both the text and the illustrations was to encourage people to view sex as natural, enjoyable, and liberating and to reject rigid either-or perspectives.

The book emphasized tenderness, experimentation, and advanced techniques of lovemaking. Explicit pen-and-ink illustrations, with Japanese and Indian themes, showed a great diversity of techniques and positions, and while controversial to some, they added much to the book's popularity. The people in the illustrations were not film-star beautiful as in most sexuality books, but this fact, along with the artistic appeal of the drawings, helped people to identify with them.

Comfort was a published scholar, having already written eleven scholarly nonfiction books, six novels, and numerous poems and plays, frequently with sexual themes. One of his books had criticized authors of previous medical sex manuals for appointing themselves as moral judges. He edited *The Joy of Sex* in two weeks and later regretted that his fame was based mostly on this book. He also was a political activist, focusing some of his attention on reforming sex laws.

Impact *The Joy of Sex* was ranked number four on the best-seller charts in 1973 and became very popular in many countries. It was a popular coffee-table book, symbolizing the growing acceptance of open discussion of sexuality. Occasionally it was called educated pornography, but overall, it received very little criticism. The book discussed the physical side of sex, but because of its tremendous acceptance, two years later, Comfort edited *More Joy: A Lovemaking Companion to "The Joy of Sex,"* which dealt with the relationship aspects of sex. It, too, became a best-seller. Ultimately, Comfort's books had a tremendous positive effect on sexual openness for women and men during the 1970's.

Further Reading

Chang, Jolan, and Joseph Needham. *The Tao of Love and Sex.* New York: Penguin, 1977.

Friday, Nancy. *Women on Top: How Real Life Has Changed Women's Fantasies.* New York: Simon & Schuster, 1993.

Gerhard, Jane F. *Desiring Revolution: Second-Wave Feminism and the Rewriting of Twentieth-Century American Sexual Thought, 1920-1982.* New York: Columbia University Press, 2001.

Abraham D. Lavender

See also *Everything You Always Wanted to Know About Sex but Were Afraid to Ask*; *Hite Report, The*; Homosexuality and gay rights; Literature in the United States; Pornography; Self-help books; Sexual revolution; Swingers.

■ Jumbo jets

Definition Large, long-distance, wide-bodied airplanes

The jumbo jets of the 1970's helped create economies of scale in the airline industry, which in turn allowed the hub-and-spoke system of airline travel that emerged in subsequent decades.

The 1970's saw many factors that brought about both the development and the eventual success of jumbo jets. Continued development in the Third

World combined with an overall increase in the world's population created an opportunity for global marketing. Moreover, the expanding world economy required that people travel for business, while an increase in income also allowed people to travel for pleasure. Thus, the need for a larger and longer-range jet aircraft arose in order to serve the "global village."

In the late 1960's, Pan American World Airways (Pan Am) began asking aircraft builders for a new generation of aircraft to replace the Boeing 707's and DC-8's in their fleet. All three major manufacturers responded. Boeing responded with the 747, McDonnell Douglass with the DC-10, and Lockheed with the L-1011. These aircraft came to be called "jumbo jets" because of their large size. They were built to fly twice as far as previous aircraft while carrying three times as many people in multilevel comfort.

In 1970, the Boeing 747 became the first of these aircraft to be put into commercial service. This plane, measuring 231 feet, was longer than the Wright brothers' flight at Kitty Hawk. Four Pratt and Whitney turbofan engines were developed especially for the jets to power them. The 747 was designed to travel at .85 Mach (565 miles per hour), yet it could land and take off from conventional airports. Over the next thirty years, it would evolve into one of the most versatile and well known of the jumbo jets.

Another of these aircraft was the McDonnell Douglas DC-10, which used a triengine design when it was launched in 1970. It had one General Electric turbofan under each wing, while a third engine was mounted on the tail. The DC-10 also evolved into a number of configurations during the 1970's, although the most successful was arguably the KC-10 Extender.

The Lockheed L-1011 also began flying in 1970 and used a tri-engine design. The plane had Rolls Royce engines under each wing, and the third was built into the top of the fuselage at the tail in an S-duct design.

Impact Many of the jumbo jets that emerged during the 1970's have been successful not only as passenger planes but also as jet freighters. This is in part because of their large lifting capacity—150,000 pounds—and long range—4,000 to 6,000 miles. The military developed its own jumbo jet during the

1970's, the C-5 Galaxy. It was also built as a freighter and could be used on conventional or even unpaved runways.

The increase in the price of fuel in 1973-1974 changed the way in which the airlines operated their jumbo jets. A hub-and-spoke system began to be used in which smaller planes would bring passengers to a central, or hub, airport and consolidate them on the jumbo jets for longer flights domestically or internationally.

Further Reading

Jacobs, Lou. *Jumbo Jets.* New York: Simon & Schuster, 1976.

Tennekes, Henk. *The Simple Science of Flight: From Insects to Jumbo Jets.* Boston: MIT Press, 1997.

Robert Stewart

See also　Aircraft; Inventions; Science and technology; Transportation.

■ Jumbo Tornado Outbreak of 1974

The Event　Multiple tornadoes hit parts of the United States and Canada

Date　April 3-4, 1974

Place　Between the Mississippi River and the crest of the Appalachian Mountains and into Ontario, Canada

The United States' worst tornado outbreak in history lasted about eighteen hours. During this period, 148 tornadoes mercilessly wreaked havoc and death in their wake.

The geographical extent of the terrifying tornado outbreak was extraordinary. Altogether, tornadoes affected thirteen U.S. states and Ontario, Canada. Six states received the majority of activity. Reports of the first twisters came from Tennessee and Georgia on April 3, around 2 P.M. Within an hour and a half,

A powerful tornado moves through Xenia, Ohio, part of the Jumbo Tornado Outbreak. (AP/Wide World Photos)

Fujita Scale of Tornado Intensity

F-Scale Number	Intensity Phrase	Wind Speed
F0	Gale tornado	40-72 mph
F1	Moderate tornado	73-112 mph
F2	Significant tornado	113-157 mph
F3	Severe tornado	158-206 mph
F4	Devastating tornado	207-260 mph
F5	Incredible tornado	261-318 mph

killer storms were popping up in Indiana, then Illinois, Ohio, Kentucky, and Alabama. Tornadoes also tore through Michigan, Mississippi, North Carolina, South Carolina, Virginia, West Virginia, and New York. One twister even crossed over into Canada from Michigan and back again. The outbreak ended about 8 A.M. the next morning.

Paths of the 148 tornadoes amounted to more than 2,500 miles of destruction. Twisters, ranging from 0 to 5 on the Fujita tornado scale, killed 330 people and injured 5,484 more. Some of the storms traveled more than 100 miles (160 kilometers)—the average path length of a tornado is 2 miles (3.2 kilometers). One deadly vortex was 5 miles wide (8 kilometers)—the average twister is one-eighth of a mile wide.

Six tornadoes were categorized on the Fujita scale as F5 tornadoes. At the outbreak's peak, fifteen tornadoes were on the ground at the same time. Xenia, Ohio, was the site of the most damaging and deadly twister, which killed 34 people, injured 1,600 others, and destroyed 1,300 homes. Deadly vortexes also struck Brandenburg, Kentucky (31 killed); Monticello, Indiana (19 killed); and Guin, Alabama (23 killed). The tornado that crossed into Canada struck the city of Windsor, Ontario, killing 8 people there.

Impact The outbreak caused more than one billion dollars in property damage. T. Theodore Fujita, creator of the Fujita Scale, conducted an aerial survey of the outbreak. His flyover observations and analysis of aerial photographs led him to discover small-scale damaging downdrafts, also called downbursts, that take place during the violent storms. Fujita also concluded that individual thunderstorms of the outburst spawned a series of tornadoes or tornado "families." The outbreak ultimately led to expansion of the National Weather Service's radio network, which would supplant a slower Teletype storm warning system.

Subsequent Events Accident investigators would recognize downbursts as the cause of several major airline crashes in the following decade. Moreover, the tornado outbreak's devastation spurred Congress to fund research that would lead to the use of Doppler radar during the 1980's in order to provide better lead times for the issue of storm warnings.

Further Reading

Fujita, T. Theodore. "Jumbo Tornado Outbreak of 3 April 1974." *Weatherwise* 27, no. 3, 116-126.

Ludlum, David M. *The American Weather Book.* Boston: Houghton Mifflin, 1982.

Richard A. Crooker

See also Natural disasters.

K

■ Kaufman, Andy

Identification   American comedian and
    performance artist
Born   January 17, 1949; New York, New York
Died   May 16, 1984; Los Angeles, California

During the 1970's, Kaufman pioneered the concept of performance art within a mass media context.

Andy Kaufman began to perform magic tricks and comedy routines at children's parties and became a paid performer by age fourteen. Early on, he developed lifelong fascinations with Elvis Presley, professional wrestling, and the fine line between performance and reality. By the early 1970's, Kaufman was confusing, and sometimes delighting, comedy club audiences with his unique brand of improvisation. His appearance as Foreign Man on the inaugural broadcast of *Saturday Night Live* in the fall of 1975 introduced Kaufman to a national audience that began to anticipate his unpredictable presence on seventeen more episodes of the live show.

Kaufman and his alter ego, the lounge singer Tony Clifton, gained a following of mostly young fans who appreciated the outrageousness of his experimental style, which was showcased in a series of live concerts, guest appearances on variety shows, and his television special *Andy's Funhouse* (1979). The closest to mainstream performance and wide popularity that Kaufman ever came was through his character Foreign Man, who developed into Latka Gravas, a regular cast member of the highly regarded television sitcom *Taxi* (1978). However, Kaufman found the restraints of scripted television comedy oppressive, preferring instead the challenges and opportunities of live performance. Attracted to the comic and dramatic possibilities of wrestling, Kaufman began a brief, ludicrous wrestling career, during which he improvised wrestling matches with women from his audiences, provoked a long-running (albeit fake) feud with World Wrestling Federation wrestler Jerry Lawler, and proclaimed himself World Intergender Wrestling Champion.

Impact   Andy Kaufman blurred the separation between guerrilla theater and popular entertainment. His legendary refusal to break character and his direct, often bizarre engagements with audiences challenged definitions of performance and the relationship between performers and their audiences.

Subsequent Events   Because Kaufman was in good physical health, not a smoker, and notorious for his elaborate hoaxes, many wrongly assumed that the announcement of his death in 1984 from lung cancer at age thirty-five was Kaufman's most outrageous stunt. Regrettably, it was not.

In 1995, the National Broadcasting Company (NBC) broadcast *A Comedy Salute to Andy Kaufman*, which contained tributes to Kaufman's inspiration, influence, and artistic courage by many leading American comedians. The biopic *Man in the Moon* (1999), produced by *Taxi* cast member Danny DeVito, directed by Milos Forman, and starring Jim Carrey in an award-winning performance, introduced Kaufman to another generation of fans who could access his original performances on syndicated television.

Further Reading

Hecht, Julie. *Was This Man a Genius? Talks with Andy Kaufman/Julie Hecht*. New York: Random House, 2001.

Zehme, Bill. *Lost in the Funhouse: The Life and Mind of Andy Kaufman*. New York: Delta, 2001.

Zmuda, Bob, and Matthew Scott Hanson. *Andy Kaufman Revealed: Best Friend Tells All*. Boston: Little, Brown, 1999.

Carolyn Anderson

See also   Comedians; *Saturday Night Live*; Sitcoms; *Taxi*; Television in the United States; Theater in the United States; Variety shows.

■ Keep America Beautiful

Identification   A coalition of nonprofit businesses and organizations that fights the nationwide litter problem

Date   Established during the 1950's

During the 1970's, Keep America Beautiful mounted a television advertising campaign educating people about what they could do to help stop litter. However, environmental groups withdrew their affiliations from Keep America Beautiful, charging that the organization's main corporate contributors pressured it to work against anti-littering legislation.

Keep America Beautiful produced the "Crying Indian" television spot, which first aired in 1971 and showed a teardrop slowly running down the face of a distraught Cherokee Indian named Iron Eyes Cody. It showed Cody sitting in a canoe or atop a horse star-

ing at garbage floating in a pristine river or at trash along a highway. The image of the crying Indian reached hundreds of thousands of homes repeatedly throughout the decade and became iconic of the environmental movement.

In 1973, Keep America Beautiful sponsored research on reasons why people litter and on the primary sources of litter. It began the Clean Community System in 1976. Funded by the U.S. Brewers Association, an affiliated member of Keep America Beautiful, the system coordinated efforts by businesses, schools, neighborhood groups, and local governments to reduce litter in neighborhoods and communities. Georgia sponsored the first Keep America Beautiful statewide program in 1978. Keep America Beautiful launched its first teacher curriculum supplement, Waste in Place, in 1979. Just as the "Crying Indian" public service announcement did, these activities focused on the importance of indi-

In 1998, Georgia launched a litter-fighting program patterned on Keep America Beautiful's "Crying Indian" public service announcement of the 1970's. (AP/Wide World Photos)

vidual responsibility in cleaning up litter. People Start Pollution, People Can Stop It became a popular Keep America Beautiful slogan.

Impact The impact of the "Crying Indian" advertisement was remarkable. In the first four months of airtime, more than 100,000 people requested a booklet on how to reduce pollution. The famous tear arguably played a role in the fledgling environmental movement. It stirred people to think twice about throwing garbage out of their car windows by reminding them that they too could help stop pollution of the landscape.

Despite the ad's success, environmental groups affiliated with Keep America Beautiful felt that the organization should focus on corporate as well as individual responsibility. Environmentalists wanted it to support state legislation requiring companies to charge deposits on beer and soft drink containers. Instead, it lobbied against container deposits, ostensibly because the organization wanted to protect profits of its corporate donors: The main contributors of money to Keep America Beautiful were companies that made nonrefillable glass, aluminum, paper, and plastic containers. In response to Keep America Beautiful's antideposit policy, the Sierra Club, the National Audubon Society, and the National Wildlife Federation withdrew their affiliation with the group by the end of the decade.

Subsequent Events Keep America Beautiful expanded its influence following the 1970's. Furthermore, the "Crying Indian" ad continued to air through 1983, with another showing in 1997. It won two Clio Awards, and *Ad Age Magazine* named it one of the top one hundred advertising campaigns of the twentieth century. Environmentalists and Keep America Beautiful remained estranged over philosophical issues.

Further Reading

Keep America Beautiful. http://www.kab.org.

Megalli, Mark, and Andy Friedman. *Masks of Deception: Corporate Front Groups in America.* Washington, D.C.: Essential Information, 1991.

Reinhardt, Forest L. *Down to Earth: Applying Business Principles to Environmental Management.* Boston: Harvard Business School Press, 1999.

Richard A. Crooker

See also Advertising; Environmental movement.

■ Kennedy, Ted

Identification U.S. senator
Born February 22, 1932; Boston, Massachusetts

Kennedy's strong support of a wide variety of progressive economic, political, and social issues allowed him to set the agenda for liberalism perhaps to a greater degree than any other politician in the 1970's.

Edward (Ted) Kennedy spent the 1970's rebuilding his political career after a tragic automobile accident in 1969 tarnished his reputation. This effort led him to take strong liberal stands on a wide range of issues to such an extent that he became the best-known liberal Democrat in the U.S. Senate.

Kennedy was the youngest son of the powerful Massachusetts multimillionaire businessman-politician Joseph P. Kennedy, Sr. His other older brothers, President John F. Kennedy and Senator Robert F. Kennedy, were assassinated in 1963 and 1968, respectively.

After graduating from Harvard University in 1956 and the University of Virginia Law School in 1959, Ted Kennedy plunged directly into politics by working in his brother's presidential campaign and then his own campaign for the Senate seat that his brother vacated upon becoming president. Elected when he had barely attained the Senate's minimum age of thirty years, he rose quickly within the Senate hierarchy to the post of Democratic majority party whip in 1969.

Later that year, while vacationing in Massachusetts, he drove his car off a bridge on Chappaquiddick Island. Mary Jo Kopeckne, a passenger in the car, was killed. The circumstances surrounding this event were never explained adequately, and his reputation was so damaged that a pall was left over his political career. In 1971, he was defeated for re-election to the post of majority whip by Senator Robert Byrd of West Virginia.

Kennedy did not quit but instead rebuilt his political career by becoming known as a national spokesman for liberal causes, such as women's rights and affirmative action. He became increasingly opposed to the Vietnam War and supported greater government spending on welfare programs for the poor, minorities, and other disadvantaged groups. He was one of the early leaders in favor of a program of national health insurance.

In 1979, he had risen to a significant Senate post

Ted Kennedy. (Burton Berinsky/Landov)

as chairman of the Senate's Judiciary Committee. As dissatisfaction grew within the liberal wing of the Democratic Party with the performance of incumbent President Jimmy Carter by the end of the 1970's, Kennedy was poised to launch his unsuccessful 1980 presidential bid against Carter.

Impact Ted Kennedy's support of liberal causes—women's rights, affirmative action, anti-Vietnam War activities, education, health care, and welfare—was so steadfast that he became the titular head of the liberal wing of the Democratic Party in Congress and the most readily identified liberal in the country. The stands that he took came to identify liberalism in America during the 1970's.

Further Reading

Clymer, Adam. *Edward M. Kennedy.* New York: Morrow, 1999.

David, Lester. *Good Ted, Bad Ted: The Two Faces of Edward M. Kennedy.* Secaucus, N.J.: Carol, 1993.

Goodwin, Doris Kearns. *The Fitzgeralds and the Kennedys.* New York: St. Martin's Press, 1991.

Hersh, Seymour M. *The Dark Side of Camelot.* Boston: Little, Brown, 1997.

Richard L. Wilson

See also Abortion rights; Affirmative action; Antiwar demonstrations; Carter, Jimmy; Congress, U.S.; Liberalism in U.S. politics; McGovern, George; Vietnam War; Voting Rights Act of 1975; Welfare.

■ Kent State massacre

The Event Students are killed at an antiwar protest
Date May 4, 1970
Place Kent State University in Kent, Ohio

The killing of antiwar protesters by National Guard troops increased opposition both to the war in Vietnam at colleges and to antiwar protests in middle America. Coming at a time when the volatile situation had seemed to be calming down, the resurgence of violent protests closed many colleges early for the year.

On May 4, 1970, the Vietnam War came home to the United States. At Kent State University, National Guard troops fired into a crowd of antiwar protesters, killing four. The events leading up to the shootings were complicated and rested partly on a fear that the general public had of the protesters, whom many older people saw as an uncontrolled mob.

Having been elected in 1968 partly on a platform of ending the Vietnam War, President Richard M. Nixon pledged to begin bringing troops home and to avoid invading Vietnam's neighboring countries. The year 1968 had been a particularly violent one, filled with troubling events: the Tet Offensive in Vietnam, the My Lai massacre of Vietnamese villagers by American soldiers (details of which emerged only later), the assassinations of Martin Luther King, Jr., and Robert Kennedy, and escalation of violence in antiwar and civil rights protests.

On April 30, 1970, President Nixon announced that troops from the Army of the Republic of Vietnam (South Vietnam) and from the United States were going into Cambodia, just across the border from Vietnam. He called this "an incursion" rather than an invasion, stating that the United States was not invading Cambodia but, rather, was trying to destroy enemy bases—those of the North Vietnamese—in Cambodia. After Nixon's announcement, college campuses all over the country, which had been relatively quiet previously, erupted. Student activists at notoriously political campuses—the University of California at Berkeley, the University of Michigan, the University of Wisconsin at Madison, Harvard,

Brandeis, and the University of Chicago—staged huge protests, but they were not alone.

At the time, approximately half the country was opposed to the war in Vietnam, while others were disgusted by the behavior of the antiwar protesters, believing that these protesters were aiding the enemy psychologically by lowering American morale. Most of the protesters were college students, people of the same age as those fighting in Vietnam. They believed that the United States had no business fighting this foreign war, one that was costly and of questionable merit.

The National Guard Reacts   The most contentious protests broke out at Kent State in Ohio and at Jackson State in Mississippi. At Kent State, the students, feeling betrayed by Nixon's actions, began protesting on campus. By May 2, the demonstrations were

peaceful during the day but rowdy at night. Some people burned the Reserve Officers' Training Corps (ROTC) building, and the mayor asked for help from the governor. The National Guard was called out, and they responded.

National Guard troops were, in many cases, people the same age as college students (in fact, some were college students) who joined the guard in order to get money for tuition, to supplement their earnings, or to avoid the draft and certain Vietnam posting. The National Guard allowed recruits to stay at home and continue with their lives, spending six weeks during the summer and one weekend a month in training while paying them.

The guard troops had been helping to calm things down at a union strike nearby, so they were tired and tense. Meanwhile, Governor James A. Rhodes believed that he was fighting communism by

Kent State student Mary Ann Vecchio screams as she kneels over the body of Jeffrey Miller, who was shot by the Ohio National Guard during an antiwar demonstration. (Hulton Archive/Getty Images)

inhibiting the protesters, so he was resolute in his arguments to thwart the activists. The mayor banned any protests, which further infuriated the students.

More than thirty years after the events, uncertainty about exactly what happened on May 4 continued to exist. What is certain is that more than sixty shots were fired into the crowd, which had thrown rocks and empty tear gas canisters in response to tear gas shot by the troops. Four people were killed, both male and female, and nine were wounded.

While members of the National Guard claimed that they heard the command to fire, those in charge denied issuing that command. The result was the same regardless. Armed troops were firing on mostly middle-class college students who were acting under the rights of free speech and free assembly.

Impact When word about the killings got out to other colleges, the violence spread. Faculty at many schools voted to condemn the war officially, and schools all over the country called for Nixon's impeachment. Opinions about the war and those protesting the war further polarized an already deeply divided country.

At Jackson State in Mississippi, where students were protesting the "police action" at Kent State and American involvement in Vietnam, white state troopers fired at black students, killing two who were watching from a window.

Further Reading

Gitlin, Todd. *The Sixties: Years of Hope, Days of Rage.* New York: Bantam, 1987. Gitlin, a founder of Students for a Democratic Society, traces the events of the antiwar movement from the perspective of an active participant in many of the events. As a sociologist, he brings the tools of academic research to this book.

Heineman, Kenneth J. *Campus Wars: The Peace Movement at American State Universities in the Vietnam Era.* New York: New York University Press, 1993. Details the events leading up to, during, and after the massacre at Kent State.

Viorst, Milton. *Fire in the Streets: America in the 1960's.* New York: Simon & Schuster, 1979. Viorst focuses his book on the violent demonstrations throughout the days of protest.

Tracy E. Miller

See also Antiwar demonstrations; Cambodia invasion and bombing; Nixon, Richard M.; Vietnam War; Weather Underground.

■ King, Billie Jean

Identification American tennis player
Born November 22, 1943; Long Beach, California

King is recognized as one of the most successful women's tennis players in the history of the game. She was largely responsible for the increased popularity of women's tennis and contributed significantly to the struggle for women's rights in and outside the sport.

Billie Jean King dominated women's tennis during the 1970's. She won three singles, five doubles, and three mixed doubles titles at Wimbledon. She also won singles titles at the U.S. Open in 1971 and 1974, with a total of thirteen U.S. Open titles in all. By the time that she finished playing competitively in 1984, she had won seventy-one singles championships. King was the first female athlete to win more than $100,000 in prize money in a single season, and in 1972 she was named *Sports Illustrated*'s Sportsperson of the Year, the first woman to be so honored.

King is also known for her highly publicized tennis exhibition match against aging male champion Bobby Riggs. The match, played on September 20, 1973, and billed as "The Battle of the Sexes," drew more than thirty thousand people to the Houston Astrodome and was watched on television by more than fifty million viewers around the world. King beat Riggs in straight sets 6-4, 6-3, and 6-3 and took the prize money of $100,000. More important, at a time when women's tennis was not as prestigious as men's, her success over a male competitor gave instant credibility to the women's game.

In addition to playing a pivotal role in advancing equality between the sexes, King was also responsible for publicizing gay and lesbian rights. Her bisexuality became front-page news when she was sued for palimony stemming from a lesbian affair with her personal secretary and lover Marilyn Barnett. King was the first American athlete to acknowledge a homosexual relationship publicly.

Impact Billie Jean King was at the center of the changes taking place in women's athletics during the 1970's. In addition to her outstanding play, she championed a move toward equal prize money for men and women. Outraged at the disparity between men's and women's prizes at major tournaments, King spearheaded the drive to create a separate tour for women's professional tennis players, which came to be known as the Virginia Slims Tour. King's activities helped to legitimize women's professional tennis. She was integral in the development of the Women's Tennis Association, and she cofounded World Team Tennis, America's only professional coed team sport. She became the first woman to coach a professional team with men when she served as player/coach for the Philadelphia Freedoms of World Team Tennis.

King's social activism, in and outside the world of professional tennis, along with the passage of Title IX of the Education Amendments of 1972, significantly enhanced the number of girls and women participating in sports.

Further Reading

Lipsyte, Robert. *Idols of the Game.* Atlanta: Turner, 1995.

Lumpkin, Angela. "The Contribution of Women to the History of Competitive Tennis in the United States in the Twentieth Century." In *Her Story in*

Sport: A Historical Anthology of Women in Sports, edited by Reet Howell. West Point, N.Y.: Leisure Press, 1982.

Mary McElroy

See also   Ashe, Arthur; Battle of the Sexes; Connors, Jimmy; Evert, Chris; Feminism; Homosexuality and gay rights; Sports; Tennis; Women's rights.

■ King, Stephen

Identification   American writer of horror fiction
Born   September 21, 1947; Portland, Maine

During the 1970's, King revolutionized books by making the horror novel acceptable to a wider audience.

Until the publication of Stephen King's first novel, *Carrie* (1974), the market for horror stories consisted almost entirely of reprints of classic stories by authors such as Edgar Allan Poe and Nathaniel Hawthorne. Novels were even rarer and, with the exceptions of best-sellers such as Ira Levin's *Rosemary's Baby* (1967) and William Peter Blatty's *The Exorcist* (1971), they did not make an impact with audiences. *Carrie* changed everything and opened the door for new horror novelists such as Anne Rice and Clive Barker, almost single-handedly creating a market for horror novels that book publishers were eager to fill.

King's approach—writing stories about average people encountering unspeakable horror in everyday surroundings—struck a chord with readers because King's protagonists were Everymen like themselves. King told stories like a friend around the campfire, easing the reader in until the terror happens. King placed every effort on storytelling, and it showed.

King often was accused of making his writing too commercial, and King himself noted that his stories are like fast-food meals rather than a gourmet dinner. King avoided highly educated words when simple ones would do, making him that much more accessible to the public at large. In every story, no matter what the subject, King wrote from a character's personal perspective rather than from an unemotional perspective about the horror itself. King's writing style was also unusual: Descriptions interrupted with stream of consciousness became his trademark.

The film version of *Carrie*, directed by Brian De Palma, opened in 1976 to critical acclaim.

Billie Jean King. (Volvo Women's Tennis Cup)

King's novels and the films that they inspire seemed to go hand in hand. People who had never read King's work soon wanted to do so, and book readers were curious if the films would be as good as the books; the combination added to King's popularity. As King's yearly book turnaround time became known, he quickly gained a reputation as someone on whom readers could depend on year after year to spin a good and terrifying tale.

Impact King wrote six books during the 1970's, and they cemented his reputation as a writer who not only knew the traditions of horror but also took horror to new levels of acceptability. King became the world's most sucessful writer, with more than forty books published by the early twenty-first century and two or more titles often competing on best-seller lists concurrently.

Further Reading

Bloom, Harold, ed. *Modern Critical Views: Stephen King*. Philadelphia: Chelsea House, 1998.

King, Stephen. *On Writing: A Memoir of the Craft*. New York: Scribner, 2000.

Winter, Douglas E. *Stephen King: The Art of Darkness*. New York: New American Library, 1984.

Kelly Rothenberg

See also Book publishing; *Exorcist, The*; Horror films; Literature in the United States.

■ KISS

Identification American hard-rock band
Date Formed in 1972

KISS was one of the most influential rock-and-roll bands of the 1970's, as the group's music and performance style had a significant impact on the development of popular music in the United States.

In 1972, rhythm guitarist Paul Stanley and bass guitarist Gene Simmons recruited drummer Peter Criss and lead guitarist Ace Frehley to form the rock-and-roll band KISS. The band made its first appearance in August, 1973, in New York City. Shortly thereafter, following its second performance in Manhattan, the group was offered a management contract. Within two weeks, KISS had signed a recording contract with Casablanca Records. The group would become

KISS in 1976. (AP/Wide World Photos)

known for wearing elaborate black-and-white character makeup and costumes and for using ornate stage sets.

In 1974, the band released three albums, *KISS*, *Hotter than Hell*, and *Dressed to Kill*, all of which were moderately successful. The group's fourth album, *Alive* (1975), went platinum and included its first U.S. hit single, "Rock and Roll All Nite." The next album, *Destroyer* (1976), was equally successful and earned the group its first Top 10 single on the music charts. In 1976 and 1977, KISS produced three more albums, *Rock and Roll Over*, *Love Gun*, and *Alive II*, all of which turned platinum and catapulted the group to major recording-artist status in the music industry. In 1979, the band released its final album of the decade, *Dynasty*, which featured the worldwide hit single "I Was Made for Lovin' You."

KISS's appeal to audiences lay in its bigger-than-life stage sets with pyrotechnic displays, its glitzy costumes, and its rock anthems. Throughout the 1970's, the group's popularity continued to multiply, and by the end of the decade, the group's fans—known as the "KISS Army"—had grown to hundreds of thousands of people. In 1977, KISS was named the most popular band in the United States in a Gallup poll. Taking advantage of this popularity, the group also launched an enormous marketing campaign, selling countless consumer items such as makeup kits, masks, and board games. The members even starred in a science-fiction film, *KISS Meet the Phantom of the Park* (1978), and Marvel Comics published two superhero cartoon books about the band.

Impact   During the 1970's, KISS rose to superstar status, in large part because of its explosive live shows, outrageous costumes, and hard-rock anthems. The group's legions of fans became almost cultlike. Enthusiasts formed KISS-like bands, complete with costumes and flashy stage shows. Attendance records at stadium concerts were consistently broken as millions of people attended KISS shows. In essence, the group became a cultural phenomenon of the 1970's that defined rock-and-roll music for a generation of teenagers. Equally important, the band's influence on music and the music industry was far-reaching. Its music had a significant impact on the development of heavy-metal music, its stage shows redefined concert standards, and the selling of its image created a whole new marketing industry for musicians.

Further Reading

Abbott, Waring, Gene Simmons, and Paul Stanley. *KISS: The Early Years.* New York: Crown, 2002.

Elliott, Paul. *KISS—Hotter than Hell: The Stories Behind Every Song.* New York: Thunder's Mouth Press, 2002.

Bernadette Zbicki Heiney

See also   Hard rock and heavy metal; Music; Radio.

■ Kissinger, Henry

Identification   National security adviser and secretary of state in the Nixon and Ford administrations

Born   May 27, 1923; Fürth, Bavaria, Germany

Kissinger was instrumental in shaping and implementing U.S. foreign policy, especially the United States' exit from Vietnam, an effort for which he won a Nobel Peace Prize. He was also a key player in Cold War diplomacy with the Soviet Union, opening China to U.S. diplomats, and shaping peace in the Middle East.

With the election of President Richard M. Nixon in 1968, Henry Kissinger went from being a Harvard professor of political science to national security adviser, one of the most important members of a president's administration. Despite political differences, Kissinger became Nixon's most powerful and valuable aide and was given a great deal of latitude in implementing American foreign policy. Nixon wanted a peaceful world, and Kissinger strove to bring it about.

In early 1969, Kissinger believed that a negotiated peace could be achieved in Vietnam within six months. In fact, negotiations would drag out over nearly four years as diplomats in Paris tried to balance the interests of Washington, South Vietnam, and North Vietnam. Kissinger rejected the notion of an American military victory but recognized the role of American military power in forcing the North Vietnamese to the table. Thus, he supported the interdiction bombings in Cambodia beginning in March, 1969. After attending the negotiations in Paris in early 1970 and seeing the diplomatic logjam, he supported the invasion of Cambodia by Americans and South Vietnamese troops at the request of Cambodian leader General Lon Nol in April, 1970. This move, and the student deaths at an antiwar demonstration at Kent State University in May, alienated many of his friends and colleagues in academia. Moreover, the Kent State event weighed very heavily on the conscience of Kissinger, a Jewish refugee from Adolf Hitler's Germany.

Kissinger ventured to Paris again as Nixon's personal negotiator in September, 1970, and again in May, 1971. After a massive invasion of North Vietnamese regular troops in late March, 1972, Kissinger returned to Paris seeking a cease-fire and prisoner exchange that would lead to a complete and orderly withdrawal of all U.S. troops. Though North Vietnam's main negotiator, Le Duc Tho, had always demanded imposition of a communist-type government in Saigon as his principal war aim, he reduced this to a coalition government in August. After another bombing campaign of the North after Nixon's reelection in November, 1972, the two sides achieved a cease-fire agreement, called the Paris Peace Accords, and "peace with honor" on January 27, 1973. For this, Kissinger shared with Le Duc Tho the Nobel Peace Prize for 1973, a recognition he repudiated after the brutal fall of Saigon to the communists in the spring of 1975.

Cold War and China Kissinger's role in opening relations with communist China and smoothing them with the Soviet Union were less ambivalent. Beginning in early 1969, at Nixon's behest, Kissinger began informal, secret negotiations with members of the Chinese government with the aim of normalizing a relationship that had been frozen for twenty years. On July 15, 1971, Nixon announced that he would visit Mao Zedong and Premier Zhou Enlai in Beijing, a promise that he kept the following February. It took a staunch anticommunist such as Nixon to make such a bold move and a tireless diplomat such as Kissinger to prepare the way.

Kissinger's stature and skills served his president well. Three months later, Nixon became the first U.S. president to visit Moscow, where he signed the original Strategic Arms Limitation Treaty (SALT I), another diplomatic coup made possible by Kissinger's efforts.

Henry Kissinger. (Library of Congress)

Secretary of State In August, 1973, in the midst of the Watergate crisis, Nixon appointed Kissinger as secretary of state in the hope of maintaining a stable foreign policy in the face of an unpredictable future. In fact, he would retain the position until the inauguration of President Jimmy Carter in early 1977. Much of Kissinger's time and energy was absorbed with the aftermath of the Yom Kippur War of October, 1973. Beginning on November 5, he carried out what was dubbed "shuttle diplomacy," personally traveling between Washington, D.C., Tel Aviv, Israel, and Damascus, Syria, in order to broker a military disengagement of, and settlement between, Israel and hostile Arab states. He achieved this with an agreement signed on May 31, 1974, a success that bolstered his already stellar reputation.

After Nixon's resignation on August 9, 1974, Kissinger continued to serve President Gerald R. Ford, maintaining most elements of Nixon's foreign policy and its implementation. After leaving office on January 20, 1977, Kissinger took to the lecture circuit while serving as a consultant and writing his memoirs, which first appeared in 1979.

Impact Henry Kissinger enabled Richard Nixon to claim major foreign policy advances in China and the Soviet Union and to fulfill his promise to Americans of ending the U.S. role in Vietnam. Moreover, his shuttle diplomacy defused a highly volatile standoff in the Middle East. Kissinger acted deftly on the world's stage and earned the world's recognition as the foremost diplomat of the decade.

Further Reading

Burr, William. *Kissinger Transcripts: The Top Secret Talks with Beijing and Moscow.* New York: New Press, 1999. State Department documents that provide behind-the-scenes material on Kissinger's dealings with Soviet and Chinese leaders during the Nixon and Ford years.

Hanhimaki, Jussi M. *The Flawed Architect: Henry Kissinger and American Foreign Policy.* New York: Oxford University Press, 2004. Respectful but highly critical analysis of Kissinger's foreign policy.

Isaacson, Walter. *Kissinger: A Biography.* New York: Simon & Schuster, 1992. Highly detailed and balanced account of Kissinger's life up to the early 1990's; aside from Kissinger's own memoirs, arguably the fullest account available to date.

Israel, Fred. *Henry Kissinger.* New York: Chelsea House, 1986. Biographical account that focuses on his career in the cabinet and State Department; for younger readers.

Kissinger, Henry. *Ending the Vietnam War: A History of America's Involvement in and Extraction from the Vietnam War.* New York: Simon & Schuster, 2003. Kissinger's own examination of American involvement in the Vietnam conflict and American departure from it through his own perspective.

_____. *The White House Years.* Boston: Little, Brown, 1979. Kissinger's memoirs of his career as presidential adviser and cabinet member.

Joseph P. Byrne

See also Antiwar demonstrations; Cambodia invasion and bombing; China and the United States; Cold War; Ford, Gerald R.; Foreign policy of the United States; Israel and the United States; Kent State massacre; Middle East and North America; Nixon, Richard M.; Nixon's visit to China; Nobel Prizes; Paris Peace Accords; SALT I and II treaties; Soviet Union and North America; Vietnam War.

■ Knievel, Evel

Identification American motorcycle daredevil
Born October 17, 1938; Butte, Montana

Knievel used his self-promotional skills and colorful personality to become a popular culture hero in the 1970's.

Evel Knievel began his career as a motorcycle daredevil in the mid-1960's. His rapid rise to fame inspired a 1971 film biography, *Evel Knievel*, starring George Hamilton. In 1977, Knievel played himself in the film *Viva Knievel!* Although some questioned whether he was an athlete, Knievel was a fixture on the American Broadcasting Company (ABC) television program *Wide World of Sports* during the 1970's and appeared on the cover of *Sports Illustrated* magazine in 1974. Young fans made the Ideal Toy Company's line of Knievel merchandise a huge success. His likeness appeared on everything from lunch boxes to T-shirts, and his exploits were celebrated in comic books and country music songs.

Appearing throughout the United States and Canada during the decade, Knievel often attempted jumps over rows of cars and buses. His successes included a 1971 jump over nineteen cars in Ontario, Canada, that set a world record. However, Knievel's accidents and injuries were perhaps more famous. A 1972 stunt in San Francisco ended with a broken back and a concussion. After jumping thirteen buses in London, England, in 1975, Knievel broke his pelvis and announced his retirement, but he returned to the daredevil circuit later that year. Another serious injury in 1976 put an end to his major appearances.

Knievel's most anticipated and disappointing event in the 1970's did not involve a motorcycle. In September, 1974, Knievel tried to jump the Snake River Canyon in Idaho in a rocketlike vehicle called the Sky Cycle X-2. Extensive media coverage and Knievel's multimillion-dollar fee overshadowed the stunt itself, which ended with Sky Cycle's parachute malfunctioning and the vehicle crashing. Knievel did further damage to his image when he served prison time for assaulting a former publicist in California in 1977. By the end of the 1970's, age, injury, and bad publicity had taken a toll on Knievel, who trained his son Robbie to carry on his legacy as a daredevil.

Evel Knievel warms up on his motorcycle in 1971. (AP/Wide World Photos)

Impact Individualistic, seemingly indestructible, and dressed in red, white, and blue, Evel Knievel catered to American appetites for risk-taking. His motorcycle symbolized both rebellion and freedom, but Knievel rejected comparisons to motorcycle gangs such as the Hell's Angels or the protagonists in the 1969 film *Easy Rider.* Although he appealed to youth with his antidrug, self-confident image, Knievel was also a hard-drinking, pugnacious figure. His greatest talent may have been self-promotion, with the Snake River Canyon spectacle an early example of hype—a phenomenon in which an event is secondary to its advertisement and publicity.

Further Reading

Mandich, Steve. *Evel Incarnate: The Life and Legend of Evel Knievel.* London: Sidgwick & Jackson, 2000.

Saltman, Sheldon. *Evel Knievel on Tour.* New York: Dell, 1977.

Ray Pence

See also Advertising; Fads; Hobbies and recreation; Sports; Television in the United States; Toys and games.

■ Koch, Ed

Identification New York City mayor, 1977-1989
Born December 12, 1924; Bronx, New York

Koch revitalized New York City during a period of fiscal crisis and civic problems.

Ed Koch, an active reformer who served from 1968 to 1970 in the U.S. House of Representatives, ran in New York City's Democratic mayoral primaries in 1977 against such candidates as Mayor Abraham Beame and New York State's lieutenant governor, Mario Cuomo, against whom he won the runoff election by a narrow margin. His Republican opponent was Bella Abzug, a colorful member of the House of Representatives.

When Koch became its mayor, New York City was in dire shape. Mayor John Lindsay had accumulated huge deficits during his term immediately before Beame became mayor in 1973. Beame was a respected financial authority. In 1975, however, two years into his term, such a dire financial crisis overtook the city that a declaration of bankruptcy seemed

Ed Koch addresses reporters at a press conference in 1977 after his victory in New York City's mayoral race. (AP/Wide World Photos)

imminent, and the city's bonds were sharply downgraded. A further complication occurred on July 13-14, 1977, when a power outage left the city without electricity for more than twenty-four hours. Widespread looting occurred, and much of the blame for the civil chaos of that evening was heaped upon Beame's administration.

As mayor, Koch immediately tackled the city's most pressing problems. A liberal Democrat through most of his life, he sought office as a fiscal conservative and financial reformer. Conservative Jewish, Italian, and Irish voters in Brooklyn, Queens, and Staten Island supported his candidacy. Because he needed help from financial moguls in order to restore New York's financial integrity, he cultivated the help of notable figures such as David Rockefeller and Donald Trump, who had vested interests in the city's economic recovery.

Koch emphasized a law-and-order agenda. He defended the death penalty, and he opposed public unions and the unpopular Vietnam War. An energetic public servant—he often asked his constituents, "How'm I doing?"—Koch was not blindly loyal to his party. He had, however, an unquestionable devotion to New York's citizens. He served three terms but lost when he ran for a fourth.

Impact   When New York City's future seemed hopeless, Ed Koch undertook the Herculean task of reviving the city's economy and restoring its stability. Practicing fiscal restraint and enlisting the assistance of prominent people with much to gain from the city's recovery, he stabilized New York's economy and restored the troubled metropolis as the robust commercial and cultural center it had historically been.

Further Reading

Koch, Edward, with Daniel Paisner. *Citizen Koch: An Autobiography.* New York: St. Martin's Press, 1985.

Mollenkopf, John H. *A Phoenix in the Ashes: The Rise and Fall of the Koch Coalition in New York City Politics.* Princeton, N.J.: Princeton University Press, 1992.

Mollenkopf, John H., and Manuel Castells, eds. *Dual City: Restructuring New York.* New York: Russell Sage Foundation, 1991.

R. Baird Shuman

See also   Byrne, Jane; Daley, Richard J.; Feinstein, Dianne; Jackson, Maynard, Jr.; Liberalism in U.S. politics; Moscone, George; New York City blackout of 1977.

■ *Kramer vs. Kramer*

Identification   Motion picture
Director   Robert Benton (1932-   )
Date   Released in 1979

Kramer vs. Kramer showed the effects of divorce with greater depth, sensitivity, and honesty than had been depicted previously on film.

In *Kramer vs. Kramer,* Joanna Kramer (played by Meryl Streep) is a frustrated woman, unhappy in her marriage and insecure in her parenting skills. She leaves her husband, Ted (Dustin Hoffman), a New York City advertising executive, and seven-year-old son, Billy (Justin Henry), in order to regain her

Dustin Hoffman (left) and Justin Henry play father and son in the film Kramer vs. Kramer. *(Museum of Modern Art/Film Stills Archive)*

sense of self. Her departure creates difficulties for Billy and Ted: Billy blames himself for his mother's desertion, while Ted has to act both as father and as mother to his son, forcing him to devote less time to his job. The two eventually develop a close relationship and a better understanding of Joanna's departure.

Their newfound happiness is short-lived. Joanna, who has spent time in California undergoing therapy, returns to New York. She has found a job and regained her self-esteem. She wants to take Billy back, but Ted vows to fight for custody. To complicate matters further, Ted is fired from his job because his boss is displeased with his decreased productivity. Ted needs employment in order to gain custody of Billy, so he takes a new job at a lower salary, earning less money than Joanna. Subsequently, Ted and Joanna become embroiled in an ugly court battle for custody. The judge rules in Joanna's favor, but she realizes that Billy is happy with Ted and allows Ted to keep the boy.

Kramer vs. Kramer recounted these events with intelligence, perception, and wit, taking pains to develop a balanced portrait of both parents and showing each with flaws as well as virtues. Its story and characters resonated with viewers who had experienced the pain of divorce and child-custody disputes. The film earned high praise from film critics and was a box-office success.

However, the film fared less well with some feminists, who maintained that Ted was portrayed more sympathetically than was Joanna. Ted, they argued, stays home and sacrifices his job in order to care for his son, while Joanna selfishly abandons her child to pursue her own interests.

Kramer vs. Kramer was nominated for nine Academy Awards and received five Oscars at the ceremony held April 14, 1980. The film captured Best Picture honors, and Robert Benton received one award for his direction and another for his screenplay. Hoffman won his first award for Best Actor; Streep was named Best Supporting Actress.

Impact   *Kramer vs. Kramer* offered filmgoers a realistic and nuanced view of a family confronting divorce and child-custody battles. Its success showed that there was a market for character-driven films and for films depicting the problems shared by contemporary audiences.

Further Reading

McCreadie, Marsha. *The Casting Couch and Other Front Row Seats: Women in Films of the 1970's and 1980's.* Westport, Conn.: Greenwood Press, 1990.

Magill, Frank Northen, Patricia King Hanson, and Stephen L. Hanson, eds. *Magill's Survey of Cinema: English Language Films, First Series.* 4 vols. Englewood Cliffs, N.J.: Salem Press, 1980.

Osborne, Robert. *Seventy-five Years of the Oscar: The Official History of the Academy Awards.* New York: Abbeville Press, 2003.

Rebecca Kuzins

See also   Academy Awards; Child support and custody; Film in the United States; Hoffman, Dustin; Marriage and divorce; Streep, Meryl; Women's rights.

L

■ Lafleur, Guy

Identification Canadian hockey player
Born September 20, 1951; Thurso, Quebec, Canada

Lafleur was one of the most exciting and prolific scorers in the National Hockey League (NHL). He was a primary force in the Montreal Canadiens' capture of five Stanley Cups during the decade.

Drafted first by the Montreal Canadiens in the 1971 NHL amateur draft, Guy Lafleur moved easily from a spectacular career in the Quebec Junior Hockey League to the professional league. Although teammate goalie Ken Dryden beat out Lafleur for the rookie of the year award in 1972, Lafleur's twenty-nine goals, scintillating skating, and passing abilities signaled a bright future.

After three solid but somewhat disappointing seasons, the right wing broke out in 1974-1975 with fifty-three goals and sixty-six assists. In each of the next three seasons, Lafleur scored the most points and won the NHL's Art Ross Trophy. For the remainder of the 1970's, Lafleur had fifty goals or more in each season, with his best season coming in 1977-1978, when he scored sixty goals. From 1975 to 1980, Lafleur was named to the first All-Star Team. In 1977 and 1978, "The Flower," as he was nicknamed—*fleur* means "flower" in French—won the Hart Trophy as the most valuable player.

Lafleur was a major contributor to Montreal's postseason successes. In 1975, he scored twelve goals in just eleven playoff games. In the four consecutive years that the Canadiens won the Stanley Cup, Lafleur led all scorers three times.

In a decade of turmoil for hockey, the Montreal Canadiens and Lafleur consistently overwhelmed opponents with team speed. Lafleur's skating ability and scoring instincts stood in contrast to the violence used by less talented teams. According to one teammate, the six-foot-tall Lafleur played with "dazzling abandon" as his speed protected him from the physical tactics of desperate defenders. With his long blond hair flowing behind him, Lafleur's fluid, rink-long dashes repeatedly brought hockey fans to their feet. He did not take success for granted, and his longtime coach, Scotty Bowman, observed that Lafleur always was obsessed to be better. His achievements and poised demeanor made Lafleur popular with the English- and French-speaking communities of Canada. Proud of his Quebec roots and loyal to the Montreal organization, Lafleur best symbolized the tradition of French Canadian excellence in the NHL.

Impact Guy Lafleur represented the best of hockey's artistic appeal. His style and career served as a bridge between the success of players Bobby Hull and Gordie Howe before the 1970's and Wayne Gretzky and Mario Lemieux in the 1980's. His incredible accomplishments on ice led to Lafleur's induction into the Hockey Hall of Fame in 1988, shortly after his retirement.

Further Reading

Dryden, Ken. *The Game.* New York: John Wiley & Sons, 2003.

MacInnis, Craig. *Remembering Guy Lafleur.* Vancouver: Raincoast Books, 2004.

M. Philip Lucas

See also Hockey; Sports.

■ Language Poets

Definition A group of writers whose work foregrounds the materiality of linguistic formations and procedures

The Language Poets became a prominent literary force in the San Francisco and New York City areas during the 1970's. These poets had a tremendous impact on American poetry to the extent that their work intersected with more mainstream poetic movements as a critique of the Vietnam conflict. At the same time, the Language Poets extended the Beat Poets' critique of American culture in general.

The official beginning of the Language Poetry movement is generally considered 1971 because the first issue of *This*, a magazine dedicated to avant-garde poetry and fiction and edited by Barrett Watten and Robert Grenier, was published in that year. Among the poets published in the issues of *This* during its existence from 1971 to 1978 were Ron Silliman, Charles Bernstein, Bernadette Mayer, Hannah Weiner, and the editors themselves. Although some poets emphasized the different poetic strategies used by individual writers, the Language Poets as a whole viewed their work as the completion of the modernist project, which had emphasized the medium itself as the subject matter of artistic production. Self-consciously following this modernist tradition that led back to nineteenth century poet Emily Dickinson and included early twentieth century avant-garde writers such as Gertrude Stein, Ezra Pound, and the Objectivists, the Language Poets rejected the bardic tradition of the other major nineteenth century American poet, Walt Whitman. This rejection had culminated in the semi-religious invocations of Allen Ginsberg and the Beats beginning in the 1950's.

Radically politicized by the Vietnam War, poets such as Watten and Silliman emphasized nonrepresentational writing and formal experimentation as a strategy against the voice-based lyric and narrative tradition that dominated creative writing programs in universities from the early to the late twentieth century. At the same time, these poetic strategies sought to undermine the ideological abuse of language by an American presidential administration seeking support for its intervention in the Vietnam conflict.

Adopting continental literary theory to denaturalize the "conversational" discourse of mainstream poetry, the Language Poets argued that the use of "nonpoetic" discourse by the Beats and other countercultural poetic movements—including certain tendencies within ethnopoetics, Deep Image poetics, and black aesthetics—functioned to reinforce the predominant discourse of a government and its institutions that they allegedly opposed. Thus, for the Language Poets, avant-garde linguistic structures and syntax that emphasized the materiality of writing, such as the work of Weiner, and orality, such as the sound-texts of Steve McCaffery, constituted another weapon to be deployed against the rhetoric of the ruling class.

Impact Although they began as small core of writers on the West and East Coasts, the Language Poets had an impact disproportionate to their numbers. Through a multitude of small literary magazines such as *Avec, Chain,* and *L=A=N=G=U=A=G=E*; small publishers such as the Figures, Telephone Books, and Roof Books; and reading series in San Francisco, Milwaukee, Chicago, Philadelphia, and New York City, the Language Poets greatly altered the landscape of American poetry during this era.

Further Reading

Andrews, Bruce, and Charles Bernstein, eds. *The L=A=N=G=U=A=G=E Book.* Carbondale: Southern Illinois University Press, 1984.

Reinfield, Linda. *Language Poetry.* Baton Rouge: Louisiana State University Press, 1992.

Williman, Ron. *In the American Tree: Language, Realism, Poetry.* Orono: University of Maine, 1986.

Tyrone Williams

See also Black Arts Movement; Literature in Canada; Literature in the United States; Poetry.

■ *Last Tango in Paris*

Identification Motion picture
Director Bernardo Bertolucci (1940-)
Date Released in 1972

Last Tango in Paris was an important film during the decade for both its depiction of explicit sexual activity and its tortured portrait of human relationships.

Last Tango in Paris was filmed on location in Paris by the Italian director Bernardo Bertolucci and was a joint Italian, American, and French production. The cast includes the legendary American actor Marlon Brando as Paul and the young French actor Maria Schneider as Jeanne. Paul is a middle-aged American who is despondent over the recent suicide of his French wife, Rosa. Jeanne is a twenty-year-old French woman who is about to marry her filmmaker boyfriend. Paul and Jeanne meet accidentally in a vacant Paris apartment that is for rent. Out of desperation, they begin a three-day anonymous affair. Paul is a tortured soul who has sadomasochistic tendencies. The apartment becomes a sanctuary for the couple. While Jeanne is the innocent in the relationship, Paul has scars that he wishes to cleanse. When Paul finally expresses a need to know Jeanne outside the

Marlon Brando and Maria Schneider in a scene from the controversial motion picture Last Tango in Paris. (Museum of Modern Art/Film Stills Archive)

confines of the apartment, she becomes frightened and shoots him with her father's revolver. Unfortunately, the cocoon of the apartment could not save either of the characters from themselves or from the cruel world outside.

Last Tango in Paris jarred American audiences for its critical examination of the nature of love and the fragility of human relationships. The film was first shown in the United States at the 1972 New York Film Festival. The influential film critic of *The New Yorker*, Pauline Kael, stated that the film had a "jabbing eroticism" and went so far as to claim that *Last Tango in Paris* "must be the most powerfully erotic movie ever made." Because of the explicit sexual nature of *Last Tango in Paris*, the film was given an X rating by the Motion Picture Association of America (MPAA) board in 1973.

Impact   Although considered an art house film, *Last Tango in Paris* did relatively well at the box office and was one of the top-grossing films of 1973. The New York Film Critics and the National Society of Film Critics named Marlon Brando the Best Actor of 1973 for his portrayal of Paul. He also received a 1973 Academy Award nomination for Best Actor. The film was such an important media topic of its time that it became the cover story of both *Time* magazine and *Newsweek*. *Time* received more than twelve thousand protest letters against having *Last Tango in Paris* as a cover story, a record number for the magazine. Some American communities refused to allow the film to be shown. Ultimately, the collaboration of Bertolucci, the veteran Brando, the newcomer Schneider, and the rest of those involved with the making of *Last Tango in Paris* had produced a motion picture about which critics and filmgoers alike would argue for years to come.

Further Reading

Bertolucci, Bernardo. *Bernardo Bertolucci: Interviews.* Edited by Fabien S. Gerard, T. Jefferson Kline, and Bruce Sklarew. Jackson: University Press of Mississippi, 2000.

Lev, Peter. *American Films of the '70's: Conflicting Visions.* Austin: University of Texas Press, 2000.

Lewis, Jon. *Hollywood v. Hard Core: How the Struggle over Censorship Saved the Modern Film Industry.* New York: New York University Press, 2002.

Tonetti, Claretta Micheletti. *Bernardo Bertolucci: The Cinema of Ambiguity.* New York: Twayne, 1995.

Jeffry Jensen

See also Academy Awards; Brando, Marlon; Censorship in the United States; Film in the United States.

■ Latchkey children

Definition Unsupervised children who regularly engage in self-care at home alone or with underage siblings

The growing number of latchkey children during the 1970's raised awareness of a national day care crisis in the United States and brought attention to conflicts regarding work schedules and family obligations as more families became dual worker or single-parent families.

The term "latchkey" refers to the old-fashioned method of lifting a door latch to enter a home. The concept of latchkey children was first used in the United States to refer to children who supervised themselves at home alone during World War II because their fathers were away and their mothers worked outside the home.

The phenomena of latchkey children grew tremendously during the 1970's. Estimates suggest that between five and ten million children at one time regularly cared for themselves before or after school, on weekends, during summer vacations, and on holidays or unexpected school closings while their parents worked. In 1976, the Census Bureau reported that 18 percent of children aged seven to thirteen routinely cared for themselves.

During the decade, the women's movement and difficult economic conditions led to a rise in families with two parents working outside the home. Addi-tionally, rising divorce rates created more single-parent families in which the sole parent had to work. Increased social mobility coupled with a decline in assistance from other relatives led to a national lack of affordable, adequate child care. Consequently, the child-care model of latchkey children reemerged as a substantial number of children stayed home alone engaging in self-care. Parents adopted self-care when alternative child care was inadequate or too expensive, a single parent was involved, the parents perceived the neighborhood as safe for their children, and children were older, more mature, and presumably better able to take of themselves.

The outcomes of children in self-care received attention as part of broader changes in child-rearing practices during the 1970's. Latchkey children tended to be similar to adult-supervised children in terms of independence, self-esteem, social adjustment, and interpersonal relationships, but self-care was also linked to levels of fearfulness and anxiety.

Impact The number of latchkey children in the 1970's led to a reexamination of child care in the United States. As teachers and principals noticed students protecting the house keys worn on strings around their necks, self-care became the center of controversy about child-care policies and practices.

Child advocacy movements worked to meet the needs of latchkey children, and latchkey assistance programs that were developed in the 1970's continued to provide services for children in self-care in later decades. The Boy Scouts and Girls Scouts of America, the American Red Cross, and Campfire, Inc. offered classes to help parents and children adapt to self-care. Communities and local organizations such as libraries, recreation centers, and churches also developed latchkey enrichment programs that might include emergency training or survival guides.

Further Reading

Long, Lynette, and Thomas Long. *The Handbook for Latchkey Children and Their Parents.* New York: Berkley Books, 1983.

Robinson, Bryan E., Bobbie H. Rowland, and Mike Coleman. *Latchkey Kids.* Lexington, Mass.: Lexington Books, 1986.

Barbara E. Johnson

See also Child support and custody; Demographics of the United States; Flex time; Marriage and divorce; Women in the workforce.

■ *Late Great Planet Earth, The*

Identification   Best-selling book
Author   Hal Lindsey (1929-   )
Date   Published in 1970

This work, based upon biblical prophecy and current events, postulated that the battle of Armageddon, or World War III, would involve a Russian invasion of the Middle East. It became a phenomenal best-seller and was made into a film in 1978.

The Late Great Planet Earth focuses on "the end times" and posits the Rapture of Christian believers who will be taken from Earth to Heaven in the immediate future. The key catalyst for author Hal Lindsey's themes was the creation of the modern nation of Israel in 1948—all other conclusions stem from his belief that this event marked the beginning of the end of the world, a view reinforced by Israel's capture of Jerusalem in the Six-Day War in 1967. By fusing biblical prophecy and political events, he reached an audience beyond Christians of an evangelical or Fundamentalist persuasion.

Using forty years as the duration of a generation, Lindsey writes that the future events he describes will happen within a generation of the founding of Israel, or by 1988. He cites Matthew 24:34 in support. The end times will begin when an Arab African alliance of Libya (Put), Ethiopia (Cush), and Iran (Persia) invades Israel, and Russia (the Magog of Ezekiel 38:2)—supported by the Iron Curtain countries of Eastern Europe (Gomer) and southern Russian people (Togarmah) and led by a commander referred to as Gog in Ezekiel 38:15,16—seeks both to grab Israel's vast mineral wealth in the Dead Sea Basin and to secure the "land bridge" in the Middle East. This scenario is illustrated by maps in the book.

Once the Russian intervention is under way, the Russians will double-cross their Arab African allies, and then the Antichrist leader of a united Western Europe—the beast with ten horns referenced in Daniel 7:24—originally supported by China, will attack the Russians. China will betray the Antichrist and march against him with 200 million troops, and to stop this onslaught, the Antichrist will use nuclear weapons. During this time, the Jews will convert en masse to Christianity, and Christ will return and destroy all the armies.

Following his interpretation of the Book of Revelation, Lindsey outlines how history and time will come to an end. He writes that Christ will separate surviving believers from unbelievers and establish his one-thousand-year reign on Earth, the millennium. At its end, an attempted rebellion by unbelievers will be led by Satan, but Christ will destroy them and then create the "new heaven and new earth."

As a postscript, Lindsey offers predictions about religious, political, and social trends. Some of these offered no surprises, including a predicted movement away from institutionalized churches and disbelief within church leadership. However, he also notes that the United States would lose its dominant position in the Western world and experience tremendous increases in drug usage, crime, unemployment, poverty, mental illness, and illegitimacy.

Impact   Written in a very plain and simple style, the book paved the way for many similar works in the 1970's and following decades, and interest in biblical prophecy, international relations, and Middle Eastern politics was heightened. Lindsey himself continued writing in this vein.

Further Reading

Boyer, Paul S. *When Time Shall Be No More: Prophecy Belief in Modern American Culture*. Cambridge, Mass.: Harvard University Press, 1992.
Clouse, Robert G. "Late Great Predictions." *Christian History* 18, no. 1 (1999): 40, 41.
Lindsey, Hal. *The Late Great Planet Earth*. Grand Rapids, Mich.: Zondervan, 1970.

Mark C. Herman

See also   Christian Fundamentalism; Literature in the United States; Middle East and North America; Religion and spirituality in the United States.

■ Latin America

Definition   The countries south of the United States

Peaceful and violent revolutions, right-wing coups, and the growing influence of Cuban communism all posed great challenges to the military, economic, and diplomatic presence of the United States in Latin America during the 1970's.

Political upheaval in Latin America during the 1970's confronted the United States with tremendous risk in a region vital to American national security. Revolutions in Nicaragua and El Salvador led many American diplomats to fear socialist revolution in the region, while a series of military coups installed pro-American regimes that committed horrendous human rights abuses.

South America   In Chile, a coalition of socialists, communists, and moderate voters elected Salvador Allende, the Western Hemisphere's first Marxist president, in 1970. Dubbed the Peaceful Road to Socialism by his supporters, Allende's tenure in office was cut short, however, when his program of nationalizing Chilean copper and other industries ignited the wrath of U.S. president Richard M. Nixon and his national security adviser, Henry Kissinger. The Central Intelligence Agency (CIA) fomented labor strikes against Allende and funneled money to opposition parties during congressional elections in 1972, thereby enabling a *coup d'état* in 1973. The new regime of General Augusto Pinochet Ugarte later was held responsible by human rights organizations such as Amnesty International for executing thousands of political prisoners and imprisoning tens of thousands more.

The relationship between the United States and Latin America was dominated in the 1970's by the presence of Fidel Castro's communist regime in Cuba. (AP/Wide World Photos)

A copycat coup in Uruguay that same year likewise received favorable treatment from the U.S. government, which had trained the Uruguayan military and police in stifling civil disobedience. Neighboring Argentina also witnessed agonizing political and economic chaos in the early 1970's. The urban-guerrilla Montonero Peronist Movement, commonly known as the Montoneros, attempted to seize power through armed struggle. Former president Juan Perón briefly returned to office in 1973, died in 1974, and left the presidency to his wife, Isabela. Her disastrous performance set the stage for a military coup in 1976 and the "dirty war" that followed, during which thousands of trade unionists, teachers, and students were imprisoned, tortured, and killed at the hands of death squads formed by the army and navy. Kissinger, secretary of state under President Gerald Ford, took the position that the Argentine crisis was an internal manner and hushed criticism of the military junta before the U.S. Congress.

Nixon, Kissinger, and Ford all promoted good relations with Brazil, the economic giant of the continent, but the military regime in power after 1964 strongly objected to the administration of president Jimmy Carter after he publicly scolded its country, a longtime American ally, over human rights violations.

Central America and the Caribbean   From 1970 to 1979, all of the Central American republics, except Costa Rica, suffered under military rule. Honduras, Guatemala, El Salvador, and Nicaragua appeared politically stable, and the United States helped control regional affairs by occupying the Panama Canal. Domestic strife between the very rich and the 70 percent of Central Americans who lived below the poverty line existed, however. This socioeconomic disparity came to a head in 1979, when the leftist Sandinista National Liberation Front (FSLN) overthrew the American-backed dictatorship of Anastasio Somoza Debayle in Nicaragua in July. During the same period, Salvadoran rebels rallied against the U.S.-supported military regime installed by a set of junior officers in October, sparking a civil war. President Jimmy Carter funneled millions of dollars in military aid into El Salvador, Guatemala, and Honduras to stem a tide of revolution deemed harmful to the security of Mexico, which by then was a major oil-exporter to the United States. Carter helped diffuse another potential crisis by signing a treaty with Panamanian strongman Omar Torrijos to give sovereignty of the Panama Canal back to the country by 1999.

The United States suspected that Cuban president Fidel Castro was behind many of the region's revolutions of the decade. By 1979, Castro had spent twenty years in power. The American trade embargo against Cuba remained in place, but by the end of the decade, most Latin American governments had defied the U.S. government and had restored diplomatic ties with the communist nation. Although he offered some material support to guerrillas in Nicaragua and El Salvador, Castro generally remained preoccupied with Africa. Tens of thousands of Cuban troops fought in defense of Marxist regimes in Angola and Ethiopia, tipping the scales in the Cold War in favor of the Soviet Union on that contested continent. A revolution on the tiny Caribbean island of Grenada in 1979 headed by the radical New Jewel Movement granted Cuba a strategic, though politically insecure, regional ally.

Impact The polarization of Latin American politics during the 1970's between the revolutionary Left and military rulers sympathetic to the United States begat a schizophrenic foreign policy toward a region many Americans had long ignored. Officially, the United States government favored democracy and peaceful reform, but covertly—and at times overtly—it championed dictatorship and maintenance of the socioeconomic status quo, leaving most Latin Americans trapped in poverty and repression.

Further Reading

Kissinger, Henry. *Years of Renewal.* New York: Simon & Schuster, 2000. Kissinger offers his rationale for supporting anticommunist dictatorships in Latin America and containing Cuban expansionism in Africa from 1974 to 1977. He was both a participant in and a historian of the events he describes, making his account biased but highly valuable.

Kornbluh, Peter, ed. *The Pinochet File: A Declassified Dossier on Atrocity and Accountability.* New York: New Press, 2003. A frightening and revealing look at how the United States undermined democracy in Chile. Kornbluh himself assisted in the declassification of thousands of State Department, White House, and CIA documents that detail U.S.

complicity in the overthrow of Salvador Allende and connivance in covering up the atrocities that followed the coup of 1973.

LaRosa, Michael, and Frank O. Mora, eds. *Neighborly Adversaries: Readings in U.S.-Latin American Relations.* Lanham, Md.: Rowman & Littlefield, 1999. An extensive collection of primary sources from both U.S. and Latin American policymakers and historians sheds light on the perpetual swing between neglect and intrusion that seems to mark U.S. foreign policy toward Latin America, especially during the 1970's.

Julio César Pino

See also Carter, Jimmy; Central Intelligence Agency (CIA); Cold War; Ford, Gerald R.; Foreign policy of the United States; Kissinger, Henry; Mexico and the United States; Nixon, Richard M.; Panama Canal treaties.

■ **Latinos**

Definition Americans originating fully or partially from Spanish-speaking countries

During the 1970's, Latinos took sizable steps to ensure their educational, economical, and political success in the United States. They began opening doors to the American Dream.

The term "Latino" is used to describe groups of very diverse people who are joined by the language they share, Spanish. Among intellectuals and artists, it is a preferred term to identify those who had migrated to the United States from the Iberian Peninsula or from Latin America. "Latino" is mostly used as a political term; it is a term developed by Spanish-speaking groups in the United States.

"Hispanic," on the other hand, is a term invented by the government in the 1970's to group Spanish-speaking people into one category. A group of officials was asked to produce a term to unify Spanish-speaking groups in order for them to be identified more easily by the U.S. Census Bureau. As it became widely used by the Census, in work applications, and by the media, many people in the United States began confusing the term "Hispanic" as denoting a race. "Latino" and "Hispanic" are not racial terms but rather indicate ethnicity, that is, people who may have African, Arabic, Jewish, Native American, or European cultural backgrounds but are grouped together solely because of linguistic heritage.

Education The 1970's brought the implementation of educational organizations to serve the Latino community. After the development of the first department of Chicano studies in the United States at California State University at Los Angeles in 1968, a series of Latino studies programs emerged across the country. Carmelo Mesa-Lago, a scholar at the University of Pittsburgh, founded the *Cuban Studies Newsletter*, marking the emergence of Cuban studies as an academic discipline in 1970. That same year, two programs were instituted: Marta P. Cotera and her husband established Colegio Jacinto Treviño in Mercedes, Texas, as the first Mexican American College in the United States, and the Chicano Studies Research Center at the University of California at Los Angeles (UCLA) was founded to conduct research, house a library, and publish the journal *Aztlán*.

In 1971, the Center for Chicano-Boricua Studies, the first Hispanic ethnic studies program established in the Midwest, began at Wayne State University in Detroit. Later that year, Deganawidah-Quetzalcoatl University (DQU) near Davis, California, became the first Native American and Chicano university. Later in 1973, Antonia Pantoja, an educator and social worker, founded Universidad Boricua in Washington, D.C. The university was developed to provide bilingual and career-oriented programs for professionals as well as other workers. The Center for Puerto Rican Studies was also founded at Hunter College of the City University of New York (CUNY) during the same year.

A series of foundations and organizations followed to support Latino studies and education in general. They included the Latino Institute in the Midwest; the National Hispanic Scholarship, which was supported by the Catholic Church; and the National Association for Bilingual Education (NABE), serving teachers, administrators, and communities.

Bilingual Education Title VII of the Elementary and Secondary Education Act started the bilingual movement in 1968. Its hope was to reduce the dropout rate and sensitize people in the United States to the rich and diverse cultures and traditions of Latinos. However, few schools experimented with bilingual education around the country.

In 1972, Aspira, Inc., a national grassroots educational services organization, brought a suit against the New York City school system. It maintained that tens of thousands of Latino students in New York City were receiving inadequate education in their first language. On August 29, 1974, Aspira obtained a consent decree to offer bilingual education in the schools.

The Equal Educational Opportunities Act passed by the U.S. Congress in 1974 was developed to create equality in public schools by making bilingual education available to Latino youth. However, it was not until later that year, with the Supreme Court decision *Lau v. Nichols*, that laws required that students be given instruction in their first language. The decision was a cornerstone for providing bilingual education across the nation. Also during the same year, the U.S. Congress passed the Bilingual Education Act to finance the preparation of bilingual teachers and development of curriculum.

Film and Television Two Chicano documentary films were made in 1971. *Requiem 29*, made by David Garcia, described the Chicano moratorium on the Vietnam War. Jesús Salvador Treviño's *América Tropical* dealt with the whitewashing of a David Alfaro Siqueiros mural in Los Angeles. In 1978, the documentary *Agueda Martinez: Our People, Our Country*, by Esperanza Vázquez and Moctezuma Esparza, was nominated for an Academy Award. Cheech Marin and Tommy Chong formed a duo called Cheech and Chong that entertained people through various comedy films.

However, one of the most successful cinematographers during the 1970's was Cuban-born Néstor Almendros, who won an Academy Award for Best Cinematography in 1978 for his film *Days of Heaven*. Among the most notable films that he made during the era were *Chinatown* (1974) and *Kramer vs. Kramer* (1979). In 1979, the hit Cuban American film *El Súper* won awards. Based on the play written by Cuban Iván Acosta, the film depicted the life of a working-class Cuban American in New York and his adjustment and culture shock to living in the United States.

On television, *Chico and the Man* became a successful Latino sitcom from 1974 through 1978 for a total of eighty-eight shows. However, the success of the show was cut short when Freddie Prinze, a costar, committed suicide in January, 1977.

Literature In literature, Latinos entered the publishing market and obtained many prestigious prizes. In 1971, Rudolfo A. Anaya's novel *Bless Me, Ul-*

tima became a best-selling Chicano novel after winning the prestigious Premio Quinto Sol National Chicano Literary Award in 1972. *Bless Me, Ultima* became one of the first Latino books to reach non-Latino readers in the United States.

In 1973, Nicholasa Mohr published her first book, *Nilda*, which won the Jane Addams Children's Book Award and became the first book by a Latina to be published by a major publishing house. Her books, written for children and adults, are based on her experience of growing up female, Latina, and a minority in New York City. Her *El Bronx Remembered* (1975) won *The New York Times* Outstanding Book Award in teenage fiction as well as the Best Book Award from the *School Library Journal* and was a finalist for the National Book Award in 1975. In 1977, the National Council of Social Studies and the Children's Book Council named Mohr's third book, *In Nueva York* (1977), a Notable Trade Book in the Field of Social Studies.

Chicano poet Gary Soto won the nationally prestigious Academy of American Poets Prize and the Nation's Discovery Award in 1975. In 1977, he won the United States Award of the International Poetry Forum for his book *The Elements of San Joaquín*. Also in 1977, Rolando Hinojosa, another Chicano writer, won the Premio Casa de las Américas from Cuba for his novel *Klail City y sus Alrededores* (1976; *Klail City: A Novel*, 1987). Nicolás Kanellos received a monetary prize for being named Outstanding Editor from the Coordinating Council of Literary Magazines for work on *Revista Chicano-Riqueña*.

Politics In 1971, Henry Cisneros, who later became the mayor of San Antonio, Texas, became the youngest White House fellow in history. He earned degrees from Harvard University and George Washington University. In 1972, Ramona Acosta Bañuelos became the first Latina U.S. treasurer. She had also been named Outstanding Business Woman of the Year in Los Angeles a few years earlier. In 1973, Puerto Rican Maurice Ferré became the first Latino mayor of Miami, and Jerry Apodaca became the first Latino governor of New Mexico in fifty years. Later, in 1975, Raúl Castro became the first Latino governor of Arizona. In addition to becoming governor, Castro served in various ambassador positions. Polly Baca-Barragán was elected to the Colorado state senate in 1978. She was the first Latina to be elected to this position.

La Raza Unida (The United Race) was the first successful third political party in Texas. José Angel Gutiérrez and others founded the party in 1970. The party was able to elect Roel Rodríguez, a write-in candidate, as a county commissioner in La Salle County, Texas. In 1977, La Raza Unida elected Frank Shaffer-Corona to the District of Columbia school board. This victory proved that the party could bring success outside its Mexican American districts.

Civil Rights In the late 1960's, Latino civil rights groups appeared throughout the United States. These groups included La Raza Unida, the Mexican American Legal Defense and Educational Fund, National Chicano Youth Liberation Conference, and the Young Lords, a militant politicized party founded in New York City and similar to the African American organization of the Black Panthers. The Cuban American Legal Defense and Education Fund, the National Conference on Puerto Rican Women, National Image, and the Puerto Rican Legal Defense and Education Fund were also founded in 1972, and the Congressional Hispanic Caucus was created in 1975. These groups were formed to end discrimination, especially in the workforce, as well as to improve civil rights for all Latinos.

In 1970, in Los Angeles, the first national march for Mexican Americans took place. The National Chicano Moratorium on the Vietnam War was a protest against both the high casualty rates in the Vietnam War and the lack of civil rights within the country for Mexican Americans. It became the largest demonstration in U.S. Latino history when it gathered close to thirty thousand marchers from throughout the Southwest. As police dispersed them, some marchers were killed in the process, and the moratorium became a watershed in the Chicano Civil Rights movement. Rubén Salazar, a well-known Chicano journalist, was killed and chosen as a martyr for the movement. In 1975, Congress approved to expand the U.S. Voting Rights Act to include Mexican Americans. When initially approved in 1965, the act had only included African Americans and Puerto Ricans.

In 1973, the United Nations recognized Puerto Rico as an official protectorate of the United States. In addition, the right of the Puerto Rican people to decide their own future as a nation was approved. This brought support to the independence movement in Puerto Rico and in the United States, although Puerto Rico remained a commonwealth into

Members of the United Farm Workers (UFW) march in support of a grape boycott against the Gallo winery in 1975. In the 1970's, the Latino community fought for better wages and housing conditions, limits to pesticide use, and the right to unionize and strike. (Lou Dematteis)

the twenty-first century, whereby Puerto Ricans in the United States do not have full rights of citizenship.

In the labor movement, César Chávez became very well known during the 1960's and 1970's. By 1965, he had founded the largest farmworkers union, the United Farm Workers (UFW), in Delano, California. In 1975, mainly because of his efforts, the California legislature passed the California Labor Relations Act. It provided for secret ballot union elections for farmworkers. Chávez continued to boycott and strike for lettuce and grape agricultural workers throughout the 1970's. Better wages, health, and housing conditions; limited use of pesticides; and the right to unionize and strike were improvements Chávez obtained for farmworkers in California, Arizona, and later, nationally.

Sports Golf star Nancy Lopez was rookie of the year in 1977 and Ladies Professional Golf Association (LPGA) Player of the Year for 1978-1979. Other notable Latino sports figures of the era included Venezuelan shortstop Luis Aparicio, who won many Gold Gloves as the best American League shortstop in the history of baseball. From 1964 to 1971, the Minnesota Twins' Pedro "Tony" Oliva made all-star teams and led his team in hits. Roberto Clemente was the first Puerto Rican baseball player to be admitted to the Hall of Fame. He was the four-times National League batting champion and awarded twelve Gold Gloves, among other records.

Impact Latinos made significant contributions to the United States in various areas such as education, government, and civil rights during the 1970's. It was a decade for demanding and defending equal rights, building a better life, and integrating into mainstream society.

Further Reading
Crawford, James. *Hold Your Tongue: Bilingualism and the Politics of "English Only."* Reprint. Reading,

Mass.: Addison-Wesley, 1993. This is a comprehensive study of opposing sides in the language debate, including the movements related to bilingualism and "English Only."

Kanellos, Nicolás. *Hispanic Firsts: Five Hundred Years of Extraordinary Achievement.* New York: Visible Ink Press, 1997. This readable book about the contributions and achievements of Latinos in the United States is written in chronological order and listed by specific themes.

Stavans, Ilan. *Latino U.S.A.: A Cartoon History.* New York: Basic Books, 2000. This book, done entirely in cartoons, is a historical view of major Latino groups in the United States from the Conquest through the modern era.

Suárez-Orozco, Marcelo M., and Mariela Paez. *Latinos: Remaking America.* Berkeley: University of California Press, 2002. This book covers issues on immigration, race, labor, health, language, education, and politics related to Latinos in the United States.

Telgen, Diane, and Jim Kamp, eds. *¡Latinas! Women of Achievement.* Foreword by Nicholasa Mohr. New York: Visible Ink Press, 1996. This book gives detailed autobiographical information about seventy well-known Latinas who have triumphed as activists, artists, authors, educators, politicians, and athletes, among many other occupations.

José A. Carmona

See also Anaya, Rufolfo A.; Castañeda, Carlos; Chávez, César; Cheech and Chong; Chicano movement; *Chico and the Man*; Equal Opportunity Act of 1972; *Lau vs. Nichols*; Lopez, Nancy; Puerto Rican nationalism.

■ *Lau v. Nichols*

Identification U.S. Supreme Court decision
Date Decided on January 21, 1974

The Supreme Court's unanimous ruling established educational rights for non-English-speaking students and mandated that school districts with a large number of pupils who speak little or no English must provide special language and education instruction so as not to deny those students access to an equal opportunity for a meaningful education.

Kinney Kinmon Lau and twelve other non-English-speaking pupils filed a lawsuit in U.S. District Court in March, 1970, on behalf of nearly three thousand Chinese-speaking students. The plaintiffs alleged that San Francisco school board president Alan Nichols and other officials failed to create adequate programs in the city's school district that would allow recent immigrant Chinese children to receive special instruction in the English language. School officials responded that even with federal Health, Education, and Welfare (HEW) Department monies and state financial assistance, San Francisco's school board was obligated to provide for only about 30 percent of Chinese-speaking students to get special bilingual-language instruction because of insufficient funds and few Chinese-speaking teachers.

Both the U.S. District Court and the Ninth Circuit Court of Appeals ruled that Lau's claims of discrimination did not amount to a violation of the Civil Rights Act of 1964 or the Fourteenth Amendment. These decisions meant that the San Francisco schools' responsibility did not go beyond that of providing Chinese students with the same facilities, textbooks, teachers, and teaching materials that it provided to other children.

Because of the public importance of this issue, however, the U.S. Supreme Court granted review. On January 21, 1974, the U.S. Supreme Court ruled that students who are not proficient in the English language are denied an opportunity for a meaningful education. California policy required all school districts to ensure the mastery of English by their pupils. Therefore, the Court argued that if Chinese-speaking students do not understand English, then equal treatment is not occurring in the classroom simply by providing the same teachers, texts, and curriculum. Denial of a meaningful opportunity to participate in the educational program is discrimination banned by section 601 of the Civil Rights Act and HEW guidelines that prohibit racial discrimination in federally assisted San Francisco schools. Affirmative steps were required to reach language proficiency. The *Lau* case was sent back to the federal district court, and the district judge ruled that a suitable remedy to the case was bilingual education.

Impact Because of the *Lau* decision and subsequent court rulings and state legislative enactments during the 1970's, nearly 360 American school districts chose or were pressured to introduce bilingual, bicultural, or English-immersion programs to meet the needs of limited-English-speaking students. Moreover, in 1975, the Voting Rights Act was amended to require the use of bilingual ballots in areas of certain states with high percentages of limited-English-speaking voters.

Further Reading

Crawford, James. *Bilingual Education: History, Politics, Theory, and Practice.* 3d ed. Los Angeles: Bilingual Educational Service, 1995.

McPherson, Stephanie. *Lau v. Nichols: Bilingual Education in Public Schools.* Berkeley Heights, N.J.: Enslow, 2000.

Wang, Ling-Chi. "*Lau v. Nichols*: History of a Struggle for Equal and Quality Education." In *The Asian American Educational Experience: A Source Book for Teachers and Students*, edited by Don T. Nakanishi and Tina Nishida. New York: Routledge, 1995.

Steve Mazurana

See also Affirmative action; Asian Americans; Congress, U.S.; Education in the United States; Immigration to the United States; Racial discrimination; Supreme Court decisions.

■ Lava lamps

Definition Decorative lamps, each of which consisted of a glass cylinder on a cone-shaped base containing water, wax, and other ingredients that rise and fall in a hypnotic motion when exposed to heat

Date First produced in Great Britain in 1963; brought to the United States in 1965

Lava lamps are relics of the psychedelic age and prime examples of late 1960's and early 1970's decorative kitsch.

Little is known about the man who built the first "motion lamp," save that his name was Mr. Dunnett. His creation was discovered in a Hampshire pub by an Englishman named Edward Craven-Walker shortly after World War II. Craven-Walker purchased the unique lamp, which was made out of a cocktail shaker and other assorted items, and brought it home with him, determined to figure out how it worked. It took fifteen years to solve the mystery, but once he had it, he created the Crestworth Company, in Dorset, England, and began marketing what he called the astro lamp in 1963.

The design was imported to the United States in 1965 after two American entrepreneurs saw one at a German trade show. They negotiated a deal to manufacture and retail a version of the astro lamp in

North America. The original manufacturer was the Haggerty Company, based in Chicago. The first U.S. version of the newly renamed lava lamp was the Century model, which featured a gold base with star-shaped holes. The 52-ounce globe was available with yellow or blue liquid and red or white solid material. Many models followed, including one with plastic flowers and greenery and another made of wrought iron.

The science is simple, even if the combination of ingredients is not. A sealed glass container is placed atop a metal base and heated with a 40-watt bulb. When the special wax mixture is heated, it rises within the carrier liquid, forming lavalike shapes. When cold, the wax mixture is denser than the carrier liquid, but once it is heated by the light bulb, it becomes less dense and rises to the top, only to cool and float back down again. The glass container gives off an aquarium-like glow, and the process is repeated as long as the bulb remains lit.

Impact By the mid-1970's, the popularity of lava lamps had faded, but they never stopped selling. A nostalgia boom in the mid-1990's brought a sales resurgence, as the next generation rediscovered psychedelia.

Further Reading

Hemingway, Wayne, and Keith Stephenson. *Cocktail Shakers, Lava Lamps, and Tupperware: A Celebration of Lifestyle Design from the Last Half of the Twentieth Century.* Gloucester, Mass.: Rockport, 2004.

Stern, Jan, and Michael Stern. *The Encyclopedia of Bad Taste.* New York: HarperCollins, 1990.

P. S. Ramsey

See also Fads; Hippies; Home furnishings; Mood rings; Toys and games.

■ Leaded gasoline ban

Definition Environmental policy
Date First reductions standards issued in 1973

The banning of leaded gasoline is considered one of the most effective environmental policies ever adopted in the United States. The ban is responsible for tangible health benefits, especially in reducing the symptoms of elevated blood lead levels in children.

Charles F. Kettering and Thomas A. Midgley are credited with developing leaded gasoline in the 1920's. Kettering was vice president of research at

General Motors, and Midgley was Kettering's research assistant. The discovery of leaded gasoline was driven in part by the desire to eliminate the rackety sound (knocking) of early, inefficient automobile engines. The specific discovery that tetraethyl lead functions as a near perfect "antiknock" agent for gasoline engines is dated to December 9, 1921.

The adverse health effects of leaded gasoline were recognized soon after its invention. The first line of evidence came from symptoms of lead poisoning suffered by Midgley and his coworkers in the laboratory. Beginning in 1922, scientific experts voiced concerns about the insidious nature of lead poisoning and the potential risks to the public if tetraethyl lead were to be used widely in automobiles. Surgeon General Hugh Cumming and the Public Health Service added to the warnings, and the Bureau of Mines was commissioned to conduct a health assessment. Despite these public concerns, large-scale manufacture of tetraethyl lead commenced around 1923, and a new company, Ethyl Gasoline Corporation, was created in August, 1924, to synthesize and distribute the additive worldwide.

By the 1970's, leaded gasoline had become ubiquitous and so had extensive lead poisoning of the general population. On January 10, 1973, the U.S. Environmental Protection Agency (EPA) issued a regulation recognizing that leaded gasoline compromised the integrity of the newly required automobile emission control installations. An additional EPA regulation issued on December 6, 1973, specifically addressed the EPA's finding that lead particle emissions from automobiles presented a significant risk to the health of urban populations, particularly children. Altogether, the ban on leaded gasoline is chronicled in at least eleven federal regulations in the 1970's.

Impact The ban on leaded gasoline is responsible for more than a 90 percent decrease in the blood lead concentration of the average American. Despite the apparent success of the cluster of regulations initiated in the 1970's, lead poisoning from the legacy of leaded gasoline continued to be a public health concern worldwide in later years. However, increasing awareness about lead poisoning and intensified research into safer alternative materials have helped address the problems related to lead in later years.

Further Reading

Environmental Protection Agency. "Prohibition on Gasoline Containing Lead or Lead Additives for Highway Use." *Federal Register* 61, no. 23 (1996): 3832-3838.

Rosner D., and G. Markowitz. "A 'Gift of God'? The Public Health Controversy over Leaded Gasoline During the 1920's." *American Journal of Public Health* 75 (1985): 344-352.

Oladele A. Ogunseitan

See also Air pollution; Clean Air Act of 1970; Environmental movement; Environmental Protection Agency (EPA); Occupational Safety and Health Act of 1970; Safe Drinking Water Act of 1974.

■ LED and LCD screens

Definition Electronic devices that can project data and images onto a screen

The development of screen displays using light-emitting diodes (LEDs) and liquid crystal displays (LCDs) in the 1970's led to myriad applications ranging from digital watches to jumbo televisions.

An LED screen is a semiconducting material that emits light when electrical current flows through it in one direction. The color of the light depends on what semiconducting material is used. The first visible-spectrum LED was invented in 1962 by Nick Holonyak, Jr. By the early 1970's, LEDs were being manufactured by General Electric and Motorola for calculator and watch displays. Most LED displays of that time were very small, requiring that a bubble magnifying lens be mounted above each displayed digit to enlarge the numerals for viewing. During the early to mid-1970's, most watch and calculator displays in the United States were using gallium arsenide LEDs, which produced a deep-red color. By 1973, the Soviets had developed silicon carbide LEDs, which emitted a greenish-yellow color. By the later 1970's, LED displays were being used in electronic games, such as Mattel's Missile Attack and Baseball.

An LCD screen consists of a layer of voltage-sensitive liquid solution that is encased between two sheets of polarizing material. When a small voltage is applied, the liquid changes color. The first operational LCDs were developed in the late 1960's. In 1971 and 1972, Rockwell, Sharp, and Texas Instruments released some bulky portable calculators with

LCD displays that were lit from behind. For pocket-sized calculators that were rapidly being developed during the early to mid-1970's, LED displays were utilized. However, since LCDs consumed less power than LEDs, LCD development was pursued. Between 1976 and 1977, LCD technology advanced to the point that LCDs became the choice for calculator and watch displays. The first LCD pocket calculator displays used a yellow filter to protect the display surface, which was sensitive to ultraviolet (UV) light. Most used one or two replaceable miniature batteries for power. By 1979, the UV problem was solved, yielding LCD calculators with gray-colored display surfaces. That same year, Milton Bradley released the first handheld game system with interchangeable cartridges, Microvision, which used a monochrome LCD screen.

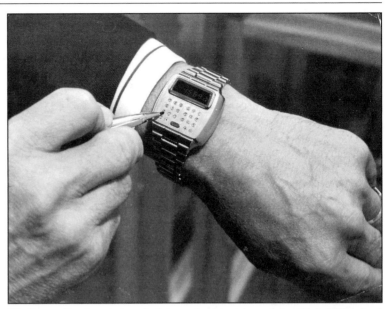

The first combined computer-calculator and wristwatch, made possible by LCD technologies, is displayed in 1977. (Hulton Archive/Getty Images)

Impact During the 1970's, digital quartz watches were developed that used LEDs or LCDs instead of gears that turned numbered cards. Pocket calculators that consumed little power evolved from the development of LED and LCD displays. The 1970's marked the development of LED and LCD displays that continued to replace the once widely used cathode ray tube (CRT) for screen displays. LCD and LED screens came to be used in a multitude of applications that continued to grow, ranging from cellular phones to pocket-sized portable television sets and laptop computers to jumbo television displays. Display screens using LCDs coupled with LEDs continued to be developed for a variety of applications.

Further Reading

Bloomfield, Louis A. *How Things Work: The Physics of Everyday Life.* New York: John Wiley & Sons, 1997.

Fukuda, Mitsuo. *Reliability and Degradation of Semiconductor Lasers and LEDs.* Boston: Artech House, 1991.

Lueder, Ernst. *Liquid Crystal Displays.* New York: John Wiley & Sons, 2001.

Alvin K. Benson

See also Atari; Computers; Inventions; Science and technology; Toys and games; Video games.

■ Led Zeppelin

Identification British hard-rock band
Date Formed in 1968

Led Zeppelin was one of the premier rock acts in the United States during the 1970's.

Led Zeppelin was formed in 1968 by studio guitar virtuoso Jimmy Page, who had joined the Yardbirds as Eric Clapton's replacement. Page attempted to keep the disintegrating act running by recruiting fellow studio musician John Paul Jones to play bass and Birmingham unknowns Robert Plant and John Bonham on vocals and drums, respectively. The Yardbirds name was dropped in favor of Led Zeppelin, named after an early twentieth century German airship, supposedly after a joke by the Who's Keith Moon, although other versions of the legend exist. By the beginning of the new decade, energetic manager Peter Grant had successfully cultivated the band's image as a first-rate live act and targeted the vast American market in favor of the group's homeland audience.

U.S. fans responded enthusiastically to Grant's efforts. *Led Zeppelin III* was released in 1970, an album that continued to showcase the act's ability to intermingle hard rock with blues and folk music, often inspired by Dark Age and Celtic themes. For example, the album contained the thunderous "Immigrant Song," an ode to wandering Vikings. Few other major bands were exploring such diverse subject matter. Although touring was a key element of its success, the rising popularity of the band could cause challenges, such as a riot that left forty people injured at a concert in Milan, Italy.

While the first three Led Zeppelin albums enjoyed strong sales, their fourth outing would prove to be their most successful, making it one of the best-selling rock albums in U.S. history. The untitled 1971 work, generally known as *Led Zeppelin IV*, contains the haunting megahit "Stairway to Heaven," which became the band's best-known song. The varied interests of the group were reaffirmed on this album, which contained traditional hard-rock classics such as "Black Dog," "Rock and Roll," a *Lord of the Rings*-inspired piece titled "The Battle of Evermore,"

and nods to American blues, such as "When the Levee Breaks."

Led Zeppelin continued to intersperse ever-growing U.S. tour bookings with new studio work such as 1973's *Houses of the Holy*. In particular, songs such as the strange and anguished "D'yer Mak'er" and the brilliant and pondering "Over the Hills and Far Away" showed that band members' songwriting talents were far from tapped. The unbroken streak continued in 1975 with the two-record compilation titled *Physical Graffiti*, which held further classics such as "Trampled Under Foot" and "Kashmir."

Some might speak of Led Zeppelin's next few years as the band's twilight, as it slid a bit from the stratospheric heights it had reached earlier in the decade. While *Presence* (1976) and *In Through the Out Door* (1979) generated strong sales, by previous standards, they were disappointing. The group also ex-

Led Zeppelin, with guitarist Jimmy Page and singer Robert Plant, perform in 1970. (DPA/Landov)

perienced disruption after Plant sustained severe injuries in a car wreck and then suffered the tragic loss of his young son to illness in 1977. Ultimately, it was another misfortune, not a lack of fan support, that led to the end: The band chose to break up when Bonham died after a drinking binge on September 24, 1980.

Impact By the middle of the 1970's, Led Zeppelin had charted a remarkable course. Its fresh releases had also inspired new American fans to go back and buy the band's earlier works. Five of the first six albums would eventually sell more than ten million copies each, and the band is generally estimated to be one of the highest-selling musical acts in history.

Further Reading

Davis, Stephen. *Hammer of the Gods*. London: Pan Books, 1995.

Schaffner, Nicholas. *The British Invasion*. New York: McGraw-Hill, 1982.

Welch, Chris. *Peter Grant: The Man Who Led Zeppelin*. London: Omnibus Press, 1996.

Roger Pauly

See also Hard rock and heavy metal; Music.

■ Léger, Jules

Identification Governor-general of Canada, 1974-1979

Born April 4, 1913; Saint-Anicet, Quebec, Canada

Died November 22, 1980; Ottawa, Ontario, Canada

Léger held office in very tumultuous and conflicted times for Canada, especially for his own French Canadian people.

Jules Léger was born into a large and pious Roman Catholic family—his older brother, Paul-Émile, later became cardinal archbishop of Montreal. As did many French Canadian politicians of his generation, Léger began his career as a journalist. However, he quickly became interested in diplomacy, joining the Ministry of External Affairs in 1940 and rising to ambassadorial rank in 1953. As ambassador to Mexico, he strengthened Canada's hemispheric ties, which had long played second fiddle to ties with Great Britain and Europe. During the 1960's and 1970's, he held ambassador positions in Europe, serving in Italy, France, and Belgium.

Following the retirement of Roland Michener in 1974, many felt that Canada needed another French-speaking governor-general in the light of the growing nationalist stirrings in Quebec. Léger's diplomatic poise and wide set of acquaintances made him the natural candidate.

The role of the governor-general in Canadian politics is limited, serving as the representative of the Crown in Canada other than on the rare occasions when the sovereign is actually physically present in the country, as was Elizabeth II in 1976, when she opened the Montreal Summer Olympic Games. The governor-general opens Parliament, makes many official speeches, and undertakes an arduous schedule of public appearances across the country.

Unfortunately, Léger suffered a stroke six months into his term while speaking at the University of Sherbrooke. Though he made a quick recovery, he was never quite up to his best form. Nonetheless, aided by his widely admired wife, Gabrielle, Léger resumed his official duties. In 1976, another tragedy struck when La Citadelle, the governor-general's second residence in Quebec City, was severely damaged by fire. Again, Gabrielle Léger took much of the role in the restoration efforts. Though Léger left office before the 1980 Québec referendum—a measure to make the province a separate country—his clear pro-federal position was a boost to the "No" side in that vote.

During his tenure, Léger took a particular interest in art and music, and his patronage of artists such as Alfred Pauline codified a certain late-modernist taste in Canadian culture.

Impact The governor-generals of Canada are not the most important of politicians, as they typically serve only a ceremonial and official role. Nonetheless, Léger's serene and genial presence during years of great change and instability in Canada made him a unifying figure during the 1970's.

Further Reading

Malcolmson, Patrick, and Richard Myers. *The Canadian Regime: An Introduction to Parliamentary Government in Canada*. Guelph, Ont.: Broadview Press, 2001.

Noonan, James. *Canada's Governors General at Play: Culture and Rideau Hall*. Ottawa: Borealis, 2002.

Nicholas Birns

See also; Canada and the British Commonwealth; Charter of the French Language; Francophonie, La; Michener, Roland.

■ Legionnaires' disease

The Event Pneumonia outbreak caused by a
  newly recognized infectious agent
Date July, 1976

*Identification of the cause of an outbreak of Legionnaires'
disease by the Centers for Disease Control (CDC) in 1977
marked the beginning of a new era of epidemiology and led
to the recognition that infectious diseases had not been van-
quished by vaccines and antibiotics.*

In July, 1976, 221 people attending a convention for
former service personnel in Philadelphia became ill
with fever, chills, and a cough that developed into an
unusual form of pneumonia. Thirty-four people
died. Since most of those individuals affected were
members of the American Legion, the disease
quickly became known as Legionnaires' disease. A
major effort to identify the source of the outbreak
began, involving federal, state, and local health authorities and coordinated by the CDC.

In January, 1977, the bacterium that causes Legionnaires' disease, *Legionella pneumophila*, was isolated. The source of the infection was determined to
be the cooling tower that provided water for the air-
conditioning system at the hotel. Although the first
cases of Legionnaires' disease were identified in
1976, analysis of samples from unidentified pneumonia cases confirmed the presence of *Legionella*
from as far back as 1947.

The Legionnaires' disease bacterium is found in
creeks, ponds, and soil, as well as hot water tanks, air-
conditioning cooling towers, evaporative condens-
ers, and whirlpool spas—anywhere warm water can
stagnate. *Legionella pneumophila* cells often form
biofilms, or communities of microorganisms at-
tached to a solid surface, on the lining of water tanks
and cooling towers. Bacteria within these biofilms
are generally more resistant to bactericidal agents
such as chlorine, making elimination of *Legionella*
difficult.

There is no evidence that Legionnaires' disease

*Members of the American Legion attend a hearing on the deadly pneumonia outbreak three months earlier dubbed "Legionnaires'
disease." (AP/Wide World Photos)*

can be passed directly from one person to another. Rather, the causative organism is inhaled in tiny droplets of liquid such as those emitted by air-conditioning systems or aerosols generated by whirlpools and hot tubs, showers, or fountains. Researchers determined that outbreaks most commonly occur in large buildings with central air-conditioning systems. Such tightly sealed, air-conditioned buildings were becoming common in the 1970's in response to the energy crisis. The Legionnaires' disease outbreak in 1976 was one of the first indications that newly constructed, energy-efficient buildings might encourage outbreaks of airborne infectious organisms.

Impact   Legionnaires' disease was one of the first identified "modern plagues." The 1930's, 1940's, and 1950's are often considered the golden age of medicine, particularly because of the triumphs over infectious disease. However, emerging infectious diseases such as Legionnaires' disease, as well as infectious agents discovered in subsequent decades, such as human immunodeficiency virus (HIV), Ebola, hantavirus, hepatitis C, and West Nile virus, alerted the medical community that infectious diseases were not a thing of the past and required well-coordinated epidemiological surveillance efforts to identify and curb outbreaks.

Further Reading

Karlen, Arno. *Man and Microbes: Disease and Plague in History and Modern Times.* New York: Simon & Schuster, 1995.

Thomas, Gordon, and Max Morgan-Witts. *Anatomy of an Epidemic.* 1984. Garden City, N.Y.: Doubleday, 1982.

Lisa M. Sardinia

See also   Acquired immunodeficiency syndrome (AIDS); Health care in the United States; Medicine; Science and technology; Smallpox eradication; Toxic shock syndrome.

■ Leisure suits

Definition   Casual attire for men

Leisure suits were a major fashion movement for casual and business apparel for men during the 1970's.

Leisure suits, also known as sports or casual suits, featured a variety of design details and fabrics. The coat was designed as a shirtlike garment, worn with or without a belt or as a short baseball jacket. Collars were created either as semi-roll, shirt, or stand similar to the Nehru look. Jackets often featured a Western-style yoke, pleats, tucks, and patch pockets with top stitching of silk twist or similar thread highlighting the design features. Pants had a traditional waistband but without pleats and legs that were narrow to the knees and then flared into a bell-bottom shape at the hemline. Cuffs were featured on some pants.

Popular fabrics for the suits included jacquard double-knit, suede, corduroy, and twill. The fabric designs and colors were often bold and bright, and suits appeared in solids, tartan plaids, paisleys, and florals. Pastel tints of blues, greens, and yellows were favored for the warmer seasons, with dark blues, browns, grays, and blacks for the colder weather. Bolder colors such as chartreuse, red, orange, and purple also were used. Designers and manufacturers often coordinated fabrics such that one piece of the suit featured boldly designed fabric and the other piece featured a solid color.

The fibers and fabrics used in leisure suits were a reflection of the explosion in textile development during the 1970's. The discoveries of the stabilization of knits and textured yarns lead to the popularity of polyester and other manufactured fibers for leisure suits. The crease-resistant fibers and fabrics discovered in the 1970's eliminated the structural-support fabrics needed to maintain the pressed and tailored image in traditional suits. The new fabrics also lowered the cost of production and care of menswear. The discovery of artificial suede, such as the upscale Ultra Suede, provided a look that led the way for leisure suits to be worn as business attire.

Leisure suits also served as crossover fashion. They crossed established fashion lines from haute couture to high fashion to the masses. Designers such as Ralph Lauren and Perry Ellis marketed exclusive designer suits and ready-to-wear suits. Leisure suits also blurred social and work settings by becoming acceptable both for casual and for business wear. While the traditional three-piece suit never was eliminated completely in the 1970's, the leisure suit did provide an acceptable alternative for men in business settings. In addition, the leisure suit became one of the first garments to provide a look that crossed gender lines. The design of the leisure suit for men and the pantsuit for women were similar and provided a unisex look. Designer Tommy Netter gained fame for his unisex design suits for Mick and Bianca Jagger during the 1970's.

Impact Leisure suits, unique in design and fabric, quickly rose to the level of fashionable garb for men during the 1970's and just as quickly fell from popularity when the masses returned to traditional casual and business attire by 1980.

Further Reading

Bigelow, Marybelle S. *Fashion in History.* 2d ed. Minneapolis, Minn.: Burgess, 1979.

Payne, Blanche, Geital Winakor, and Jane Farrell-Beck. *The History of Costume.* New York: Harper-Collins, 1992.

Sue Bailey

See also Bell-bottoms; Fads; Fashions and clothing; Platform shoes; Polyester.

■ Lévesque, René

Identification Canadian politician
Born August 24, 1922; New Carlisle, Quebec, Canada
Died November 1, 1987; Montreal, Canada

During the 1970's, Lévesque was the face of Quebec nationalism. For a time, it seemed as if he would preside over what people had once thought inconceivable—the assumption by Quebec of full sovereignty.

René Lévesque was born on Quebec's Gaspe Peninsula. As a teenager, he began to work as a radio announcer, eventually working in radio for the U.S. Army during the latter stages of World War II. Returning to Quebec, he worked for the Canadian Broadcasting Company (CBC), where he helped lead a 1958 strike that made him more politically aware. During the 1960's, Lévesque entered politics as a liberal and was active in promoting what came to be called the Quiet Revolution, a period during which Quebec was swiftly modernized. Lévesque, however, was one of the few prominent public figures in his era to espouse full sovereignty for Quebec. After the October Crisis of 1970, in which a group of Québécois terrorists murdered Pierre Laporte, a provincial cabinet minister, Lévesque had become the representative of mainstream Québec nationalism and led a new party, the Parti Québécois (PQ).

Lévesque led the PQ to victory in the November 15, 1976, elections, a win that stunned the vast majority of observers. For a French-speaking population that had long felt oppressed and disenfran-

René Lévesque. (Library of Congress)

chised, the PQ's success was truly epochal. Once in office, Lévesque swiftly moved to make the French language dominant on public signs and in government communication, moving Bill 101, called the Charter of the French Language, through the National Assembly. He also significantly expanded social services, making the Quebec government into perhaps the most comprehensive welfare state in North America.

Late in the decade, Lévesque proposed a referendum in which Quebec citizens would decide whether to vote for sovereignty. Though he carefully avoided the word "independence" in the referendum question, using "sovereignty-association" instead, in fact the proposal would have given Quebec the full rank and power of an self-governing nation, with only an economic association remaining with the rest of Canada. Lévesque galvanized much of Quebec behind his ideas. However, he alienated some Quebec citizens, such as older French-speaking women, who did not want to disturb traditional ties with Canada. Moreover, despite his pro-American stance,

Lévesque never quelled the fears of American conservatives and centrists that an independent Quebec would become "the Cuba of the North." At a time of international instability with the crises in Iran and Afghanistan, American policy makers were satisfied with the referendum's defeat on May 20, 1980, by a 40-60 margin.

Undaunted by defeat, Lévesque gave, that night, one of the great speeches of twentieth century political history, saying that the voters of Quebec had said *À la prochaine*—until next time.

Impact   René Lévesque served as Quebec's prime minister for five more years, even winning one more election. He is best known as the great leader of Quebec nationalism. However, his economic and social policies were also very important, as he nationalized the province's power industry and presided over its transition from a church-dominated society to a largely secular and liberal one.

However, when he died of cardiac arrest at the age of sixty-five, his dream of Quebec sovereignty was still unfulfilled. After his death, Dorchester Boulevard, in downtown Montreal, was renamed Boulevard René Lévesque.

Further Reading

Fraser, Graham, and Ivon Owen. *René Lévesque and the Parti Québécois in Power.* 2d ed. Montreal: McGill-Queen's University Press, 2001.

Pauklin, Marguerite. *René Lévesque: Charismatic Leader.* Richmond Hill, Ont.: Fitzhenry and Whiteside, 2005.

Nicholas Birns

See also   Canada and the United States; Charter of the French Language; Elections, Canadian; Francophonie, La; October Crisis; Quebec Charter of Human Rights and Freedoms.

■ Liberalism in U.S. politics

Definition   A political ideology often associated with the Democratic Party and certain political movements and policy positions, such as feminism, environmental protection, affirmative action, and abortion rights

The liberalism that emerged during the 1970's differed from the economic-based, New Deal liberalism that dominated American politics and the Democratic Party from 1932 to 1968. In particular, it intensified differences between the Republican and Democratic Parties and among American voters, especially on noneconomic issues such as foreign policy, civil rights, crime, environmental protection, and the role of women in American society.

The Democratic National Convention of 1968 was the most divisive, controversial national party convention in modern American history. The nomination of Vice President Hubert H. Humphrey for president and the convention's adoption of a platform plank on the Vietnam War that generally reflected President Lyndon B. Johnson's policies angered many antiwar delegates and demonstrators in Chicago. Televised violence between demonstrators and police in Chicago conveyed the impression to many Americans that the antiwar movement was radical and dangerous. This impression contributed to Richard M. Nixon's defeat of Humphrey in the 1968 presidential election.

The events and immediate effects of the 1968 Democratic National Convention greatly influenced the characteristics of liberalism during the 1970's. In preparing for the 1972 presidential election, the Democratic Party changed its delegate selection processes so that presidential candidates had to be nominated through binding primaries and caucuses in the states and so that there would be a substantial increase in the percentages of women, young adults, and racial minorities chosen as delegates for future Democratic national conventions, beginning in 1972.

1972 Presidential Campaign   As a major influence in the Democratic Party's adoption of these procedural reforms, Senator George McGovern of South Dakota quickly emerged as a leading candidate for the Democratic presidential nomination of 1972. McGovern's advocacy of the most liberal positions on the Vietnam War—namely, an immediate, complete American military withdrawal and amnesty for draft evaders—attracted the support of the most liberal, antiwar Democrats and college students. More moderate, rival Democratic presidential candidates Humphrey, Edmund Muskie, and Henry Jackson criticized McGovern's liberal positions on foreign and defense policies and social issues such as court-ordered busing as extreme and irresponsible. Nevertheless, the new party rules that benefited liberal activists enabled McGovern to secure the nomination.

With his recent diplomatic visit to China and nuclear arms control treaty with the Soviet Union, Nixon appeared to be a moderate, unifying candidate compared to McGovern. In his landslide reelection, Nixon won more than 60 percent of the popular vote and carried forty-nine of the fifty states in the electoral college. The Democrats retained control of Congress, but, for the remainder of the 1970's, the Democratic Party was plagued by the following dilemma: How can the Democratic Party nominate presidential candidates and adopt platforms that not only satisfy liberal activists and interest groups but also can win general elections by attracting independent and moderate Democratic voters?

Issues and Movements   The nature, meaning, and political impact of liberalism in the 1970's were also affected by social and cultural changes in American society that occurred beyond two-party politics and policy differences over how to end the Vietnam War. At the time, liberal positions concerning civil rights for African Americans included affirmative action and court-ordered busing occurring outside the South. Liberalism in criminal justice was more strongly identified with opposition to the death penalty and support for greater protection of the civil liberties of criminal suspects and defendants, better living conditions and rehabilitation for convicts, and gun control. More popular, less controversial liberal policy positions included environmental protection, energy conservation, workplace safety, campaign finance reform, and consumer protection. Liberal interest groups, such as Public Citizen and Common Cause, lobbied for new laws and agencies, such as the Environmental Protection Agency (EPA) and the Occupational Safety and Health Administration (OSHA).

Determined to protect the abortion rights established by the Supreme Court's 1973 decision in *Roe v. Wade*, the feminist movement also grew in size and influence as a major aspect of liberalism in the 1970's. With the National Organization for Women (NOW) as its largest interest group, the feminist movement advocated new laws favorable to women on issues such as job discrimination, sexual harassment, maternity leave, and divorce. Throughout the 1970's, feminists tried, but eventually failed, to secure ratification of the proposed Equal Rights Amendment (ERA). In foreign policy, the liberalism of the 1970's sought to reduce defense spending and

end the draft, continue and improve détente with the Soviet Union, improve American relations with the Third World, and strengthen human rights in Latin America.

Impact   The effects of liberalism during the 1970's were immediate and enduring. Liberal policy positions, especially on social issues, appeared to be extreme and controversial to many white, middle-class Americans during the 1970's. They contributed to the landslide reelection of President Nixon in 1972, the unexpectedly narrow election margin of Jimmy Carter—a moderate southern Democrat—in the 1976 presidential election, and the decisive victory of conservative Republican nominee Ronald Reagan in 1980. The liberalism of the 1970's also contributed to the proliferation in the number and variety of interest groups and movements devoted to one or more liberal policy positions and of new federal agencies and regulations. Even decades later, Democratic presidential candidates generally avoided identifying themselves as liberals because of liberalism's controversial legacy of the 1970's.

Further Reading

Brinkley, Alan. *Liberalism and Its Discontents.* Cambridge, Mass.: Harvard University Press, 1998. A comprehensive analysis of how and why liberalism became controversial after the 1960's.

Scammon, Richard M., and Ben J. Wattenberg. *The Real Majority.* New York: Capricorn, 1971. A study based on polling data which claims that social issues will dominate future presidential elections.

White, Theodore H. *The Making of the President, 1972.* New York: Atheneum, 1973. An extensive examination of the 1972 presidential campaign, including the influence of liberalism on the Democratic nomination and general election.

Sean J. Savage

See also   Abortion rights; Affirmative action; Busing; Carter, Jimmy; Conservatism in U.S. politics; Elections in the United States, midterm; Elections in the United States, 1972; Elections in the United States, 1976; Environmental movement; Feminism; McGovern, George; National Organization for Women (NOW); Nixon, Richard M.; Occupational Safety and Health Act of 1974; Reagan, Ronald; *Roe v. Wade*; Women's rights.

■ Liddy, G. Gordon, and E. Howard Hunt

Identification   Nixon reelection campaign operatives who masterminded the Watergate break-in

G. Gordon Liddy

Born   November 30, 1930; Hoboken, New Jersey

E. Howard Hunt

Born   October 9, 1918; East Hamburg, New York

Liddy and Hunt are most famous as the planners with the most direct responsibility for the bungled break-in that led to the Watergate scandal and the subsequent resignation of President Richard M. Nixon.

E. Howard Hunt was in the Office of Strategic Services (OSS) during World War II and served in the Central Intelligence Agency (CIA) from 1949 to 1970. Despite his official resignation from the CIA in 1970 in order to join the White House staff, suspicions continued for many years that he in fact remained a CIA operative given his frequent, continuing contacts with the agency.

Graduating from Fordham University in 1950, G. Gordon Liddy joined the U.S. Army and served two years in Korea. Returning to Fordham, he graduated from its law school in 1957 and joined the Federal Bureau of Investigation (FBI) for five years until he resigned to practice law and become a prosecutor in New York. After running unsuccessfully for the Republican Party's 28th District congressional nomination in 1968, he ran the Nixon presidential campaign in that district. After Nixon won, Liddy became a U.S. Treasury Department lawyer and later moved to the White House staff before joining Nixon's Committee to Re-elect the President (CRP).

Both Hunt and Liddy were recruited to operate a "Special Investigations Group," informally known as the "Plumbers," to stop leaks from the Nixon administration. In that capacity, they organized a break-in of the psychiatrist who treated Daniel Ellsberg, the man responsible for leaking the Pentagon Papers to *The New York Times*, and attempted to get information with which to discredit Ellsberg. That the break-in was a failure did not discourage Liddy and Hunt from planning an even riskier break-in of the Democratic National Committee headquarters in the Watergate office complex in Washington, D.C. Directing the break-in from across the street, they were easily linked to the burglars, who were apprehended on the premises and arrested. Hunt initially refused to implicate the White House but cracked after federal judge John J. Sirica imposed a severe sentence on him. Meanwhile, Liddy never revealed anything while in prison and served more than four years—longer than any other Nixon administration official—until his sentence was commuted by President Jimmy Carter.

Impact   The serious bungling of the two burglaries at the hands of G. Gordon Liddy and E. Howard Hunt set in motion a chain of events that led to the impeachment process initiated against Richard M. Nixon and resulted in his ultimate resignation as president of the United States.

Subsequent Events   After serving thirty-three months in jail, Hunt was released, and he returned to writing spy novels, as he had done early in his career. He declared bankruptcy in Florida in 1995. After prison, Liddy wrote his autobiography and appeared on television game shows and the series *Miami Vice*. He subsequently became a syndicated radio talk show host and a highly paid celebrity on the lecture circuit.

Further Reading

Bernstein, Carl, and Woodward, Bob. *All the President's Men.* 2d ed. New York: Simon & Schuster, 1987.
Liddy, G. Gordon. *Will: The Autobiography of G. Gordon Liddy.* Rev. ed. New York: St. Martin's Press, 1991.

Richard L. Wilson

See also   Committee to Re-elect the President (CRP); Nixon, Richard M.; Nixon tapes; Nixon's resignation and pardon; Pentagon Papers; Scandals; Sirica, John J.; Watergate.

■ Literature in Canada

Definition   Fiction and nonfiction by Canadian authors

In the 1970's, Canadian literature in English and French reached a noteworthy level of technical experimentation while consolidating features of regional and national identity.

This decade witnessed important trends in biography and memoir, fiction, poetry, and drama in both official languages of Canada, English and French.

Biography and Memoir   The vast quantity of biographies and memoirs in English during the 1970's tended to have an academic slant. The most notable biographies were of historical or political eminences such as journalist William Lyon Mackenzie; naturalist Grey Owl; prime ministers Robert Borden, Lester B. Pearson, and Mackenzie King; and politicians Sir Joseph Flavelle, Clarence Decatur Howe, and Robert Stanfield. Literary biography was dominated by academics and journalists, with C. F. Klinck writing about poet Robert Service, Douglas Day about writer Malcolm Lowry, Kathleen Coburn about poet Samuel Taylor Coleridge, Doug Fetherling about novelist and screenwriter Ben Hecht, and Maria Tippett about author and artist Emily Carr.

Memoirs in English cut a wide swath and usually showed more literary flair than did the academic biographies. The most noteworthy were John Glassco's *Memoirs of Montparnasse* (1970), although much of it turned out to have been fabricated; Dorothy Livesay's *A Winnipeg Childhood* (1973) and her later collage of documentary memories *Left Hand Right Hand* (1977); and Hugh Garner's *One Damn Thing After Another* (1973), which was punchy, racy, and raw. The most elegantly written memoirs came from Charles Ritchie, who won the Governor General's Award for *The Siren Years: A Canadian Diplomat Abroad, 1937-1945* (1974) and followed it with *An Appetite for Life: The Education of a Young Diarist, 1924-1927* (1977).

On the French side, history and politics were not neglected, as books on Joseph-Charles Taché, Maurice Duplessis, Louis-Joseph Papineau, Lionel Groulx, Pierre Trudeau, and René Lévesque received significant press. Because of increasing scholarly interest in French Canadian writers and artists, there was a plethora of literary biographies and studies. Figures such as Gabrielle Roy, Paul-Émile Borduas, Marcel Dube, and Alfred Pellan received their share of scrutiny. An interesting cross-fertilization of the literary essay and biography took place in Victor-Lévy Beaulieu's *Pour saluer Victor Hugo* (1971), *Jack Kerouac* (1972), and *Monsieur Melville* (1978).

Fiction   Perhaps because of the vast size of the land and the concentration of cultural power in a few metropolises, novels and short stories in Canada tended to have more of a regional than a continental character. Therefore, it was possible to speak of Acadian literature, Western fiction, Maritime poetry, or Québécois drama. Political and social history fed these categories. For example, the destruction of the French settlement of Acadia by the British in the eighteenth century was seen as a paradise lost to an evil political agenda. Antonine Maillet became the leading voice for the Acadians with her novel *La Sagouine* (1972), which expressed both the suffering and the triumphal strength of her people. Dramatists Laval Goupil and Germaine Comeau and poet Raymond LeBlanc investigated the weapons required to empower those who were incapable of collective revolt.

French Canada boldly addressed its conflicted relationship with English Canada in novels such as Claude Jasmin's *La Petite Patrie* (1972), Jacques Godbout's *D'Amour, P.Q.* (1972), Réjean Ducharme's *L'Hiver de force* (1973), Yves Beauchemin's *L'Enfirouapé* (1974), Michel Tremblay's *La Grosse Femme d'à côté est enceinte* (1978), Pierre Turgeon's *Un, deux, trois* (1970), André Major's *Histoires de déserteurs* trilogy (1974-1976), Roger Fournier's *Les Cornes sacrées* (1977), and the translations of Roch Carrier's *La Guerre, Yes Sir!* (1968; English translation, 1970) and *Floralie, ou es-tu?* (1969; *Floralie, Where Are You?*, 1971).

French Canadian nationalism made a proud case for the use of *joual*, Quebec's peculiar dialect, and though many authors focused on small communities, they used interesting techniques—nonlinear narrative, mosaic composition, mythic and poetic elements, metafictional devices—and universal subjects—feminist concerns, social injustice—by which to enlarge the appeal of their stories.

English Canada had its own historical and nationalist themes, such as Mennonite suffering and the tragedy of Riel and the Metis in Rudy Wiebe's *The Blue Mountains of China* (1970) and *The Scorched-Wood People* (1977) or colonialism and revolution in Dave Godfrey's *The New Ancestors* (1970). However, though survival was a dominant cultural symbol and theme—especially as identified in Margaret Atwood's seminal thematic survey of Canadian literature, *Survival* (1972)—novelists and short-story writers tended to have other preoccupations.

The 1970's saw works by noteworthy feminists such as Atwood, Margaret Laurence, Alice Munro, Audrey Thomas, Marian Engel, Jane Rule (English Canada's answers to Quebec's Nicole Brossard), Hélène Ouvrard, and Madeleine Ouellette-Michalska. There were mythmakers (Jack Hodgins and Robertson Davies), social realists (Matt Cohen, Ray Smith,

Brian Moore, Timothy Findley, Morley Callaghan, Mavis Gallant, and Hugh MacLennan), satirists (Atwood, Davies, Mordecai Richler, John Metcalf, John Mills, W. O. Mitchell, and Robert Kroetsch), and mannerists (Metcalf, Daphne Marlatt, Norman Levine, Michael Ondaatje, and Hugh Hood). These categories were flexible, and writers often crossed from one to another. There were also the "one-shot wonders" such as Adele Wiseman, Wayland Drew, Robert Harlow, and Chris Scott, writers who made a significant impact with a single book but who did not notably enlarge their contribution to the genre afterward.

French Canada had innovators such as Beaulieu, Gérard Bessette, Jacques Poulin, Yves Theriault, and Jean-Yves Soucy who could easily negotiate links between narrative technique and history—as in Anne Hébert's *Kamouraska* (1970), Pierre Chatillon's *Le Fou* (1975), or Jacques Lanctôt's *Rupture de ban* (1979)—or who could express the strange interplay between reason and the subconscious or delirium, including Jacques Brossard, Yvon Rivard, and Jacques Garneau. English Canada also did not lack literary ambition and scope. Hood, who had made a case for modernism with his short-story collections, began his epic twelve-part New Age series, an emblematic sequence of novels about history, politics, art, economics, geography, sociology, family life, and religion. Though influenced by Coleridge, William Wordsworth, Marcel Proust, James Joyce, Anthony Powell, and Honoré de Balzac, he launched into a new kind of documentary fantasy that defied neat definition. Clark Blaise turned out novels and short stories that explored the dark sides of reality in extraordinary images. Davies completed his Deptford Trilogy (1970-1975) with the panache of one who easily mingled Jungian psychology with sharp social satire.

By and large, however, the Canadian novel in English was still struggling to find its niche on the world scene. Things were a little more advanced in the area of the short story, where writers were quickly establishing themselves as writers of the first rank by publishing their stories in little magazines, journals, anthologies, short-story annuals, and foreign magazines. Atwood, Hodgins, Thomas, and W. D. Valgardson won praise for their stories, but the leading collections of the genre were Laurence's *A Bird in the House* (1970); Alistair MacLeod's *The Lost Salt Gift of Blood* (1978); Munro's award-winning *Who Do You*

Think You Are? (1978); Hood's *The Fruit Man, the Meat Man, and the Manager* (1971) and *Dark Glasses* (1976); Gallant's *From the Fifteenth District* (1979); Austin C. Clarke's *When He Was Free and Young and He Used to Wear Silks* (1971); Blaise's *A North American Education* (1973) and *Tribal Justice* (1974); Levine's *Selected Stories* (1975); and Metcalf's *The Lady Who Sold Furniture* (1970) and *Girl in Gingham* (1978).

These collections caught their writers at relatively early stages in their careers, yet at a point that showed surprising literary maturity, range, and sophistication. Laurence's semiautobiographical short stories about young Vanessa MacLeod were told in the character's adult voice and captured the special flavor of Laurence's fictional setting during the Depression. MacLeod's elegiac and lyrical tones, Hood's emblematic epiphanies, Munro's remarkable textures, Gallant's complex structures, Clarke's social realism inflected with dialect, Blaise's rich prose style, Levine's delicate minimalism, and Metcalf's elegant wit and deflationary structure all pointed to impressive achievements by writers who would keep growing in stature over subsequent decades.

Poetry Canadian poetry in English became less nationalistic than it had been in the 1960's, despite the rise of Quebec nationalism and the Trudeau era that often exacerbated political conflict between English and French Canada. Nevertheless, there were politics in Dennis Lee's *Civil Elegies, and Other Poems* (1972), Milton Acorn's *More Poems for People* (1972), Irving Layton's many volumes, and Bill Bissett's *Nobody Owns th [sic] Earth* (1971), but usually of populist sentiment, international import, or satire.

Instead, Canadian poetry in English kept its focus on other subjects for meditation and experimentation. It manifested its variety in the travel poems of Layton, Atwood, Eli Mandel, Earle Birney, Al Purdy, and Patrick Anderson; the biographical collage of Ondaatje's *The Collected Works of Billy the Kid* (1970); the documentary fantasy of Atwood's *The Journals of Susanna Moodie* (1970); the genre specialization of Kroetsch in *The Ledger* (1979) and *Seed Catalogue* (1978), John Newlove in *Lies* (1972), and Phyllis Webb in *Selected Poems, 1954-1965* (1971); the colloquial, conversational tone of George Bowering's poems in *George, Vancouver* (1970) and *Touch: Selected Poems, 1960-1970* (1971); the humane character sketches of Alden Nowlan in *I'm a Stranger Here Myself*

(1974), the sometimes arcane mythology of Gwendolyn MacEwen's *The Armies of the Moon* (1972); and the concrete and sound experiments of B. P. Nichol in *Still Water* (1970) and *Unit of Four* (1973) and in his edited collection *The Cosmic Chef* (1970).

On the French Canadian side, poetry had a more distinct political cast. The Quiet Revolution of the 1960's was over because the October Crisis and the subsequent War Measures Act of 1971 served as catalysts for inflammatory political poetry by Gérald Godin (who became a Parti Québécois minister), Paul Chamberland, Michele Lalonde, Monique Bosco, and Marie Laberge. This political fervor extended to poet-singers such as Claude Péloquin, Raoul Duguay, Gilles Vigneault, Félix Leclerc, Yvon Deschamps, and Gilbert Langevin.

The idea of politics has a wide compass, so even poetry about feminism, jazz, and the counterculture in Quebec had strong radical sentiments, principally influenced by an aesthetic called *barre du jour* that demanded the dismantling of lyricism and the sabotaging of text. Quebec poets manifested strong individuality, and, in the process of releasing primitive impulses and flouting social conventions, they were able to be more linguistically adventurous than their English or European counterparts. Whatever the politics driving their poetry, these poets were able to express instincts for freedom, eroticism, and community. Quebec poetry always showed a national identity, and some of its greatest exemplars in the 1970's were Gaston Miron, Fernand Ouellette, Jacques Brault, and Michel Garneau.

Drama   The early 1970's saw the addition of several new regional theaters to the alternative theater movement and the founding in 1972 of Playwrights' Co-op (now Playwrights Canada) that was the main publishing source for new plays. Documentary drama, often in the form of collective collaborations among actors, directors, and writers, was the chief staple—such as *The Farm Show* (pr. 1976), *Paper Wheat* (pr. 1978), Wiebe's *Far as the Eye Can See* (pr. 1977), and Rick Salutin's *1837: William Lyon Mackenzie and the Canadian Revolution* (pr. 1976)—which had characters and stories drawn from history or contemporary events. Other plays were more technically advanced. Salutin's *Les Canadiens* (pr. 1977) used the metaphor of hockey to analyze Quebec history, Sharon Pollock used vaudeville and cabaret in *The Komagata Maru Incident* (pr. 1976) in an indict-

ment of racism, Ken Gass employed a comic-book style to lampoon fascism in *Hurray for Johnny Canuck* (pr. 1975), Hrant Alianak wrote short plays influenced by film noir, and George F. Walker spoofed theatrical and film conventions in *Zastrozzi, the Master of Discipline* (pr. 1977).

The dominant dramatic form was realism, as in the cases of David French, David Freeman, Tom Walmsley, Joanna Glass, Margaret Hollingsworth, and David Fennario. There were also remarkable essays in poetic parable and Brechtian technique (Michael Cook), melodramatic opera (Ken Mitchell), impressionism (John Murrell), and surrealism (Lawrence Russell).

Nothing in English Canadian drama, however, matched Michel Tremblay's poetic use of *joual* (rhythmic, often braided dialogue and chorus), Robert Gurik's Brechtian allegories, Jean-Claude Germain's political satire, Jean Barbeau's powerful social and existential studies, Michel Garneau's musical structures and poetic critiques of politics, or Roch Carrier's dramatic parables. French Canadians seemed to write about the body politic and the politics of sex, history, religion, culture, and family life. Their plays showed that, in Quebec, drama was not simply an entertainment but a driving force in the expression and consolidation of identity.

Impact   During the 1970's, a land that had been a nation for slightly over a century was able to start staking its claims in world literature. French Canada was ahead of English Canada in fiction, nonfiction, and drama, perhaps because it concentrated more on its own history and culture in defining itself. The decade marked the beginning of a dialogue between the two official cultures as writers found their works translated into each other's language.

Further Reading

Atwood, Margaret, ed. *The Canadian Imagination: Dimensions of a Literary Culture.* Cambridge, Mass.: Harvard University Press, 1977. Discusses French Canadian literature and surveys Canadian fiction, poetry, drama, and individual authors.

Benson, Eugene, and L. W. Conolly, eds. *The Oxford Companion to Canadian Theatre.* Toronto: Oxford University Press, 1989. Contains more than seven hundred entries by contributors from across Canada.

Keith, W. J. *Canadian Literature In English.* New York: Longman, 1985. Argues that the concept of "Canadian tradition" is neither a theme (survival) nor an abstraction, but one that gradually evolves from literary works.

Toye, William, ed. *The Oxford Companion to Canadian Literature*. Toronto: Oxford University Press, 1983. The first comprehensive anthology of biographies and essays on the breadth of Canadian literature in both official languages. Offers long articles on drama, the novel, short stories, and poetry by expert scholars and nonacademics.

Keith Garebian

See also Atwood, Margaret; Censorship in Canada; Children's literature; *Ecotopia*; Journalism in Canada; Literature in the United States; Mowat, Farley; Poetry; Richler, Mordecai; Roy, Gabrielle; Theater in Canada.

■ Literature in the United States

Definition Fiction and nonfiction by American authors

In the 1970's, U.S. literature continued to experience the turbulent renaissance of critical thought that began in the 1960's.

At this moment in American literature, there were important challenges to the modernist concept of form, extreme experimentation in styles, and a blurring of the boundaries traditionally set around genres of all kinds, along with a major increase in and recognition of minority and women's writing.

In the 1970's in the United States, postmodernist subversions of the Western scientific and rationalistic heritage were challenging modernist certainties, phenomenological approaches seeking to identify the essence of the subject, and formalist or social realist approaches to literature. Influences such as the Beat counterculture of the 1950's, existentialist philosophy, and imports of Russian and French theories of language all contributed to this critique of modernist assumptions, which included a belief in progress in linear time, a celebration of reason, a belief in the stability of language, an assumption that the author is sole creator, and the possibility of a single unified aesthetic.

Postmodernists focused on the act of reading as a form of *jouissance*, a French word for a kind of "play" in criticism that is supposed to be pursued for its own pleasure, not for any social agenda. In contrast with

T. S. Eliot's statement that there is no creative criticism, postmodernism placed the burden of play and creativity on the reader, who was expected to be a critic, identifying marginalized ways of knowing and being within literature and culture. Besides advocating *jouissance*, however, postmodernist criticism also claimed a politically sophisticated insight: Like language, the world is composed entirely of "difference," of others whose perspectives are independent of the reader's sense of truth. Therefore, in contradiction to modernist belief that there can be a universal explanation of literature and culture, postmodernism holds that no single truth can describe the whole of a culture.

National and international politics also had much to do with the course of American literature in the 1970's. Fears surrounding the United States' role in the nuclear age and technological warfare after World War II had fueled an increasing sense of malaise, horror, and suspicion, as short-story writers and novelists contemplated the absurdity of institutions and beliefs that had previously been trusted guides. Around the end of the decade, formalism returned to prominence, at the same time that strong conservative trends in the nation reflected a yearning for a return to core values. It is doubtful, however, that the return to realism fully reflected the political conservatism of the nation, since literary styles did not necessarily identify political loyalties. Radical liberal writers used realism, and political conservatives and even reactionaries were involved in postmodern agendas. For instance, although radically aware of the cultural nightmare, Saul Bellow hewed to social realism and rejected the cult of the absurd, whereas the credentials of at least one critic who was a leading architect of postmodernism, Paul de Man, have proven to be tainted by fascism.

New and vibrant literatures of minority groups emerged that were frequently, but not always, grounded in realistic modes. During the 1970's, these writings were becoming sufficiently central to American literature to influence the direction of criticism and to mandate reviews of the literary canon, which had been previously held sacrosanct.

Postmodernism in the 1970's Postmodernist theory was grounded in the world-weary disgust of the Beats in the 1950's and in the existential ennui of European philosophers of language in later decades. By the beginning of the 1970's, postmodernists were in full revolution against formalism. A cornucopia of new approaches emerged that were intended to render the content of texts ever more fluid, such as the increase in the introspective style of "metafiction" or "surfiction," which anticipated postmodernist writing's tendency to call attention to itself as a text for its own sake.

This type of writing had existed long before the 1970's, as in the subtle jest implied by the extensive footnotes in James Joyce's fictional *Finnegans Wake* (1939). By the 1970's, established experimental writers continued from their earlier work, such as John Barth in *Chimera* (1972) and with his conscious erosion of boundaries between high and low culture and pastiche in *Letters* (1979) and Doris Lessing in *Briefing for a Descent into Hell* (1971) and *The Memoirs of a Survivor* (1974).

The 1970's responded dramatically to these strategies of irreverence in the face of a fearsome, complex world. Newer writers in this tradition came to prominence in the 1970's. Thomas Pynchon, the author of *The Crying of Lot 49* (1966), again showed his mastery of the absurdist novel with *Gravity's Rainbow* (1973). Donald Barthelme's Freudian *The Dead Father* (1975) embodied pastiche or parody of others' works. Kurt Vonnegut, Terry Southern, John Hawkes, and others also practiced absurdist principles in writing. The 1970's marked the end of the modernist cult of individualism and a breakdown of signification (especially of language) that moved in extreme instances toward an end to coherence.

Postmodernism also continued to attack the concept that literature should be personal and purely literary. As postmodernism turned its gaze inward onto the liberalism of previous ages while attempting to maintain a stance in opposition to more conservative literary agendas, mimetic stances based on Emersonian liberalism or the nationalistic optimism of a Walt Whitman were as subject to postmodernist literary scrutiny as were the more recent agendas of neoconservative anticommunism. Criticism reflected this political mood of the literature, sometimes critiquing, sometimes adapting, and sometimes appropriating and reimagining overtly political positions such as Marxism, feminism, and perspectives from writers of minority groups. This display of dark humor, artifice, and skill rejected the possibility of human progress and redemption. Skepticism was not, however, the only trend, as formalism reinvented itself and staged a return.

Formalism vs. Postmodernism   Before the advent of postmodernism, formalist approaches to literature had relied on a modernist sense of "purity" that required integrity both of the genre and of the medium of expression. In the 1970's, the older school of realism continued its productions and success, with writers such as John Updike in *Rabbit Redux* (1971) and Bellow in *Humboldt's Gift* (1975) approaching the human condition with compassion rather than through the darker lens of avant-garde sensibility. Lionel Trilling's book of criticism *Sincerity and Authenticity* (1972) attempted to reclaim primacy for realism by establishing connections between the old term "sincerity" and the new term "authenticity."

Yet realism persisted in Bellow and other Jewish American writers, and African American novelists such as James Baldwin led the way for black realistic writing with *Go Tell It on the Mountain* (1953) and continuing to *Just Above My Head* (1979). These were socially conscious novels tempered with compassion. Postwar Southern writers in the mold of William Faulkner also contributed 1970's novels, such as Eudora Welty's *The Optimist's Daughter* (1973). These writers continued to rely on traditional methods of mimesis, verisimilitude, and reportorial representation in order to focus attention on the realities of meanness, corruption, and oppression.

Meanwhile, postmodernist thought asked realism to reinvent itself, to reexamine its roots and reclaim its vitality in the 1970's. In many instances, writers of diverse ethnic and cultural backgrounds changed the realistic novel to suit the needs of an era of ethnic and minority awakening. African American novelist Toni Morrison exhibited postmodern tendencies in *The Bluest Eye* (1970) and *Sula* (1973) when she introduced elements outside the pale of verisimilitude, such as Western mythology, fairy tales, and black folk culture. The impact of postmodernist critiques can also be seen in the Magical Realism of Latino writers and in the blending of myth and the horrors of the nuclear age and its wars in Native American Leslie Marmon Silko's *Ceremony* (1977).

Meanwhile, serious science fiction (as opposed to the special-effects-laden films that began to dominate the mass market), such as Robert A. Heinlein's *I Will Fear No Evil* (1970), made the traditionally realistic genre of science fiction psychologically strange. The modified use of mimesis and other devices in feminist fiction are also examples of the vital transformation of this neorealistic writing.

Traditional writers of realistic fiction were changing, too. Norman Mailer had developed from the tradition of John Dos Passos's social protest into dark fantasies such as *The Armies of the Night* (1968). John Cheever wrote *Falconer* in 1977, and Updike published *The Coup* in 1978.

In the area of nonfiction, the memoirs of Vietnam veterans also worked to perpetuate realism. The revival of realism also owes an essential debt to novels by populists, immigrants, and ethnic groups, including the beginning of a great body of thoughtful writing by Asian Americans, Native Americans, Jewish Americans, African Americans, Latinos, women, and new immigrants.

Feminists and Minorities The second wave of the American feminist movement emerged out of the civil rights struggle of the 1960's, and it reflected some of the separatist conclusions from the violent loss of leadership in these movements. The 1970's saw not only the rise of feminist separatist writers such as Adrienne Rich but also a separatist feminist critical movement. Elaine Showalter's *A Literature of Their Own* (1977) and Sandra Gilbert and Susan Gubar's *The Madwoman in the Attic* (1979) are the pioneering works of gynocriticism, the exclusive study of women writers. Gynocritics focused on the history of middle-class white women's writing as it responds to a masculine literary tradition.

The work of Joyce Carol Oates is one example of gynocritical opposition to Harold Bloom's theory that there is only "influence" left in letters, resisting male-centered mythology and reclaiming female roots in Western writing. Gynocriticism created its own canon by identifying an oppressed "voice" throughout the history of Western women's literature.

By the 1980's, however, French feminists such as Toril Moi would point out that a modernist unified "self" had been assumed to exist within the idea of an identifiable voice. The binary oppositions implied by gynocentric criticism that failed to take into account homosexual relationships were also attacked as an unexamined construct of traditional white male critical structure. One pioneering example of this critique is Audre Lorde's "An Open Letter to Mary Daly" (1979). Thus, as white feminist second-wave criticism emerged out of the civil rights struggle of the 1960's, this new wave of minority feminism answered back, structuring a new direction to criticism that was gaining ground by the 1980's.

Lesbian feminism, which experienced hostility from conventional feminists, developed in parallel ways to other marginalized groups in the 1970's. In the early 1970's, Rich, a poet and cultural critic, downplayed sexuality and included women who chose not to have sex. Rich received the National Book Award for her book of poems *Diving into the Wreck* (1973). She shared her acceptance statement with fellow nominees Lorde and Alice Walker, two other writers who dealt with lesbianism, "in the name of all women whose voices have gone and still go unheard in a patriarchal world." Lorde's poems from the 1960's and 1970's were collected in *Chosen Poems, Old and New* (1982), while Walker published *The Third Life of Grange Copeland* (1970), *In Love and Trouble: Stories of Black Women* (1973), and *Meridan* (1976).

Ethnic minorities in the 1970's tended toward a humanistic optimism that a realistic, historical approach could best transform the culture. As in previous decades, however, this optimism was tempered by a sense of alienation. Minority writers were also beginning to explore in greater depth the chaos that confronted them and to affirm more specifically their conflicts with the dominant white culture, an activity that incidentally revealed common ground between modern and postmodern writing and criticism.

While an important facet of minority authorship in the 1970's was the independence and wealth of diverse writing and responses to mainstream American culture, there was some common ground, including the treatment of social issues, the theft or undermining of cultural identities by the dominant culture, and the development of critiques of feminist minorities that demanded greater awareness of the literatures of different ethnic groups. Neomythological tropes and Magical Realism were also popular styles, and music often provided a basic aesthetic in writing, especially in poetry.

African American writers who emerged out of the racial unrest of the 1960's helped to push the focus toward a more militant view in the 1970's. Ralph Ellison's *Invisible Man* (1952) and Richard Wright's *Native Son* (1940) had demonstrated a willingness to address the negative impact of racism on African Americans. The militant critique of the white aesthetic in the Black Arts movement of the late 1960's and early 1970's, led by LeRoi Jones (Amiri Baraka) and other proponents of a black aesthetic, mandated a redemptive approach to literature that did not address the disruptive effect of racism but focused on black power.

African American women writers tended to pass over this male-oriented black aesthetic, favoring a new appreciation and criticism of African American literature as a whole. Lorde, Walker, and Morrison were in this group; a later triumph was Morrison becoming the first African American and only the eighth woman to win the Nobel Prize in Literature, in 1993. Other distinguished newer male writers such as Ishmael Reed, with *Mumbo Jumbo* (1972), did not fit into the black aesthetic; Reed was a leader in the postmodernist movement and a pioneer of ethnic postmodernism.

Among Latino writers, the 1970's began a large and continuing output of Spanish and English works, with some focal points being oral heritage, problems of bilingualism, and pressures of the contemporary world on Latino culture. Latino authors and titles in the 1970's followed in abundance the groundbreaking 1972 novel *Bless Me, Ultima* by Rudolfo A. Anaya; others were Oscar Zeta Acosta's *The Revolt of the Cockroach People* (1973) and Nash Candelaria's *Memories of the Alhambra* (1977).

In the tradition of seventeenth century writer Sor Juana Inés de la Cruz, Latina and Chicana writers found themselves in resistance to traditionalist assumptions of this militant male-dominated way of defining culture, but they also resisted acultural white feminism. Pioneers in Latina feminist writing included Estela Portillo-Trambley with *Rain of Scorpions, and Other Writings* (1975), Bernice Zamora with *Restless Serpents* (1976), Ana Castillo with *i close my eyes (to see)* (1976), and Alma Villanueva with *Bloodroot* (1977) and *Poems* (1977). Out of the challenges that Latina and other minority women writers met in the 1970's, Cherríe Moraga and Gloria Anzaldúa edited *This Bridge Called My Back* (1981), a watershed work demanding more attention for the writings of women of color.

Other groups of minority writers were also emerging. *Aiiieeeee! An Anthology of Asian-American Writers* (1974), edited by Frank Chin and others, formalized a classification of "Asian American" writing, which focused on the social history of Asian Americans. The response was complicated by diversity within the Asian community. For instance, Chin bitterly criticized the postmodernist elements in Maxine Hong Kingston's *The Woman Warrior* (1976). By the 1980's, however, opponents had made a case that Chin's was a predominantly masculine and traditionalist construction of the vast and diverse area of Asian American writing that had overlooked much of importance, especially with regard to Asian women's writing in general, which had been experimenting with concepts of postmodern fragmentation as a way of expressing the reality of Asian loss of family traditions in the United States. The perspectives of these authors is as varied as Asian culture: Japanese Americans singled out for concentration camps in the United States during World War II had a different experience from Chinese immigrants who built the American railroads, the experience of race on which Chin had focused. Some critics are trying to reconsider Chin as a precursor whose work successfully resists and critiques racial stereotypes.

"Art for art's sake" does not generally apply to Native American writing. N. Scott Momaday's Pulitzer Prize-winning 1968 novel *House Made of Dawn* brought attention to indigenous cultural issues and literature in the 1970's. *The Blue Cloud Quarterly* offered a 1970's venue to Native American writers. The early work of Silko, such as *Ceremony*, continued the Momaday tradition of politicized writing, but it dealt uniquely with the issues of mixed blood Native Americans. Silko also differs from other women writers in that she successfully supports both male and female aspects of Laguna Pueblo culture.

Native American poetry had not been published much before 1972. Anthologies such as *The Whispering Wind* (1972), edited by Terry Allen, included much that was not good but also called attention to worthwhile authors. Another anthology featuring a distinguished group of poets was Duane Niatum's *Carriers of the Dream Wheel* (1975). One particularly important poet who emerged in the 1970's was Joy Harjo, whose postmodern poetic *The Last Song* (1975), *What Moon Drove Me to This?* (1980), and *She Had Some Horses* (1983) have been widely praised. These writers and others anticipated and contributed to a flowering of indigenous writing in the 1980's.

Impact Historians of literature offer diverse perspectives of the canonical challenges in the 1970's, some favoring an emphasis on authors who worked inside the canon and some eager to bring forth new perspectives. All, however, agree that it is not possible to reduce this complex decade to a few simple concepts. Instead, the 1970's continued and expanded considerably on a postwar trend of defying attempts to conjure up a unified literature, culture, or criticism for America—or even attempts to construct unity within its social and ethnic groups. This trend has endured as new visions of literary possibility continue to inform American thought, and as ethnic and other minority writing has been institutionalized in the curricula and programs of leading universities.

Further Reading

Davidson, Cathy N., and Linda Wagner-Martin. *The Oxford Companion to Women's Writing in the United States*. New York: Oxford University Press, 1995. A thorough discussion of U.S. women's writing. An essential reference for the 1970's development of feminist criticism.

Elliott, Emory, ed. *Columbia Literary History of the United States*. New York: Columbia University Press, 1988. The final chapters consist of essays by various important critics on major literary trends in the United States after 1945.

Lauter, Paul, and Richard Yarborough, eds. *The Heath Anthology of American Literature*. Boston: Houghton Mifflin, 2002. This anthology offers the best inclusion of ethnic and minority literature.

Perkins, George B., and Barbara Perkins, eds. *The American Tradition in Literature*. 10th ed. Boston: McGraw-Hill, 2002. A frequently referenced anthology that offers significant general overviews of postwar literature.

Suzanne Araas Vesely

See also Anaya, Rudolfo A.; Angelou, Maya; Black Arts movement; Blume, Judy; Bombeck, Erma; Broadway musicals; Censorship in the United States; Children's literature; *Chorus Line, A*; *Culture of Narcissism, The*; Durang, Christopher; *Everything You Always Wanted to Know About Sex but Were Afraid to Ask*; *Fear of Flying*; Feminism; Giovanni, Nikki; *Gravity's Rainbow*; *Greening of America, The*; *Hite Report, The*; *I'm OK, You're OK*; *Jesus Christ Superstar*; *Jonathan Livingston Seagull*; Journalism in the United States; *Joy of Sex, The*; King, Stephen; Language Poets; *Late Great Planet Earth, The*; Literature in Canada; Mailer, Norman; Mamet, David; Morrison, Toni; Oates, Joyce Carol; *Our Bodies, Ourselves*; *Passages*; Poetry; *Population Bomb, The*; Rich, Adrienne; Robbins, Harold;

Self-help books; Shange, Ntosake; Shaw, Irwin; Simon, Neil; Sondheim, Stephen; Steinem, Gloria; Theater in the United States; Thompson, Hunter S.; *Torch Song Trilogy*; Updike, John; Vonnegut, Kurt; Wilson, Lanford; Wolfe, Tom; *Woman Warrior, The*; Woodward, Bob, and Carl Bernstein; *Zen and the Art of Motorcycle Maintenance*.

■ Little League participation by girls

The Event Little League officials end boys-only baseball teams

Date Became law on December 26, 1974

Children, age eight through twelve, gained access to Little League baseball teams regardless of their gender.

When Carl Stotz established Little League baseball in 1939, he did not specify gender restrictions but intended eligibility only for boys. By 1951, Little League headquarters officially ruled to exclude girls. Two decades later, Little League executives still considered girls too weak to play baseball. They stated that because Congress had granted the Little League's 1964 federal charter, only those legislators could approve changes. Officials justified the exclusionary policy by describing Little League as an essential training phase for boys to perfect skills and gain experience to pursue college scholarships and professional careers unavailable to females. Advocates for girls in Little League emphasized that baseball should be recreational and help children develop teamwork skills, and they stressed that girls were athletically capable. Some communities established coed teams to replace Little Leagues. The Mother's March on the Little League lobbied Congress.

When parents filed discrimination lawsuits, most state courts said that they had no jurisdiction over Little League. Maria Pepe's lawsuit was the catalyst for change. Invited by a coach, she tried out for Little League in Hoboken, New Jersey, in 1971. Selected as team pitcher, Pepe played in three games before opposing teams complained to Little League headquarters. Officials warned that the team would be penalized if Pepe remained on the roster. The National Organization for Women (NOW) filed a civil rights suit, declaring that Pepe had suffered sexual discrimination in the use of public facilities, which was addressed in Title IX—the 1972 legislation that protected gender equality in education and prohibited use of federal funds to support discriminatory practices.

In early 1974, New Jersey's Division of Civil Rights and State Superior Court said that Pepe's equal rights had been unlawfully denied and demanded that Little League start allowing girls to play baseball. The state assembly defeated a Little League effort to delay inclusion of female players. Approximately 2,000 teams representing 150,000 players quit in protest. Court representatives warned national officials of possible fines and imprisonment. On June 12, 1974, Little League headquarters stated that girls could try out for teams. However, few girls benefited immediately because this rule change occurred after spring tryouts and team assignments; Pepe was too old to participate. Little League asked Congress to reword its charter. After the bill passed, President Gerald Ford signed it into law on December 26, 1974.

Impact The Little League decision enhanced improvements in females' athletic opportunities and increased participation. Little League officials introduced a girls-only Little League softball program in 1974. Approximately 29,000 girls participated during its inaugural season. By 1977, the number of girls playing Little League baseball peaked, representing 1 percent of 2.25 million team members in 31 countries. Revised instruction manuals incorporated girls' photographs.

The Little League change began to be reflected in popular culture as well. Novels based on real cases included Isabella Taves's *Not Bad for a Girl* (1972) and Bill J. Carol's *Single to Center* (1974). Tatum O'Neal starred as a Little League pitcher in the film *The Bad News Bears* (1976), and a similar television sitcom premiered in 1979.

Further Reading

Pogrebin, Letty Cottin. "Baseball Diamonds Are a Girl's Best Friend." *Ms. Magazine* 3, 3 (September, 1974): 79-82.

Van Auken, Lance, and Robin Van Auken. *Play Ball! The Story of Little League Baseball.* University Park: Pennsylvania State University Press, 2001.

Elizabeth D. Schafer

See also Baseball; National Organization for Women (NOW); Sports; Title IX of the Education Amendments of 1972; Women's rights.

■ Littlefeather, Sacheen

Identification Native American actor and activist
Born 1947; California

Littlefeather made headlines when she rejected an Academy Award on behalf of Marlon Brando at the ceremony held on March 27, 1973.

Marlon Brando refused the 1973 Academy Award for Best Actor in *The Godfather* in order to protest the film and television industries' inaccurate portrayal of American Indians and to emphasize grievances associated with the ongoing occupation of Wounded Knee. In his place, he sent Sacheen Littlefeather, an actor born Maria Cruz of mixed Apache, Yaqui, Pueblo, and Caucasian ancestry.

Sacheen Littlefeather shows the media the note from Marlon Brando declining his Academy Award for Best Actor in the name of Native American rights. (AP/Wide World Photos)

At the awards ceremony, Littlefeather said,

> I'm representing Marlon Brando this evening and he has asked me to tell you . . . that he . . . very regretfully cannot accept this very generous award. . . . I beg at this time that I have not intruded upon this evening and that we will, in the future . . . our hearts and our understanding will meet with love and generosity. Thank you on behalf of Marlon Brando.

A few people in the audience applauded, but many more jeered until Littlefeather walked off the stage. Later in the evening, Clint Eastwood wondered whether he should present the award for Best Picture "on behalf of all the cowboys shot in John Ford Westerns over the years." Raquel Welch said "I hope the winner doesn't have a cause" before announcing the recipient of the Best Actress award. Cohost Michael Caine criticized Brando for "letting some poor little Indian girl take the boos" instead of "[standing] up and [doing] it himself."

After the ceremony, Littlefeather shared the text of Brando's statement with the press. Brando wrote, "[T]he motion picture community has been as responsible as any for degrading the Indian. . . . I, as a member in this profession, do not feel that I can as a citizen of the United States accept an award here tonight." Brando wrote of American Indians:

> When they laid down their arms, we murdered them. We lied to them. We cheated them out of their lands. We starved them into signing fraudulent agreements that we called treaties which we never kept. We turned them into beggars on a continent that gave life for as long as life can remember.

Impact Sacheen Littlefeather's brief appearance on behalf of Brando produced a few film roles for her, as well as an appearance in *Playboy* magazine. She continued as an activist encouraging Native Americans to work in Hollywood; fighting to combat alcoholism, obesity, and diabetes among Native Americans; and caring for Native Americans with acquired immunodeficiency syndrome (AIDS), including her brother.

Further Reading

Brando, Marlon. "The Godfather: That Unfinished Oscar Speech." *The New York Times*, March 30, 1973. Available at http://www.nytimes.com/packages/html/movies/bestpictures/godfather-ar3.html.

Johnson, Troy, and Joane Nagel, and Duane Cham-

pagne, eds. *American Indian Activism: Alcatraz to the Longest Walk.* Champaign: University of Illinois Press, 1997.

Bruce E. Johansen

See also Academy Awards; American Indian Movement (AIM); Brando, Marlon; Film in the United States; *Godfather* films; Native Americans; Peltier, Leonard; Trail of Broken Treaties; Wounded Knee occupation.

■ Lopez, Nancy

Identification Latina professional golfer
Born January 6, 1957; Torrance, California

Lopez was the first female golfer to be considered a superstar. She was a standout athlete who drew widespread attention to the achievement of women in her sport.

Mexican American Nancy Lopez was introduced to golf early in her life by her father, Domingo. He moved the Lopez family to Roswell, New Mexico, where, partially to improve his wife Marina's medical condition, the family took up golf. Domingo encouraged Nancy to enter the New Mexico Women's Ama-

Nancy Lopez. (Ralph W. Miller Golf Library)

teur Championship, which she won at the age of twelve in 1969. She forged an impressive record of amateur and junior championships, and in 1975, she decided to compete as an amateur in the primarily professional U.S. Women's Open. Lopez's swing was technically unusual, but it generated extraordinary power. Lopez stunned the entire tournament by tying for second place overall. That same year, she enrolled at the University of Tulsa, which she attended for two years before turning professional in 1977.

In the spring of 1978, Lopez garnered headlines across the sports world when she won five tournaments in a row and nine overall for the year. She became a household name, earning publicity both for herself and for her entire sport. She continued her success in 1979, winning eight tournaments, including the Ladies Professional Golf Association (LPGA) tournament. Though her older counterparts on the women's golf tour, such as Mickey Wright and JoAnne Carner, might have been expected to be jealous, they realized that Lopez's visibility bode good things for all women golfers and they generally admired her. Despite all her achievements, however, she never won the U.S. Women's Open, the sport's most famous tournament.

Impact The LPGA had been in existence since 1950, but few Americans recognized women's golf as a high-level sport until the beginning of Nancy Lopez's fame. Her telegenic quality, marketability, and consistent winning led to a wider visibility for women's golf, as well as contributing to the greater attention given to female athletes in previously male-dominated sports. Although Lopez never again towered over the sport as she did in the late 1970's, she remained a consistent force on the tour during the subsequent two decades before retiring in 2003.

Further Reading

Burnett, Jim. *Tee Times: On the Road with the Ladies Professional Golf Tour.* New York: Scribners, 2002.

Lopez, Nancy, with Peter Schwed. *The Education of a Woman Golfer.* New York: Simon & Schuster, 1979.

Marvis, Barbara J., and Theresa S. Swanson. *Famous People of Hispanic Heritage: Pedro José Greer, Jr., Nancy Lopez, Rafael Palmeiro, Hilda Perera.* Elkton, Md.: Mitchell Lane Multicultural Biography Series, 1996.

Nicholas Birns

See also   Golf; Nicklaus, Jack; Sports.

■ Love, American Style

Identification   Television comedy series
Date   Aired from 1969 to 1974

This anthology of miniplays and sketches—all dealing with lighthearted, sentimental, or family-centered understandings of romance—offered airtime opportunities to a wide range of celebrity guest stars while giving the program's network a chance to promote actors appearing on its own sitcoms.

Love, American Style was the only anthology programming of its day that focused on short romantic comedy. Airing on the American Broadcasting Company (ABC) network, the program featured hour-long episodes divided into two, three, four, or five segments. Each episode used different casts and directors and began with a title, "Love and the . . . ," which set the night's theme. Although the series was cut back to just half an hour for sixteen episodes during the second season, it returned to its original format when it was moved to Friday night in 1971 and kept that format and time slot until its cancellation.

The theme song, performed by the Cowsills in the first season and then by the Charles Fox Singers, might not have done very well on the charts, but it left a lasting impression on viewers, who would henceforth associate the music with the visuals of fireworks exploding on screen, representing the power and majesty of love. To enhance this connection, in the last two seasons, fireworks sound effects were added to the opening titles. The same brass bed was used repeatedly in episode after episode, despite the different settings or circumstances, in order to provide a recurring motif that fans could identify.

Sometimes, real-life celebrity couples, such as Sonny Bono and Cher, Jerry Stiller and Anne Meara, or Steve Allen and Jayne Meadows, would play fictional couples on the show. The program also provided a venue for recurring visits from such comedic actors as Judy Carne, Alice Ghostley, Kaye Ballard, Charles Nelson Reilly, and Larry Storch. Guest stars could be as varied as Agnes Moorehead, Vincent Price, Milton Berle, Burt Reynolds, Edward Everett Horton, and Sissy Spacek. One-minute blackout skits, often starring character actor Stuart Margolin, were sometimes used as filler between segments.

Impact Although it never ranged higher than number twenty-five in the Nielsen ratings, *Love, American*

Style paved the way for more successful romantic comedy programming for ABC that used television celebrities and guest stars within a more structured format, including Aaron Spelling's *Love Boat* (1977-1986) and *Fantasy Island* (1978-1984). It also spawned three diverse spin-offs: *Barefoot in the Park* (1970-1971), the animated *Wait Till Your Father Gets Home* (1972-1974), and, most notably, the very successful sitcom *Happy Days* (1974-1984).

Further Reading

Brooks, Tim, and Earle F. Marsh. *The Complete Directory to Prime Time Network and Cable TV Shows: 1946-Present.* 8th ed. New York: Ballantine, 2003.

McNeil, Alex. *Total Television.* 4th ed. New York: Penguin, 1996.

Marc, David. *Comic Visions: Television Comedy and American Culture.* 2d ed. Malden, Mass.: Blackwell, 1997.

Scot M. Guenter

See also *Happy Days*; Sitcoms; Television in the United States; Variety shows.

■ Love Canal

Identification   Neighborhood used as a dumping ground for chemical by-products
Date   Came to public attention in 1978
Place   Niagara Falls, New York

The events at Love Canal were a significant cause of the American public's heightened fears of chemical pollution and of the exorbitantly expensive Superfund cleanup project embarked upon by the U.S. federal government.

In the 1940's, Hooker ElectroChemical Corporation owned land in the Love Canal area of Niagara Falls, New York, that it used as a dump for chemical manufacturing by-products. The site had been used before as a dump by the city and the U.S. Army. Hooker tested the site before use and found it to be safe; local and state-level government inspectors approved the site and issued the appropriate permits. Hooker then used the dump site from 1942 until the early 1950's, at which time it discontinued dumping, sealed the site with an impermeable clay covering, and left it alone.

In the early 1950's, the Niagara Falls Board of Education was looking for a site to build a new school. It approached Hooker and expressed interested in purchasing the Love Canal site. Hooker refused to sell, pointing out that the site was a chemical dump and not appropriate for a school. The Board of Education persisted and overrode Hooker's refusal by threatening to have the local government condemn the property and force the sale.

Hooker then sold the property to the city for one dollar in 1953. In the sale contract and in other public forums, Hooker made explicit the property's history, expressed its opposition to the city's plans, urged that the property be used only for a parking lot or a park, and made clear that under no circumstances should the clay barrier be breached. The city then developed the property, putting in sewer lines and having a school built upon the chemical dump. In 1957, it also sold a parcel of the land to real estate developers, who built a number of homes upon it.

About twenty years later, many Love Canal residents noticed seepage in their basements and notified authorities, who identified the seepage as toxic chemicals. Upon learning this, the residents were frightened and outraged, and these sentiments became national and international as reporters converged upon the area and the story went public. In August, 1978, President Jimmy Carter declared Love Canal a disaster area. Approximately nine hundred families were evacuated.

Determining Culpability   Very quickly, Hooker faced widespread public condemnation and more than two billion dollars in lawsuits. Consumer activist Ralph Nader denounced Hooker as a "callous corporation" that dumped chemicals into the environment without regard to public safety. A 1979 *Atlantic Monthly* article attacked Hooker, asking whether anyone could expect privately owned corporations to act responsibly and suggesting that their profit motive would naturally lead them to put monetary concerns above health concerns. The U.S. federal government's Environmental Protection Agency (EPA) proceeded to enact many new regulations governing how corporations were to handle their waste products.

Less attention was given to the role of the school board and the local government. Some critics argued that the Love Canal disaster was being mishandled and that the wrong lessons were being learned. They pointed out that Hooker had acted appropriately and that the media and state and federal governments were ignoring the real culprits. The school board had ignored Hooker's repeated warnings, the local government had used its power of condemnation to force the sale against Hooker's will, and the sales contract stated explicitly that upon the sale of the property, all responsibility for its proper maintenance shifted to its new owner, the city of Niagara Falls.

However, there was a sense that it was hard to fault the city's motive of wanting to build a school inexpensively. There was also the challenge of assigning legal liability to nonprofit organizations acting in the public interest. The difficulty of mounting legal challenges against the power of government was well understood, and there was little precedent for singling out individual members of school boards or local government officials who used their legally granted powers. Additionally, there was no possibility that the local government would be able to pay the hundreds of millions of dollars in anticipated liability and cleanup costs, so attention focused on finding deeper pockets from which to extract the funds.

Impact   While long-term studies showed no increase in rates of cancer, birth defects, or other ailments among residents of the area since the 1970's, toxic chemicals were nonetheless exposed and released into the environment. As a result, residents of the area were frightened, were dislocated, and suffered large losses of property value; hundreds of millions of dollars were spent on cleanup and litigation; and there was little agreement about who was responsible or how to prevent future exposures.

Subsequent Events   From the late 1970's until early 2004, when the Love Canal area was declared clean and safe again, millions of dollars were spent on cleanup, a result of a 1980 approval by Congress of the Superfund bill sponsored by Senator Al Gore. The event contributed to the increased amount of government regulation of waste disposal and the creation of projects such as Superfund as well as to ongoing debates in politics and economics about whether private or public institutions are more likely to behave responsibly with respect to the proper handling of potentially dangerous waste.

Residents of Love Canal in New York attend a neighborhood protest. (AP/Wide World Photos)

Further Reading

Beauchamp, Tom. "Hooker Chemical and Love Canal." In *Cases in Society, Business, and Ethics.* Upper Saddle River, N.J.: Prentice-Hall, 1998. A clear survey of the Love Canal events, highlighting the ethical and political controversies involved.

"Love Canal." *The Atlantic Monthly,* December, 1979. An early journalistic reaction to the events at Love Canal, blaming Hooker Chemical and other corporations for causing a toxic waste crisis in New York and around the nation.

New York State Department of Health. *New York State Department of Health Newsletter,* April, 2002. New York State's announcement of the findings of its long-term study of the health effects on residents.

Whalen, Robert P. *Love Canal—Public Health Time Bomb: A Special Report to the Governor and the Legislature.* New York State Department of Health, September, 1978. Physician Whalen's official report on the disaster

Zuesse, Eric. "The Truth Seeps Out." *Reason*, February, 1981. An early journalistic and detailed history of Love Canal highlighting the roles of the school board and of local government.
Stephen R. C. Hicks

See also Carter, Jimmy; Environmental movement; Environmental Protection Agency (EPA); Nader, Ralph.

■ Love Story

Identification Motion picture
Director Arthur Hiller (1923-   )
Date Released in 1970

This tragic drama appealed to an audience seeking love, not war, but who were nonetheless reconciled to unhappy endings.

Erich Segal turned his script for *Love Story* into a novel, which appeared at the same time as the film and became a best-seller, which added to the impact of the motion picture. Like most great love stories, the film ends tragically, but it also contains romantic elements of William Shakespeare's *Romeo and Juliet* and the fairy tale of Cinderella. Jenny Cavalleri (played by Ali MacGraw), a Radcliffe student, is the daughter of an Italian American baker. Oliver Barrett IV (Ryan O'Neal), a hockey-playing student from Harvard, is the son of a wealthy lawyer whose family connection to Harvard is reflected in the name of Barrett Hall on the Harvard campus.

Jenny is daunted by the socioeconomic disparity between herself and Oliver. Oliver, whose attraction to her is partly based on his desire to rebel against his father, is determined to bridge the class gap. The theme of true love overcoming class differences and parental opposition has long appealed to mass audiences, and the theme of youthful rebellion against father figures and all forms of authority appealed to a generation of filmgoers concerned about the war in Vietnam and rights for black Americans and women.

When Oliver defies his father and is on his own, he marries Jenny, who now has her "prince," but the fairy tale lacks a "happily ever after" ending. Jenny is diagnosed with a fatal illness and dies after the couple move from Cambridge to New York City, where Oliver has a job with a prestigious law firm. For the film's audience, this tragic ending seemed to relate to the situation in Vietnam: In addition to acknowledging the death of the young and the beautiful, the film also implied that, just as in the Vietnam War, things do not always end happily. Moreover, the film's conflict between generations (Oliver and his father) was paralleled by the very real conflict in American society between the young people protesting in the streets and the establishment figures in power. Jenny tried to reconcile Oliver and his father, but while Juliet's death brought together the Montagues and the Capulets in *Romeo and Juliet,* Jenny's death is not enough to bring the two men together. Their failure to relate is essentially a failure to communicate, a situation mirrored in American politics and society.

Impact In addition to being the top-grossing film of 1970, *Love Story* received an Academy Award for Best Musical Score and garnered several additional nominations, among them Best Picture and Best Director for Arthur Hiller, who also won a Golden Globe for directing. *Oliver's Story*, a 1978 sequel, met the fate of most sequels—failure at the box office.

Further Reading

Emery, Robert J. *The Directors: Take Two.* New York: Watson-Guptil, 2000.

Lieman, Sergio. *Robert Wise on His Films.* Los Angeles: Directors Guild, 1995.

Phillips, Gene. *Major Film Directors of the American and British Cinema.* Bethlehem, Pa.: Lehigh University Press, 1999.
Thomas L. Erskine

See also Film in the United States.

M

■ McGovern, George

Identification American politician
Born July 19, 1922; Avon, South Dakota

In addition to being the presidential nominee of the Democratic Party in 1972, McGovern was arguably the leading public voice in opposition to the Vietnam War and a tireless advocate for eradicating hunger.

As a student at Dakota Wesleyan University, McGovern put his education on hold in 1943 to enlist in the U.S. Army Air Force during World War II. For his service as a bomber pilot in the European theater of the war, McGovern was awarded the Distinguished Flying Cross, returning to his hometown of Mitchell, South Dakota, a hero. After finishing his college degree in 1946, McGovern briefly considered following in his father's footsteps, enrolling in a theological seminary in Illinois. However, he transferred to Northwestern University, where he earned his Ph.D. in history in 1953.

The same year that he completed his Ph.D., McGovern undertook the challenge of organizing the moribund Democratic Party in South Dakota. As a result of his grassroots efforts, several Democrats were elected at all levels of government in the once Republican-majority state. One of those elected was McGovern himself, who, in 1956, won a seat in the U.S. House of Representatives. After two terms as representative and an unsuccessful bid for the U.S. Senate in 1960, McGovern joined the administration of John F. Kennedy as director of the Food for Peace program.

Thus began a new chapter in the prairie statesman's life: crusader for the hungry. McGovern revolutionized not only the Food for Peace program but also the way in which the country dealt with agricultural surpluses and food aid throughout the 1960's and 1970's. He emerged as the leader of the anti-hunger movement worldwide, work he would continue during his long tenure in the Senate and after his political career ended. From school lunches to nutritional programs, from support for the domestic farmer to international agricultural exports, McGovern's fingerprints were evident on the full range of U.S. food programs.

Senator and Presidential Candidate In 1962, McGovern was successful in his bid to win a seat in the U.S. Senate, where he would serve three terms, being reelected in 1968 and 1974. In 1969, McGovern chaired the Commission on Party Structure and Delegate Selection, which instituted sweeping reforms—making the process more democratic and open to all people—in the way that the Democratic Party selected its presidential nominees. Fittingly, in 1971, the reform leader became the first Democrat to announce candidacy for the 1972 presidential campaign. Presidents Lyndon B. Johnson and Richard Nixon continued to escalate U.S. involvement in Vietnam, and the United States grappled with the meaning of this new kind of war. From his seat in the U.S. Senate and in lecture halls on college campuses across the country, McGovern became the voice and conscience of the antiwar movement. He introduced legislation to limit American involvement in Vietnam and demanded answers to questions that two White Houses avoided.

By the standards of the day, McGovern's announcement of his presidency campaign came very early. However, the early announcement, tireless grassroots organizing, his notoriety as a leading critic of the Vietnam War, and his following in the youth movement on college campuses across the country helped him secure his party's nomination among a crowded, competitive field.

The campaign suffered a setback when McGovern's vice presidential selection, Senator Thomas F. Eagleton of Missouri, was discovered to have been hospitalized for mental health problems in the previous decade. McGovern was forced to replace Eagleton, after pledging to stand by his side, ultimately selecting R. Sargent Shriver, former director of the Peace Corps and a Kennedy relative. Although Mc-

Govern lost to incumbent Richard M. Nixon by one of the largest margins in presidential election history—winning only Massachusetts and the District of Columbia—he did earn 38 percent of the popular vote and succeeded in building support for ending the war in Vietnam.

Impact George McGovern's antiwar stance and his troubles with his running mate likely cost him his seat in the Senate and the presidency. It is equally likely, however, that his public actions aided the antiwar movement and hastened the ending of the Vietnam War. His idealism, compassion, and liberalism influenced the Democratic Party during the decade, just as his life's work continued to inspire the peace and antihunger movements.

Subsequent Events The former presidential candidate lost his bid for a fourth term in the Senate in 1980 and briefly campaigned for the presidency again in 1984. McGovern's "retirement" from politics freed up time for him to pursue a host of other interests, all the while continuing his work for peace and against hunger. He continued to publish books and editorials at a prolific rate. He served as the head of the Middle East Policy Council from 1991 to 1998, and he was appointed U.S. ambassador to the United Nations' Food and Agricultural Organization in 1998. McGovern's life work was recognized in 2000 when he was awarded the Presidential Medal of Freedom by President Bill Clinton. One year later, the United Nations appointed McGovern as the first global ambassador on hunger with its World Food Programme.

Further Reading

Anson, Robert Sam. *McGovern: A Biography.* New York: Holt, Rinehart & Winston, 1972. Gives interesting insight into McGovern's activities during the decade.

Knock, Tom. "Come Home, America: The Story of George McGovern." In *Vietnam and the American Political Tradition: The Politics of Dissent,* edited by Randall B. Woods. Cambridge, U.K.: Cambridge University Press, 2003. Notes McGovern's important role within the antiwar movement.

George McGovern campaigns for president in January, 1972. (Barry Sweet/Landov)

McGovern, George. *An American Journey: The Presidential Campaign Speeches of George McGovern.* New York: Random House, 1974. Gives good insight into McGovern's rhetoric and the issues that he used to galvanize support.

_____. *Grassroots: The Autobiography of George McGovern.* New York: Random House, 1977. McGovern's life and politics in his own words.

Watson, Robert P., ed. *George McGovern: A Political Life, a Political Legacy.* Pierre: South Dakota State Historical Society, 2004. Essays discuss such topics as McGovern's upbringing, military service, and congressional and senatorial terms.

Robert P. Watson

See also Antiwar demonstrations; Eagleton, Thomas F.; Elections in the United States, 1972; Liberalism in U.S. politics; Nixon, Richard M.; United Nations; Vietnam War.

■ Mailer, Norman

Identification   American novelist and nonfiction
writer
Born   January 31, 1923; Long Branch, New Jersey

*Mailer, a renowned novelist and nonfiction essayist by
the 1970's, blended both literary approaches and became
an important representative of the New Journalism movement.*

By the 1970's, American novelist Norman Mailer became one of the foremost practitioners of what
writer and social critic Tom Wolfe popularized as
"The New Journalism." Employing the techniques
that Wolfe and others were developing, Mailer dis-
carded any pretense at complete journalistic neutrality and described his own internal emotions. He
used this approach in his National Book Award- and
Pulitzer Prize-winning book *The Armies of the Night*
(1968).

His observations on the antiwar demonstrations
and political conventions of the late 1960's provided
a launching base for his 1970's journalism. In 1969,
Mailer wrote a long article on the Apollo Moon landing for *Life* magazine. The resulting book, *Of a Fire on
the Moon* (1970), explored the cultural and philosophical meanings of that space venture. Speaking
as Aquarius, the observer, he discussed the technological aggressiveness of the space program as being
a reflection of a white Anglo-Saxon domination of
the United States.

In 1971, Mailer returned to two other favorite
themes, boxing and sexuality. In *King of the Hill*, he
analyzed the Muhammad Ali-Joe Frazier heavyweight boxing match, continuing his longtime personal and literary interest in pugilism, a theme he
featured again in *The Fight* (1975). *The Prisoner of Sex*
(1971) served as a rejoinder to the women's liberation movement and to feminist attacks on his writings by lambasting what he considered fallacies in
feminist viewpoints.

Existential Errands (1972) mixed miscellaneous
political writing and cultural criticism in the fashion
of Mailer's previous collections, dating back to *Advertisements for Myself* (1959). In it, he examined such
subjects as filmmaking and photography, Black
Power, interstate highways, the Vietnam War, the
John F. Kennedy assassination, and his own run for

mayor of New York in 1969. *St. George and the Godfather* (1972) reprised his political reporting format
begun in 1960, when he covered the Kennedy election. Much like *Miami and the Siege of Chicago* (1969),
which reported on the Republican and Democratic
Conventions of 1968, Mailer updated the technique
to chronicle the George McGovern and Richard
Nixon presidency campaigns.

Mailer detoured from his journalistic style to de-
liberate on the life of film icon Marilyn Monroe. A
beautiful book combining photographs and Mailer's provocative text, *Marilyn* (1973) paid homage
to the Hollywood star and elevated her to a cultural
symbol of the age. In 1974, in *The Faith of Graffiti*, he
made a strong case for graffiti both as an exuberant
expression of individualism and as an important art
form and not simply a defacement of private and
public property.

In 1979, Mailer delivered another Pulitzer Prize-
winning book, *The Executioner's Song*. Mailer related
the tale of Gary Gilmore, the Utah murderer executed in 1977. The story allowed Mailer ample opportunity to explore the role of personal and institutional violence in American society.

Impact   Stylistically, *The Executioner's Song* and Norman Mailer's other 1970's journalism puzzled critics, who wondered whether it represented a retreat
from the brash stances of the New Journalism or
whether it signified the most subtle blending of fiction and fact. In either case, Mailer during this decade fortified his claim as a preeminent cultural
critic.

Further Reading

Lennon, J. Michael, ed. *Conversations with Norman
    Mailer.* Jackson: University Press of Mississippi,
    1988.
Merrill, Robert. *Norman Mailer Revisited.* New York:
    Twayne, 1992.
Wenke, Joseph. *Mailer's America.* Hanover, N.H.: Uni-
    versity Press of New England, 1987.

Thomas L. Altherr

See also   Antiwar demonstrations; Apollo space
program; Boxing; Death penalty; Elections in the
United States, 1972; Feminism; Gilmore, Gary; Graffiti; Journalism in the United States; Literature in
the United States; New Journalism; Wolfe, Tom.

■ Mamet, David

Identification American playwright and director
Born November 30, 1947; Chicago, Illinois

During his rise to prominence during the 1970's, Mamet became known as one of the most distinctive voices in American theater.

David Mamet began writing for the stage in Chicago in the early 1970's and became associated with that city and with American regional theater. Many of his earliest produced plays were works of children's theater, a fact somewhat surprising to those familiar with his better-known adult plays, which are often vulgar and disturbing. Among his earliest successes was the one-act _Duck Variations_ (pr. 1972), a play about two elderly Jewish men sitting on a bench in Chicago, speculating about the nature of life and the universe while they watch the ducks on Lake Michigan.

The first of Mamet's plays to be performed in New York was _Sexual Perversity in Chicago_ (pr. 1974). As the title suggests, the play is an exploration of the problems and loneliness inherent in human relationships conducted primarily on the physical level. The next of his plays to open in New York was the very successful _American Buffalo_ (pr. 1975), set in a junk shop and tracing an ill-fated robbery attempt by three inept, small-time crooks. The play contains several elements characteristic of much of Mamet's work—a grubby setting, working-class (or even criminal-class) male characters, and stylized, vulgar dialogue. Both _Sexual Perversity in Chicago_ and _American Buffalo_ won prestigious Obie Awards for Off-Broadway theater in 1976, securing Mamet's reputation as an important new voice on the American stage.

In addition to the Obies, Mamet won a number of other important awards in the mid- and late 1970's, including a Rockefeller Foundation Grant (1976), a Columbia Broadcasting System (CBS) fellowship to the Yale School of Drama (1976-1977), a New York Drama Critics Circle Award for _American Buffalo_ (1977), and an Outer Critics Circle Award (1978). He also served as a visiting lecturer and artist-in-residence at several institutions, including Marlboro College (1970), Goddard College (1971-1973), the Illinois Council for the Arts (1974), and the University of Chicago (1975-1976 and 1979). His other contributions to the stage in this period included directing plays (his own and those of other playwrights) and serving as founder, artistic director, and board member of regional theaters in Chicago.

Impact David Mamet's dark and disturbing view of American society became an important force in the theater world during the 1970's. His original voice and vision were from the start characterized by rapid-fire, highly stylized language, heavily laced with profanity and evoking a deeply masculine world of competition and anxiety. In later years, he continued writing and directing plays and also went on to expand his writing talents into other media, most notably screenplays and essays.

Further Reading

Bigsby, C. W. E. _David Mamet._ London: Methuen, 1985.

Carroll, Dennis. _David Mamet._ New York: St. Martin's Press, 1987.

Kane, Leslie, ed. _David Mamet: A Casebook._ New York: Garland Press, 1991.

Janet E. Gardner

See also Theater in the United States.

David Mamet. (Brigitte Lacombe)

■ Manilow, Barry

Identification American singer-songwriter
Born June 17, 1946; Brooklyn, New York

A pop-music superstar during the mid- to late 1970's, Manilow began the decade as accompanist and music director for Bette Midler and ended it with several of his own number-one hit singles under his belt.

During the 1970's, Barry Manilow's career developed from that of accompanist and commercial jingle writer to superstar. During the early part of the decade, he played piano as backup for Bette Midler in New York's Continental Baths, a Turkish bath house for gay men. He was invited to become Midler's music director and worked with her for the next three years. Manilow's musical arrangements of such songs as "Chapel of Love," "Delta Dawn," and "Leader of the Pack" helped Midler win her first Grammy Award for Best New Artist for her album *The Divine Miss M* (1972). Meanwhile, Manilow was still earning money as a commercial jingle writer and singer. Well-known songs for McDonald's, Dr. Pepper, Band-Aids, and State Farm Insurance, among many others, were written, performed, or arranged by Manilow.

Manilow came into his own with his first hit single, "Mandy," which appeared on his album *Barry Manilow II* (1974) and reached number one on the *Billboard* pop music chart in 1975. Other hits soon followed, including "I Write the Songs," "Even Now," "Looks Like We Made It," and his disco hit "Copacabana (at the Copa)." Following the release of "Mandy," Manilow became popular to a more mainstream audience. Teenage girls and homemakers alike enjoyed his music. He began playing concerts to sold-out crowds, and, despite some negative reviewers who found his work too saccharine, his records continued to make it to the top of the charts. In 1976, he won the Song of the Year Grammy Award for "I Write the Songs." "Copacabana (at the Copa)" earned him his second Grammy Award for Best Male Pop Vocal Performance in 1978. His Broadway engagement titled *Barry Manilow on Broadway* won him a Tony Award.

By 1979, Manilow had produced eight albums, including his *Live* album and his *Greatest Hits Volume I.* Additionally, the American Broadcasting Company (ABC) network produced three television specials for him between 1977 and 1979. In 1977, *The Barry Manilow Special* won an Emmy Award for Best Special of the Year.

Impact Barry Manilow's broad appeal during the decade and his talent for arranging and composing a variety of music, including old swing songs, pop music, and show tunes, launched him into superstardom. He remained popular in the 1980's and continued to perform into the twenty-first century.

Further Reading

Butler, Patricia. *Barry Manilow: The Biography.* New York: Music Sales, 2002.
Manilow, Barry. *Sweet Life: Adventures on the Way to Paradise.* New York: McGraw-Hill, 1987.

Pamela Hayes-Bohanan

See also Disco; Music; Singer-songwriters.

■ Manson Family

Identification A religious cult led by Charles Manson

The brutal murder of seven wealthy Los Angeles residents by cult leader Manson and his brainwashed, drug-ravaged followers delivered a wake-up call to the United States to take stock of its violent pop culture.

Charles Manson was a bearded, charismatic spiritual leader who viewed himself as both Christ and Satan. He managed to persuade his followers—or, as they came to be known, his "Family"—to take part in a mass murder in an attempt to set off a racial armageddon. Manson, who saw himself as "the fifth angel" and the enormously popular Beatles as the other four, called his radical philosophy "Helter Skelter," after the Beatles' song from the *White Album* (1968). Manson believed that the American black population needed to be shown how to bring about "Helter Skelter," and it was up to the Manson Family to show them how to carry it out.

The Crime On the evening of August 9, 1969, Manson and his entourage went on a killing spree and brutally massacred twenty-six-year-old Hollywood actor Sharon Tate, who was the wife of film director Roman Polanski and eight months pregnant. The group also killed twenty-five-year-old coffee heiress Abigail Folger, her thirty-two-year-old boyfriend Voytek Frykowski, and the thirty-six-year-old famous hair stylist Jay Sebring at Tate's home on Cielo Drive in the canyons just above Beverly Hills, California.

Tate's housekeeper, Winifred Chapman, arrived the following morning to find one body on the lawn, another in a parked car (who turned out to be the caretaker's teenage friend), and pools of blood inside the house. Police found the word "Pig" written in blood on the front door.

During the same night, Leno and Rosemary LaBianca, residents of the Los Feliz neighborhood, were similarly murdered by Manson's gang. The word "War" had been carved in Leno's flesh, and his wife had been stabbed forty-one times. "Death To Pigs," "Rise," and "Helter Skelter" had been scrawled throughout the house.

The Trial A bloody fingerprint belonging to one of the Manson Family found at the Tate home and a wallet belonging to Rosemary LaBianca helped convict Manson and his followers: Susan Atkins, Patricia Krenwinkel, and Leslie Van Houten. Manson, who appeared in court with an "X" carved into his forehead, defended himself. His followers, seemingly unperturbed about the consequences of their crime, made every effort to ensure Manson went un-

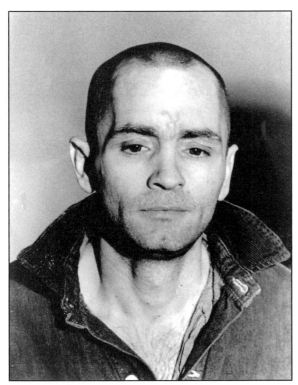

Charles Manson in 1971, just before his death sentence was announced. (AP/Wide World Photos)

harmed. Throughout the trial, Manson created disturbances in the courtroom, and at one point, while his female followers chanted in Latin, he yelled at the judge that someone should cut his head off.

It took twenty-two weeks for the prosecution to present its case. However, the only sentence that defense lawyer Ronald Hughes recited was "Thank you, your Honor, the defendants rest." In response, Manson's followers yelled that they, but not Manson, had indeed committed the murders. Hughes's body was found shortly after.

On January 24, 1971, after nine days of deliberation, all defendants, including Manson, were found guilty of murder. The death penalty was imposed. The women shaved their heads in protest and threatened to murder the jury. The trial of another family member, Charles "Tex" Watson, was delayed, but he was later found guilty of murder, and other Family members, including Robert Beausoleil, Charles Watson, Bruce Davis, and Steve Grogan, were convicted for the murders of other victims. However, the death penalty was abolished in 1972, and the Manson Family was given life sentences instead. Another Manson follower named Lynette "Squeaky" Fromme attempted to assassinate President Gerald R. Ford in Sacramento, California, in 1975, but she was thwarted by the Secret Service.

Impact The Manson Family cult gained prominence in American popular culture by bringing to light its indulgence in free love practices, pseudoreligious rituals, and use of the hallucinogen LSD and through its extreme violence. *Rolling Stone* magazine called Manson "the villain of our time." The murder trial was a media sensation that gave American society reason to pause during the 1970's. What, the country asked, could have brought about such brutal crimes?

Although the media initially labeled the murders as "random and senseless," the victims later came to be regarded as specific targets of the Manson Family by representing, in the cult's mind, everything loathsome and poisonous about American culture. Manson himself is often quoted as saying, "I am only what you made me. I am a reflection of you." Manson and his outrageous "family" cast a dark shadow on the hippie ideal of free love and flower power and brought about the distrust of anyone who smoked pot or wore long hair.

Manson maintained some influence on defiant

Manson Family members Susan Atkins, Patricia Krenwinkel, and Leslie Van Houten are led to the courtroom in 1970 during their trial for the Tate-LaBianca murders. (AP/Wide World Photos)

youth and received more mail than any other United States inmate in the years to come. Seen as the ultimate antiestablishment hero, his face adorned T-shirts and posters, and he remained the ongoing subject of popular films.

Further Reading

Bugliosi, Vincent. *Helter Skelter: The True Story of the Manson Murders.* New York: W. W. Norton, 2001. Written by the prosecuting attorney in the Manson trial, the book expertly details Manson's horrific background and his charismatic hold over his "family." Includes fifty pages of photographs.

King, Greg. *Sharon Tate and the Manson Murders.* New York: Barricade Books, 2000. Biography of Tate, rising Hollywood starlet and Manson Family victim, including her burgeoning career, her marriage to director Roman Polanski, and her role as a member of the Hollywood elite. Describes the search for her killers and the resulting trial. The book focuses on Manson's victims rather than on Manson himself.

Manson, Charles. *Manson in His Own Words.* New York: Grove Press, 1988. Manson describes his childhood and resultant life of crime while providing harsh insight into the making of a deadly criminal mind. Factually relates the Tate-LaBianca murders that sent him to prison. Sixteen pages of photographs.

M. Casey Diana

See also   Cults; Death penalty; Drug use; Ford assassination attempts; Hippies.

■ Marley, Bob

Identification   Jamaican reggae musician
Born   February 6, 1945; Nine Miles, St. Ann Parish, Jamaica
Died   May 11, 1981; Miami, Florida

Marley, popularly known as "the King of Reggae," brought international exposure to Jamaican reggae music and Rastafarianism, the religion from which the music draws inspiration.

Bob Marley, Peter McIntosh, Bunny Livingston, and rhythm players Carlton and Aston Barrett formed the Wailers in the early 1960's. The group obtained regional acclaim with many single recordings. The Wailers became known internationally in 1972 with the Island Records release of *Catch a Fire*, their first commercially successful album. The band's popularity in the United States and Great Britain followed its performance tours, and the band changed its name to Bob Marley and the Wailers.

The second album, *Burnin'* (1973), included the song "I Shot the Sheriff," which created instant fame in the United States as a cover hit by Eric Clapton. By 1975, original members McIntosh and Livingston had left to pursue solo careers, and Marley became an international celebrity. In 1976, the album *Rastaman Vibration* was released, and the Wailers were honored with the *Rolling Stone* Album of the Year Award. In November, 1976, Marley, his wife, Rita, and visitors were attacked by gunmen at his Kingston home two days before giving a free performance at the Smile Jamaica concert. In 1977, another top-selling album, *Exodus*, was listed in the U.S. Top 30 as Americans bought reggae albums despite the widespread popularity of disco.

At the One Love Peace concert in April, 1978, Marley welcomed both Jamaican president Michael Manley and the Opposition party leader Edward Seaga to the stage, where audience members watched as the two political leaders shook hands. On June 15, 1978, Marley was awarded the Peace Medal of the Third World from the United Nations.

Kaya, released in 1978, was somewhat controversial in the U.S. market because of references to Marley's Rastafarian beliefs about the closeness to God (Jah) that could be achieved through smoking ganja (marijuana). Rastafarianism, a Christian religious movement originating in Jamaica's impoverished and oppressed communities, was a lifestyle represented by Marley and other "dreads," as they were called because they wore their hair in dreadlocks. In the last year of his life, Marley contracted cancer but could not be fully treated because of his religious beliefs. He died in a Miami hospital.

Impact   Bob Marley was considered by many to be the first international black superstar. His influence in the United States could be heard throughout the decade as many American musicians, including Johnny Nash, Paul Simon, and Blondie, imported reggae rhythms into their own songs to make their music sound exotic. Marley's contributions to the world peace movement included efforts in Ethiopia and Kenya as well as Jamaica. His funeral in 1981 was attended by hundreds of thousands of mourners, including Jamaica's prime minister.

Further Reading

Marley, Rita, with Hettie Jones. *No Woman, No Cry: My Life with Bob Marley.* New York: Hyperion Books, 2004.

White, Timothy. *Catch a Fire: The Life of Bob Marley.* New York: Henry Holt, 2000.

Susan W. Mills

See also   Drug use; Music; Progressive rock; Religion and spirituality in the United States.

■ Marriage and divorce

Definition   Social institution under which a man and a woman become legally united and the legal dissolution thereof

Delaying of, and alternatives to, traditional marriage, along with increasing instances of divorce, had a significant impact on family life in the 1970's. Subsequently, this foundational element of society changed fairly dramatically during the decade.

Americans have long held the belief that a mercurial emotion such as romantic love should serve as the basis for entry into the institution of marriage. Popular televisions shows of the 1970's such as *Love, American Style* reinforced that message. Another popular show, *Happy Days*, portrayed the American ideal of family life during the 1950's. However, a hit movie of the 1970's, *Love Story* (1970), also showed that love did not always have a fairy-tale, happy ending.

Marriage   Many Americans also held long-standing beliefs that marriage was the only proper context for childbearing and for family formation. Consequently, sex before marriage traditionally was frowned upon. The sexual revolution, which many experts agree ran from the mid-1960's to the mid-1970's and was the second such revolution in the United States during the twentieth century, changed that notion. This revolution was facilitated by more reliable methods of birth control and greater access to abortion that the landmark 1973 Supreme Court case *Roe v. Wade* provided. Premarital sexual alternatives of various sorts were at least implicit in popular television shows such as *Three's Company.*

With more premarital sex occurring, many people delayed getting married, and the fact that more people were seeking even higher levels of education also contributed significantly to this trend. At the beginning of the 1970's, the average ages at first marriage for men and women were 23.2 and 20.8 years, respectively. By the end of that decade, these ages had increased to 24.7 and 22.0 years.

The practice of cohabitation—popularly referred to as "living together"—also contributed to delayed marriage. According to census data, the number of households that appeared to be cohabitational increased by 300 percent during the decade. While living together appeared to be a new phenomenon to many, others viewed it merely as a variation on a traditional American option of common-law marriage. This option was prevalent during the nineteenth century westward movement of pioneer settlers who wanted to start families but had outdistanced gov-

ernment licensing and even religious authorities. Consequently, states retroactively considered people who lived as if they were married to be so legally bound. This type of common-law marriage began to be recognized more widely during the 1970's. While many of those in states that did not recognize common-law marriage did not intend to be legally married when they began to live together, during this period, an increasing number of legal marriages were preceded by cohabitation prior to making these unions legal.

The number of single Americans rose during this period as a result of the combination of social trends. For example, at the beginning of the 1970's, the proportions of twenty- to twenty-four-year-old men and women who were still single were 36 percent and 55 percent, respectively. By the end of that decade, these proportions were 50 percent and 69 percent. For men and women aged twenty-five to twenty-nine, the respective proportions that were still single went from 11 percent and 19 percent

Although some couples chose alternative lifestyles and the divorce rate rose, most young people in the 1970's continued to embrace the concept of marriage and to hold traditional weddings. (NARA)

Number of marriages per 1,000 unmarried women age 15 and older

1960	87.5
1970	76.5
1975	66.9
1980	61.4

Number of divorces per 1,000 unmarried women age 15 and older

1960	9.2
1965	10.6
1970	14.9
1975	20.3
1980	22.6

at the beginning of the decade to 21 percent and 33 percent at decade's end.

Additionally, increased singleness was an inevitable outcome of the positions taken and promoted by such organizations as the National Organization for Women (NOW) and the National Lesbian and Gay Rights Organization. With the increasing independence of women, they were less likely to jump into marriage. Similarly, as those whose attraction was to their same sex received more social legitimacy, they were less likely to marry opposite-sex partners than they may have been previously.

The sexual revolution that had such a large impact on premarital relations also influenced extramarital relations in a variety of ways. There were small but significant increases in the numbers of men and women who reported that they engaged in some form of sex with someone other than their spouses. This ranged from the traditional secret affairs, to consensual "swinging," to the new notion of "open marriage"—in which spouses were free to pursue emotional and sexual attachments with outsiders as long as the marital relationship took precedence.

The delaying and deferring of marriage during the 1970's in favor of the various forms of singleness reflected a sea change in social attitudes. At the height of the baby boom—approximately 1957—more than half of a representative sample of U.S. adults agreed that someone who did not want to get married was selfish, immature, peculiar, or morally flawed. However, two decades later, those who agreed with such descriptions were less than one-third of those polled.

Divorce During this period, the factors that induced people to delay and defer marriage in the first place, as well as to seek various forms of extramarital sexual relations, were also culpable in causing people to end the marriages into which they ultimately entered. While Census statistics show that the legal ending of marriages had been increasing since the bureau first began to measure the trend in 1860, the incidence of divorce reached new highs not previously seen before, or equaled since, the 1970's. The previous year of high divorce rates—1946, as many hurried marriages due to World War II and the deportation of soldiers ultimately broke up—was equaled in 1973 and was exceeded in the following years. The rate peaked around 1978 and 1979, with twenty-three divorced women for every one thousand adult women in the U.S. population, and declined in subsequent years. In 1970, the rate had been eighteen divorced adults per one thousand. Fully one-quarter of the marriages begun in the first year of the decade had ended by 1977.

The incidence of divorce had begun to accelerate during the 1960's. It did so even more dramatically with the introduction of no-fault divorce, which made divorce considerably easier to obtain. Research has shown that the easier it is to obtain a divorce, the more likely it is to happen. When men are less likely to be held responsible for a divorce, they are also less likely to be required to pay alimony, and thus, more likely to consider divorce a viable option.

Another important factor that helped increase the prevalence of legal marital dissolution during this decade was the implications of the women's movement, which asserted that women should not need men and impelled greater movement of women into the paid labor force. Women who can support themselves are far less likely to stay in what they consider an unhappy marriage than those who are economically dependent.

While the 1970's began with more than 70 percent of U.S. households being composed of the traditional nuclear family, divorce had made single-parent families much more common by its end. Single-parent families long had been common in American society, but in the past, they were more likely to be due to the death of a parent.

Divorce became a popular topic in entertainment. The Public Broadcasting System (PBS) aired one of television's first "reality shows" with *An American Family*, which, among countless story lines, had the mother, Pat Loud, telling her husband that she wanted a divorce. A popular film of that decade, *Kramer vs. Kramer* (1979), depicted the difficulties of marital dissolution on adults as well as children.

Remarriage With the increased prevalence of divorce that characterized the 1970's, it was only natural that remarriage would become more prominent in that decade as well—many of those who divorced perhaps were disenchanted with their own particular marriage and not the idea of marriage itself. In the latter part of that decade, almost 90 percent of remarriages involved divorced people, with 28 percent of all U.S. women getting married in 1978 having been previously divorced. Consequently, some sociologists began commenting on what they referred to as a variation on traditional monogamy: serial monogamy, or one partner at a time.

During the 1970's, for those who married young and divorced quickly—those under age twenty-five—more than one-third had remarried within the next year. However, the percentages that remarried quickly declined as age increased, often because there were more likely to be children involved at older ages. The presence of children—and thus, the creation of what academicians refer to as blended or reconstituted families—often slows the remarriage process, but it tends not to suppress ultimate rates of remarriage. Nevertheless, blended families rarely run as smoothly as they did in *The Brady Bunch* television show. Those of the dominant racial categories in the United States (white Americans) remarried more quickly and more often than those of the largest racial minority, African Americans. The gap between these rates grew during the 1970's.

Impact While changes in marriage, including lower rates and later starts, and a growing rate of divorce during the 1970's reshaped the look of the American family, the trends were not entirely new and, in fact, resembled historical trends of families within the United States. This objective reality ran counter to popular perceptions of the "good old days" of American families.

Further Reading

Cherlin, Andrew. "The Trends: Marriage, Divorce, and Remarriage." In *Family in Transition*, edited by Arlene S. Skolnick and Jerome H. Skolnick. 6th ed. Glenview, Ill.: Scott, Foresman, 1989. A prominent sociologist details demographic changes in Americans' marital status.

Coontz, Stephanie. *The Way We Never Were: American Families and the Nostalgia Trap*. New York: Basic Books, 1992. A well-known historian debunks popular misconceptions of families of the past.

_____. *The Way We Really Are: Coming to Terms with America's Changing Families*. New York: Basic Books, 1997. In a follow-up to her acclaimed initial offering, Coontz clarifies the contemporary circumstances of U.S. families.

Davis, James A. "Did Growing Up in the '60's Leave a Permanent Mark on Attitudes and Values? Evidence from the General Social Survey." *Public Opinion Quarterly* 68 (2004): 161-183. A sociologist examines the results of questionnaire research relevant to marital status in the era.

Duvall, Evelyn, M., and Brent C. Miller. *Marriage and Family Development*. 6th ed. New York: Harper & Row, 1985. A classic text written by a pioneer of family studies and one of her students.

Furstenberg, F., Jr., et al. "Growing Up Is Harder to Do." *Contexts* (Summer, 2004): 33-49. A sociological examination of changes in family structure written for lay audiences.

Model, John. *Into One's Own: From Youth to Adulthood in the United States, 1920-1975*. Berkeley: University of California Press, 1989. A prominent historian explores changes in trends such as marital status that are relevant to the transition to adulthood.

Reiss, Ira L., and Gary R. Lee. *Family Systems in America*. 4th ed. New York: Holt, Rinehart and Winston, 1988. A classic sociological text about all aspects of U.S. families written by an expert of sexual studies and one of his students.

Thornton, Arland, and Linda Young-DeMarco. "Four Decades of Trends in Attitudes Toward Family Issues in the United States." *Journal of Marriage and the Family* 63 (2001): 1009-1037. A historical study of opinion research relevant to family issues such as marriage and divorce.

Scott Magnuson-Martinson

■ Martin, Steve

Identification American comedian and actor
Born August 14, 1945; Waco, Texas

At a time when most popular comedians were known for their politically or socially confrontational humor, Martin emphasized the traditional slapstick virtues of split-second timing and unpredictable absurdity, a combination that proved hugely successful in his records, television shows, radio performances, books, and films.

When Steve Martin burst onto the national entertainment scene in 1976 as a white-suited, prematurely gray, banjo-playing "wild and crazy guy," few in his audience knew that he had already spent years honing his craft by writing for popular television comedy shows—including *The Smothers Brothers Comedy Hour* and *The Glen Campbell Good Time Hour*—and paying the dues of an itinerant performer. To viewers, his emergence had all the trappings of overnight success. As one of the first comedians to benefit from the exposure of a Home Box Office (HBO) special and a guest-host slot on *Saturday Night Live*, Martin quickly joined the likes of George Carlin and Richard Pryor in a relatively select group of stand-up comedians who enjoyed large-scale celebrity status.

What made Martin unique was not only his unthreateningly dapper appearance and manic spontaneity but also the fact that his entire act was essentially a parody of the acts of other comedians, specifically the lugubriously self-congratulatory nightclub variety. He was also the decade's first "multithreat" comedian, enhancing his routines with lowbrow sight gags (such as a false arrow through the head) and song parodies, often used simultaneously.

By 1978, he had earned two platinum albums for *Let's Get Small* (1977) and *A Wild and Crazy Guy* (1978), had a gold single with "King Tut," and had written the best-selling book *Cruel Shoes* (1977). He had also popularized, with Dan Aykroyd, the "Festrunk Brothers"—two haplessly hip Czechoslovakians obsessed with "swinging" who soon became among the best-loved recurring characters on *Saturday Night Live*.

Ironically, it was Martin's very popularity that brought about the end of his live performances, as the growth of his audience and its increasing proportion of adolescents required him to abandon the intimacy of nightclubs and theaters and to play stadium-sized venues inhospitable to any but the broadest of his routines. His starring role in the film comedy *The Jerk* (1979), rather than representing a detour, indicated the direction that his career would take in subsequent years.

Impact The enthusiasm that greeted Steve Martin's unapologetic silliness opened the door for comedians of a similar inclination, including Robin Williams, Andy Kaufman, Martin Mull, and Howie Mandel, and helped establish the *Saturday Night Live* guest-host slot as an influential launching pad for comic talent. Moreover, his success in a variety of genres helped increase the professional opportunities for comedians of all persuasions and to broaden the very definition of the word "comedian" itself.

Further Reading

Martin, Steve. *Cruel Shoes*. New York: G. P. Putnam's Sons, 1977.
Miller, James A., and Tom Shales. *Live from New York: An Uncensored History of "Saturday Night Live," as Told by Its Stars, Writers, and Guests*. New York: Little, Brown, 2002.
Walker, Morris Wayne. *Steve Martin: The Magic Years*. New York: S.P.I. Books, 2001.

Arsenio Orteza

■ Marvin v. Marvin

Identification Legal case regarding cohabitation
Date Decided on December 27, 1976
Place California Supreme Court

The Marvin *case began a trend that recognized the right of unmarried cohabitants to enter into express contracts to pool resources and acquire property. Express agreements between unmarried adults living together are unenforceable only to the extent that they are based explicitly on unlawful "meretricious" (sexual) services.*

Plaintiff Michelle Triola Marvin, a Las Vegas dancer and supper club singer, met actor Lee Marvin and moved in with him in 1964. When they split up seven years later, she claimed that she had cooked and cleaned for him and had taken care of him after he had been drinking. She claimed that he told her, "What I have is yours and what you have is mine," that they agreed to hold themselves out to the general public as husband and wife, and that he agreed to support her.

California law required that married persons split the assets of their marriage (community property). Although the Marvins were not formally married, Michelle believed that she was entitled to money from Lee because she fulfilled her obligations under the agreement and gave up her career as an entertainer in order to devote herself to the defendant. When Lee disagreed, the dispute went to court. Celebrity divorce lawyer Marvin Mitchelson asserted Michelle's claim to Lee Marvin's earnings of more than one million dollars. The so-called palimony suit produced widespread media publicity.

The case demonstrated that courts may inquire into the conduct of the parties in order to determine whether it indicates an implied contract or implied agreement of partnership or joint venture, thereby setting an important legal precedent. Moreover, a nonmarital partner may recover in *quantum meruit* (the reasonable value) of the household services rendered minus the reasonable value of support received if he or she can prove that the services were rendered with the expectation of monetary reward. The suit relied on a doctrine in contract law known as "quasi" or "implied" contract, in which courts may infer a legally enforceable agreement from the circumstances of the parties' dealings, even though they had not entered into any written agreement.

Impact A spouse's right to support or property arises from the spouse's status as a married person. The *Marvin* court case expressly declined to treat unmarried cohabitants like married persons. Rather, it ruled that a nonmarital partner's right to support or to property is dependent upon proof of some underlying basis, such as the existence of an express or implied contract or some other legal claim. Although the case applied specifically only in California, other states have since applied the same principles to con-

tracts between unmarried couples, both heterosexual and homosexual.

Subsequent Events The case was sent back to the trial court for further proceedings. In 1981, the trial court in *Marvin II* found that the parties had never agreed to share their property and that Lee Marvin did not agree to support Michelle. Nonetheless, the court awarded Michelle $104,000 for the purpose of rehabilitation or training to learn new employable skills.

Further Reading

Ball, Howard. *The Supreme Court in the Intimate Lives of Americans: Birth, Sex, Marriage, Childrearing, and Death.* New York: New York University Press, 2002.

Booth, Alan, and Crouter, Ann C., eds. *Just Living Together: Implications of Cohabitation for Children, Families, and Social Policy.* Mahwah, N.J.: Lawrence Erlbaum, 2002.

Marcia J. Weiss

See also Cohabitation; Marriage and divorce.

■ *Mary Hartman, Mary Hartman*

Identification Television comedy series
Producer Norman Lear (1922-   )
Date Aired from 1976 to 1977

The satiric soap opera became a hit in syndication after being rejected by the major networks for its black humor.

Mary Hartman, Mary Hartman was developed by Norman Lear, the producer of *All in the Family,* who hoped that his new program would air as a daytime soap opera. When the three television networks found its dark humor too controversial, Lear sold it into syndication. The show quickly became a hit, with thirty-minute episodes running five nights a week after the late news in most major markets. Most of the first twenty episodes were directed by Emmy Award-winner Joan Darling, television's first female director.

The series revolved around Mary Hartman, a suburban housewife in fictional Fernwood, Ohio. Each episode opens with the syrupy theme song of soaring violins, punctuated by Mary's mother, Martha Shumway (played by Dody Goodman), calling "Mary Hartman. Mary Hartman!" Mary was played by Louise Lasser (the former wife and early costar of Woody Allen). With pageboy bangs and long braids, she lurches wide-eyed and dazed from one bizarre crisis to the next, often with a cigarette in her hand. Her husband, Tom (Greg Mullavey), is impotent with her but contracts a venereal disease while having an affair. Their sullen daughter, Heather (Claudia Lamb), is kidnapped by a mass murderer. Mary's younger sister, Cathy (Debralee Scott), is rude and promiscuous; their grandfather (Victor Kilian) is the Fernwood Flasher.

Mary's best friend, Loretta Haggers (Mary Kay Place), a buxom blond with a heart of gold who aspires to become a country-western star, is paralyzed after a car accident involving a station wagon full of nuns. When Mary brings an ill neighbor a bowl of her chicken soup, the man, who has been washing his medicine down with whiskey, becomes sleepy and drowns in the soup while Mary and his wife chat. Through all of life's crises, Mary frets over such domestic challenges as the possibility of waxy yellow buildup on her kitchen floor.

Frustrated and depressed, Mary is flattered by the attentions of Dennis Foley (Bruce Solomon), a local police sergeant who is madly in love with her. She skittishly resists his interest at first; when they finally begin an affair, he has a heart attack. In the first season's finale, Mary has a nervous breakdown on a talk show on which she represents an average housewife.

Citing the strain of appearing in a daily television show, Lasser left the show during its second season. Her absence was explained by having her desert Tom and Heather to run off with Sergeant Foley. The show continued under the name *Forever Fernwood*, but without Mary the ratings declined and the series was cancelled six months after Lasser left.

Impact *Mary Hartman, Mary Hartman* was a darkly comic parody of soap operas and consumerism. The show's lead character was a constant viewer of such fictional shows as *Tears of Our Years*, and her life was guided by advertising slogans. Unlike in typical soap operas, the characters were lower-middle-class factory workers and aproned housewives. Heather was unlike the perky but mischievous children usually seen on television, and Cathy's open promiscuity was daring for television in the 1970's.

Further Reading

Marc, David. *Comic Visions: Television Comedy and American Culture.* 2d ed. Malden, Mass.: Blackwell, 1997.

Marc, David, and Robert J. Thompson. *Prime Time, Prime Movers: From "I Love Lucy" to "L.A. Law"—*

America's Greatest TV Shows and the People Who Created Them. Boston: Little, Brown, 1992.

Ozersky, Josh, et al. *Archie Bunker's America: TV in an Era of Change, 1968-1978.* Carbondale: Southern Illinois University Press, 2003.

Irene Struthers Rush

See also *All in the Family*; Allen, Woody; *Mary Tyler Moore Show, The; Maude; Rhoda*; Sitcoms; Television in the United States.

■ *Mary Tyler Moore Show, The*

Identification Television situation comedy
Date Aired September, 1970, to September, 1977

This highly successful television show featured a single, professional woman as the lead character.

When it first aired in 1970, *The Mary Tyler Moore Show* was the only major television show featuring a single woman in the starring role. It was a situation comedy that relied on the relationships of the ensemble cast to develop the plots. Mary Tyler Moore portrayed the main character, Mary Richards, a woman in her thirties who had just ended a live-in relationship with a boyfriend. Richards was a television producer at WJM-TV, a mediocre television station in Minneapolis, and she lived alone in an apartment.

Richards's emotional and social life revolved around the people with whom she interacted at work: news director Lou Grant (played by Ed Asner), newswriter Murray Slaughter (Gavin MacLeod), anchorman Ted Baxter (Ted Knight), and Sue Ann Nivens (Betty White), the man-hungry "Happy Homemaker." She also shared experiences with two women in her apartment building: her best friend, Rhoda Morgenstern (Valerie Harper), and her landlady, Phyllis Lindstrom (Cloris Leachman).

Although *The Mary Tyler Moore Show* was primarily a comedy, the show also dealt with a number of serious issues, including premarital sex, divorce, and freedom of the press. The character, in some ways, mirrored the desires of feminist women in the 1970's. However, the show also stimulated disagreement among feminist critics because of its contradictory messages. Richards enjoyed her independence, liked her job, and led an active social life. At the same time, however, her character often seemed weak and childlike. For example, Richards was the only character on the show who referred to her boss as "Mr. Grant." Her independent image seemed to

Mary Tyler Moore as Mary Richards and Ed Asner as Lou Grant from The Mary Tyler Moore Show. (CBS/Landov)

wither when her character was confronted by strong characters on the show. At work, she acted more like a sister or mother than a producer when interacting with her male coworkers.

Impact   Despite having some critics, *The Mary Tyler Moore Show* was embraced by many Americans and earned twenty-nine Emmy Awards, including three for Outstanding Comedy Series and numerous others for the actors, writers, and directors. Three of the characters from the show became the stars of the successful spin-offs: *Rhoda, Phyllis,* and *Lou Grant. The Mary Tyler Moore Show* set the pace for the many ensemble comedies that would come after it, including *Taxi, Cheers,* and *Friends.* It continued to air in syndication years after its debut.

Further Reading

Douglas, Susan J. "The Rise of the Bionic Bimbo." In *Where the Girls Are.* New York: Random House, 1994.

Dow, Bonnie. "Hegemony, Feminist Criticism, and *The Mary Tyler Moore Show." Critical Studies in Mass Communication* 7, no. 3 (September, 1990): 261-275.

Rabinovitz, Lauren. "Sitcoms and Single Moms: Representations of Feminism on American TV." *Cinema Journal* 29, no. 1 (Fall, 1989): 3-19.

Sherri Ward Massey

See also   Feminism; Sitcoms; *Taxi*; Television in the United States; Women in the workforce.

■ **M*A*S*H**

Identification   American television series
Date   Aired from September, 1972, to February, 1983

M*A*S*H was television's first dark comedy, combining comic irreverence with the serious subjects of war—in this case, the Korean War—and death.

The television series *M*A*S*H* began as a book, written by Richard Hornberger (under the pen name Richard Hooker) and based on his one-and-a-half-year experience as a surgeon with a Mobile Army Surgical Hospital (MASH) unit in Korea. The novel, rejected seventeen times until William Morrow Publishing saw its promise, became a best-seller. Filmmaker Robert Altman produced a highly successful film version in 1970, which led to Twentieth Century-Fox's decision to create a pilot for television and eventually a series. With Gene Reynolds as producer-director, Larry Gelbart as writer, and Burt Metcalfe as casting director and associate producer, the basic concepts behind the success of *M*A*S*H* the film were translated into *M*A*S*H* the television series.

The Actors   Playing the part of chief surgeon Captain Benjamin Franklin "Hawkeye" Pierce was Alan Alda. Both Reynolds and Gelbart felt that Alda was the only choice for this key role. Gelbart described Alda, with his humor and humanism, as "the linchpin" holding the show together. After reading Gelbart's script for the pilot, Alda remarked, "It was the best pilot script I had ever read." His only reservation was that the subject of war not be taken lightly. Alda was one of the three cast members who stayed with the show for its duration. Over the course of the series, Alda also directed and wrote a number of episodes.

Other cast members were McLean Stevenson,

playing Lieutenant Colonel Henry Blake, commander in charge of the 4077th M*A*S*H unit. Unhappy with working conditions, Stevenson left the show at the end of its third season. The manner of his character's departure from the show provoked more comment than perhaps any television show to date. Although the cast knew that Stevenson was leaving, they did not know that his character would die on his way back home. As Corporal Walter "Radar" O'Reilly (Gary Burghoff) reads the telegram announcing Blake's death, the shock on the faces of the cast is real. In *TV Guide*'s survey of the "One Hundred Greatest Episodes of All Time," this *M*A*S*H* episode, titled "Abyssinia, Henry," was number twenty. Blake's job was filled by Colonel Sherman T. Potter, played by Harry Morgan. Hawkeye's fellow surgeon and partner in mischief was Captain "Trapper John" McIntyre, played by Wayne Rogers. Rogers left the show after four years, and his role as Hawkeye's sidekick was assumed by Captain B. J. Hunnicut, played by Mike Farrell.

Larry Linville played the part of Major Frank Burns, who served as the butt of the pranks and jokes of Pierce, Trapper John, and later Hunnicut. His pettiness and "stick to the rules" mentality made him the perfect vehicle to show the humanity and caring of Pierce and others who saw the war as grim reality, not an opportunity to "flex one's rank." Linville was perfect as the "ferret-faced" Major Burns and once said that he developed his character by thinking of "every idiot I've ever known." Linville left the show after five years; the surgeon who took his place at the 4077th was Major Charles Emerson Winchester III, played by David Ogden Stiers. The only female lead role was that of Major Margaret "Hot Lips" Houlihan, played by Loretta Swit. A multifaceted character who changed from a martinet officer to a more warm and caring individual, Houlihan was a frequent opponent of Pierce. Swit remained with the show for its entire run.

Rounding out the cast of regular characters were Radar, Father Francis Mulcahy (William Christopher), and Corporal Maxwell Klinger (Jamie Farr). Burghoff, the only actor who was in the film, again played Radar. As company clerk, he had a sixth sense about what someone was going to say or when wounded would be coming. Burghoff left the show after seven years. His job was taken over by Farr. Originally Farr was cast for only one episode, playing a cross-dresser bucking for a Section 8 discharge. His character, clad in a dress that showed his hairy legs and talking like a regular soldier, was a hit; Farr was written into the show as a permanent cast member and stayed with the show until it ended.

Wayne Rogers (left) played Trapper John and Alan Alda was Hawkeye Pierce in the celebrated series M*A*S*H. *(CBS/Landov)*

Broadcast History The first showing of *M*A*S*H* in September, 1972, received a poor review in *Time* magazine, which stated that "The show, which began as one of the most promising series of the new season, is now one of its biggest disappointments." The program aired on Sunday at 8 P.M. on the Columbia Broadcasting System (CBS) network, but low ratings initially put the show in danger of cancellation. However, the following season, the network switched the show from Sunday to Saturday, between "America's favorite sitcom" *All in the Family* and the highly rated *Mary Tyler Moore Show.* Audiences discovered *M*A*S*H* and loved the show, making it the fourth-most-watched series of the season. When CBS again moved *M*A*S*H* to a new night, Tuesday, the audience followed. *M*A*S*H* maintained its high ratings for the next decade.

Impact *M*A*S*H* aired 251 episodes and won many Emmy Awards for writing, directing, and editing. Alda won two Emmys in 1974 for acting, and Burghoff, Morgan, and Swit won Emmys for Outstanding Supporting Actor or Actress.

Over the years, *M*A*S*H*, which had begun with an antiwar scenario, evolved into more of a study of the characters and how they changed. The series was first aired during American involvement in Vietnam, and the increasing antiwar attitudes within the United States in the early 1970's are reflected in the portrayal of war in *M*A*S*H*. However, by the second half of the 1970's, the country had become a more conservative place, and, leaving behind the fierce liberalism of its early days, *M*A*S*H* reflected this change.

As a result of its comic treatment of serious subjects, innovative and multilayered story lines, and depiction of believable characters, *M*A*S*H* became one of the most widely syndicated television shows in history. The final episode, a 150-minute program, aired in February, 1983, to an audience of more than 125 million people.

Further Reading

Gehring, Wes. "*M*A*S*H* Turns Thirty." *USA Today*, September, 2002, 66-70. A comprehensive overview detailing how the series evolved.

Gelbart, Larry. *Laughing Matters: On Writing "M*A*S*H," "Tootsie," "Oh, God!", and a Few Other Funny Things*. New York: Random House, 1998. A view of *M*A*S*H* from the writer's perspective.

Kalter, Suzy. *The Complete Book of "M*A*S*H."* New York: Abrams, 1984. Full of pictures, with detailed information about the actors.

Marcia B. Dinneen

See also *All in the Family*; *Mary Tyler Moore Show, The*; Sitcoms; Television in the United States.

■ *Maude*

Identification Television situation comedy
Producer Norman Lear (1922-   )
Date Aired from 1972 to 1978

Maude was television's answer to the women's liberation movement—a program about an outspoken woman involved in situations that had previously been off-limits for situation comedy.

The character of Maude Findlay made her first television appearance on December 11, 1971, on an episode of *All in the Family.* Maude was Edith Bunker's cousin and the polar opposite of Edith's husband, Archie. In contrast to Archie, a conservative, working-class male chauvinist, Maude was liberal, upper middle class, and an opinionated feminist. As played by Beatrice Arthur, a five-foot-nine woman with a deep bass voice, Maude was nothing like the demure housewives and mothers that traditionally had been characters in television comedies. Maude proved so popular during two appearances on *All in the Family* that the show's producer, Norman Lear, spun off a situation comedy (sitcom) for her. *Maude* debuted on the Columbia Broadcasting System (CBS) network on September 12, 1972.

Maude lived in suburban Tuckahoe, New York, with her fourth husband, Walter (played by Bill Macy), her divorced daughter, Carol (Adrienne Barbeau), and her grandson, Phillip (Kraig Metzinger). Maude dealt with a variety of crises during her six years on the air. She experienced menopause and had a face-lift. Walter suffered with alcoholism, a nervous breakdown, and the bankruptcy of his appliance store. In a two-part episode, forty-seven-year-old Maude learned that she was pregnant. She decided to have an abortion, and Walter supported her decision. These shows initially aired in November, 1972, and drew protests from right-to-life groups; the controversy grew even more heated when the episodes were repeated the following August. The U.S. Catholic Conference convinced some of CBS's affiliates not to run the programs, and Lipton Tea pulled its advertising. CBS aired the programs despite the complaints.

Maude earned high ratings in its first four seasons. Many baby boomers considered the show's depiction of family life more realistic than the perfect families portrayed in earlier sitcoms. The program's feminist leanings resonated with viewers during the heyday of the women's liberation movement. By its fifth year, however, the show no longer placed among the twenty-five top-rated programs. In a final attempt to salvage the show, Maude moved to Washington, D.C., to work for a Democratic congressman. The congressman died, and Maude was chosen to complete his term. However, after three episodes of this format, Arthur decided to leave the show. *Maude*'s final episode aired on April 29, 1978.

Impact   *Maude* dealt with social issues and domestic situations that earlier sitcoms ignored. The show set new standards for content, language, and the depiction of women. *Maude*'s success made it more acceptable for other television programs to feature strong-minded, independent women characters.

Beatrice Arthur (left) portrayed the tough-talking Maude. She is shown here with Esther Rolle, whose character Florida Evans was later given her own series, Good Times. (CBS/Landov)

Further Reading

Cowan, Geoffrey. *See No Evil: The Backstage Battle Over Sex and Violence on Television.* New York: Simon & Schuster, 1979.

Dow, Bonnie J. *Prime-Time Feminism: Television, Media Culture, and the Women's Movement Since 1970.* Philadelphia: University of Pennsylvania Press, 1996.

Jones, Gerald. *Honey, I'm Home! Sitcoms, Selling the American Dream.* New York: Grove Weidenfeld, 1992.

Marc, David. *Comic Visions: Television Comedy and American Culture.* 2d ed. Malden, Mass.: Blackwell, 1997.

Rebecca Kuzins

See also   Abortion rights; *All in the Family*; Feminism; *Mary Tyler Moore Show, The*; Sitcoms; Television in the United States; Women's rights.

■ May Day demonstrations of 1971

The Event   Anti-Vietnam War protesters descend on the U.S. capital
Date   May 3-5, 1971
Place   Washington, D.C.

Demonstrators' attempts to disrupt government activity in the U.S. capital were countered by indiscriminate arrests that violated civil liberties, resulting in the largest mass detentions in U.S. history.

Two weeks before the May Day peace demonstrations in Washington, D.C., more than 250,000 people had marched in that city to protest the war in Vietnam. The May Day demonstrations, beginning Monday, May 3, were carried out by a much smaller and more militant group of protesters, whose stated goal was to close down the federal government by blocking the city's traffic flow. A loose-knit organization called the Mayday Collective organized the event and publicly announced twenty-one sites where demonstrators would gather. District police and federal government officials decided that the capital would be kept open at all costs and determined that this could be accomplished only by suspending normal arrest and detention procedures.

When about 12,000 protestors moved into position Monday morning, they were met by 5,100 city police and 1,400 National Guard soldiers, with 10,000 more Army and Marine troops held in reserve. About 7,200 arrests were made that day, and many who were arrested had nothing to do with the demonstrations. Most of those detained had no real arrest information recorded and were charged with "disorderly conduct." They were held at makeshift detention facilities without adequate food, water, and sanitation, and the majority were released by the next day by posting a ten-dollar collateral. By midday on Tuesday, even the collateral requirement was abandoned, and the rest were released without being processed.

On Tuesday, the demonstrators changed tactics and 3,000 gathered at the Justice Department to listen to speeches. Police announced that anyone who did not leave would be arrested, and about 1,500 were taken to jail. Another 1,200 protesters marched from the Mall to the Capitol Building. This gathering was called an "unlawful assembly" by the chief of police, and 1,146 people were arrested. Standard arrest procedures were followed, and the charges were more serious. There were a couple of small protests later in the week, but nothing on the scale of the first two days.

Altogether, more than 13,000 protesters were arrested during the May Day demonstrations. Almost all detained on the first day had charges dropped, and litigation on subsequent arrests resulted in rulings that protesters' rights of free speech and assembly had been violated, and their charges were also dropped.

Impact The May Day peace demonstrations of 1971 marked the end of large-scale protests against the war in Vietnam. The constitutionally guaranteed rights of free speech, assembly, and due process were affirmed by the courts, rendering invalid the argument made by government officials that the need for social order overrode the rule of law. The United States withdrew all combat troops from Vietnam in 1972 and signed a peace treaty with North Vietnam in 1973.

Further Reading

Hixson, Walter L. *The Vietnam Antiwar Movement.* New York: Garland, 2000.

Nicosia, Gerald. *Home to War: A History of the Vietnam Veterans' Movement.* New York: Crown, 2001.

Wells, Tom. *The War Within: America's Battle over Vietnam.* New York: Henry Holt, 1996.

Jerry Shuttle

See also Antiwar demonstrations; Kent State massacre; Vietnam Veterans Against the War; Vietnam War.

■ "Me Decade"

Definition   Phrase coined to describe the self-absorption of 1970's

The "Me Decade" was a well-known catchphrase describing social and psychological developments in the 1970's in which expectations and values emphasized personal choice and gratification rather than social obligations, family responsibilities, or community affiliations.

The phrase "Me Decade" was introduced by journalist Tom Wolfe in an influential article in *New York* magazine, published in 1976 and titled "The 'Me' Decade and the Third Great Awakening." Declaring that the 1970's represented a period of sweeping change that amounted to a "third great awakening in American history," Wolfe predicted that the 1970's would come to be known as the "Me Decade." He suggested that the political activism and community spirit of earlier decades had shifted to an emphasis on individual happiness and personal economic well-being. Wolfe pointed out that most people, historically, have not positioned themselves as single, self-maximizing individuals outside the orbit of their families or communities. However, the changes during the 1970's represented a great sea change in manners and morals in which traditional values and loyalties were abandoned in favor of a new, more hedonistic, rebellious, and emotional approach which gave top priority to self-esteem, self-fulfillment, and self-invention. The decade's new emphasis on the individual was also associated with a wish to be released from conformist social pressures, a loss of trust in the federal government in the wake of the Vietnam War and the Watergate scandal, and an unprecedented thirty-year period of prosperity.

Wolfe's catchphrase came to be seen as a fitting description of a period in which the role of the family was diminishing and in which feminist, gay rights, and racial equality movements emphasized the entitlements of the individual. The "Me Decade" especially came to stand for an emphasis on personal choice, which was said to account for the high divorce rate and the erosion of family values. Moreover, it was also associated with a new concern with the body, especially with regard to exercise, food, and sexual freedom. Despite its association with physical health and psychological well-being, however, the phrase was generally deployed pejoratively and was often used in association with a conservative critique of a permissive liberal morality.

Impact The "Me Decade" was adopted by the culture as an apt label for the 1970's. It was put into general use almost immediately as a pithy summary of one of the era's important trends and was especially favored by political and social commentators of the time. It also reverberated in decades following the 1970's, with many critics suggesting that it continued to aptly describe a continuing cultural emphasis on self-fulfillment rather than community involvement or political activism.

Further Reading

Frum, David. *How We Got Here: The '70's: The Decade That Brought You Modern Life—For Better or Worse.* New York: Basic Books, 2000.

Lasch, Christopher. *The Culture of Narcissism.* New York: Warner Books, 1991.

Wolfe, Tom. "The 'Me' Decade and the Third Great Awakening." In *Mauve Gloves and Madmen, Clutter and Vine, and Other Stories, Sketches, and Essays.* New York: Bantam Books, 1999.

Margaret Boe Birns

See also *Culture of Narcissism, The*; Fitness movement; Human potential movement; *I'm OK, You're OK*; New Age movement; *Our Bodies, Ourselves*; Self-help books; Slogans and slang; Wolfe, Tom.

■ Medicine

Definition Medical discoveries and advances during the decade

Much of the work in the medical field during this period involved development and adaptations of new technologies. In a sense, medical research was coming of age.

The application of ultrasonography and computed tomography (CT) techniques, or CAT scans, represented some of the first applications of emerging computer technology in diagnosis of disease and provided a noninvasive methodology for three-dimensional imaging of tissue.

Ultrasonography, also referred to as ultrasound scanning, had its origins in World War II using principles of sonar utilized by ships in submarine detection. The process involved the use of very high frequency sound waves projected into or through a medium such as water or the body. When the waves pass through objects of varying density, they are re-flected. The first medical application of ultrasound technology utilized an ultrasonic reflectoscope. In the early 1950's, Dr. Inge Edler, director of cardiology at University Hospital in Lund, Sweden, and Carl Hertz, a graduate student there, utilized the procedure for analysis of mitral valve function.

During the 1970's, ultrasonic scanning was applied in procedures for fetal monitoring. A handheld transducer was placed over the uterus, allowing a real-time observation of a developing fetus. While the images obtained could be considered crude if compared with twenty-first century technology, it was nevertheless possible to observe fetal movements as well as cardiac activity and fetal development.

In the 1950's and 1960's, Allan Cormack, a South African-born physicist working at Harvard University, and Godfrey N. Hounsfield, an engineer working at Electrical and Musical Instruments Limited (EMI) in Great Britain, developed a method by which an X-ray scan could be used to develop a three-dimensional image of body tissue. The principle, known as computed axial tomography (CAT), involved using X rays to "slice" through thin sections of tissue from different angles. Differing densities of tissue could be displayed on a computer screen, producing a three-dimensional image.

The technique was first applied in 1972, when a patient at Atkinson Morley's Hospital in Wimbledon, England, was diagnosed with a brain tumor on the basis of the first clinically described CT procedure. The technique initially was applied only for the diagnosis of disorders involving the head, and images could take several hours for development. Between 1974 and 1976, however, an increasing number of machines were installed in hospitals, and the technique was applied to the body as a whole. Within a few years, the technology underwent rapid improvement, and the entire CT process could be completed in a matter of seconds. In 1979, Cormack and Hounsfield were awarded Nobel Prizes in Physiology or Medicine.

Recognition of Emerging Diseases While some of the more significant infectious illnesses either were eradicated (smallpox) or at least brought under control (childhood diseases), the 1970's also found the appearance of new diseases, or at least the earliest recognition that such diseases may be found in the population. Acquired immunodeficiency syndrome (AIDS) as a distinct disease entity would be defined during the 1980's. However, its origins probably came about some years before. In 1978 and 1979, four individuals from Zaire had appeared in a hospital in Antwerp, Belgium, suffering from a variety of unusual microbial infections; at least one appeared to have developed a rare lung disease caused by the protozoan *Pneumocystis carinii*. All exhibited an underlying immunodeficiency. Some years later, after the AIDS virus had been isolated, analysis of frozen blood samples from these patients confirmed that they were among the earliest victims of this growing plague.

In the weeks following the July, 1976, meeting of the American Legion at the Bellevue-Stratford Hotel in Philadelphia, Pennsylvania, an increasing number of the members began developing an unusual form of pneumonia. By the end of August, 182 cases would be reported, with more than two dozen deaths. The illness, which would shortly be known as Legionnaires' disease, was determined to be caused by a soil organism named for its place of discovery, *Legionella*. The disease was not new; subsequent analysis indicated that cases had appeared as early as the 1940's. However, the Philadelphia outbreak provided further proof that certain diseases have always been endemic in populations.

Some diseases entered the population not so much from carriers, but rather followed the encroachment of civilization into areas not encountered previously by large numbers of persons. This was particularly true in Africa. During the latter part of 1969 into the early months of 1970, dozens of persons working as hospital staff or missionaries in the western African country of Sierra Leone, as well as local villagers, developed an illness characterized by high fever and severe hemorrhaging. The Lassa virus, named by Dr. Jordi Casals-Ariet for the village in Nigeria from which it was isolated in 1969, was maintained in nature as an endemic infection in rodents. However, as humans encroached on these isolated areas, they came into increasing contact both with the carrier and with the virus itself. By the end of the decade, it became clear that human infection was much more common than originally realized; several hundred thousand persons a year are probably infected. Fortunately, the virus appears to be poorly transmitted between humans, limiting the scope of an epidemic.

Understanding of the role of lifestyle and disease also began a maturation phase. A link between high levels of cholesterol and heart disease was established during this period. While the specific reports centered on unusually high levels of cholesterol with a genetic basis, the clear implication was that a diet high in fat could be a contributing factor to heart problems. Sexually transmitted diseases associated with viruses began to increase, reflecting the changes in sexual mores of the period. At least one form of cancer, cervical cancer, was linked to infectious agents transmitted from sexual partners. Meanwhile, the first vaccine for another sexually transmitted virus, hepatitis B, was developed.

Genetic Engineering   During the 1950's and 1960's, scientists studying infection of bacteria by viruses noted a phenomenon called "restriction": Bacterial viruses (bacteriophages) grown on certain strains of bacteria would not grow on other, similar strains. The basis for restriction was determined in the 1960's when it was discovered that restrictive strains of bacteria produce enzymes that degrade the viral deoxyribonucleic acid (DNA); the term "restriction enzymes" was coined to describe these molecules.

The usefulness of many of these enzymes was a result of their ability to cut DNA at specific sites, often resulting in a staggered cut. As a result, different DNA could be sliced with the same enzyme. Since they all contained the same cut, they could be considered as "sticky." DNA from different sources could be spliced together, making possible a new field of genetic engineering.

In 1972, Herbert W. Boyer, a biochemist at the University of California, and Stanley Cohen, a professor of medicine at Stanford, began a collaboration using the newly developed techniques in molecular biology to clone specific genes and reported their first results a year later. The technique was quite simple in theory. Isolated genes were inserted into circular pieces of DNA called plasmids. Plasmids in turn could be placed into bacteria, which would produce whatever gene product, including human proteins, was encoded in the DNA. In 1979, human insulin could be produced by the bacterium *Escherichia coli*, the first of many human products synthesized in large quantities by bacteria as a result of genetic engineering.

"Test-Tube" Babies   Fallopian tube blockage represents one of the most common reasons for infertility in women. Eggs are produced normally, but because they cannot travel through the tube, fertilization cannot occur. During the late 1960's, Dr. Patrick Steptoe from Oldham General Hospital in England and Dr. Robert Edwards, a physiologist at Cambridge, began a collaboration in which they attempted to isolate oocytes from a woman and to carry out fertilization in laboratory dishes.

During the early 1970's, Steptoe and Edwards performed their first experiments in what would become known as in vitro fertilization. Between 1972 and 1975, they were able to implant developing embryos into approximately eighty women, but none proved successful.

In 1976, the procedure was modified. Rather than using hormone treatment to regulate embryonic development and implantation, Steptoe and Edwards decided to rely on the woman's own hormonal cycle. In November, 1977, an eight-cell embryo was implanted into Lesley Brown, a Bristol, England, woman who had attempted for nearly a decade to become pregnant. On July 25, 1978, Steptoe delivered a healthy five-pound, twelve-ounce baby through a cesarean section. Louise Joy Brown represented the first successful "test-tube" baby. Another such baby was delivered successfully by a woman in Glasgow, Scotland, six months later.

Cancer Research and Treatment   The "War on Cancer" declared by President Richard M. Nixon began to demonstrate some success in the 1970's, albeit in an unusual fashion. In December, 1971, the president signed the National Cancer Act for funding into cancer research. The former biological warfare laboratories at Fort Detrick, Maryland, were converted into research facilities for this purpose. However, it was soon discovered that rather than being due to viral infection—the premise on which the "war" was based—most cancers were the result of improper regulation of genetic material called oncogenes.

First discovered in a class of viruses associated with animal cancers, the normal human counterparts of these so-called oncogenes were discovered to regulate cell reproduction. Only when these genes were mutated or inappropriately expressed would the result be a cancer. The first of these human oncogenes, the sarcoma gene, was reported in 1976; within two decades, nearly one hundred human oncogenes were identified.

Research into treatment of cancer also benefited from ongoing research. Prior to the 1970's, surgery to remove cancerous tumors, as well as radiation or chemotherapy, represented the limited methods of choice for treatment. Other than the replacement of radical mastectomy by a more modified surgical procedure in 1979, little had changed in treatment choices since the 1950's. In 1975, Georges Kohler and César Milstein in Cambridge, England, reported a procedure by which antibody proteins could be produced that would target specific molecules. Known as monoclonal antibodies, such proteins could be directed specifically against the surfaces of cancer cells. By attaching radioactive substances or anticancer chemicals to the monoclonal antibodies, physicians could apply immunotherapy against the desired target rather than using a previous random process.

While immunotherapy proved a promising method to treat a variety of cancers, research continued to produce or test a new generation of drugs for chemotherapy: cisplatin in 1971, doxorubicin in 1974, and tamoxifen and interferon in 1978.

Impact   During the decade, the application of new technologies allowed for noninvasive techniques to be utilized in diagnosis of disease. People were then able to be observed on an outpatient basis, reducing costs and freeing space in hospitals. More rapid and more accurate diagnosis became possible.

The burgeoning field of molecular biology entered a maturation phase. The discovery of restriction enzymes along with methodologies for isolation and insertion of genes opened the way for the new field of genetic engineering. Within a few years, it became possible to isolate and clone dozens of genes, with applications in providing inexpensive and pure human gene products such as insulin and various other hormones. "Test-tube technology" provided hope for persons who were unable to conceive children, and coupled with molecular biology, it provided methodologies for the study of genetic disease.

Further Reading

Bishop, J. Michael. *How to Win the Nobel Prize*. Cambridge, Mass.: Harvard University Press, 2003. Autobiography of the Nobel laureate author. Bishop describes the research into understanding the molecular basis of cancer and gives anecdotal stories of research over the years.

Boon, Jo-Ellen. "Allan Cormack." In *The Nobel Prize Winners, Physiology or Medicine*, edited by Frank N.

Magill. Pasadena, Calif.: Salem Press, 1991. A brief biography of the person who developed many of the mathematical principles used in CT scans.

_____. "Godfrey Newbold Hounsfield." In *The Nobel Prize Winners, Physiology or Medicine*, edited by Frank N. Magill. Pasadena, Calif.: Salem Press, 1991. A brief biography of the person primarily involved in applying technology utilized for CT scans.

Edwards, Robert, and Patrick Steptoe. *A Matter of Life*. New York: William Morrow, 1980. A description of events leading up to this medical team's work on in vitro fertilization, the work which resulted in the first test-tube baby.

Garrett, Laurie. *The Coming Plague*. New York: Penguin Books, 1994. A discussion on the problems of emerging diseases by a Pulitzer Prize-winning author. Emphasis is placed on the role of sociology in the spread of such diseases.

Thomas, Gordon, and Max Morgan-Witts. *Anatomy of an Epidemic*. Garden City, N.Y.: Doubleday, 1982. Popular account of the 1976 Legionnaires' disease outbreak and the discovery of the etiological agent behind it.

Richard Adler

See also Acquired immunodeficiency syndrome (AIDS); Cancer research; CAT scans; Genetics research; Legionnaires' disease; Science and technology; Smallpox eradication; Test-tube babies; Toxic shock syndrome; Ultrasonography.

■ Metric system conversion

Definition A legislated effort to convert the measurement system

During the 1970's, the United States and Canada attempted nationwide conversions to the metric system, which was used by the majority of nations worldwide. With the entire world using the same system, international business, science, and communication would be simplified.

The need for a coordinated measurement system was recognized as early as 1670, and the first metric system was developed in France a century later. By 1900, thirty-five nations, including Europe and most of South America, officially accepted the metric system. In the United States, an 1866 act of Congress legalized the use of the metric system for business and legal matters, and the metric standards were officially adopted by 1893. The Canadian parliament legalized the use of the metric system in 1871. The majority of citizens, however, continued to use the inch-pound system for measurement.

In 1971, the U.S. National Bureau of Standards released a report that urged a carefully coordinated national program to make the United States predominantly metric within ten years. During President Gerald R. Ford's term, Congress passed the Education Amendments of 1974, which encouraged educational institutions to prepare students in the use of the metric system. The Metric Conversion Act of 1975 established the United States Metric Board, whose mission was to coordinate and plan the use and voluntary conversion to the metric system. The act did not establish a target date for conversion, however, and the board was disbanded in 1982.

In 1971, the Canadian government, led by Pierre Trudeau, introduced the *White Paper on Metric Conversion*. By 1975, weather forecasts were in metric, and schools began teaching metric exclusively. By 1977, all road signs were metric, and new cars had to have metric speedometers and odometers. In 1978, timetables were established to convert the sale of motor fuels, retail foods, and home furnishings to metric by 1980. With the change in government in 1979, however, the conversion became voluntary and slowed down.

Impact The drive to convert to the metric system during the 1970's and 1980's lost momentum, and Canada and the United States continued to use the dual measurements of the metric and inch-pound systems into the twenty-first century. Neither government required that only the metric system be used or strictly enforced existing laws regarding metric use.

Subsequent Events Following the 1970's, the United States and Canada continued a gradual change to the metric system, starting with the stock exchange, governmental offices, temperature reports, and legal documents. Many large and small industries—especially those in the automotive, agricultural, scientific, and medical equipment manufacturing industries—voluntarily converted to metric use because of economic factors. Because the majority of the world uses only the metric system, the United States and Canada must label and produce products in metric units in order to be competitive in foreign markets.

Further Reading

Chapman, Michael. "Metrics: Mismeasuring Consumer Demand." *Consumers' Research*, February, 1994, 24-27.

Condon, Erin. "Still a Matter of Inches." *Insight on the News* 17, no. 36 (September 24, 2001): 22.

Fong, Diana. "Make Mine Metric." *Forbes* 143, no. 13 (June 26, 1989): 106.

Virginia L. Salmon

See also Business and the economy in Canada; Business and the economy in the United States; Education in Canada; Education in the United States; Science and technology.

■ Mexico and the United States

Definition Diplomatic relations between neighboring countries

Benefiting from considerable oil wealth, Mexico maintained a foreign policy exceptionally independent from the United States during the decade. Of mutual economic importance were the jobs created in Mexican border factories known as maquiladoras, which were built by American investment attracted to Mexican low wages.

Relations between Mexico and the United States during the 1970's spanned several different presidential administrations in each country. In Mexico, there were the presidencies of Gustavo Díaz Ordaz (1964-1970), Luis Echeverría (1970-1976), and José López Portillo (1976-1982). In the United States, there were those of Richard M. Nixon (1969-1974), Gerald R. Ford (1974-1977), and Jimmy Carter (1977-1981).

During the presidency of Díaz, an event occurred that would have far-reaching consequences for the ideological and foreign policy directions of Mexico during the following decade. In 1968, the army fired on a student demonstration in downtown Mexico City, resulting in a massacre. The cabinet minister responsible for security, Echeverría, would become president two years later.

Echeverría's Independence In order to counter criticism of his administration as reactionary, Echeverría reoriented Mexican foreign and domestic policy in a more leftist and independent direction. At the time, the main concerns of the United States in relation to Latin America were the containment or removal of the communist regime of Fidel Castro

in Cuba, who came to power in 1959, and the Marxist regime of Salvador Allende in Chile, who was inaugurated in 1970. President Nixon and his secretary of state, Henry Kissinger, supported the military overthrow of Allende in 1973.

Asserting his independence from U.S. policy, Echeverría welcomed Chilean political exiles to Mexico and made a state visit to Cuba. He opposed American-backed military regimes in Latin America, as well as the racist policy of apartheid in South Africa and the repression of Palestinian nationhood by Israel—situations in two regions of the world that the United States supported. He increased restrictions on foreign capital, which was primarily American, and nationalized portions of the landowning, electrical, and mining sectors, in which such capital was often invested. Finally, by ending the fixed exchange rate of the Mexican peso and the U.S. dollar, Echeverría radically devalued the peso in relation to American currency.

During Carter's presidency, U.S. foreign policy became more reflective of Mexican criticism. The United States became more alert to Latin American regimes that violated human rights. Moreover, it reduced the interventionist character of the United States in the region by sponsoring a treaty to return the Panama Canal to the country of Panama.

Oil, Trade, and Labor Issues The great international economic crisis of the 1970's was the rapid rise in the price of oil, causing critical waves of inflation around the world, which seriously affected the U.S. economy. In the middle of the decade, by an extraordinary stroke of good fortune, Mexico discovered, in its southern regions, some of the largest reserves of oil in the world. The world's largest consumer of oil and one of the world's largest producers of oil were now neighbors.

Mexican oil exports to the United States in the late 1970's began to alter radically the balance of trade between the two countries, which had always been negative for Mexico. Moreover, Mexican manufactured exports to the United States dramatically increased. American and other foreign manufacturers began to build assembly plants along Mexico's northern border, taking advantage of low labor costs. Known as maquiladoras, the plants numbered several hundred at the beginning of the decade and had tripled by the end of the period. Maquiladoras kept jobs in Mexico, in contrast to previous decades when the U.S.-sponsored bracero program had allowed Mexican contract labor to enter the United States. This growth of a Mexican population in the United States gave birth to a cultural consciousness known as the Chicano movement, which flourished during the 1970's.

Mexican government spending during the 1970's created considerable national debt. The accumulation of this debt occurred within a government foreign policy that was increasingly assertive of an independent Mexican role in international politics. This policy often antagonized international investors and policy makers, especially those from the United States.

Impact Large government spending programs dissipated the wealth that Mexico accrued from discoveries of exceptional reserves of petroleum. Such indebtedness made the country more vulnerable to the United States and other foreign countries, thereby curbing its autonomous economic and independent international policies.

Subsequent Events Mexican oil and manufactured exports to the United States allowed Mexico, by the mid-1980's, to improve considerably its balance of trade profile with the United States. Ultimately, this income allowed Mexico to buy more U.S. goods. However, its rapidly expanding national debt and vulnerable international financial position prompted it to adopt a foreign policy less independent and critical of the United States in subsequent decades. While during the 1970's, political populism dominated the Mexican presidency, during the remainder of the twentieth century, candidates for the Mexican presidency presented credentials based more on economic expertise and stable relations with the United States.

Further Reading

Coatsworth, John H., and Carlos Rico, eds. *Images of Mexico in the United States.* La Jolla: University of California at San Diego, 1989. Collection of papers on U.S. perceptions of Mexico prepared for the Bilateral Commission on the Future of United States-Mexican Relations at the Center for U.S.-Mexican Studies of University of California at San Diego.

Domínguez, Jorge I., and Rafael Fernández de Castro. *The United States and Mexico: Between Partnership and Conflict.* New York: Routledge, 2001. Examines how relations between the United States and Mexico occur within a context of their international and bilateral institutions and systems and their respective internal dynamics.

Glade, William P., and Cassio Luiselli, eds. *The Economics of Interdependence: Mexico and the United States.* La Jolla: University of California at San Diego, 1989. Details financial, commercial, technological, and organizational aspects of U.S.-Mexico economic relations for the period.

Krauze, Enrique. *Mexico—Biography of Power: A History of Modern Mexico, 1810-1996.* New York: HarperCollins, 1997. A leading Mexican analyst places events of recent decades in Mexico within their historical context since the independence of the country.

Paz, Octavio. *The Other Mexico: Critique of the Pyramid.* New York: Grove Press, 1972. A famed Mexican Nobel laureate examines the formative aspects of his country's national characteristics at the beginning of the 1970's.

Edward A. Riedinger

See also Chicano movement; Foreign policy of the United States; Latin America; Latinos; Oil embargo of 1973-1974; Panama Canal treaties.

■ Michener, Roland

Identification Governor-general of Canada, 1967-1974
Born April 19, 1900; Lacombe, Northwest Territories (later Alberta), Canada
Died August 6, 1991; Toronto, Ontario, Canada

As a dignified and active governor-general, Michener helped represent Canada to the world.

The son of a senator, Daniel Roland Michener won a Rhodes scholarship in 1920, which took him to Hertford College, Oxford. He also qualified as a barrister. These years had a definitive impact on Michener's eventual career, cementing personal connections that would shape his later contributions to Canadian public life. While at Oxford, Michener formed a lifelong friendship with Lester B. Pearson, Canada's prime minister from 1963 to 1968. The two played on Oxford's Canadian-dominated ice hockey team, which won consistent lopsided victories over rivals. On his return to Canada, Michener practiced law in Toronto. He entered politics and served as a Progressive Conservative at the provincial level from

1945 to 1948 and as a federal member of Parliament (MP) between 1953 and 1962. He was also speaker of the House of Commons from 1957 to 1962 and Canadian high commissioner in India in the mid-1960's.

Liberal prime minister Pearson appointed Michener governor-general of Canada in 1967. This became an especially important post as the centennial year celebrations brought an unprecedented number of distinguished visitors to Canada. The Micheners oversaw extensive improvements to Rideau Hall, Canada's government house. The same regal dignity and political impartiality that had made Michener an effective speaker of the House of Commons served him well as governor-general. He developed a good rapport with Pierre Trudeau, Pearson's successor. Michener presided over the first Order of Canada Awards and eliminated some outmoded vestiges of colonialism, most notably the obligatory curtsy to the governor-general. His multilingual wife, Norah, who had a Ph.D. in philosophy and was the author of several books, helped to fulfill social duties, which included official visits throughout Canada and abroad.

While the British queen is Canada's head of state, the governor-general represents the monarch in Canada. Michener, with the queen's approval, made foreign visits as Canada's head of state throughout the late 1960's and early 1970's. Some monarchists resented this supposed erosion of the queen's role, but others welcomed the "Canadianization" of the Crown.

Michener also was a keen sportsman, encouraging Canadians to take up fitness pursuits and promoting the "participation" program. He personally went running with groups of schoolchildren. Furthermore, the governor-general made numerous trips to the Arctic, drawing attention to Canada's North. Michener was succeeded as governor-general by Jules Léger in 1974.

Impact Michener's term as governor-general marked a shift to a greater "Canadianization" of the role. While the queen remained Canada's head of state, when traveling abroad she represents Britain. Michener's official visits to foreign countries were made as Canada's resident head of state, a further development in the evolution in the governor-general's role that raised questions about the status of the monarchy during the 1970's. Michener re-

mained active into his eighties—jogging, playing tennis, and even mountain climbing—and lived to be ninety-one.

Further Reading

Michener Rohr, Joan, with Terrence Heath. *Memories of a Governor General's Daughter.* Toronto: Bedford House, 1990.

Stursberg, Peter. *Roland Michener: The Last Viceroy.* Toronto: McGraw Hill Ryerson, 1989.

Barbara J. Messamore

See also Canada and the British Commonwealth; Léger, Jules; Trudeau, Pierre.

■ Microprocessors

Definition Single silicon chips containing all the processing circuitry of a computer

The progressive development of microprocessors during the 1970's led to the personal computing transition to microcomputers and the eventual availability and widespread use of computers throughout the world.

By the late 1960's, the technology for making large-scale integrated circuits that contained thousands of electronic components was available. In 1970, Texas Instruments (TI) invented the single-chip microprocessor. As a result of functional problems, it was never marketed. Later in 1970, Federico Faggin of Intel configured a central processing unit (CPU) chip that became known as the 4004 4-bit microprocessor, meaning that it could process data internally in 4-bit words. The 4004 could perform 60,000 operations per second.

In 1972, Intel announced the 8008 microprocessor, an 8-bit chip that started the microcomputer industry with the production of the French Micral microcomputer in 1973. In 1974, Intel introduced the 8080 microprocessor, an 8-bit chip that used the N-channel metal oxide semiconductor (NMOS) technology. It contained 5,000 transistors, could perform 290,000 operations per second, and was used in the Altair 8800 microcomputer in 1975.

By 1975, other companies besides Intel were producing microprocessors competitively. Motorola released the MC6800 microprocessor, the first to use a single five-volt power supply. Zilog marketed the Z-80, which was faster than the Intel 8080. In November, 1976, Intel countered with a faster 8-bit chip, the 8085 microprocessor. In the meantime, Metal Oxide

Semiconductor (MOS) Technology had developed the inexpensive 8-bit MOS 6502 microprocessor: It charged twenty-five dollars rather than the hundreds of dollars charged by competitors. The Apple II, the Atari 400 and 800, and the Commodore PET microcomputers all used the MOS 6502.

After development difficulties and a variety of delays, Intel released the 8086 microprocessor in June, 1978. It was a 16-bit chip containing 29,000 transistors, and it could execute one-third of a million instructions per second. Around the same time, Motorola produced the MC6801 microprocessor, the first to contain 35,000 transistors. In late 1978, it marketed the MC6809 microprocessor, a 16-bit chip. By mid-1979, Intel had upgraded its 8086 microprocessor to the faster 8088, which is the chip that was selected by International Business Machines (IBM) Corporation to produce its personal computer (PC) in 1981. In late 1979, Motorola released the MC68000 microprocessor, which could process data in 32-bit words. It was chosen by Apple for the Lisa computer and for the production of the Macintosh personal computer.

Impact Microprocessor development during the 1970's revolutionized the computer industry, leading to the production of small personal computers and portable terminals. Competition between a number of companies, particularly Intel, Motorola, and MOS Technology, led to rapid development of faster, cheaper microprocessors during the 1970's and set the stage for the production of the IBM PC and the Apple Macintosh in the early 1980's.

Further Reading

Brey, Barry B. *The Intel Microprocessors: Architecture, Programming, and Interfacing.* Upper Saddle River, N.J.: Prentice Hall, 2000.

Crisp, John. *Introduction to Microprocessors and Microcontrollers.* Oxford, England: Newnes, 2003.

Alvin K. Benson

See also Apple Computer; Communications in the United States; Computer networks; Computers; Inventions; Microsoft; Science and technology.

■ Microsoft

Identification Software company that would later become the largest software company in the world

Date Founded in 1976

During the 1970's, Microsoft introduced a business model for high-technology firms that revolutionized the computer industry. This model included entering into strategic partnerships that were advantageous to Microsoft, buying companies that had software needed to complete a major Microsoft product, and hiring the best employees to develop software that customers wanted.

Bill Gates and Paul Allen began working on computers together at Lakeside School in Seattle, Washington, around 1973 and became adept at programming in the computer language BASIC during this time. Both Gates and Allen were at Harvard in December, 1974, when they saw an article in *Popular Electronics* describing a personal computer called the MITS Altair 8800. In 1975, Gates and Allen contacted MITS, located in Albuquerque, New Mexico, and offered to write a BASIC interpreter for the Altair. They finished the BASIC interpreter later in 1975, and they licensed it to MITS. Allen went to work for MITS, while Gates continued to work on improving their BASIC interpreter.

In 1976, Gates and Allen decided to sell an improved version of the Altair BASIC to other microcomputer companies, but Altair objected. Allen left MITS and joined Gates in full-time software development. In November, 1976, they registered a company named Microsoft with the Office of the Secretary of the State of New Mexico.

By early 1977, Microsoft was licensing its BASIC to a number of microcomputer companies, and later that year, MITS dropped its contention that it had an exclusive licensing agreement with Microsoft. In July, 1977, Microsoft released its second computer language, FORTRAN, and in April, 1978, Microsoft announced its third computer language, Microsoft COBOL. In January, 1979, Microsoft moved its offices from Albuquerque, New Mexico, to Bellevue, Washington. While Microsoft was still a small company, it was on its way to becoming the software giant it would become in subsequent decades.

Impact The software that Microsoft developed during the 1970's revolutionized the computer industry by demonstrating that a company could be a success if it specialized in developing computer software. Moreover, Microsoft's interpretive BASIC and DOS popularized the microcomputer during this period and helped propel it into the prominent position that it held in later decades.

Subsequent Events   In 1980, Microsoft began talking to International Business Machines (IBM) Corporation about developing a complete software system for the new IBM personal computer (PC). To facilitate this development, Microsoft acquired an operating system, QDOS, and upgraded it to MS DOS. In August, 1981, IBM introduced its PC, which used Microsoft's DOS, assembler, BASIC, FORTRAN, and COBOL. The success of the IBM PC catapulted Microsoft into a leadership position in the microcomputer software industry, which it continued to hold into the twenty-first century.

Further Reading

Manes, Stephen, and Paul Andrews. *Gates: How Microsoft's Mogul Reinvented an Industry—and Made Himself the Richest Man in America.* Carmichael, Calif.: Touchstone Press, 1994.

Wallace, James, and James Erickson. *Hard Drive: Bill Gates and the Making of the Microsoft Empire.* Carmichael, Calif.: HarperCollins, 1993.

George M. Whitson III

See also   Apple Computer; Computer networks; Computers; Inventions; Microprocessors; Science and technology.

■ Middle East and North America

Definition   Diplomatic relations between two world regions

Overarching superpower conflicts set the stage for a turbulent decade in Middle East and North American relations.

In the decade immediately following the turbulent but decisive Six-Day War in 1967 between Israel, on one hand, and Egypt, Jordan, and Syria, on the other, relations between the Middle East and North America were tempered by the hostilities and frustration that overwhelmed the Arab nations in the region. The Islamic revolt in Iran, which was orchestrated with the siege on the American embassy in Tehran and the subsequent hostage crisis in late 1979, was further proof of troubled relations between the region and the West, particularly the United States. The crisis in the region was centered on the Arab-Israeli conflict, in which the defeated Arab nations blamed not only Israel for their humiliation in the battlefield but also Western powers— including the United States, Great Britain, and France—for helping Israel.

Conflict over Israel   The tiny state of Israel, created in Palestine by the United Nations in 1947, had scored a victory twenty years later over the combined military assault of the neighboring Arab states. In efforts to regain their lost possessions, the Arab states of Egypt and Syria made a spirited attempt at retaliation in a surprise attack during the Jewish holiest holiday, Yom Kippur, in 1973. According to most analysts, the Yom Kippur War was launched to regain not only land but also Arab pride, which was badly bruised during the Six-Day War.

Thereafter, a stalemate ensued, leaving the dispute over Palestine still unsolved. The liberation struggle for the freedom of Palestine ultimately fell upon the leadership of the Palestine Liberation Organization (PLO), which resorted to various terrorist techniques to secure Palestine's freedom. As expected, condemnations from nations sympathetic to the Arab cause soon polarized the global community on both sides of the conflict. The United Nations was compelled to take steps in order to negotiate peace between the warring parties.

Canada and the United States adopted some similar as well as different strategies in dealing with Middle East conflicts. Both nations, as members of the United Nations, accepted in principle the creation and survival of Israel, but from most estimates, the United States became more forceful and blatant in its support for Israel than did Canada during the course of the conflicts. The United States also played a more visible role than Canada in a series of diplomatic mediations to assuage the feelings of Arabs and bring them to a peaceful negotiation with Israeli officials.

One of the highest points in peace negotiations was the Camp David Accords in 1978. Under the administration of U.S. president Jimmy Carter, the leaders of Israel and the PLO met and agreed on various peace initiatives, which raised high hopes for peace before the close of the 1970's.

A Divided Global Community   During the decade, a political and ideological battle occurred within the United Nations regarding the Middle East, and two distinct alliances emerged to take sides with the warring factions. In the climate of the Cold War, it soon became evident that superpower politics would become a major organizing framework around which the opposing camps would rally. Consequently, an Arab-Soviet-Third World bloc joined to form what amounted to a pro-Palestinian lobby at the United Nations. Its influence was most felt in the General Assembly, where it frequently voted to pass resolutions opposing Israel while supporting the fledgling PLO. The bloc's effort paid off when, in 1974, the U.N. General Assembly invited PLO chairman Yasser Arafat to address the organization.

Through the strategy of bloc voting in the United Nations, the pro-PLO lobby was able to establish the Committee on the Inalienable Rights of the Palestinian People in 1975. The panel became, in effect, part of the PLO apparatus, issuing stamps, organizing meetings, and preparing films and draft resolutions in support of Palestinian rights. In 1976, the committee recommended "full implementation of the inalienable rights of the Palestinian people, including their return to the Israeli part of Palestine." It recommended that November 29—the day that the United Nations voted to partition Palestine in 1947—be declared an International Day of Solidarity with the Palestinian People.

United Nations Resolutions   The Arab-Soviet-Third World bloc also tried to oppose Western support for Israel by insisting on the full implementation of various U.N. resolutions. For example, the United Nations Resolution 338, dated October 22, 1973, was unanimously adopted. It called for an immediate cease-fire and termination of all military activities in the Middle East and called upon the concerned parties to start, immediately after the cease-fire, the implementation of Security Council Resolution 242 (1967) in all of its parts. Negotiations would start, immediately and concurrently with the cease-fire, between the parties concerned under appropriate patronage aimed at establishing a just and durable peace in the Middle East.

Resolution 446 was adopted on March 22, 1979, with three countries abstaining—Norway, Great Britain, and the United States. The resolution determined that the policy and practices of Israel in establishing settlements in Palestinian and other Arab territories occupied since 1967 had no legal validity

PLO chairman Yasser Arafat addresses the United Nations in 1974, declaring "I have come bearing an olive branch and a freedom fighter's gun. Do not let the olive branch fall from my hand." During the 1970's, the situation in the Middle East was dominated by the "Palestinian question." (AP/Wide World Photos)

The United States took an active role in promoting peace in the Middle East when President Jimmy Carter (center) brought together Israeli prime minister Menachem Begin (left) and Egyptian president Anwar Sadat to sign the Camp David Accords in 1978. (National Archives)

and constituted a serious obstruction to achieving a comprehensive, just, and lasting peace in the Middle East. It called upon Israel, as the occupying force, to abide by the 1949 Fourth Geneva Convention, to rescind its previous measures, and to desist from taking any action that would result in changing the legal status and geographical nature of the Arab territories occupied since 1967, including Jerusalem.

American Initiatives As a result of the global bipolar superpower conflicts that dominated the decade, many of the initiatives made by U.S. foreign policy makers were largely decided after calculating what strategic and military advantages could be gained over the Soviet Union. According to some analysts, nearly everything that the United States has done in the Middle East can be understood as contributing to the protection of its long-term access to Middle Eastern oil and, through that control, the United States' claim to world leadership. The Ameri-

can buildup of Israel and Iran, and U.S. aid given to "moderate," pro-Western Arab regimes—such as those in Saudi Arabia, Kuwait, and Jordan—were intended to keep the region in friendly hands and uphold "regional stability."

The Nixon, Ford, and Carter administrations demonstrated their commitment to the underlying principles of the Cold War era by adopting variations of foreign policy that were most compatible with their larger ideological visions for securing American national interests in the region. Under the Nixon administration, many of the U.S. Middle East initiatives were conducted under the plan of Secretary of State William Rogers and Henry Kissinger's "shuttle diplomacy."

While the Rogers Plan represented only one side of the Middle East policy of the Nixon administration, albeit the weaker side, Kissinger's diplomacy reflected the stronger and competing side of interventionist policy. According to some analysts, Rogers's efforts were to broker a solution and Kissinger's efforts were to thwart and stall the solution.

In both instances, they were consistent with the Nixon Doctrine, articulated by the president in July, 1969. Under that doctrine, the United States would rely on local powers to keep internal regional order and furnish "military and economic assistance when requested and appropriate." The United States would continue to provide a nuclear umbrella to deter Soviet intervention. In other words, client states such as Israel and Iran would police their regions in order to prevent upheavals by forces inimical to U.S. interests.

Upon assuming office, President Gerald R. Ford expressed concerns over Israeli intransigence and announced a "reassessment" of U.S. policy. For nearly six months, no new arms agreements with Israel were concluded. However, a strong Israeli lobby spearheaded by seventy-six senators sent a letter to Ford demanding that he declare that the United States "stands firmly with Israel" in future negotiations. Consequently, the United States undertook a series of measures which included military aid, an end to pressure for Israeli withdrawal from the West Bank, a promise to defend Israel if the Soviets went to war against it, and a pledge not to talk to the PLO until it recognized Israel and accepted relevant U.N. resolutions.

When President Jimmy Carter came into office in 1977, he was no less committed to the U.S.-Israeli relationship than his predecessors had been, but he showed a remarkable difference and a greater concern for the Palestinian cause. In a departure from the Kissinger-led initiative, the Carter administration opened consultations with the Soviet Union to outline a comprehensive resolution of the Arab-Israeli conflict. The plan included Israeli withdrawal from occupied Arab lands, a resolution of the Palestinian issue, normalization of relations between Israel and the Arab states, and international guarantees provided at least in part by the United States and the Soviet Union.

The effort to move toward some kind of settlement induced Carter into negotiations that ultimately led to the Camp David Accords signed in 1978 between Egyptian president Anwar Sadat and Israeli prime minister Menachem Begin. Two agreements came out of the conference, a "Framework for Peace in the Middle East" and a "Framework for the Conclusion of a Peace Treaty Between Egypt and Israel."

Canadian Initiatives   Generally, the Western powers, including the United States and Canada, were unanimous and committed to the U.N. resolution that created the state of Israel and by implication, its survival. However, the countries shared some differences in the conceptualization and implementation of their policies toward conflicts in the region.

Unlike the United States, Canada failed to recognize permanent Israeli control over territories occupied in 1967: the Golan Heights, the West Bank, East Jerusalem, and the Gaza Strip. Canadian officials also stated their opposition to all unilateral actions that might prejudice the outcome of negotiations, including the establishment of settlements in the territories, along with moves to annex East Jerusalem and the Golan Heights.

Impact   Relations between North America and the Middle East in the 1970's were largely determined by the overarching currents in the global superpower conflicts. Within this context, the conflict between Israel and Arabs became a subtext to the larger bipolar conflict, with supporters or opponents lining up at different points on the ideological spectrum. An Islamic revolt in Iran and the hostage crisis involving fifty-two Americans in Tehran brought significant instability to the U.S.-Middle East relationship in 1979.

Further Reading

Ambrose, Stephen E. *The Rise to Globalism: American Foreign Policy, 1938-1980.* New York: Penguin Books, 1980. Some of the consequences of the age of globalization are considered along with U.S. reaction to the phenomena.

Bill, James A. *The Eagle and the Lion: The Tragedy of American-Iranian Relations.* New Haven, Conn.: Yale University Press, 1988. A chronicle of the troubling relations between the United States and Iran through the Cold War era.

Fromkin, David. *A Peace to End All Peace: The Fall of the Ottoman Empire and the Creation of the Modern Middle East.* New York: Avon Books, 1989. A historical analysis of the currents of political forces that reshaped the Middle East after the fall of the Ottoman Empire.

Laqueur, Walter, and Barry Rubin, eds. *The Israel-Arab Reader: A Documentary History of the Middle East Conflict.* New York: Penguin Books, 1984. A comprehensive and historical narrative on the origins and prospects of the Israel-Arab conflicts, with suggestions for resolutions.

Lenczowski, George. *American Presidents and the Middle East.* Durham, N.C.: Duke University Press, 1990. A historical overview of the role and policies of various U.S. presidents toward the Middle East.

_____. *The Middle East in World Affairs.* 3d ed. Ithaca, N.Y.: Cornell University Press, 1962. Provides good discussion of accusations of Western betrayal of the Arabs after World War I and resulting relations with Arabs in the decades that followed.

Liggio, Leonard P. "Oil and American Foreign Policy." *Libertarian Review,* July/August, 1979, 65. A discussion about the effect of oil in forging American foreign policy.

Austin Ogunsuyi

See also Camp David Accords; Cold War; Foreign policy of Canada; Foreign policy of the United States; Iranian hostage crisis; Israel and the United States; Kissinger, Henry; Oil embargo of 1973-1974; Soviet Union and North America; United Nations.

Harvey Milk. (AP/Wide World Photos)

■ Milk, Harvey

Identification San Francisco gay activist and politician
Born May 22, 1930; New York, New York
Died November 27, 1978; San Francisco, California

As the first openly gay man elected to the San Francisco Board of Supervisors, Milk was a symbol of the emerging gay rights movement both in San Francisco and in the United States.

Harvey Milk's election to the San Francisco Board of Supervisors in 1977 was hailed as a defining moment in American politics as an openly gay candidate won a city council seat in one of the nation's largest cities. Although he served as San Francisco supervisor for only eleven months before being assassinated along with Mayor George Moscone by a former member of the city council, Milk's political career left an indelible impact on the 1970's.

Becoming active in community affairs in San Francisco after moving there and opening a camera shop, Milk made several unsuccessful runs for public office. In 1973, he sought a seat on the Board of Supervisors but lost that race by more than seventeen thousand votes. Determined to continue with his political career, Milk took a leading role in organizing a neighborhood group, the Castro Valley Association. Eventually, his actions drew recognition from San Francisco's political establishment, and Milk was appointed to the San Francisco Board of Permit Appeals by Mayor Moscone in 1975. Despite this appointment, however, Milk lost his campaign for a seat in the California state legislature in 1976 to Art Agnos, a future mayor of the city. In 1977, Milk finally achieved his goal of being elected to a post in San Francisco city government when he won a seat on the Board of Supervisors.

As supervisor, Milk enjoyed a good working relationship with Mayor Moscone and the president of the Board of Supervisors, future United States senator Dianne Feinstein. During his tenure, the city council approved a gay rights ordinance banning discriminatory practices in employment.

On November 27, 1978, former supervisor Dan White, who asked Mayor Moscone to reappoint him to the city council, grew despondent over the unwillingness of the mayor to make such a decision. The situation was made more complex by the widespread awareness that White had resigned the office and now was putting Mayor Moscone in an awkward position by asking for a reappointment to his old job. White's despondency led him to murder Mayor Moscone in his city hall office and then assassinate Supervisor Milk in his office.

White was convicted of the lesser charge of manslaughter and received an eight-year sentence. White's defense team argued that his severe depression led to an excessive consumption of junk food (including Twinkies snack cakes) on the day of the murders, thus deepening his depression and contributing to a loss of control over his actions. This argument became known as the "Twinkie defense."

Impact The election of Harvey Milk was a bright spot during an antigay backlash in the late 1970's. Singer Anita Bryant had led a vigorous antigay crusade in Florida against efforts in Miami-Dade County to enact protections for members of the gay community. The unfortunate circumstances of Milk's death had positive effects, wuch as the creation of schools, community organizations, and public facilities in his memory.

Further Reading

Shilts, Randy. *The Mayor of Castro Street: The Life and Times of Harvey Milk.* New York: St. Martin's Press, 1981.

Weiss, Mike. *Double Play: The San Francisco City Hall Killings.* Reading, Mass.: Addison-Wesley, 1984.

Michael E. Meagher

See also   Bryant, Anita; Feinstein, Dianne; Homosexuality and gay rights; Moscone, George; National Lesbian and Gay Rights March of 1979; White Night Riots.

■ Miniseries

Definition   Television format in which a unified story is told in two or more episodes broadcast in close succession, often on consecutive evenings

The success of the miniseries and the soap-opera series that they spawned had a profound impact on television storytelling: Episodic television became less fragmented and featured continuous plot lines that carried across several episodes or even seasons.

The miniseries emerged from American television's experimentation with storytelling forms other than the half-hour or one-hour weekly program, which had constituted the norm of prime-time network programming following the emergence of television in the late 1940's. From that time through the late 1960's, if writers and producers wished to tell a longer, more complex story than was possible in the traditional formats, their only option was the two-part episode—one story told over two episodes, each broadcast in the series's usual weekly time slot.

In the late 1960's and early 1970's, American television began to expand its repertoire of formats by producing a few ninety-minute series and by developing ninety-minute and two-hour made-for-television films. However, it was the success of the Public Broadcasting Service (PBS) network in the early 1970's in importing from British television several limited-run series, which told lengthy stories over a set number of episodes, that ultimately inspired the American miniseries. Most of these were based on literature or on history. Not surprisingly, then, the first two miniseries broadcast on American television, both produced by the American Broadcasting Company (ABC) network in the early and mid-1970's, were based on novels and dealt with history: *QB VII* (1974), based on a novel by Leon Uris, and the very popular *Rich Man, Poor Man* (1976), based on a novel by Irwin Shaw.

Though both of these miniseries drew high ratings, neither of them could rival the sheer epic sweep and astronomically high ratings of ABC's miniseries adaptation of Alex Haley's *Roots,* a tale about his African American ancestors' experiences in the days of slavery and their aftermath. *Roots,* running for eight consecutive nights in January, 1977, attracted almost 100 million American viewers, became a pop-culture phenomenon, swept the Emmy nominations that year, and caused a widespread national discussion of slavery and race relations. It also inspired a sequel, *Roots: The Next Generations,* which ran for eight consecutive nights on ABC in February, 1979.

Impact Miniseries became a staple of American television, during the 1970's and after. However, as the novelty of the new format wore off—and production costs rose—numbers of episodes within the typical miniseries began to drop to two or three, down from the seven or eight of the 1970's. However, the success of the miniseries format arguably helped inspire another, similar experimentation with narrative device, the resurrection of the nighttime soap opera, with one of the first being *Dallas*, which premiered in early 1978.

Further Reading

Brooks, Tim, and Earle Marsh. *The Complete Directory to Prime Time Network and Cable TV Shows: 1946-Present.* 8th ed. New York: Ballantine, 2003.

Haley, Alex. *Roots: The Saga of an American Family.* Garden City, N.Y.: Doubleday, 1976.

Ozersky, Josh, et al. *Archie Bunker's America: TV in an Era of Change, 1968-1978.* Carbondale: Southern Illinois University Press, 2003.

Thomas Du Bose

See also *American Family, An; Roots;* Television in the United States.

■ Minorities in Canada

Definition A term used by Canadian public policymakers to distinguish between the English majority and those non-Caucasian in race, nonwhite in color, and whose first language is not English; includes aboriginals (First Nations), the Québécois French, and individuals with origins in the Caribbean, Asia, Central and South America, the Middle East, and Africa

In the 1970's, policy initiatives increasingly began to acknowledge the segment of Canadian society deemed minorities. Such initiatives accepted the necessity for the government to define a path by which minorities would be treated equally in the political, social, and economic life of Canada.

Throughout the decade, Canadian public policy makers created policy initiatives that were to redefine both institutions and society for minorities. These initiatives were an acknowledgment of some important realities. Changes to Canada's immigration laws in the years 1962 and 1967 resulted in the arrival of large numbers of people from areas of the world other than Europe. By the 1970's, this trend resulted in a change in the demographics of the population, giving a new dimension to Canada's cultural diversity, as the increase in individuals with origins in

the Caribbean, Central and South America, Africa, the Middle East, and especially Asia can attest.

Like most culturally plural democracies, Canada struggled to ensure that all citizens were accorded just and inclusive treatment within institutions. Canada was not unused to diversity, given that earlier immigrants, though predominantly from Europe, came from diverse cultural, historical, and linguistic traditions. Nonetheless, Canadian institutions were still largely unfamiliar with diversity that was non-European in character. Therefore, it was necessary to create an environment of inclusiveness and equality for all Canadians, notwithstanding their cultural heritage, in anticipation of even greater growth within this demographic.

Changes to Immigration Laws As the 1970's progressed, Canada indeed witnessed major growth in the non-European segment of the population. This was aided by the fact that in 1977 further revisions to Canada's immigration laws literally opened the borders to the world and reinforced the previous departure from earlier legislation, which had encouraged immigration to Canada primarily from Britain and Europe. The 1977 revisions were instrumental in extending citizenship to immigrants from diverse cultural, linguistic, racial, historical, and ethnic backgrounds.

However, as large waves of migration brought people who did not conform to Anglo-Saxon culture and physical appearance and the character of Canada's population became increasingly culturally plural, minorities experienced systemic intolerance that was devastating to their social, economic, and political progress within the country. In order to improve this situation, the Canadian government introduced and implemented policies and legislation that were to exemplify how all Canadians, including minorities, should be treated within institutions and society.

Official Multiculturalism In 1971, for example, Prime Minister Pierre Trudeau announced a plan to introduce an official policy on multiculturalism, acknowledging increased cultural pluralism and defining an institutional framework in which to foster and facilitate the fair and inclusive treatment of minorities.

Debates questioning Trudeau's motives for introducing multiculturalism abounded. Some suggested that official multiculturalism was really intended to curb the rising demands of the French minority to secede from Canada by making French claims just another minority concern, rather than the primary concern. Other interpretations acknowledged that though there might be partial truth in these arguments, in terms of minority rights, an official policy on multiculturalism would give credibility to minority complaints of systemic discrimination; most important, it would legitimize the minority presence within Canadian society.

In order to solidify Canada's new commitment to equity, the Canadian Human Rights Act was passed in 1977. It created equal opportunity for those who, like minorities, faced discrimination in the education system, the health care system, the workplace, and other areas of life.

Impact The 1970's saw great progress for minorities in Canada. It was in this decade that diversity emerged and expanded within Canadian society. New public policy initiatives attempted to create an equitable path for minorities, but preexisting groups such as aboriginals and the Québécois French balked at being placed within the same category as new arrivals. These two groups felt that their status within Canadian society was more rooted in the tradition of the land, and as a result they wanted to be acknowledged in a more prominent light than were recent immigrants. Therefore, in the 1970's minority reaction to these initiatives was polarized. While some groups hailed the changes as having helped to alleviate societal strains, aboriginals and French Canadians claimed that policies such as official multiculturalism worked to undermine their interests, not protect them.

Further Reading

Abu-Laban, Yasmeen, and Daiva Stasiulis. "Unequal Relations and the Struggle for Equality: Race and Ethnicity in Canadian Politics." In *Canadian Politics in the Twenty-first Century,* edited by Michael Whittington and Glen Williams. 5th ed. Scarborough, Ont.: Nelson Thomson Learning, 2000. This chapter thoroughly explicates minority treatment in Canadian public life throughout several decades, including the 1970's. The authors question whether policy initiatives, such as those carried out in the 1970's, truly improved the status of minorities within Canadian society.

Bothwell, Robert, Ian Drummond, and John English. *Canada Since 1945: Power, Politics, and Provincialism.* Rev. ed. Toronto: University of Toronto Press, 1989. A comprehensive history of Canadian politics that thoroughly covers each decade. One of the more important aspects of this volume is its look at influential figures, such as Prime Minister Pierre Trudeau, who helped to shape public policy for minorities in the 1970's.

Elliott, Jean Leonard, and Augie Fleras. *Engaging Diversity: Multiculturalism in Canada.* 2d ed. Scarborough, Ont.: Nelson Thomas Learning, 2002. This volume looks at diversity in Canada, going back to the 1970's, arguably one of the most influential decades in terms of the introduction of significant policy initiatives affecting minority induction into Canadian life. Includes debates questioning the substantive value of official multiculturalism for minorities in Canada.

Krauter, Joseph, and Norris Davis. *Minority Canadians: Ethnic Groups.* Toronto: Methuen, 1978. An outline of the history of minority experiences in Canada that explores such issues as institutional and societal discrimination. Provides a background on why multicultural policies are important in culturally plural societies.

Esmorie J. Miller

See also Canadian Citizenship Act of 1977; Canadian Human Rights Act of 1977; Demographics of Canada; Foreign policy of Canada; Immigration to Canada; Multiculturalism in Canada; National Indian Brotherhood; Quebec Charter of Human Rights and Freedoms; Trudeau, Pierre.

■ Miss Manners column

Identification Syndicated newspaper column
Author Judith Martin (1938-   )
Date First published in 1978

Martin redefined the purpose of etiquette for a constantly changing society and created a uniquely witty persona through which to express her views.

For Judith Martin, etiquette makes it possible for humans to enjoy the ceremonies of life, whether family meals or weddings, and avoid unpleasant confrontations with others, whether in the family, the workplace, or traffic. As the daughter of Jacob Perlman, an economist for the United Nations, she traveled extensively, seeing the differing forms of etiquette in other cultures and recognizing the urgent need for good manners. A Wellesley College graduate (1959) and, beginning in 1960, a reporter for *The Washing-*

ton Post, she was committed to social change as well as outspoken. *Washington Post* owner Katharine Graham in her 1997 memoir *Personal History* recalled seeing Martin pushing a baby carriage in a 1972 picket line to protest the exclusion of women as members from the prestigious Gridiron Club. Likewise, because of previous comments about President Richard M. Nixon and his family, Martin was the only reporter barred from covering the 1971 White House wedding of Nixon's daughter Tricia. Martin briefly recalled this incident in a collection of newspaper columns, *The Name on the White House Floor,* published in 1972.

In 1978, she created her advice column, which incorporated both her sense of the importance of good manners and her acceptance that changing conditions create the need for changing manners; unlike most previous etiquette writers, she was not locked into maintaining the rigid rules of a vanished elite. Her editors were not enthusiastic about the column's potential because etiquette seemed a dead issue after the social changes of the 1960's, but the flood of letters in response to Martin's column assured her success. Her column was quickly syndicated, appearing in more than two hundred newspapers.

The success of the column was in part the result of the "Miss Manners" persona that Martin adopted for her column. Miss Manners was a legendary figure used to educate earlier generations in the refinements of etiquette ("What would Miss Manners say?"). Martin wrote as if she were that figure. Her prose style, reminiscent of the style of nineteenth century British novelist Jane Austen, whom she admired, combined unusually impeccable grammar and sentence structure and generally clear and simple word choice. Her responses were spiced by irony, modern idioms, and the occasional Victorianism or reference to a Victorian figure, such as author Anthony Trollope, as if Martin and that Victorian were contemporaries. The result was a highly original comic style attractive to general readers as well as those interested in specific points of etiquette.

Impact Judith Martin quickly became the most influential writer in her field. The overwhelming response to her column resulted in a series of bestselling books, beginning with *Miss Manners' Guide to Excruciatingly Correct Behavior* (1982), *Common Courtesy: In Which Miss Manners Solves the Problems That Baf-*

fled Mr. Jefferson (1985), and *Miss Manners' Guide to Rearing Perfect Children* (1984).

Further Reading

Caldwell, Mark. *A Short History of Rudeness: Manners, Morals, and Misbehavior in Modern America.* New York: Picador USA, 2000.

Koeppel, Geri. "Judith Martin." In *Newsmakers: The People Behind Today's Headlines.* Issue 4. Detroit: Gale Group, 2000.

Betty Richardson

See also Bombeck, Erma; Journalism in the United States.

■ *Missions of the College Curriculum*

Identification   Higher education national study
Date   Published in 1977

This national study of higher education, published by the Carnegie Foundation for the Advancement of Teaching, called for the reform of general education courses in the typical undergraduate college major, emphasizing a variety of core curriculum courses to broadly educate students.

During the 1970's, there was a growing concern about American students' declining levels of general knowledge and analytical skills. General dissatisfaction with the condition of the learning environment in higher education led many institutions to seek ways to restore earlier curricular models and the values they embodied. In 1977, the *Missions of the College Curriculum* was published by the Carnegie Foundation for the Advancement of Teaching, a leading higher education think tank based in New York City. The report praised the careful development of the college major but referred to college general education requirements as a "disaster area." At that time, general education curriculums were fragmented and incoherent. The report emphasized that the undergraduate core curriculum could serve as a major statement of each higher education institution's unique contribution to the intellectual development of students. Furthermore, the report argued that general education courses deserved greater attention from colleges than had been paid in the previous decade.

During the 1960's and 1970's, most U.S. colleges and universities had moved away from an emphasis on general education or core programs in response to external pressures in order to allow students more freedom in course selection and to emphasize vocational and professional preparation. These developments largely eroded core curriculum programs as a central focus of U.S. higher education. In response to these developments, the Carnegie Foundation's report called for structuring college courses as part of a new core curriculum initiative to contribute to the intellectual development of students and to reflect what higher education institutions considered important in their mission to American society. General education concerns should have a higher priority in colleges and universities, argued the foundation, so that curriculum content could be generated by sustained thought and institutional input and less as a consequence of current social trends and external pressures.

This report served as the basis for curriculum reform nationwide, such as the *Harvard Core Curriculum Report* of 1978. Faculty and academic administrators from the American colleges and universities engaged in dialogue, seeking to identify means for improvement of general education requirements. Examples of core curriculum areas include a concern with the way society gains and applies knowledge and an understanding of the universe, as well as emphasis placed on basic aptitude in communication skills, classical and modern literature, art, music, history, the social sciences, and mathematical, physical, and biological sciences. At most American four-year colleges and universities, the core curriculum amounted to approximately one-third of the undergraduate program during the 1970's.

Impact   As a result of the *Missions of the College Curriculum* report, beginning in the late 1970's, the pendulum began to swing back in favor of more developed core curriculum requirements in U.S. colleges and universities. The report also ushered in a period of intense debate on the issue, reflected in such books as Allan Bloom's *The Closing of the American Mind* (1987) and Dinesh D'Souza's *Illiberal Education* (1991), arguing for a specific core of knowledge that a student should master. Ultimately, the report influenced U.S. colleges and universities to pursue a common educational experience, develop a community of learners, provide opportunities for sharing of viewpoints and ideas, and encourage a discovery and transmission of knowledge to enhance intellectual growth.

Further Reading

Boyer, Ernest L. *College: The Undergraduate Experience in America.* New York: Harper & Row, 1987.

Carnegie Foundation for the Advancement of Teaching. *Missions of the College Curriculum.* San Francisco: Jossey-Bass, 1977.

Gaff, Jerry, and James Ratcliff, eds. *Handbook of the Undergraduate Curriculum: A Comprehensive Guide to Purposes, Structures, Practices, and Change.* San Francisco: Jossey-Bass, 1997.

J. B. Watson, Jr.

See also   Education for All Handicapped Children Act of 1975; Education in Canada; Education in the United States; Title IX of the Education Amendments of 1972.

■ Mississippi River flood of 1973

The Event   The Mississippi River floods more than seventeen million acres along its valley

Date   Began on March 15, 1973

The Mississippi flood left people homeless, killed wildlife, and led President Richard M. Nixon to declare the region a disaster area.

The Mississippi River and its tributaries drain an area of about 3.2 million square kilometers (1.23 million square miles) in the center of the United States. In general, it has its greatest flow in the spring, when snow melts in the drainage basins of the Missouri and Ohio Rivers, and the high discharge from the snowmelt combines with spring precipitation.

In the spring of 1973, the Mississippi River reached its highest level in more than 150 years. The stage for the 1973 flood had been set in the late fall and winter of 1972, when heavy rainfall all along the Mississippi River and its tributaries was followed by equally heavy snowfall in the North and West. The month of February was unusually warm, and the snowmelt collected in a drainage basin that was already saturated. On March 13, following a warm spell that rapidly melted the snow in the northern part of the drainage basin, flooding conditions were reported on the Missouri River. The flooding was worsened by heavy rainfall in which some areas of the drainage basin received more than fourteen inches of rainfall in forty-eight hours.

Because the Mississippi River floods annually, the Army Corps of Engineers had previously built a series of structures that would allow the diversion of excess water to the Atchafalaya River, a shorter route to the Gulf of Mexico. The Low Sill Structure north of Baton Rouge, Louisiana, built of reinforced concrete and comprising eleven floodgates, was part of this system of floodways, levees, and channels connecting the Mississippi and Atchafalaya Rivers. On March 15, a large scour hole began to develop under the Low Sill Structure. Emergency repairs attempted while the river continued at flood levels were not successful, necessitating the first and only opening of the gates at the Morganza Combined Control Structure located about thirty-five miles north of Baton Rouge. The Low Sill Structure was saved, though repairs after the flood cost more than $15 million.

Impact Unfortunately, the flood control system was overwhelmed by the magnitude of the event, which was the worst flood in the region since 1927. In the lower Mississippi River valley, 17 million acres were inundated, as well as 600,000 acres in the delta. The flood caused more than $180 million in property damage and took a terrible toll on the wildlife living in the delta during the flood. It also left thirty-five thousand people homeless and caused more than thirty deaths. President Nixon declared all of the counties bordering the Mississippi River south of St. Louis, Missouri, as disaster areas. The floodwaters did not completely recede until June.

Further Reading

Ambrose, Stephen E., and Douglas Brinkley. *The Mississippi and the Making of a Nation: From the Louisiana Purchase to Today.* Washington, D.C.: National Geographic, 2002.

Barry, John M. *The Great Mississippi Flood of 1927 and How It Changed America.* New York: Touchtone, 1997.

Denyse Lemaire and David Kasserman

See also Natural disasters.

■ **Mister Rogers' Neighborhood**

Identification Children's television series
Creator Fred Rogers (1928-2003)
Date Aired from 1968 to 2001

The preschoolers of the 1970's were the first generation to become a part of Mister Rogers' Neighborhood. *While most children's television shows at the time were filled with hyperactivity and violence, Mr. Rogers calmly and qui-*

Fred Rogers, the host of the children's television show Mister Rogers' Neighborhood. *(AP/Wide World Photos)*

etly made his way into the homes and hearts of American children.

Fred Rogers, host and producer of the show, often said that the reason he went into television was because he hated it so. The first time he ever saw a television set was at his parents' home in 1951. Dissatisfied with what he saw, he immediately decided to go into television in order to make it better.

In 1968, one year after Congress passed the Public Broadcasting Act, the Public Broadcasting Service (PBS) network included *Mister Rogers' Neighborhood* in its first schedule of programs. By that time, Rogers had completed a degree in music composition from Rollins College, a Bachelor of Divinity from Pittsburgh Theological Seminary, and graduate studies in child development from the Arsenal Family and Children's Center.

From the beginning, *Mister Rogers' Neighborhood* was unique; the pace was unusually calm and low-key, with no hype or animations. Rogers wrote the songs and scripts for the show and served as chief puppeteer. The goal of the series was to help strengthen children's self-esteem. In each episode,

Rogers talked openly about issues that concerned children such as death, divorce, going to the doctor, moving to a new house, or going to school. By allowing for quiet pauses and slow transitions, he gave children time to think about, and respond to, what he had to say. Each episode was meticulously planned and included predictable routines such as the opening with Rogers entering his television living room, singing the theme song, and changing into his cardigan sweater and sneakers.

Impact   *Mister Rogers' Neighborhood* became the longest-running program on public television. The show temporarily stopped production in 1976 but resumed again in 1983 because of popular demand. Through this series, Fred Rogers profoundly touched generations of children; he gave them a glimpse of how to make the world a better place.

Subsequent Events   After 1983, about twelve new episodes were produced each year and simply mixed in with the earlier shows. Through the years, the set changed very little and *Mister Rogers' Neighborhood* always seemed to live perpetually in the early 1970's.

By the time of his death on February 27, 2003, Rogers had received virtually every children's television award for which he was eligible, including two George Foster Peabody Awards, several Emmy Awards, and a variety of Lifetime Achievement Awards from the National Academy of Television Arts and Sciences. He also received honorary degrees from more than thirty-five colleges and universities including Yale, Middlebury, and North Carolina State Universities.

Further Reading

Collins, Mark, and Margaret Mary Kimmel, eds. *"Mister Rogers' Neighborhood": Children, Television, and Fred Rogers.* Pittsburgh: University of Pittsburgh Press, 1996.

Rogers, Fred. *The World According to Fred Rogers: Important Things to Remember.* New York: Hyperion, 2003.

Stewart, David. "Mister Rogers in His Neighborhood." In *The PBS Companion: A History of Public Television.* New York: TV Books, 1999.

Joy M. Gambill

See also   Children's television; Education in the United States; Public Broadcasting Service (PBS); Television in the United States.

■ Mitchell, John

Identification   U.S. attorney general
Born   September 15, 1913; Detroit, Michigan
Died   November 9, 1988; Washington, D.C.

While serving as chairman of the Committee to Re-elect the President (CRP), Mitchell became involved in planning, approving, and covering up the break-in at the Watergate office complex. The scandal resulted in Mitchell's disgrace, conviction, and imprisonment.

After a lengthy career as a lawyer, John Mitchell became involved during the 1960's with the housing agenda of New York governor Nelson Rockefeller, and he contributed to the development and passage of the U.S. Housing and Urban Development Act during the next year. In 1967, Mitchell's law firm merged with that of Richard M. Nixon, and the two men began to develop a close professional relationship. In 1968, Nixon persuaded Mitchell to take on the management of his presidential campaign; Mitchell's strategy and efforts contributed to Nixon's close victory over Democrat Hubert H. Humphrey. Nixon then asked Mitchell to join his cabinet as attorney general.

John Mitchell testifies in front of the Senate Watergate Committee in July, 1973. (Dennis Brack/Landov)

During his tenure as attorney general, Mitchell took a tough stand on crime; however, his use of wiretaps and other practices resulted in discrediting the Nixon administration's anticrime agenda. Nonetheless, Mitchell continued to use electronic surveillance, and he wired the phones of thirteen members of the National Security Council who were suspected of "leaking" details about Nixon's Vietnam policy. However, Mitchell failed in his efforts to stop the publication by *The New York Times* of Daniel Ellsberg's Pentagon Papers. On February 15, 1972, Mitchell stepped down as attorney general in order to manage Nixon's reelection campaign.

Meanwhile, White House aides E. Howard Hunt and G. Gordon Liddy were arrested in connection with a break-in of Democratic Party headquarters at the Watergate complex on June 16, 1972. It soon became apparent that Mitchell knew of the plans for the break-in. Within two weeks, Mitchell resigned as chair of the CRP. Nixon was reelected in a landslide victory, but the issue of Watergate emerged during the months after the election. Mitchell was implicated in the break-in and its cover-up by his estranged wife, Martha, and White House aides such as Jeb Stuart Magruder.

Mitchell was indicted in May, 1973, for conspiracy, obstruction of justice, and perjury. On January 1, 1975, he was convicted on all charges. After a delay for appeals, Mitchell served nineteen months in a federal prison. His efforts to expand the powers of the Justice Department were reversed by legislation during the 1970's, but some of the investigative powers that he sought were reinstated with the Patriot Act in 2002.

Impact John Mitchell's involvement in the Watergate scandal contributed to the collapse in confidence among Americans in the Nixon administration and the resignation of President Nixon on August 9, 1974.

Further Reading

Oudes, Bruce. *From the President's Secret Files.* New York: HarperCollins, 1989.

Woodward, Bob, and Carl Bernstein. *All the President's Men.* 2d ed. New York: Simon & Schuster, 1994.

_____. *Final Days.* Reprint ed. Cutchogue, N.Y.: Buccaneer Books, 1994.

William T. Walker

See also Committee to Re-elect the President (CRP); Elections in the United States, 1972; Liddy, G. Gordon, and E. Howard Hunt; Nixon, Richard M.; Pentagon Papers; Watergate.

■ Mitchell, Joni

Identification Canadian singer-songwriter, musician, poet, and painter

Born November 7, 1943; Fort Macleod, Alberta, Canada

Mitchell's compositional output, ranging from introspective folk-pop songs to jazz-influenced works, motivated musicians and songwriters during the 1970's and proved influential in later decades.

In the early 1970's, rock music was influencing the acoustic folk quality of Joni Mitchell's compositions. In March, 1970, she received the Grammy Award for Best Folk Performance of 1969 for her album *Clouds*. *Ladies of the Canyon*, released in April, 1970, was her third collection of original compositions. The album went platinum and yielded the hit single "Big Yellow Taxi." The album *Blue*, released in June, 1971, was an instant commercial and critical success, peaking in the Top 20 on the *Billboard* album charts in September, 1971. A classic album from the 1970's, *Blue* was inducted later into the Grammy Hall of Fame. *For the Roses*, released in October, 1972, was her first album to incorporate orchestral arrangements into her evolving folk-pop sound. The album, another critical success, included the hit single "You Turn Me On (I'm a Radio)."

Court and Spark, released in January, 1974, became her highest-charting album to date. In March, 1974, the single "Help Me" became a Top 10 single. This album demonstrated musical growth from a simple, acoustic style to a contemporary pop style. A series of shows at Los Angeles's Universal Amphitheater in the summer of 1974 was recorded for a live album, released as a two-record set in December of that year and titled *Miles of Aisles*. The jazz-influenced *The Hissing of Summer Lawns*, released in 1975, was not greeted enthusiastically by critics. Although the album sold well and remained on the *Billboard* album charts for seventeen weeks, *Rolling Stone* named it the worst album of 1975.

The mood of *Hejira*, released in November, 1976, is more subdued and personal. The album climbed to number thirteen on the *Billboard* charts, reaching

Joni Mitchell in 1972. (AP/Wide World Photos)

gold status three weeks after its release. *Don Juan's Reckless Daughter,* released in December, 1977, was her first studio double album. This experimental album received mixed reviews, although it peaked on the *Billboard* charts at number twenty-five and went gold within three months.

Mitchell's performed her the song "Coyote" during the Band's farewell concert, which was released in April, 1978, on record and on film. Titled *The Last Waltz,* the film was a critical success and gave Mitchell widespread exposure. *Mingus,* released in June, 1979, was Mitchell's most daring and controversial project and the biggest change in her music. It began as a collaboration with jazz bassist Charles Mingus. *Mingus* received a relatively positive response, but album sales were low and it received little radio air time.

Impact   Joni Mitchell influenced musicians and audiences alike with her reflective, autobiographical poetry and songwriting. Her music reflected the social issues of the 1970's, never compromising to popular trends or fashion. Although her transition from folk to jazz-influenced music was not considered a critical success, her base of fans remained loyal to her evolving vision.

Further Reading

Luftig, Stacy. *The Joni Mitchell Companion: Four Decades of Commentary.* New York: Schirmer Books, 2000.

O'Brien, Karen. *Joni Mitchell: Shadows and Light—The Definitive Biography.* London: Virgin, 2003.

P. Brent Register

See also   Band, The; Jazz; Music; Radio; Singer-songwriters.

■ *Mon Oncle Antoine*

Identification   Canadian film
Director   Claude Jutra (1930-1986)
Date   Released in 1971

This motion picture marked the beginning of what was expected to be the "new wave" of Canadian feature films, when exciting new directors were just starting to create a Canadian film mythology. Jutra's film provided important insights into the lives of rural French Canadians during the grim, repressive era before Quebec's Quiet Revolution of the 1960's, when a Liberal government improved the image and reality of French Canada.

Still widely regarded as one of the best feature films ever made in Canada, *Mon Oncle Antoine* (my uncle Antoine) is a poignant study of teenage Benoit (played by Jacques Gagnon) as he discovers his world and family in Black Lake, a small Quebec asbestos-mining town in the 1940's. Director Claude Jutra forsakes his penchant for abstract style—as seen in his 1964 autobiographical film *À tout prendre* (take it all)—in favor of narrative simplicity, characterization, and a strong sense of milieu. The story is told through the eyes of Benoit, and it follows events and experiences in the lives of his family members, especially his uncle (Jean Duceppe), an alcohol-loving store owner and undertaker whom the boy reluctantly helps in delivering a coffin to a family that has lost a son during preparations for Christmas.

Fundamentally a rite-of-passage tale, the film, shown in French with English subtitles, depicts Benoit's religious irreverence (he secretly consumes a Communion wafer and wine), burgeoning sexuality, ability to look death in the face, discovery of his aunt's (Olivette Thibault) infidelity with her clerk, and his uncle's pessimism and self-contempt. The film also affords a glimpse into the rancid relationships between working-class French Canadian miners and their British bosses, while also capturing the harsh beauty of a Quebec winter landscape through Michel Brault's remarkable cinematography. The film was shot on location in mostly natural light and without cranes, dollies, or klieg lights.

Moreover, the feature scores political points without strident rhetoric. By concentrating, for example, on Joseph Poplin (Lionel Villeneuve), who bitterly quits the mine to work in the bush, and on an episode during which the rich mine manager throws cheap toys to children in the street during a carriage ride, the film depicts a grumbling, often grim and biased society. The film makes clear that the local French Canadians know that they are being exploited by Americans and English-speaking Canadians who take advantage of their cheap labor and resources without giving much back in return.

Impact   One of the most honored Canadian films of all time—it won eight Etrog Awards, including Best Film and Direction–*Mon Oncle Antoine* is distinguished from most of its forerunners and contemporaries by virtue of its fresh observation, uncompromising realism, lack of narrative artifice, strong characterization, and humor in the midst of oppression and pain. Jutra does not sanitize anything in telling his story (for which he wrote the screenplay with the help of Clement Perron), and he ensures that the boy's point of view is not diluted or altered by an adult bias.

Further Reading

Feldman, Seth, ed. *Take Two: A Tribute to Film in Canada.* Toronto: Irwin, 1984.

Knelman, Martin. *Home Movies: Tales from the Canadian Film World.* Toronto: Key Porter Books, 1987.

Wine, Bill. *"Mon Oncle Antoine."* In *Magill's Survey of Cinema: Foreign Language Series*, edited by Frank N. Magill. Vol. 5. Englewood Cliffs, N.J.: Salem Press, 1985.

Keith Garebian

See also   Film in Canada; Francophonie, La.

■ *Monday Night Football*

Identification   Television broadcasts of prime-time professional football games
Date   Began airing in September, 1970

Monday Night Football *increased the popularity of the National Football League (NFL) and became a cultural phenomenon.*

Monday Night Football was the brainchild of Pete Rozelle, NFL commissioner, and Roone Arledge, an executive of the American Broadcasting Company (ABC) television network. Arledge envisioned football as part of a year-round schedule of Monday night television events that would include professional basketball, films, and family-oriented variety shows. Long after other programs fell by the wayside, *Monday Night Football* moved beyond sports programming to the status of cultural phenomenon.

The first broadcast team consisted of Keith Jackson, Don Meredith, and Howard Cosell. The banter between Meredith, who was folksy and spontaneous, and Cosell, who was bombastic and sardonic, sparked as much viewer interest as the games themselves. Jackson languished, despite the fact that he was the only team member with previous football broadcasting experience. Jackson was replaced by Frank Gifford, who would work the Monday night games from 1971 to 1998.

Along with the personalities in the booth, the camera work and onscreen graphics introduced on *Monday Night Football* set a high standard for other sports broadcasts; for example, slow-motion replays first appeared on *Monday Night Football*. According to some accounts, however, the drive for flawless video production took a heavy toll on the technical crew, who were worn down by the demands of capturing every detail of the games.

As the broadcasters gained in fame, their relationship with the football fans became a major ingredient of the Monday night spectacles. Cosell in particular delighted in goading fan hatred with his venomous criticism of popular players. As the 1970's went on, the fans at every game would brandish anti-Cosell posters. Cosell read all the hate mail, baited his detractors, and thoroughly enjoyed his role as the most despised person on television. Even half-time shows were not immune from Cosell's acid tongue. During a New Orleans Saints game, he launched into a lengthy diatribe questioning the reenactment of the 1814 Battle of New Orleans on the field and blasting it as an inappropriate promotion of militarism.

Although the banter among Gifford, Meredith, and Cosell kept fans watching, the tension in the booth grew with each game. Gifford disliked the razzle-dazzle camera techniques and playing straight man to the Cosell-Meredith comic feud. Meredith felt inadequate and left the team in 1974 but returned in 1977. Cosell never learned much about football and, as time went on, made frequent mistakes that disrupted his partners.

Impact Despite the internal feuds, the popularity of *Monday Night Football* grew steadily. A long list of officials and celebrities lined up for the opportunity to be interviewed at halftime on Monday night. Bars developed elaborate activities to lure in customers to watch the games. American presidents were reluctant to schedule speeches or press conferences on Monday nights during football season for fear of angering millions of fans. Through a combination of luck, timing, and innovation, *Monday Night Football* became a sports phenomenon. Ultimately, it led to major changes in the way in which sporting events were broadcast and helped make sports commentators major celebrities.

Further Reading

Arledge, Roone. *Roone*. New York: HarperCollins, 2003.

Gunther, Mark. *Monday Night Mayhem*. New York: HarperCollins, 1988.

Michael Polley

See also Cosell, Howard; Football; Sports; Television in the United States.

■ Monty Python

Identification British troupe of sketch comedians
Date Formed in 1969

During the 1970's, Monty Python introduced a new brand of absurdist humor to Americans, which occasionally pushed the boundaries of what was considered acceptable.

Monty Python's roots sprang from Great Britain's elite universities at Oxford and Cambridge, where generations of undergraduates performed humorous sketches in revues. Monty Python members Graham Chapman, John Cleese, Eric Idle, Terry Jones, and Michael Palin were part of these revue troupes at Oxford or Cambridge. Terry Gilliam, the only American-born member, provided animations for their signature comedy show, *Monty Python's Flying Circus*.

The structure of *Monty Python's Flying Circus* was taken directly from the university revues: one humorous sketch following another with little or no connecting material. The sketches were typically satirical but not political in any narrow, partisan sense.

They were also highly innovative for the time, with the humor following more from outrageous characters in outlandish situations rather than the traditional set up-punchline format of traditional comedy.

The group combined an absurdist quality with sometimes daring subject matter, which included poking fun at self-important pretensions, the British class system, and even religion. Even the structure of the show broke the rules, often running the closing credits halfway through the show or playing the opening theme music at the show's conclusion.

Monty Python's Flying Circus originally aired on the BBC from 1969 to 1974, and it was later picked up by a number of Public Broadcasting Service (PBS) affiliates in the United States beginning in 1974. The group also produced a number of films, including a compilation of sketches from the television show titled *And Now for Something Completely Different* (1971), as well as *Monty Python and the Holy Grail* (1975) and *Life of Brian* (1979).

Impact *Monty Python's Flying Circus* earned a cult following in Britain and perhaps especially in the United States. Such American and Canadian shows as *Saturday Night Live* and *SCTV* owed a debt to the anarchic, intellectual-yet-silly sketch comedy pioneered by Monty Python. Comedians of a later generation, including Robin Williams and Steve Martin, often cite Monty Python as an influence on their writing and performance.

Subsequent Events The group did not perform together following Chapman's death in 1989, although they appeared at a number of comedy festivals. The surviving members of the troupe remained active, producing, writing, directing, and appearing in films and situation comedies in both Britain and the United States. *Spamalot*, a Broadway musical show based on *Monty Python and the Holy Grail* and written by Idle, appeared in 2005.

Further Reading

Morgan, David. *Monty Python Speaks*. San Francisco: Perennial Currents, 1999.

Ross, Robert. *The Monty Python Encyclopedia*. New York: TV Books, 1999.

Christopher Berkeley

See also Comedians; Film in the United States; Public Broadcasting Service (PBS); *Saturday Night Live*; Television in the United States.

■ Mood rings

Definition Inexpensive pieces of costume jewelry
featuring crystals that supposedly changed color
based on the wearer's mood
Date First produced in 1975

*Mood rings were the perfect symbol of the "Me Decade," an
external indicator of the wearer's mood for all to see.*

The mood ring originated as a result of the study
of biofeedback. In biofeedback, external devices
are used to monitor bodily functions like heart or
blood pressure, in hopes that these functions can be
brought under voluntary control. Thirty-three-year-
old Joshua Reynolds, a pioneer in the field, was involved in several projects to monitor brain waves before settling on the idea of a portable, inexpensive
biofeedback device. Reynolds was also a marketing
expert and quickly realized the sales potential of
his new creation. He garnered the support of the
Faberge cosmetic company, and the first mood ring
entered the market in 1975.

The ring's popularity began in New York City but
quickly spread throughout the United States. Mood
rings were a fun fad because the color of the surface
was supposed to reflect a person's mood. Dark purple signified happiness, contentment, or arousal. A
blue ring meant that the wearer was calm or relaxed,
while blue-green showed that the wearer was merely
content. Green was considered average, and amber
meant that one was a little nervous or ill at ease. Gray
signified anxiety, and black demonstrated stress or
tension.

In reality, the surface of the ring responded to
skin temperature, not mood. The crystals contained
within the glass shell were sensitive to temperature
and changing position as the temperature of the
glass surface altered. This, in turn, changed the way
in which light reflected off the crystals, causing the
surface to change colors. What was considered an
"average" mood actually meant the temperature of
the crystal was 82 degrees Fahrenheit. The colors
therefore correlated to skin temperature. If a person
is passionate or excited, his or her skin tends to become flush. If that same person is nervous or upset,
then the blood flow to the skin lessons, the skin temperature drops, and the ring changes color.

Impact As with most fads, the popularity of mood
rings was fleeting. Imposters quickly appeared, and

"impulse rings" and "persona rings" glutted the market. After a few years, the crystals no longer functioned and settled into the black configuration permanently.

This was not the last fad for Joshua Reynolds; he
also created the Thigh-Master, an exercise device
popularized by infomercials starring former *Three's
Company* actor Suzanne Somers during the 1980's.

Further Reading

Feinstein, Stephen. *The 1970's: From Watergate to
Disco.* Berkeley Heights, N.J.: Enslow, 2002.
Stern, Jan, and Michael Stern. *The Encyclopedia of Bad
Taste.* New York: HarperCollins, 1990.

P. S. Ramsey

See also Astrology; Atari; Bell-bottoms; CB radio;
Fads; Fashions and clothing; Hippies; Lava lamps;
Pet rocks; Pyramid power; Rubik's cube; Streaking;
Toys and games.

■ Moonies

Identification Members of the Unification Church

*When the Reverend Sun Myung Moon, founder of the Uni-
fication Church, moved his headquarters from Korea to
Tarrytown, New York, in 1971, the Moonies movement
gained momentum. However, the organization also caused
a whirlwind of controversy everywhere it went for being
cultlike in its activities.*

Sun Myung Moon was born in Korea on January 6,
1920, and raised in the Presbyterian Church. However, he claimed that on Easter Day, 1936, Jesus appeared to him and chose him for the mission of establishing his Kingdom of Heaven on Earth. Over
the next nine years, Moon received many revelations
through prayer, the study of religious Scriptures,
and spiritual communications with leaders such as
Moses, Buddha, and God himself. These revelations
were later translated into English and published as
the *Divine Principle*, the text used as the official doctrine of the Unification Church.

In 1954, after spending several years in prison for
heresy and for evading the draft, Moon founded the
Holy Spirit Association for the Unification of World
Christianity, also known as the Unification Church.
Missionaries from the Church were sent to the
United States beginning in 1959, but little headway
was made until 1971, when Moon completed his

third world tour and returned to the United States to make New York his headquarters.

Before 1971, Moon had never spoken in the West, but during the early 1970's, he was seen and heard by thousands of people across North America and Europe. In order to fund the evangelistic speaking tours and to purchase real estate needed for the Church's mission, members began selling peanuts, candles, and flowers on the streets. Through extensive media coverage, Moon became a household name and his followers became known as "Moonies." Parents became alarmed and formed an anticult movement when their children left college and careers to spend up to eighteen hours a day on the streets soliciting donations for the Church.

Impact Many scholars consider the Unification Church to be one of the most controversial religions in history. During the 1970's, the Moonies gained notoriety as they supported Richard M. Nixon's presidency at the time of Watergate. They also came to be known for their mass weddings in which hundreds of couples were "blessed" by Moon. The church also invested in a variety of nonprofit and business organizations including a ballet academy, the Unification Theological Seminary, several newspapers, and a pharmaceutical company during the decade.

Subsequent Events As of 2004, the Church claimed to have 30,000 members in the United States, with approximately 200,000 worldwide. They owned an expanded network of businesses and educational enterprises, including *The Washington Times*, Paragon Press, and the University of Bridgeport in Connecticut. Moon continued to draw controversy through his organization called the Family Federation for World Peace and Unification.

Further Reading

Barker, Eileen. *The Making of a Moonie: Choice or Brainwashing?* New York: Basil Blackwell, 1984.

Chryssides, George D. *The Advent of Sun Myung

The Reverend Sun Myung Moon (right) is applauded by noted British physicist R. V. Jones after delivering the opening address at the International Conference on the Unity of Sciences, one of Moon's many front organizations, in 1977. (AP/Wide World Photos)

Moon: The Origins, Beliefs, and Practices of the Unification Church. New York: St. Martin's Press, 1991.

Mickler, Michael L. "Unification Church ('Moonies')." In *Odd Gods: New Religions and the Cult Controversy,* edited by James R. Lewis. Amherst, N.Y.: Prometheus Books, 2001.

Joy M. Gambill

See also Cults; Religion and spirituality in the United States.

■ Mopeds

Definition Bicycles propelled by small motors

The moped was a gas-efficient mode of transportation that people could use to travel short distances, usually within the confines of urban areas.

The two-wheeled moped, first produced by BMW in Germany in the 1920's, was a hybrid combining the shape, size, and pedal-power of a regular bicycle with a 50 cubic centimeter motor and a hint of the heft and styling of a motorcycle. Its name derived from "motor" (mo) and "pedal" (ped). The mopeds' small engine and consequent low speeds (40 miles per hour at best) meant that they were not allowed on limited-access public roads during the 1970's. Mopeds had a mechanism called a centrifugal clutch that allowed the rear wheels to be powered by either the pedals or the motor. The rider used the pedals to initiate the machine's forward movement until the motor could take over. They could attain maximum speeds on a smooth flat surface, but the pedals were usually necessary to make it up a steep hill.

Inexpensive to purchase and operate—they could go as much as 150 miles on one gallon of gasoline—mopeds were popular with teenagers not yet licensed to drive a car. They came equipped with single- or double-size saddles, optional windshields, lockable telescopic front forks, and luggage racks. Moreover, some adults concerned with fuel efficiency found mopeds a handy mode of transportation: The oil and gasoline shortages during the 1970's meant that conserving gas and saving money took on greater importance. By 1977, mopeds reached fad status.

Though they came in bright, even gaudy, colors, with lots of chrome, they were often made of cheap materials. They had inadequate power for some circumstances, and because they also had poor brake and suspension systems, they were generally considered unsafe. On highways or city streets, they were hard to see, thus creating another safety concern.

Impact   For young people who wanted to be able to come and go as they pleased to malls, theaters, and sports arenas, the moped was a fashionable transportation alternative to skateboards, roller skates, or walking. Motor scooters, perennially popular in parts of Europe, had more power and higher status, but they were more expensive, and their higher speed capability required the riders to have licenses in many states.

Further Reading

Bennett, Jim. *The Complete Motorcycle Book.* 2d ed. New York: Facts On File, 1999.

Skelton, Richard. *Funky Mopeds: The 1970's Sports Moped Phenomenon.* Dorcester, England: Veloce, 2004.

Jane L. Ball

See also   Energy crisis; Fads; Roller skating; Skateboards; Transportation.

■ Mormon Church lifting of priesthood ban for African Americans

The Event   The decision that male African Americans could have the power and authority to act in the name of God based on individual moral worthiness

Date   Announced on June 9, 1978

The decision to allow African Americans to receive the blessings associated with holding the priesthood helped increase African American participation in the Mormon Church and alleviated claims of racism lobbed at Mormons.

Joseph Smith, the first president and prophet of the Church of Jesus Christ of Latter-day Saints (commonly referred to as the Mormon or LDS Church) in the nineteenth century, was a strong advocate of equal rights for African Americans. During his lifetime, two African Americans, Elijah Abel and Walker Lewis, were ordained to the priesthood in the church. According to other church leaders, the priesthood policy was clarified during the latter part of Smith's life. Based on verses in LDS scripture known as *The Pearl of Great Price*, any male descendant of Noah's son Ham could not hold the priesthood in the LDS Church. Smith believed that African Americans were descendants of Cain through the lineage of Ham, which would disqualify them from holding the priesthood. When Brigham Young succeeded Joseph Smith as the leader of the Mormons in 1844, he followed this so-called priesthood ban policy, pointing out that the policy would remain in force until revelation from the Lord dictated otherwise. All LDS prophets who followed Young continued with the same policy until 1978. Although African Americans could be members of the church, males were restricted from holding the priesthood.

During the latter 1960's and into the mid-1970's, the Mormon Church was criticized in the media for its priesthood policy. Mormons were targeted as being racist. Numerous protests and demonstrations were conducted at sporting events involving LDS-owned Brigham Young University (BYU). Some institutions declined to schedule any further athletic competitions with BYU. Concerts presented by the eminent Mormon Tabernacle Choir were boycotted. Nonetheless, the number of African American members of the Mormon Church increased.

In 1971, under the direction of LDS president Joseph Fielding Smith, the Genesis Group was formed for the purpose of fellowshipping African American Mormons. After Spencer W. Kimball became president of the Mormon Church in 1973, he reiterated the priesthood ban policy for African Americans, stating that it would take a revelation from the Lord to change the policy.

The Revelation　As worldwide membership in the Mormon Church escalated, more and more people of African ancestry joined the church. Due to the growing number of Mormons in Brazil during the 1960's and 1970's, the LDS Church began building a temple in São Paulo in 1978. When completed, worthy priesthood holders and female members of the church who were not of the Hamitic lineage could participate in the higher ordinances of the gospel of Jesus Christ that are administered in a Mormon temple. However, due to the mixing of races in Brazil, it was nearly impossible to determine who was of Hamitic ancestry. Consequently, it would be almost impossible to know whom to exclude from the priesthood or who to restrict from temple attendance. In 1977, LDS missionaries were also successful in Ghana, resulting in many Ghanaians joining the Mormon Church. The priesthood ban policy was becoming increasingly complex to administer and enforce.

In early 1978, Mormon Church leaders, under the direction of Kimball, spent weeks carefully discussing the priesthood-ban issue. On June 1, 1978, President Kimball fervently prayed for the guidance and direction of the Lord concerning admittance of worthy African American Mormons to the priesthood. After spending considerable time praying, Kimball and other church leaders who met with him reported that the spirit of the Lord confirmed to them that the priesthood was to be made available to all worthy male members of the church, regardless of color or race. The priesthood ban had been lifted.

On June 9, 1978, an announcement of President Kimball's revelation was issued to the media. All the major television networks featured the announcement. *The New York Times*, the *Washington Post*, and the *Los Angeles Times* carried the story on their front pages. The vast majority of Mormons throughout the world were elated with the news. African Americans now had all the privileges and blessings available to them that are associated with full membership in the Mormon Church. According to church records, Joseph Freeman, Jr., who had been a member of the church since 1956, was the first African American to be ordained to the priesthood after the 1978 revelation.

Impact　One of the most important revelations in the history of the Church of Jesus Christ of Latter-day Saints was given to President Spencer W. Kimball in 1978. It allowed worthy African American males to hold the priesthood and made available to all worthy members of the church all the blessings that the gospel of Jesus Christ affords, including participation in the higher ordinances in Mormon temples. As a result, African American membership in the Mormon Church increased dramatically. White Mormons, who had been accused of racial discrimination, generally were relieved to have the new policy in force.

Further Reading

Bringhurst, Newell G., and Darron T. Smith, eds. *Black and Mormon.* Urbana: University of Illinois Press, 2004. Explores the history of African Americans in the Mormon Church, including the priesthood ban policy, racial relations within the church, and life for African American Mormons after the 1978 revelation lifted the priesthood ban.

Embry, Jessie L. *Black Saints in a White Church: Contemporary African American Mormons.* Salt Lake City: Signature Books, 1993. Embry unveils answers about the Mormon priesthood ban policy, as well as a comprehensive history of African Americans in the Mormon Church, with an emphasis on how African Americans were assimilated into the church after the 1978 revelation.

Martins, Helvecio, and Mark Grover. *The Autobiography of Elder Helvecio Martins.* Salt Lake City: Aspen Books, 1994. The intriguing story of Helvecio Martins, the first African American called as a general authority in the Mormon Church after the priesthood ban was lifted. His struggles, his spiritual experiences, his devotion, and his dedication before and after receiving the priesthood are documented.

Alvin K. Benson

See also　African Americans; Episcopal Church ordination of women; Johnson, Sonia; Racial discrimination; Religion and spirituality in the United States.

■ Morrison, Toni

Identification African American writer
Born February 18, 1931; Lorain, Ohio

In her dual roles as an editor and emerging writer, Morrison actively encouraged the publication and widespread acceptance of African American literature during the 1970's.

As a newly single mother, Toni Morrison joined the editorial staff of Random House, eventually rising to the position of senior editor. During a period of growing public interest in minority cultures, she oversaw production of an early anthology that introduced Americans to contemporary African writers. She inspired and was largely responsible for the publication of Middleton Harris's seminal *The Black Book* (1974), a pictorial history of three hundred years of African American life, which included the face of Morrison's mother in the cover montage. Morrison also edited the autobiographies of celebrities Muhammad Ali and Angela Davis, but she was particularly enthusiastic about publishing and promoting the work of new authors, such as Gayl Jones and Toni Cade Bambara. At the same time, she was teaching African American literature at Howard and Yale Universities.

With the publication of three novels, Morrison launched her own distinguished literary career as well. She remarked that she wrote the first two because they were the sort that she had hoped to read yet could never find, but in all of them she questioned the American status quo. *The Bluest Eye* (1970) revealed how an uncritical acceptance of a "white" ideal of beauty destroyed a little black girl and her mother. *Sula* (1973) explored the ways in which the lifelong friendship between two black women, traditional Nel and rebellious Sula, challenged their community.

Morrison's third book, *Song of Solomon* (1977), was her breakout novel, the first of many best-sellers and the first by a black writer to become a Book-of-the-Month Club main selection since Richard Wright's *Native Son* (1940). It was awarded the National Book Critics Circle Award and serialized in *Redbook*, a popular women's magazine. In *Song of Solomon*, she established a characteristic narrative voice that linked African American idioms with traditional storytelling, interweaving a young man's classical quest with elements of modern black culture. With this book, Morrison gained full control of her powers by combining realism with myth, the mundane world with the supernatural.

Impact By the end of the decade, Toni Morrison was becoming a significant literary force as she sought to nurture new voices and resurrect the silenced stories of black life. The future 1993 Nobel Prize winner was likewise influential in broadening African American writing to include more female protagonists and perspectives, even as she emphasized the crucial importance of a shared heritage and the dignity of ordinary people. In her own work, her fascination with the richness of the spoken language and the solemn weight of ancestors, folklore, and tradition added a new dimension to American literature.

Further Reading

Als, Hilton. "Ghosts in the House." *The New Yorker* 79 (October 27, 2003): 64-75.

Denard, Carolyn. "Toni Morrison." In *Black Women in America: An Historical Encyclopedia*, edited by Darlene Clark Hine. Brooklyn, N.Y.: Carlson, 1993.

Samuels, Wilfred D., and Clenora Hudson-Weems. *Toni Morrison*. Boston: Twayne, 1990.

Joanne McCarthy

See also African Americans; Ali, Muhammad; Book publishing; Davis, Angela; Literature in the United States.

■ Moscone, George

Identification Mayor of San Francisco, 1976-1978
Born November 24, 1929; San Francisco, California
Died November 27, 1978; San Francisco, California

The assassination of Moscone in 1978 reignited the gay rights movement, and ensuing riots demonstrated the gay population's unwillingness to accept further discrimination.

George Moscone earned a law degree, and before becoming San Francisco's mayor, he served in the state senate, where he was an ally of California governor Jerry Brown. While in the senate, he was elected senate majority leader, marched with farmworker activist César Chávez, and shepherded a bill through the legislature providing for funding for three-quarters of a million students to have school lunches.

Mayor George Moscone (right) with San Francisco supervisor Harvey Milk at the signing of the city's gay rights bill in 1977. Both men would be assassinated a year later. (AP/Wide World Photos)

He was elected San Francisco mayor in 1976 and served until his death.

As mayor, Moscone brought changes to San Francisco's city supervisor system that required supervisors to live in the districts in which they served. The large gay constituency in the Castro district helped local politician and Castro resident Harvey Milk run a successful campaign for, and get elected as, the first openly gay city supervisor. Moscone's main claim to political notoriety was his support for Milk's bill banning housing discrimination against gays. It was this bill that caused another city supervisor, Dan White, to resign.

Two days after his resignation, White asked for his seat back. When Moscone refused this request, most gay rights activists believe that White decided to take revenge. White, however, later claimed in court proceedings that severe depression—both evidenced and worsened by his eating of junk food—had caused him to lose control of his own actions and to shoot Moscone and Milk to death. This defense was generally accepted at his trial and became known as the "Twinkie defense." White was convicted of manslaughter and received a sentence of only seven years. This light sentence resulted in massive protests, leading to the White Night Riots in May, 1979.

Impact The assassinations of George Moscone and Milk, the widespread reactions to them, and White's light sentence marked a shift in the gay rights movement from a social to a more political movement. This shift would become even more apparent as the acquired immunodeficiency syndrome (AIDS) crisis emerged in the early 1980's. The date of the assassinations has been commemorated in subsequent years in San Francisco with a gay rights march, and the National Lesbian and Gay Rights March of 1979 commemorated their deaths. Moscone was followed in office by Dianne Feinstein, who later became a U.S. senator.

Further Reading

Hinckle, Warren. *Gayslayer! The Story of How Dan White Killed Harvey Milk and George Moscone and Got*

Away with Murder. Virginia City, Nev.: Silver Dollar Books, 1985.

Salter, Kenneth W., ed. *The Trial of Dan White.* El Cerrito, Calif.: Market and Systems Interface, 1991.

Shilts, Randy. *The Mayor of Castro Street: The Life and Times of Harvey Milk.* New York: St. Martin's Press, 1982.

Weiss, Mike. *Double Play: The San Francisco City Hall Killings.* Reading, Mass.: Addison-Wesley, 1984.

Jessie Bishop Powell

See also Acquired immunodeficiency syndrome (AIDS); Bryant, Anita; Byrne, Jane; Daley, Richard J.; Feinstein, Dianne; Homosexuality and gay rights; Jackson, Maynard, Jr.; Koch, Ed; Liberalism in U.S. politics; Milk, Harvey; National Gay and Lesbian Rights March of 1979; White Night Riots.

■ Mowat, Farley

Identification Canadian writer and environmentalist

Born May 12, 1921; Belleville, Ontario, Canada

By focusing attention on the extermination of wildlife and the desecration of wilderness lands, Mowat advanced environmental causes in Canada and throughout the world.

During the 1970's, Farley Mowat continued to publish prose works castigating his countrymen and his government for their indifference toward nature and its creatures. In *A Whale for the Killing* (1972), he described his attempts to save a beached, pregnant whale from the tortures inflicted on it by the people of Burgeo, Newfoundland, where Mowat was then living, and from the indifference of the government officials and the scientists who could have saved its life. *Wake of the Great Sealers* (1973), the story of Newfoundland's seal hunts, also showed human beings at their worst; so too did the memoir *And No Birds Sang* (1979), a graphic account of Mowat's combat experiences in Italy and Sicily during World War II.

Mowat also continued to warn about dire consequences if measures were not taken to protect the Arctic, the theme of *The Great Betrayal: Arctic Canada Now* (1976), a sequel to *Canada North* (1973). His fascination with the Far North took Mowat and his wife, Claire, to Siberia in 1966 and again in 1969; the result was *Sibir: My Discovery of Siberia* (1970), drawn largely from the journals that Claire kept during their visits. *Tundra: Selections from the Great Accounts of*

Arctic Land Voyages (1973), edited by Mowat, was the first of three books containing firsthand accounts by Arctic explorers. Throughout all these works, Mowat emphasized the beauty of the Far North, while admitting how hostile the region could be to human beings. In *The Snow Walker* (1975), a collection of short stories set in the tundra, he expressed his sympathy for ordinary people living in an uncompromising environment and trying desperately to preserve their simple lifestyle against the inroads of so-called progress.

Impact Throughout the decade, Mowat remained the best-known spokesperson for Canada's Green Movement and a never-failing irritant to the establishment. He also became increasingly pessimistic as to whether the warnings that he voiced had any effect. However, one of the works published during this period did have specific results: *A Whale for the Killing* is credited with focusing attention worldwide on the plight of whales and with motivating a number of efforts to save them, both as individuals and as a species. As one of Canada's best-known authors and one who appealed to people of all ages, during this period, Mowat was in a position to mold public opinion, thus contributing immeasurably to a growing sensitivity about environmental issues.

Further Reading

King, James. *Farley: The Life of Farley Mowat.* South Royalton, Vt.: Steerforth Press, 2002.

Orange, John. *Farley Mowat: A Biography.* Toronto: E. C. W. Press, 1993.

Rosemary M. Canfield Reisman

See also Environmental movement; Greenpeace; Literature in Canada.

■ *Ms.* magazine

Identification Feminist periodical

Date First published in January, 1972

Ms. magazine was a vital part of the 1970's feminist movement and was the first national feminist women's magazine that became iconic of feminist publications.

Limited by the male domination in journalism, the publication of feminist articles was rare in mainstream periodicals prior to 1972. Although there were nearly five hundred smaller feminist publications, none acquired a large mainstream audience. Gloria Steinem founded *Ms.* because of her inability

Gloria Steinem, the publisher of Ms. magazine, reveals the cover of the January, 1977, issue rating President Jimmy Carter's first year in office. (AP/Wide World Photos)

to place articles about women's issues with male editors and publishers; she edited *Ms.* from its inception until 1988. In 1963, she had written an exposé about her experience as a Playboy Bunny, which helped her become a visible spokeswoman of the feminist movement. Her subsequent travels connected her with women in rural and urban areas, whose concerns and issues were not being addressed by existing periodicals. Finding the audience for *Ms.* from this experience, as well as from her work with the Women's Action Alliance, she approached her cofounder at *New York* magazine, Clay Felker, for backing.

Exceeding the publisher's expectations, the preview issue sold out its 300,000 run within the first eight days of the periodical's publication. By 1973,

there were approximately 200,000 subscribers who were under thirty-five, college educated, and employed in white-collar work. Addressing the real condition of women's lives, the magazine secured a loyal audience who was ready for social change.

Ms. magazine captured the energy and concerns of the women's movement and employed feminist values in its organization, operation, and content. Its female staff collaborated on editorials, on layout, and in writing and soliciting articles. *Ms.* also refused to include sexist advertising or articles about fashion, food, and typical subjects of women's magazines—its serious exposés attracted politically minded readers. Moreover, the magazine modeled a new relationship between reader and publisher with its extended letters column, thus ensuring that a multiplicity of voices and concerns were acknowledged. Finally, self-help articles helped empower women to assume new levels of personal responsibility in their own social, economical, and educational endeavors.

Peaking with a circulation of 500,000 in 1976, *Ms.* was heavily in debt by 1979, partly because of its policy of restricting advertisers and also because of competition from a new spate of women's magazines. Publishing industry consultants reported to the editorial board in 1978 that other magazines had co-opted the successful formula of *Ms.*, which lessened its distinctiveness. Moreover, popular feminism and intellectual feminism diverged at the end of the decade; readers preferred popular aspects of the movement, but the editorial board strengthened their commitment to intellectual feminism. Although Steiner's operation was reorganized as the nonprofit Ms. Foundation, the magazine's circulation never increased, a fact many attributed to the organization's focus on ideals, not profit.

Impact   *Ms.* magazine paved the way for other feminist women's magazines, and its reporting on topics such as rape, domestic violence, and job discrimination broke journalistic bounds.

Further Reading

Farrell, Amy Erdman. *Yours in Sisterhood: "Ms." Magazine and the Promise of Popular Feminism.* Chapel Hill: University of North Carolina Press, 1998.

Scott, Linda. "Imagining Feminism in the Marketplace: Linda Scott Interviews Gloria Steinem." *Advertising and Society Review* 4, no. 4 (2003).

Rebecca Tolley-Stokes

See also Feminism; Journalism in the United States; National Organization for Women (NOW); *Our Bodies, Ourselves*; Self-help books; Sexual revolution; Steinem, Gloria; Women's rights.

■ Muldowney, Shirley

Identification American drag racer
Born June 19, 1940; Schenectady, N.Y.

Muldowney was the first woman ever licensed to drive National Hot Rod Association (NHRA) Top Fuel drag racers, but her achievement goes well beyond this "first." During the 1970's, she excelled at this overwhelmingly male sport, not only in competing with men but also in beating them at their own game.

Shirley "Cha Cha" Muldowney began racing cars at age eighteen, and by 1965, she had earned her license from the NHRA to drive gasoline-powered dragsters. She began the 1970's by racing the dangerous "funny cars," winning her first major meet in 1971. After three years racing funny cars and surviving four fires caused by engine failure, she decided to move up to compete in the Top Fuel class, becoming the first woman to be licensed for Top Fuel racing in the NHRA.

In 1975, Muldowney became the first woman to qualify for the Top Fuel finals and the first woman to break the five-second time barrier. This impressive showing during the 1975 season earned her a place on the American Auto Racing Writers and Broadcasters Association's All American Team. In 1976, she won her first NHRA national event, was named Top Fuel driver of the year by *Drag News*, and was again named to the All American Team.

Muldowney reached a new peak in 1977, becoming only the second person to exceed 250 miles per hour and winning the NHRA Spring Nationals, the NHRA Summer Nationals, and the NHRA Molson Grand Nationals in Canada. She completed the season by becoming the first woman to win the Winston World Championship for points in Top Fuel. Once

again, she was named Top Fuel Driver of the Year by *Drag News* and was named Person of the Year by *Car Craft*. She was also awarded an Outstanding Achievement Award from the U.S. House of Representatives.

Impact Shirley Muldowney did not merely break the gender barrier in drag racing—she demolished it. During the 1970's, she went beyond excelling as a woman in the sport and began surpassing the men, proving that women are capable of competing with men on a level playing field. She was the best-known female drag racer, and, at least to the general public, she held the most recognizable name in the sport. Honored by the New York State Senate as one of Thirty Women of Distinction, along with such figures as Susan B. Anthony and Eleanor Roosevelt, she changed the way in which Americans look at women and their sporting accomplishments. In 1983, the film *Heart Like a Wheel* dramatized her life.

Further Reading

Miller, Ernestine. *Making Her Mark: Firsts and Milestones in Women's Sports.* McGraw-Hill, 2002.

Muldowney, Shirley, and Bill Stevens. *Shirley Muldowney's Tales from the Track.* Sports, 2004.

Mary Virginia Davis

See also Automobiles; Feminism; Little League participation by girls; Sports; Title IX of the Education Amendments of 1972; Women's rights.

■ Multiculturalism in Canada

Definition The recognition and preservation of ethnic and racial identities within a bilingual framework

Federal legislation in the 1970's paved the way for new policies and programs intended to protect the country's ethnic and racial groups and their identities. The policy reinforced the country's founding "cultural mosaic" philosophy.

Multiculturalism is a national policy that supports and advocates mutual respect and accommodation of ethnic and racial groups. The concept is roughly equivalent to pluralism, or "cultural mosaic," and stands in contrast to the perception of conformity in the American melting pot model.

Before the 1960's, Canada's immigration policy was highly restrictive, and immigrants came primarily from the Americas and Europe. The 1960's were a time of sweeping immigration reform that forever changed the ethnic face of the country. Legislation swung open the doors for immigrants from non-European countries, especially in Asia and Latin America.

In 1969, the Canadian government assembled a Royal Commission on Bilingualism and Biculturalism and assigned it to hold public hearings across the country in order to study and better understand the country's social fabric. By gathering public sentiments, the commission concluded that the old immigration policy of assimilation was neither popular nor just. The ensuing report reiterated earlier governmental commitments to helping people from all ethnic groups across society, regardless of birthplace. It recommended a more powerful version of a multicultural policy than the one actually implemented a few years later. The Immigration Act of 1976 abolished discrimination on the basis of race, ethnicity, religion, gender, and national origins. Beginning in the 1970's, Canada welcomed large numbers of Asians, Latinos, and Africans into its national mosaic.

The 1960's were also years of bad feeling between Canada's English- and French-speaking elements. The separatist issue in Quebec and the underlying current of French nationalism were key motivators in the development of Canada's multiculturalism policy.

An Official Policy   On October 8, 1971, Prime Minister Pierre Trudeau announced a new national multicultural policy in the House of Commons, thus giving formal recognition to Canada's pride in pluralism.

Multiculturalism became the focus of prolonged and heated policy debates. Proponents argued that multiculturalism was a positive condition that would strengthen Canadian identity. Support for the policy was strongest in the most culturally diverse areas, such as urban settings (especially Toronto and Vancouver), and weakest in rural areas and small towns. Opponents argued that it would undermine Canadian unity and threaten the very existence of the Canadian state. Some feared the dilution of British and French cultures, especially in Quebec, where nationalism had flared violently.

In the long run, however, provincial governments followed the lead of the national government and implemented multicultural policies within their jurisdictions. Multiculturalism fit the Québécois mind-set of "separate and distinct," and Quebec bureaucrats eventually developed programs similar to those in other provinces. Ethnic groups long established in Canadian society saw the new policy as an opportunity for cultural enrichment, a means for building pride in heritage. New immigrants, on the other hand, saw multiculturalism as a way of fighting racial prejudice and discrimination and securing jobs, education, and housing. These differing perspectives often clashed on the national scene.

Canada was also to be a multicultural state within the framework of bilingualism. French and English had been legally designated as the country's two official languages in 1969. All Canadians would conform to Canada's official languages in the country's public institutions but be encouraged to pursue and maintain ethnic languages in the private realm. Government grants were made available for projects to recognize, celebrate, and preserve ethnic heritage. At least 130 groups are given special attention today in the heritage program. With federal and provincial backing, schools and communities began teaching "heritage languages" such as Chinese, Korean, and Croatian, in addition to the country's two official languages.

Impact   Multicultural programs emphasized institutional change, citizen participation, and improvement of relations between the races. Critics argued that a formal policy of multiculturalism encouraged immigrants to segregate themselves from their host society, an argument often tied to xenophobia and anti-immigrant feeling.

As early as 1981, federal officials established a unit for handling race relations in the country, a concern that subsequently became a priority of the multicultural policy. Government programs were heavily cultural in the first implementation phase but subsequently shifted to issues of education, human rights, and social services.

Subsequent Events   The country's Charter of Rights and Freedoms and Constitution in 1982 reinforced cultural pluralism as the essence of Canadian identity. The Act for the Preservation and Enhancement of Multiculturalism in Canada, passed in 1988, was the country's first parliamentary framing of a multiethnic and racial policy. It encouraged all Canadians to join in recognizing and celebrating pluralism while also identifying fully as Canadians. A new cabinet post, the minister of multiculturalism, was created in 1991.

The future of Canada's multiculturalism policy is likely to hinge on the tenor and content of its immigration policy. Immigrants will continue to arrive, and, as they do, it is likely that a multicultural policy will continue to foster a unified national identity while encouraging pride in ethnic and racial distinctiveness.

Further Reading

Cameron, Elspeth. *Multiculturalism and Immigration in Canada: An Introductory Reader.* Toronto: Canadian Scholars' Press, 2004. A basic history of immigration in Canada and how it influenced the framing of multicultural policy.

Day, Richard J. F. *Multiculturalism and the History of Canadian Diversity.* University of Toronto Press, 2000. An analysis of the discourse on multiculturalism and the influence of multicultural policy on the cohesion of the state.

Driedger, Leo, ed. *The Canadian Ethnic Mosaic: A Quest for Identity.* Toronto: McClelland and Stewart, 1978. Examines ethnic identity within the legal context of multiculturalism.

Li, Peter S. *Race and Ethnic Relations in Canada.* 2d ed. New York: Oxford University Press, 1999. An overview of racial and ethnic groups, multicultural policy, and contemporary issues.

Migus, Paul M., ed. *Sounds Canadian: Languages and Cultures in Multi-ethnic Society.* Toronto: Peter Martin Associates, 1975. Examines language patterns and challenges within the context of an evolving mosaic society.

Ann M. Legreid

See also   Canadian Citizenship Act of 1977; Canadian Human Rights Act of 1977; Demographics of Canada; Education in Canada; Immigration Act of 1976; Immigration to Canada; Minorities in Canada; Trudeau, Pierre.

■ Munich Olympics terrorism

The Event   Palestinian kidnappers, aligned with the extremist group Black September, attack Israeli athletes; more than one dozen people eventually die

Date   September 5-6, 1972

The Israeli Olympic team takes part in the opening day ceremonies on August 26, 1972. (AP/Wide World Photos)

A hooded member of Black September appears on the balcony of a building in the Olympic Village where the terrorist group holds Israeli athletes hostage on September 5, 1972. (AP/Wide World Photos)

The Munich Games incident was the first blatant act of terror at the Olympics. A Palestinian group broke into the Olympic Village and fatally shot an Israeli coach and athlete. A tense all-day standoff began, and it ended with a failed rescue attempt at a nearby airfield. Nine additional Israelis, one German police officer, and five terrorists died.

The 1972 Munich Olympics were in their second week of competition when they were tragically interrupted. In the overnight hours of September 5, 1972, a group of Palestinian terrorists called Black September entered the Munich Olympic Village and moved toward the complex housing Israeli athletes. They fatally shot two Israelis and kidnapped nine others. The terrorists demanded that more than two hundred of their comrades held in Israeli prisons be freed. Israel's prime minister, Golda Meir, refused the demands, and she alerted the Germans that she and her government supported any efforts that they were making to free the hostages. The International Olympic Committee (IOC) mandated that the Games continue, and already-scheduled Olympic events continued for several hours without interruption. The IOC was criticized harshly for adopting that position, and the Israeli government was infuriated.

Negotiation and Crisis   A series of negotiations involving the kidnappers and German officials began. Meanwhile, on multiple occasions, German officials requested that they be allowed to replace the Israelis as hostages. The kidnappers refused. Late in the day, the Palestinians agreed to a plan that called for them and the hostages to be taken in two helicopters to a nearby airfield and flown on a plane to a Middle Eastern country.

The Germans had no intention of allowing the kidnappers and their hostages to leave the country. A plan to attack the Palestinians was hatched, and it involved the use of police sharpshooters, who would fire on the terrorists at the airfield. One problem was immediately identified: The German police thought that there were only five terrorists, instead of eight, and therefore did not have enough sharpshooters at the airfield. There was a second problem: Inadequate lighting at the airfield meant that the snipers could not see the terrorists easily and could not get a clean shot at them. A firefight began soon after the helicopters landed and lasted for more than an hour. It was falsely reported that the hostages had been rescued. Instead, the terrorists used a grenade to kill several of the hostages in one of the helicopters. Others shot dead the Israelis in the second helicopter.

IOC president Avery Brundage, a United States citizen, stood before athletes, officials, journalists, and others at the Olympic Stadium on September 6, one day after the murders, and insisted that the Games go on. Speaking on behalf of a unified IOC leadership, which had made the decision the night before to resume the Games, Brundage said that terrorists should not be allowed to destroy the international goodwill that was part of the Olympics. A day of mourning was declared, and the Games resumed one day later. Brundage, who planned to retire at the conclusion of the Munich Olympics, had long been a lightning rod for criticism because of his personal beliefs regarding the Olympic Games and the role that they played in the world. In the long hours of confrontation at Munich, he held a series of meetings with the crisis team that was trying to end the standoff. In doing so, he ignored the wishes of other members within the IOC hierarchy, who asked him to steer clear of the delicate negotiations.

Impact The Olympic Games, brought back to life at the end of the nineteenth century, survived the Munich massacre, but they would never be the same. Media interest in security preparations increased at subsequent Games. The fear of similar attacks also ensured that Olympic organizers in each host city would earmark large amounts of money toward security efforts. The Olympics—representing opportunities for people from all over the world to gather in friendly and peaceful athletic competitions—were forever scarred.

Further Reading

Espy, Richard. *The Politics of the Olympic Games.* Berkeley: University of California Press, 1979. Espy charts the intertwining of politics and the modern Olympics from their beginnings through the 1970's.

Groussard, Serge. *The Blood of Israel: The Massacre of the Israeli Athletes—The Olympics, 1972.* New York: William Morrow, 1975. A powerful account of the events connected with the kidnapping and hostage crisis.

Guttmann, Allen. *The Games Must Go On: Avery Brundage and the Olympic Movement.* New York: Columbia University Press, 1984. An excellent analysis of the man who was determined not to allow the terror attacks to stop the ongoing Games.

Mandell, Richard. *A Munich Diary: The Olympics of 1972.* Chapel Hill: University of North Carolina Press, 1991. Provides the reader with Mandell's thoughts about the whole of the 1972 Summer Games, not just the terror.

Reeve, Simon. *One Day in September: The Full Story of the 1972 Munich Olympics Massacre and the Israeli Revenge Operation "Wrath of God."* New York: Arcade, 2000. Well-detailed account of what happened in Munich. Perhaps the strongest element of this book is the chapter outlining the roots of the Black September organization, and how and why it targeted the Olympics.

Anthony Moretti

See also Israel and the United States; Middle East and North America; Olympic Games of 1972; Sports; Symbionese Liberation Army (SLA); Terrorism.

■ Muppets, The

Identification Puppets that starred in a variety of television shows and films

Jim Henson's lifelike puppets—showcased in television, films, and cartoons—became some of the most lovable characters in American popular culture during the decade.

The Muppets were the creations of Jim Henson, who worked as a puppeteer in college and had his own show in the Washington, D.C., area during the 1950's. His Muppets were a cross between marionettes and hand puppets: Their mouths were usually worked by hand and their arms and legs often moved by strings. The puppeteer was usually situated below the Muppet. Henson even built special stages so that there was room for the puppeteers to move, which added to the illusion that the Muppets were real.

Comedian Bob Hope appears in The Muppet Movie *with Gonzo. (AP/Wide World Photos)*

Though certain Muppet characters had appeared on a variety of shows throughout the 1960's, Henson's creations became widely known once he joined the production staff of *Sesame Street*. Creating Big Bird, Bert, Ernie, Kermit the Frog, and a host of others to mix with the live cast members of the show, Henson used the Muppet characters to help deliver the educational content of the show. Muppets also were "guests" on a variety of shows and even had a segment on *Saturday Night Live.*

Henson wanted the Muppets to have their own show that would appeal to the whole family and not just to children. In 1976, *The Muppet Show*, produced in Great Britain, hit American airwaves. The Muppets, led by Kermit the Frog, hosted a live guest star each week who performed in vaudevillian type sketches with the Muppets. Other popular characters included Miss Piggy, performed by Frank Oz, who also acted as Fozzie Bear, Gonzo the Great, the Swedish Chef, and a variety of others. An array of celebrities, including Bob Hope, Elton John, Christopher Reeve, and Brooke Shields, appeared on the show. *The Muppets Show* became successful with adults and children by incorporating the funny characters with social and cultural satire; for instance, in one skit, singing woodland animals had to dodge zealous hunters. Since Muppets came in all sizes, shapes, and colors, acceptance was another theme that Henson and the writers tried to emphasize through the show. Henson made 120 episodes before ending production in 1980. By then, the Muppets had already become film stars with the debut of *The Muppet Movie* in 1979.

Impact   Jim Henson is second only to Walt Disney in the creation of popular lovable characters that have had an enduring impression on American culture, as well as in making a lasting impact on children's television and puppeteering.

Further Reading

Aaseng, Nathan. *Jim Henson, Muppet Master.* Minneapolis: Lerner, 1988.

St. Pierre, Stephanie. *The Story of Jim Henson, Creator of the Muppets.* Milwaukee: Gareth Stevens, 1997.

P. Andrew Miller

See also   Children's television; *Saturday Night Live*; *Sesame Street*; Television in the United States; Variety shows.

■ Music

Definition   The many styles of popular music and its subgenres

During the 1970's, music—particularly the most popular strains such as rock and soul—continued its rise in culture, spawning a plethora of subgenres and becoming big business in the process.

The 1960's icons of rock and pop music still had a strong bond with the public at the beginning of the new decade, and many of them were able to become even bigger than before. Upon their breakup in the spring of 1970, the Beatles became four successful solo artists. The Who and the Rolling Stones achieved new levels of success; their albums *Who's Next* (1971) and *Exile on Main Street* (1972), respectively, were massively popular and critically hailed, and they solidified their positions as rock superstars and top concert draws. For much of the early 1970's, however, Bob Dylan remained an enigma—keeping out of the public eye and releasing albums that confounded his audience in their apparent lack of ambition.

Taking a few cues from Dylan's musical legacy were singer-songwriters. Artists such as Jackson Browne, James Taylor, Joni Mitchell, and "supergroup" Crosby, Stills, Nash, and Young made contemplative music using acoustic guitars and pianos, musing on personal, autobiographical matters with poetic lyrics. On the other side of the coin, the rise of British bands Led Zeppelin and Black Sabbath pointed to the increasing popularity of heavy, loud music—hard rock, which would later mutate into heavy metal. This music was wildly popular with one of rock's target audiences: teenage boys.

Glam rock shared with hard rock a propensity for loud guitars, but the similarities ended there. Whereas hard rock emphasized the performers' masculinity, glam purposely courted androgyny and theatricality. It remained mainly a British obsession, but one of glam's progenitors, David Bowie, would emerge as one the decade's most innovative stars. Some bands took it upon themselves to build on the ambition and classical pretensions of 1960's albums such as the Beatles' *Sgt. Pepper's Lonely Hearts Club Band* (1967). Yes, Genesis, and King Crimson played what became known as progressive rock. They filled their music with complex time signatures and extended instrumental showcases, and their songs regularly went into double digits in minutes.

While many rock bands in the 1970's strove to push boundaries—musical, sexual, or otherwise—other pop acts succeeded by catering to mainstream tastes, with melodic songs that were often either mellow and easygoing or cheeringly upbeat. Among these acts were John Denver, the Carpenters, and Barry Manilow. Occasionally, an artist would emerge who somehow managed to touch on a number of elements of 1970's rock, such as the British piano player Elton John, who dominated the charts in the early 1970's just as the Beatles had in the previous decade.

Artists Rise and Listeners Rebel   Rock had become big business. The prices of tickets and albums were rising. The blockbuster album became parlance: Two prominent examples were the Eagles' *Hotel California* (1976) and Fleetwood Mac's *Rumours* (1977). Though both bands were based in California and specialized in a soft, pop-friendly sound, they were fairly divergent. The Eagles' roots were in country rock, and *Hotel California* was a social commentary on decadence in Los Angeles. Fleetwood Mac had evolved considerably from its origins as a British blues band. Now the members crafted impassioned pop songs that detailed the romantic melodramas occurring within the group. Also the British rock band Pink Floyd scored two massive sellers in the 1970's with its meditations on war, paranoia, and stardom: *Dark Side of the Moon* (1973) and *The Wall* (1979). The band's spectacle-sized live shows—complete with state-of-the-art lights, film projections, and giant inflatable props—were equally popular.

Though they attracted legions of devotees, Fleetwood Mac, the Eagles, and Pink Floyd had their detractors. Some rock fans felt that their meticulous navel-gazing betrayed the music as self-indulgent works of complacent millionaires. Meanwhile, artists such as Journey, Meat Loaf, and Peter Frampton were derided as "corporate rock"—slick, bombastic, and superficial.

Many fans found saviors in the original avatars of American punk rock: New York-based acts such as the Ramones, Patti Smith, and Talking Heads. Others, threatened more by the rise of disco, pinned their hopes on the slightly more conventional Bruce Springsteen. Springsteen managed to combine all of his inspirations—Roy Orbison, Phil Spector, Dylan, and more—to create something seemingly new. He wrote often-sprawling story-songs about working-class dreamers and became famous for his marathon, high-energy concerts.

Jazz and Country Rock Out   Rock's influence was such that its sound began to permeate other genres, most notably jazz and country.

The use of electric instruments—not just plugged-in guitars, basses, and pianos, but synthesizers as well—was once rare in jazz. In the 1970's, it practically became de rigueur. An innovator in this development—as with so many jazz developments—was trumpeter Miles Davis. His late 1960's albums had kicked off the renaissance of jazz-rock, also known as fusion. Once into the next decade, he wasted no time in continuing this path. Davis solidified his standing as a true jazz superstar, although some critics found his albums in the 1970's to be increasingly inconsistent. Despite his success, health and drug problems caused Davis to spend the entire second half of the decade out of the spotlight.

Several veterans of Davis's electric bands became leading lights of fusion in the 1970's: keyboardist Herbie Hancock, tenor sax player Wayne Shorter and keyboardist Joe Zawinul with their successful jazz-rock group Weather Report, British guitarist John McLaughlin with Mahavishnu Orchestra, and pianist Chick Corea with Return to Forever. Not all of the top fusion musicians were Davis veterans—guitarist Pat Metheny and latter-day Weather Report bassist Jaco Pastorious became name players as well.

Though fusion dominated the jazz sound in the 1970's, acoustic instrumentation did not vanish entirely. Keith Jarrett was another former member of Davis's electric groups, but upon leaving he renounced electric keyboards and synthesizers and dedicated himself fully to acoustic piano, in solo or group settings. His 1975 *The Koln Concert* was a double album of a solo piano performance entirely improvised, and it was both a critical and commercial success.

Despite, or maybe because of, fusion's popularity, a backlash was inevitable, as some musicians and fans felt that jazz musicians were too eagerly courting mainstream acceptance by favoring technology and pop-friendly melodies over musical skill and improvisation. However, this backlash would not assume full force until the next decade.

The country-rock hybrid had also begun at the end of the 1960's, via artists such as Dylan and the Byrds. This trend continued in the new decade, thanks to Byrds offshoot the Flying Burrito Brothers (and the subsequent solo career of the group's singer, Gram Parsons), and Michael Nesmith of the Monkees, with his First National Band. However, these acts were not nearly as successful as Linda Ronstadt and the former members of her backing band who became the Eagles. Neil Young's country-rock album *Harvest* (1972) became one of his most successful.

Though Willie Nelson had written Patsy Cline's signature song "Crazy" and others in the 1960's, in 1970 he moved from Nashville—country music's home base—back to his home state of Texas and began holding annual Fourth of July picnics with musicians young and old performing. Nelson also began releasing albums that were much starker than what was coming out of Nashville, and he brought the rock innovation of the concept album to country with *Red Headed Stranger* (1975). Like Nelson's picnics, the Nitty Gritty Dirt Band brought young and old country musicians together on its hit triple album *Will the Circle Be Unbroken?* (1972), on which the group invited many of its country forebearers to perform.

Soul to Funk   Some of the 1960's soul stars became even more famous and influential in the 1970's. Two Motown giants, Marvin Gaye and Stevie Wonder, paved the way. They broke from the Detroit label's precise rules regarding record making to become more autonomous and daring. Another Motown act, the Jackson 5, provided the label with some of its biggest hits of the 1970's thanks to the impossibly exuberant and emotive vocals of its lead singer, a pre-pubescent Michael Jackson.

Some of the biggest soul hits of the early 1970's came out of Philadelphia through the songwriter-producers Kenny Gamble and Leon Huff of the record label Philadelphia International. With help from arranger Thom Bell, they created lush hits for artists such as the O'Jays ("Love Train"), Billy Paul ("Me and Mrs. Jones"), and Harold Melvin and the Blue Notes ("If You Don't Know Me by Now").

Working out of Memphis, Al Green scored hit after romantic hit with songs such as "Let's Stay Together" and "Tired of Being Alone." He was no stranger to controversy, however, most notably when a spurned lover tried to kill him by dosing him with hot grits before killing herself. Not too long after that incident, Green rediscovered his gospel faith and abandoned secular music. Another unique ro-

mantic character of 1970's soul was Barry White, a corpulent figure with a big beard and a bottomless, deep singing voice who somewhat incongruously became a major sex symbol. He was also a gifted songwriter, arranger, and producer.

Among the most prominent developments in soul music this decade was funk, which strived to be more danceable and wilder than anything that the genre had yet provided. Funk took its cues from James Brown, who in the 1960's revolutionized music by emphasizing the beat rather than the melody. Another 1960's hit maker, Sly and the Family Stone, helped helped refine funk in the 1970's, although the group's mastermind, Sly Stone, would flame out mid-decade as a result of increasing drug use. George Clinton built on their foundation. With his two groups, Parliament and Funkadelic, Clinton combined funk with psychedelia, jazz, and other sounds and developed a bizarrely humorous, elaborate stage act with sights such as a giant spaceship and musicians performing in diapers. Yet he also addressed the tumult that African Americans faced in the United States. Just as popular, but otherwise very different, was Earth, Wind, and Fire, which specialized in a cleaner brand of funk, both musically and lyrically, dominated by distinctive horns and singer Phillip Bailey's falsetto.

All the developments and advances made by soul music would be deeply felt by the end of 1970's, as the genre spawned first disco, then hip-hop.

The Rise and Fall of Disco   Totems of the disco era such as the Bee Gees, Donna Summer, and John Travolta dancing in his white suit in the 1977 film *Saturday Night Fever* are used constantly to evoke the 1970's as a whole. "Disco" is a shortened form of "discotheque," a term referring to clubs where records are played for the explicit purpose of dancing. While these clubs had been in existence since the 1960's, they became increasingly popular the following decade, especially in New York City and especially with the gay community. By the mid-1970's, an aesthetic to disco music was beginning to emerge, honing in on the throbbing, unwavering beat. Disco's main goal was to get people dancing. The disc jockeys (DJs) at the clubs were always searching for the perfect segues, a way of moving from one song to another without an audible change in tempo, ensuring that everyone kept moving.

When it came to making disco music, musicians,

At the end of the 1970's, popular musical styles encompassed both the easy listening pop tunes of Barry Manilow (far right) and the energetic disco beat of the Bee Gees, composed of brothers Barry, Maurice, and Robin Gibb (left-right). (AP/Wide World Photos)

songwriters, and even singers to a degree were less important than producers, who were responsible for melding all the ingredients to create the ideal, utterly danceable disco song. Most of the architects of the disco sound were producers such as Giorgio Moroder. Nevertheless, a few artists managed to distinguish themselves, one way or another. Summer, one of Moroder's charges, gained notoriety for her seventeen-minute-long "Love to Love You Baby," in which she did little more than moan the title suggestively for the song's duration. She proved to be one of the more successful and distinctive of disco divas, with big hits such as "Last Dance" and "Bad Girls."

Disco provided an unlikely career resurgence for Australian pop fraternity the Bee Gees. The veteran group, consisting of brothers Barry, Maurice, and Robin Gibb, contributed several songs to *Saturday*

Night Fever, starring Travolta. The soundtrack sold thirty million copies and yielded the Bee Gees' most recognizable songs, "Stayin' Alive," "You Should Be Dancing," and "How Deep Is Your Love"—seminal disco numbers all.

Saturday Night Fever brought disco well and truly into the mainstream. Another successful act was Chic, led by guitarist Nile Rodgers and bassist Bernard Edwards. Chic was one of the few disco bands that was also a functioning unit, rather than a front for session musicians. At the same time, the genre wound up spawning some truly curious novelty knock-offs, such as "Disco Duck" by Los Angeles radio DJ Rick Dees, a disco record from show tune warbler Ethel Mermen, and a disco version of the theme from *Star Wars* (1977). Then there was the Village People: five men dressed up as gay male stereotypes—biker, construction worker, cop, Native American, and cowboy—singing songs such as "Y.M.C.A." and "Macho Man." The group, a fabrication by producer Jacques Morali, became hugely successful, if only for a time.

By this point, rock stars were getting into the act and reaping benefits, as popular disco-flavored songs from the Rolling Stones ("Miss You") and Rod Stewart ("Do Ya Think I'm Sexy") helped the aging rock gods appear current. Nevertheless, many rock fans were less than appreciative of disco, especially when it seemed to co-opt their favorite bands. Soon enough the "Disco Sucks" backlash began, and shortly after the end of 1970's, the whole phenomenon seemed forever encapsulated as a relic of its decade (although *Off the Wall*, a 1979 disco-flavored album by Michael Jackson, sold spectacularly well and proved that the former Jackson 5 star had something of a future).

The Early Days of Hip-Hop   Despite not coming into its own commercially and artistically until later decades, hip-hop and rap had their roots and genesis firmly entrenched in the 1970's. By the middle of the decade, in the Bronx neighborhood of New York City, many of the major aspects of hip-hop were already almost fully formed. Unlike disco DJs, who strived to keep the beat moving by blending seamlessly from one track to another, Bronx DJs—playing at house parties, schools, community centers, and the like—were interested in the breaks, or drum fills. These DJs used turntables to stretch out those breaks, playing them over and over. They would use two copies of the same song, each on its own turntable. Soon the DJs were performing in tandem with MCs (emcee, master of ceremonies, or mic controller), who would provide spoken-word accompaniment.

Along with the equally burgeoning graffiti culture among African Americans living in New York City, hip-hop was a strikingly innovative underground phenomenon, one that built on established aspects of black culture and spun them into something modern yet timeless. At the very end of the decade, the genre had its first taste of mainstream popularity with the 1979 hit single "Rapper's Delight," by the Sugar Hill Gang.

Broadway Musicals and Classical Music   The 1970's saw the rise of one of Broadway's most her-

alded composers, Stephen Sondheim. He had his first flush of fame as the lyricist for Leonard Bernstein's classic *West Side Story* in 1957. In the 1970's, his musicals such as *Company* (1970), *A Little Night Music* (1973), and *Follies* (1974) broke new ground with psychologically acute plots and characters and artfully constructed songs. With their pretensions to high art, though, Sondheim's musicals often garnered critical praise without doing terribly well at the box office. Still, he managed to contribute a few Broadway standards during this time, with *A Little Night Music*'s "Send in the Clowns" and *Company*'s "The Ladies Who Lunch."

In contrast to Sondheim, British composer Andrew Lloyd Webber helmed flashy, rock-flavored musicals that often delighted audiences and disgusted critics. He had successes in the 1970's with *Jesus Christ Superstar* (1971) and *Evita* (1978). In 1975, *A Chorus Line*, one of the biggest successes on Broadway, opened. Conceived by director-choreographer Michael Bennett, the show documented the struggles of aspiring dancers.

If overshadowed by popular music, classical music still managed to innovate, nodding to both tradition and modernity. Established composers such as Aaron Copland and Benjamin Britten (who died in 1976) wrote their final major works. The more avant-garde wing was represented by John Cage and Karl Stockhausen. One major composer who emerged during this decade was Philip Glass. His arrival on the scene was announced with his 1976 opera *Einstein on the Beach*. Glass's lulling, repetitive textures, known as minimalism, garnered some controversy; some found his work too simplistic.

Impact   Music became increasingly diverse and popular throughout the decade, reverberating in film, fashion, and other social arenas. Consumers were presented with an unprecedented amount of choice in the music that they could purchase, which led to inevitable backlashes against some music.

Subsequent Events   Many popular musicians of the 1970's were unable to sustain their careers into the next decade. Some, however, from Michael Jackson to Bruce Springsteen to Andrew Lloyd Webber, became even more successful. Despite the rebellions of genres such as punk rock, music in the next decade would continue to evolve into something larger, louder, and more lucrative.

Further Reading

Breithaupt, Don, and Jeff Breithaupt. *Night Moves: Pop Music in the Late '70's.* New York: St. Martin's Press, 2000.

_____. *Precious and Few: Pop Music of the Early '70's.* New York: St. Martin's Press, 1996. These two volumes offer a fond look back at the most popular artists and songs of the decade.

Coryell, Julie, and Laura Friedman. *Jazz-Rock Fusion: The People, the Music.* Milwaukee: Hal Leonard, 2000. In-depth look at the most popular style of jazz in the 1970's.

Toop, David. *Rap Attack #3.* London: Serpent's Tail, 2000. An updated edition of the early, seminal look at the history of hip-hop.

Michael Pelusi

See also Aerosmith; Ballet; Band, The; Bee Gees, The; Bowie, David; Broadway musicals; Carpenters, The; *Chorus Line, A*; Classical music; Concert for Bangla Desh; Cooper, Alice; Country music; Dance, popular; Denver, John; Disco; Discotheques; Eagles, The; Earth, Wind, and Fire; Fleetwood Mac; Gaye, Marvin; Hard rock and heavy metal; Heart; Hip-hop; Jazz; *Jesus Christ Superstar*; Joel, Billy; John, Elton; KISS; Led Zeppelin; Manilow, Barry; Marley, Bob; Mitchell, Joni; Pink Floyd; Presley, Elvis; Progressive rock; Punk rock; Queen; Radio; Ramones, The; Reddy, Helen; Rush; Singer-songwriters; Soul music; Springsteen, Bruce; Studio 54; Summer, Donna; Up with People; Van Halen; Village People, The; Watkins Glen rock festival; Who, The; Wonder, Stevie.

N

■ Nader, Ralph

Identification American consumer activist
Born February 27, 1934; Winsted, Connecticut

Nader introduced a watchdog mentality to the American consumer public and advocated for the public interest in opposition to unaccountable corporate and bureaucratic power.

Ralph Nader began his life's work as an advocate for accountability during the 1960's through his penchant for freelance muckraking in the tradition of such turn-of-twentieth-century notables as George Seldes and Upton Sinclair. In the 1970's, Nader transcended his role as mere tattletale to become a true leader of an astoundingly successful popular movement. He managed to attract, inspire, organize, and arrange for the support of hundreds of "Nader's Raiders" to examine and publish unprecedented and hard-hitting exposés of corporate and government activities that had previously been ignored or hidden from public scrutiny. He also established a nongovernmental organization (NGO) called Public Citizen in order to advocate for the people as consumers of corporate and government products and programs.

Nader founded the Center for Study of Responsive Law in 1969 and staffed it with two hundred Nader's Raiders selected from thirty thousand applicants. Seventeen books had been published by this group by 1972. These works provided the United States with its first pervasive source of investigative journalism, in which mainstream newspapers and periodicals had previously been reluctant to engage. The books meticulously documented the performance of, among others, federal agencies, private banking groups, land developers and speculators, agricultural suppliers, and private service providers. They "named names" and exposed motivations and outcomes of these operations from the perspective of the average citizen, which made the books very popular. Some examples of these titles include *Poli-*

tics of Land (1973), by Robert C. Fellmeth; *Water Wasteland* (1971), edited by David Zwick and Marcy Benstock; and *Old Age: The Last Segregation* (1971), by Claire Townsend.

Nader's work throughout the 1970's, however, was primarily focused on establishing as many "watchdog" types of organizations as he could. These "Nader Groups" were not interested in pontificating theoretical approaches to American economic and political problems but favored instead to point out inconsistencies, inefficiencies, and inappropriateness among producers. In doing so, they hoped to empower consumers through widespread and acces-

Ralph Nader. (Library of Congress)

sible information and knowledge, which Nader followers held to be the key ingredient in getting the market and bureaucracy to generate unbiased and allocative solutions; in other words, to make the citizen-consumer sovereign in these transactions.

Public Citizen was the primary instrument in Nader's consumer movement. It served as an umbrella for six affiliated organizations with membership of more than 150,000: Congress Watch, the Health Research Group, the Litigation Group, the Critical Mass Energy Project, Global Trade Watch, and Buyers Up. Each group acted as a watchdog by publishing the results of its examinations of various corporate and government institutions. These organizations were credited with inspiring numerous consumer protection laws and regulatory agencies designed to reveal the inner workings of production and bureaucratic processes for public scrutiny.

Nader also founded numerous groups outside the realm of Public Citizen, such as the Project on Corporate Responsibility, the Public Interest Research Group, and the Study Group on Antitrust Law Enforcement. The purpose of each group was similar: to alert citizens of the range of threats that they faced in using consumer products and services so that they could use them more wisely or demand more useful products and services.

Impact   During the Carter administration, the consumer movement recorded its greatest impact on American society as several heads of Nader Groups were awarded roles in various leading federal regulatory agencies.

Further Reading

Marcello, Patricia Cronin. *Ralph Nader.* Westport, Conn.: Greenwood Press, 2004.

Nader, Ralph. *The Ralph Nader Reader.* New York: Seven Stories Press, 2000.

James Knotwell

See also   Child product safety laws; Consumer Product Safety Act of 1972.

■ National Air and Space Museum

Identification   Branch of the Smithsonian Institution that holds the world's largest collection of spacecraft and aircraft
Date   Opened July 1, 1976
Place   National Mall, Washington, D.C.

The "space race" during the 1960's made Americans interested in all matters of flight, and in the early to mid-1970's, the museum earned a new name and a new home, as well as finding itself the sponsor of important historical-scientific research and various symposia on the broad topic of flight.

A part of the Smithsonian Institution, the National Air and Space Museum first came into existence as the National Air Museum by an act of Congress on August 12, 1946. Its collections were culled from Smithsonian holdings and could be traced back to the 1876 Centennial Exposition in Philadelphia, at which time the Chinese government donated a group of kites. As for airplane artifacts, the Stringfellow engine of 1889 was the first to be accessioned formally into the collection. Over subsequent years, a selection of aviation artifacts was on view in the Smithsonian's Arts and Industries Building and on "rocket row" outside the Smithsonian Castle, both on the National Mall. The most famous artifacts then were arguably Charles Lindbergh's *Spirit of St. Louis*, which curator Paul Garber requested by telegram from Lindbergh as the latter was flying across the Atlantic, and the 1903 *Wright Flyer* of the Wright Brothers, which was displayed from 1948 onward.

The advent of the space race rekindled interest in all matters of flight, and in 1958 and 1966 respectively, Presidents Dwight D. Eisenhower and Lyndon B. Johnson signed laws calling for the construction of a building and the inclusion of spaceflight in the collection.

The renamed National Air and Space Museum got its first director in 1971—Apollo 11 astronaut Michael Collins. The following year, Congress appropriated some forty million dollars for the construction of the new building. The design came from Gyo Obata of Hellmuth, Obata and Kassabaum architects and consisted of several building blocks linked together by glass atriums. Groundbreaking took place on November 20, 1972. The site chosen, along Constitution Avenue, was the second-to-last spot available on the National Mall.

Most of the museum's collection was housed in a series of warehouses at Silver Hill in Suitland, Maryland, on the outskirts of Washington, D.C. The decision on what to include in the museum's exhibit area depended in part on gifts received. For example, the Federal Republic of Germany gave the museum a Zeiss VI planetarium instrument with an automatic control system. In so doing, it made the museum's Albert Einstein planetarium the only one of its type to be fully automated.

Construction took three and a half years. Beginning in February, 1976, artifacts were installed in the museum, including the *Spirit of St. Louis*, the *Wright Flyer*, and the Apollo 11 command module. President Gerald R. Ford inaugurated the museum on July 1, 1976. Within six weeks, attendance was breaking the two million mark.

Because most of the collection still remained in Suitland, the museum arranged to begin guided tours there in 1977. It also began the practice of sponsoring major conferences on aerospace themes, as well as public events for the enjoyment of all. In the first year of operation, these conferences included a symposium celebrating the fiftieth anniversary of Lindbergh's transatlantic flight and a Frisbee festival on the Mall.

The following year, the general aviation gallery opened. Meanwhile, Collins stepped down as director. The late 1970's marked a shift toward historical and scientific research. The Charles A. Lindbergh Chair of Aerospace History was established in 1977, and Charles Harvard Gibbs-Smith, Keeper Emeritus of the Victoria and Albert Museum in London, became the first occupant. Various symposia on figures such as Lindbergh, the Wright Brothers, and Amelia Earhart were held, and the General Electric Lecture Series began.

Impact By the end of the decade, the National Air and Space Museum was among the most visited museums in the world, and discussion began about possibly expanding its exhibit surface. Such plans would not become reality for another two decades, when a new annex at Dulles Airport was established.

Further Reading

Boyne, Walter J. *The Aircraft Treasures of Silver Hill*: New York: Rawson, 1982.

Brian, C. D. B. *The National Air and Space Museum.* New York: Harry N. Abrams, 1979.

Guillaume de Syon

See also Aircraft; Apollo space program; Pioneer space program; Science and technology; Space exploration.

■ National Indian Brotherhood

Identification Canadian organization
Date Founded in 1970

The story of the National Indian Brotherhood (NIB) is that of the particular struggles of the First Nations peoples of Canada. These struggles involved how to maintain their individual identities, cultures, dignity, and right for self-determination.

One of the greatest barriers to attempts to form a national organization for the First Nations with any national presence was been the issue of unity. The size of Canada and the various cultures within the country contributed to this monumental endeavor.

Centuries of change and resulting treaties meant loss of land and liberty. The Indian Act of 1876 affected education directly, as did the Indian Act of 1927, which compounded these issues by denying the first inhabitants of Canada the right to speak their native language or practice any traditional religion. It forced children from their homes to boarding schools, where they were subjected to horrendous conditions including severe punishment when they exhibited even the slightest tradition from their native culture. In addition, this act made it illegal for First Nations people to form any political organizations. The history of government treatment of the First Nations peoples meant that they were left out of Canada's formal political process.

Several attempts were made to form a national Indian organization after both world wars and again in 1961. In 1969, the Trudeau government issued a white paper policy to abolish the Indian Act and treat the First Nations as any other minority, rather than as a distinct group. The peoples of the First Nations knew that they had to unite, and widespread Indian opposition to the white paper across Canada provided the necessary motivation. The result was the first meeting of the NIB, held in Vancouver on August 21, 1970. The first president was George Manuel, from the Shuswap Nation, a well-known and highly respected activist.

More than fifty First Nations were represented by the NIB. While the First Nations had diverse locations, history, and cultures, they had common needs, including health, education, and economic development, as well as land and treaty issues. Manuel traveled more than 100,000 miles in the first year to meet with the people in the communities, not just their local and provincial leaders. During the early years of the NIB, there was little if any funding, and those in leadership paid tremendous personal prices. Offices were housed in spaces donated by member First Nations, with phones sometimes cut off because of lack of funding.

After the NIB listened to people from all levels, consensus was built and a plan of action was developed. The organization's response to the government's white paper policy was the 1972 *Indian Control of Indian Education* policy paper, called the red paper policy. In 1975, under Manuel, the NIB was also involved in the international community, as it took a leadership role in the formation of the United Nations World Council of Indigenous People.

Impact The National Indian Brotherhood gained government support and proved to have an influential political voice. However, it was not without some controversy. Changes were made in the organization, and the NIB became the Assembly of First Nations in 1982.

Further Reading

Assembly of First Nations. *Traditions and Education: Towards a Vision of Our Future: A Declaration of First Nations Jurisdiction over Education.* Ottawa, Ont.: Author, 1988.

Cardinal, Harold. *Rebirth of Canada's Indians.* Edmonton: Hurtig, 1977.

McFarlane, Peter. *Brotherhood to Nationhood: George Manuel and the Making of the Modern Indian Movement.* Toronto: Between the Lines, 1993.

Connie H. Rickenbaker

See also Demographics of Canada; Education in Canada; Minorities in Canada; Multiculturalism in Canada; Native Americans.

■ *National Lampoon's Animal House*

Identification American film
Director John Landis (1950-)
Date Released in 1978

This hit movie inspired a number of subversive comedies and continued the tradition of comic films set on college campuses.

The concept for *National Lampoon's Animal House* grew from the college experiences of the three writers: Douglas Kenney, an alumnus of the *Harvard*

John Belushi in a scene from National Lampoon's Animal House. *(Hulton Archive/Getty Images)*

Lampoon and founding editor of the *National Lampoon* magazine; Chris Miller; and Harold Ramis, an alumnus of The Second City comedy troupe of Chicago. Although the original script was turned down by Warner Bros., Universal Studios accepted it because of Kenney's connection with the popular *National Lampoon.* John Landis, then only twenty-seven years old, was the last choice for director. He took the script, originally full of racism and gratuitous cruelty, and asked the writers to omit some of the grosser aspects. The result is a funny and literate screenplay.

With the exception of veteran actor Donald Sutherland, playing the jaded English professor, all the actors were virtually unknown. Kevin Bacon made his screen debut in the film, but John Belushi, playing John "Bluto" Blutarsky, is the most memorable character. Ramis knew Belushi through their involvement in The Second City and wrote the part with Belushi in mind. Although Landis took away much of his dialogue, Belushi still managed to steal any scene in which he appeared with a raised eyebrow, a drunken grin, or a leer. His few lines are legend—for example, his comment on being kicked out of school, "Seven years down the drain." Other actors included Tom Hulce as Pinto, Stephen Furst as Flounder, Tim Matheson as Otter, and Karen Allen as Katy.

The film had a low budget of $2.5 million and, to cut costs, was shot almost entirely on the University of Oregon campus. The university was reluctant about using the campus and gave the crew thirty days to complete filming. Cast and crew worked six-day weeks and finished in twenty-eight days. Seven weeks after release, the film had generated $45 million at the box office.

Set at fictional Faber College, the time period is 1962, before the John F. Kennedy assassination and the turmoil of the later 1960's. There are no "issues" to be aired. Major concerns are Jell-O slurping, toga parties, and drinking beer. The conflict in the film is between the establishment-supporting "goody-goodies" of Omega House and the fun-oriented, reprobate brothers of Delta House. All the positives about fraternity life are aspects of Delta; negative aspects were represented by the Nazi-like Omega. The result was a film full of fun and energy, supported by exuberant music, including "Shout" and "Twistin' the Night Away."

Impact With its sense of freedom and anarchy, *National Lampoon's Animal House* tapped into nostalgia for a simpler time. Its antiestablishment humor had a wide appeal, and the toga party became a national craze on college campuses. The film won the 1979 People's Choice Award for Favorite Non-musical Motion Picture. In 2002, it was inducted into the Library of Congress's National Film Registry of motion pictures that are "culturally, historically, or aesthetically" significant to American film.

Further Reading

Mitchell, Elvis. "Critic's Notebook: Revisiting Faber College." *The New York Times*, August 25, 2003, p. E1.

Shah, Diane, and Ron Labrecque. "Toga, Toga, Toga." *Newsweek*, October 2, 1978, 74.

Sigoloff, Marc. *Films of the Seventies: A Filmography of American, British, and Canadian Films, 1970-1979.* Jefferson, N.C.: McFarland, 2000.

Marcia B. Dinneen

See also Belushi, John; Blockbusters; Comedians; Film in the United States; *Saturday Night Live.*

■ National Lesbian and Gay Rights March of 1979

The Event National march commemorating the tenth anniversary of the Stonewall Inn riots
Date October 14, 1979
Place Washington, D.C.

This march signaled the convergence of power at the height of the gay and lesbian revolution. It was the first national-level political gathering of the gay and lesbian communities.

The year 1979 marked the tenth anniversary of the riots at the Stonewall Inn in Greenwich Village, New York, that sparked the gay and lesbian revolution, and the community wanted to commemorate the event. It also wanted to memorialize the 1978 murders of San Francisco city supervisor Harvey Milk and Mayor George Moscone by former San Francisco city supervisor Dan White. White, who was homophobic, received an extremely light sentence for the murders. Though the White Night Riots in San Francisco that followed his sentence did express the gay and lesbian communities' outrage, there remained a lingering sense of malaise surrounding the event at the national level. Milk had repeatedly suggested a march on the nation's capital before his assassination, so organizers felt that such an event would capture some of his spirit. However, the groups organizing the march initially had trouble gathering support from the greater gay and lesbian community.

Objectors feared that the march would not draw many participants. They also feared that a strong national statement like a march would garner the same kind of backlash that Dade County, Florida, encountered when it passed a gay rights law. Indeed, much of the nation was still influenced by anti-gay-rights activist Anita Bryant and her followers, and the influence of the Moral Majority and an anti-gay backlash was sweeping across the nation. However, the march ultimately attracted more than a hundred thousand participants, and people came from throughout the United States and ten additional countries to join in solidarity. Among the groups formed as a result of the march was the National Coalition of Black Lesbians and Gays.

Impact The march drew a large number of attendees and thereby strengthened the gay and lesbian rights movement at the national level.

Subsequent Events On October 11, 1987, the Second National March on Washington for Gay and Lesbian Rights drew between 500,000 and 650,000 participants.

Further Reading

Dynes, Wayne R., and Stephen Donaldson. *Homosexuality and Government, Politics and Prisons.* New York: Garland, 1992.

Rayside, David Morton. *On the Fringe: Gays and Lesbians in Politics.* Ithaca, N.Y.: Cornell University Press, 1998.

Riggle, Ellen D. B., and Barry L. Tadlock. *Gays and Lesbians in the Democratic Process: Public Policy, Public Opinion, and Political Representation.* New York: Columbia University Press, 1999.

Smith, Raymond A., and Donald P. Haider-Markel. *Gay and Lesbian Americans and Political Participation: A Reference Handbook.* Santa Barbara, Calif.: ABC-Clio, 2002.

Jessie Bishop Powell

See also Bryant, Anita; Homosexuality and gay rights; Milk, Harvey; Moscone, George; White Night Riots.

■ National Maximum Speed Limit

Identification National speed limit on highways and interstates of fifty-five miles per hour
Date Imposed in 1974

Emerging from a congressional act to alleviate the fuel shortages imposed by the OPEC oil embargo, the National Maximum Speed Limit helped improve safety standards on U.S. highways.

In the mid-1970's, energy consumption continued to soar, domestic oil production was in decline, and government officials feared the onset of recession. Congress passed the Emergency Highway Conservation Act, which lowered state and interstate highway speeds to fifty-five miles per hour, in January, 1974. This act originally was intended to be a temporary measure that would conserve fuel—an estimated 200,000 barrels of oil per day—in order to offset the effects of the oil embargo by the Organization of Petroleum Exporting Countries (OPEC). The embargo resulted in an energy shortage that caused long lines at gas stations throughout the United States.

However, within the first year of the act's passage, officials noted that fatal crashes and highway deaths dropped by nine thousand nationwide. Tests conducted by the Federal Highway Administration and General Motors concluded that fifty-five miles per hour was the most-fuel-efficient speed for trucks and most vehicles and that crashes doubled once speeds reached sixty miles per hour or higher. With the reduction in highway fatalities, Dr. James Gregory of the National Highway Traffic Safety Administration contended that the lowered speed limit contributed to the decline in highway fatalities and was advantageous to Americans from a safety perspective.

President Jimmy Carter also began to endorse the idea of legislation for improving safety on the nation's highways, and by the end of 1974, Congress passed the National Maximum Speed Limit to make the fifty-five miles per hour speed permanent. The limit was the first government-imposed national speed limit since World War II. In order to ensure compliance with the new law, a provision within the act specified that states that failed to lower the speed limit within sixty days of enactment would not receive federal aid to fund highway projects.

Impact The National Maximum Speed Limit proved to be controversial throughout the subsequent two decades. Politically charged debates began almost immediately over whether the reduced speed limit actually contributed to the decline of roadway accidents, fatalities, and medical costs. Advocates for highway and automobile safety, such as Ralph Nader, provided statistical data that supported the benefits of a lower speed limit. However, in 1978, several states introduced legislation to defy the congressional act; those efforts failed. In 1987, however, Congress amended the law to allow sixty-five miles per hour on some interstates, and in September, 1995, it revoked the National Maximum Speed Limit.

Further Reading

Cerrelli, Ezio. *Estimating the Safety Effects of the 55 MPH National Speed Limit.* Washington, D.C.: National Highway Traffic Safety Administration, 1977.

Heckard, R. F. *Safety Aspects of the National 55 MPH Speed Limit: Final Report.* Washington, D.C.: Federal Highway Administration, 1976.

U.S. Department of Transportation. *55 MPH Fact Book*. Washington, D.C.: National Highway Traffic Safety Administration, 1979.

Gayla Koerting

See also Automobiles; Carter, Jimmy; CB radio; Energy crisis; Gas shortages; Nader, Ralph; Oil embargo of 1973-1974.

■ National Organization for Women (NOW)

Identification Organization founded to advocate women's rights
Date Started in 1966

NOW was the first women's organization to demand equal employment opportunities for women based on Title XII of the Civil Rights Act of 1964. During the decade, as it grew to become the largest women's rights organization in the United States, its major goal became passage of the Equal Rights Amendment (ERA).

NOW was founded by twenty-eight women who were attending the Third National Conference of the Commission on the Status of Women in Washington, D.C. These women were frustrated by the Equal Employment Opportunity Commission's inattention to the plight of women, as well as the conference leaders' refusal to allow them to present resolutions regarding discriminatory practices in employment. Betty Friedan, author of *The Feminine Mystique* (1963), was made president of the new organization, while cofounder Pauli Murray became the first African American female Episcopalian priest in the United States. Within a year, three hundred men and women had become charter members, and NOW had published a Bill of Rights for Women, which, among other things, called for an equal rights amendment, equal job opportunities for women, and reproductive rights for women.

Modeling their operational tactics on those of the National Organization for the Advancement of Colored People (NAACP), the founders of NOW decided to make the enforcement of Title VII of the Civil Rights Act of 1964 their first prior-

ity. NOW worked to end sex-segregated advertising in newspapers and lobbied to end protective labor legislation. In 1969, NOW's efforts resulted in a U.S. Fifth Circuit Court decision that women could not be barred from jobs that required heavy lifting, such as those in the construction industry.

Beginning in 1967, NOW supported legalized abortion, but its major campaign during the 1970's was focused on passage of the ERA to the U.S. Constitution. As part of the ERA campaign, NOW called attention to the male-female wage gap in the United States by distributing buttons that read "59 cents." On August 26, 1970, Friedan organized a mass march and strike of women workers that she called the Women's Strike for Equality. NOW also became in-

The National Organization for Women (NOW) distributes literature at its fourth annual conference in March, 1970. NOW later called for a mass march and strike of women workers, called the Women's Strike for Equality. (AP/Wide World Photos)

volved in political party platforms and in establishing close ties with other organizations and labor unions. The ERA was approved by the U.S. Senate in March of 1972; within a year, thirty of the required thirty-eight states had ratified the amendment.

Friedan left office as president of NOW in 1970 and was succeeded by Wilma Scott Heide, a leader more sympathetic to the concerns of lesbians. In 1971, NOW included a statement of lesbian rights in its agenda and strengthened its position on abortion rights. In a number of cities, NOW was the chief initiator of women's consciousness-raising groups.

A New Phase   Between 1972 and 1978, NOW began its second stage of development. With a membership of more than fifteen thousand, NOW became a well-established political group with growing numbers, regular funding, and articulated strategic goals. NOW developed its lobbying capabilities, established a legislative office, and began the process of establishing political action committees (PACs). Although national leaders had divided into factions, they were able to elect Karen DeCrow as president in 1974 under the slogan Out of the Mainstream and Into the Revolution. Hoping to keep peace among its factions, in 1976 DeCrow led the organization in redistributing power among its national, regional, and state levels, giving more autonomy to local and state chapters.

In 1978, Eleanor Smeal was elected president of the organization. Smeal persuaded NOW leaders to declare an ERA "state of emergency." The opponents of ERA had mounted a ferocious campaign against its ratification as a resurgent Far Right political movement determined to defeat progressive reforms relating to the rights of women. Moreover, ERA ratification had come to a standstill by 1978, with three states needed to complete the process. NOW leaders raced against the 1982 deadline for ratification, with NOW spending as much as 25 percent of its entire budget to complete the ratification process.

Impact   Although the ERA was not ratified by the states, NOW established political structures and strategies that became very effective in other campaigns during the decade. The struggle for the ERA also drew more women into the political arena and led to more female elected officials. Between 1970 and 1979, NOW's membership increased from about 3,000 to 100,000, due in part to its commitment to ratification of the ERA as well as its support of lesbian and reproductive rights.

Subsequent Events   Although the ERA was reintroduced several times following 1982, it was not passed. NOW remained the most influential women's rights organization in the United States, growing to more than 500,000 members and holding chapters in all fifty states and the District of Columbia. The group's tactics changed after the defeat of the ERA: Instead of working to influence those already in elected office, NOW backed political candidates for federal offices and for state and local offices. The organization used lobbying and litigation to address issues such as child care, pregnancy leave, abortion, sexual harassment in the workplace, and lesbian rights. NOW has also campaigned for passage of state equal rights amendments and continued its struggle for a national ERA.

Further Reading

Barakso, Maryann. *Governing NOW: Grassroots Activism in the National Organization for Women.* Ithaca, N.Y.: Cornell University Press, 2005. Barakso examines NOW's origins, organizational structure, and goals, as well as the strategies it used to reach those goals. She explains the organizational movement beginning with the ERA and its failure to electoral politics and beyond.

Buechler, Steven M. *Women's Movements in the United States: Woman Suffrage, Equal Rights, and Beyond.* New Brunswick, N.J.: Rutgers University Press, 1990. Contains a section "Classes and Race" that discusses the creation of NOW and its early priorities and goals, as well as its biases that were to deeply affect and split the organization.

Carden, Maren Lockwood. *The New Feminist Movement.* New York: Russell Sage Foundation, 1974. Among many other discussions, the book provides an analysis and critique of the methods and aims of feminism as a whole.

Hole, Judith, and Ellen Levine. *Rebirth of Feminism.* New York: Quadrangle Books, 1971. The authors include a section on the formation and early history of NOW, describing it as "the first militant feminist group in the twentieth century to combat sex discrimination in all spheres of life."

Yvonne Johnson

See also   Abortion rights; Equal Rights Amendment (ERA); Feminism; Homosexuality and gay rights; National Lesbian and Gay Rights March of 1979; Steinem, Gloria; Women in the military; Women in the workforce; Women's rights.

■ National Public Radio (NPR)

Identification A not-for-profit radio network
  providing commercial-free news and
  entertainment programming to public radio
  stations across the United States
Date Founded in 1970; launched in 1971

By the 1970's, U.S. commercial radio had lost its voice, being pushed aside by commercial television. NPR sought to revitalize radio by producing news programs that would bring Americans, who had fallen out of the habit of listening to radio, back to the medium.

National Public Radio (NPR) was founded on February 24, 1970, with ninety public radio stations as charter members. In contrast to commercial radio, NPR carried very little advertising, except for brief statements from major donors. Since NPR would not be dependent on advertising revenue, it could be free from the ratings-driven decision making of commercial media and, therefore, could produce news programming that would be less sensationalistic. NPR was designed to be an alternative to commercial media by using good journalistic skills to promote personal growth rather than corporate gain and to speak with "many voices and many dialects."

Even though NPR's goal was to set itself apart from the commercial media, it was criticized because it did not sound like commercial network radio stations. Critics also charged NPR with liberal bias and elitism. A 1978 survey showed that NPR's audience was 90 percent white; 49 percent of listeners were college educated, and 18 percent earned more than $25,000 per year in income.

Two technical advances in the mid-1970's helped NPR make enormous strides: broadcast satellites and FM radios in cars. With satellite transmission, NPR's sound was clean, clear, and accessible, and quality sound production became the signature of NPR. Producers and engineers created subtle mixes of sounds, voices, and ambient noises to create pictures in listeners' minds. Before satellite broadcasts, NPR was limited to a small band of listeners, but once NPR began broadcasting from space, its audience increased dramatically. With FM car radios, NPR became a companion to millions of commuters nationwide.

All Things Considered NPR's first flagship program, *All Things Considered*, debuted on May 3, 1971, as a ninety-minute, weekday afternoon public affairs program that emphasized interpretations and investigative reporting. The program was designed to do more than simply transmit information: It also conveyed the experience of people and institutions from a wide variety of backgrounds and locations. *All Things Considered* shied away from the sixty-second news spots that were the standard fare on commercial network radio. Instead, the NPR program modeled itself after the Canadian Broadcasting Company's *This Country in the Morning*, which used long-form news reports with a combination of narratives, taped interviews, and ambient sound.

When *All Things Considered* first aired, 104 stations in thirty-four states and Puerto Rico had subscribed to receive NPR programming. *All Things Considered*'s first broadcast included nearly one hour of excerpts from the May Day protests by Vietnam veterans in Washington, D.C., and a sixteen-minute report in which a nurse vividly described her experiences as a heroin addict. Early station reactions to *All Things Considered* were uniformly negative. After a series of changes in program cohosts and producers, the program improved and won a Peabody Award for excellence in radio journalism in 1972.

Other Programming In April, 1971, NPR created public radio's first full-time, national, live interconnection system by providing to its affiliates live coverage of the Senate Foreign Relations Committee hearings on Vietnam. In February, 1978, NPR broadcast the Panama Canal treaty debate live from the Senate floor. For thirty-seven days, correspondent Linda Wertheimer covered the treaty debate from gavel to gavel, the first time an outside microphone had been allowed in a Senate session.

On November 5, 1979, NPR launched its second news and public affairs program, *Morning Edition.* As the title implied, *Morning Edition* was a weekday-morning public affairs program that ran for two hours, with stations having the option of repeating one or both hours. A typical *Morning Edition* program included newscasts and in-depth reports, interviews, profiles, commentaries, human-interest features, and segments on science, the arts, business, sports, and politics.

By the late 1970's, NPR was attracting a sophisticated listening audience with a range of cultural programming. By 1979, *Jazz Alive!*—a weekly program of taped, live performances—had the largest audience of any jazz program on the network. NPR's other cultural offerings included *Shakespeare Festival*, a package of drama, musical specials, and lectures, and *Masterpiece Radio Theatre*, a fifty-two-week drama series produced by the British Broadcasting Corporation (BBC) and station WGBH in Boston.

Impact National Public Radio was once described as one of the best-kept secrets in U.S. broadcasting. In the early 1970's, only one in five Americans had ever tuned in to one of its shows, and those who did rarely remembered NPR's name. However, by the end of the 1970's, NPR had finally gained national acclaim. Its flagship news programs, *All Things Considered* and *Morning Edition*, later became two of the most popular radio programs in the United States. Despite its struggles during the 1970's, NPR was able to reclaim the creativity of the golden age of radio by developing innovative news and cultural programming that would become part of mainstream American radio.

Further Reading

Collins, Mary. *National Public Radio: The Cast of Characters*. Washington, D.C.: Seven Locks Press, 1993. A lighthearted (with some profanity) history of NPR's coverage of memorable news stories and the correspondents who covered them.

Looker, Thomas. *The Sound and the Story: NPR and the Art of Radio*. Boston: Houghton Mifflin, 1995. A history of NPR with detailed descriptions of its daily operations and biographies of NPR personalities.

McCourt, Tom. *Conflicting Communication Interest in America: The Case of National Public Radio*. Westport, Conn.: Praeger, 1999. A scholarly critique of NPR and its effect on U.S. culture without using interviews with the principal figures involved in NPR's development.

Wertheimer, Linda, ed. *Listening to America: Twenty-five Years in the Life of a Nation, as Heard on National Public Radio*. Boston: Houghton Mifflin, 1995. Gives a selection of transcripts from *All Things Considered* from 1971 to 1994.

Eddith A. Dashiell

See also Journalism in Canada; Journalism in the United States; Public Broadcasting Service (PBS); Radio.

■ Native Americans

Definition Members of any of the aboriginal peoples of the United States

A history of broken promises and lives of poverty and hopelessness brought forth a new Indian militancy that created a series of protests and confrontations between law enforcement and Native Americans during the 1970's.

The American Indian Movement (AIM) was founded in 1968 in Minneapolis. In the words of Jane Wilson, an Ojibwe woman who was an early member of the group, "We just had to do something." Wilson's statement reflects two important facts of Native American life in the United States. The history of Native American and U.S. government relations has long been strained by broken treaties and broken promises. For example, the 1868 treaty granting to the Lakota Sioux Indians the Black Hills of the Dakotas "in perpetuity" was rescinded in 1877 by the Black Hills Act, thereby opening sacred Sioux land to white miners and settlers. This betrayal was central to many of the American Indian protests of the 1970's. As a consequence of this betrayal and countless others, Native Americans have never felt an equal partnership in American democracy. Moreover, since the Sioux, Cheyenne, Cherokee, and other bands were forced onto reservations in the nineteenth century, Native American life in the United States has been bleak. Native Americans have long been the portion of the American population that has the highest rates of poverty, unemployment, and alcoholism. It was in such a context that AIM rose to prominence in the 1970's.

The initial purpose of AIM was to garner for Indians and indigenous communities the same sort of attention that the "War on Poverty" was focusing on poverty throughout the United States in general. Termination and relocation programs had forced thousands of Native Americans off the reservations and into cities, where they could find no work.

In the early 1970's, the movement became much more overtly political. AIM adopted an upside-down American flag as its symbol. Though many members of white and Indian communities saw this symbol as un-American, members of AIM had other meanings in mind. Dennis Banks, one of founding members of AIM, later noted that the upside-down flag, which historically signified an international sign of distress, was a symbol of the ugly reality of Indian life in

America: "No one could deny that Indians were in bad trouble and needed help."

Indian Awareness and Protest   The first half of the decade was a watershed period for American Indian awareness. Anglo-American historian Dee Brown published *Bury My Heart at Wounded Knee* in 1970, a very popular, groundbreaking history of the United States' encroachment upon Indian lands in the West. Meanwhile, AIM activities and influence began to make headlines. From November, 1969, until June, 1971, Native Americans of various tribes occupied Alcatraz Island in San Francisco Bay. Issuing a proclamation "To the Great White Father and All His People," the occupiers reclaimed the island "by right of discovery," stating that the isolation, prison building, lack of modern facilities, rocky soil, and other limitations made the island resemble "most Indian reservations." During the fall of 1970 and the spring of 1971, AIM protested the Lakota Sioux loss of the Black Hills in the broken treaty of 1868 by setting up a camp at Mount Rushmore. They symboli-

cally reclaimed the land that the United States had taken, thereby emphasizing the irony that the famous faces of George Washington, Thomas Jefferson, Abraham Lincoln, and Theodore Roosevelt were carved into stone on land that had been bequeathed to the Sioux "in perpetuity." On Thanksgiving Day in 1970, Wampanoag leader Frank James spoke at Plymouth Rock, Massachusetts, renaming Thanksgiving "a national day of mourning."

In 1972, the protests became more intense. Echoing the Civil Rights movement's March on Washington in 1963, Indian activists organized the Trail of Broken Treaties March, arriving in Washington, D.C., on Friday, November 3, 1972, four days before the presidential election on Tuesday, November 7. Organized by AIM and seven other Native American groups, the procession stretched for four miles. Leaders of the group planned to present to authorities in Washington a twenty-point proposal in order to improve the United States' relationship with Indian tribes within its borders. When neither the president nor the vice president agreed to meet with

An American Indian encampment in Washington, D.C., in 1978 as part of the Longest Walk protest. (Library of Congress)

the marchers, various members of the group barricaded themselves into the Bureau of Indian Affairs (BIA) building, staying for five days and causing extensive damage.

This event did not play well with the Federal Bureau of Investigation (FBI) or or with many of those residing in Native American communities. The results were increased vigilance on the part of the FBI concerning Indian activities and a clear split among Indians themselves. Some Indians saw AIM members as troublemakers, viewing the activists' insistence on adhering to traditional Indian practices, such as the sweat tents and the Sun Dance, as obstacles to integrating the Indian community into the larger American community. They also saw the activists' increasingly violent protests as counterproductive. It was in such a context that the strange events of the mid-1970's began to unfold on the Pine Ridge Reservation in South Dakota.

The Events at Pine Ridge Pine Ridge contained within its borders significant Native American history. Part of the Black Hills was within its borders, as well as the famous site of the massacre of Native Americans at Wounded Knee in 1891. After two white men allegedly killed two Indians in 1973 on or near the reservation with little punishment for the perpetrators, there was a riot of AIM supporters at the courthouse in nearby Custer, South Dakota. This was followed quickly by the AIM occupation of Wounded Knee. The occupation lasted seventy-one days, ending in May, 1973. Between one and two hundred Indians held Wounded Knee, demanding that the U.S. government agree to discuss reinstating the treaty of 1868. They were surrounded by armed FBI agents with whom they exchanged gunfire. An FBI sniper eventually killed Buddy Lamont, a member of the occupying force.

The conflict at Wounded Knee reflected a large split in Pine Ridge politics. Richard Wilson, the president of the Pine Ridge Tribal Council, was decidedly against AIM and worked for and with the BIA. He reflected the feelings of many of those on the Pine Ridge Reservation that AIM was too radical. In the years between 1972 and 1975, a quiet war developed between Wilson and his supporters and the AIM leadership and its supporters. Meanwhile, the FBI had decided that AIM was harboring communist sympathizers and stepped up its surveillance of the group. Such a move created a warfare mentality on

Native American reservations, particularly at Pine Ridge.

On June 25, 1975, two FBI agents came to Pine Ridge with an arrest warrant for Jimmy Eagle, a Native American who was wanted on charges of theft and assault. Not finding him, the agents returned the next day. They approached dwellings belonging to the Jumping Bull family, residences they had searched the day before. Soon gunfire erupted, and agents Ron Williams and Jack Coler were killed. After their murder, the roads in and out of the reservations were blocked, and several Indians on the scene noticed helicopters circling overhead. Indians in various buildings near the shooting began to seek cover. Others attempted to get off the reservations. One of the groups of Indians that successfully passed through the FBI lockdown was led by AIM activist Leonard Peltier.

Great controversy continues to exist concerning who fired first. Indians near the shooting claim that the FBI agents began firing on the cabins without provocation. Further, many Indians on the reservation saw the entire situation as a prefabricated attack. They use as evidence the unusually quick appearance of roadblocks and the presence of helicopters. They argued that such force would not have been present if the FBI were not planning an attack. FBI agents discount this version of events, stating that they were simply serving a warrant and that AIM members were waiting to fire upon them.

AIM activist Peltier was eventually convicted of killing the agents in March, 1976. His conviction was controversial and widely questioned by world leaders and social activists, including several Hollywood actors.

The Death of Anna Mae Pictou-Aquash The other famous casualty of the conflict between AIM and the U.S. government during this era was that of Anna Mae Pictou-Aquash. Pictou-Aquash, a Mi'kmaq woman from Nova Scotia, was an active member of AIM and a devout supporter of returning to the traditional Indian ways. She heroically smuggled food to those AIM members who occupied Wounded Knee. On February 24, 1976, cattle rancher Roger Amiotte found Pictou-Aquash's body at the bottom of a thirty-foot ravine. Though the FBI agents who investigated the case had recently questioned Pictou-Aquash concerning AIM activities, none of them recognized the badly decomposed body. An autopsy yielded no fingerprints for the body, so the FBI instructed the lab to cut the hands off and send them to Washington, D.C., for more precise fingerprinting. Meanwhile, the corpse was buried in a pauper's grave, and the coroner listed the cause of death as "exposure." When Washington authorities identified the body as that of Pictou-Aquash, the FBI had the corpse exhumed, and a second autopsy revealed the cause of death to be a bullet wound behind her ear.

Many Indians blamed the FBI for the killing, citing the cutting off of hands and the botched autopsy as attempts to hide evidence. Others blamed AIM, citing evidence that some in AIM thought that Pictou-Aquash was an FBI informant.

Impact   The 1970's were a watershed era for American Indian activists, who fought in various ways to gain representation for their communities as well as recognition for their long history of struggle. Some of these efforts paid off as important legislation was passed in order to protect critical aspects of Native American culture—for example, the American Indian Religious Freedom Act of of 1978—and to assist Indians in their pursuit of self-determination and education—the Indian Self-Determination and Education Assistance Act of 1975.

Subsequent Events   In the Peltier case, despite repeated calls for a new trial, Peltier remained in prison as of 2005. Peter Matthiessen's book *In the Spirit of Crazy Horse* (1983) gave Peltier near martyr status, tying him to the great Lakota hero Crazy Horse. Not everyone shared Matthiessen's view: Some Indians were insulted that Matthiessen would tie Peltier, whom they consider a villain, to the great Crazy Horse. The book also provoked a libel suit from the FBI agents and former governor of South Dakota William Janklow. Their suit kept the book off the shelves from 1983 until 1991, when Matthiessen won a suit by appealing to his First Amendment rights.

By 1999, Russell Means, a prominent AIM official, stated that he believed that AIM officials ordered the killing of Pictou-Aquash on the suspicion of her being an FBI informant. Since then, former AIM members John Boy Graham and Arlo Looking Cloud have been charged with her murder. Looking Cloud was convicted of murder in February, 2004, and sentenced to life in prison. Graham's case was pending

in 2005. Meanwhile Pictou-Aquash's two daughters, children at the time of her death, have led a tireless campaign seeking justice for their mother. On June 21, 2004, Pictou-Aquash's body was given final burial in Nova Scotia.

Further Reading

Banks, Dennis, with Richard Erdoes. *Ojibwa Warrior: Dennis Banks and the Rise of the American Indian Movement.* Norman: University of Oklahoma Press, 2004. Banks's autobiography, which includes historical information on AIM.

Brown, Dee. *Bury My Heart at Wounded Knee.* Thirtieth anniversary ed. New York: Henry Holt, 2000. Using important primary resources, including photos and letters written by Native Americans, Brown traces the struggle at Wounded Knee in the last decades of the nineteenth century. Provides excellent context for understanding the events of the 1970's.

Grant, Bruce. *Concise Encyclopedia of the American Indian.* New York: Random House, 1989. An A-Z reference book that traces the history of the American Indian in the United States from the 1500's to the late twentieth century.

Matthiessen, Peter. *In the Spirit of Crazy Horse.* New York: Penguin, 1992. The controversial book that details the Lakota's long-standing struggle with the U.S. government.

Smith, Paul Chaat, and Robert Allen Warrior. *Like a Hurricane: The Indian Movement from Alcatraz to Wounded Knee.* New York: The New Press, 1996. Members of the Comanche and Osage tribes write a narrative on American Indian activism and the rise of AIM.

H. William Rice

See also   American Indian Movement (AIM); American Indian Religious Freedom Act of 1978; Indian Self-Determination and Education Assistance Act of 1975; Littlefeather, Sacheen; Peltier, Leonard; Trail of Broken Treaties; Wounded Knee occupation.

■ Natural disasters

Definition   Destructive events of nature that cause major damage to property or injury and loss of life to humans; includes earthquakes, volcanic eruptions, floods, droughts, blizzards, tsunamis, hurricanes, and tornadoes

During the 1970's, natural disasters killed about twenty-eight hundred people and destroyed or damaged billions of dollars worth of homes, businesses, crops, and infrastructure (sewers, streets, schools, hospitals, banks, electricity and water supplies) in the United States and Canada. Several calamities spurred the U.S. and Canadian governments to improve disaster prevention and preparedness in hazardous areas.

Natural disasters can be divided into geological events (such earthquakes, sinkholes, and landslides) and weather-related incidents (such as storms and floods). North America is at high risk for both kinds of disasters.

Geological Disasters Nine earthquakes occurred during the decade with a magnitude of 6.0 or greater on the Richter scale, two in populated areas. The first major geological disaster during the decade was the Sylmar earthquake which took place on February 9, 1971. This temblor was centered in Sylmar, California, a suburban community in the San Fernando Valley near Los Angeles. The quake registered a magnitude 6.7. The ground shook for about one minute, but in that brief span of time, the quake killed sixty-five people, injured more than two thousand, and incurred $505 million in property damage within a 30-mile radius. Nearly everyone felt the temblor in San Diego 120 miles away.

Next came the opening of a sinkhole in the Canadian village of St.-Jean-Vianney, Quebec, on May 4, 1971. Heavy rains caused the gaping hole that induced a mudslide which killed thirty-one people and swallowed up thirty-five homes, a school bus, and several cars.

A third major geological disaster took place in the Imperial Valley of California on October 15, 1979, when a powerful 6.4 earthquake injured ninety-one people and caused an estimated $30 million in property damage. The most severe property damage was to buildings in El Centro, California.

Weather-Related Disasters Much of the western United States experienced severe drought conditions in the late 1970's, while precipitation levels were above normal in the rest of North America. Most people who lived through the 1970's east of the Rockies remember the decade for the widespread impact of cold winters (particularly the devastating blizzards), the floods accompanying Hurricane Agnes, and the Jumbo Tornado Outbreak of 1974.

Blizzards are heavy snowstorms with blinding whiteouts and severely cold winds. Four such storms of the 1970's stand out for their ferocity: Montreal's "Snowstorm of the Century" in 1971, the U.S. Midwest blizzards in 1975 and 1977, and the U.S. Northeast's "nor'easter" blizzard of 1978.

Earthquakes with Magnitude 6.0+ in the United States and Canada in the 1970's

Date	Location	Magnitude
June 24, 1970	South of Queen Charlotte Islands	7.4
February 9, 1971	San Fernando Valley, California	6.7
July 30, 1972	Sitka, Alaska	7.6
February 2, 1975	Near Islands, Alaska	7.6
March 28, 1975	Eastern Idaho	6.1
July 29, 1976	West of Vancouver Island, Canada	7.1
February 28, 1979	Mt. St. Elias, Alaska	7.6
May 20, 1979	Alaska Peninsula	7.0
October 15, 1979	Imperial Valley, Mexico-California border	6.4

Richter Scale of Earthquake Magnitude
1.0-3.0: Recorded on local seismographs, but generally not felt
3.0-4.0: Often felt, no damage
5.0: Felt widely, slight damage near epicenter
6.0: Damage to poorly constructed buildings and other structures within 30 miles (50 kilometers)
7.0: "Major" earthquake, causes serious damage up to about 60 miles (100 kilometers)
8.0: "Great" earthquake, great destruction, loss of life over several hundred kilometers
9.0+: Rare great earthquake, major damage over a large region (more than 1,000 kilometers)

The Snowstorm of the Century, Montreal's worst snowstorm on record, took place on March 4, 1971. It killed seventeen people and dumped 19 inches (47 centimeters) of snow. Winds reaching 69 miles (110 kilometers) per hour blew snowdrifts as high as second-story windows. The powerful wind snapped power lines and cut electricity for ten days. The city hauled away thousands of truckloads of snow.

In the Midwest blizzard from January 10-12, 1975, frigid conditions killed thousands of cattle, and low visibility, snowdrifts, and icy roads stranded countless motorists. Eight people died in the storm in South Dakota, with other deaths in surrounding states. The January, 1977, Midwest blizzard was part of the coldest winter month of the decade. Record low temperatures stretched from northeast Texas to New Jersey and Florida. Snow fell as far south as the Florida Keys, and freezing temperatures caused severe damage to the state's citrus crops.

The nor'easter blizzard of 1978 came to life on February 5 over South Carolina and moved northeast, following the U.S. East Coast, on February 6-7. (Meteorologists call such coastal storms nor'-easters because they travel in a northeasterly direction.) The storm dumped up to 3 feet (1 meter) of snow across the U.S. Northeast and caused ninety-nine deaths. Snowfall, ice, tidal flooding, beach erosion, and high winds caused about $600 million in property losses to Massachusetts, New York, New Jersey, and New Hampshire.

Hurricanes are storms that usually make landfall (come onshore) along the Gulf Coast (from Texas to western Florida) and the U.S. East Coast. A rare landfall occurred in Canada when Hurricane Beth slammed into Nova Scotia on August 15, 1971. U.S. shores were struck by twelve hurricanes in the 1970's, fewer hurricanes than in any other decade of the twentieth century. Four storms stand out for their destruction: Celia (1970), Eloise (1975), Agnes (1972), and Frederic (1979).

Hurricanes in the United States and Canada in the 1970's

Date of Landfall	Hurricane Name	Category	Location of Landfall
August 3, 1970	Celia	3	Texas
August 15, 1971	Beth	1	Canada
September 10, 1971	Fern	1	Texas
September 16, 1971	Edith	2	Louisiana
October 1, 1971	Ginger	1	Virginia
June 19, 1972	Agnes	1	Florida
October 8, 1974	Carmen	3	Louisiana
September 23, 1975	Eloise	3	Alabama
October 10, 1976	Belle	1	New York
September 6, 1977	Babe	1	Louisiana
September 2, 1979	David	2	Florida
September 10, 1979	Bob	1	Louisiana
September 13, 1979	Frederic	3	Alabama

Saffir-Simpson Hurricane Scale
Category 1: 74-95 mile per hour (mph) winds
Category 2: 96-110 mph winds
Category 3: 111-130 mph winds
Category 4: 131-155 mph winds
Category 5: winds greater than 155 mph

Agnes was a Category 1 hurricane; the others were much stronger Category 3 hurricanes. Nevertheless, Hurricane Agnes is famous for its broad geographical impact. It made landfall along the Florida Panhandle, crossed the coastal plain, and came back over the Atlantic off North Carolina. After regaining strength again, Agnes came onshore as a tropical storm over Long Island, New York, and then moved westward in an arc over southern New York and into north-central Pennsylvania, where severe flooding took place. Hurricane Agnes was the costliest natu-

Chronological List of Major Weather-Related Disasters in the United States and Canada in the 1970's

Date	Disaster	Location	Description
September 25, 1970	Fires, Santa Ana winds	Southern California	Wind-fanned fires; 1,000 structures destroyed
January 4, 1971	Blizzard	Kansas to Wisconsin	27 deaths; property damage
February 21, 1971	Tornadoes	Louisiana and Mississippi	4 tornadoes; 121 deaths; 1,600 injuries
March 4, 1971	Blizzard	Montreal	17 deaths; property damage
August, 1971	Floods	New Jersey and Pennsylvania	$138 million property damage
February 26, 1972	Floods	West Virginia	Heavy rains; broken dam; 118 deaths
June, 1972	Floods	Eastern United States	$3.1 billion property damage; 122 deaths
June 9-10, 1972	Flood	Black Hills, South Dakota	238 deaths; $164 million property damage
Spring, 1973	Flood	Mississippi River	33 deaths; $1.2 billion property damage
May, 1973	Flood	South Platte River	$120 million property damage
April 3-4, 1974	Tornadoes	Ontario to Georgia	Super outbreak of 148 tornadoes; 330 deaths; 5,484 injuries; widespread property damage
January 10-12, 1975	Blizzard	Minnesota ("Storm of the Century" for the state)	35 deaths; property damage
July, 1975	Flood	Red River, North Dakota, and Canada	4 deaths; $273 million property damage
September, 1975	Floods	New York and Pennsylvania	9 deaths; $296 million property damage
July 31, 1976	Flood	Big Thompson Canyon, Colorado	139 deaths; $35.5 million property damage
October, 1976	Floods	Southern California and Arizona	$160 million property damage
January, 1977	Cold wave	Ontario, Canada, to southern Florida	Record-setting snowfalls; snowflakes in Miami
April, 1977	Floods	Kentucky	22 deaths; $424 million property damage

(continued)

Date	Disaster	Location	Description
July, 1977	Flood	Johnstown, Pennsylvania	76 deaths; $200 million property damage
September, 1977	Floods	Kansas City creeks	23 deaths; $5 million property damage
November 6, 1977	Flood	Taccoa, Georgia	Heavy rains; dam failure; 38 deaths
February-March, 1978	Flood	Southern California	20 deaths; $100 million property damage
April, 1978	Floods	Pearl River (Louisiana and Mississippi)	15 deaths; $1 billion property damage
August, 1978	Floods	Southeastern Texas	33 deaths; $100 million property damage
April, 1979	Floods	Southeast Texas	1 death; $500 million property damage
April 10, 1979	Tornadoes	Texas and Oklahoma	23 tornadoes; 56 deaths; widespread property damage
July, 1979	Floods	East Texas	1 death; $750 million property damage

Note: Dollar values not adjusted for inflation

ral disaster in U.S. history at the time: It caused an estimated $3.1 billion in damage and claimed at least 122 lives.

During the 1970's, the general pattern of monthly occurrences of tornadoes, vicious rotating columns of air, was typical of previous decades, except for a spike in April, 1974. On April 3-4, 1974, the worst eighteen-hour period of tornadoes in U.S. history occurred. It was called the Jumbo Tornado Outbreak. In total, 148 tornadoes produced about 900 square miles (2,300 square kilometers) of damage in thirteen states: Michigan, Indiana, Illinois, Ohio, New York, Kentucky, West Virginia, Virginia, Tennessee, North Carolina, Mississippi, Alabama, and Georgia. One tornado also traveled from Michigan into Canada.

Impact   During the 1970's, more than 90 percent of the natural disasters in the United States and Canada resulted from weather or climate extremes. Countless people required government aid. In response to flooding caused by Hurricane Agnes, the U.S. Congress passed the Flood Disaster Protection Act of 1973. This act offers flood insurance to those communities that adopt and enforce floodplain management ordinances.

In response to the Sylmar earthquake, the California legislature strengthened building codes by passing the Alquist Priolo Special Studies Zone Act in 1972. This act prohibits the location of most structures for human occupancy across the traces of active faults.

In response to the growing number of people affected by natural disasters, the U.S. Congress created the Federal Emergency Management Agency (FEMA) in 1979 to merge many state and local disaster programs. Canada began the Disaster Financial Assistance Arrangements Program in 1970 to help Canadian provinces cover the cost of disaster recovery. Canada also instituted the Flood Damage Reduction Program in 1975.

Subsequent Events   In the decades that followed, population growth in North America exposed more people to natural hazards. More people began to suffer from floods and hurricanes because of the ex-

A view of Main Street in Johnstown, Pennsylvania, on July 20, 1977, after floodwaters from heavy rain and a broken dam started to recede. (AP/Wide World Photos)

pansion of homes and businesses into flood-prone and hurricane-prone areas. Similarly, more tornadoes were reported, as more people were living in their paths. Fortunately, annual death rates due to natural disasters did not increase, as a result of better disaster preparedness, the development of Doppler radar and satellite technology, and improved storm and flood warning systems.

Further Reading

Amdahl, Gary. *Disaster Response: GIS for Public Safety.* Redlands, Calif.: ESRI Press, 2001. An illustrated guide to using geographic information systems to aid in responding to natural disasters.

Bryant, E. A. *Natural Hazards.* New York: Cambridge University Press, 1991. An excellent primer on a wide range of climatic and geological hazards.

Ludlum, David M. *The American Weather Book.* Boston: Houghton Mifflin, 1982. Ludlum's book lists extreme U.S. weather and weather-related phenomena for each day of the year up to the date of the book's publication.

National Climate Data Center. U.S. Storm Events Data Base. http://www4.ncdc.noaa.gov/cgi-win/wwcgi.dll?wwEvent~Storms. This search-based Web site allows access to reports on virtually every type of U.S. extreme weather event on record.

National Oceanic and Atmospheric Administration. Climatic and Weather Extremes. Http://lwf.ncdc.noaa.gov/oa/climate/severeweather/extremes.html. This Web site includes information about extreme U.S. weather events, such as hurricanes and tornadoes, with damage costs.

Richard A. Crooker

See also Disaster films; Environmental movement; Jumbo Tornado Outbreak of 1974; Mississippi River flood of 1973; Sylmar earthquake.

■ *Network*

Identification Motion picture
Director Sidney Lumet (1924-)
Date Released in 1976

As much documentary as satiric fantasy, Network *powerfully analyzes how the anger captured in its unforgettable tagline—"I'm mad as hell and I'm not going to take this anymore"—is cultivated by mass media and turned into profit by the corporations that govern people's lives.*

Network begins with a fleeting look at the "golden age of television," as Max Schumacher (played by William Holden) and Howard Beale (Peter Finch) reminisce about the days of Edward R. Murrow, when reporting the news was handled seriously and responsibly. Those days are over, and the network is controlled by people raised by television—such as Diana Christensen (Faye Dunaway), brought up on Bugs Bunny cartoons—and corporate culture, which guarantees that they and the shows they produce will be devoid of human feeling and have no concern for the public interest. Max and Howard are out of place in this new network, and each responds with a kind of craziness.

Max is fired because he clings to the idea that news should be insulated from television's relentless drive to entertain and make a profit. Nevertheless, he has an affair with Diana, although he knows that she will preside over the network's ruin and perhaps his ruin as well. Max ultimately escapes by leaving Diana, even as she is throwing him out. Perhaps the function of this odd coupling in the film is to celebrate its failure, allowing screenwriter Paddy Chayefsky and director Sidney Lumet to dramatize Max's realization that the painful world of intimacy and awareness is far preferable to the anesthetizing world represented by Diana, who is described as "television incarnate." The one defines the human; the other destroys it.

Howard is even crazier than Max. He is initially fired because of poor ratings, but when he announces that he will kill himself on the air, he suddenly becomes the enormously popular "mad prophet of the airwaves" speaking to and for a mass audience that, like him, is "mad as hell." He is encouraged by the network, which is firmly in the hands of corporate executive Frank Ruddy (Robert Duvall). Traditional journalistic ethics and conventional standards and practices vanish in the pursuit of higher ratings, which mean higher profits. *The Howard Beale Show*, a blend of ranting and rabble-rousing, becomes the anchor of a network lineup that also includes a regular program composed of footage filmed by the radical Ecumenical Liberation Army, a clear allusion to the real-life Symbionese Liberation Army (SLA) that kidnapped Patty Hearst.

The success of the network is meteoric but short-lived, largely because of the perversity of the corporate system: The corporation that took over the network is itself taken over by a larger group, which turns Howard into a spokesperson not for anger and protest but for obedience to the corporate interests that rule the world. His viewers become dispirited

and start tuning out. The network executives coolly decide that their best strategy, selfish and amoral as always, is to arrange for Howard's assassination on his own show. The film ends with this surprisingly undramatic event, shown first fullscreen and then on a grid of four television monitors, which present it as only one inconsequential image among many others to a jaded, desensitized audience.

Impact   *Network* gives a strikingly accurate picture of troubled and tumultuous mid-1970's America, where the population had many reasons to be "mad as hell," stirred up by angry talk shows and tabloid journalism, confused and betrayed by revelations about corporate involvement in political disruptions and assassinations outside the United States and about governmental corruption within the United States, culminating in Watergate.

Network also proved to be stunningly prophetic: The dangers of corporate control of the media accelerated, television news became increasingly focused on profit and entertainment, and a powerful and omnipresent visual media intensified concerns about how such an environment threatens to turn people into what the film calls "humanoids," incapable of deep feeling and living life by acting out "scripts" handed to them by image and story makers. *Network* warns its audience about the "shrieking madness" that is at the heart of television as a medium and an incarnation of corporate culture.

Further Reading
Boyer, Jay. *Sidney Lumet.* New York: Twayne, 1993.
Considine, Shaun. *Mad as Hell: The Life and Work of Paddy Chayefsky.* New York: Random House, 1994.
Sidney Gottlieb

See also   Academy Awards; Censorship in the United States; Dunaway, Faye; Film in the United States; Hearst, Patty; Journalism in the United States; Symbionese Liberation Army (SLA); Talk shows; Television in the United States.

■ Neutron bomb

Definition   A type of nuclear weapon intended to destroy life but minimize damage to structures

The development of the neutron bomb created a political and moral dilemma about the use of atomic weapons on specific targets and in specific areas.

An enhanced radiation warhead (ERH), better known as the neutron bomb, is a specialized type of nuclear weapon intended to avoid the negative military side affects of typical nuclear weapons. Whereas conventional nuclear weapons produce a massive blast effect and create lingering radioactivity, the United States developed the ERH to cause damage less through blast than by a brief but massive dose of radiation that would then immediately dissipate. The result is a large number of dead enemy personnel but minimum damage to physical structures, such as buildings or bridges, in the blast area.

The U.S. military developed the neutron bomb in the late 1970's as a reflection of the military realities facing the North Atlantic Treaty Organization (NATO). First, the Soviets had a huge preponderance in tanks and other armored forces. Second, in accordance with NATO's nonpreemption policy, war with the Soviet Union would begin only with a Soviet invasion of Western Europe, meaning that the war would be fought on NATO soil in Germany, an important U.S. ally. Presuming that outnumbered NATO forces could not contain a conventional Soviet attack, military planners envisioned the ERH as a means of destroying a large number of concentrated Soviet tanks but without massive physical damage to the German countryside.

Antiwar and antinuclear groups immediately protested the U.S. plan to develop and field the ERH. Critics charged that the neutron bomb made nuclear war more, rather than less, likely because field commanders had a sense that the weapons could be used with impunity. Moreover, they argued, the Soviets were likely to respond with similar nuclear weapons of their own. Finally, the neutron bomb was labeled a weapon of capitalist imperialism by critics since it gave the United States the ability to kill its enemies while leaving factories, infrastructure, and other means of production intact. Some NATO members also objected to the weapon, especially the Germans, who were faced with the potential liberal use of the ERH on their soil.

Impact The neutron bomb, eventually fielded in small numbers with the U.S. military in the early 1980's, demonstrated the difficulties of dealing with the Soviet military threat in Europe without expending large amounts of resources to match the Soviets in conventional power.

Further Reading

Cohen, Samuel. *The Truth About the Neutron Bomb: The Inventor of the Bomb Speaks Out.* New York: William Morrow, 1983.

Wasserman, Sheri L. *The Neutron Bomb Controversy: A Study in Alliance Politics.* New York: Praeger Press, 1983.

Steven J. Ramold

See also Anti-Ballistic Missile (ABM) Treaty; Antinuclear movement; Cold War; Foreign policy of the United States; SALT I and II treaties.

■ New Age movement

Definition A social movement centered on spirituality

The New Age movement allowed members of the baby boom generation and others to maintain a spiritual commitment based on personal experience, while also salvaging those aspects of "establishment" religions that were important to them and discarding that which they considered outmoded or irrelevant.

The New Age movement takes its name from the astrological age of Aquarius, the beginning of a new two-thousand-year cycle that was slated to arrive at the end of the twentieth century, and which, in the 1960's, was considered the herald of major changes in human life on Earth. The tremendous cultural changes that took place in the United States as the 1960's turned into the 1970's lent reality to these anticipated events. The New Age movement was largely a middle-class movement of those attracted to a variety of non-Western religious elements that they incorporated into their own belief systems.

Origins Rooted in movements and events of the past such as Gnosticism, spiritualism, and the human potential movement, the New Age movement was nevertheless a direct response to changing conditions within U.S. society. In the 1970's, as the war in Vietnam wound down and the United States experienced economic recession, loyalty to establishment religions waned as more baby boomers came of age. Most churches lost membership, as they were considered by many to be out of touch with contemporary concerns. It was not that Americans had less faith but rather that they thought churches had become increasingly irrelevant.

As the decade began, disillusionment with religious institutions matched the low view held by many Americans of most social institutions, largely because of the realization that formal religion had not been instrumental in solving critical social problems such as civil rights, the war in Vietnam, and the participation of women in leadership roles. Young people questioned religious authority. A 1978 study found that strong religious beliefs did not entail membership in an established church. Instead, high levels of faith manifested themselves in new and personal approaches to religion, many of them found in New Age religion.

From Disillusionment to the New Age   Faith remained relatively high among American youth, but they found innovative outlets for their spirituality by adding new elements based on a variety of experiences and practices. Some of this interest was related to the altered states of consciousness discovered by young people through the use of hallucinogenic drugs. In some cases, drug use led indirectly to the formation of new religious communities based on Eastern religions such as Zen Buddhism or yoga: Meditation techniques practiced in these religions often became a replacement for a dependency on drugs. Others were motivated by a shift in the field of psychology and its emphasis on self-actualization and self-fulfillment. Whatever the motivation, the New Age movement concentrated on spirituality rather than formal religion.

The New Age movement was not a religious movement in the formal sense of the word, because it had no particular doctrine or dogma and no discrete membership. However, it became a spiritual movement because of its transcendental concerns and its emphasis on personal experience as a key to spirituality. Furthermore, this movement precipitated the development of individual interest in mysticism and magic as ways of knowing, thereby ushering in new interests in astrology, tarot cards, and magical practices such as spells and incantations, channeling, and divination.

The spiritual elements of the New Age movement were often accompanied by practical or secular activities, such as a move toward holistic medicine and the rediscovery of folk medicine for health and healing. An interest in non-Western medical practices, such as acupuncture and the use of herbs, took its place alongside a renewed interest in vegetarianism (often related to Eastern religious practices) and eventually even in a particular style of music.

Impact   The New Age movement generated interest in ancient religions and spiritualities and the religions of native peoples around the world, as well as opened the door to new understandings of Eastern religious traditions. While producing new interpretations of Christianity and Judaism, it also forced mainstream churches to reexamine themselves and adapt to a more contemporary environment. The New Age movement served as a repository of spiritual interest that eventually led many people back to mainstream religion but continued to provide a place for those who sought out the new.

Further Reading

Heelas, Paul. *The New Age Movement.* Boston: Blackwell, 1996. A scholarly analysis and comprehensive treatment of the New Age movement within the context of modernity.

Lewis, James R., and J. Gordon Melton, eds. *Perspectives on the New Age.* Albany: State University of New York Press, 1992. An excellent collection of essays that trace the origins and characteristics of the New Age movement, as well as articles about New Age communities.

Roof, Wade Clark. *Spiritual Marketplace.* Princeton, N.J.: Princeton University Press, 1999. In this book, a religious scholar examines New Age religion in the context of the varieties of American religious forms.

Whitworth, Belinda. *New Age Encyclopedia.* Franklin Lakes, N.J.: New Page Books/Career Press, 2003. This alphabetically arranged compendium of the New Age movement defines and explains everything from "Abduction by Aliens" to "Zero Balancing." It also includes a list of resources and an extensive bibliography for writings about the New Age movement.

Wuthnow, Robert. *Experimentation in American Religion.* Berkeley: University of California Press, 1978. Provides an interesting look at New Age religion as it was developing in the 1970's and a consideration of its effects on mainstream religions.

Susan Love Brown

See also   Acupuncture; Astrology; Buddhism; Castañeda, Carlos; Cults; Drug use; Human potential movement; Jesus People Movement; Religion and spirituality in Canada; Religion and spirituality in the United States; Scientology; Wiccan movement; *Zen and the Art of Motorcycle Maintenance.*

■ New Journalism

Definition   A style of journalism that takes on
devices of literary fiction

*Emerging from a 1960's movement in which some young
journalists wrote columns and articles from a subjective
viewpoint and used techniques that had previously been
seen only in fiction, New Journalism was further identified
and defined during the 1970's in conferences, anthologies,
and media discussion.*

New Journalism represents a significant development in American popular culture and is sometimes
called "literary journalism" or "creative nonfiction";
that is, reporting published in magazines and books
that is written in a more captivating style than traditional journalism. Certain writers and their books
were influential in creating recognition for and acceptance of the New Journalism. Although Joan
Didion's collection of essays *Slouching Towards Bethlehem* came out in 1968, it went through many reprints
and set a standard for New Journalism as it was defined in the 1970's. The essays were previously published in such magazines as *The New York Times Magazine, Holiday, The American Scholar,* and *The Saturday
Evening Post.* Truman Capote's *In Cold Blood,* the
story of two merciless killers who murdered a prosperous Kansas farm family, first appeared in *The New
Yorker* and came out as a book in 1966. Capote
claimed it as a new literary genre, the nonfiction
novel, and it became enormously successful. The
book's fame led journalists to emulate the techniques of the increasingly popular new style.

Tom Wolfe started his career as a journalist for
The New York Herald Tribune, where Jimmy Breslin was
later hired to work as a feature writer. Breslin arrived
on the scene of his story early in order to get background material and used "novelistic details" in his
stories, unheard of techniques in journalism at the
time. Wolfe, after years of perfecting his journalism
in articles and books such as *The Electric Kool-Aid Acid
Test* (1968), publicized the term "the New Journalism" in his book of that name that appeared in 1973
and included an anthology edited by Wolfe and
E. W. Johnson. *Esquire* magazine also encouraged
the work of Wolfe, Breslin, and Gay Talese, another
early practitioner of New Journalism.

Techniques   In his landmark book, *The New Journalism,* Wolfe defines four techniques that had pre-

viously been used in writing the realistic novel and
suggests that journalists were now using these techniques in nonfiction, a genre that had previously
been limited to a linear, objective style of reporting.
The writers of this new style hoped to achieve the ab-
sorbing quality and emotional intensity that had
long been a hallmark of novels.

The first of Wolfe's techniques was scene-by-scene
construction, rather than straight narrative. The basic reporting unit was no longer the datum, or piece
of information, but the scene. The New Journalists
tried to embed themselves in the events and then
stay there long enough to see and hear things that
were not meant for their eyes and ears. This approach also required dialogue, the second technique, which was recognized by the journalists as
that which engages readers more than any other. Dialogue is a powerful way of creating character and
will often reveal more about a character than
lengthy description.

The third device listed by Wolfe is the "third-
person point of view"—that is, exploring characters'
emotions and thoughts by interviewing them. This

*Joan Didion, one of the practitioners of New Journalism in the
1970's. (Quintana Roo Dunne)*

technique requires dialogue and helps the reader identify with the character. The final technique that Wolfe finds significant is the recording of all the appurtenances, objects, and distinctive habits of a character, that which he calls the character's "status life." Although Wolfe does not mention them, simile and metaphor are often used in the New Journalism to give more impact to the topic.

One of the results of the combination of these techniques was that the narrator, or reporter, also became part of the scene. The old ideal of the objective reporter who had no responsibility but to deliver the information began to erode into the subjective, first-person narrator. The New Journalists maintained this approach by reporting the mood, tone, and feelings of a story as well as the facts, and in doing so, they could convey to the audience the underlying truth of what was happening.

Some authorities believe this shift in journalism arose from the television talk shows that large segments of the population watched during the 1960's and 1970's. Writers began to realize the connection between popular culture and news and between immediate events and commercialism. Talk show personalities such as Jack Paar and Johnny Carson questioned their guests and delivered their own impressions of the answers with a lifted eyebrow or a smirk. Writers wanted to do the same thing in print.

Impact   The most important impact of the New Journalism was the creation of the first new literary genre in more than a century, which became an established and accepted component of American writing and in turn, influenced other styles. Perhaps the most well-known of these offshoots was "gonzo" journalism and creative nonfiction. Hunter S. Thompson invented gonzo and was the major practitioner of it in books such as *Fear and Loathing in Las Vegas* (1971) and numerous articles in magazines such as *Rolling Stone* and *Playboy*. His writing has been called both fiction and the best New Journalism ever written. Thompson defined gonzo as writing that depends on spontaneity, with no rewriting allowed, from a writer who is as personally involved in the story as possible. Creative nonfiction is a term used to identify nonfiction that utilizes the techniques of fiction and became, following the 1970's, much more mainstream, with new magazines devoted to the style alone and older, more traditional journals finding a place for it in their pages.

Further Reading

Fishwick, Marshall, ed. *New Journalism*. Bowling Green, Ohio: Bowling Green University Popular Press, 1975. A collection of essays by different authors, each dealing with a separate aspect of New Journalism. It offers a variety of styles, from scholarly to amusing, and illustrates how controversial New Journalism is.

Johnson, Michael L. *The New Journalism*. Lawrence: University of Kansas Press, 1971. One of the first and most influential books on New Journalism, it is used as a research resource by numerous writers and scholars.

Wolfe, Tom. *The New Journalism*. New York: Harper & Row, 1973. With an anthology edited by Wolfe and E. W. Johnson. The landmark book that defines New Journalism in terms that have been accepted in the years since. It is also rich in examples of the genre.

Sheila Golburgh Johnson

See also   *Doonesbury*; Journalism in the United States; Literature in the United States; "Radical Chic"; Talk shows; Thompson, Hunter S.; Wolfe, Tom.

■ New York City blackout of 1977

The Event   A power failure plunges New York City into darkness
Date   July 13-14, 1977

The 1977 blackout forced utility companies to devise ways to prevent recurrences and forced public officials to develop new protocols for dealing with such events.

At 9:43 P.M. on a sultry Wednesday evening, July 13, 1977, a massive power failure hit New York City and its boroughs. With temperatures in the mid-nineties and the humidity high, New Yorkers sweltered, and, before power was restored at 10:14 P.M. on the following evening, the city was without power for more than twenty-five hours.

Civil Unrest   This was not the first time New York City had experienced a major power outage. Nine years earlier, a similar event kept the city dark for more than thirteen hours, and New Yorkers coped with the situation peacefully. The 1965 outage blacked out 80,000 square miles in New England and in New York, New Jersey, and Pennsylvania. Ironically, just three days before the power outage of 1977, Charles Luce, chairman of the Board of Consolidated Edison, the major supplier of electrical power to New York City, appeared before the United States House of Representatives' Subcommittee on Energy and Power to guarantee that power outages like that of 1965 would never happen again.

Whereas the 1965 outage had brought out the best in New Yorkers, many of whom knocked on the doors of neighbors they scarcely knew to make sure they were safe, the 1977 outage ended in a rash of burglaries and lootings. Under the cover of darkness, vandals broke into stores and hauled away everything movable. Sounds of breaking glass permeated the city's streets. A mob psychology began to prevail as people decided it was their right to steal what they could from unprotected businesses throughout the city.

The violent response was arguably one that reflected the social and civil discontent of the mid-1970's. Civil unrest had engulfed much of the country, particularly in urban areas. Unease over the war in Vietnam, an energy crisis, and disenchantment with government following the Watergate scandal and the subsequent resignations of President Rich-

ard M. Nixon and Vice President Spiro T. Agnew all encouraged massive civil disobedience. New York City was virtually bankrupt when the power outage added yet another dimension to its staggering problems.

Mayor Abraham Beame, in the Bronx when the outage hit, returned to his office in City Hall through darkened streets and ordered more than twenty-five thousand civil employees, mostly firefighters and police, to report to work immediately. About half of these employees were unable to do so, often because of disabled public transport. New York State governor Hugh Carey sent state police officers into the city to assist overtaxed local officers, who were attempting to restore order to such hard-hit areas as Brooklyn's Bushwick and Williamsburg neighborhoods and to Manhattan's Harlem, where the looting was particularly intense. City officials hoped that the situation would quiet down after sunrise, but in some areas, daylight led to even more widespread looting. By sunset, with power still off, more pillaging occurred; however, by that time, little was left to steal.

The sun rises on July 14, 1977, over New York City, still without power after a massive blackout. (AP/Wide World Photos)

Extent of the Damage   The outage and the resulting violence left New York and, indeed, the state and nation reeling. When the losses from the 1977 power outage were tallied, it was estimated that cash-strapped New York City had incurred an estimated one billion dollars in damage. More than four thousand looters were arrested; untold thousands escaped apprehension.

More than four hundred police officers and about sixty firefighters were injured during the melee. The police received more than 67,000 calls during the outage, four times the usual number. A total of 1,037 fires were set; many were allowed to burn out of control because firefighters were too overburdened to fight them.

Three months after the power outage, President Jimmy Carter visited the South Bronx and was astounded by the devastation still evident there. He pledged federal aid to the city but also declared his resolve to work toward long-term solutions to New York City's problems and to offer federal loan guarantees, earlier rejected by President Gerald Ford, so that the city could begin to rebuild.

Impact   The 1965 power outage revealed that when interconnecting power grids are packed too tightly together, they can fail when hit by overloads, subsequently resulting in power outages covering wide geographic areas. In the 1977 outage, however, the problem occurred because the New York area was not connected closely enough to the Canada-United States Eastern Interconnection. With three major power plants out of commission, Consolidated Edison needed to supply more power than its facility could provide. The 1977 outage was made worse because a thunderstorm passed over New York City immediately before the outage. Although utility companies strive to prevent massive outages, widespread blackouts continued to occur into the twenty-first century.

An unanticipated impact of the blackout occurred about nine months later when metropolitan hospitals found that their maternity wards suddenly were swamped. Many babies were conceived on July 13 and 14, 1977.

Further Reading

Curvin, Robert, and Bruce Porter. *Blackout Looting! New York City, July 13, 1977.* New York: Gardner Press, 1979. Focuses on looting and pillaging during the 1977 blackout.

De Angelis, Therese. *Blackout! Cities in Darkness.* Berkeley Heights, N.J.: Enslow, 2003. Provides juvenile readers with an accessible overview of the 1977 power outage.

Grossman, Peter Z. *In Came the Darkness: The Story of Blackouts.* New York: Simon & Schuster, 1981. Solid presentation aimed at adolescent readers.

McLeish, Ewan. *Energy Resources: Our Impact on the Planet.* Austin, Tex.: Raintree Steck-Vaughn, 2002. Broad consideration of environmental issues.

R. Baird Shuman

See also   Carter, Jimmy; Energy crisis; Natural disasters.

■ Nicholson, Jack

Identification   American film actor
Born   April 22, 1937; Neptune, New Jersey

Nicholson became recognized as one of the leading American actors during the 1970's through his powerful portrayals of antihero characters.

The film that established Jack Nicholson as an actor who was ready for stardom was the 1969 counterculture feature film *Easy Rider.* He was asked to play the role of George Henson by Dennis Hopper and Peter Fonda. For his portrayal of the small-town southern lawyer, Nicholson won the Best Supporting Actor Award from the New York Film Critics Circle and the National Society of Film Critics. He also received a 1969 Academy Award nomination for Best Supporting Actor. Because of *Easy Rider,* Nicholson no longer had to do B-movies or guest spots on television programs.

In 1970, Nicholson starred in *Five Easy Pieces,* a film directed by Bob Rafelson. The film garnered praise, and Nicholson proved that he could be counted on to deliver a stellar performance as the lead actor of a feature film. For his performance as a man out of touch with the world around him, Nicholson earned his first Academy Award nomination as Best Actor and solidified his position as one of the most respected actors working in Hollywood.

In 1971, he starred in the controversial film *Carnal Knowledge.* Directed by Mike Nichols, this sexually charged film presented Nicholson with a chance to play a darkly serious character with what would become his trademark ironic sense of humor.

He received his second Academy Award nomination for Best Actor in 1973 for the film *The Last Detail.*

A third nomination came the next year for his extraordinary performance in Roman Polanski's period film *China-town* (1974). The film received critical acclaim and was a major hit at the box office.

Nicholson's best year of the decade was arguably 1975. He appeared in four films, including *The Passenger, Tommy, The Fortune,* and *One Flew over the Cuckoo's Nest.* It was his portrayal of Randle McMurphy in *One Flew over the Cuckoo's Nest* that established Nicholson as one of the most popular screen stars working in the 1970's. For his portrayal, he finally won an Academy Award for Best Actor, and the film won a total of five awards, including Best Picture.

Impact　Along with Dustin Hoffman, Robert De Niro, Al Pacino, and Gene Hackman, Jack Nicholson ushered in a new breed of Hollywood leading men during the 1970's. These actors could brilliantly portray characters who did not fit in with the society around them and who were damaged in some way. These and other prominent American actors of the 1970's did not follow in the footsteps of the "common man" heroes that Henry Fonda, Jimmy Stewart, or Gregory Peck played in earlier decades. They also did not play the John Wayne type of larger-than-life hero. Instead, they were drawn to roles in which they portrayed antiheroes, and perhaps no actor was better at playing the outsider and the rebellious, free-spirited character than Nicholson.

Further Reading

Amburn, Ellis. *Jack, the Great Seducer: The Life and Many Loves of Jack Nicholson.* New York: Harper-Entertainment, 2004.

Brode, Douglas. *The Films of Jack Nicholson.* Secaucus, N.J.: Citadel Press, 1987.

McGilligan, Patrick. *Jack's Life: A Biography of Jack Nicholson.* New York: W. W. Norton, 1994.

Thompson, Peter. *Jack Nicholson: The Life and Times of an Actor on the Edge.* Secaucus, N.J.: Carol, 1997.

Jeffry Jensen

See also　Academy Awards; *Chinatown*; De Niro, Robert; Film in the United States; Hoffman, Dustin; *One Flew over the Cuckoo's Nest*; Pacino, Al.

Jack Nicholson accepts his Academy Award for Best Actor in 1976 for his performance in One Flew over the Cuckoo's Nest. *(AP/Wide World Photos)*

■ Nicklaus, Jack

Identification　American professional golfer
Born　January 21, 1940; Columbus, Ohio

Nicklaus was a major force in professional golf during the 1970's, winning eight major titles, including three Professional Golfers Association (PGA) tournaments, two Masters, two British Opens, and one U.S. Open. He also set earnings records both in money earned in a single year and in career totals.

Prior to the 1970's, Jack Nicklaus, an Ohio State University graduate, already had become a premier golfer by winning the U.S. Amateur twice (1959, 1961), the Masters three times (1963, 1965, 1966), the U.S. Open twice (1962, 1967), the British Open once (1966), and the Professional Golfers' Association (PGA) Championship once (1963).

During the 1970's, Nicklaus captured nine majors and finished second in six majors. He won the 1970 British Open in a playoff after tying Doug Sanders at 283 at St. Andrews, Scotland. After coming in second behind Charles Goody in the 1971 Masters with 281, Nicklaus lost a playoff to Lee Trevino in the 1971 U.S. Open at Ardmore, Pennsylvania. He won the 1971 PGA Championship by two strokes with a 281 at Palm Beach Gardens, Florida, becoming the first golfer to conquer every major twice. Nicklaus nearly attained the Grand Slam in 1972, taking the Masters by three strokes with a 286 and the U.S. Open by three strokes with a 290 at Pebble Beach, California, and losing the 1972 British Open by just one stroke to Trevino at Gullane, Scotland. Nicklaus secured one major in 1973, winning the PGA by four strokes with a 277 at Cleveland, Ohio.

At the 1974 PGA in Winston-Salem, North Carolina, Trevino edged Nicklaus by one stroke. Nicklaus conquered two majors in 1975, taking the Masters by one stroke with a 276 and the PGA by two strokes with a 276 at Akron, Ohio. He made the most impressive shot of his storied career at the 1975 Masters, hitting a one-iron 246 yards to the fifteenth green in the final round. Nicklaus finished second to Johnny Miller in the 1976 British Open and to Tom Watson in both the 1977 Masters and the 1977 British Open. His last major victory of the decade came at the 1978 British Open, which he captured with a 281 at St. Andrews, Scotland. He came in second behind Spanish golfer Seve Ballesteros in the 1979 British Open at Lytham, Great Britain.

Impact Jack Nicklaus dominated golf during this decade. During his career, he became the only golfer to win twenty majors and every major at least three times, and he finished in the top five in fifty-six major tournaments. He earned seventy tour victories, second only to Sam Snead, and he averaged 71.0 strokes per round. He also ranked first in the amount of money earned eight times—in 1964, 1965, 1967, 1971, 1972, 1973, 1975, and 1976—and was runner-up in that category six times. Nicklaus was named PGA Player of the Year five times—1967, 1972, 1973, 1975, and 1976—and the *Sports Illustrated* Sportsman of the Year in 1978. He was elected to the World Golf Hall of Fame in 1974.

Subsequent Events Nicklaus secured his final three majors during the 1980's. He won the 1980 U.S. Open and the 1980 PGA. In the 1986 Masters, the most dramatic victory of his entire career, he ranked eighth after three rounds. He shot a 65 in the final round, tallying 35 on the front nine and 30 on the back nine. Nicklaus eagled the fifteenth and birdied the sixteenth and seventeenth to edge out Greg Norman and Tom Kite by one stroke. He received the Golfer of the Century Award in 1988 and designed more than two hundred golf courses in the United States and abroad.

Further Reading
Nicklaus, Jack. *Golf My Way.* New York: Simon & Schuster, 1974.
Nicklaus, Jack, and Ken Bowden. *Jack Nicklaus: My Story.* New York: Simon & Schuster, 1997.
Sounes, Howard. *The Wicked Game: Arnold Palmer, Jack Nicklaus, Tiger Woods, and the Story of Modern Golf.* New York: HarperCollins, 2004.
David L. Porter
See also Golf; Lopez, Nancy; Sports.

■ Ninety-day freeze on wages and prices

The Event President Richard M. Nixon freezes wages and prices in order to address rapid inflation in the economy
Date Announced on August 15, 1971

Nixon's failure to solve the problem of stagflation detracted from his successes in the area of foreign policy, so he made the decision to break a campaign promise not to impose price and wage controls on Americans.

One of President Nixon's most pressing domestic problems in 1971 was the rate of price inflation in the economy. Expanded government spending on the war in Vietnam and increased social programs in the United States during the 1960's and early 1970's had resulted in the classic recipe for inflation. While presidents and other elected officials ardently desire both low inflation and low unemployment, in the short run, the cost of lowering one is raising the other. Actions that fight inflation, including a reduction in the growth of the money supply, increase unemployment in the economy; actions that fight unemployment, such as higher government spending, tend to increase the rate of inflation.

During Nixon's first term as president, both unemployment and inflation had risen dramatically. This combination—called stagflation—was previously not considered possible by postwar economists who believed in a fixed trade-off between unemployment and inflation. Nixon's economic advisers were as confused about what to do about stagflation as anyone else. Surely, given the rate of deficit spending required by the war in Vietnam and increased social programs at home, unemployment should not be so high. As part of the Republican Party's platform in the 1968 presidential election, and in June, 1971, Nixon had promised that he would not impose wage or price controls on Americans.

Few other remedies for stagflation presented themselves, however, and on Sunday evening, August 15, 1971, President Nixon addressed Americans on television and announced the imposition of a ninety-day price and wage freeze designed to bring inflation down to a rate of 2 to 3 percent growth in the price level per year. Critics charged that the timing of the announcement, specifically the need to make the announcement before the financial markets opened the next morning and the reluctance to interrupt the popular show *Bonanza* for the announcement, was better thought out than the freeze itself.

Impact   The wage and price freeze was moderately successful and brought inflation down to an annual rate of 4 percent throughout its duration. The move by Nixon was seen by many as decisive and on the following day, the Dow Jones Industrial Average rose by 32.9 points—its largest one-day rise until that time. When the freeze was lifted in mid-November, 1971, however, inflation continued unabated. A series of mandatory wage and price guidelines over the next eighteen months did not bring inflation below 5 percent, and a second wage and price freeze was instituted in June, 1973, to an American public already dealing with shortages caused by the wage and price guidelines. The entire Nixon wage and price control apparatus was abolished in April, 1974, and Nixon resigned the presidency on August 8, 1974, as the rate of inflation topped 12 percent.

Further Reading

Nixon, Richard. *RN: The Memoirs of Richard Nixon.* New York: Simon & Schuster, 1990.

Rockoff, Hugh. *Drastic Measure: A History of Wage and Price Controls in the United States.* Cambridge, England: Cambridge University Press, 2004.

Betsy A. Murphy

See also   Business and the economy in the United States; Elections in the United States, 1972; Gas shortages; Income and wages in the United States; Nixon, Richard M.; Unemployment in the United States.

■ Nixon, Richard M.

Identification   U.S. president, 1969-1974
Born   January 9, 1913; Yorba Linda, California
Died   April 22, 1994; New York, New York

Nixon, despite notable successes in foreign policy, is the only United States president forced to resign in order to avoid being tried on impeachment charges.

When the 1970's began, Richard Milhouse Nixon was completing his first year as president of the United States. Scoring a slim victory over his opponents in the elections of 1968, Nixon received 43.7 percent of the popular vote. In 1970, the nation was torn by civil strife connected with the prolonged and unpopular Vietnam War. It had a relatively high unemployment rate and mounting inflation. At the time Nixon was inaugurated, the Vietnam War had claimed the lives of more than thirty thousand American troops and more than one million Vietnamese citizens. As a presidential candidate, Nixon had vowed he would end the war.

Nixon surrounded himself with aides whom he charged with protecting him from those he considered his enemies. H. R. Haldeman was his chief of staff and John Ehrlichman was his aide for domestic affairs. Henry Kissinger was the national security and foreign policy adviser.

Notable for his paranoid personality, Nixon directed John Dean and Charles Colson to compile an Enemies List, and people listed were excluded from White House functions. Some had their income tax returns audited by the Internal Revenue Service (IRS) on orders from Nixon and his aides. In some cases, they were, on Nixon's orders, shadowed by detectives that the White House employed. The president ordered a voice-activated recording system installed in the Oval Office to give him a record of everything that transpired there.

Kent State   Protests against the Vietnam War were widespread in 1970. In Washington, D.C., the preceding October, 200,000 antiwar protesters had marched. Nixon, attempting to counter such demonstrations, made his famous "silent majority" speech—claiming that most Americans supported the war objectives in Vietnam—which went over well. However, by the spring of 1970, antiwar protests had resumed nationwide on college and university campuses.

On May 4, 1970, administrators at Ohio's Kent State University brought in the National Guard to control demonstrations that had disrupted the campus for three days. Protesters hurled stones at members of the guard, who fired into the crowd, killing four students and injuring nine. This disaster ignited new waves of protests, which were intensified when a reporter, overhearing Nixon refer to the Kent State protesters as "bums," published his statement.

The Pentagon Papers   On June 13, 1971, *The New York Times* published parts of the Pentagon Papers, a secret study that the Department of Defense had commissioned on the war in Vietnam. This classified document revealed that the government had deceived Americans about many details relating to the war. When this story broke, the White House reverted to a siege mentality.

Kissinger feared that a leak involving such sensitive, classified documents would cause the United States to lose the confidence of the countries with which he was trying to broker a Vietnam peace agreement, notably the Soviet Union, China, and North Vietnam. Government attorneys filed lawsuits against *The New York Times* to prevent continued publication of the Pentagon Papers.

The Supreme Court heard the case and, citing constitutional guarantees of freedom of speech and of the press, ruled 6-3 in favor of the newspaper. Thwarted in attempts to withhold these papers from the public, Nixon sought vengeance against Daniel Ellsberg, who had leaked the papers hoping that their circulation would pressure the administration into ending the war quickly.

Fearing that additional leaks might occur, Nixon directed his aides to prepare a daily list of what newspapers and television news programs throughout the country were reporting. He scrutinized this list every morning and gave Colson the responsibility of ferreting out and dealing with leaks that his surveillance uncovered.

Nixon also formed a group to deal with those he considered his enemies. This group was designated "the Plumbers." High on Nixon's list of enemies was Ellsberg. The Plumbers' Unit sought to discredit him by demonstrating that he was mentally unsound. Two of the Plumbers, G. Gordon Liddy and E. Howard Hunt, broke into the office of Ellsberg's psychiatrist on September 3, 1971. Discovering

nothing among the psychiatrist's files to establish Ellsberg's mentally instability, they trashed the office, making it appear that addicts seeking drugs had committed the break-in. Questioned months afterward, Nixon said that he did not think this action was wrong or excessive in light of what Ellsberg had done to compromise national security.

The Outlook for 1972   Nixon feared that he might lose the presidency in the 1972 elections. The Vietnam War dragged on, inflation loomed, unemployment was high, and the energy crisis, which had peaked late in 1971, persisted. On January 5, 1972, Nixon formed the Committee to Re-elect the President (CRP) to organize his campaign. Attorney General John Mitchell resigned his cabinet post in order to direct CRP.

During the preceding year, Nixon had, to the dismay of some conservatives, established the Environmental Protection Agency (EPA) and the Occupational Safety and Health Administration (OSHA). He also enacted wage and price freezes to stem the growing inflation. Nixon also sent American troops into Cambodia, a neutral country bordering Viet-

Richard M. Nixon. (Library of Congress)

nam that the communists in North Vietnam used as a base from which to attack South Vietnam. General Lon Nol, a staunch anticommunist, had taken control of Cambodia. Because the North Vietnamese were attacking Lon Nol's forces, Nixon sent troops to defend Cambodia's anticommunist government. Nixon's unpopularity grew as troop casualties in Cambodia and Vietnam mounted.

These events hurt Nixon in the polls, and he knew that public opinion had to be turned around—his reelection seemed doubtful. Mitchell and his CRP colleagues raised millions of dollars, much of it illegally, to finance the upcoming campaign. They pressured major industries to contribute to Nixon's war chest in return for favorable treatment by the administration. The president had a secret slush fund on which he could draw at will. To regain public support, however, the president needed to do something dramatic.

China Visit and Soviet Union Summit Communist North Vietnam received support from China and the Soviet Union to fight South Vietnam. The United States had no diplomatic relations with the People's Republic of China (PRC) in 1972 and was engaged in the Cold War with the Soviet Union. Nixon, thoroughly anticommunist, decided to make an official visit to communist China, the first American president to do so.

Excerpt from Richard M. Nixon's question-and-answer session at the Annual Convention of the Associated Press Managing Editors Association on November 17, 1973:

"Let me just say this, and I want to say this to the television audience: I made my mistakes, but in all of my years of public life, I have never profited, never profited from public service—I have earned every cent. And in all of my years of public life, I have never obstructed justice. And I think, too, that I could say that in my years of public life, that I welcome this kind of examination, because people have got to know whether or not their president is a crook. Well, I am not a crook. I have earned everything I have got."

The visit was the most brilliant tactical move of Nixon's career, because it forced the Soviet Union, fearful of a United States-China alliance, to adopt a conciliatory attitude toward the United States. The tactic worked exactly as Nixon and his foreign affairs adviser, Kissinger, had anticipated.

In May, 1972, largely as a result of his February mission to China, Nixon arranged a summit meeting in Russia with Soviet leader Leonid Brezhnev, during which an accord, the Strategic Arms Limitation Treaty (SALT), was reached, bringing about the reduction of nuclear arsenals in both countries.

Immediately before the summit with the Soviets, the North Vietnamese intensified their attacks on South Vietnam. The administration understood that if the United States failed to take aggressive action, the Vietnam War would most likely be lost to the communists. Ignoring the counsel of his advisers, who feared that taking such action would derail the delicate negotiations under way with the Soviets, Nixon argued that failing to retaliate against North Vietnam would make the United States seem weak.

Nixon ordered around-the-clock bombing of Hanoi, North Vietnam's capital, and cut off Haiphong, its major seaport, with mines. This gamble succeeded because it forced the Soviets to acknowledge America's power. This turn of events served to solidify the president's political base and led to his winning the 1972 election with 60.7 percent of the popular vote.

Watergate Even as Nixon's supporters celebrated his victory in 1972, the greatest threat to his presidency was threatening to spin out of control. Prior to the election, on June 17, 1972, District of Columbia police had arrested five men caught breaking into the Democratic National Committee's headquarters in the Watergate office complex. The break-in, engineered by the CRP, appeared to be an attempt by anticommunist refugees from Fidel Castro's Cuba to discredit George McGovern, who would be Nixon's opponent in the forthcoming elections and who had advocated normalizing relations with Cuba. Nixon knew nothing of the break-in until the following morning, when he read about it in the newspaper. However, he was not concerned, dismissing it as an ill-advised aberration.

On June 23, in an Oval Office conversation with Nixon, Haldeman expressed fear that Federal Bureau of Investigation (FBI) scrutiny into the break-in could embarrass the administration. He suggested that the FBI be misled by making investigators think that the break-in had been engineered by the Central Intelligence Agency (CIA). Haldeman also recommended that the administration pay legal expenses and certain living expenses for the Watergate defendants. Nixon agreed, saying that he had secret discretionary funds that he could use for the payoffs. This was Nixon's first direct involvement in what turned into the Watergate scandal that eventually destroyed his presidency. At this point, the president clearly intended to obstruct justice, an impeachable offense.

The Watergate investigation continued until August, 1974. The June 23 conversation with Haldeman had been recorded by the Oval Office's taping system. Nixon's attempts to withhold the incriminating tapes were thwarted when the Supreme Court by a unanimous vote ordered him to surrender them to investigators. Two years later, when the so-called smoking gun tape of June 23, 1972, became public, Nixon realized that he must resign the presidency, which he did on August 9, 1974.

Gerald R. Ford, whom Nixon appointed vice president when Spiro T. Agnew was forced to resign in 1973, succeeded Nixon. One month later, Ford granted Nixon a full pardon. More than seventy of the former president's associates were convicted of crimes associated with Watergate, and many were imprisoned for these crimes. Nixon alone escaped punishment.

Impact   Richard Nixon returned to California a defeated man. Eventually, however, he recovered and began to reconstruct his life. He made speeches and wrote his memoirs, the first volume of which sold briskly in 1978. He then had four television interviews with journalist David Frost, earning $540,000 for them.

Nixon's greatest impact was in foreign affairs, particularly in ending the Cold War with the Soviet Union and the Vietnam War. However, he will probably be forever remembered as the first American president forced to resign in order to avoid conviction in an impeachment trial. A major outcome of the scandals of the Nixon administration was a heightened accountability in all levels of government, particularly at the highest levels.

Nixon leaves the White House on August 9, 1974, after resigning the office of president. (Nixon Presidential Materials Project)

Subsequent Events   In 1980, Nixon moved to New York City and later to Park Ridge, New Jersey. Every subsequent president sought counsel from him. After his death in 1994, Nixon's body was returned to California for internment near the Richard Nixon Library and Birthplace, established in Yorba Linda in 1990. President Bill Clinton and every living former president attended Nixon's funeral.

Further Reading

Friedman, Leon, and William F. Levantrosser, eds. *Watergate and Afterward: The Legacy of Richard Nixon.* Westport, Conn.: Greenwood Press, 2000. A balanced collection of essays assessing Nixon's presidency.

Gergen, David. *Eyewitness to Power: The Essence of Leadership—Nixon to Clinton.* New York: Simon & Schuster, 2000. Well-presented view of Nixon's presidency compared with those of his successors.

Marquez, Heron. *Richard M. Nixon.* Minneapolis: Lerner, 2003. Offers an honest evaluation of

Nixon's presidency. Recommended for young adult readers.

Nixon, Richard M. *In the Arena: A Memoir of Victory, Defeat and Renewal.* New York: Simon & Schuster, 1988. Nixon's retrospective account of his presidency and ultimate disgrace.

_____. *RN: The Memoirs of Richard Nixon.* New York: Grosset & Dunlap, 1978. Reflects the pain that accompanied Nixon's resignation.

Schuman, Michael. *Richard M. Nixon.* Springfield, N.J.: Enslow, 1998. Presents essentials of Nixon's political legacy. For young adult readers.

Whittington, Keith E. *Constitutional Construction: Divided Powers and Constitutional Meaning.* Cambridge, Mass.: Harvard University Press, 1999. See especially the chapter titled "Richard Nixon and the Leadership of the Modern State."

R. Baird Shuman

See also Agnew, Spiro T.; Central Intelligence Agency (CIA); Cold War; Cox, Archibald; Dean, John; Ehrlichman, John; Enemies List; Federal Bureau of Investigation (FBI); Ford, Gerald R.; Haldeman, H. R.; Kissinger, Henry; Liddy, G. Gordon, and E. Howard Hunt; Nixon tapes; Nixon's resignation and pardon; Nixon's visit to China; Pentagon Papers; Vietnam War; Watergate.

■ Nixon tapes

Definition Audiotapes of conversations that took place in the White House during the presidency of Richard M. Nixon

As historical artifacts, the Nixon tapes provide a rare look at a president's behind-the-scenes conduct. They also assumed crucial legal significance because they constituted evidence of presidential complicity in the Watergate scandal.

Taping systems had been used in the White House during most of the 1960's by presidents John F. Kennedy and Lyndon B. Johnson in order to record selected meetings and telephone calls, but in February, 1971, a new voice-activated system was installed for President Richard M. Nixon's use. The system captured all conversations in the Oval Office and certain other locations, eventually producing more than four thousand hours of tapes on a wide variety of topics.

After the Watergate burglary occurred in June, 1972, key discussions between Nixon and his aides on the ensuing scandal were recorded without the knowledge of most of the participants. These candid conversations revealed, among other things, Nixon's efforts to divert the Federal Bureau of Investigation (FBI) from investigating the break-in, the payment of "hush money" to Watergate burglars, and fears that earlier break-ins, aimed at Pentagon Papers figure Daniel Ellsberg, might be revealed. During the first year of the unfolding scandal, the tapes recorded Nixon's growing involvement in the ongoing cover-up, as new strategies were plotted for deflecting blame away from the president.

Public Disclosure of the Tapes In July, 1973, presidential aide Alexander Butterfield revealed the existence of the tapes during testimony before Senator Sam Ervin's investigating committee, prompting White House chief of staff Alexander Haig to order the taping system removed and the tapes sequestered. After receiving competing advice from his lawyers on whether to destroy or preserve the tapes, Nixon decided to retain them in the hope that they would ultimately serve to exonerate him. Once their existence became known, however, the tapes eagerly were sought as evidence by Senate investigators and the courts, and Nixon campaigned against their release on the grounds that executive privilege protects the confidentiality of communication between the president and his advisers.

In October, 1973, a federal court of appeals ordered Nixon to turn over nine tapes to District Judge John J. Sirica. The White House sought to arrange a compromise in which transcripts of Watergate-related conversations would be prepared by the White House and certified as accurate by Senator John Stennis, but Special Prosecutor Archibald Cox refused to approve the compromise and was subsequently fired on Nixon's orders in what became known as the Saturday Night Massacre. When it was revealed in December, 1973, that the tape of a conversation held soon after the Watergate break-in had an eighteen-and-a-half-minute gap, suspicion grew that it was Nixon's conniving hand and not an accident that had destroyed crucial evidence.

After Nixon finally relented in the face of public opinion and legal pressure and released more than one thousand pages of tape transcripts in April, 1974, his presidential image was tarnished seriously when the transcripts revealed his use of swear words and his behind-the-scenes scheming. The White House strategy shifted from portraying Nixon as innocent to averting his impeachment, but this strategy was imperiled in late July, 1974, when the Supreme Court ordered the release of sixty-four additional tapes, including the "smoking gun" tape of June 23, 1972, in which the impeding of the FBI's investigation was discussed by Nixon.

Realizing that impeachment was inevitable, Nixon resigned in August, 1974, and after leaving office, he worked out an agreement with the federal government that, if implemented, would have required the destruction of all the tapes. This agreement was overturned when Congress passed and President Gerald R. Ford signed the Presidential Recordings and Material Preservation Act of 1974, which placed the tapes under government control and mandated that any information in the tapes about presidential abuse of power would be made public as soon as possible.

Impact   Beyond the key role that the tapes played in bringing about the political downfall of a president, they also redefined President Nixon's character and conduct in the eyes of the American public. Without the tapes, Nixon might have not only clung to office but also preserved his public image of rectitude and honesty. Beyond this, the tapes spelled an end to presidents recording their conversations, as Nixon's successors saw in his experience a chilling lesson in the political dangers posed by such tapes. The drawn-out legal battle that followed Nixon's resignation prevented the release of many of the tapes until long after the 1970's, but the realization that crimes and cover-ups could occur in the White House increased the credibility gap between public and government and laid the foundation for Congressional investigations of other abuses of power during the 1970's.

Excerpt from the "smoking gun" tape of June 23, 1972:

H. R. HALDEMAN: Okay—that's fine. Now, on the investigation, you know, the Democratic break-in thing, we're back to the—in the, the problem area because the FBI is not under control, because Gray doesn't exactly know how to control them, and they have, their investigation is now leading into some productive areas, because they've been able to trace the money, not through the money itself, but through the bank, you know, sources—the banker himself. And, and it goes in some directions we don't want it to go. Ah, also there have been some things, like an informant came in off the street to the FBI in Miami, who was a photographer or has a friend who is a photographer who developed some films through this guy, Barker, and the films had pictures of Democratic National Committee letterhead documents and things. So I guess, so it's things like that that are gonna, that are filtering in. Mitchell came up with yesterday, and John Dean analyzed very carefully last night and concludes, concurs now with Mitchell's recommendation that the only way to solve this, and we're set up beautifully to do it, ah, in that and that . . . the only network that paid any attention to it last night was NBC . . . they did a massive story on the Cuban . . .

RICHARD M. NIXON: That's right.

HALDEMAN: . . . thing . . .

NIXON: Right.

HALDEMAN: . . . that the way to handle this now is for us to have Walters call Pat Gray and just say, "Stay the hell out of this . . . this is ah, business here we don't want you to go any further on it." That's not an unusual development.

NIXON: Um huh.

HALDEMAN: And, uh, that would take care of it.

NIXON: What about Pat Gray? Ah, you mean he doesn't want to?

HALDEMAN: Pat does want to. He doesn't know how to, and he doesn't have, he doesn't have any basis for doing it. Given this, he will then have the basis. He'll call Mark Felt in, and the two of them . . . and Mark Felt wants to cooperate because . . .

NIXON: Yeah.

HALDEMAN: . . . he's ambitious.

NIXON: Yeah.

HALDEMAN: Ah, he'll call him in and say, "We've got the signal from across the river to, to put the hold on this." And that will fit rather well because the FBI agents who are working the case, at this point, feel that's what it is. This is CIA.

Further Reading

Haig, Alexander. _Inner Circles: How America Changed the World—A Memoir._ New York: Warner Books, 1992. This autobiography of Nixon's chief of staff provides extensive detail on how the tapes complicated the president's handling of the Watergate scandal.

Hoff, Joan. "The Endless Saga of the Nixon Tapes." In _A Culture of Secrecy: The Government Versus the People's Right to Know_, edited by Athan Theoharis. Lawrence: University Press of Kansas, 1998. Describes the fate of the tapes as historical artifacts, which Nixon and his family sought to control after his presidency.

Kutler, Stanley. _Abuse of Power: The New Nixon Tapes._ New York: Free Press, 1997. A compilation of transcripts of many of the tapes, including those released after the publication of the author's first book on the tapes, with editorial comments.

_____. _The Wars of Watergate: The Last Crisis of Richard Nixon._ New York: Alfred A. Knopf, 1990. A comprehensive history of the Watergate scandal and the role played by the tapes.

Larry Haapanen

See also _All the President's Men_; Committee to Re-elect the President (CRP); Congress, U.S.; Cox, Archibald; Dean, John; Deep Throat; Ehrlichman, John; Enemies List; Ervin, Sam; Haldeman, H. R.; Liddy, G. Gordon, and E. Howard Hunt; Mitchell, John; Nixon, Richard M.; Nixon's resignation and pardon; Pentagon Papers; Saturday Night Massacre; Sirica, John J.; Watergate.

■ Nixon's resignation and pardon

The Event   Richard Nixon resigns the presidency and subsequently is pardoned by his successor, Gerald R. Ford

Date   August 9 to September 8, 1974

Nixon, facing impeachment, becomes the only U.S. president to resign from office. His successor, Gerald Ford, must decide whether to pardon him.

November 7, 1972, should have been a happy day for President Richard Nixon. He had just won election to his second term as president of the United States, scoring a landslide victory over George McGovern. Nixon took 60.7 percent of the popular vote and carried every state except Massachusetts. As members of his administration celebrated, however, Nixon brooded because he realized that he was being drawn irrevocably into the quickly developing Watergate scandal.

The president had no direct involvement in the

Excerpt from Richard M. Nixon's resignation speech, delivered on August 8, 1974:

"In all the decisions I have made in my public life, I have always tried to do what was best for the nation. Throughout the long and difficult period of Watergate, I have felt it was my duty to persevere, to make every possible effort to complete the term of office to which you elected me.

....

I would have preferred to carry through to the finish whatever the personal agony it would have involved, and my family unanimously urged me to do so. But the interest of the nation must always come before any personal considerations.

From the discussions I have had with congressional and other leaders, I have concluded that because of the Watergate matter I might not have the support of the Congress that I would consider necessary to back the very difficult decisions and carry out the duties of this office in the way the interests of the nation would require.

I have never been a quitter. To leave office before my term is completed is abhorrent to every instinct in my body. But as president, I must put the interest of America first. America needs a full-time president and a full-time Congress, particularly at this time with problems we face at home and abroad.

To continue to fight through the months ahead for my personal vindication would almost totally absorb the time and attention of both the president and the Congress in a period when our entire focus should be on the great issues of peace abroad and prosperity without inflation at home.

Therefore, I shall resign the presidency effective at noon tomorrow. Vice President Ford will be sworn in as president at that hour in this office."

President Gerald R. Ford addresses the nation on September 8, 1974, to announce his pardon of former president Richard M. Nixon. (Library of Congress/Courtesy Gerald R. Ford Library)

break-in at Democratic National Headquarters in the Watergate office complex in June, 1972. He first learned of the event the morning after it happened. His guilt was in trying to cover up the crime that involved some of his aides who were active in the Committee to Re-elect the President (CRP).

Grounds for Impeachment The burglars were indicted on September 15, 1972, and received bribes from the president's CRP funds in exchange for taking the blame. The decision to pay bribes was reached a week after the break-in. In a meeting in the Oval Office with his aide H. R. Haldeman on June 23, Nixon accepted Haldeman's suggestion to mislead the Federal Bureau of Investigation (FBI) by making the break-in look like a Central Intelligence Agency (CIA) operation. Haldeman recommended paying the legal fees and living expenses of the Watergate defendants in return for their support of the story that Haldeman was concocting.

The June 23 conversation was captured on a re-

cording system that Nixon had installed in the Oval Office in 1970. It was not until July 16, 1973, however, that the deputy assistant to Nixon, Alexander Butterfield, revealed to the Watergate investigators the existence of the recording system and the damning tapes that eventually destroyed Nixon's presidency.

Nixon fought to withhold these tapes from the Senate Watergate Committee, but on July 24, 1974, the Supreme Court voted 8-0 that the tapes be turned over. On August 5, Nixon had to provide a transcript of the most incriminating tape, his June 23, 1972, conversation with Haldeman, often called the "smoking gun." The tape demonstrated that the president participated in obstructing justice. Ten days earlier, the House Judiciary Committee had approved, by a 27-11 vote, going forward with the first article of impeachment, obstruction of justice.

Having lost what support he had before releasing the smoking gun transcript, Nixon, acknowledging that impeachment was inevitable and conviction a strong possibility, submitted his resignation as president effective at noon on August 9, 1974.

On August 9, Gerald R. Ford became the thirty-eighth president of the United States. Ford was the only vice president who had not won election to the office—he was appointed by Nixon after Vice President Spiro T. Agnew was forced to resign following his *nolo contendere* (no contest) plea to charges of tax evasion in October, 1973.

The Aftermath The Watergate scandal demoralized the nation. An electorate that gave Nixon a landslide victory became cynical about government. Ford's most pressing task initially was to heal a nation torn asunder by the events precipitating Nixon's resignation.

White House chief of staff Alexander Haig served as intermediary between Nixon and Ford shortly before the resignation, suggesting that Ford might consider pardoning Nixon to avoid litigation that could drag on for years. Despite what some cynics assumed, however, no deal had been struck between Nixon and Ford before Nixon appointed him to the vice presidency, nor did Nixon approach Ford when resignation seemed unavoidable.

Several members of Nixon's cabinet hoped that a pardon would be offered. Ford, on the day he assumed office, however, had not reached a decision about granting one. He sought professional advice regarding the legality of pardoning Nixon and was assured that it was within his power. Ford realized the risk he could run in pardoning Nixon. He knew that collusion would be suspected, although none had occurred. Nevertheless, he was convinced that the legitimate business of government would be impeded if the Nixon prosecution dragged on. Therefore, on September 8, 1974, he pardoned Nixon.

In part his proclamation read

> I, Gerald R. Ford, President of the United States, . . . have granted and by these presents do grant a full, free, and absolute pardon unto Richard Nixon for all offenses against the United States which he, Richard Nixon, has committed or may have committed or taken part in during the period from January 20, 1969, through August 9, 1974.

> Excerpt from President Gerald R. Ford's remarks on signing a proclamation granting pardon to Richard M. Nixon, delivered on September 8, 1974:
>
> "My conscience tells me clearly and certainly that I cannot prolong the bad dreams that continue to reopen a chapter that is closed. My conscience tells me that only I, as President, have the constitutional power to firmly shut and seal this book. My conscience tells me it is my duty, not merely to proclaim domestic tranquillity but to use every means that I have to insure it.
>
> I do believe that the buck stops here, that I cannot rely upon public opinion polls to tell me what is right.
>
> I do believe that right makes might and that if I am wrong, ten angels swearing I was right would make no difference.
>
> I do believe, with all my heart and mind and spirit, that I, not as President but as a humble servant of God, will receive justice without mercy if I fail to show mercy.
>
> Finally, I feel that Richard Nixon and his loved ones have suffered enough and will continue to suffer, no matter what I do, no matter what we, as a great and good nation, can do together to make his goal of peace come true."

Nixon's acceptance of the pardon clearly constituted an admission of guilt.

Impact The Watergate debacle established that high crimes and misdemeanors, even when committed by a public figure as powerful as the U.S. president, will be punished. This outcome demonstrated that the federal government can continue to function even in the face of an upheaval caused by such cataclysmic events as the resignations of both the president and the vice president.

The nation, although seriously demoralized by the Watergate scandal, tried to emerge from it with a renewed strength. The constitutional form of government on which the United States was founded had survived this most difficult of challenges.

Further Reading

Cannon, James. *Time and Chance: Gerald Ford's Appointment with History.* New York: HarperCollins, 1994. Penetrating insight into Ford's relationship with Nixon.

Emery, Fred. *Watergate: The Corruption of American Politics and the Fall of Richard Nixon.* New York: Simon & Schuster, 1994. A thorough investigation of the Watergate scandal.

Greene, John Robert. *The Presidency of Gerald R. Ford.* Lawrence: University Press of Kansas, 1995. A compassionate account of Ford's agonizing decision to pardon Nixon.

Marquez, Heron. *Richard M. Nixon.* Minneapolis: Lerner, 2003. Detailed account of the Watergate scandal written for young adult readers.

R. Baird Shuman

See also   Agnew, Spiro T.; Deep Throat; Elections in the United States, 1972; Ford, Gerald R.; Nixon, Richard M.; Nixon tapes; Watergate.

■ Nixon's visit to China

The Event   A visit by the American president to China that signaled a diplomatic breakthrough in relations between China and the United States

Date   February 21-28, 1972

President Richard M. Nixon's visit to China reversed two decades of hostilities and began an era of détente that led to the establishment of diplomatic relations between the two nations.

On July 15, 1971, President Richard Nixon announced that he had accepted an invitation by Chinese premier Zhou Enlai to visit China. The communist victory in the Chinese civil war in 1949 had been followed in 1950 by an alliance between the new government of the People's Republic of China (PRC) and the Soviet Union. The leader of the Chinese Communist Party, Mao Zedong, called this a policy of "leaning to one side," that of the communists. The Korean War that began in 1950 pitted the United States and China on opposing sides as each aided its respective ally, communist North Korea and pro-Western South Korea. A series of treaties ensued with the Taiwan-based Republic of China (ROC) and others in which the United States worked to contain and isolate China. The United States also blocked PRC from membership in the United Nations, maintaining that the ROC was the true legal government representing China. During the Vietnam War, China gave to communist North Vietnam massive aid but not combat troops, and the United States provided aid and military support to South Vietnam, a situation that further exacerbated relations between the two nations.

After his election victory in 1968, Republican president Nixon and his National Security Adviser Henry Kissinger began a process of global realignment in order to achieve a new balance of power that included withdrawing U.S. troops from Vietnam and improving relations with China. Meanwhile, the initial Chinese-Soviet alliance had deteriorated as a result of a rivalry between the two communist powers. Faced with threats from and border conflicts with the Soviet Union and a general international diplomatic isolation, China was ready for rapprochement with the United States. A secret visit by Kissinger to Beijing early in July, 1971, to prepare the groundwork culminated in President Nixon's announcement of his visit on July 15, 1971.

Nixon in Beijing   On February 21, 1972, President Nixon arrived in the Chinese capital of Beijing accompanied by First Lady Pat Nixon, Secretary of State William Rogers, Kissinger, and others. The visit and negotiations culminated in the Shanghai Communique, issued on February 21. It pledged both sides to seek peaceful coexistence through mutual respect, equality, and noninterference in each other's internal affairs. It also sought to work toward the lessening of international tensions; to establish exchanges in scientific, cultural, and other realms; and to work toward the full normalization of relations between the two nations. On the crucial question of Taiwan, the United States acknowledged that there was one China, that Taiwan is a part of China, and affirmed its interest in an eventual peaceful unification of China. Further negotiations were slowed by U.S. domestic problems resulting from the Watergate affair that mired the second term of President Nixon and ended in his resignation from office. The restoration of full diplomatic relations took place in 1979 under President Jimmy Carter.

Impact   President Nixon's visit to China ended two decades of confrontation between the two nations on two battlegrounds: Korea and Vietnam. It was a result of changing international relations, most notably the Sino-Soviet split in the 1960's that ended the Western fear of a monolithic communist bloc. It also reflected a new alignment of world powers from the bipolarization of the post-World War II era to a multilateral world consisting of the United States, Soviet Union, Western Europe, China, and Japan.

President Richard M. Nixon stands on the Great Wall during his historic visit to China in 1972. (National Archives/Nixon Project)

With the Soviet Union posing a greater danger to both China and the United States, improved U.S.-China relations promised to benefit both countries in their dealings with the Soviet Union.

The visit began a détente between China and the United States that reduced the possibility of war between China and the Soviet Union and weakened the latter country's international position, in turn making it more anxious to negotiate agreements with the United States. It also led to the opening of China and an increase in trade and other exchanges between China and the Western world, most notably with the United States and Japan.

Another result of the Nixon visit was the withdrawal of U.S. opposition to seating the PRC in the United Nations as a permanent member of the Security Council. Many nations that had not recognized the PRC, especially Japan, followed the U.S. shift to establish diplomatic relations with Beijing and sever relations with the ROC on Taiwan, which was forced to withdraw from the United Nations.

Subsequent Events   Taiwan was affected most adversely by Nixon's reversal of policy. After 1979, the United States had no formal diplomatic relations or military alliance with the ROC (Taiwan), but the two nations maintained informal diplomatic relations, authorized by the Taiwan Relations Act passed by the U.S. Congress. The many treaties and agreements between the United States and ROC also remained in effect. The United States continued its stand that the unification of the two Chinas should be pursued through peaceful means.

Further Reading

Garver, John. *China's Decision for Rapprochement with the United States, 1968-1971.* Boulder, Colo.: Westview Press, 1982. Provides interesting analysis and historical analysis of the era.

Kissinger, Henry. *White House Years.* Boston: Little, Brown, 1979. Provides excellent insight of the topic by a man who was the strategist of a new world order and worked to bring it about.

Li Zhishui. *The Private Life of Chairman Mao.* Translated by Tai Hung-chao. New York: Random House, 1994. A revealing book published on Mao Zedong by his personal physician and confidant.

Nixon, Richard M. *The Memoirs of Richard Nixon.* New York: Warner Books, 1978. The work of a staunch anticommunist who then orchestrated the reversal of U.S. foreign policy.

Wu, Fu-mei Chiu. *Richard M. Nixon Communism, and China.* Washington, D.C.: University Press of America, 1978. An analysis of Nixon's China policy.

Jiu-Hwa Lo Upshur

See also China and the United States; Détente; Foreign policy of the United States; Kissinger, Henry; Nixon, Richard M.

■ Nobel Prizes

Definition   Prizes awarded each year for achievements in chemistry, economics, literature, peace, physics, and physiology or medicine

The Nobel Prize is a significant sign of international praise. Nobel laureates bring prestige to their home countries and institutions and attract the interest of students and funding bodies to their work.

During the 1970's, the Nobel Prizes in science and economics were dominated overall by researchers born or working in the United States, while Americans won only two awards in the categories of literature and peace.

Chemistry   The chemistry prizes of the decade honored diverse achievements. Herbert C. Brown, the winner for 1979, was a pioneer in the use of boron hydrides in synthesizing organic compounds, while William N. Lipscomb, the 1976 laureate, developed methods for understanding the chemical bonds in polyhedral boron hydrides. The 1971 prizewinner, Gerhard Herzberg, blended theory with experiment in his studies of molecular spectra, particularly those of free radicals (species with odd numbers of electrons). The 1974 laureate Paul J. Flory's work led to a better understanding of the synthesis and properties of macromolecular compounds, which are important commercially and in life processes. Christian B. Anfinsen, Stanford Moore, and William H. Stein were honored in 1972 for fundamental studies of the enzyme ribonuclease.

Literature and Peace   The American prizewinners for literature were Saul Bellow, in 1976, and Isaac Bashevis Singer, in 1978. Bellow's novels include *Herzog* (1964) and *Mr. Sammler's Planet* (1970). Singer, who immigrated from Poland, often wrote in Yiddish. Some of his best-known works are *Der Sotan in Gorey* (1935; *Satan in Goray,* 1955) and *A Friend of Kafka, and Other Stories* (1970).

Peace prizes went to U.S. secretary of state Henry Kissinger in 1973 and plant pathologist and environmental activist Norman Borlaug in 1970. Kissinger was honored for helping to negotiate the end of the Vietnam War. Borlaug, known as the founder of the Green Revolution, earned his prize by developing new types of crops, particularly wheat, for developing countries.

Physics   In physics, John Bardeen (winning his second Nobel Prize), Leon N. Cooper, and John Robert Schrieffer were honored in 1972 for their theoretical treatment of superconductivity—a significant phenomenon for energy-saving technology. Ben R. Mottelson and L. James Rainwater shared a prize in 1975 for their work on the structure of the atomic nucleus. Burton Richter and Samuel Ting, winners in 1976, discovered the psi/J particle. James H. Van Vleck and Philip W. Anderson shared a prize in 1977 for their work on magnetic and disordered systems in condensed matter. The 1978 laureates Arno A. Penzias and Robert W. Wilson discovered cosmic microwave background, which is significant in cosmology because it supports the big bang theory of creation. Sheldon L. Glashow and Steven Weinberg shared the last prize of the decade for their theoretical work on unifying the weak and electromagnetic interactions.

Physiology or Medicine   Julius Axelrod won a Nobel Prize in 1970 for his work on humoral transmitters at nerve terminals, while Earl Wilbur Sutherland, Jr., was honored in 1971 for studies of hormones. Gerald M. Edelman, the 1972 laureate, discovered the chemical structures of antibodies. Christian de Duve and George E. Palade elucidated the structural and functional organization of the cell and shared the prize in 1974. David Baltimore, Renato Dulbecco, and Howard M. Temin, joint prizewinners in 1975, studied tumor viruses and genes. The prize was split in 1976 between Baruch S. Blumberg and D. Carleton Gajdusek, who discovered new mechanisms for the origin and spread of infectious diseases, including hepatitis and prion diseases such as kuru, Creutzfeldt-

American Nobel Prize Winners, 1970-1979

Year	Chemistry	Economics	Literature	Peace	Physics	Physiology or Medicine
1970		Paul A. Samuelson		Norman Borlaug		Julius Axelrod*
1971	Gerhard Herzberg	Simon Kuznets				Earl Wilbur Sutherland, Jr.*
1972	Christian B. Anfinsen Stanford Moore William H. Stein	Kenneth J. Arrow*			James Bardeen Leon N. Cooper John Robert Schrieffer	Gerald M. Edelman*
1973		Wassily Leontief		Henry Kissinger*		
1974	Paul J. Flory					Christian de Duve* George E. Palade*
1975					Ben R. Mottelson* L. James Rainwater*	David Baltimore Renato Dulbecco Howard M. Temin
1976	William N. Lipscomb	Milton Friedman	Saul Bellow		Burton Richter Samuel Ting	Baruch S. Blumberg D. Carleton Gajdusek
1977					Philip W. Anderson James H. Van Vleck	Roger Guillemin Andrew Victor Schally Rosalyn Yalow
1978		Herbert A. Simon	Isaac Bashevis Singer		Arno A. Penzias Robert W. Wilson	Daniel Nathans* Hamilton O. Smith*
1979	Herbert C. Brown*	Theodore W. Schultz Arthur Lewis			Sheldon L. Glashow* Steven Weinberg*	Allan M. Cormack*

*Prize shared with non-American

The American Nobel Prize winners for 1976 (left-right): Burton Richter, D. Carleton Gajdusek, William N. Lipscomb, Saul Bellow, Samuel Ting, Milton Friedman, and Baruch S. Blumberg. (AP/Wide World Photos)

Jakob syndrome, and bovine spongiform encephalopathy (mad cow disease).

Roger Guillemin and Andrew Victor Schally shared half of the 1977 prize for their studies of peptide hormones in the brain; the other half went to Rosalyn Yalow, who developed radioimmunoassay, a method for analysis of hormones such as insulin. She was the only woman awarded a prize for physiology or medicine in the decade. Daniel Nathans and Hamilton O. Smith shared a prize in 1978 for their work on restriction enzymes, which are important for the analysis of deoxyribonucleic acid (DNA), and Allan M. Cormack shared an award in 1979 for developing computed axial tomography (CAT scans), an important tool for diagnosis.

Economic Sciences First awarded in 1969, the economics prize is administered separately from the other prizes. Cambridge, Massachusetts, and Chicago were home to six of the eight American Nobelists during the 1970's.

Paul A. Samuelson of the Massachusetts Institute of Technology (MIT), the 1970 laureate, developed static and dynamic economic theory, while at Harvard University Kenneth J. Arrow, the 1972 winner, and Wassily Leontief, the 1973 winner, developed economic equilibrium theory and input-output methods, respectively. The 1971 laureate Simon Kuznets, also of Harvard, pioneered an experimentally based economic growth interpretation.

At the University of Chicago, Milton Friedman was honored in 1976 for consumption analysis and monetary history. Theodore W. Schultz, the 1979 laureate, studied economic development and developing countries, as did his cowinner Sir Arthur Lewis at Princeton University. At Carnegie-Mellon

University, 1978 laureate Herbert A. Simon conducted research into decision-making processes in economic organizations.

Impact The American winners of the Nobel Peace Prize were influential. Henry Kissinger and North Vietnamese negotiator Le Duc Tho shared the 1973 prize, but the latter declined it. Kissinger himself could not attend the award ceremony and later donated his prize money to war orphans. Norman Borlaug's work helped to alleviate hunger by improving the crops available to developing countries.

The achievements of the American science winners varied from arcane discoveries in particle physics, to invention of the CAT scanner, which revolutionized medical diagnosis. The discovery of cosmic microwave background provided significant evidence supporting a hot, dense start to the universe. New insights into disease mechanisms, such as the genetic basis of cancer, and prion diseases provided new possibilities for diagnosis and therapy.

Further Reading

Bellow, Saul. *To Jerusalem and Back: A Personal Account.* New York: Penguin, 1985. Bellow reveals much about himself and about Arab-Israeli relations in this travel narrative.

Bishop, J. Michael. *How to Win a Nobel Prize.* Cambridge, Mass.: Harvard University Press, 2003. Gives basic information on how the awards are made and offers the personal reminiscences of a 1989 prizewinner.

Feldman, Burton. *The Nobel Prize: A History of Genius, Controversy, and Prestige.* New York: Arcade, 2000. Lists the prize winners by year and nationality. Describes some of the controversies that have arisen in nominating and awarding the prizes.

Grinstein, Louise S., Rose K. Rose, and Miriam H. Rafailovich, eds. *Women in Chemistry and Physics: A Biobibliographic Sourcebook.* Westport, Conn.: Greenwood Press, 1993. Provides a biography and publications for Rosalyn Yalow.

James, Laylin K., ed. *Nobel Laureates in Chemistry, 1901-1992.* Washington, D.C.: American Chemical Society, Chemical Heritage Press, 1993. Details of the life and work of the laureates.

Lindsten, Jan, ed. *Nobel Lectures in Physiology or Medicine 1971-1980.* River Edge, N.J.: World Scientific, 1999. Contains the lectures of all the recipients except for Julius Axelrod.

Singer, Isaac Bashevis, and Richard Burgin. *Conversations with Isaac Bashevis Singer.* Garden City, N.Y.: Doubleday, 1985. The writer discusses his philosophy and creative processes.

John R. Phillips

See also Cancer research; CAT scans; Foreign policy of the United States; Genetics research; Green Revolution; Inventions; Kissinger, Henry; Literature in the United States; Medicine; Paris Peace Accords; Science and technology; Vietnam War.

■ Noise Control Act of 1972

Identification Noise emission standards for commercial products, aircraft, railroads, and trucks

Date Signed into law on October 27, 1972

Recognizing that noise pollution, just as air or water pollution, can be harmful to health, Congress enacted this law as an attempt to regulate and control noise.

Noise, like other forms of pollution, increased steadily with advances in technology. During the first half of the twentieth century, noise levels increased exponentially, but no coordinated effort at regulation existed because noise was not generally perceived as being a problem. Defining noise as any unwanted sound, however, indicates that the problem is pervasive and epidemic. People began to recognize, for example, that the extremely loud sounds experienced in industrial environments would eventually lead to permanent hearing loss, yet the much lower levels of sound encountered daily by average citizens were considered a mere annoyance. However, experts soon realized that noise is more than mere annoyance; even relatively low levels can adversely affect an individual's physical and mental health. Noise interferes with sleep stages, can impair performance of difficult tasks, produce anxiety, and increase stress. Chronic exposure may cause such adverse physiological effects as elevated blood pressure and increased hormone excretion.

Experts also began to understand that noise is particularly problematic to the young, the infirm, and the elderly. Children constantly surrounded by excessive environmental noise learn to tune it out; after entering school, they need to be trained to listen and focus their attention. For the ill, noise lengthens recuperation time and often results in extended medical treatments.

During the 1960's, various studies documented the dangers of high-decibel noise and the concealed risks of long-term exposure to lower levels. As environmental awareness increased as the 1970's began, citizens became increasingly more concerned about attempting to control environmental noise pollution. Pressured by environmental groups and concerned citizens, Congress enacted the Noise Control Act in 1972. This legislation set noise emission standards for commercial products, aircraft, and ground vehicles. The act also required the Environmental Protection Agency (EPA) to coordinate all federal programs relating to noise research, control, and regulation. The EPA was authorized to require environmental impact studies for new highways and industrial sites. It was also mandated to finance research on noise control, provide technical assistance to state and local governments, and disseminate public information about noise hazards.

Impact   As a consequence of the act, the EPA prepared model noise ordinances specifying maximum allowable sound levels for various regions—residential, commercial, and industrial—for different times of day. Because of this act, much more attention was given to land use planning and creating quieter residential areas. Housing developments began to be kept separated from industrial areas, and concrete noise-reducing barriers were routinely installed along interstate highways passing near residential areas.

Further Reading

Baron, Robert Alex. *The Tyranny of Noise.* New York: St. Martin's Press, 1970.

Strong, William J., and George R. Plitnik. *Music, Speech, Audio.* Provo, Utah: Soundprint, 1992.

George R. Plitnik

See also   Environmental movement; Environmental Protection Agency (EPA).

Oates, Joyce Carol

Identification American writer and scholar
Born June 16, 1938; Lockport, New York

As a prolific writer of novels, short stories, book reviews, essays, poems, and plays, Oates was a constant presence in the literary climate of the 1970's.

Joyce Carol Oates's exploration of the subconscious gained her a reputation for an unflinching willingness to explore what are often considered the less desirable aspects of the human experience, such as violence and its tragic effects. The 1970's were a particularly productive time for Oates as her books were published at the rate of two or three per year. Although some critics equated this with automatic writing and implied that Oates was privileging quantity over quality, she attributed her rate of completion and publication of books to a highly disciplined routine of writing and teaching (full-time at the University of Windsor in Canada) according to a daily schedule, eliminating what she considered any unwanted distractions from her life. Oates explained that combining mutually rewarding activities such as writing and teaching helped her sustain her enthusiasm and motivation for both.

In novels such as *Wonderland* (1971), *Do with Me What You Will* (1973), *The Assassins* (1975), *Childwold* (1976), *Son of the Morning* (1978), and *Unholy Loves* (1979), Oates presented characters whose lives are guided by obsession, self-delusion, and isolation. During the decade, she developed the style of realism combined with grotesque elements that gave her work its appeal to the subconscious. She also combined her interests in literature and psychology in college courses that she developed and taught at this time.

The short stories that Oates wrote at this time also showed an interest in psychologically complex characters who do not know themselves nearly as well as the reader comes to know them through Oates's descriptive and revealing details. Collections of these stories include *The Poisoned Kiss* (1975) and *All the*

Good People I've Left Behind (1978). In her seemingly limitless energy for writing and its different forms, Oates also managed to have four books of poetry published in this decade: *Love and Its Derangements* (1970), *Angel Fire* (1973), *The Fabulous Beasts* (1975), and *Women Whose Lives Are Food, Men Whose Lives Are Money* (1978). Although her poetry received less acclaim than her fiction, it did satisfy her desire to experiment with language and imagery in a different, more concentrated style than her sprawling novels.

Impact In the 1970's, Joyce Carol Oates built her reputation as one of the United States' most prolific and influential writers and scholars. By exploring the terrain of the human psyche and portraying the struggles and triumphs of sometimes tragically flawed characters, she delved more deeply into the subconscious than many other writers of the time dared. Although this approach made her work controversial for its time, it also established Oates both as a writer who was not afraid to confront the darker side of human nature and as one committed to writing not only as a career but also as a way of life.

Further Reading

Johnson, Greg. *Invisible Writer: A Biography of Joyce Carol Oates.* New York: Plume, 1998.

Oates, Joyce Carol. *The Faith of a Writer: Life, Craft, Art.* New York: HarperCollins, 2003.

Holly L. Norton

See also Literature in the United States; Poetry.

Occupational Safety and Health Act of 1970

Identification U.S. federal legislation
Date Signed into law on December 29, 1970

The Occupational Safety and Health Act was designed to ensure the safety and health of American workers. It established the Occupational Safety and Health Administration (OSHA) and transformed the enforcement of safety and health standards from a state function to a federal one.

Growing out of labor-management disputes and resistance, OSHA was created by legislation in 1970 to set specific industry standards strengthened by its oversight provisions. OSHA had two principal functions: setting standards and conducting workplace inspections to ensure that employers were complying with the standards and providing a safe and healthful workplace for their employees. The act extended to all employers and their employees in the fifty states, the District of Columbia, Puerto Rico, and all other territories under federal government jurisdiction. The act did not cover self-employed persons; farms that employed immediate family members of the farmer; working conditions regulated by other federal agencies, such as mining, nuclear energy and nuclear weapons manufacture, and many segments of the transportation industry; and employees of state and local governments.

OSHA standards sometimes required employers to adopt certain practices to protect workers on the job. It would be the employer's responsibility to become familiar with applicable standards and to comply with them. States with OSHA-approved job safety and health programs were to set standards at least as effective as the equivalent federal standard.

Federal OSHA standards for all industries required that employees have access to their medical records maintained by the employer regarding employees' exposure to toxic substances. Each industry segment had to provide employees with personal protective equipment designed to protect them against certain hazards, such as helmets to prevent head injuries in construction, eye shields and ear protection for welders, and gauntlets for ironworkers. Manufacturers and importers of hazardous materials had to conduct hazard evaluations of the products that they manufactured. If a product was found to be hazardous under the terms of the standard, then containers had to be labeled appropriately and accompanied by a material safety data sheet. Employees had to be trained to recognize and avoid the hazards.

Under OSHA, employees were granted certain rights: to contact the administration about safety and health conditions in their workplaces and have their confidentiality maintained, to contest the time period that OSHA allows for correcting standard violations, and to participate in OSHA workplace inspections.

In order to enforce its standards, OSHA selected compliance and safety officers, chosen for their knowledge and experience in the occupational safety and health area, who were authorized to conduct workplace inspections of establishments covered by the act. States with their own occupational safety and health programs could conduct inspections using qualified state inspectors. Fines and sanctions could be assessed for violations of the act, depending on the severity of the violation. Citations and penalties were reviewable and could be appealed by employees and employers.

Impact   Since its creation in 1970, OSHA has used its resources to stimulate management commitment and employee participation in comprehensive workplace safety and health programs. Its standards have created enforcement mechanisms to protect workplaces and workers.

Further Reading

MacAvoy, Paul W., ed. *OSHA Safety Regulation: Report of the Presidential Task Force.* Washington, D.C.: American Enterprise Institute for Public Policy Research, 1977.

Mendeloff, John. *Regulating Safety: An Economic and Political Analysis of Occupational Safety and Health Policy.* Cambridge, Mass.: MIT Press, 1979.

Northrup, Herbert R., et al. *The Impact of OSHA: A Study of the Effects of the Occupational Safety and Health Act on Three Key Industries—Aerospace, Chemicals, and Textiles.* Philadelphia: Industrial Research Unit, Wharton School, University of Pennsylvania, 1978.

Marcia J. Weiss

See also   Business and the economy in the United States; Unions in the United States; Women in the workforce.

■ October Crisis

The Event   Canadian government's reaction to terrorist kidnappings in Quebec Province
Date   Lasted from October 5 to December 4, 1970

Reacting strongly to two kidnappings by violent secessionists, Prime Minister Pierre Trudeau imposed the War Measures Act, which temporarily suspended many of the liberties guaranteed by the Canadian Bill of Rights.

From the beginning of the Canadian confederation, many French-speaking citizens in Quebec desired an independent country and resented domination by the English-speaking majority. By 1970, the idea of an independent Quebec was becoming increasingly popular in the province. During the 1960's, the Front de Libération du Québec (FLQ), a secret organization advocating a combination of secession and radial socialism, was responsible for seven deaths and some two hundred acts of terrorism. Twenty-three members of the FLQ were caught and sent to prison. In February and June, 1970, police in the region of Montreal successfully intercepted FLQ plots to kidnap consuls from Israel and the United States.

On October 5, four armed members of the "liberation cell" of the FLQ kidnapped British trade commissioner James Cross. In return for his freedom, the kidnappers demanded publication of the FLQ's manifesto, release of all FLQ members from prison, $500,000 in gold, and safe-conduct out of the country. Five days later, four militants of the FLQ's Chénier cell kidnapped Quebec's vice premier and minister of labor, Pierre Laporte.

Government Reaction From the beginning of the crisis, Canadian prime minister Trudeau, in consultation with the recently elected prime minister of Quebec, Robert Bourassa, decided not to make any significant concessions to the kidnappers, especially not to release any FLQ prisoners. When the Canadian Broadcasting Corporation (CBC), ignoring Trudeau's personal request, had the FLQ's manifesto read over the radio and television, it ironically increased the public's hostility toward the kidnappers.

On October 12, Trudeau ordered the army to protect important people and government buildings in Ottawa. In a famous press conference the next day, he said that he would ignore the "bleeding-hearts" and take any action necessary to combat "a parallel power which defies the elected power." When asked how far he would go, he answered, "Well, just watch me." In Montreal, Bourassa and the members of his cabinet stayed in the Queen Elizabeth Hotel under armed guard. On October 15, Bourassa and other provincial leaders formally asked Trudeau to impose martial law under the War Measures Act. Their request warned of an attempt by a minority "to destroy social order through criminal action."

Early in the morning of October 16, the federal cabinet proclaimed application of the act, outlawing the FLQ and providing the police with special pow-

ers of search, arrest, and detention without warrant or probable cause. The police quickly arrested hundreds of communist supporters and radicals suspected of supporting the FLQ. On October 17, the Chénier cell announced that Laporte had been executed, and the next day his body was found in a car trunk in Saint Hubert.

On November 6, as a result of extensive investigations, the police in Montreal arrested one of those responsible for Laporte's murder. A month later, Francis Simard and two others were arrested on Montreal's south shore. The four men were convicted and sentenced to life imprisonment, but they were paroled within twelve years.

On December 3, the police located Cross, who was being held by about ten kidnappers in a northern Montreal apartment. Unable to escape, the kidnappers agreed to release Cross in exchange for safe-conduct to Cuba for themselves and their families. The next day, after they were flown to Cuba, Cross was released. Within fifteen years, almost all FLQ members who had fled the country returned to face justice in Canada, generally receiving sentences of less than two years.

During the October Crisis, a total of 468 persons were arrested under the War Measures Act. Only ten of these suspects were convicted of wrongdoing, while 435 were released without any charges being filed. Many prominent citizens, including newspaper editor Claude Ryan, strongly criticized the emergency measures. Defenders of the policy argued that most of the periods of detention were relatively short, that all suspects were provided with legal counsel, and that innocent persons were later given monetary compensation for their time in jail. In December, a Gallup poll indicated that 87 percent of the Canadian people approved the application of the act.

Impact In the Province of Quebec, the dramatic events and publicity of the October Crisis galvanized opposition to terrorist violence. Partly as a result of the crisis, the FLQ ceased to exist. In contrast to the many bombings and deaths of the 1960's, virtually no terrorist acts would occur in Quebec during the next several decades.

Although the majority of Canadians approved of Trudeau's handling of the crisis, his policies were significantly less popular in Quebec than in the rest of the country. Moderate Quebec nationalists resented the arrests and detentions of their more radical colleagues. Following the crisis, support for Quebec secession appeared to increase rather dramatically, and memories of the October events appeared to help the separatist Parti Québécois take power in the provincial elections of 1976.

The invocation of the War Measures Act continued to be controversial long after the crisis had passed. Most civil libertarians insisted that the policy was unnecessarily oppressive and a dangerous precedent. For other observers, however, the main lesson of the crisis was that the use of emergency powers is sometimes the most effective way to combat terrorism.

Further Reading

Coleman, Ronald. *Just Watch Me: Trudeau's Tragic Legacy.* Victoria, B.C.: Trafford, 2003. A critical interpretation of Trudeau's policies, especially the way in which he dealt with the October Crisis.

Coleman, William. *Independence Movement in Quebec, 1945-1980.* Toronto: University of Toronto Press, 1984. An excellent historical account of the separatist movement in Quebec.

Fournier, Louis. *FLQ: The Anatomy of an Underground Movement.* Toronto: NC Press, 1984. A study of the terrorist organization responsible for the crisis of 1970.

Pelletier, Gérard. *The October Crisis.* Translated by Joyce Marshall. Toronto: McClellan & Stewart, 1971. A standard account by Trudeau's close friend and cabinet member.

Saywell, John. *Quebec Seventy: A Documentary Narrative.* Toronto: University of Toronto Press, 1971. A valuable collection of documents dealing with the October Crisis.

Simard, Francis. *Talking It Out: The October Crisis from the Inside.* Translated by David Homel. Montreal: Guernica, 1987. The later reflections of a major leader of the Chénier cell that kidnapped and murdered Laporte.

Vallières, Pierre. *The Assassination of Pierre Laporte: Behind the October 1970 Scenario.* Translated by Ralph Wells. Toronto: J. Lorimer, 1977. An account of the crisis written by a prominent Quebec separatist.

Thomas Tandy Lewis

See also   Censorship in Canada; Charter of the French Language; Francophonie, La; Journalism in Canada; Minorities in Canada; Quebec Charter of Human Rights and Freedoms; Terrorism; Trudeau, Pierre.

■ Oil embargo of 1973-1974

The Event   Refusal of Arab countries to sell oil to pro-Israeli countries

Date   October 17, 1973-May 17, 1974

In the midst of the fourth Arab-Israeli war, Arab countries decreased oil production and placed an embargo on shipments of crude oil to countries with close ties to Israel, especially the United States and the Netherlands.

On October 6, 1973, which was the Jewish holy day of Yom Kippur, Egypt and Syria conducted a surprise attack against Israel. The Soviet Union provided assistance for the invasion. At first it appeared that the two Arab nations might defeat the Israelis. However, on October 14, U.S. president Richard M. Nixon responded by ordering a massive airlift of weapons and supplies to Israel, and the airlift continued for a full month. It included approximately fifty-six combat aircraft, and 28,000 tons of equipment, enabling Israel to recover and then to prevail in the conflict.

The economies of almost all industrialized countries were highly dependent on imported oil. Even

---

Member States of the Organization of the Petroleum Exporting Countries (OPEC) During the 1970's

Founding members:
Iran
Iraq
Kuwait
Saudi Arabia
Venezuela

Additional members and the years they joined:
Qatar (1961)
Indonesia (1962)
Libya (1962)
United Arab Emirates (1967)
Algeria (1969)
Nigeria (1971)
Ecuador (1973)
Gabon (1975)

the United States, while less vulnerable than Western Europe, was importing 35 percent of its energy needs. Most of the major exporting countries belonged to the Organization of Petroleum Exporting Countries (OPEC), an international cartel established to regulate the supply and prices of oil. The Arab members of the cartel, including Saudi Arabia, Iraq, Libya, and the Arab Emirates, together produced more than half of the world's oil.

On October 17, the Arab oil ministers announced a cut in oil production and a rolling oil embargo on supporters of Israel. Two days later, after Nixon pledged $2.2 billion in aid to Israel, Saudi Arabia and other Arab countries announced a total embargo against the United States. Soon thereafter, the Arab embargo was extended to the Netherlands, which was the largest entrance point for oil flowing into Western Europe.

During the five months of the embargo, oil prices rose to unprecedented levels—from less than $3 a barrel to a high of $11.65 in January, 1974. This increase significantly harmed the industrial counties and contributed to an international recession. Secretary of State Henry Kissinger made numerous trips to the Middle East in order to negotiate an end to the conflict. On January 18, 1974, Egypt and Israel entered into a disengagement agreement. On May 17, the Arab oil ministers, with the exception of Libya, finally agreed to end the embargo.

Impact Ultimately, the Arabs failed to achieve their political demands because of the cash-flow needs of OPEC countries with large populations, especially non-Arab countries such as Venezuela, Nigeria, and Indonesia. Even though the embargo resulted in price increases and long lines to purchase gasoline in the United States, it never substantially disrupted the supply of oil. For about a decade, the OPEC countries, especially those of the Middle East, gained substantial wealth as a result of the "oil shock." The price of oil, however, declined because of the discovery of new fields, the enhanced production of older

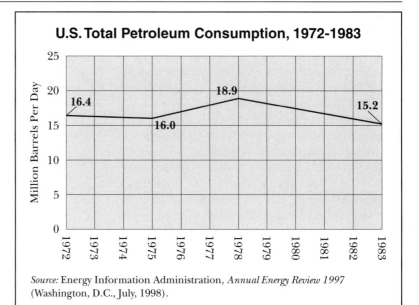

U.S. Total Petroleum Consumption, 1972-1983

Source: Energy Information Administration, *Annual Energy Review 1997* (Washington, D.C., July, 1998).

fields, and the conservation activities of the importing countries.

Although the Arab embargo had limited influence on the diplomatic policies of Western Europe and Japan, it did not substantially affect the pro-Israeli commitment of the United States. As a result of the embargo, American policy makers became more determined to seek a settlement in the Arab-Israeli conflict. The countries of Israel and Egypt, moreover, emerged from the Yom Kippur War with large debts and a growing reliance on American assistance. For these reasons, the war and the embargo helped make possible the Camp David Accords of 1978.

Further Reading

Congressional Quarterly Editors. *The Middle East.* 9th ed. Washington, D.C.: CQ Press, 1999.

Little, Douglas. *American Orientalism: The United States and the Middle East Since 1941.* Raleigh: University of North Carolina Press, 2004.

Rabinovich, Abraham. *The Yom Kippur War: The Epic Encounter That Transformed the Middle East.* New York: Schocken Books, 2004.

Thomas Tandy Lewis

See also Camp David Accords; Energy crisis; Foreign policy of the United States; Gas shortages; Inflation in the United States; Israel and the United States; Middle East and North America.

■ Olympic Games of 1972

The Event   The 1972 staging of winter and
summer international athletic competitions,
held every four years

Date   Winter Games, February 3-13, 1972;
Summer Games, August 26-September 11, 1972

Place   Winter Games, Sapporo, Japan; Summer
Games, Munich, West Germany

*While featuring several record-breaking performances of
notable international athletes, the Olympic Games of 1972
were mired in controversy surrounding issues of amateurism and sportsmanship. The Summer Games gained unfortunate infamy following the terrorist acts committed by the
Palestinian Black September group.*

The eleventh Winter Olympic Games featured 1,006
competing athletes—205 women and 801 men—
who represented thirty-five nations. The United
States had the largest contingent with 118 athletes—
91 men and 27 women. The Games of Sapporo were
the first to be held outside Europe or the United
States. For the Winter Games, American broadcast
rights were $6.4 million compared with the $2.5 million for the 1968 Grenoble, France, Games.

Controversy of Amateurism   Three days prior to
the commencement of the Games in Sapporo, retiring president of the International Olympic Committee (IOC), Avery Brundage, threatened to disqualify
forty alpine skiers for professionalism. On the average, alpine skiers were able to draw salaries of fifty
thousand dollars a year by representing the trademarks associated with the skiing industry. Brundage
had a strong disapproval of athletes using the Games
as a means to advertise commercial interests of
the sports industry. In 1968, during the Grenoble
Games in France, Brundage ordered that any photographs taken of skiers would be without the presence of any ski manufacturers' trademarks.

As a response to Brundage's threat, members of
the Federation Internationale de Ski (FIS) threat-

Anne Henning (left) of the United States captured the gold medal in 500-meter speed skating at the 1972 Winter Olympics. (AP/Wide
World Photos)

ened to boycott the 1972 Olympics. Without the main attraction of alpine skiing, the Olympics would be a disaster. The executive committee of the IOC decided to make an example out of the sport's most commercialized star, Karl Schranz, voting 28-14 to disqualify him. Schranz had earned more than fifty thousand dollars annually by testing ski equipment. Schranz was the most outspoken critic of Brundage and the hypocrisy of amateurism in the Olympics. He criticized Brundage for not going after the Soviet bloc nations and their state-sponsored Olympic athletes. Ultimately, Schranz became the scapegoat for this controversy, although he urged his fellow alpine skiers not to boycott. He ended his skiing career never having won an Olympic gold medal.

The question of amateurism came under further protest when Canada refused to send a hockey team to the Olympics. Canadian officials protested the use of "professional amateurs" by Soviet bloc nations.

Medal Counts and Notable Athletes The United States won a total of eight medals: three gold, two silver, and three bronze. American women athletes captured seven medals, while the American men captured one medal, the silver in ice hockey. Twenty-year-old Dianne Holum from Northbrook, Illinois, won the 1,500-meter ice skating event, thereby setting an Olympic record. This was the first Olympic ice skating event won by an American woman. Holum would go on to win the silver medal in the 3,000-meter ice skating event. Sixteen-year-old Anne Henning, also from Northbrook, Illinois, won the 500-meter sprint in speed skating. Twenty-one-year-old Barbara Cochran captured the third gold medal won by Americans at these Olympics, this time in the slalom. It was the first gold medal for any American in alpine skiing in twenty years.

The sport heroes of the Olympics were Ard Schenk of Holland, who won three gold medals in speed skating, and Galina Kulacova of the Soviet Union, who captured three gold medals in cross-country skiing. Perhaps the biggest surprise of the Olympics was the performance of alpine skier Francisco Ochoa of Spain, who won the gold medal in the slalom—the first Spaniard to win a gold medal in the Winter Olympic Games. In addition, Japan made a clean sweep of the 70-meter ski jump. The gold

Leading Medal Winners of the 1972 Summer Olympics, Men

Total	Athlete	Country	Sport	Gold-Silver-Bronze
7	Mark Spitz	United States	Swimming	7-0-0
5	Sawao Kato	Japan	Gymnastics	3-2-0
4	Jerry Heidenreich	United States	Swimming	2-1-1
4	Roland Matthes	East Germany	Swimming	2-1-1
4	Akinori Nakayama	Japan	Gymnastics	2-1-1
4	Shigeru Kasamatsu	Japan	Gymnastics	1-1-2
4	Eizo Kenmotsu	Japan	Gymnastics	1-1-2
3	Valery Borsov	Soviet Union	Track and Field	2-1-0
3	Mitsuo Tsukahara	Japan	Gymnastics	2-0-1
3	Steve Genter	United States	Swimming	1-2-0
3	Viktor Klimenko	Soviet Union	Gymnastics	1-2-0
3	Mike Stamm	United States	Swimming	1-2-0
3	Vladimir Bure	Soviet Union	Swimming	0-1-2

Leading Medal Winners of the 1972 Summer Olympics, Women

Total	Athlete	Country	Sport	Gold-Silver-Bronze
5	Shane Gould	Australia	Swimming	3-1-1
5	Karin Janz	East Germany	Gymnastics	2-2-1
4	Olga Korbut	Soviet Union	Gymnastics	3-1-0
4	Lyudmila Tourischeva	Soviet Union	Gymnastics	2-1-1
4	Tamara Lazakovitch	Soviet Union	Gymnastics	1-1-2

medal won by Yukio Kasaya in this event was the first gold medal won by Japan in the Winter Games; the only medal that the country had won previously in the Winter Games was a silver medal in 1956.

Summer Olympics   The 1972 Summer Olympic Games were attended by a total of 7,123 athletes— 6,065 male and 1,058 women—the most of any previous Olympic Games. The Olympic program was expanded to twenty-one sports with the addition of archery, team handball, and judo for a total of 195 events. Broadcasting rights for the Games in the United States were set at $7.5 million, an increase of $4 million from the 1968 Mexico City Games.

In preparation for the Games, the West German government invested more than $640 million to construct new sports stadiums, swimming pools, and sports halls. In addition, improvements were made at airports, subways, and cultural centers with the intention to showcase West Germany and stimulate tourism.

Terrorism at the Games   Unfortunately, organizers of the twentieth Olympiad never anticipated the horrific terrorist event that would plague their Olympics. In the early morning of September 5, eight members of the Palestinian Black September terrorist organization broke into the Munich Olympic Village, executed two Israeli athletes, and took nine Israeli athletes hostage. By 5:30 A.M., the leader of the organization made the group's demands: the release of two hundred Palestinian prisoners held in Israeli jails and the provision of an airliner to provide passage to Egypt. Twenty-three hours later, as the terrorists boarded a plane, a shootout between German police and the terrorists took place. All nine hostages were killed, as well as five of the

terrorists, a police officer, and a helicopter pilot.

Following the horrific terrorist attack, the question of whether to complete the Games came under discussion. The Israeli ambassador requested that the Games be canceled; athletes from the Arab states of Egypt, Kuwait, and Syria left the Games because of fear of possible reprisals. A number of Norwegian and Dutch athletes refused to compete, suggesting that the Games should be halted. American swimming champion Mark Spitz left, fearing for his life because of his Jewish American identity. However, a majority of athletes felt that the Games should continue. A memorial service was held on the morning of September 6 in the Olympic Stadium in front of a crowd of eighty thousand. At the service, IOC president Brundage announced that the Games must go on. They were extended by one day, to be completed by the eleventh of September.

Controversy   A number of incidents that displayed poor athletic behavior occurred during the Games. After losing a water polo match to the Soviets, Yugoslavian water polo athletes mobbed the Cuban referee, throwing water bottles and spitting on him. Members of the Pakistani field hockey team attacked the referees after their loss to West Germany. The team members were suspended from any future competition in the Olympics. Similarly, Vince Matthews and Wayne Collett of the United States were suspended from future Olympics competition following their behavior after the 400-meter track event in which they stood disrespectfully on the victory stand during the playing of the national anthem.

Controversy also developed during the gold-medal basketball contest between the United States and the Soviet Union. The men's basketball team lost for the first time in the Olympics in a controversial contest that ended 51-50. With the U.S. team trailing 49-48 with a few seconds left to play, Doug Collins stole the ball from a Soviet player and broke down court for a lay-up. Collins was fouled and went to the free-throw line and scored both free throws to put the United States ahead 50-49. With three seconds on the clock, the Soviets tried to inbound the ball but failed. The Soviets were given two more chances to inbound the ball, and they finally scored. The United States appealed to the IOC, feeling it had been wronged. The appeals were denied, and the U.S. team declined to accept the silver medal and refused to attend the medals ceremony.

A number of mishaps plagued American athletes during the 1972 Games. Sixteen-year-old Rick De-Mont, the gold medalist in the 400-meter freestyle swimming event, had his medal taken away when it was discovered that he was taking a prescription for his asthma that included a drug banned in the Olympics. He had listed the prescription drug that he had been taking for years on his medical form, but the team doctors of the United States neglected to provide the information to the IOC prior to his event. Moreover, two of the United States' fastest sprinters, Eddie Hart and Raynaud Robinson, failed to attend their semifinal heats as a result of being given the wrong starting times by the U.S. sprint coach. Each had tied the world record prior to the Olympic Games, and in all likeliness, both would have contended for the gold medal. American pole-vaulter Bob Seagren, who had won a gold medal in the 1968 Games, was informed that because of a new rule, he would not be permitted to use his fiberglass pole.

Performances and Heroes   Aside from the controversies that emerged during the Games, there were a number of heralded performances. The 1972 Olympics resulted in thirty world records and eighty Olympic records. American athletes dominated the swimming events, winning seventeen gold medals out of twenty-nine swimming events. A fifteen-year-old Australian female swimmer, Shane Gould, won five medals in women's swimming.

However, it was the performance of Mark Spitz that captured widespread attention in swimming. After he won five gold medals at the 1967 Pan-American Games, great things were expected of Spitz at the 1968 Olympic Games, but he surprisingly failed to win an individual event. At the 1972 Olympics, however, he set an Olympic record by winning seven gold medals, all of them in world-record time.

American wrestlers gave their best performances ever in wrestling, winning six medals—three gold, a silver, and two bronze medals. Wayne Wells and Ben Peterson joined Dan Gable, considered to be the United States' greatest wrestler, in winning gold medals.

In the marathon, American Frank Shorter won the gold medal. It was the first time that an American won this event since 1908. In 1976, Shorter won the silver medal and became the first American to win two Olympic medals in the marathon. Shorter often has been credited as being responsible for the late 1970's running boom in the United States. Gymnast Olga Korbut of the Soviet Union won a gold medal in the floor exercise and the balance beam that sparked a worldwide fad in her sport. Lasse Viren of Finland became only the fourth Olympian in history to win the 5,000- and 10,000-meter races within the same Games. Despite falling down in the

Top Ten Standings for the 1972 Winter Olympics

Medals Won	Country	Gold	Silver	Bronze
16	Soviet Union	8	5	3
14	East Germany	4	3	7
12	Norway	2	5	5
10	Switzerland	4	3	3
9	Holland	4	3	2
8	United States	3	2	3
5	West Germany	3	1	1
5	Italy	2	2	1
5	Austria	1	2	2
5	Finland	0	4	1

finals of the 10,000-meter race, Viren was able to recover and run the final mile in a time of 4:01. Teofilo
Stevenson won his first gold medal in the heavyweight boxing division. After the Olympics, he was
pursued with lucrative multimillion dollar contracts
to turn professional, but he refused to be lured with
these offers and went on to win gold medals in the
1976 and 1980 Olympics.

The Soviet Union compiled a total of ninety-nine
medals (fifty gold, twenty-seven silver, and twenty-
two bronze) during the 1972 Summer Olympics,
its best showing since entering the Games in 1952.
The United States had a total of ninety-four medals (thirty-three gold, thirty silver, and thirty-one
bronze).

The Olympic organizers had planned a festive
conclusion for the Games, but because of the unfortunate events that unfolded, the closing ceremony
lasted only forty-five minutes, with a brief period of
silence for the eleven murdered Israeli athletes.

Impact The Olympics of 1972 raised a number of
issues dealing with the principles of amateurism and
the difficulty to regulate it; the question was put to
rest with the 1992 Barcelona Games, when all contes-
tants, amateur and otherwise, were allowed to compete in most of the events on the Olympic program.
The use of the Olympics to stage political statements
would continue in subsequent Olympic Games but
with greater attention to security. Nevertheless, the
Olympics continued to be a major international athletic attraction as prices for the Games television
rights increased during the latter part of the decade.

Further Reading

Espy, Richard. *The Politics of the Olympic Games.* Berkeley: University of California Press, 1979. The author provides a historical account of the political,
economic, social, and philosophical forces that
have influenced the conduct of the Olympic
Games.

Killanin, Lord, and Rodda John, eds. *The Olympic
Games: Eighty Years of People, Events, and Records.*
New York: Collier Books, 1976. Includes a collection of articles dealing with various aspects
surrounding the Olympic movement such as amateurism and the development of the various
sports that appear on Summer and Winter programs. Also, reviews each Olympiad up to 1972.

Mallon, Bill, and Ian Buchanan. *Quest for Gold: The*

Encyclopedia of American Olympians, New York: Leisure Press, 1984. Provides brief biographical review of American Olympic athletes.

Alar Lipping

See also Basketball; Boxing; Canada Cup of 1976;
Commonwealth Games of 1978; Hamill, Dorothy;
Hockey; Jenner, Bruce; Munich Olympics terrorism;
Olympic Games of 1976; Soccer; Spitz, Mark; Sports.

■ Olympic Games of 1976

The Event The 1976 staging of winter and
summer international athletic competitions,
held every four years
Date Winter Games, February 4-15, 1976;
Summer Games, July 17-August 1, 1976.
Place Winter Games, Innsbruck, Austria;
Summer Games, Montreal, Canada

*Despite prohibitive financial costs and political disruptions
and boycotts, the Winter and Summer Olympic Games of
1976 were largely successful and highlighted a number of
prominent athletes to an international audience, including Bill Koch, Rosi Mittermaier, Dorothy Hamill, Nadia
Comaneci, Bruce Jenner, Edwin Moses, Kornelia Ender,
and Leon Spinks.*

Following the 1972 Olympic Games, Avery Brundage, who had served as the president of the International Olympic Committee (IOC) since 1952,
stepped down, and Lord Michael Killanin of Ireland
became the new head of the IOC. The 1976 Olympics would be the first for Lord Killanin's administration. In 1972, the IOC awarded the 1976 Winter
Games to Denver, Colorado, but in 1972, Colorado
voters rejected a five-million-dollar bond issue to finance the undertaking. As a result, Denver withdrew, and Innsbruck, Austria, stepped in to host the
Winter Games, as it had in 1964.

The twelfth Winter Olympic Games were represented by thirty-seven nations and 1,123 athletes:
231 women, 892 men. The Olympic program featured thirty-seven events, including a new one, ice
dancing. The Austrians had constructed twin Olympic cauldrons, and for the first time in Olympic history, two flames were lit, one in each cauldron. One
cauldron represented the previous time that the
Olympics were held in Innsbruck, and the other represented the present Games. As a result of the terrorist event during the 1972 Munich Games, during
which eleven Israeli athletes were killed, the Games

were conducted under extreme security that included uniformed guards with submachine guns.

Controversy and Performances Before the Games, the Soviet bloc made objections to the IOC regarding the broadcasting rights that were provided to Radio Free Europe to cover the Games. The IOC responded to the Soviet objection and disallowed Radio Free Europe the rights to air the Games. Secretary of State Henry Kissinger stated his disapproval of IOC's caving in to the Soviet bloc.

On the first day of competition, Bill Koch, from Guilford, Vermont, became the first American to win a medal in cross-country skiing by placing second in the 30-kilometer race. The United States would compile three gold medals. Sheila Young, of Detroit, won the 500-meter ice skating sprint, and Peter Mueller, of Mequon, Wisconsin, won the 1,000-meter ice skating event. Nineteen-year-old Dorothy Hamill from Connecticut won the gold medal in figure skating. Her performance was flawless, and she received resounding applause from the nine thousand spectators in the Olympic Ice Stadium.

Rosi Mittermaier of West Germany won two gold medals in alpine skiing: downhill and the slalom. She needed a victory in the giant slalom to win the coveted grand slam, which no woman had ever won. She won the silver medal in the giant slalom, placing second to Canada's Kathy Kreiner and losing her bid to win the grand slam by twelve-hundredths of a second.

Summer Olympic Games The twenty-first Summer Olympic Games had a total of 6,028 athletes—4,781 men and 1,247 women—representing ninety-two nations. The Olympic program included twenty-one sports and 198 events, with new events for women in basketball, team handball, and rowing.

When Montreal accepted the hosting of the Games, Mayor Jean Drapeau gambled on making the games self-financing. The original budget estimate was $310 million. Drapeau's organizing committee thought the costs for hosting the games would be balanced from the $25 million in television rights from the American Broadcasting System (ABC) and the corporate advertising rights bought by Coca-Cola, Pitney-Bowes, and Adidas. However, the growing global inflation coupled with labor disputes resulted in the cost for staging the Olympics growing to $1.5 billion. The Olympic Park alone cost $800 million and the stadium another $650 million, and security expenses stood at $100 million. The escalating cost of the Games resulted in the Quebec provincial government taking over the construction from Mayor Drapeau. The $1 billion debt earned from the Games took twenty-two years to pay off.

Political Controversy Five hours before the opening ceremonies, twenty-two African nations and three from Asia refused to participate in the opening ceremonies. The Supreme Council for Sport in Africa (SCSA) was calling for a boycott to protest the inclusion of New Zealand to participate in the Games.

Leading Medal Winners of the 1976 Summer Olympics, Men

Total	Athlete	Country	Sport	Gold-Silver-Bronze
7	Nikolai Andrianov	Soviet Union	Gymnastics	4-2-1
5	John Naber	United States	Swimming	4-1-0
5	Mitsuo Tsukahara	Japan	Gymnastics	2-1-2
4	Jim Montgomery	United States	Swimming	3-0-1
3	John Hencken	United States	Swimming	2-1-0
3	Sawao Kato	Japan	Gymnastics	2-1-0
3	Eizo Kenmotsu	Japan	Gymnastics	1-2-0
3	Rüdiger Helm	East Germany	Canoeing	1-0-2

Leading Medal Winners of the 1976 Summer Olympics, Women

Total	Athlete	Country	Sport	Gold-Silver-Bronze
5	Kornelia Ender	East Germany	Swimming	4-1-0
5	Nadia Comaneci	Romania	Gymnastics	3-1-1
5	Shirley Babashoff	United States	Swimming	1-4-0
4	Nelli Kim	Soviet Union	Gymnastics	3-1-0
4	Andrea Pollack	East Germany	Swimming	2-2-0
4	Lyudmila Tourischeva	Soviet Union	Gymnastics	1-2-1
3	Ulrike Richter	East Germany	Swimming	3-0-0
3	Annagret Richter	West Germany	Track and Field	1-2-0
3	Renate Stecher	East Germany	Track and Field	1-1-1
3	Teodora Ungureanu	Romania	Gymnastics	0-2-1

The SCSA claimed that New Zealand violated the Olympic sanction of South Africa to participate in the Games by having a New Zealand rugby team tour South Africa earlier in the year. New Zealand claimed that the rugby team had no affiliation with any Olympic organization since rugby was not an Olympic sport. Furthermore, New Zealand officials cited that an American women's softball team had toured South Africa and that during the present Olympic Games there was a South African cricket team touring Canada. The IOC saw no grounds to disallow New Zealand from participating. The SCSA protest against New Zealand resulted in the boycott of the Olympics of twenty-nine African nations and 690 athletes. Among the countries were Kenya, Tanzania, Nigeria, and Zambia. Kenya, with a delegation of 132, had several gold-medal prospects among its thirty-two track-and-field athletes. The long-awaited contest between John Walker of New Zealand and Filbert Bayi of Tanzania, who traded record times in the 1,500-meter track event throughout the previous four years, did not occur.

In 1970, Canada instituted a one-China policy in which the People's Republic of China (PRC), not Taiwan, was recognized as China. The IOC had recognized Taiwan as the Republic of China for the 1976 Olympic Games, and it stated that the PRC was not a member of the IOC. The Canadian government, led by Prime Minister Pierre Trudeau, stood fast with recognizing only one China. The U.S. government opposed the Canadian stand. The United States Olympic Committee debated whether to compete in the Olympics if Taiwan was refused the right to be recognized as China. A compromise between the IOC and the Canadian government was offered: The athletes from the PRC could compete under their flag but would have to be recognized as athletes from Taiwan (the Republic of China). On July 16, the delegation from the Republic of China refused the compromise solution and did not participate. The United States was so opposed to the decision that U.S. secretary of state Kissinger refused to attend the Games.

Athletic Performances In light of the political disruptions, the Games continued with eighty-eight participating nations. A fourteen-year-old Romanian schoolgirl named Nadia Comaneci overshadowed the storied performance of Olga Korbut during the 1972 Games. On July 19, Comaneci received the first perfect score of 10 in Olympic gymnastics. In total, she scored seven perfect scores of 10 en route to her three gold medals, one silver, and one bronze. In men's gymnastics, Nikolai Andrianov won four individual gold medals in floor exercise, vaulting horse, rings, and combined. In addition to his four gold medals, Andrianov won two silver medals and one bronze for a total of seven medals.

American men dominated the swimming events. The team won twelve out of thirteen gold medals, losing out only to David Wilkie of Great Britain in the 200-meter breaststroke. Out of the thirty-three medals for individual events, American men captured twenty-five. John Naber collected a total of four gold medals and one silver medal. Every event in men's swimming had a world record set except for the 100-meter butterfly.

In 1912, women's swimming was introduced as an Olympic sport, and American female swimmers first appeared in 1920. Following 1920, the United States women swimmers had been the most dominant force in the Olympics. However, in 1976, swimmers from East Germany overwhelmed the United States. Of the thirteen swimming events, East German women won eleven gold medals, and the U.S. won one gold medal. Leading the East German swimmers was Kornelia Ender, who earned four gold medals and established three world records and equaled one.

The Montreal Games were a banner Olympics for American boxing. U.S. boxers won five gold med-als—the most since 1952. Gold-medal winners for the United States included Leo Randolph (flyweight), Howard Davis (lightweight), Sugar Ray Leonard (light welterweight), Michael Spinks (middleweight), and Leon Spinks (light heavyweight). However, it was Teofilo Stevenson of Cuba who won the heavyweight gold medal, as he did in 1972 and 1980.

In track and field, Edwin Moses won the gold medal in 400-meter hurdles in world-record time of 47.64, winning by 8 meters in front of second-place finisher Michael Shine, also of the United States. Missing from the event, because of the African nation boycott, was John Aki Bua of Uganda, who had the world record in the 1972 Olympics. Alberto Juantorena of Cuba won gold medals in the 400-meter and 800-meter events, establishing a world record of 1:43.50. Lasse Viren of Finland continued to do what he did in the 1972 Olympic Games by winning both the 5,000-meter and 10,000-meter events. In the 100-meter race, the first-ranked American, Harvey Glance, came in fourth; for the first time

The U.S. and Soviet hockey teams square off at the 1976 Winter Olympics. (AP/Wide World Photos)

since 1928, the United States failed to medal in the 100-meter race. Hasely Crawford of Trinidad won the gold. In field events, Mac Wilkins of the United States won the discus, and John Powell won the bronze. In the long jump, Americans Arnie Robinson won the gold medal and Randy Williams won the silver medal. The decathlon was won by Bruce Jenner of the United States in world-record points of 8,617.

The medal standings at the conclusion of the Montreal Olympic Games had the Soviet Union winning a total of 125 medals: 49 gold, 41 silver, and 35 bronze. The German Democratic Republic (GDR) had a total of ninety medals: forty gold, twenty-five silver, and twenty-five bronze. The United States had more medals than the GDR with ninety-four but held six less in gold, with a total of thirty-four.

Top Ten Standings for the 1976 Winter Olympics

Medals Won	*Country*	*Gold*	*Silver*	*Bronze*
27	Soviet Union	13	6	8
19	East Germany	7	5	7
10	United States	3	3	4
10	West Germany	2	5	3
7	Norway	3	3	1
7	Finland	2	4	1
6	Austria	2	2	2
6	Holland	1	2	3
5	Switzerland	1	3	1
4	Italy	1	2	1

Impact The economic turmoil that surfaced during the 1976 Montreal Games frightened many countries from considering hosting subsequent Olympics events. Following the 1976 economic disaster of the Montreal Games, only one city offered to bid on the 1984 Olympic Games, Los Angeles. The use of the Olympic Games as a means to express political protest would continue in the 1980 Olympics in Moscow, when President Jimmy Carter ordered the United States Olympic Committee to boycott the Moscow Olympic Games in order to protest the Soviet Union's invasion of Afghanistan. As a response, the Soviet bloc nations boycotted the 1984 Los Angeles Olympic Games.

Further Reading

Espy, Richard. *The Politics of the Olympic Games.* Berkeley: University of California Press, 1979. The author provides a historical account of the political, economic, social, and philosophical forces that have influenced the conduct of the Olympic Games.

Mallon, Bill, and Ian Buchanan. *Quest for Gold: The Encyclopedia of American Olympians.* New York: Leisure Press, 1984. Provides brief biographical review of American Olympic athletes.

Preuss, Holger. *The Economics of the Olympic Games: Hosting the Games, 1972-2000.* Petersham, N.S.W.: Walla Walla Press, 2001. Reviews the economic costs encountered in hosting the Olympic Games and outlines the revenue generated during the Olympic Games.

Wallechinsky, David. *The Complete Book of the Summer Olympics.* Woodstock, N.Y.: Overlook Press, 2000. Gives facts and statistics on important athletes and all sports involved in the Summer Games.

Alar Lipping

See also Boxing; Canada Cup of 1976; Commonwealth Games of 1978; Hamill, Dorothy; Hockey; Jenner, Bruce; Munich Olympics terrorism; Olympic Games of 1972; Soccer; Spitz, Mark; Sports.

■ *One Flew over the Cuckoo's Nest*

Identification Motion picture
Director Milos Forman (1932-   )
Date Released in 1975

One of the most popular motion pictures of the decade, One Flew over the Cuckoo's Nest *attacked and exposed hypocrisies on topics such as sanity, drugs, sex, control, and society.*

Jack Nicholson (center) in a scene from One Flew over the Cuckoo's Nest. (Museum of Modern Art/Film Stills Archive)

Based on Ken Kesey's 1962 novel of the same title, although made without the author's permission, *One Flew over the Cuckoo's Nest* is arguably one of the most-watched and studied films of the decade. Preying on residual angst from the 1960's, the film expressed collective, entrenched fears of its 1970's viewers. The main conflict is between Randle Patrick McMurphy (played by Jack Nicholson) and "Big Nurse" Ratched (Louise Fletcher). McMurphy, who has chosen life in a mental ward instead of prison after pleading guilty to charges of statutory rape, confronts Big Nurse, the "control freak" mother figure in charge of the Combine, which is the term McMurphy uses for the mental ward to imply the all-powerful governmental system that controls citizens everywhere.

The American Indian narrator of the story, Chief Bromden (Will Sampson), represents the silent, all-knowing, repressed minority in American society—he is one who sees everything and copes with reality by feigning the inability to talk. This depiction of Chief Bromden was timely, coming after African Americans and other minorities had received a modicum of rights with civil rights laws passed in the previous decade, which were being enacted or struggled over during the 1970's. It raised the question of whether, and to what extent, society would actualize equality and allow its members to achieve dignity and self-worth. Similarly, scenes in the film depicting sex (McMurphy arranges for two prostitutes to visit the mental ward) and drugs and alcohol (also brought into the facility) address concerns of viewers. Although newfound social freedoms and legal rights for those who had never truly had them were ostensibly available, the film made viewers ponder just how far the country would go toward realizing them in a meaningful way.

The film gives a mixed, bittersweet answer to this question: On one hand, Chief Bromden does triumph and chooses to leave the mental ward to make a life on his own terms. On the other hand, Mc-Murphy is given electroshock treatments until he is totally void of the ability not only to resist Big Nurse but also to have any identity that is his own.

Impact   In 1976, *One Flew over the Cuckoo's Nest* was the first film in more than two decades to receive Academy Awards for Best Picture, Best Director, Best Actor, Best Actress, and Best Screenplay. Its most enduring effect on audiences was the realization that the Combine—symbolizing ruthless, mechanized government—would eventually win in the daily lives of people. Those running society would cruelly ensure that rebellion would not win over conformity at all cost.

Further Reading

Ferrell, William K. *Literature and Film as Modern Mythology.* Westport, Conn.: Praeger, 2000.

Porter, M. Gillen. *"One Flew over the Cuckoo's Nest": Rising to Heroism.* Boston: Twayne, 1989.

Carl Singleton

See also   Academy Awards; Film in the United States; Nicholson, Jack.

■ Open marriage

Definition   A married couple who agrees that each is free to seek other intimate relationships

Open marriages reflected changing social norms and values in the United States during the 1970's. They changed the nature of traditional marriage by making marriage a personal contract between partners, lessening social restrictions on married couples, and decreasing gender role stereotypes in marriage.

Rising divorce rates of the 1970's contributed to the popularity of open marriage, a term coined in the 1970's in response to young adults searching for both intimacy and growth in a committed relationship similar to, but without the limitations of, traditional marriage. Young people recognized the instability of traditional marriages and adopted open marriages in an effort to avoid divorce. Open marriages offered a definite contrast to "closed" marriages, which many felt involved ownership of one's mate, denial of the self, rigid roles determined by sex, and absolute fidelity. Closed marriage focused on a couple as one fused identity, while open marriages built on the concept of synergy. Practitioners argued that marital bonds grew when each partner

contributed individual, personal strengths to the relationship.

Open marriages made each marriage unique and designed to meet every couple's specific needs. The concept was furthered by Nena and George O'Neill's 1972 book *The Open Marriage.* In it, the O'Neills provide eight strategies for establishing an open marriage. The guidelines included living for now, privacy, flexibility in roles, open companionship, and open, honest communication. These guidelines helped give partners individual freedom and provided for personal growth while maintaining a supportive, primary relationship. The couple bond was meant to remain central, but each partner demonstrated responsibility for the self and respect toward the other. These principles of open marriage helped partners communicate with each other in order to develop a consensus about living together as a couple.

Infidelity, or extramarital sexual relationships, was widely associated with open marriages during this time, which made it a controversial topic. In an open marriage, sex outside of marriage is acceptable if both spouses agree, but it is not essential to the concept of open marriage. Open marriage differs greatly from extramarital relationships, free love, or polygamy. In an open marriage, sexual relationships outside the primary bond exist only with the full knowledge and consent of the other partner.

Impact   While discussed extensively in the popular media during the 1970's, open marriages did not become a prominent lifestyle, probably because of the association with infidelity. Subsequent research suggested that most marriages established under the explicit premise of open marriage were short-lived. The concept of open marriage did, however, change social definitions of, and expectations in, marriage from a legal contract with rigid role expectations to a psychological, personal bond.

Further Reading

Macklin, Eleanor. "Nontraditional Family Forms: A Decade of Research." *Journal of Marriage and Family* 42 (1980): 905-922.

O'Neill, Nena, and George O'Neill. *Open Marriage: A New Life Style for Couples.* New York: Avon Books, 1972.

Barbara E. Johnson

See also   Cohabitation; Feminism; *Hite Report, The*; Marriage and divorce; Sexual revolution; Swingers.

■ Operation PUSH

Identification   Civil rights organization
Date   Founded in 1971

Operation PUSH was started to increase economic opportunities for African Americans, but during the 1970's its mission grew into one that also included the goals of achieving international peace and social justice for all minorities and women.

After the assassination of Martin Luther King, Jr., in 1968 in Memphis, Tennessee, the Civil Rights movement began to lose its momentum without its leader. The focus of the movement was further compromised because the United States was focusing on the Vietnam War. In an effort to revive the movement, the Reverend Jesse Jackson founded Operation PUSH, which continued to do the work that King had left unfinished. PUSH stands for People United to Serve Humanity, and its primary concern is empowerment, peace, and social justice.

The organization's original purpose was to strengthen the economic security of African Americans and other disadvantaged individuals. PUSH organized boycotts for black consumers, worked to provide jobs for minorities, and supported black businesses. Operation PUSH also asked American companies to set up black distributorships and to advertise in black newspapers and magazines as a show of support for the businesses of African Americans.

Operation PUSH soon extended its purposes to national concerns, such as politics and education. In the late 1970's, Operation PUSH brought national attention to minorities within the educational system and to raising money for elementary education. In 1977, Jackson formed an offshoot of Operation PUSH known as PUSH for Excellence. At this time, forced busing of students to integrate schools was under way, and minority education was a contentious subject. During this time, an initiative to offer low-cost college educations to minorities was also in place. An abundance of financial aid was offered to

Black Panther leader Bobby Seale (left) confers with Operation PUSH founder Jesse Jackson at the National Black Political Convention in 1972. (AP/Wide World Photos)

people of color as well as other disadvantaged populations. Persons of color could attend college during the decade and pay very little for their education, and the efforts of Operation PUSH helped realize this goal.

Impact The efforts of Jackson and Operation PUSH had many positive effects on the lives of people of color during the 1970's, as well as other disadvantaged Americans. Jackson's personality gained national exposure for the organization and helped call attention to disparities within the United States.

Further Reading

Haskins, James. *Jesse Jackson: Civil Rights Activist.* Berkeley Heights, N.J.: Enslow, 2000.

Rainbow/PUSH Coalition. www.rainbowpush.org.

Starletta Barber Poindexter

See also Affirmative action; African Americans; Busing; Education in the United States; Racial discrimination.

■ Orr, Bobby

Identification Canadian hockey player
Born March 20, 1948; Parry Sound, Ontario, Canada

Perhaps the most powerful and graceful skater in the history of the National Hockey League (NHL), Orr played for the Boston Bruins from 1966 to 1976 and the Chicago Blackhawks from 1976 to 1978.

When *The Hockey News* celebrated its fiftieth anniversary in 1997, it polled hockey experts for their opinion regarding the fifty best hockey players of all time. Three names led the rest by a wide margin: Gordie Howe, Wayne Gretzsky, and Bobby Orr.

Drafted by the Boston Bruins at the mere age of fourteen, Orr fulfilled the team's expectations by leading the Bruins to Stanley Cup championships in 1970 and 1972, each time scoring the winning goal and being chosen the most valuable player (MVP) in the playoffs. He won the Rookie of the Year award his first year in Boston, finishing second as Best Defenseman, an award that he would win every following year until 1975. No defenseman before or since Orr had ever won a season-scoring championship, a feat that he achieved twice, in 1970 and 1975. He was the National Hockey League's MVP in 1970, 1971, and 1972.

Orr's superstardom gave him considerable economic clout. He became one of the first NHL players to obtain an agent, Alan Eagleson, to negotiate contracts on his behalf. Not surprisingly, Orr obtained the largest salary ever paid to a hockey player, which helped raise the salaries of underpaid rank-and-file players. Orr and Eagleson were instrumental in forming the National Hockey League Players Association (NHLPA), the first union of professional hockey players.

Orr's career was cut short by a series of knee injuries that ended his dominance in hockey after the 1975-1976 season. He played only twenty-six games for the Chicago Blackhawks before finally retiring in 1978. Unfortunately, Eagleson had used his position as Orr's agent and head of the NHLPA to defraud both Orr and the union (for which he eventually served jail time), leaving Orr practically bankrupt at the end of what should have been an extremely lucrative career.

Impact Orr had a major impact not only on how the game was played but on the business of professional hockey in North America as well. He revolutionized the game by transforming how defensemen played. Before Orr, defensemen stayed close to their goaltender and rarely pressed the attack in the offensive zone. Orr created a new model defenseman who transitioned quickly from defense to offense, often carrying the puck himself into the offensive zone. This opened up hockey, providing a faster, higher-scoring, and more entertaining game for fans.

Further Reading

Dryden, Steve. *The Hockey News Century of Hockey: A Season-by-Season Celebration.* Foreward by Bobby Orr. Toronto: McClelland & Stewart, 2001.

MacInnis, Craig. *Remembering Bobby Orr.* Toronto: Stoddart, 1999.

Christopher Berkeley

See also Hockey; LaFleur, Guy; Sports; Unions in Canada.

■ *Our Bodies, Ourselves*

Identification Book about women's health written by women
Author Boston Women's Health Collective
Date Published in 1973

Our Bodies, Ourselves *was a feminist initiative to give women greater understanding of their bodies and greater control over their health.*

The Boston Women's Health Collective was an organization of women founded explicitly to improve women's understanding of their bodies and, through education, to provide them with more informed access to health care. It developed from an informal meeting about women's health at a 1969 feminist conference. At the meeting, several participants expressed their dissatisfaction with the available medical services for women. Based on the number of stories that circulated at the conference, it became evident that there was a need for women to learn more about their bodies' functions, specifically with regard to reproductive and sexual health. However, the challenge was to devise an effective method for implementing this education.

Eventually, the activist group decided to create a course for women based on feminist principles, including a teaching method called collaborative learning. They compiled their ideas into a 1970 booklet that was called *Women and Their Bodies*. Based on the interest in their work, the group reorganized into the Boston Women's Health Collective in 1972 and updated their booklet into *Our Bodies, Ourselves*, which was published in 1973 and soon became a best-seller.

The first commercially published edition of *Our Bodies, Ourselves* was received with mixed reviews. Feminists and health workers saw the book as a wonderful resource for adolescent girls and adult women, both of whom desperately needed more information about their body functions. *Our Bodies, Ourselves* celebrated women's health and dispelled myths about menstruation, birth, and menopause, all of which traditionally had been presented as problems to be overcome rather than as uniquely female and life-enhancing traits. However, the publication was also highly controversial since it provided information about contentious topics, including birth control, lesbian sexuality, and masturbation. During the 1970's, some libraries that placed *Our Bodies, Ourselves* on their circulation shelves were the recipients of public protests from religious and conservative groups.

Impact *Our Bodies, Ourselves* demonstrated that women without medical training could educate themselves and others about women's health issues. The success of this publication and other activities by the collective contributed to the developing women's health movement of the decade. Moreover, the publication continued in subsequent decades to satisfy an educational need: Bookstores continued to stock updated editions, which eventually became available in several dozen foreign languages.

Further Reading

Cherry, Susan Spaeth. "Book on Women Creates Controversy for Libraries Nationwide." *American Libraries* 9, no. 1 (January, 1978): 21-22.

Morgen, Sandra. *Into Our Own Hands: The Women's Health Movement in the United States, 1969-1990.* Piscataway, N.J.: Rutgers University Press, 2002.

Norsigian, Judy, et al. "The Boston Women's Health Book Collective and *Our Bodies, Ourselves*: A Brief History and Reflection." *Journal of the American Medical Women's Association* 54, no. 1 (Winter, 1999): 35-39.

Susan J. Wurtzburg

See also Feminism; Health care in Canada; Health care in the United States; *Joy of Sex, The*; *Ms.* magazine; National Organization for Women (NOW); Sanitary napkins with adhesive strips; Self-help books; Sexual revolution; Women's rights.

P

■ Pacino, Al

Identification   American film and stage actor
Born   April 25, 1940; New York, New York

As the star of several of the decade's most successful films, Pacino became one of the era's most powerful new screen presences.

Al Pacino, a high-school dropout who worked at menial jobs while studying acting, had appeared in several Off-Broadway plays and won a Tony Award for playing a drug addict in *Does a Tiger Wear a Necktie?* (pr. 1969) when he was cast in his first important film role as another junkie in *The Panic in Needle Park* (1971). Though few saw this film, director Francis Ford Coppola was impressed enough to battle Paramount Studios executives for the right to cast Pacino in the pivotal role of Michael Corleone in *The Godfather* (1972). Paramount preferred a name actor such as Robert Redford for the part. With his portrayal of the reluctant Mafia boss, Pacino instantly became a major star. With *The Godfather, Part II* (1974), one of the rare sequels to match the quality of the original film, Pacino continued Michael Corleone's descent into the lies, corruption, and murder he had foresworn as a young man.

Pacino's penchant for sensitive, brooding, antiheroes can be seen in Sidney Lumet's *Serpico* (1973). Based on the true story of New York police officer Frank Serpico's efforts to expose corruption in the police department, the film offered Pacino another chance to play a smoldering loner. In *Dog Day Afternoon* (1975), another true story directed by Lumet, Pacino had his first truly flamboyant role as a manic, bisexual bank robber.

Pacino chose his roles carefully, not making many films and always looking for something different. As a result, some of his films were much less successful than his four hits, all of which earned him Academy Award nominations. He also was nominated for his role as a grandstanding trial lawyer in *And Justice for All* (1979), though some critics saw this role as evidence of Pacino's unfortunate tendency for overacting at times.

Pacino's acting talent is displayed in several classic film scenes, including the young Michael Corleone's nervous resolve to assassinate his father's enemies in *The Godfather*; Michael's realization that his brother Fredo has betrayed him in *The Godfather, Part II*; Michael's closing the door on his wife at the end of that film; and his bank robber in *Dog Day Afternoon* frantically shouting "Attica," a reference to a recent mishandling of a prison riot, to incite spectators to support him and not the police. Pacino became a master at conveying both subtle and extreme emotions.

In 1977, Pacino returned to the stage in David Rabe's antiwar play *The Basic Training of Pavlo Hummel* and won another Tony Award. He continued alternating between the theater and films thereafter.

Impact   Al Pacino continued the Actors Studio tradition of performers such as Marlon Brando and Paul Newman by combining sensitivity and diversity in a variety of roles and for striving for realism and depth in his performances.

Further Reading

Schoell, William. *Films of Al Pacino*. New York: Carol, 1995.

Yule, Andrew. *Life on the Wire: The Life and Art of Al Pacino*. New York: Donald I. Fine, 1991.

Michael Adams

See also   Academy Awards; Attica prison riot; Blockbusters; Brando, Marlon; De Niro, Robert; Film in the United States; *Godfather* films; Theater in the United States.

■ Palmer, Jim

Identification   American baseball player
Born   October 15, 1945; New York, New York

Palmer won more games than any other major league pitcher in the 1970's, leading the Baltimore Orioles to three

American League pennants and the World Series championship in 1970.

By 1969, Jim Palmer had recovered from serious arm injuries to emerge as a star on a baseball dynasty. With his trademark high fastball and slow curve, the right-handed pitcher was remarkably consistent through the decade. He led the American League in wins three times and earned run average (ERA) twice. Palmer won the Cy Young Award as best pitcher in the league in 1973, 1975, and 1976. During the decade, he was chosen for six American League All-Star teams and started in four of them. From 1970 to 1972, Palmer pitched eight scoreless innings against the National League's best players. His excellent fielding earned him four Gold Glove awards in the late 1970's.

Surrounded by excellent Oriole pitchers such as Dave McNally, Mike Cuellar, and Mike Flanagan, Palmer emerged as the most dominant. He led the Orioles to five Eastern Division championships and American League pennants in 1970, 1971, and 1979. Palmer's victory over the mighty Cincinnati Reds in the opening game of the 1970 World Series led the Orioles to their second-ever world championship. His election to baseball's Hall of Fame in 1990 is testimony to his career accomplishments.

In a decade when players gained more control over their careers and salaries, Palmer was known for his independence and his professionalism. His battles with manager Earl Weaver were legendary. Both were highly intelligent perfectionists driven to win. Weaver usually dismissed Palmer's complaints about physical ailments, which led to more public arguments and, ironically, to more Baltimore victories. Palmer's work ethic, however, was unquestioned. Weaver noted that between pitching assignments, Palmer sat on the bench intensely studying opposing pitchers and hitters. In the late 1970's, the six-foot-three-inch Palmer used his movie star good looks to advertise Jockey underwear, adding to his fame. Nevertheless, Palmer remained loyal to the Orioles, forgoing significant salary offers from wealthier clubs. His thoughtfulness and charm made him a popular figure across the nation.

Impact Baseball fans in the 1970's witnessed a changing game and the early chapters of labor turmoil. Jim Palmer was both a charismatic figure and a symbol of stability. He led a very good pitching staff and kept the Baltimore Orioles one of the premier teams throughout the decade.

Further Reading

Eisenberg, John. *From Thirty-third Street to Camden Yards: An Oral History of the Baltimore Orioles.* New York: McGraw Hill, 2001.

Palmer, Jim, and Jim Dale. *Together We Were Eleven Foot Nine.* Kansas City: Andrews and McMeel, 1996.

M. Philip Lucas

See also Baseball; Sports.

■ Panama Canal treaties

Identification Bilateral treaties between the United States and Panama
Date Went into effect on October 1, 1979

The pair of treaties provided a twenty-year timeline in which control of the Panama Canal would pass from the United States to Panama, and they ensured the permanent neutrality of the Canal Zone.

In 1903, the Hay-Bunau-Varilla Treaty gave the United States the right "in perpetuity" to construct and operate a canal in the newly created nation of Panama on the isthmus between Central and South America. The permanency of the treaty chafed Panamanian sensibilities, and reacquiring rights to the Canal Zone became the primary goal of Panamanian foreign policy in the following decades. Despite continual pressure, the United States refused to consider transferring control of the canal until a violent riot swept through the Canal Zone in 1964. After the riot, the Johnson administration agreed to discuss a new canal treaty, but a 1968 military coup in Panama delayed the negotiation process.

By 1971, General Omar Torrijos Herrera firmly controlled Panama, and he renewed pressure on the United States for a treaty. Initially, the Nixon administration ignored requests for negotiations begun during the Johnson years, but in 1973, Torrijos took the issue to the United Nations. In an attempt to avoid international disapproval, Secretary of State Henry Kissinger consented to talks with Panama, and in February, 1974, he and Panama's foreign minister, Juan Antonio Tack, agreed to a set of eight principles that would guide the negotiation process. These principles included the extension of Panamanian sovereignty over the Canal Zone, improved economic benefits for Panama, and the establishment of a fixed date for transfer of control of the canal from the United States to Panama. However, before the negotiations went very far, the Nixon administration collapsed under the weight of the Watergate scandal.

Congressional Opposition After Gerald R. Ford became president, treaty discussions resumed, but U.S. congressional opposition to the treaty slowed the process. Opponents claimed that the United States had paid for construction of the canal and that Panama lacked the political stability to ensure continuous operation. Republican senator Strom Thurmond led the resistance, which primarily consisted of conservative Republicans and southern Democrats. To demonstrate his and others' defiance, Thurmond obtained thirty-eight signatures on a resolution declaring that the United States had to retain permanent control of the Canal Zone. Treaties require a two-thirds vote in the Senate, so the opposition only needed thirty-four votes to de-

feat a treaty. The treaty seemed doomed before it was even drafted. Furthermore, discontent spilled over into the House of Representatives, which controlled the fiscal aspects of the negotiation process. In order to appease Congress, Kissinger declared that the United States needed to maintain a permanent right to defend the canal. The statement met with instant disapproval in Panama, and six hundred disgruntled students stoned the American embassy.

Congressional opposition and the demonstration in Panama caused the treaty negotiations to be an important issue in the 1976 presidential race. Ford shared many of Thurmond's views, but he and Kissinger also believed in the importance of meeting Panama at the negotiating table. As a result, Ford ran into trouble with several influential members of his own party. The conflict, combined with Ford's abnormal rise to the presidency once Nixon resigned, left him vulnerable in the 1976 primaries, and Ronald Reagan seized upon the canal issue as a means to challenge for the Republican presidential

U.S. president Jimmy Carter (left) shakes hands with Panama's head of government, General Omar Torrijos Herrera, on September 7, 1977, after they signed the Panama Canal treaties. (AP/Wide World Photos)

nomination. Reagan waged a fierce campaign and exploited the canal issue for his own personal benefit, but prominent Republican senator Barry Goldwater eventually sided with Ford and helped secure his nomination. Ford then faced Jimmy Carter in the 1976 campaign, during which the canal treaties remained an issue. However, Carter's views differed little from those of Ford, and the matter lacked the importance that it had in the Republican primary.

The Treaties Upon winning the election, Carter made finalization of the Panama Canal treaties his chief foreign policy goal. Building on the work of previous administrations, the State Department negotiated two treaties. The first, known as the Panama Canal Treaty, abrogated the 1903 treaty and provided for the return of the canal to Panama on December 31, 1999. In the intervening years, the treaty also compelled the United States to increase payments to Panama for the privilege of operating the canal. The second treaty, called the Neutrality Treaty, stated that the canal would always remain neutral in times of war. The Neutrality Treaty also gave the United States the permanent right to defend the canal. This point created discontent in Panama, and later discussion restricted the United States from interfering in Panama's domestic affairs. Diplomats completed negotiations by August, and on September 7, 1977, Carter and Torrijos met in Washington, D.C., to sign the treaties.

Panama quickly ratified the treaties by a national vote, but in the United States, they still faced substantial Senate opposition. Debates on the issue were fierce and lasted several months, but Carter made it his mission to ensure passage of the treaties. The president lobbied hard for them, and largely because of his efforts, they both barely passed with a 68-32 vote. After ratification, the treaties went into effect on October 1, 1979.

Impact The most obvious effect of the treaties on American life in the 1970's was their connection to politics and the 1976 presidential election. Opposition to negotiations with Panama catapulted Reagan into a position of national political importance, and President Carter's successful negotiations with Panama and the U.S. Congress provided him with an early victory that enhanced his administration. Though unpopular with many Panamanians, the treaties nonetheless improved U.S.-Panamanian relations by finally settling an issue that had soured affairs between the two nations for more than sixty years. Finally, both nations honored the treaty, and the United States peacefully returned the canal to Panama as planned on December 31, 1999.

Further Reading

Conniff, Michael L. *Panama and the United States: The Forced Alliance.* 2d ed. Athens: University of Georgia Press, 2001. A detailed overview of the role of the canal in the history of U.S.-Panamanian relations.

Kaufman, Burton I. *The Presidency of James Earl Carter, Jr.* Lawrence: University Press of Kansas, 1993. This assessment of the Carter presidency cites the Panama Canal treaties as one of his greatest achievements.

LaFeber, Walter. *The Panama Canal: The Crisis in Historical Perspective.* Rev. ed. New York: Oxford University Press, 1990. This concise study discusses the political debates over the canal treaties in the 1970's from the American and Panamanian perspectives. Especially good for providing historical context.

John K. Franklin

See also Carter, Jimmy; Conservatism in U.S. politics; Congress, U.S.; Elections in the United States, 1976; Foreign policy of the United States; Ford, Gerald R.; Kissinger, Henry; Latin America; Reagan, Ronald.

■ Paris Peace Accords

Identification Peace treaty ending U.S. military involvement in the Vietnam War

Date Signed on January 27, 1973

The treaty between the United States, the Republic of Vietnam (South Vietnam), the Democratic Republic of Vietnam (North Vietnam), and the Provisional Revolutionary Government of Vietnam (the Viet Cong) provided for a cease-fire, withdrawal of the United States troops within sixty days, return of prisoners of war (POWs), an account of soldiers missing in action (MIAs), and legal recognition of the Republic of Vietnam. It allowed North Vietnamese troops to remain in South Vietnam and provided an end to the war on a compromise basis.

After Richard M. Nixon's inauguration in January, 1969, secret negotiations between National Security Adviser Henry Kissinger for the United States and Le Duc Tho for North Vietnam began in Paris. They

The Paris Peace Accords ending the Vietnam War were negotiated by North Vietnam delegate Le Duc Tho (left) and U.S. National Security Adviser Henry Kissinger. (AP/Wide World Photos)

proceeded tortuously as the North Vietnamese hoped that American public opinion would force the Nixon administration to make concessions favorable to the North Vietnamese and the Viet Cong.

An agreement very similar to the final one was almost finalized in October, 1972, but President Nguyen Van Thieu of South Vietnam raised objections, and Nixon sought to convince Thieu to accept it; the North Vietnamese initially wanted the agreement signed by October 31, 1972, in order to secure what they perceived as advantages. However, the North Vietnamese suggested proposed changes in language that referred to a "coalition" government in South Vietnam. Although Kissinger made his famous statement that "peace is at hand" on October 26, 1972, the agreement was not signed and additional talks in November and December, 1972, were unsuccessful as well. To bring the North Vietnamese back to the negotiations, Nixon ordered massive bombing of North Vietnam between December 18

and 29, 1972. When talks resumed on January 8, 1973, Kissinger and Le quickly reached agreement by January 13, 1973; Nixon assented two days later. Although Thieu had reservations, he acquiesced. The arrangement was ratified on January 23, 1973, and it was formally signed and took effect on four days later.

The Paris Peace Accords consisted of nine chapters, twenty-three articles, and three protocols signed subsequent to the main agreement. In addition to the aforementioned provisions, the treaty created the Joint Military Commission and the International Commission on Control and Supervision—formed by Poland, Hungary, Canada, and Indonesia—to supervise the cease-fire and troop withdrawal. In order to monitor elections in South Vietnam, a National Council of National Reconciliation and Concord was established; the 1954 Geneva Convention was reaffirmed with regard to the Demilitarized Zone (DMZ) as a provisional boundary between North and South Vietnam, which were to undertake talks on peaceful reunification.

Impact Despite persistent violations of the treaty by North Vietnam, the United States did not intervene both because Congress had cut off funding to do so and because of the Watergate scandal. Tremendous controversy developed over whether North Vietnam had made a complete accounting of POWs and MIAs. The final drama played out on April 30, 1975, when the North Vietnamese completed their successful conquest of South Vietnam, reunifying the country as a communist dictatorship.

Further Reading

Davidson, Phillip B. *Vietnam at War: The History, 1946-1975.* New York: Oxford University Press, 1991.

Kimball, Jeffrey. *Nixon's Vietnam War.* Lawrence: University Press of Kansas, 1998.

Mark C. Herman

See also Antiwar demonstrations; Foreign policy of the United States; Kissinger, Henry; Nixon, Richard M.; Nobel Prizes; POWs and MIAs; Vietnam War.

■ *Partridge Family, The*

Identification　Television family series
Date　Aired from 1970 to 1974

This series depicted a single mother raising five children in California, driving a multicolored school bus, performing in concerts with her children, and helping her children work through a variety of early adolescent experiences.

Popular with young viewers and successful in ratings and modeled after the popular 1960's family singing group the Cowsills, *The Partridge Family* appealed to young adults with its use of music and the depiction of adolescent experiences. The show's members were widowed mother Shirley (played by Shirley Jones); sons Keith (David Cassidy), Danny (Danny Bonaduce), and Chris (first Jeremy Gelbwaks, later Brian Forster); and daughters Laurie (Susan Dey) and Tracy (Suzanne Crough). David Madden played the family's manager and agent, Reuben Kincaid.

Each week, a family member would face some sort of social dilemma that was eventually resolved, and the family would sing a song that related to the experience. Only two actors in the series, Jones and her real-life stepson Cassidy, actually sang the songs; the other actors lip-synched to background music performed by professional singers. Danny played guitar, Chris played drums, Laurie played keyboard, and Tracy played the tambourine.

Although *The Partridge Family* was a fictional singing group, the show's producers used creative marketing to promote the show before it actually aired. Some of the songs were released by the studio early and played on teen radio stations in order to generate interest in the show. The most popular songs, such as "I Think I Love You" and "I Woke Up in Love This Morning," hit the *Billboard* charts and sold millions of records.

The Partridge Family was originally broadcast on the American Broadcasting Company (ABC) network on Friday evenings after the popular *The Brady Bunch* series. It was often compared to *The Brady Bunch* show especially during the later seasons when the Brady children formed their own singing group.

Impact　The early marketing success of the series helped the series become a huge hit with young viewers. Many ancillary products, including books, toys, and lunch boxes, were marketed, and they sold well. Moreover, David Cassidy became an idol to millions of teenage fans worldwide. He performed in live concerts on many weekends and between filming of the series. After four years of juggling acting and concerts, Cassidy decided to focus his talents on a solo singing career and declined to do a fifth season.

After ninety-six episodes, the series was canceled. A cartoon sequel titled *The Partridge Family, 2200 A.D.* aired on Saturday mornings in 1974-1975 and included the voices of some of the original cast members. In this spin-off, the Partridge Family traveled in outer space to perform concerts.

Further Reading

Cassidy, David. *C'mon Get Happy.* New York: Warner Books, 1994.

Green, Joey. *The Partridge Family Album: The Official Get Happy Guide to America's Television Family.* New York: HarperCollins, 1994.

Noreen A. Grice

See also　*Brady Bunch, The*; Children's television; Music; Television in the United States.

The Partridge Family proved so popular with children that merchandizing followed, such as this lunchbox with a picture of the bus from the television series. (Hulton Archive/Getty Images)

■ Passages

Identification Best-selling nonfiction book
Author Gail Sheehy (1937-   )
Date Published in 1976

At 933 pages, Passages *was a lengthy but very popular foray into psychological journalism that identified, defined, and described the major phases and critical turning points in adult life in American culture.*

Turning thirty-nine in 1976, journalist Gail Sheehy was experiencing her own midlife crisis. Because she felt her situation mirrored that of many of her own generation entering "middlescence" during the 1970's, she decided to study the crisis of "coming of age" in American culture. She had studied psychological literature by scholars as varied as Carl Gustav Jung, Sigmund Freud, Carl Rogers, and Erik Erikson, and for her book, *Passages: Predictable Crises of Adult Life*, Sheehy interviewed 115 educated, middle-class Americans between the ages of eighteen and fifty-five.

Sheehy's intention was to do for adulthood what other scholars had done for childhood: provide a case-study format about stages or "times of transition" encountered in adult life. First, she identified the "pulling up roots" stage, which occurs around the age of eighteen when one leaves home to find one's place in the broader society through higher education, the military, or employment. Next came the "trying twenties," when one experiments with the various roles available in order to discern how they fit in to one's "life plan." The "catch 30" time follows, defined as the end of adolescence when one is filled with a "yearning for change" and may ask whether life holds more possibilities. Sheehy defined the fourth stage as "rooting and extending," which occurs during the early thirties and serves as a time of trying to feel settled in marriage, family, faith, community, and career. The "deadline decade" of the mid-thirties follows, when one might feel that time is running out, options are decreasing, and life feels more fixed than fluid. Sheehy argues that if "re-evaluation" is to occur, this is the stage when it ought to happen. Finally, the last stage, during the mid-forties, finds an individual in a period of renewal or resignation, when one comes to terms with the fact that one's life is now largely determined and lived.

Impact Gail Sheehy's *Passages*, an essay on maturation in the United States, quickly had the appeal of similar self-help books by authors such as Norman Vincent Peale and Dale Carnegie. Sheehy captured the mood of the mid-1970's, when concern for the self was central and self-fulfillment was an important goal for millions. While *Passages* proved to be Sheehy's landmark best-seller, its sequel, *Pathfinders: Overcoming the Crises of Adult Life and Finding Your Own Path to Well-Being* (1981) also did well. The far-reaching importance of *Passages* was evident in a 1991 survey by the Book of the Month Club that placed *Passages* ninth in a list of the ten most-influential books having an impact on people's self-understanding.

Further Reading
"Gail Sheehy." In *Current Biography Yearbook, 1993*, edited by Judith Graham. New York: H. W. Wilson, 1993.

Sheehy, Gail. *Passages: Predictable Crises of Adult Life.* New York: E. P. Dutton, 1976.

_____. *Pathfinders: Overcoming the Crises of Adult Life and Finding Your Own Path to Well-Being.* New York: William Morrow, 1981.

C. George Fry

See also Book publishing; *Culture of Narcissism, The*; Demographics of the United States; Human potential movement; *I'm OK, You're OK*; Journalism in the United States; Literature in the United States; Psychology; Self-help books.

■ Patton

Identification Motion picture
Director Franklin J. Schaffner (1920-1989)
Date Released in 1970

This film about World War II American war hero General George S. Patton won eight Academy Awards, including Best Picture.

Many historians and film critics praised the historical and political accuracy, attention to detail, and battle scenes of *Patton*. Charismatic and flamboyant, the real General Patton believed he was a reincarnated warrior with multiple past lives. His brilliance, rebellious nature, self-confidence, and volatile personality were so well represented by American actor George C. Scott that Scott won the Academy Award for Best Actor. The film's other Academy Awards included Best Screenplay, Best Director, Best Art Direction, Best Sound, and Best Film Editing.

Patton was based on the autobiography of General Omar N. Bradley, who was both one of Patton's subordinates and one of his superior officers during World War II. General Bradley was still alive during the film's production and provided in-person advice for the planning, writing, and actual scene shooting; American actor Karl Malden played his role.

Much of the filming was done in Spain, and the Spanish army and air force provided soldiers and military equipment, including American-built 1950's- and 1960's-era battle tanks. Even with the liberal use of later-built military equipment, the detailed accuracy of the soldiers, equipment, and battle scenes was considered excellent by critics. Other filming locations included Great Britain, Morocco, and Greece.

One unique aspect that set the film apart from other films was its ability to withstand the scrutiny of war, film, and political critics alike. It provided drama; large-scale, re-created battle scenes; historical accuracy; detailed production locations; and inspirational acting. Many earlier World War II films could not withstand fair criticism from historians and veterans.

Scott was a gifted actor, and many film experts believe that his lead role as Patton was the highlight of his career. He brilliantly researched and immersed himself into the role and possessed additional realistic traits similar to those of Patton, such as physical appearance, mannerisms, and speech pattern.

Critics also noted that *Patton* redefined the American war film during the Vietnam War—a time when war films were considered unmarketable. Some political historians believe that U.S. president Richard M. Nixon was influenced by the motion picture to the extent that it affected his Vietnam War decisions and policies.

Impact The film *Patton* proved to the film industry that war films could be made that are historically accurate, entertaining, and financially successful at the box office. Many people were educated about the history of World War II and the personal sacrifice made by soldiers during the war. The film stimulated study of George S. Patton's aggressive leadership style and resulting battlefield success.

Further Reading

Bradley, Omar Nelson. *A General's Life: An Autobiography.* New York: Simon & Schuster, 1983.

D'Este, Carlo. *Patton: Genius for War.* New York: HarperCollins, 1995.

Hirshon, Stanley P. *General Patton: A Soldier's Life.* New York: HarperCollins, 2002.

Patton, George S. *War As I Knew It.* New York: Houghton Mifflin, 1975.

Alan P. Peterson

See also Academy Awards; Film in the United States.

■ Payton, Walter

Identification African American football player
Born July 25, 1954; Columbia, Mississippi
Died November 1, 1999; Barrington, Illinois

During the 1970's and 1980's, Payton was considered one of the premier running backs in the National Football League (NFL). He spent his entire thirteen-year football career playing for the Chicago Bears.

The name "Walter Payton" and jersey number 34 are synonymous with the Chicago Bears' professional football team. The African American Payton began playing high school football for a segregated high school, John T. Jefferson in Columbia, Mississippi. As a result of high school integration, he played for Columbia High School. He began his stellar football career as a student-athlete while attending Jackson State University. During his four-year tenure on the college football team, Payton earned All-American status and rushed for 3,563 yards. His additional college football achievements included leading scorer (160 points) and National Collegiate Athletic Association (NCAA) all-time scorer (464 points) in 1973. His unique running style, coordination, speed, power, quickness, balance, and agility led to the nickname "Sweetness."

The Chicago Bears recognized Payton's college football prowess and drafted him in the first round in 1975. His professional football career, in which he played 190 games, can be described as spectacular. Payton broke O. J. Simpson's single-game rushing record (275 yards) and, in 1989, passed Jim Brown's all-time rushing record. Payton's remarkable rushing achievements also included most all-purpose running yards (21,802), most rushing yards (16,726), and 110 touchdowns. In addition to his outstanding

Walter Payton. (AP/Wide World Photos)

rushing records, Payton also demonstrated an ability to grab passes coming out of the backfield, catching a total of 492 passes and making 15 touchdowns.

Impact Walter Payton was one of the NFL's most gifted and durable running backs. His numerous college and professional football awards included National Football Conference (NFC) Player of the Year in 1976 and 1977, and NFL Player of the Year in 1977 and 1985. In recognition of his outstanding football talent, he was inducted into the Professional Football Hall of Fame in 1993.

Throughout his professional career, Payton remained an excellent role model, public servant, father, and husband. He retired from the NFL in 1987, became an Indy car owner, and supported youth programs. Payton died at the age of forty-five as a result of liver disease.

Further Reading
Payton, Walter, and Don Yaeger, eds. *The Autobiography of Walter Payton.* New York: Villard Books, 2000.

Wiggins, David K., ed. "Payton, Walter." In *African Americans in Sports.* Vol. 2. Armonk, N.Y.: Sharpe Reference, 2004.

Dana D. Brooks

See also African Americans; Football; *Monday Night Football*; Simpson, O. J.; Sports.

■ PCB ban

Definition Regulations concerning the use of polychlorinated biphenyls (PCBs)
Date Issued on April 19, 1979

The PCB ban was a landmark event in the response to, and recognition of, human health risk and ecosystem damage resulting from a widespread family of manufactured chemicals that persist in the environment.

Marking a long struggle by environmentalists and consumer activists, the Toxic Substances Control Act was enacted on October 11, 1976, in order to regulate toxic chemicals in the environment. A major consequence of this act was to ban the manufacture of a group of chemicals known as PCBs. The U.S. Environmental Protection Agency (EPA) was charged by the act with developing a set of regulations governing the ban, use, and disposal of PCBs. On April 19, 1979, the EPA issued a set of final rules banning further manufacturing of all PCBs and introducing a phased elimination of almost every PCB use.

PCBs, because of their stability, insulating qualities, and resistance to fire, were widely used as insulating fluids in electrical equipment and were found in most power plants, factories, transit systems, elevators and mining equipment, hydraulic and heat transfer systems, and in almost all large buildings. A host of products, such as hydraulic fluid, pumps, compressors, and pigments, contained PCBs. Oil-filled capacitors laden with PCBs were used in a variety of "white goods" such as air conditioners, fluorescent light ballasts, photocopiers, and other electronic gear. Accordingly, an outright ban was deemed to be too costly for industry and other electrical equipment users. The United States' sole producer of PCBs, Monsanto, had already responded to mounting environmental concern and public pressure by voluntarily ceasing production in 1977, but thousands of tons of PCBs remained in existing equipment.

Among the risks of exposure to PCBs are increased cancers and reproductive abnormalities in various species. Estrogen-like synthetic chemicals such as PCBs have been found to cause hermaphroditic development in fish and birds and to reduce sperm count in human males. Moreover, PCBs are soluble in fat, not water, and therefore resist environmental degradation, accumulating in organic tissues and becoming biologically amplified in food chains and webs. Many thousands of tons of PCBs were already in the environment by this decade, rapidly accumulating in bottom sediments of lakes and other surface waters.

Impact   The PCB ban responded to public environmental awareness and helped spur further research into the dangers of PCBs. Among the requirements of the new EPA regulations was the stipulation that, at the end of its life span, electrical equipment had to be replaced with other gear that did not use PCBs. Moreover, since PCB-contaminated waste oil had been used as a dust control agent on roads, that use also ceased immediately with the regulations, as did a number of other risky activities associated with PCBs.

Further Reading

Crawford, Ronald L., and Don L. Crawford, eds. *Bioremediation: Principles and Application.* New York: Cambridge University Press, 1996.

Hutzinger, Otto, S. Safe, and V. Zitko. *The Chemistry of PCBs.* Boca Raton, Fla.: CRC Press, 1974.

Wagner, Travis P. *The Complete Guide to the Hazardous Waste Regulations.* 3d ed. New York: John Wiley & Sons, 1999.

Robert M. Sanford

See also   Chlorofluorocarbon ban; DDT ban; Environmental movement; Environmental Protection Agency (EPA); Leaded gasoline ban; Water pollution.

■ Pelé

Identification   Brazilian soccer player
Born   October 23, 1940; Três Corações, Minas Gerais, Brazil

Widely acknowledged as the finest athlete player ever to play soccer, Pelé enjoyed a meteoric career in Brazil and helped popularize the game in North America during the 1970's.

Born Edson Arantes do Nascimento in a remote Brazilian village, Pelé developed exceptional soccer skills as a boy and began playing professionally when he was a teenager. In 1958, at the age of seventeen, he created an international sensation by scoring six goals while leading Brazil to the World Cup championship in Sweden. An injury kept him out of the 1962 finals—which Brazil again won—but he returned to lead Brazil to a third World Cup title in 1970.

Pelé retired from international competition in 1971 and from his Brazilian club team in 1974. By then, he held the world record for total goals scored and had been, for a brief period, the world's highest-paid team athlete. Renowned for his stylish skills, brilliant playmaking, and devotion to team play, Pelé also possessed a radiant smile and personality that made him, at that moment, one of the world's most famous and beloved people.

After retiring, Pelé soon experienced financial setbacks that drove him back to the field. In 1975, he announced his wish to help develop soccer in North America, where the game had long struggled to find fans, and he signed a multimillion-dollar, three-year contract with the New York Cosmos of the North American Soccer League (NASL). His impact on North American soccer was dramatic. During his first season, he helped lead the Cosmos to the top of their division and was named the league's most valuable player. He dramatically boosted attendance figures wherever he played. In New York, average attendance at Cosmos games rose above forty thousand—an unprecedented figure for American soccer attendance. Pelé's presence in the NASL also helped to attract to the league other international soccer stars, including Germany's Franz Beckenbauer, who joined Pelé on the Cosmos.

Pelé remained with the Cosmos through two and one-half seasons. On October 1, 1977, he played his final game in New York's Giants Stadium, where the Cosmos faced his former Brazilian club, FC Santos, in an exhibition match. Pelé played the first half for the Cosmos and the second half for Santos. The attention that unusual game drew was further proof of Pelé's popularity: 77,200 people, including 650 journalists, attended the game, which was broadcast in thirty-eight nations.

After retiring for good from playing, Pelé worked for several years as a broadcaster in the United States and continued to promote North American soccer. In 1981, he played a Trindadian prisoner of war in Germany in Sylvester Stallone's World War II film *Victory*, in which Allied prisoners play a soccer game against German soldiers.

Impact The impact that Pelé had on North American soccer during the 1970's was great. His radiant personality and reputation as the world's finest player drew unprecedented attention to the sport. After he retired from the scene, however, soccer fell back into the doldrums, and the NASL itself folded in 1985. Nevertheless, Pelé is credited with helping to bring the World Cup competition to the United States in 1994. Three years later, he became minister of sports in Brazil.

Further Reading

Harris, Harry. *Pelé: His Life and Times.* New York: Parkwest, 2002.

Machin, Noel. *Pelé: King of Soccer.* New York: Longman, 1984.

Pelé, with Robert L. Fish. *My Life and the Beautiful Game: The Autobiography of Pelé.* Garden City, N.Y.: Doubleday, 1977.

R. Kent Rasmussen

See also Soccer; Sports.

■ Peltier, Leonard

Identification Ojibwa-Sioux activist and political prisoner

Born September 12, 1944; Grand Forks, North Dakota

The controversial conviction of Peltier in 1977 of aiding and abetting in the deaths of two Federal Bureau of Investigation (FBI) agents on the Pine Ridge Indian Reservation in South Dakota was decried as a gross injustice by several national and international groups and individuals.

Leonard Peltier became an American Indian activist in the 1960's and 1970's, following decades of intense Native American protests regarding mistreatment of Native Americans and violations of federal Indian policies and treaties. He joined the American Indian Movement (AIM) and participated in several demonstrations, including the Trail of Broken Treaties march on Washington, D.C., in November, 1972. More than five hundred demonstrators participated, and they presented a twenty-point document to federal officials that demanded a redress of grievances and a recognition of Indian rights. The Bureau of Indian Affairs (BIA) building was then occupied by Indian protesters for several days. Federal officials agreed to study the twenty demands and al-located transportation funds to help the protesters return to their homes.

Because of AIM's militant activities, the Nixon administration, using the justification of threats to national security, increased FBI involvement, through its Counterintelligence Program (COINTELPRO), against AIM and its leaders. During the early 1970's, accusations against this program included its providing false evidence, bringing phony charges against people, and initiating physical confrontations. COINTELPRO activities were especially questionable on the Pine Ridge Indian Reservation, where Peltier was living.

Pine Ridge was a powder keg ready to explode because of charges by AIM and Indians living on the reservation of corruption and graft against the tribal government and its leadership. On June 26, 1975, two FBI agents were killed outside a home on the reservation. According to the FBI, the agents were issuing an arrest warrant for an occupant in the house when gunfire commenced. Others claim, however, that the agents wanted a confrontation with AIM. Although numerous FBI agents, BIA police, and other law enforcement personnel quickly arrived at the scene, those involved in the incident successfully eluded them.

The FBI launched a massive manhunt, and four Indians were finally indicted for the murder of the two agents. One was released because of weak evidence, and two were acquitted by a jury verdict of self-defense in 1976. Peltier was the only one of the four men found guilty of aiding and abetting in the deaths of the FBI agents. He was sentenced to two consecutive life terms in June, 1977.

Much of the evidence presented at his trial was circumstantial. In addition, Peltier and his supporters claim that the FBI manufactured and suppressed evidence. Although additional evidence was discovered following his conviction that Peltier supporters claim should exonerate him, Peltier remained incarcerated and was denied a new trial or parole on several occasions.

Impact To many groups and individuals worldwide, Leonard Peltier became a symbol of injustice toward minority people by a powerful government bent on punishing him for a crime based on questionable evidence. Peltier continued to maintain his innocence in the crime in later years and claimed he was a victim of racial discrimination.

Further Reading

Hentoff, Nicholas. "The Peltier Case." *The Nation* 240 (June 22, 1985): 756.

Melmer, David. "Peltier Lawyers Ask for FBI Probe." *Indian Country Today*, April 7, 2004, A1, A3.

Messerschmidt, Jim. *The Trial of Leonard Peltier*. Boston: South End Press, 1989.

Raymond Wilson

See also American Indian Movement (AIM); Federal Bureau of Investigation (FBI); Native Americans; Racial discrimination; Trail of Broken Treaties; Wounded Knee occupation.

■ Pentagon Papers

Identification Secret, multivolume set that detailed American involvement in Vietnam

Date Published in 1971

The Pentagon Papers demonstrated decades-long dedication within the executive branch to the "domino theory" of resistance to communism, as well as a perception of Indochina as a vital element in U.S. security. Once published, they fueled the antiwar movement and contributed to growing unease about the power of the executive branch.

Commissioned by Secretary of Defense Robert S. McNamara in 1967, the seven-thousand-page *History of U.S. Decision-Making Process on Vietnam, 1945-1968*, better known as the Pentagon Papers, was completed in 1969. A mere fifteen copies were distributed: They went to those with very high security clearances. The Pentagon Papers consist of forty-seven volumes, of which three thousand pages are narrative history and analysis, written through the joint efforts of thirty-six civilian and military authors. In addition, four thousand pages of actual documents are appended, originating in the Office of the Secretary of Defense and the State Department, with some additional materials from the Central Intelligence Agency (CIA). The document's authors did not have access to White House files and were instructed not to do interviews.

The Pentagon Papers revealed that the Truman, Eisenhower, Kennedy, and Johnson administrations all chose the path of misrepresenting facts concerning U.S. presence in Vietnam both to the American public and to Congress. For example, the Johnson administration in 1964 rushed Congress into voting to increase the war effort by withholding full information about what was represented as an "unpro-

voked" attack on American vessels. The executive branch did not act upon reports from the U.S. intelligence community that indicated the unlikelihood of eventual American military or political success.

Papers Are Leaked On June 13, 1971, Daniel Ellsberg, one of the document's thirty-six authors, leaked photocopied excerpts from the Pentagon Papers to *The New York Times*. Ellsberg, a former Marine, was an employee of both the Pentagon and the RAND Corporation. In a 1998 interview made under the auspices of the Institute of International Studies at the University of California, he explained his decision to leak the document as being the result of reading it in its entirety for the first time in 1969. This complete overview made him deeply aware of how past administrations had been given information and advice indicating that the United States should get out of the war and yet ignored them. Ellsberg concluded that a new form of pressure must be applied to the executive branch. With help from a former RAND analyst named Tony Russo, Ellsberg spent months attempting unsuccessfully to get antiwar members of Congress, including William Fulbright and George McGovern, to make public the illegal photocopies that he offered to them. Only after this attempt failed did he send additional photocopies to the newspapers.

After publication of three initial articles in a projected series based on the documents, the U.S. Justice Department obtained a temporary restraining order against the newspaper from the Federal Court for the Southern District of New York. The government argued that further publication would threaten the national security. At a subsequent point in the legal battles surrounding publication of the documents, the government argued further that publication would endanger national security because it would diminish the constitutional power of the president over the conduct of foreign affairs and his authority as commander in chief.

When publication began, Ellsberg went underground in order to avoid arrest for what the U.S. Espionage Act defines as a criminal offense. On June 18, 1971, *The Washington Post* also published portions of the document. A government attempt to get another injunction to prevent further publication by that newspaper failed. As legal battles continued, an additional fifteen U.S. newspapers published materials based on the documents. On June 29, Senator

Katharine Graham, the publisher of The Washington Post, *and Ben Bradlee, the newspaper's editor, celebrate a legal victory in their efforts to publish the Pentagon Papers.* (AP/Wide World Photos)

Mike Gavel of Alaska succeeded in getting the document into the public record.

Supreme Court Involvement   On June 25, the U.S. Supreme Court took up *The New York Times* and *The Washington Post* cases together. On June 30, 1971, in *New York Times Co. v. United States,* the Court voted 6-3 to remove all prior restraints on free expression made in lower courts. The Court noted that "security" is an overly broad and vague term, which cannot cancel out such a fundamental law as the First Amendment. The two newspapers resumed publication.

In January, 1973, the Ellsberg-Russo trial began. The disclosure of illegal White House wiretaps led to the dismissal of the charges against them. In 1973, U.S. involvement in the war in Vietnam officially ended.

Impact   Senator Gavel described the significance of the publication of the Pentagon Papers and the legal

battles that ensued as being important, effective responses to the growing power of the executive branch of government, which seemed to have growing and sophisticated technologies and specialists to use in hiding state secrets. The Pentagon Papers also contributed additional fuel to an already intense debate about the war. The break-in to Ellsberg's psychiatrist's office, during a White House-sponsored effort to personally discredit him, helped feed the movement leading to Richard M. Nixon's removal from the presidency in 1974.

Further Reading

Ellsberg, Daniel. *Secrets: A Memoir of Vietnam and the Pentagon Papers.* New York: Viking, 2002. Ellsberg tells the story of his decision to release the Pentagon Papers and the aftermath.

Kimball, Jeffrey. *The Vietnam War Files: Uncovering the Secret History of Nixon-Era Strategy.* Lawrence: University Press of Kansas, 2004. Calls on more than 140 official print documents and taped White

House conversations to elucidate Nixon-era strategy in Vietnam.

The Pentagon Papers: The Defense Department History of United States Decisionmaking on Vietnam. 5 vols. Boston: Beacon Press, 1971-1972. A noncopyright version of the complete document, based on the official record of the U.S. Senate Subcommittee on Public Buildings and Grounds.

Barbara Roos

See also   Foreign policy of the United States; Journalism in the United States; McGovern, George; Nixon's resignation and pardon; Supreme Court decisions; Vietnam War.

■ Pet rocks

Definition   Cultural fad
Date   Introduced in 1975

The pet rock instantly became a fad and one of the most sought-after items of 1975 by offering the consumer a "quiet, well-behaved" companion that required no care, no vet bills, and asked nothing of its owner.

Part of the appeal of pet rocks, a quintessential 1970's fad, was the packaging. (Hulton Archive/Getty Images)

In 1975, thirty-eight-year-old Gary Dahl accidentally created one of the largest crazes of the 1970's while in a bar with friends in Los Gatos, California. The out-of-work freelance advertising man came up with the idea for the pet rock while listening to his friends complain of the expense and responsibility of pet ownership. Dahl described his idea of a perfect pet: one that required nothing from its owner, did not make a mess, cost nothing to maintain, and was loyal and obedient. Dahl later presented each of his friends with a smooth beach rock to jokingly illustrate this perfect pet.

Met with his friends' unexpected enthusiasm and financial backing, Dahl imported more than three tons of Mexican beach stones and marketed the pet rock, ranging in price from $3.89 to $5.00 in top department stores and gift boutiques across the country. After being on the market for only one month before Christmas, the pet rock immediately became one of the hottest-selling holiday items in December, 1975, selling more than fifteen thousand per week. The pet rock came in its own carrying case, complete with airholes and straw padding. Also included was an owner's manual for the "care and training of your pet rock." The manual described how to train the pet rock to do tricks such as playing dead, rolling over, and tumbling down hills. It also explained how pet rocks could be trained to be "guard rocks," since they could easily be concealed in one's pocket to be used against an attacker.

Like all fads, the pet rock craze was short-lived. By 1977, there were many variations of decorated and personalized pet rocks, along with accessories such as pet rock food (a chunk of rock salt) and pet rock shampoo (ordinary detergent). However, with more than five million pet rocks sold, interest began to dwindle. With this decline in popularity, the country saw a rise in pet rock burials and cemeteries. These last rite ceremonies were generally fund-raisers or publicity stunts for businesses.

Impact   The pet rock was a quintessential 1970's craze that met all fad criteria: It was useless, desirable, short-lived, and above all, profitable—Dahl received ninety five cents for every rock sold. While many critics were appalled by its success, some argued that after the Vietnam War, Watergate, and a decade of social unrest, the country needed the lightness and humor that the pet rock offered.

Further Reading

Johnson, Richard A. *American Fads.* New York: Beech Tree Books, 1985.

Panati, Charles. *Panati's Parade of Fads, Follies, and Manias.* New York: HarperPerennial, 1991.

Sann, Paul. *American Panorama.* New York: Crown, 1980.

Sara Vidar

See also   Fads; Lava lamps; Mood rings; Toys and games.

■ Photography

Definition   Artistic, journalistic, and commercial use of photos

The 1970's saw photography increasingly become an American medium, and the decade is considered by many as the golden age of American photography. The movement pervaded pop culture, print media, journalism, and museums by departing from its traditional relationships with advertising, photojournalism, and documentation in provocative new ways.

In the decades immediately after World War II, the market for picture magazines declined, and television news diminished the need for most documentary or photojournalistic images. As these markets decreased, so did the dominance of spontaneous-witness photographers. Where before images used for commercial, documentary, or artistic purposes were filled with a sense of photojournalism, postwar photography chose to see itself as a blossoming art form.

By the mid-1970's, photography had become a major component of critical contemporary art practices, assimilated and absorbed into the mainstream art world, with many nonphotographer artists integrating photographic media into their works. Many mixed-medium artists began to explore cameras in exciting new ways to extend and test traditional mediums such as painting and printmaking. Documentary and photojournalism began to be blended into a hybrid photographic style that was served as art

more than spontaneous-witness images. Fashion and portraiture photography began to adopt the techniques and styles from art photography, and many art photographers looked to fashion and photojournalism for methods of making their own social commentary.

Use in Art   During the 1970's, advertising photography began to take on themes of social commentary by using the techniques of documentary photography. By the middle of the decade, museums and art collectors began to look at photographs with the seriousness once reserved for paintings, printmaking, and drawing. The era saw the most rapid growth of photographic acquisitions by museums.

At the same time, photography became pivotal in the postmodern art movement. Postmodernists believed that originality and personal expression were invalid artistic goals in a world filled with available reproductions. They felt all visual images were merely copies, and since photography was the source of most reproductions, postmodernism hailed photography as the most influential and important medium of contemporary art.

Another major movement during this time was a shift in landscape imaging, called the New Topographics. Previous landscape photographers had focused primarily on producing dramatic, beautiful images of the natural world. New Topographic photographers emphasized the tension between the traditional beauty of natural lands and human-induced alterations to the landscape.

Use in Print Media   Though the decade of the 1970's saw the demise of picture magazines such as *Look* and *Life*, other print magazines emphasizing social commentary, lifestyles, and fashion began to use photographic images as a means to propel stories. Women's specialty and lifestyle magazines began to hire renowned photographers to shoot fashion and interview illustrations. The rock-and-roll publication *Rolling Stone* became a training ground for some of the finest portrait and documentary photographers of the later twentieth century.

One of the most prominent advances in photography during the 1970's was the rise of the photographic book. Many photographers began to work on series of images from their life experiences, trips, and observations. The scope of an image series usually was dramatized by the photographer's perspective or involvement with the subject matter. In these types of books, the photographer, rather than an editor, became the one to make decisions over presentation order. Moreover, many of the photographers began to write their own commentary to contextualize their photographs, another sea change in publication decision making.

Photography for the Masses After World War II, postwar prosperity fueled a migration of Americans from cities to suburbia. The suburban lifestyle, with its emphasis on leisure activities, combined with the rise of a certain amount of disposable income for many families, allowed color photography to become a widespread hobby among the public.

Certain innovations in the field during this period made the hobby gain more appeal for even the most novice of photographers. Film development processes became globally standardized around the Kodak system. It thus became possible to take both black-and-white and color photographs in very low light conditions and feel assured of a successful negative that was capable of providing a useable print. With the introduction of Cibachrome printing papers in 1975, print colors could be better preserved, and the fading and color inconsistency of previous processes were eliminated. As a result of these kinds of developments, between 1970 and 1980, the sales of black-and-white film dropped annually from 80 million rolls to 30 million.

One of the biggest advancements in photography during the 1970's was the widespread availability of affordable 35 millimeter cameras. Japanese camera companies, especially Nikon, Canon, and Pentax, provided the market with high-quality cameras and lenses, at a range of prices most consumers could afford. As a result, the nonprofessional photographer could access equipment capable of recording quality images on high-grade film stocks. During the 1970's, the 35-millimeter camera also became a standard travel fashion accessory. At the same time, development of stable Polaroid films resulted in a marked increase in sales of "instant" or "self-developing" cameras.

Impact Technical advances and standardization practices during the 1970's made it possible for amateur and professional photographers to choose from a number of cameras, lenses, and films, an option not previously available. Cameras with integral light meters and capable of using sensitive films became an industry standard. Quality equipment at reasonable prices also became available at this time, and the processing of a variety of films—black-and-white and color negatives, as well as color positives—could be printed and enlarged within a new growing type of photographic business, the fast print service. Such advances during the 1970's expanded photography's impact during the last half of the twentieth century, increasing its capacity to grow as an art form and making a camera a must-have family possession.

Further Reading

Garner, Gretchen. *Disappearing Witness: Change in Twentieth Century American Photography.* Baltimore: Johns Hopkins University Press, 2003. Written for a scholarly audience, this book chronicles the factors of change in photography over the last half of the twentieth century.

Jeffrey, Ian. *Photography: A Concise History.* New York: Oxford University Press, 1981. This book tells the story of photography by documenting the contributions and influences of specific photographers.

Lemagny, Jean-Claude, and André Rouillé, eds. *A History of Photography: Social and Cultural Perspectives.* New York: Cambridge University Press, 1986. The history of photography as an art form and its role as a social and cultural record.

Marien, Mary Lou. *Photography: A Cultural History.* New York: Harry N. Abrams, 2002. Provides richly illustrated text with a fascinating timeline comparing historical events with major photographic works.

Szarkowski, John. *Looking at Photographs: One Hundred Pictures from the Collection of the Museum of Modern Art.* New York: New York Graphic Society and Rapoport, 1976. Images and text documenting the art of photography; commentary by one of photography's most well-known critics.

Randall L. Milstein

See also Advertising; Art movements; Journalism in Canada; Journalism in the United States; Pop art.

■ Pink Floyd

Identification British rock band
Date Formed in 1965

Pink Floyd was one of the most original and innovative groups to appear in the U.S. rock market during the 1970's.

Amalgamating its name from American blues legends Pink Anderson and Floyd Council, Pink Floyd gained a dedicated local following as London's premiere acid rock band in the late 1960's. By the beginning of the 1970's, the group—which included Nick Mason on drums, Roger Waters on bass, and Richard Wright on keyboards—had gotten rid of its increasingly unstable founder and frontman, Syd Barrett. His place on lead guitar was filled by an old personal friend, David Gilmour. Although all members made important contributions to writing and vocals, Waters would soon emerge as the key architect of a new, more structured Pink Floyd style.

One significant change was the manner in which the band began to concentrate on longer projects and abandon the pursuit of singles. They provided background music for several film and television projects and released a flurry of full-length albums, including *Atom Heart Mother* in 1970 and *Meddle* in 1971. Pink Floyd finally made the transatlantic leap in 1973, bursting onto the U.S. pop charts with the hit album *Dark Side of the Moon*, produced in part by engineering wizard Alan Parsons. The album hit number one in 1973 and stayed on *Billboard* magazine's top-100 chart until 1988, the longest album run in history.

Pink Floyd's follow-up U.S. tour in 1973 was also an enormous success as sold-out events demonstrated the band's legendary showmanship to a new American audience. Perhaps as a continuation of the group's acid rock origins, the concerts were noted for extensive lighting, smoke, and combustible special effects.

The middle of the decade saw new releases such as *Wish You Were Here* (1975), an extensive tribute to Barrett, and *Animals* (1977), an Orwellian analysis of the world order according to the band. The band made headlines when, while the cover for *Animals* was being shot, a large inflatable pig broke loose from its moorings and drifted through the airspace of London's Heathrow Airport.

During various tours in this period, the group's stage show grew, but Waters had also sensed a growing gulf of alienation and isolation between the audience and himself in the role of rock performer. For all intents and purposes, there might just as well have been a wall between them. At the end of the decade, this theme became the basis of Pink Floyd's most successful venture, *The Wall*, released late in 1979. Loosely connected to events in Waters's own life, the double album tells the story of a fictional rock star named Pink Floyd who becomes isolated by

a metaphorical wall of parental loss, bullying teachers, drugs, and the pressures of stardom. A very limited concert tour followed, visiting only four cities, which included the construction of a thirty-foot wall during the stage show.

Impact The American rock market responded enthusiastically to Pink Floyd's *Dark Side of the Moon*, with its haunting, electronically driven melodies intermixed with gospel-choir backup vocals and sound effects such as ringing cash registers. *The Wall* proved equally popular, and the total revenue from the album even surpassed that of *Dark Side of the Moon*, eventually selling more than twenty million copies worldwide. The film *Pink Floyd The Wall*, written by Roger Waters and directed by Alan Parker, was released in 1982. Waters apparently found it an increasing challenge to continue the status quo, however, and left the band in 1985.

Further Reading

Fitch, Vernon. *The Pink Floyd Encyclopedia*. Burlington, Ont.: Collector's Guide, 1999.

Schaffner, Nicholas. *The British Invasion*. New York: McGraw-Hill, 1982.

_____. *Saucerful of Secrets*. New York: Harmony Books, 1991.

Roger Pauly

See also Hard rock and heavy metal; Led Zeppelin; Music.

■ Pioneer space program

Identification Space missions to investigate Venus, Jupiter, and Saturn
Date Pioneer 10 launched on March 2, 1972; Pioneer 11 launched on April 5, 1973; Pioneer 12 launched on May 20, 1978; Pioneer 13 launched on August 8, 1978

Pioneer 10 was the first space probe to fly by Jupiter, while Pioneer 11 was the first to fly by Saturn. The Pioneer Venus space mission returned data that unveiled the complex atmosphere of that planet.

Launched on March 2, 1972, Pioneer 10 passed through the asteroid belt and flew by Jupiter in December, 1973, capturing the first close-up images of that planet. The data returned from Pioneer 10 revealed the magnetic field of Jupiter, provided a map of its radiation belts, and suggested that Jupiter is primarily composed of liquid rather than gas. Pioneer 10 was aimed so that Jupiter's gravitational field deflected the space probe out of the plane of the solar system and into interstellar space, becoming the first human-made object to exit the solar system.

On April 5, 1973, Pioneer 11 was launched into space, flying by Jupiter in December, 1974. Images returned by Pioneer 11 showed Jupiter's Great Red Spot embedded in a broad white zone that dominated the planet's southern hemisphere. The probe recorded temperatures of Jupiter's atmosphere, located its magnetic field, and provided pictures of its polar regions. Continuing on its mission, Pioneer 11 flew past Saturn in September, 1979. It returned data indicating Saturn's strong magnetic field, as well as glimpses of Saturn's atmosphere.

In the late 1970's, two Pioneer spacecraft probed Venus. The Pioneer Venus Multiprobe (Pioneer 13) consisted of four probes that were released into the Venusian atmosphere in late 1978. As they descended, they revealed the circulation patterns of the atmosphere and showed that the clouds lie primarily in a high layer about 48 to 58 kilometers above the surface. After reaching the surface of Venus, one probe unexpectedly continued operation for about forty-five minutes. The other spacecraft, the Pioneer Venus Orbiter (Pioneer 12), was put into orbit around Venus on December 4, 1978. It collected evidence for the existence of active volcanoes on Venus. In the early 1980's, it sent back numerous images showing that the upper levels of the planet's atmosphere rotate around the planet in just four days.

Impact   The Pioneer space program provided astronomers with data and images of Venus, Jupiter, and Saturn that encouraged more intense study and investigation of these and other planets. The accomplishments of Pioneer 10 and Pioneer 11 provided the impetus and funding for the Voyager missions that were launched in 1977 to explore the outer planets.

Subsequent Events   The Pioneer Venus missions established the foundation for developing more sophisticated instrumentation for the Galileo flyby of Venus in 1990. The Pioneer 10 mission was ended on March 31, 1997. The last data received from the probe was on January 23, 2003.

Further Reading

Kranz, Gene. *Failure Is Not an Option: Mission Control from Mercury to Apollo 13 and Beyond.* New York: Simon & Schuster, 2000.

Leverington, David. *New Cosmic Horizons: Space Astronomy from the V2 to the Hubble Space Telescope.* Cambridge, England: Cambridge University Press, 2001.

Alvin K. Benson

See also   Apollo space program; Astronomy; Science and technology; Skylab; Space exploration; Viking space program; Voyager space program.

■ Platform shoes

Definition   Footwear with thick soles and often high heels designed for added height

Platform shoes were a major fashion trend during the 1970's. From practical to outlandish styles for both men and women, platform shoes were so popular that they became an identifying image or symbol of the decade.

Platform shoes existed as early as the 1600's, when Venetian women wore high-soled "chopines" to indicate high social status. Although they were worn in earlier decades in the United States, it was during the 1970's that platform shoes became a pervasive fashion trend and reached the height of their popularity. For the first time, men also wore platform shoes. In 1971, a Milwaukee store sold 1,300 pairs of high-heeled men's platform shoes in just three months.

The platform shoes of the early 1970's had one-inch soles. By 1975, two-inch or higher soles and five-inch heels were common. Eventually, there were seven- or eight-inch or higher stacked heels.

Designers were experimental and creative, so platform shoes appeared in various styles and colors. Materials included colored leather, suede, fabric, snake skin, and wood. Soles were made from plastic, cork, wood, or rubber. Shoes were often decorated with psychedelic designs, rhinestones, jewels, or sequins. However, simple and durable Scandinavian style clogs with wooden soles were also popular.

While some shoes were designed for practical, everyday wear, others shoes were created for shock value, especially for celebrities. The superstar Elton John was known for his flamboyant stage antics, oversize platform boots, extravagant apparel, and wild sunglasses. Among his platforms was a pair of shiny

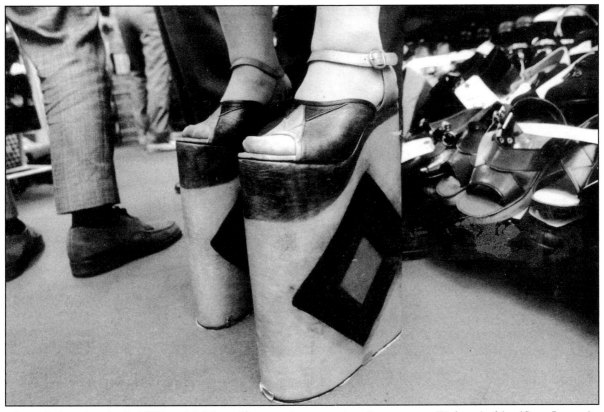

Some platform shoes in the 1970's took height to the extreme in an attempt to be outrageous. (Hulton Archive/Getty Images)

silver leather boots with red-and-white striped soles and large red "E" and "J" monograms. The famous heavy metal rock group KISS wore platform shoes that were monstrous, metallic, and threatening.

Platform shoes were also worn at discotheques, another cultural trend of the 1970's. In the classic 1977 film *Saturday Night Fever,* John Travolta set the disco style with his famous white suit and platform shoes. For the disco look, women chose platform heels with straps.

Impact Platform shoes were an integral part of the world of fashion and popular culture of the 1970's. They symbolized the decade's spirit of experimentation and rebellion against tradition. Paralleling other trends in clothing and gender issues, platform shoes of the 1970's were worn by men as well as women. They were popular across social classes, with styles for the workplace, as well as for disco dancers, rock musicians, and hippies. The shoes complemented bell-bottoms, hot pants, miniskirts, and other fashion fads.

Further Reading

Ellsworth, Ray. *Platform Shoes: A Big Step in Fashion.* Atglen, Pa.: Schiffer, 1998.

Panati, Charles. *Panati's Parade of Fads, Follies, and Manias.* New York: Harper, 1991.

Pendergast, Sara, Tom Pendergast, and Sarah Hermsen. *Fashion, Costume, and Culture: Clothing, Headwear, Body Decorations, and Footwear Through the Ages.* Detroit: UXL, 2004.

Alice Myers

See also Bell-bottoms; Dance, popular; Disco; Discotheques; Fads; Fashions and clothing; Hippies; John, Elton; KISS; *Saturday Night Fever;* Travolta, John.

■ Poetry

Definition A form of concentrated expression through meaning, sound, and rhythm

During the 1970's, poetry flourished both in the United States and in Canada. The decade was a time of expansion, experimentation, and of increasing diversity.

Although it is customary to describe poets who began writing after World War II as "contemporary," thus differentiating them from the "modern poets" of the prewar period, some of the important American poets of the 1970's continued to write much like the modernist New Critics. Richard Wilbur, Howard Nemerov, and John Hollander, for example, all wrote from a detached, ironic standpoint and used tightly controlled forms. Other poets, such as Elizabeth Bishop, Robert Hayden, and Amy Clampitt, reflected the restraint of the modernists, while like the newer poets, they experimented with form and a more personal kind of expression.

By contrast, contemporary poets had two objectives: the rejection of fixed forms, verse, and meter in favor of "open" prosody and the substitution of the poet's most intimate experiences and emotions for the objectivity of the formalists. Though by the 1970's some of the groups of contemporary poets that had evolved during the 1950's and 1960's were no longer active, others remained strong. For example, the New York school of poets, whose most prominent member at the time was John Ashbery, utilized their knowledge of contemporary art to expand the possibilities of verse. Under the influence of Surrealist art and their reading of the Latin American Surrealist poets, the Deep Image poets deliberately avoided logical structure in their visionary poetry, and late in the decade, a group called the Language Poets voiced its belief that words were incapable of expressing anything.

During the 1970's, the Confessional Poets continued to write intensely personal poems, recording and analyzing their tumultuous inner lives. One of the most important of these writers, Robert Lowell, had frequent mental breakdowns, necessitating institutionalization, and early in the decade, two others, John Berryman and Anne Sexton, took their own lives. Other Confessional Poets, however, were energized by the new freedom of expression. Adrienne Rich, for example, could now explore all of her experiences, whether as a woman, as a mother, or as a lesbian.

Identity and Diversity Both in the United States and in Canada, the 1970's was a time when new voices were being heard. The women's rights movement had encouraged many more women to begin writing, believing that at last their works would be judged on the same basis as those of men. It became much easier for a woman to publish her poetry, though perhaps still difficult to attain real recognition. Between 1970 and 1979 in Canada, for example, the annual Governor General's Literary Award for poetry went to only two women.

After the Civil Rights movement empowered African American writers, the more radical Black Power movement went beyond a demand for justice, insisting that African Americans should take pride in their own identity. The resulting Black Arts movement was led by LeRoi Jones, also known as Amiri Baraka. His poems not only focused on the experience of African Americans but also utilized the rhythms of blues, jazz, and vernacular speech. The Black Arts movement produced a number of outstanding poets, many of them women, and it was a major influence even on already established poets such as Gwendolyn Brooks.

Canadian poets, too, were concerned about identity, but for them, the decade was primarily a time of cultural nationalism. They took pride in becoming culturally independent of Great Britain as well as pride in resisting cultural domination by the United States. They had also begun to define identity as attachment to a particular locale in their country, but, as the Canadian poet and novelist Margaret Atwood pointed out, it was still difficult for this nation of immigrants, who had survived such hardships, to feel fully rooted to their land. Moreover, it is not surprising that in the poetry of the 1970's, the themes of solitude and alienation, which Atwood believes characterize Canadian literature, are readily found.

However, in Canada, as well as in the United States, the decade was also marked by an explosion of identity-centered poetry written by various ethnic minorities. In Canada, Quebec separatists used street language to voice their rebellion against convention and authority, while in the southwestern United States, Chicano and Chicana poets felt that bilingual works best reflected their unique identity. In both countries, descendants of the original Americans relived the past and revived their spiritual heritage, while recent immigrants from Asia brought their own traditions to poems written in English.

Impact By maintaining a wide diversity in form, tone, subject matter, and language, the poets of the 1970's reflected and affirmed the poetic revolution that had taken place in the two previous decades. The very fact that they spoke in so many different voices, expressing so many different viewpoints, meant that later poets would have far more options open to them. They could choose to write poems that were formal or seemingly formless, traditional or experimental, linguistically controlled or wholly idiomatic. Thus, the very diversity of the poetry written in the United States and in Canada during the 1970's served to strengthen the tradition of freedom of expression that both nations hold dear.

Further Reading

Atwood, Margaret, ed. *The New Oxford Book of Canadian Verse in English.* Toronto: Oxford University Press, 1982. Atwood's introduction provides an excellent overview of Canadian poetry.

Bayard, Caroline. *The New Poetics in Canada and Quebec: From Concretism to Post-modernism.* Toronto: University of Toronto Press, 1989. Points out how critical theories resulted in the writing of Canadian experimental poetry.

Beach, Christopher. *The Cambridge Introduction to Twentieth-Century American Poetry.* Cambridge, England: Cambridge University Press, 2003. Contains concise descriptions of the poetic movements that dominated the 1970's. Includes bibliographical notes, a glossary, and an index.

Hamilton, Ian, ed. *The Oxford Companion to Twentieth-Century Poetry in English.* Oxford, England: Oxford University Press, 1994. Substantial essays on poets, along with entries on poetry journals, poetic movements, and critical terms.

New, W. H. *A History of Canadian Literature.* 2d ed. Montreal: McGill-Queen's University Press, 2003. Relates works and writers to cultural and social history. Includes a chronological table.

Rosemary M. Canfield Reisman

See also African Americans; Angelou, Maya; Atwood, Margaret; Black Arts movement; Feminism; Giovanni, Nikki; Language Poets; Literature in Canada; Literature in the United States; Rich, Adrienne.

■ Police and detective shows

Definition Crime-solving television programs

During the 1970's, police and detective programs continued to be popular with the American public, especially with the introduction of several eccentric characters that rose to mythic stature.

Police and detective programs have been a staple of American television since the late 1940's. In 1952, the program *Dragnet*, which had been popular on radio, made its successful debut on television. Jack Webb, who starred as Joe Friday, also directed the show and was the creative force behind it. Webb believed in presenting police work in a no-nonsense approach. This style would be copied by future police dramas, including *The F.B.I.* (1965-1974) and *Adam-12* (1968-1975). Other police shows began their run during the 1960's and continued to be aired into the 1970's, such as *Hawaii Five-0* (1968-1980), *Ironside* (1967-1975), and *The Mod Squad* (1968-1973).

Police Shows *Adam-12* was produced by Webb and took its inspiration from what he had done on *Dragnet.* The show starred Martin Milner and Kent McCord as patrol officers who encountered a variety of crime scenarios each week. *The F.B.I.*, which starred Efrem Zimbalist, Jr., presented actual Federal Bureau of Investigation (FBI) cases.

While *Adam-12* and *The F.B.I.* followed in the footsteps of *Dragnet*, other police dramas owed their success to eccentric leading characters. In 1971, the American television audience was introduced to the character of Columbo. Played by Peter Falk, Lieutenant Columbo wore a rumpled trench coat and drove a car that was ready for the junkyard. *Columbo* was part of *The NBC Mystery Movie* series on the National Broadcasting Company (NBC). This anthology series also included *McCloud*, starring Dennis Weaver, and *McMillan and Wife*, starring Rock Hudson. Columbo solved murder cases by outsmarting the murderer. Each episode began with the audience witnessing the murder, so there was no mystery as to who committed the crime. The fun of the program was to watch Columbo go through his seemingly disheveled approach to crime solving.

While Columbo had his rumpled trench coat, the character of Kojak had his lollipop. *Kojak* ran from 1973 until 1978, and in it veteran actor Telly Savalas created one of the most unique police detectives ever to appear on television. Savalas played New York police lieutenant Theo Kojak. The character became famous for sucking on a lollipop and using the expression "Who loves ya, baby?" The series was a success, and Kojak became an international icon.

Hawaii Five-0, starring Jack Lord as Steve McGarrett, was filmed on location in Hawaii. The combination of scenery and action made the series extremely popular. One of the most poignant police shows of the 1970's was in actuality a sitcom called *Barney Miller* (1975-1982). Starring Hal Linden and a remarkable cast, this half-hour comedic police show interjected a humanity that few other crime-solving programs could match. Other police shows with loyal followings during the 1970's included *The Streets of San Francisco* (1972-1977), *Police Story* (1973-1977), *Starsky and Hutch* (1975-1979), and *CHiPs* (1977-1983).

Detective Shows Private detectives, or private investigators (PIs), have been popular television characters since the 1940's. In 1967, *Mannix* first aired, starring Mike Connors as a hard-hitting and ruggedly handsome PI; the series would stay on the air until 1975.

While Joe Mannix was quick to solve problems with his fists, the character of Jim Rockford did his best to avoid violence. *The Rockford Files* (1974-1980) starred James Garner as private detective Jim Rockford, a wisecracking PI who can best be described as an antihero. Rockford was a regular guy who wanted no part of "guns and glory." The series was well written and included a fine supporting cast. All these elements helped to make *The Rockford Files* one of the best-loved detective shows of its time, and the show remained popular in reruns.

Rockford was not the only character who did not fit the standard mold of the heroic private detective. David Janssen played a cynical PI in the series *Harry O* (1974-1976). Unfortunately, the show was canceled before it could fully develop its leading character. William Conrad played a heavyset private detective in *Cannon* (1971-1976), and Buddy Ebsen played a retirement-age PI in *Barnaby Jones* (1973-1980). In 1976, *Charlie's Angels*, starring Kate Jackson, Farrah Fawcett-Majors, and Jaclyn Smith as sexy female detectives, became a huge success and a cultural phenomenon. After only one season, the popular Fawcett-Majors left the series and was replaced by Cheryl Ladd, and other cast changes followed. Nevertheless, the formula remained the same, and *Charlie's Angels* remained on the air until 1981.

Impact Many crime-solving programs were introduced to American television audiences during the 1970's. It was a decade for the unconventional cop and private detective. While Falk's character of Columbo and Garner's Jim Rockford probably stand out as the most memorable and critically acclaimed, other unconventional characters left their mark, including Robert Blake as Tony Baretta, Savalas as Theo Kojak, Weaver as Sam McCloud, Conrad as Frank Cannon, and Ebsen as Barnaby Jones.

Because of the popularity of police and detective dramas during the decade, however, there was arguably an oversaturation of the genre. Also, television networks were criticized for including too much violence in a number of these shows. Another trend that was criticized—while being popular with a large segment of the male viewing public—was the introduction of what came to be known as "jiggle TV." Through the success of such shows as *Charlie's Angels*, it became commonplace for female characters to wear revealing outfits.

Some of the most memorable police and detective dramas in the history of television were aired during the 1970's, and the selling of sex and violence have remained trends in television programming.

Further Reading

Lichter, S. Robert, Linda S. Lichter, and Stanley Rothman. *Prime Time: How TV Portrays American Culture.* Washington, D.C.: Regnery, 1994. Part IV of the book, "Crime and Punishment," looks at how violence has been portrayed in police and detective programming.

Meyers, Ric. *Murder on the Air.* New York: Mysterious Press, 1989. A detailed look at how crime solving has been portrayed on television.

_____. *TV Detectives.* San Diego, Calif.: A. S. Barnes, 1981. A thorough history of the detective drama.

Rose, Brian G., ed. *TV Genres: A Handbook and Reference Guide.* Westport, Conn.: Greenwood Press, 1985. Includes a chapter on police shows and another one on detective shows.

Settel, Irving. *A Pictorial History of Television.* 2d enlarged ed. New York: Frederick Ungar, 1983. Includes many photographs of popular 1970's shows and a solid overview of the importance of detective and police shows.

Jeffry Jensen

See also *Charlie's Angels*; *Get Christie Love*; *Hawaii Five-0*; Television in the United States.

■ Polyester

Definition Manufactured textile fiber

Fabrics made from polyester fibers were common in cloth-ing items that represented major fashion trends of the 1970's.

Polyester fibers, originally manufactured in En-gland, were introduced in the United States in 1951 by DuPont and given the trade name Dacron. Polyes-ter had many other properties that made it attractive to consumers. It had high resiliency (ability to re-turn to its original dimensions after bending or twist-ing), both wet and dry, and excellent dimensional stability. It was machine washable, easy to pack, and very durable, with excellent abrasion resistance. Polyester had high elongation, which meant that it could be stretched without breaking or tearing eas-ily. The fiber was also resistant to sunlight and unaf-fected by acids or alkalis. It could be bleached using chlorine or oxygen bleach. For all these reasons, polyester was dubbed "the miracle fiber."

Among the first uses of polyester fibers was knit shirts for men and woven blouses for women. Dur-ing the 1970's, as more women began working out-side the home, clothing that was convenient and easy to care for became increasingly important. A major fashion item of the 1970's was the pantsuit for women and the leisure suit (a more casual form of the dress suit) for men. Polyester double knit fabrics were popular with consumers because of their ability to be folded, packed, and easily laundered.

As the decade came to a close, however, many consumers no longer appreciated the aesthetics of polyester clothing and thought of the fabric as lower quality and uncomfortable. Polyester is still trying to recover from the poor image created by the polyes-ter double knits of the 1970's.

Impact The fiber polyester revolutionized the tex-tiles and apparel industries in the 1970's, and it re-mains the most widely used manufactured fiber to-day. Numerous fiber modifications to the original polyester have occurred. It is extremely versatile and can be manufactured to simulate other fibers, such as silk or wool. Polyester is also a common fiber for blends, especially with cotton. It is commonly seen in apparel and home furnishings products and in both woven and knitted fabrics.

Further Reading

Collier, Billie J., and Phyllis G. Tortora. *Understand-ing Textiles*. 6th ed. Upper Saddle River, N.J.: Prentice Hall, 2001.

Kadolph, Sara J., and Anna L. Langford. *Textiles*. 9th ed. Upper Saddle River, N.J.: Prentice Hall, 2002.

Payne, Blanche, Geitel Winakor, and Jane Farrell-Beck. *The History of Costume: From Ancient Mesopota-mia Through the Twentieth Century*. New York: Long-man, 1992.

Robinson, J. S., ed. *Manufacture of Yarns and Fabrics from Synthetic Fibers*. Park Ridge, N.J.: Noyes Data Corp, 1980.

Leigh Southward

See also Disco; Fads; Fashions and clothing; Lei-sure suits.

■ Pop art

Definition An art movement in which artworks incorporated images from popular culture and techniques of mass production

Pop art was, by the 1970's, established as one of the most in-fluential and widely recognized art movements of the later twentieth century. Pop art questioned the division between high art and mass culture by incorporating popular culture images and commercial art techniques.

Pop art drew on popular culture imagery—primar-ily advertising, comic books, and commercial prod-ucts. The artworks challenged the separation of the world of high art from the broader culture and, after almost a century of increasing abstraction, repre-sented a return of imagery to mainstream art.

The movement began in Great Britain during the mid-1950's, but even in its early stages in Europe, it was inspired by a fascination with American popular culture. The movement quickly attracted artists in the United States, where its most famous works—Andy Warhol's repeated images of Campbell's soup cans and Marilyn Monroe, Claes Oldenburg's gi-gantic stuffed sculptures of common objects, Roy Lichtenstein's oversized comic book paintings, Jas-per Johns's flag paintings, and Robert Rauschen-berg's collages and sculptures—were created.

Pop art critiqued the notion that the works from the preceding art movement, abstract expression-ism, captured the emotions of the artists directly on the canvas. The use of familiar subject matter drew attention away from the images themselves and toward the transformation of the image into art. The viewer was confronted with the degree to which paintings are, in fact, stylized arrangements of paint and other materials on canvas. At the same time, pop art extended certain themes of abstract expressionism: The extension of the painting to cover the entire canvas equally rather than centering on a subject or focal point, and the revelation of the canvas as a plane within which the artist worked.

By the early 1970's, the dominance of the two leading art movements of the 1960's—pop art and minimalism—had begun to dissipate. However, throughout the 1970's, the leading artists of the pop art movement, including Warhol, Lichtenstein, Oldenburg, Rauschenberg, and Johns, continued creating work that incorporated popular culture images and explored the issues of representation addressed by the pop art movement.

Significant Pop Artists Warhol had created many of the defining images of pop art in the 1960's. His images of Marilyn Monroe and Campbell's soup cans successfully redefined popular culture images as a valid subject for art. He concentrated on portraiture for much of the 1970's. The portraits were mainly of famous people; their images, either created by methods of mass production such as photography or silk screen or reproduced numerous times, emphasize that celebrities had become a type of commodity.

While for the most part not critical of mass culture itself, pop art images forced a consideration of how popular culture images are seen. Indeed, Warhol's repetition of portraits made evident the transformation of celebrity images into icons. Many versions of the same image, a technique used, for example, in a series of portraits of Mao Zedong in 1972, illuminated the loss of impact of images after many viewings; displayed together, the images are reduced to pattern.

In the 1970's, Roy Lichtenstein created paintings based on earlier art styles, such as cubism. Whereas

Artist Andy Warhol unveils his pop art exhibition in 1971 in front of his double portrait of Marilyn Monroe. (AP/Wide World Photos)

his earlier pop art works based on comic books had transformed popular images into high art, the works of the 1970's showed how revered works of high art had become part of the popular culture. The exaggerated size of the works allowed viewers to see the stylization of the artistic conventions, and Lichtenstein's ability to copy the style and the works critiqued the notion of style as unique to a particular artist.

Claes Oldenburg created colossal public sculptures of common objects, from 1976 onward, in collaboration with Coosje van Bruggen. *Lipstick (Ascending) on Caterpillar Tracks* (1969-1974) combined an enormous lipstick with the base of a military tank for display on the campus of Yale University. *Clothespin* (1976) was constructed for a site in downtown Philadelphia. The sculptures amused and sometimes shocked viewers as the objects often took on new associations when enlarged to such a degree. For example, the phallically shaped lipstick combined with a military apparatus drew criticism of the work as a symbol of male aggression.

Through the 1970's, Robert Rauschenberg created collages and sculptures that incorporated or consisted of found objects. His works included a series of found cardboard boxes; they were displayed unfolded, leaning against the gallery wall, without added paint. He also created a series of paintings of animal feed bags with titles such as *Goat Chow* (1977) and *Hog Chow* (1977). Finally, Jasper Johns returned to some of his earlier pop art themes, again creating works based on American flags and targets.

Impact The more famous works of the pop art movement became as recognizable as the mass-produced items they depicted. While the works were generally politically neutral, they drew attention to the increasing commercialization of American culture. Pop art influenced later art movements by reintroducing figuration into painting; the subject matter and media for art increasingly broadened with the influence of pop art as well.

Further Reading

Archer, Michael. *Art Since 1960*. 2d ed. New York: Thames and Hudson, 2002. This book provides a thorough and comprehensive study of art movements beginning with pop art, with a useful discussion of the influence of pop art on the movements that followed.

Hughes, Robert. *The Shock of the New*. New York: Alfred A. Knopf, 1991. This popular account of twentieth century art contains a largely negative but influential discussion of pop art.

Sandler, Irving. *Art of the Postmodern Era: From the Late 1960's to the Early 1990's*. New York: HarperCollins, 1996. Concentrating mainly on the movements that followed pop art, this book shows the later development of concerns important to the movement.

Joan Hope

See also Art movements; Chicago, Judy; Feminist art; Hockney, David; Segal, George.

■ *Population Bomb, The*

Identification American nonfiction book
Author Paul R. Ehrlich (1932-)
Date Published in 1968; revised in 1971

The Population Bomb was the first book to argue strongly that people and governments should start taking action to curtail the world's overpopulation.

This pocket-sized book, written in an alarmist manner with the goal of motivating people to make drastic changes in population size and the environment, received the Bestsellers Paperback of the Year Award in 1970. The book was written in an elemental style and with few statistics in the hope of reaching a mass market. The foreword was by the executive director of the Sierra Club. A revised and expanded version of the book was published in 1971, with updated facts and 30 percent new material.

Paul R. Ehrlich, a biologist, was founder and the first president of Zero Population Growth. He wrote that, about a decade before his book, world population had surpassed the ability of the earth to produce sufficient food for the world's people. The direct cause of this, he argued, was the baby boom that followed World War II. Ehrlich noted that the world population was growing exponentially, and doubling time was decreasing, now taking only thirty to forty years. He predicted that the world would undergo vast famines sometime between 1970 and 1985, with hundreds of people starving to death before then unless they died of other catastrophes, such as plagues or thermonuclear war. He also argued that it was too late to change his prediction completely but that corrective efforts should begin immediately. To this end, pressure should be exerted to reduce population size drastically in both Third World and industrialized countries, including compulsory birth control in the United States if voluntary efforts did not work.

Ehrlich was also concerned with technological and biological changes, including the use of pesticides,that were being used to increase food production. He argued that destruction of the environment could cause more world turmoil and deaths than overpopulation. He supported the environmental movement but said that population control was the first threat. Ehrlich thought that scientists from multiple disciplines should be involved in civic and political activities and included in his book samples of forceful letters that had been written by other activists. He appeared on popular television talk shows to help increase public awareness. Even though he acknowledged that he might be overstating the case, he stressed that the issue was significant.

Impact Paul Ehrlich's severe criticism of modern technology and his "doomsday" predictions were challenged by some scientists and activists, especially activists in the Green Revolution—a movement to increase agricultural yields through technological and biological means. Other critics said that the situation was more complex, while some said that the inaccuracy of his predictions over massive famine led to decreased concern over the population explosion. Increased emphasis on birth control in the United States did occur, however, and the birth rate in Third World countries underwent major decreases during the 1970's and beyond.

Further Reading

Carson, Rachel. *Silent Spring*. Reprint. Boston: Houghton Mifflin, 2002.

Mazur, Leslie Ann, ed. *Beyond the Numbers: A Reader on Population, Consumption, and the Environment*. Washington, D.C.: Island Press, 1994.

Abraham D. Lavender

See also Environmental movement; Green Revolution; Science and technology.

■ Pornography

Definition Sexually explicit material; obscenity is the legal definition of pornography that appeals to prurient interests, offends, and lacks serious artistic, political, or scientific value

The 1970's was a time during which the United States struggled for a definition of obscenity, fought political and criminal battles over pornography, and worried about the degradation of women in pornographic material.

Historically in the United States, "pornography" has been difficult to define, and during this decade, the Supreme Court was similarly challenged when faced with the task of defining and applying some type of legal standard to material that offended the public and was therefore considered obscene. In *Jacobellis v. Ohio* (1964), a case that considered the charges of pornography in the 1958 film *Les Amants* (the lovers), Justice Potter Stewart received criticism when he stated simply, "I know it when I see it, and the motion picture involved in this case is not that." However, his nebulous remark demonstrated the difficulties associated with identifying pornographic materials as obscene. Obscenity had been defined by the Court in 1957 as a form of expression that deserved no constitutional protection, such as protection under the First Amendment as free speech, because it is, "utterly without redeeming social importance."

However, in 1973, the Court gave a more concise and somewhat less vague interpretation, one that would last in subsequent decades as the test for obscenity. In *Miller v. California* (1973), it stated that a work can be found as obscene only if one of three qualities exists: The average person, applying contemporary community standards, would find that the work, taken as a whole, appeals to the prurient interest; the work depicts or describes, in a patently offensive way, sexual conduct specifically defined by the applicable state law; and the work, taken as a whole, lacks serious literary, artistic, political, or social value.

In 1974, a local theater owner in Albany, Georgia, was prosecuted after showing Jack Nicholson's film *Carnal Knowledge* (1971), thereby challenging the Miller ruling in *Jenkins v. Georgia* (1974). The film, although it did reveal nudity and had suggestive sounds, did not depict any sexual acts. A local jury, however, applied their "community standards" and found the film obscene and the theater owner guilty of showing pornographic material. The high court became involved and had to decide if the film had any redeeming value. In this case, the Court held that *Carnal Knowledge* had artistic worth and was, therefore, entitled to protection under *Miller*.

Protesters outside a porn theater in 1972 demand that the explicit film Deep Throat *be banned.* (AP/Wide World Photos)

Pornography and Organized Crime   In the 1970's, the Federal Bureau of Investigations (FBI) began investigating Mafia ties to the pornography industry when the Paraino family out of Brooklyn, a branch of the Columbo crime family, made the explicit film *Deep Throat* (1972) for $22,500; their eventual gross exceeded 100 million dollars. The film's success led the Paraino clan to develop a legitimate film studio in Hollywood. They never actually made a motion picture, but they did distribute several violent films, one of them being *The Texas Chainsaw Massacre* (1974). After investigating the Parainos for some time, the FBI decided that it would attempt to prosecute them on obscenity violations in Florida. Worried over issues of free speech, many members of Hollywood's elite became involved, including Nicholson and Warren Beatty. The age-old argument of artist's rights versus the public's right to be protected from immorality were alive and well during the 1970's.

President's Commission on Pornography   Concerns over the effects of pornography began build-

ing in the 1960's with the rise of the sexual revolution, and from those concerns, the President's Commission on Obscenity and Pornography was formed. The commission was given the responsibility of understanding the effect of obscenity and pornography upon the public, particularly minors, and its relationship to crime and other antisocial behaviors.

The commission released its report in 1970 after two years of study, concluding that pornography had no harmful effects on society. The report stated that research designed to clarify the issue found nothing to suggest a link between exposure to sexually explicit content and criminal behavior in minors or adults. Moreover, the commission could not conclude that exposure to pornographic materials was a cause of sex crimes or sexual delinquency. The commission further claimed that its findings indicated that the majority of sex offenders surveyed came from sexually repressive homes, where sexually explicit material was not generally available. Many Americans, including feminists who felt that pornography was becoming more and more violent and degrading toward women during this period, objected to the findings of the commission.

The Women's Movement and Pornography In the mid-1970's, the feminist movement attempted to redirect the focus of pornography, asserting that it was a cause of harm and violence against women. The literal definition, they reminded the public, was taken from the ancient Greek root *porne*, meaning "female sexual slave" or "prostitute," and *graphos*, meaning "writings" or "graphic descriptions." Activists protested the violence and degradation of women being sold as entertainment. However, feminists were split on the issue and adopted opposing positions on pornography; two schools of thought subsequently emerged. One camp would furiously oppose pornography; the other camp held a strong anticensorship position.

Protests against pornography escalated when, in 1976, the film *Snuff* was released, in which a woman was shown being dismembered so that the audience could achieve sexual arousal and gratification. Andrea Dworkin, a long-time feminist activist, began organizing nightly protests in places where the film was being shown. Other prominent feminists, including Gloria Steinem, joined forces with Dworkin to found Women Against Pornography, and organized Take Back the Night marches through areas such as New York City's Times Square, where strip shows, massage parlors, and adult book stores were located.

Impact Until the late 1970's, pornography was available primarily in magazines, books, and 8mm films shown in theaters. Explicit items could be purchased through the mail, or in "bad parts of town." Pornography was in the spotlight during much of the 1970's, and some of the most classic, antipornography/pro-sex lines were drawn and heatedly debated among politicians, scholars, entertainers, and much of society in general.

Subsequent Events The 1980's saw the advent of videocassette recorders (VCRs), the growth of the adult entertainment industry, and the shift of pornography to private dwellings, which allowed people to view X-rated films in the safety and privacy of their own homes. The Internet, which arrived sometime later, further changed the way, at every level, that society considered pornography.

Further Reading

Dworkin, Andrea. *Pornography: Men Possessing Women.* New York: Perigree, 1981. A book that fearlessly attacks pornography but has been attacked itself as being mired in hate and lacking sound scholarship.

Hunt, Lynn, ed. *The Invention of Pornography, 1500-1800: Obscenity and the Origins of Modernity.* Cambridge, Mass.: Zone Books, 1996. The collection of essays presented here are essential for understanding current political and censorship issues surrounding pornography.

Kendrick, Walter. *The Secret Museum.* Berkeley: University of California Press, 1996. Examines how the public's attitudes toward pornography and censorship have changed from ancient Pompeii to twentieth century presidential commissions and also looks at the effect the printing press had on porn.

Kimberly A. Manning

See also Advertising; Beatty, Warren; Censorship in Canada; Censorship in the United States; Christian Fundamentalism; Conservatism in U.S. politics; Equal Rights Amendment (ERA); *Everything You Always Wanted to Know About Sex but Were Afraid to Ask*; Federal Bureau of Investigation (FBI); Feminism; Film in Canada; Film in the United States; *Hite Report, The*; *Joy of Sex, The*; *Last Tango in Paris*; Nicholson, Jack; Sexual revolution; Steinem, Gloria; Supreme Court decisions; Women's rights.

■ POWs and MIAs

Definition Prisoners of war (POWs) and missing in action (MIA) military personnel involved in the Vietnam War

During the 1970's, many Americans regarded the safety and release of American POWs and information regarding MIAs to be among the most important objectives of American participation in the Vietnam War and its aftermath.

Most of the American POWs during the 1970's, as in the 1960's, were imprisoned in North Vietnam and were pilots who had been shot down by the sophisticated air defenses of the North Vietnamese, who had deployed the latest Soviet technology. The communists in the North and South continued to detain military combatants as well as civilians, while denying that the rulings of the Geneva Convention—which the North had signed in 1957—applied to the war in Vietnam.

However, a notable departure from past practices by North Vietnam occurred early in 1970. The American POWs began to receive far better treatment by their captors than during the previous decade, including improvements in diet, access to medical treatment, better living conditions, and lighter punishments. The prospect that U.S. president Richard M. Nixon would prosecute the war to a conclusion and hold the North accountable for its war crimes may have motivated Hanoi to adopt a more lenient policy, although the evidence for this assessment is not conclusive.

Popular and Presidential Action   While conditions improved for American POWs in Vietnam during the early 1970's, many Americans at home knew little about the progress and demanded immediate action in order to better the situation of those detained. Personal stories of captivity by POWs such as Lieutenant Dieter Dengler, who had escaped, or Colonel Norris Overly, Jr., who was among the few to be released by the communists, detailed abuses and humiliations endured through the duration of confinement and subsequently incited many Americans to protest the treatment of POWs held in Southeast Asia.

Families and friends of those held in captivity were particularly active in organizing groups that demanded more humane treatment for the POWs, more information regarding MIAs, and more action by the U.S. government concerning these issues. Many wives of the POWs held in Vietnam and Laos helped form the League of Families of American Prisoners and Missing in Southeast Asia, an organization that not only raised public awareness of the plight of prisoners of war but also included activities such as sending delegations to Paris in order to pressure North Vietnamese officials to address the POW and MIA issues during the critical period of the Paris Peace Talks in 1972.

Partly in response to the public outcry for action and partly for its own reasons, the Nixon administration waged a publicity campaign against North Vietnam's policies regarding the POWs and made the POW-MIA issue central to the peace negotiations and to the withdrawal of American military forces from Vietnam. On October 7, 1970, the administration offered a complete release of all prisoners of war if the North Vietnamese officials did likewise. Undeterred by the opposition's refusal to accept the

exchange, Nixon ordered a raid on Son Tay prison camp, an effort that failed because faulty intelligence did not reveal that the camp had been evacuated previously. Hanoi countered these actions by asserting that it had treated all of its POWs humanely and that the United States and its ally, the Republic of South Vietnam, had acted inhumanely against prisoners of war despite the inspections by the International Red Cross.

Until the release of the POWs in 1973, both sides made charges and countercharges of violations of human rights—the communists focusing on the alleged brutality of American military power and related civilian casualties, the Americans focusing on the refusal of the North to accept inspections of their prisons by neutral parties.

The War Ends, POWs Return   On January 27, 1973, all sides of the conflict in Vietnam signed the Paris Peace Accords and thereby ended officially the detention of American prisoners of war. The agreement stipulated that the withdrawal of American armed forces should proceed in direct relation to the release of all American POWs. Shortly thereafter, Operation Homebound began, and the world witnessed the first group of American POWs land at Clarkfield Base in the Philippines. With only a slight delay in procedure, the other POWs arrived home. With the exception of a controversy over the Peace Committee, a group of POWs who collaborated with their North Vietnamese captors, the return marked a period of patriotic fervor in the United States. In all, 600 POWs were repatriated: 591 Americans and 9 foreign nationals. Approximately one hundred POWs died in captivity, and one hundred escaped or gained freedom through early release.

After the return of the American POWs in Operation Homebound, the issue of MIAs became paramount. The government of the United States adjusted the number of MIAs from 1,300 to 2,500 in order to include those killed in action but whose remains had not been recovered.

Impact   During the last years of American involvement in the Vietnam War, the detention of American POWs by the communist authorities in North Vietnam, Laos, and South Vietnam (Viet Cong) and the problem of accounting for the MIAs became a critical component of both the peace terms of the war and the criteria of many Americans for assessing participation in that conflict. The safe return of American POWs and information regarding MIAs became both the passion and policy of many Americans during the Vietnam War.

Subsequent Events　In 1983, amid rumors of Americans still held in captivity, American officials determined that all but a few of the MIAs were killed in action. However, the subject was debated by many and remained a point for much speculation and controversy.

Further Reading

Denton, Jeremiah A., and Edmund H. Brandt, Jr. *When Hell Was in Session.* New York: Reader's Digest Press, 1976. A riveting personal memoir by Denton, one of the United States' most distinguished POWs.

Howes, Craig. *Voices of the Vietnam POWs: Witnesses to Their Fight.* New York: Oxford University Press, 1993. A compilation of POW accounts that further illuminates the experience of captivity during the Vietnam War.

Rochester, Stuart, and Frederick Kiley. *Honor Bound: American Prisoners of War in Southeast Asia, 1961-1973.* Annapolis, Md.: Naval Institute Press, 1999. A thorough account of the history of POWs during the Vietnam War.

Scott Catino

See also　Foreign policy of the United States; Paris Peace Accords; Vietnam War.

■ Pregnancy Discrimination Act of 1978

Identification　U.S. federal legislation
Date　Enacted on October 31, 1978

The Pregnancy Discrimination Act mandated equal treatment by employers of their employees affected by "pregnancy, childbirth, or related medical conditions." Thus, it addressed the unique situation faced by many female employees and set guidelines to ensure that fair, across-the-board standards were applied both in hiring and in the workplace.

The years after World War II witnessed a steady increase in the numbers and proportion of women in the workforce. Many employers therefore were faced with unprecedented situations involving pregnancy and related conditions and responded in diverse ways. Some acted in a manner that was alleged to be

unfair and discriminatory; in the 1960's and 1970's, the emergence of a more politically active women's movement brought these issues to the forefront.

In 1978, a bill was introduced amending the Title VII section of the Civil Rights Act of 1964 by adding a provision that made it illegal for employers with fifteen or more employees to discriminate on the basis of all matters relating to pregnancy and childbirth for "all employment-related purposes." In effect, the act legally equated pregnancy and childbirth with physical disability. This legislation had been precipitated by the 1976 Supreme Court decision *General Electric v. Gilbert* in a class-action suit filed against General Electric over the company's health plan, which did not cover pregnancy and childbirth conditions. The Court ruled that this particular case did not constitute sex discrimination and that the issue was not between the sexes but between pregnant and nonpregnant individuals. The bill therefore attempted to correct this legal ambiguity by specifically defining pregnancy and childbirth as conditions falling under the provisions of the Civil Rights Act.

The major objection arose over the question of employer-supported insurance coverage for abortions. After much deliberation, the decision was made that an employer would not be obliged to pay for health benefits covering abortion, except when the mother's life was in jeopardy or in the case of subsequent complications resulting from abortion procedures. Provisions were added both to set the effective date for the law's implementation and to safeguard against employer attempts to reduce the benefits provided once the act was in place.

Impact　The Pregnancy Discrimination Act transformed employer policy over maternity issues and though many women's rights advocates criticized its provisions as not having gone far enough and of not being very effective in situations in which employers provided few or no health benefits, it was undoubtedly a breakthrough in safeguarding against a particular form of gender bias.

Further Reading

Benokraitis, Nijole V., and Joe R. Feagin. *Modern Sexism: Blatant, Subtle, and Covert Discrimination.* Englewood Cliffs, N.J.: Prentice-Hall, 1984.

Davis, Flora. *Moving the Mountain: The Women's Movement in America Since 1960.* New York: Touchstone, 1991.

Raymond Pierre Hylton

See also Affirmative action; Age Discrimination Act of 1975; Canadian Human Rights Act of 1977; Congress, U.S.; Disability rights movement; Equal Employment Opportunity Act of 1972; Equal Rights Amendment (ERA); Privacy Act of 1974; *Roe v. Wade*; Women in the military; Women in the workforce; Women's rights.

■ Presley, Elvis

Identification American rock-and-roll artist
Born January 8, 1935; Tupelo, Mississippi
Died August 16, 1977; Memphis, Tennessee

The last decade of Presley's life found him reviving his career with a Las Vegas stage show and sinking deeper into drug use.

By the beginning of the 1970's, Elvis Presley's popularity was beginning to slip. His career received a much-needed boost when his manager, Colonel

In the 1970's, Elvis Presley headlined an elaborate show in Las Vegas. (DPA/Landov)

Tom Parker, signed a five-year, five-million-dollar contract with the International Hotel in Las Vegas. Twice a year, Presley played two shows a day, seven days a week for a month, drawings crowds of two thousand at each show and wearing a white jumpsuit with a standing collar and a neckline that plunged down to the waist.

The response that the shows received was like nothing Las Vegas had seen before. Hundreds of people had to be turned away nightly. Devoted fans came from all over the world. In honor of the attendance records he set, Presley was presented with a massive gold belt by the International Hotel, which he proudly wore for several years.

Despite his success in Las Vegas and sold-out shows on the road, Presley was unhappy. Performing and touring began to get tiresome but were necessary to pay for his excessive spending. He began to increase his already heavy drug use, which helped him sleep, stay awake, and keep his weight down. Presley's drug use became so heavy that he nearly died at least four times. It was also one of the causes of his divorce from his wife, Priscilla.

In 1973, a first-of-its-kind television special, *Elvis: Aloha from Hawaii*, was aired via satellite. The program was another career-boosting success, but there were also underlying signs of trouble. Presley's drug addiction was affecting his performances. Some nights he forgot lyrics, slurred his words, and was disoriented. Several shows had to be canceled or postponed because he did not have the energy to perform or even collapsed on stage.

During the last few days of his life, Presley was depressed. He was preparing for a tour that he did not want to go on, and a tell-all book that had been written by former employees was being released. He was worried how the public and his daughter would respond to it. There was also a television special that was filmed during his last tour, which showed him overweight, glassy-eyed, and exhausted. It all may have been too much for him. Presley was found dead in his bathroom on August 16, 1977.

Impact Elvis Presley's death was as controversial as the life that he led. His death was originally declared a suicide, but it was later suggested that the cause was a bad heart weakened by drug use. His home, Graceland, began to draw thousands of visitors each year, and Presley "sightings" made news. Even in death, he continued to be a larger-than-life legend.

Further Reading

Brown, Peter Harry, and Pat H. Broeske. *Down at the End of Lonely Street: The Life and Death of Elvis Presley.* New York: Penguin Group, 1997.

Goldman, Albert. *Elvis, the Last Twenty-four Hours.* New York: St. Martin's Paperbacks, 1991.

Thompson, Charles C., III, and James P. Cole. *The Death of Elvis: What Really Happened?* New York: Delacorte Press, 1991.

Maryanne Barsotti

See also Music.

■ Privacy Act of 1974

Identification U.S. federal legislation
Date Signed into law in December, 1974

The Privacy Act was enacted to prevent unwarranted invasion of privacy by the government. Among other goals, it was intended to strengthen individuals' control of the flow of information about themselves by authorizing the dissemination of information in the possession of the government, obtaining access to it, or restricting its disclosure.

Although not explicitly mentioned in the Constitution, the right of privacy has been articulated by the Supreme Court in *Olmstead v. United States* (1928) as an individual's "right to be let alone." Poorly defined, the constitutional right of privacy comprises freedom from government surveillance and intrusion into private affairs, avoidance of disclosures of personal matters, and protection of personal autonomy in decision making in matters such as marriage, procreation, contraception, child rearing, and education. Privacy is not absolute, however, and circumstances surrounding disclosure may be considered by the courts in sustaining an invasion of privacy action.

The roots of the Privacy Act of 1974 can be traced back to 1965, when hearings were held by the House of Representatives Special Subcommittee on Invasion of Privacy. One of the more significant influences on the Privacy Act was the report of the Secretary's Advisory Committee on Automated Data Systems commissioned by the Department of Health, Education, and Welfare, as well as the report of the Privacy Protection Study Commission, which helped to articulate the case for national privacy standards for a variety of records maintained on citizens. There were five basic recommendations later incorporated into the Privacy Act: the publication of an annual public notice in the Federal Register of changes to an existing record-keeping system; permitting an individual to view and receive copies of records about themselves contained in the federal record system and an accounting of the use of such information; an opportunity to restrict disclosure of certain information; an opportunity to correct or amend a record; and finally, a requirement that federal agencies take precautions in order to prevent misuse of data.

In a movement toward more open government, Congress enacted the Freedom of Information Act as part of the Administrative Procedures Act. Section 552(a), titled the Privacy Act of 1974, is a federal mandate that governs the treatment of personal data. The Privacy Act applied only to data held by federal agencies and did not apply to that in the possession of state or local authorities. Disclosure through communication to any person or to another agency was prohibited under the act unless one of the following specific authorizations for disclosure applied: consent of the individual; a need for the information, where required by the Freedom of Information Act, for "routine use"; and law enforcement purposes.

The major weakness of the act was the lack of enforcement mechanism among the agencies, which created loopholes. Confidential information could be forced to yield to competing medical, legal, or social interests. Public policy considerations could override the confidential nature of the privileged information. There was no uniformity among the states with regard to obtaining one's medical records and no specific and articulated legal protection of health care information.

Impact The Privacy Act attempted to protect the privacy rights of individuals, permitting government access to personal data without censorship while lending protection to citizens against exploitation and control over unauthorized use. It was the only federal law to provide a framework of protection of personal data until enactment of the Health Insurance Portability and Accountability Act (HIPAA), which became effective on April 14, 2003.

Further Reading

Bushkin, Arthur A., and Samuel I. Schaen. *The Privacy Act of 1974: A Reference Manual for Compliance.* McLean, Va.: System Development Corporation, 1975.

Freedman, Warren. *The Right of Privacy in the Computer Age.* New York: Quorum Books, 1987.

Marcia J. Weiss

See also   Censorship in the United States.

■ Progressive rock

Definition   British-identified rock music style noted for its structural complexity and its emphasis on electronic effects

Often derided as pretentious, progressive rock strove to bridge the gap between classical grandeur and rock-and-roll primitivism.

The album often cited as having launched progressive rock, albeit inadvertently, is the Beatles' *Sgt. Pepper's Lonely Hearts Club Band* (1967). Although modest by what in the 1970's would become progressive rock's most obvious standards—ever-increasing song lengths, vaguely mythological and mystical motifs, instrumental virtuosity—the album did open the door to the notion that rock-and-roll, accompanied by generous helpings of "consciousness expanding" drugs, could be a massively popular vehicle for the technologically sophisticated exploration of themes and concepts not easily accommodated by the three-minute pop song.

Perhaps because of their continent's classical music heritage, the acts best known for capitalizing on these possibilities—Pink Floyd, Yes, Genesis, and Emerson, Lake, and Palmer—were British. (The only significantly successful American progressive rock group, Kansas, achieved popularity in the second half of the 1970's largely by rendering themselves stylistically indistinguishable from their British forebears.)

In addition to lavish two and three-album sets, these groups also took pride in their visually spectacular concert performances. Emerging from among clouds of dry-ice smoke and flashing strobe lights, often with a daunting array of synthesizer banks and other mammoth electronic accessories in view, the music of these groups took on a hallucinogenic power when performed in the sports arenas that were the only venues large enough to accommodate both their formidable equipment and their many fans.

However, with the emergence in 1976 of punk rock, the aggressive simplicity of which served to reawaken rock's most primal instincts, the aesthetically and financially grandiose trappings of progressive rock began to appear suspiciously elitist, especially against the backdrop of the rising unemployment and high inflation that had come to characterize life in both England and America. By 1978 the majority of the genre's biggest names found themselves commonly referred to as "dinosaurs" and were faced with either commercial extinction (Jethro Tull and Emerson, Lake, and Palmer) or the challenge of streamlining their sound and image in an attempt to reinvent themselves as contemporary pop acts (Genesis and the Moody Blues). The exception was Pink Floyd, whose definitively cosmic 1973 album *Dark Side of the Moon* remained a perennial best-seller and whose double concept album *The Wall*, released in December, 1979, yielded a number-one million-selling single ("Another Brick in the Wall") and eventually spent four months as the best-selling album in the United States.

Notable Progressive Rock Songs of the 1970's

Song	Artist
"Wish You Were Here"	Pink Floyd
"Aqualung"	Jethro Tull
"I've Seen All Good People"	Yes
"A Trick of the Tail"	Genesis
"Lizard"	King Crimson
"Lucky Man"	Emerson, Lake, and Palmer
"Closer to the Heart"	Rush
"Come Sail Away"	Styx
"Carry On Wayward Son"	Kansas

Impact Despite the abruptness with which it lost commercial momentum, progressive rock created a taste for lavish production values that in one form or another would influence nearly every style of popular music in its wake.

Further Reading

Asbjørnsen, Dag Erik. *Scented Gardens of the Mind: A Guide to the Golden Era of Progressive Rock, 1968-1980, in More than Twenty European Countries.* Wolverhampton, England: Borderline, 2000.

Macan, Edward L. *Rocking the Classics: English Progressive Rock and the Counterculture.* Oxford, England: Oxford University Press, 1996.

Smith, Bradley. *The Billboard Guide to Progressive Music.* New York: Billboard Books, 1997.

Arsenio Orteza

See also Drug use; Hard rock and heavy metal; Hippies; Led Zeppelin; Music; Pink Floyd; Who, The.

■ Pryor, Richard

Identification African American comedian
Born December 1, 1940; Peoria, Illinois

Pryor was one of the most influential stand-up comics of the 1970's. He built a reputation for riotously funny, uninhibited monologues that offered an aggressively black perspective on his life and American society in general.

Richard Pryor was raised by his grandmother, who ran several brothels in Peoria, Illinois. This early exposure to the seedier side of life shaped his views on race, sex, and entertainment. His career started on the "chitlin circuit," performing exclusively for black Americans, but he craved the success that came with a broader audience. To that end, he patterned himself after Bill Cosby, an African American comedian acceptable to white audiences.

Although he realized some success from this strategy, Pryor felt constrained by the type of material that he was forced to use in mainstream venues. He began to integrate more ethnic humor into his act, drawing on his own experiences and reflecting the changing racial environment of that era. By 1970, he abandoned his middle-of-the-road aspirations and transformed himself into a profane comic force who shocked audiences with his highly graphic accounts of crude sex, drug use, and jumbled feelings of racial pride and despair. The latter was symbolized by his

Comedian Richard Pryor performs on The Ed Sullivan Show. (CBS/Landov)

offhand, though premeditated, use of the term "nigger" in reference to himself and other characters that he developed for his act. This approach gained him notoriety, but the controversy only fueled his popularity. He continued to draw on the most harrowing aspects of his life in order to evoke laughter even as others recoiled from the brutal honesty and the psychic turmoil that this suggested about his own state of mind. Nothing was too outrageous for Pryor to address onstage, from marital discord to his attempted suicide while freebasing cocaine.

His unpredictability made many in the entertainment industry wary even as they sought to channel his creative energy and popularity into money-making projects. In 1977, the National Broadcasting Company (NBC) network gave him a prime-time variety show, but it was cancelled after only four episodes when it became evident that Pryor would not play by network rules. He did better in films. Mainstream comedies such as *Silver Streak* (1976) and *Which Way Is Up?* (1977) were popular, though Pryor's characters rarely reflected the edginess or danger associated with his stage persona. Those qualities were on display, however, in *Richard Pryor: Live in Concert* (1979), a film version of his stand-up act. He also proved an effective dramatic actor, earning critical praise for his work in *Lady Sings the Blues* (1972) and *Blue Collar* (1978). Also successful were his record albums, including *That Nigger's Crazy* (1974) and *Bicentennial Nigger* (1976).

Impact   Much like well-known comedian Lenny Bruce, Richard Pryor used comedy as a tool of discovery, confronting personal demons and social hypocrisy in a manner that entertained and challenged his audiences. His influence on stand-up comedy was immense, particularly with younger African American comedians such as Eddie Murphy and Chris Rock. He continued to perform and make films through the 1980's, though with diminishing commercial success. Two heart attacks and multiple sclerosis effectively curtailed his career by 1990.

Further Reading

Pryor, Richard, with Todd Gold. *Pryor Convictions, and Other Life Sentences.* New York: Pantheon, 1995.

Watkins, Mel. *On the Real Side: Laughing, Lying, and Signifying—The Underground Tradition of African American Humor That Transformed American Culture, from Slavery to Richard Pryor.* New York: Touchstone, 1995.

John C. Hajduk

See also   African Americans; Comedians; Film in the United States; *Saturday Night Live*; Variety shows; Wilder, Gene.

■ Psychology

Definition   The science of human behavior and mental processes and its applications

Psychology in the 1970's integrated many voices and changed as a field. Dominated at the beginning of the decade by contemporary interpretations of the classic systems of behaviorism, psychoanalysis, and humanism, psychology became increasingly cognitive, professionalized, and medicalized throughout the decade. It contributed to changing practices in parenting, education, treatment of the mentally ill, and to the erosion of constricting stereotypes.

By 1970, the writings of three seminal thinkers had filtered into every area of psychological science. The most self-conscious scientist of these, B. F. Skinner, described his approach as behaviorism. Behaviorism, which explores experimentally induced changes in the environment and consequent changes in behavior, had long been a central force in the field. During the decade, Skinner became a public figure by outlining his behaviorist views in the popular book *Beyond Freedom and Dignity* (1971). He developed a system of learning based upon the encouragement of desirable behavior by carefully choosing and sequencing rewards, or reinforcements, after correct responses.

Two other influential thinkers of the era derived their ideas from their experiences with "talking" therapies for the emotionally disturbed. Of these, Erik Erikson was the period's major interpreter of the psychoanalysis originated by Sigmund Freud. In the 1970's, selective ideas from psychoanalysis continued to influence medical psychology. Like other analysts, Erikson upheld Freud's core principle: Emotional illness results from conflicting feelings about one's earliest relationships in childhood and can be cured by the therapeutic uncovering of these conflicts. Erikson viewed maturation as a series of crises in changing social relationships which, contrary to Freud, he extended into adult life. He viewed the infant-caretaker relationship and their mutual attachment as particularly crucial to the child's establishment of trust in human relationships.

The third seminal thinker, Carl Rogers, treated psychological troubles by "humanistic" therapy. To Rogers, a good therapist is not an expert but an understanding friend. Therapy should provide a warm, empathetic listening environment where the troubled individual could authentically express innermost feelings, discover one's "true self," and "actualize" by growing into the potential of this self.

Trends and Changes Within Psychology   In the early 1970's, leaders in psychology proclaimed its relevance to the social problems of an era troubled by civil rights struggles and the Vietnam War. Considerable psychological research was directed toward these issues. Social learning researchers, critical of television violence, demonstrated how readily children imitate aggressive models and how often guilt about such aggression is rationalized by blaming victims as deserving of their fate. Research showing the substantial overlap between the distribution of characteristics of racial and ethnic groups already had undermined any "scientific" basis for discrimination. Moreover, during this period, major research refuted the core assumption behind gender stereotyping by demonstrating the variability of ability and personality traits among men and women and the substantial overlap between their distributions of traits.

The most fundamental development within the science of psychology at this time was the explosive growth of theory and research about strategies of thinking and reasoning. Borrowing from computer models of information processing, cognitive psychology differed from the older "mentalism" in that it investigated mental strategies of interpreting events by postulating verifiable consequences in behavior. In 1970, only Jean Piaget's observations about predictable age-related changes in the patterns of children's thinking was known to most psychologists. Within the decade, however, cognitive studies inspired new textbooks and journals and invaded every area of psychology. The "cognitive revolution" had begun.

Within professional psychology, the ranks of clinical psychologists who treated psychopathology grew apace until their professional concerns dominated psychological organizations. With the advent of effective therapeutic drugs and a growing awareness of the adverse effects of institutionalization, treatment of the mentally ill increasingly took place in community settings. By the late 1970's, psychotherapy was beginning to be funded by medical insurers who pressured psychologists to address specific troublesome symptoms with briefer therapies. Since the treatment of well-functioning homosexuals seemed to serve no purpose, "homosexuality" was deleted as a disease category from the standard diagnostic manual.

Impact During the 1970's, a broader and larger segment of the public was served by an expanding variety of psychotherapeutic methods. The uncovering techniques of psychoanalysis had long served best a population of verbal, well-educated neurotics. Newer behavioral techniques of well-designed reinforcement and modeling, designed to eliminate bad habits and teach adaptive behavior, could be applied to the less articulate. Humanistic approaches open to anyone who sought personal growth expanded far beyond the domain of psychology. In the human potential movement, facilitators qualified by their "empathy" guided groups of people to self-knowledge in a climate where deep longings were freely expressed. Therapy was for all.

Psychology also influenced the socialization of the young. Programmed instruction designed to meet clearly specified behavioral objectives evolved from the Skinnerian learning laboratory to educational levels ranging from first-grade arithmetic to college chemistry. The psychoanalytically based concern with the quality of the mutual attachment between an infant and a primary caretaker was reflected in the popular writings of Dr. Benjamin Spock, who defined "good" child care for many parents. Moreover, the value of humanism's self-esteem became widely accepted. For example, fostering esteem for one's unique self became a consistent theme of Fred Rogers on the children's television series *Mister Rogers' Neighborhood*. Only a few critics argued that such emphasis on self-esteem was creating a generation of obsessively self-centered narcissists and a "Me Decade."

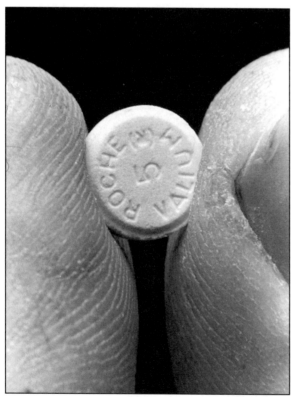

In addition to therapy, the 1970's saw a rise in the mainstream use of tranquilizers such as Valium. (AP/Wide World Photos)

Influences from the psychology of the 1970's endured in subsequent decades. Educational goals continued to be justified in terms of behavioral objectives. Open expressions of once-denied feelings became common, and women validated previously unrecognized skills with new accomplishments. Transcending temporary fads, such changes became part of the culture.

Further Reading

American Psychologist 25-35 (1970-1980). A comparison of issues early in the decade with the 1979 and 1980 issues of psychology's core publication is instructive of changes within the field during this era.

Howard, Jane. *Please Touch.* New York: Dell, 1970. A very readable account of the human potential movement from the perspective of an informed consumer.

Leahey, Thomas. *A History of Psychology: Main Currents in Psychological Thought.* Upper Saddle River, N.J.: Prentice-Hall, 2000. Chapters 14 and 15 describe the cognitive revolution and the transformation of the profession during the 1970's.

Nye, Robert D. *Three Views of Man: Perspectives from Sigmund Freud, B. F. Skinner, and Carl Rogers.* Monterey, Calif.: Brooks/Cole, 1975. The contrasting approaches to psychology pioneered by these three thinkers influenced major trends that unfolded during the decade.

Skinner, B. F. *Beyond Freedom and Dignity.* Reprint. Indianapolis: Hackett, 2002. Behaviorism's major spokesperson outlines his views and discusses their implications for society.

Thomas E. DeWolfe

See also   Children's television; Education in the United States; Homosexuality and gay rights; Human potential movement; *I'm OK, You're OK*; "Me Decade"; *Mister Rogers' Neighborhood*; *Passages*; Self-help books; Television in the United States; Women's rights.

■ Public Broadcasting Service (PBS)

Identification   Nonprofit network of public television stations

Date   Founded in 1969; began operation in 1970

Through its innovative and popular programming, PBS established itself as the leading nationwide noncommercial television network in the United States during the 1970's.

The establishment of a nationwide public broadcasting network in the late 1960's was the culmination of a decade-long push toward making standardized educational programming available to all American television viewers. PBS began operation in October, 1970, with 128 local member stations. It was created from the fledgling National Education Television (NET) network, which had been established as a means of producing and distributing programming for local educational television stations and the Corporation for Public Broadcasting (CPB), created under the Public Broadcasting Act of 1967 to promote educational television.

From its inception, PBS was distinguished from other television networks not only in its noncommercial status but also in its cooperative organization. Most of the programming broadcast on PBS was produced by member stations and typically paid for with a mixture of public and private funds. Unlike commercial networks whose programming originated from one or two "flagship" stations, PBS distributed programming produced by several local member stations, including WNET in New York, WGBH-TV in Boston, and KQED in San Francisco, as well as foreign media outlets such as the British Broadcasting Corporation (BBC) and independent producers. Funding for programming came from the CPB, the National Endowment for the Humanities (NEH), and other government sources, corporations, and private foundations, most notably the Ford Foundation. Although private companies were not allowed to advertise on PBS stations, their sponsorship of programming was expressly acknowledged on the air. Member stations paid subscription fees to PBS and assumed cooperative ownership of the network, in contrast to commercial network affiliates that exchanged commercial airtime for programming.

Programming and Technological Innovation   PBS produced and aired a wide variety of programming during the 1970's, including dramatic presentations (*Masterpiece Theatre*); programs devoted to science (*Nova* and *Cosmos*), history (*The Ascent of Man*), and public affairs (*Firing Line*); and a variety of groundbreaking documentaries, such as *An American Family* (1973). However, the network was most acclaimed for its educational programming geared toward young audiences, such as *Sesame Street, The Electric Company, Mister Rogers' Neighborhood,* and *Zoom! Ses-*

Robert MacNeil, of the PBS news program The MacNeil/Lehrer Report, *in 1978.* (AP/Wide World Photos)

ame Street, produced by the independent Children's Television Workshop (CTW), incorporated the teaching of basic language and mathematics into the traditional "nursery school" format of children's programming with its emphasis on social and recreational skills. The show utilized the innovative puppetry of Frank Oz and Jim Henson to create a fictitious neighborhood that featured a multiracial and multicultural array of characters. Lessons were often presented in both English and Spanish. *The Electric Company*, another CTW production, also featured a diverse array of characters (including a young Morgan Freeman) and used popular music and cultural iconography to appeal to a preteen audience.

In addition to its innovative programming, PBS was also on the leading edge of technological advancements in television broadcasting, pioneering the use of stereo television sound in 1972 and providing a laboratory for government-funded development of closed captioning technology during the 1970's. In 1978, the network that had begun opera-

tion by distributing programming through telephone lines became the first American television network to broadcast programming via satellite.

Impact By creating a nationwide system for producing and distributing educational programming and providing a clearinghouse for scarce financial resources, PBS permanently altered the landscape of American broadcast television in the 1970's. Educational programming, previously relegated to low-budget, local stations and "public interest" time on commercial channels, assumed an increasingly prominent role in American popular culture, as exemplified by the immense popularity of *Sesame Street*. Programs lacking sufficient financial viability or mass appeal for broadcast on commercial outlets often appeared on PBS, expanding the variety of programming available to American television viewers in the pre-cable 1970's.

Children's programming featured on the network attracted large audiences by presenting educational material in an entertaining manner, resulting in measurable increases in academic proficiency among young viewers of various ages and skill levels. The manner in which the network combined public and private funding to produce and distribute these programs provided a model for other public-private ventures in American government and society. Moreover, PBS served a vital function as a laboratory for new broadcast technology in the 1970's and beyond.

Subsequent Events In the waning decades of the twentieth century, PBS drew increasing criticism from conservatives for its perceived liberal bias and from liberals for its alleged vulnerability to corporate influence and political pressure. In addition, the network met with increased competition from cable channels specializing in educational and quasi-educational programming. However, PBS maintained a formidable presence in the American television industry with approximately 350 member stations and a variety of additional programming and services offered via satellite and the Internet.

Further Reading

Borgenicht, David. *"Sesame Street" Unpaved: Scripts, Stories, Secrets, and Songs.* New York: Hyperion Books, 1998. A light but informative behind-the-scenes history of one of the most popular and successful programs aired on PBS.

Fisch, Shalom M., and Rosemary T. Truglio. *"G" Is for Growing: Thirty Years of Research on Children and "Sesame Street."* Mahwah, N.J.: Lawrence Erlbaum, 2000. A synthesis of various research studies focusing on the impact of PBS educational programming on child development.

Jarvik, Laurence A. *PBS, Behind the Screen.* Rocklin, Calif.: Forum, 1998. A conservative critique of PBS that nevertheless provides a detailed account of the network's early history.

Ledbetter, James. *Made Possible By: The Death of Public Broadcasting in the United States.* New York: Verso, 1998. This history of American public broadcasting argues that the gradual diminution of government funding and the corresponding increase in corporate contributions has resulted in a decline in quality of PBS programming.

Ouellette, Laurie. *Viewers Like You?* New York: Columbia University Press, 2002. An analysis of the political and social issues that have shaped public television from its inception.

Stewart, David A. *The PBS Companion: A History of Public Television.* New York: TV Books, 1999. This collection of essays focuses on specific programs and personalities that contributed to the development of public television in the United States.

Michael H. Burchett

See also *American Family, An*; Children's television; Closed captioning; Education in the United States; *Mister Rogers' Neighborhood*; Muppets, The; National Public Radio (NPR); Television in the United States; *Sesame Street.*

■ Puerto Rican nationalism

Definition   Rise in Puerto Rican nationalist sentiment and the move toward independent statehood

The 1970's saw the Puerto Rican statehood movement intensify as the political parties split over the issue of the island's relationship with the United States. At the same time, violence became the tool of those seeking the island's independence.

Following the 1898 American seizure of Puerto Rico from Spain, there had been disputes over the status of the island. During the 1950's, Puerto Rico was granted commonwealth status, giving its citizens certain rights under American law. In 1967, a referendum over whether Puerto Rico should apply for statehood divided the island along political lines. By 1970, the main political party in Puerto Rico favoring continued commonwealth status, the Partido Popular Democratico (PPD), was split. A new party, the Partido Nuevo Progresista (PNP), was formed. The PNP challenged the PPD for political control, winning the governorship in 1968. In 1972, the PPD won narrowly and attempted to work with the Nixon administration to settle the status issue. However, the 1976 election for governor saw the PNP regain control by a narrow margin. The governor, Carlos Barcelo, aggressively pushed for statehood, filling the top jobs in the island government with pro-statehood followers.

Political Violence   Some Puerto Ricans were unwilling to wait for a political process to change the island's status. In 1974, a group of Puerto Rican nationalists created the Armed Forces of National Liberation (FALN) in order to conduct terrorist attacks in favor of total independence for the island. In October of that year, New York City suffered a series of bombings of major financial institutions. The bombs caused injuries and rattled the nerves of New Yorkers.

On January 24, 1975, the FALN struck the Fraunces Tavern, a New York City historical landmark where George Washington had bidden goodbye to his troops at the end of the Revolutionary War. The bombing killed five people and injured more than fifty others as they ate lunch at the popular restaurant. The bombing was tied to the FALN, which demanded the release of terrorists who had attempted to assassinate President Harry S. Truman in 1951. Throughout 1975, the FALN struck, planting bombs at major businesses, including department stores and banks in New York and Chicago. The absence of injuries was attributed more to luck than any design by the terrorists not to kill innocent people.

The bombings continued in 1976 and 1977, including one in a Puerto Rican hotel where the island's governor was meeting. The FALN continued attacking major sites in New York, killing innocent people while demanding that Puerto Rico gain its independence. The federal government responded by tracking down the terrorists and their allies and prosecuting them. In July, 1978, a break in the case occurred when New York police were called to an explosion in an apartment building. Inside they found bomb-making materials and a man who suffered ex-

tensive injuries when the bomb that he was making exploded in his face. This discovery allowed police to track down FALN members and put out of commission one of the group's most proficient bomb-makers.

The FALN was not the only group using violence on behalf of Puerto Rican independence. A group of homegrown nationalists, the Macheteros, promised to conduct a campaign of terror against the Puerto Rican government on the island. The group was not as active in the 1970's as the FALN, but it did murder two Puerto Rican police officers. The attacks on the island were usually against American military posts. Their actions included exploding a bomb planted at a Reserve Officers' Training Corps (ROTC) building as the new Puerto Rican governor was being inaugurated on January 2, 1977.

Response of American Officials   Puerto Rican politics had a limited impact on the actions of the American government. In 1972, President Richard M. Nixon formed a commission to study the status of Puerto Rico, but no legislation was proposed. The statehood question remained on the political back burner until the end of Gerald R. Ford's presidency. President Ford announced on January 1, 1977, that he supported statehood for the island. With only three weeks left in his administration, Ford could do little to make the island a state but did place pressure on the incoming Carter administration to deal with the question.

Carter responded by making ceremonial overtures toward Puerto Rico. In September, 1979, he freed four of the men who had attempted to assassinate Truman in 1951. The Carter administration also attempted to improve the island's economy by passing tax breaks for industry and banking that re-

located on Puerto Rico. The 1979 Pan-American Games were held on the island, producing controversy over whether the United States national anthem should be played at the opening of the games or if it should be replaced with the Puerto Rican anthem. A compromise was reached that allowed both to be played.

The United Nations also became involved. A special decolonization committee was established. One of its members, Cuba, was headed by the communist dictator Fidel Castro, who criticized the American government for not allowing Puerto Rico to gain independence. Castro's complaints were ignored, but the committee continued to attack the status of Puerto Rico.

Impact   The Puerto Rican nationalist movement both helped and hurt the cause for statehood and independence. The violence of the FALN and others only stiffened American resolve against bending to the demands of the groups and further slowed the process for determining the island's status.

Subsequent Events   The political divisions continued in Puerto Rico after the 1970's as the pro-statehood and pro-commonwealth parties battled for control of the government. A 1999 presidential pardon of FALN terrorists revived the controversy over the organization.

Further Reading
Malavet, Pedro. *America's Colony.* New York: New York University Press, 2004. Describes the effort of Puerto Ricans to gain independence from the United States.
Melendez, Edgardo. *Puerto Rico's Statehood Movement.* New York: Greenwood Press, 1988. Discusses the

1970's movement to make the island the country's fifty-first state.

Morris, Nancy. *Puerto Rico: Culture, Politics, and Identity.* Westport, Conn.: Praeger, 1995. Describes the changes occurring on the island in terms of its culture and political system.

Trias Monge, Jose. *Puerto Rico: The Trials of the Oldest Colony in the World.* New Haven, Conn.: Yale University Press, 1997. Discusses the difficulties faced by Puerto Rico as it remains an American commonwealth.

Douglas Clouatre

See also Chicano movement; Latin America; Latinos; Terrorism.

■ Punk rock

Definition Genre of rock music

Reacting to the overwrought spectacles that characterized much of rock music during the 1970's, punk rock brought a "do-it-yourself" aesthetic and energy back to the forefront of rock.

The British punk band the Sex Pistols in 1977. (AP/Wide World Photos)

The roots of punk rock can be traced to the previous decade. Cult urban bands such as the Velvet Underground, the Fugs, and even the more popular Doors stood out with their edgy songs about subjects such as drugs and despair. Meanwhile, garage bands across the country specialized in trashy and ragged-but-enthusiastic singles. As the 1960's became the 1970's, bands such as the New York Dolls, Iggy and the Stooges, the Modern Lovers, and the MC5 emerged with raw, energetic music that had little to do with popular music trends, such as progressive rock, singer-songwriters, or even hard rock. Their albums did not sell well and the bands soon dissolved, but they had earned small but devoted followings.

CBGBs and the New York Scene In 1974, Hilly Kristal began booking rock bands at his New York club, CBGBs. Among the earliest and most notable bands were Television, whose edgy compositions often gave way to hypnotic guitar interludes, and Patti Smith, who also often favored long songs and mixing singing with dramatic spoken-word interludes about her favorite poets, rock stars, and God.

However, it was the Ramones that called attention to the innovative genre. The Ramones were four young men from Queens, New York, who took the same false surname, dressed in leather and blue jeans, and grew their mop-top haircuts out. They played speedy, simple, and fun three-chord rock songs about boredom and girls with titles such as "Beat on the Brat" and "Sheena Is a Punk Rocker." As a whole, the music coming from CBGBs came to be known as punk rock; rock critic Dave Marsh originally coined the term in a 1970 review of a concert by garage rockers Question Mark and the Mysterians.

More significant punk bands continued to emerge at CBGBs, drawing fans looking for a new, more immediate alternative to that which was popular. Talking Heads was a quartet of intellectuals who played supple, catchy songs that sounded like little else, thanks to frontman David Byrne's neurotic, minimalist lyrics describing urban alienation. Blondie, led by former Playboy bunny Deborah Harry and her boyfriend, guitarist Chris Stein, created a stripped-down yet stylish update of early 1960's girl groups.

Anarchy in the U.K. In 1976, the Ramones toured Great Britain for the first time, inspiring young, disenfranchised youth to pick up an instrument and form a band. In Britain, punk rock had more societal implications than in the United States; the country was suffering from high unemployment, poverty, and other ills. The leading British punk rock band, the Sex Pistols, became notorious in their country for their antisocial behavior and dress, as well as songs such as "Anarchy in the U.K." The Sex Pistols' main counterparts, the Clash, encouraged a more proactive kind of revolution, endorsing self-empowerment to its audience. The word about these bands began to spread in the United States, even if the music did not exactly catch on. The Clash's 1977 debut album became the most popular import release in the United States until it finally received a domestic release two years later.

Punk Fashion Punk and fashion were more closely aligned in Britain: trademark characteristics such as torn T-shirts and leather jackets punctured with safety pins originated in a fashion store called Sex, which was co-owned by Malcolm McLaren, the future (and brief) manager of the New York Dolls and, more significantly, the Sex Pistols. In the United States, punk fashion was less distinguishable and more spartan, from Smith's ratty T-shirts to the Talking Heads' alligator shirts.

New Beginnings and Endings Record labels had begun signing the New York punk bands. Critics hailed the debut albums from Smith, Television, and the Ramones. Smith had a hit with "Because the Night," which she cowrote with Bruce Springsteen, from her third album. The Talking Heads' second album contained their first hit, a cover of Al Green's "Take Me to the River." Blondie scored with the disco-flavored "Heart of Glass."

Notable Punk Rock Songs of the 1970's

Song	Artist
"London Calling"	The Clash
"God Save the Queen"	The Sex Pistols
"Search and Destroy"	Iggy and the Stooges
"New Rose"	The Damned
"Blitzkreig Bop"	The Ramones
"Hanging on the Telephone"	Blondie
"The Modern World"	The Jam
"What Do I Get?"	The Buzzcocks
"Psycho Killer"	Talking Heads
"Personality Crisis"	The New York Dolls
"Wild Youth"	Generation X
"Gloria"	Patti Smith

However, as the decade came to a close, many of the original punk bands began to dissolve. Television broke up in 1978 after only two albums. The Sex Pistols self-destructed on their first American tour: In 1978, in the Chelsea Hotel in New York, their bassist, Sid Vicious, accidentally killed his girlfriend Nancy Spungeon and soon after died of an overdose of heroin. Smith, who had already been sidelined when she broke her neck after falling off a stage in 1977, announced her retirement in 1979 in order to marry former MC5 guitarist Fred "Sonic" Smith and start a family.

Impact Punk rock served as a reminder that one did not need to be a virtuoso or well-connected to be in a band. The do-it-yourself attitude inspired young music fans to start not only their own bands, but also their own labels, magazines, and clubs, and it encouraged them to go against the grain of what was popular.

Subsequent Events While some punk bands would experience commercial success in the 1980's—and punk's more conventional, radio-friendly cousin, new wave, became popular—for the most part, the genre remained an underground sensation. Significant punk and punk-inspired movements sprouted in cities across the United States, each in turn influencing a new group of young musicians.

Further Reading

Bowman, David. *This Must Be the Place: The Adventures of Talking Heads in the Twentieth Century.* New York: HarperEntertainment, 2001. A thorough account of one of American punk's most successful bands.

McNeil, Legs, and Gillian McCain. *Please Kill Me: The Uncensored Oral History of Punk.* 2d ed. New York: Penguin, 1997. This account collects interviews with many of the major players of punk rock's rise in the 1970's.

Ramone, Dee Dee, with Veronica Kofman. *Lobotomy: Surviving the Ramones.* 2d ed. New York: Thunder's Mouth Press, 2000. The autobiography of the Ramones' founding bassist.

Savage, Jon. *England's Dreaming: Anarchy, Sex Pistols, Punk Rock, and Beyond.* 3d ed. New York: St. Martin's Griffin, 2002. Provides an in-depth study of British punk rock's most notorious band and its contemporaries.

Spitz, Mark, and Brendan Mullen. *We Got the Neutron Bomb: The Untold Story of L.A. Punk.* New York: Three Rivers Press, 2001. Another oral history, this one focusing on the evolution of punk rock in Los Angeles.

Michael Pelusi

See also   Hard rock and heavy metal; Music; Progressive rock; Ramones, The.

■ Pyramid power

Definition   The theory that pyramid shapes generate unique powers

Pyramid power, while not a new idea, flourished during the 1970's as one of the decade's "alternative sciences." Mixing the appeal of ancient mysteries with a significant do-it-yourself component, it claimed to tap into esoteric knowledge and cosmic energy sources.

The Egyptian pyramids have always fascinated lay people and historians. The many puzzles that still surround their construction, design, and meaning have given rise to a host of highly speculative theories. As far back as 1859, a pyramidology movement was founded by mathematician John Taylor, who claimed that the measurements of the Great Pyramid of Giza were a key to foreseeing the future. In

the 1930's, the bodies of stray cats were found undecayed in the Great Pyramid. Neither phenomenon was of interest to science, and in fact, such topics remained in the shadows of even metaphysical speculation until the 1970's.

However, with the decade's growth of the New Age movement, which delved into esoteric knowledge from many sources, it was inevitable that some inquirers would seize upon the pyramids as a potential focus. Pyramid devotees claimed that any structure, large or small, built to the same proportions as the Great Pyramid could tap into biocosmic energies. Dead cats, seeds, and food were all placed in smaller pyramid shapes and said to be miraculously preserved. People, too, were urged to sleep within a pyramid to awaken with renewed energy and faster healing of injuries. Other purported effects of pyramids included keeping razor blades sharp, tenderizing meat, and even creating microwave signals that could—in the future as in the past—generate electric power.

At least two books were published during the 1970's providing detailed directions for building and aligning pyramids at home and for experiments that could be conducted using them. Some theorists suggested that "pyramid power" was known to the Egyptian pyramid builders as the key to immortality.

Impact   The long-term impact of the pyramid power movement was minimal. In many ways, its do-it-yourself aspects doomed it. Unlike such disciplines as astrology and tarot, which deal with ambiguous predictions and the highly complex field of human behavior, checking the effect of pyramids on organic matter is fairly easy. Although few scientists ever bothered to investigate the claims, during the late 1970's and early 1980's, pyramid hobbyists began to experiment with them. Most concluded that other factors—a dry microclimate or the power of suggestion—better explained the claimed results. The theory continued to have adherents, but they tended to be ignored by most in the New Age movement.

Further Reading

Dunn, Christopher P. *The Giza Power Plant.* Rochester, Vt.: Bear, 1998.

Flanagan, G. Pat. *Pyramid Power: The Millenium Science.* Reprint. Anchorage, Alaska: Earthpulse Press, 1997.

Emily Alward

See also   Fads; New Age movement.

■ Pyramid schemes

Definition A business model that involves the exchange of money for enrolling people into the scheme

Pyramid schemes proliferated during the 1970's and gained notoriety with several high-profile prosecutions and trials.

Pyramid schemes, often referred to as multilevel marketing (MLM) or network or matrix schemes, work by offering distributorships without product. The company promises, that once has signed up as a distributor, one will receive commissions for sales and recruitment for new members. However, the plan collapses once new distributors cannot be recruited, so those at the bottom levels inevitably lose money.

The origins for this type of fraud—the promise of earning big profits from a small investment—begin with Charles Ponzi during the 1920's. Ponzi made millions by speculating in international postal reply coupons. These practices gained popularity, and the Federal Trade Commission (FTC) began to investigate and challenge pyramid schemes by the 1970's. Several companies went to trial during this period. The FTC charged Glenn W. Turner, a master in network marketing, with creating two companies that were involved in pyramid schemes. In *SEC v. Glenn W. Turner, Inc.* (1973), the U.S. Ninth Circuit Court of Appeals decided that securities statues also applied to industry. Turner's "Dare to Be Great" motivational program was ruled to be an investment contract, thereby subject to securities laws and Securities and Exchange Commission (SEC) regulation.

The FTC then accused Koscot, an Orlando cosmetic company owned by Turner, of charging large membership fees, giving commissions not based upon product sales, and misleading distributors as to their earnings potential. In *SEC v. Koscot Interplane-tary, Inc.* (1975), a district court decided that pyramid schemes were a deceptive practice and violated federal securities acts of 1933 and 1934.

The FTC also accused Amway of operating an illegal pyramid in 1975, but the litigation continued for four more years. Amway prevailed in a 1979 landmark decision. The court decided that Amway's direct marketing and retail sales were a legitimate business opportunity because of company safeguards, referred to as the 70/10 rule: Amway contract provisions specified that 70 percent of the product had to be sold by retail to customers, that distributors must maintain a 10 percent base of customers, and that distributors or Amway had to buy back product inventory applicable to sales if a distributor chose to leave the company.

Impact The Koscot and Amway decisions provided the groundwork for defining unlawful pyramid schemes. States passed laws prohibiting pyramid schemes that offered to pay commissions for recruiting new distributors and not related to product sales—a legitimate multilevel marketing company will only pay commissions for retail sales.

Further Reading

Maxa, Rudy. *Dare to Be Great: The Unauthorized Story of Glenn Turner.* New York: William Morrow, 1977.

U.S. Federal Trade Commission. *Multilevel Marketing Plans: Facts for Consumers.* Washington, D.C.: Bureau of Consumer Protection, Office of Consumer and Business Education, 1996.

Walsh, James. *You Can't Cheat an Honest Man: How Ponzi Schemes and Pyramid Frauds Work and Why They're More Common than Ever.* Los Angeles: Silver Lake, 1998.

Gayla Koerting

See also Business and the economy in the United States; Scandals.

Q

■ Quadraphonic sound

Definition   Reproduced sound that achieves enhanced realism by using four channels rather than two

The advent of stereophonic sound systems in the 1950's brought an enhanced level of realism to sound reproduction, but some people felt that the sound still lacked depth. Quadraphonic, or four-channel, sound systems were an attempt to rectify this perceived deficiency.

Quadraphonic (from the Latin root *quad* meaning "four") sound systems were developed as an attempt to surround a listener completely by sound. Four independent loudspeakers, two in front and two behind the listener, were required. When the program material was stored on magnetic tape, four independent channels of sound (recorded with four independent microphones) could be utilized. For stereo vinyl discs, only two channels were available; therefore, the four recorded channels had to be encoded into two channels. This arrangement was realized in two completely different and incompatible systems, the matrix system and the discrete method. Matrix systems involved generating pseudo-independent rear speaker signals by mixing various amounts of the front left and right channels and sending the mixed signals to the rear speakers. While this method did give the impression of four separate channels, they were not independent channels. Left-right separation had to be sacrificed in order to gain a small amount of front-rear separation.

The discrete systems attempted to create four independent channels by encoding the two additional channels as information stored at frequencies well above the normal range of human hearing. A special and extremely small stylus was required to track the record groove at these high frequencies in order to receive this information, and a decoder was necessary to retrieve the information and reproduce it in the audio frequency range. Because of the technical demands of this system, the results were prone to significant levels of distortion.

Impact   Quadraphonic systems did not survive the 1970's; they remained an aberration on the path to realistic sound reproduction. The first problem was the uncritical acceptance of the assumption that if two channels are better than one, then four channels must be better than two. Quadraphonic sound was no better, and was in some cases substantially worse, than high quality stereophonic sound. A second problem was the lack of program material: Quad systems were being marketed before there was substantial public interest or many discs available. Finally, it is possible to create realistic acoustic ambiance by mixing signals from four microphones, two for direct sound and two for reverberation, into two channels. Requiring two additional channels merely to reproduce reverberant sound is superfluous.

Further Reading

Feldman, Leonard. *Four-Channel Sound.* New York: Bobbs-Merrill, 1973.

Institute of High Fidelity. *Official Guide to High Fidelity.* New York: Bobbs-Merrill, 1974.

Strong, William J., and George R. Plitnik. *Music, Speech, Audio.* Provo, Utah: Soundprint, 1992.

George R. Plitnik

See also   Dolby sound; 8-track tapes; Inventions.

■ Quebec Charter of Human Rights and Freedoms

Identification   Canadian legislation
Date   Passed on June 27, 1975; took effect on June 28, 1976

The Quebec Charter of Human Rights and Freedoms, modeled on the United Nations Universal Declaration of Human Rights, is one of the quasi-constitutional laws known as the Quebec Statutes.

The Quebec Charter of Human Rights and Freedoms was introduced by Jérôme Choquette, a strong supporter of human rights who served as the Quebec minister of justice under the Liberal government of Robert Bourassa. The charter was enacted into law by the Quebec National Assembly in 1975 and its provisions became effective one year later. It applies only to the Province of Quebec.

Each of the seven parts in the charter defines a different aspect of human rights. Part I describes the fundamental human rights and freedoms of all Quebecers. The statute contains five chapters defining these rights and freedoms: political rights, judicial rights, economic rights, social rights, and interpretative provisions. Part II establishes the Commission des Droits de la Personne et des Droits de la Jeunesse (Human Rights and Youth Commission), an institution responsible for promoting and upholding the principles of the charter. Part III defines miscellaneous rights, part IV defines rights to confidentiality, part V defines regulations that the government may adopt, and part VI establishes a human rights tribunal.

The Quebec Charter of Human Rights and Freedoms is considered quasi-constitutional, which means that no provision of any other act passed by the Quebec National Assembly can detract from its sections unless the provision explicitly states that it applies despite the charter.

A street in Montreal, the capital of Quebec, in 1979. During the decade, this French-speaking province celebrated its unique culture within Canada and sometimes threatened to declare independence. (AP/Wide World Photos)

Impact The rights covered by the Quebec Charter of Human Rights and Freedoms are extensive; the charter contains provisions not found in the Canadian Charter of Rights and Freedoms passed in 1982, such as a prohibition of discrimination on the grounds of social condition. Consequently, the Quebec legislation represents one of the world's most progressive human rights laws.

Further Reading

Canadian Legal Information Institute. Statutes and Regulations of Quebec. http://www.canlii.org/qc/laws/index.html.

Commission des Droits de la Personne et des Droits de la Jeunesse. http://www.cdpdj.qc.ca/en.

Peggy J. Anderson

See also Canadian Citizenship Act of 1977; Canadian Human Rights Act of 1977; Charter of the French Language; Education in Canada; Francophonie, La; Minorities in Canada; Multiculturalism in Canada; United Nations; Women's rights.

■ Queen

Identification   British hard-rock band
Date   Formed in 1971

Queen blended the thunderous volume of heavy metal with the decadent flamboyance of glam rock, hitting upon a commercially successful sound and pioneering the effective use of what would eventually become known as the rock video.

Queen was formed in 1971 when guitarist Brian May and drummer Roger Taylor recruited bassist John Deacon and the lead-singing pianist Freddie Mercury. By the end of the 1970's, the group had seen six of its albums sell more than 500,000 copies and two of its singles become established classics. Its early years, however, were hardly auspicious. The quartet's self-consciously arty combination of loud guitars and fanciful extravagance met with little enthusiasm. To an American public already saturated with long-haired British hard-rock "dandies," Queen's exaggeration of the mythological, apocalyptic, and sexually ambiguous pretensions of acts such as Led Zeppelin and David Bowie felt like a parody without a point.

Only with the Top 20 single "Killer Queen" in 1975 did Queen discover the secret to infiltrating American radio: coy lyrics, strong melodies, May's homemade guitar filigrees, and painstakingly overdubbed vocals. It was a formula that the group exploited with "Bohemian Rhapsody," a single from the 1975 album *A Night at the Opera*. The song defied every rule of Top 40 radio programming. Six minutes in length and comprising five stylistically distinct sections (none of which bore a resemblance to anything else on the airwaves), it made the Top 10. It also spawned an equally elaborate video clip that, because of its airing on television shows such as *The Midnight Special* and *Don Kirshner's Rock Concert*, es-

tablished Queen's image in the minds of a public that, for the most part, had yet to see them perform live. Eager to repeat this success, the group released the strikingly similar "Somebody to Love," replete with video, eighteen months later.

Apparently concerned that it was becoming trapped by its own excesses or that the stripped-down basics of punk rock might make such excessiveness appear emblematic of "Me Decade" self-indulgence, Queen returned in 1977 with the sparsely recorded *News of the World*, earning its first platinum single with the double-sided hit "We Will Rock You/We Are the Champions." *Jazz* (1978), Queen's last studio album of the decade, yielded another double-sided hit, "Bicycle Race/Fat Bottomed Girls," but it received more attention for its inclusion of an uncensored poster of the nude female bicycle race that the group staged in order to publicize the album's release.

Impact   Because Mick Jagger and Bowie had established androgyny as a rock star pose not necessarily connected with a performer's actual life, Mercury's campy homosexual mannerisms (and occasionally his lyrics) did not hamper Queen's popularity among the overridingly macho hard-rock fans, who came to expect outrageousness from the group and were seldom disappointed.

Further Reading

Freestone, Peter. *Freddie Mercury: An Intimate Memoir by the Man Who Knew Him Best.* London: Omnibus Press, 2001.

Nester, Daniel. *God Save My Queen: A Tribute.* Brooklyn, N.Y.: Soft Skull Press, 2003.

Arsenio Orteza

See also   Bowie, David; Hard rock and heavy metal; Led Zeppelin; Music; Progressive rock; Punk rock.

R

■ Racial discrimination

Definition Prejudicial action or treatment toward members of certain ethnic or racial groups

Compared with the explosive civil rights demonstrations and upheavals of the 1960's, the 1970's witnessed a moment of calm as Americans of various groups tried to adjust to newly imposed statutes that provided broader rights for minorities.

It would be naïve, if not outright overly optimistic, to assume that the landmark civil rights legislation of the 1960's automatically swept away years of acrimony and resistance that had dominated American society for decades. The 1970's, however, provided the opportunity to take stock of the progress in efforts to eliminate racial discrimination in housing, employment, public transportation, schools, other public facilities, and the implementation of the voting rights for minorities.

It was already obvious by the late 1960's that blacks were beginning to make some political gains through their increased participation in the political process. Across the board, voter registration numbers shot up upward, and several hundred African American candidates were elected into various offices in the Old South. By 1972, nearly half of southern black children were enrolled in integrated classrooms.

Consolidating the Gains During the 1970's, the U.S. Supreme Court was forced to review a number of cases in order to clarify the constitutional limits of the Equal Employment Opportunity Commission (EEOC) enforcement efforts. Many of these cases addressed the broad definition of racial discrimination, affirmative action remedies, and the rights of minorities and women, as well as the protections afforded to the freedom of religious practices.

In *McDonnell Douglas Corp. v. Green* (1973), the Supreme Court established the basic analytical framework for proving an individual case of intentional discrimination, or disparate treatment, under Title VII. The Court held that a plaintiff could prove unlawful discrimination indirectly in a hiring case by showing four facts: The plaintiff is a member of a Title VII protected group; the plaintiff applied and was qualified for the position sought; the employer rejected the plaintiff for the job; and the employer continued to seek applicants with similar qualifications after the rejection. The Court maintained that once such a bare showing has been made, in order to avoid liability an employer must articulate a legitimate, nondiscriminatory reason explaining its refusal to hire. The analytical framework of *McDonnell Douglas* has since been applied to cases brought under all of EEOC's other statutes and in one form or another to most kinds of employment decisions.

Congress also took some initiative to consolidate the legislative gains of the 1960's. It enacted the Pregnancy Discrimination Act of 1978, which amended Title VII to explicitly prohibit discrimination on the basis of pregnancy, reinstating the EEOC's interpretation of the law.

Discrimination Against Individuals It soon became clear that the Supreme Court was inclined to consolidate the spirit of civil rights legislation through various decisions in favor of dismantling previous discriminatory practices in employment and pertaining to disabilities and gender issues.

Espinoza v. Farah Manufacturing Company (1973) held that noncitizens are entitled to Title VII protection. The Court stated that a citizenship requirement for a job may violate the law if it discriminates on the basis of national origin. Following this decision, the EEOC issued revised guidelines in 1975 prohibiting the imposition of a citizenship requirement as a job criterion where it has the "purpose or effect" of excluding persons of a particular national origin.

Stating that Title VII confers an individual right to equal employment opportunities that cannot be bargained away by the union and employer, the Court in *Alexander v. Gardner-Denver Co.* (1974) held that an employee who submits a discrimination claim to arbitration under a collective bargaining agreement and loses is not precluded from suing under Title VII. In *Albemarle Paper Co. v. Moody* (1975), (1975), the Court held that when a finding of discrimination has been made, there is a presumption that back pay should be provided to make individual victims whole.

In *World Airlines, Inc. v. Hardison* (1977), the Court adapted the civil rights laws to religion and accepted EEOC guidelines that required an employer to make a reasonable accommodation for employees' and applicants' religious needs where doing so would not create an undue hardship. The Court then established a de minimis level for demonstrating undue hardship.

In *Los Angeles Department of Water and Power v. Manhart* (1978), the Court held that employers may not require female employees to make larger contributions to pension plans in order to obtain the same monthly benefits as men. The Court, agreeing with EEOC, specifically rejected a cost-justification defense that was based on the fact that women, on average, live longer than men.

Finally, favoring voluntary affirmative action programs, the Court held in *United Steelworkers of America v. Weber* (1979) that such programs are not illegal even if they include numerical goals and timetables, provided that they are intended to "eliminate a manifest racial imbalance" caused by past discrimination, are "temporary," and "do not unnecessarily trammel on interests" of or "create an absolute bar to advancement" for nonminority employees.

Attempts at Reversal   The opportunity to savor the victories of the Civil Rights movement quickly ended, however, as the Supreme Court in *Milliken v. Bradley* (1974) blindsided school desegregation advocates when it ruled that desegregation plans could not require students to move across school district lines. The decision effectively exempted suburban districts from shouldering any part of the burden of desegregation and placed the responsibility on the least prosperous districts. Boston and other cities were shaken to their foundations, as the poorest, most disadvantaged elements of the white and black communities were pitted against one another in school desegregation plans.

Affirmative action programs also remained highly controversial. Some white workers denied advancement or white students refused college admission cried out against "reverse discrimination." In *Regents of the University of California v. Bakke* (1978), the Court

ordered the Medical School of the University of California at Davis to admit white applicant Allan Bakke and stated that preference in admissions could not be based on ethnic or racial identity alone. Critics of the *Bakke* decision, including dissenting African American justice Thurgood Marshall, warned that the denial of racial preferences might sweep away years of civil rights progress, but many conservatives cheered the decision as affirming the principle that justice is color-blind.

Impact   Racial discrimination in the 1970's was largely marked by controversy arising from the landmark civil rights achievements of the preceding decade. The combined effort of both federal and state governments was needed in order to implement the statues of the 1960's. Among the groups that were able to consolidate their gains during the decade were Native Americans, women, and African Americans. The contrasting policy formulation strategies of Presidents Richard M. Nixon and Jimmy Carter helped to harden the contours and define the limits of a new civil rights era.

Further Reading

Gaffney, Edward M. "Bob Jones University: Epiphenomenon or Time Bomb?" *Journal of Social, Political, and Economic Studies* 9, no. 1 (1984): 45-57.

Jencks, Christopher. "Affirmative Action for Blacks: Past, Present, and Future." *American Behavioral Scientist* 28, no. 6 (1985): 731-760.

Kuo, Wen H. "Coping with Racial Discrimination: The Case of Asian Americans." *Ethnic and Racial Studies* 18, no. 1 (1995): 109-127.

Kusmer, Kenneth L. "African Americans in the City Since World War II: From the Industrial to the Post-Industrial Era." *Journal of Urban History* 21, no. 4 (1995): 458-504.

Surace, Samuel J. "Achievement, Discrimination, and Mexican Americans." *Comparative Studies in Society and History* 24, no. 2 (1982): 315-339.

Thompson, Walter G. "Racial Integration in U.S. Schools: The 'Busing' Controversy." *Journal of Social, Political, and Economic Studies* 7, nos. 1-2 (1982): 129-151.

Wilson, Anna Victoria. "A Black High School Student's Experience of Desegregation in Birmingham, Alabama." *Journal of the Midwest History of Education Society* 23 (1996): 117-123.

Austin Ogunsuyi

See also Affirmative action; African Americans; Asian Americans; Busing; Chicano movement; Education in the United States; Latinos; Native Americans; *Regents of the University of California v. Bakke*; Supreme Court decisions; *Swann v. Charlotte-Mecklenburg Board of Education*.

■ Racketeer Influenced and Corrupt Organizations (RICO) Act of 1970

Identification U.S. federal legislation
Date Signed on October 15, 1970

Because of the growing power of organized crime, Congress enacted the RICO statute in order to limit the Mafia's influence on legitimate businesses. American courts, however, wound up applying the RICO statute in unexpected ways.

The Racketeer Influenced and Corrupt Organizations (RICO) Act was intended to shield legitimate businesses from infiltration by organized crime. RICO was a federal response to the difficulties of rooting the Mafia out of established business enterprises, such as legalized gambling or labor unions. Using the Constitution's power to regulate interstate commerce, the statute defined violations of the law when a person or organization used racketeer-generated income to acquire influence in a business engaging in interstate commerce. Such activity included investing money in the targeted business, using racketeering to gain influence or control over a business, or using the business as a cover for other racketeering activity.

Crimes targeted by federal prosecutors using the RICO statute included such traditional organized crime activities as drug trafficking, gambling, and extortion. Single cases of such illegal activity did not qualify as a RICO violation. Rather, at least two instances of illegal activity had to take place in order to establish a pattern of behavior. If convicted, violators faced imprisonment, fines, and loss of assets gained from the illegal activity.

Bolstered by the success of the federal RICO statute in containing organized crime, most states enacted their own RICO laws for local crimes that did not cross state lines. In addition to federal cases, victims of racketeering could apply the statute to civil suits. If successful, plaintiffs in civil RICO cases could claim damages up to three times the damage suffered, plus any legal costs.

However, the penalties available in civil suits caused a major change in the application of the RICO statute. Large business concerns became the target of RICO litigation. Because of the broad definition of the statute, legitimate businesses guilty of only minor violations, such as contract violations or defective products, often faced civil RICO suits by unhappy plaintiffs. Moreover, the amount of financial compensation of three times the perceived damage was often greater than the award in typical negligence lawsuits, and critics of the RICO statutes complained that it created frivolous litigation. Other plaintiffs applied RICO against organizations engaged in social activism, such as antiabortion groups, and critics feared that the loose definition of RICO could lead to the restriction of social organization and protest.

Impact The RICO law was an effective tool against organized crime, as evidenced by the decline of the Mafia's influence after the 1970's. The broad application of the law generated critics, but the RICO statute withstood numerous Supreme Court challenges.

Further Reading

Holmes, Cameron H. *Drafting a State RICO Statute: A Comparative Analysis of Five Statutes*. Washington, D.C.: National Association of Attorney Generals, 1990.

Joseph, Gregory P. *Civil RICO: A Definitive Guide*. New York: American Bar Association, 2000.

Rakoff, Jed S., and Harold W. Goldstein. *RICO: Civil and Criminal Law and Strategy*. New York: Law Journals Seminar-Press, 2000.

Steven J. Ramold

See also Business and industry in the United States; Federal Bureau of Investigation (FBI); Hoffa disappearance; Unions in the United States.

■ "Radical Chic"

Identification Essay describing a fund-raising party for Black Panthers that was hosted and attended by elite New Yorkers
Author Tom Wolfe (1931-   )
Date Published on June 8, 1970

Wolfe's New York *magazine essay "Radical Chic: That Party at Lenny's" humorously portrayed a party in which the host—conductor Leonard Bernstein—displayed an obsession with style, racial etiquette, and the exotic allure of his Black Panther guests. By presenting the partygoers' interest in the Black Panthers as shallow and style-based, Wolfe provoked a storm of contradictory responses.*

The Bernstein party, which writer Tom Wolfe attended, was held to raise money to pay bail and legal expenses for fourteen jailed Black Panthers. Controversy over the party began when its coverage in the fashion section of *The New York Times* was carried nationally by a wire service. In an editorial about the story, *The New York Times* called the party "elegant slumming." Wolfe's essay did much more, however, to cast doubt on the host's and attendees' motives. Using the New Journalism approach of blending fact with fiction, he depicted Leonard Bernstein as hyperaware of the clothing that he and the guests wear, which hors d'oeuvres to serve and how the Black Panthers will respond to them, and the decoration of his apartment. He is acutely aware that he cannot use black servants at the party and is delighted when his wife solves the problem by procuring white South American servants. He finds appealing the Black Panthers' dress, speech patterns, hairstyles, and violent acts; they are "real men." Wolfe explains that at the heart of radical chic is a fascination with "the other"—people who are romantic, dark-skinned, primitive, but distant enough from one's location not to be "underfoot."

Reviewer John R. Coyne regretted that a work of humor polarized readers: Those who liked it were called rightists and those who hated it were dubbed left-wingers. Scholar Alan Trachtenberg accused Wolfe both of envy and of hatred of intellectuals. Literature scholar Morris Dickstein found the essay monotonous and pointed to Wolfe's many details about the wealthy partygoers' snobbishness and fashion-consciousness as a reflection of the author's own interests. In contrast, Joseph Epstein, reviewer for *Commentary*, found these details an effective comic device to showcase the elites' reliance on style, their style's incongruity for the event, and, ultimately, the lack of content in radical chic.

Impact Tom Wolfe's essay introduced "radical chic" to popular lingo and it became a catchphrase frequently used to question the middle or upper class, intellectuals, or elites when they champion radical persons or groups. Its meaning then was extended to critique middle- or upper-class white Americans who use radical methods, such as the Weather Underground, or to describe intellectuals, such as literary

and social theorists Edward Said and Jacques Derrida, whose ideas became fashionable. In later years, political correctness was called the descendant of radical chic, and literary theorist Stanley Fish linked it to his own concept, boutique multiculturalism.

Further Reading

Coyne, John R., Jr. "Sketchbook of Snobs." *National Review* 23 (January 26, 1971): 90-91.

Kuehl, Linda. "Dazzle-Dust: A Wolfe in Chic Clothing." *Commonweal* 94 (May 7, 1971): 212-216.

Staub, Michael L. "Setting Up the Seventies: Black Panthers, New Journalism, and the Rewriting of the Sixties." In *The Seventies*, edited by Sheldon Waldrep. New York: Routledge, 2000.

Glenn Ellen Starr Stilling

See also African Americans; Black Panthers; Journalism in the United States; New Journalism; Slogans and slang; Weather Underground; Wolfe, Tom.

■ Radio

Definition A wireless mode of audio communication developed in the 1920's that provides listeners with a variety of entertainment and information programming

By the 1970's, the once-dominant medium of radio had become overshadowed by the popularity of television, and radio broadcasters searched for ways in which to attract larger audiences.

The television age had replaced radio's golden era of the 1930's and early 1940's, when the airwaves were filled with fare ranging from comedy to the National Broadcasting System (NBC) Symphony Orchestra. By the 1970's, regular comedy shows and classic music had all but vanished from the nation's seven thousand radio stations. Soap operas, which were once the mainstay of daytime radio, had disappeared as well.

Because of the competition from television, radio was forced to transform itself. During the 1970's, radio became a more specialized medium, similar to the magazine business, in which programming was aimed at a particular demographic group. Instead of airing packaged music, radio stations started providing more news, discussion, sports events, live performances, and drama. Stations also began offering programs aimed at special audiences, from housewives and Latinos to homosexuals and hobbyists. Radio broadcasters used audience surveys that told them what people in various age and income groups wanted to hear. Armed with these findings, stations decided the best format with which to attract the most listeners.

During this decade, the different types of formats increased from three or four to at least two dozen. Country-and-western radio stations grew in number as well as stations that played disco, jazz, progressive rock, or songs from the 1950's and 1960's. Moreover, smaller stations could become automated by buying music, voices, and commercials in packages from the large syndicates. A manager simply could select one of a dozen formats and receive long recordings that were played over the air by machines with no announcer present in the studio.

In the early 1970's, motorists could listen only to AM radio. However, around this time, U.S. automobile manufacturers began installing FM radios in all new cars. Most of radio's growth and innovation occurred among FM stations, which emitted a higher-quality signal that was carried over shorter distances than those on the AM band. FM stations realized that they could lure more listeners and advertising dollars by turning from a predominantly classical format to a more sophisticated mix of programs, which included everything from hard and soft rock to country-western music. The better quality of FM allowed radio stations to develop more high-quality programs that attracted larger audiences.

By 1979, AM stations soon lost a sizable share of their audience to FM-stereo stations. With half the radio audience tuned to FM stereo, many AM stations found that they could no longer compete with a music format and switched to an all-news or talk format. With the talk format, listeners could call in, talk with the host, and share their views with everyone in the listening audience. Many of the talk show hosts of the 1970's included clinical psychologists, psychics, real estate experts, sex therapists, auto mechanics, sports enthusiasts, marriage counselors, and matchmakers. Some AM stations found the formula so successful that they began round-the-clock all-talk radio.

Tobacco Advertising and Indecency The 1970's also marked two government efforts to control the type of content that was aired on radio stations. Because of the health risks associated with smoking and the perceived influence advertising and broadcasting had on children, Congress passed a law in 1971 that banned all advertising for tobacco products on radio and television. Congress believed that by taking radio commercials for cigarettes off the air, the number of underage smokers and smoking-related deaths would decrease.

The federal government's desire to protect minors also prompted it to take steps to protect children from sexually explicit or profane language that aired on radio and television. The Federal Communications Commission (FCC), the federal agency responsible for overseeing radio and television, instituted regulations that required broadcasters to air indecent, but not obscene, material during a "safe harbor" time period when children were least likely to hear it. In 1978, the U.S. Supreme Court upheld the FCC's authority to regulate indecency on radio in its *FCC v. Pacifica Foundation* decision. The Supreme Court ruled that broadcasters could be fined for airing sexually explicit material during the day, when children were part of the listening audience. The issue arose after a father complained to the FCC about his young son hearing comedian George Carlin's indecent monologue about seven "dirty words" during a daytime broadcast by a New York radio station.

Impact After decades of running second best to television, radio began to experience a renaissance during the 1970's. By 1978, radio's weekly audience was at an all-time high with 166 million adult listeners, almost matching the audience for television. The amount of time the average person spent listening to radio also increased. In 1978, Americans spent about three-and-a-half hours a day listening to radio, which was half an hour more than an entire household spent listening twenty-five years earlier and only fifteen minutes less than the average for television. A widening variety of programs, from mystery dramas to shows for minorities, helped radio recreate some of its old sparkle and become a tougher competitor to television.

Further Reading

The First Fifty Years of Broadcasting: The Running Story of the Fifth Estate. Washington, D.C.: Broadcasting Publications, 1982. Detailed history of the first fifty years of radio as told through the more than two thousand issues of *Broadcasting* magazine.

Godfrey, Donald G., and Frederic A. Leigh, eds.

Historical Dictionary of American Radio. Wesport, Conn.: Greenwood Press, 1998. Alphabetical listing of terms with comprehensive definitions of a wide range of subjects related to the topic of radio in the United States.

Hilliard, Robert L., and Michael C. Keith. *The Broadcast Century: A Biography of American Broadcasting.* 3d ed. Boston: Focal Press, 2001. History of U.S. broadcast media from the 1920's through 2000.

Lackman, Ronald W. *The Encyclopedia of American Radio: An A-Z Guide to Radio from Jack Benny to Howard Stern.* New York: Facts on File, 2001. Short articles detailing the history of U.S. broadcast media from the 1920's through 2000.

Sterling, Christopher H., and John Michael Kittross. *Stay Tuned: A History of American Broadcasting.* 3d ed. Mahwah, N.J: Lawrence Erlbaum, 2001. Gives a concise history of American radio and television.

Eddith A. Dashiell

See also Advertising; Carlin, George; Censorship in Canada; Censorship in the United States; Cigarette advertising ban; Classical music; Country music; Disco; Hard rock and heavy metal; Hip-hop; Jazz; Journalism in Canada; Journalism in the United States; Music; National Public Radio (NPR); Progressive rock; Public Broadcasting Service (PBS); Punk rock; Soul music; Talk shows; Television in Canada; Television in the United States.

■ Ramones, The

Identification American pop-rock band
Date Formed in 1974

Perhaps more than any of their contemporaries, the Ramones harkened back to early 1960's and pre-Beatles American pop music. In so doing, the band returned to rock music a simplicity that emphasized melody and catchy pop hooks in an era dominated by genres that emphasized either musical virtuosity, such as blues rock and progressive rock, or production values, such as disco.

In early 1974, the Ramones formed in the Forest Hills section of Queens, New York. At first, the group consisted of Joey Ramone (Jeffrey Hyman) on drums and vocals, Johnny Ramone (John Cummings), and Dee Dee Ramone (Douglas Colvin). Soon after they began playing together, it was decided that Joey was a far better vocalist than a drummer, and the band recruited their friend Tommy

Erdelyi, who had been their manager, to take his place on drums.

The band's look of black leather jackets and straight-legged blue jeans was both an homage to 1950's rockers, such as Eddie Cochrane and a challenge to prevailing fashion trends. Whether their name was a send up to legendary pop producer Phil Ramone or a tongue-in-cheek reference to Paul McCartney's once used alias, Paul Ramone, it harkened back to Joey's heroes, the Ronnettes, as well as other girl groups from the early days of the rock era.

The band's sound suggested an earlier time as well. Solos and other self-indulgent excesses were stripped from their music. Played at what was a breakneck tempo for the mid-1970's, a typical Ramones' song rarely exceeded the two-minute mark, but all of them were counted with a "one, two, three, four" by Dee Dee. Indeed, early Ramones' shows clocked in at only twenty minutes after they had played almost a dozen songs.

The band's first three albums were recorded between 1976 and 1977: *Ramones* (1976), *Ramones Leave Home* (1977), and *Rocket to Russia* (1977). The Ramones toured constantly. After the seminal *Rocket to Russia*, however, Tommy amicably left the group in order to concentrate on music production, and his first effort was the band's subsequent album, *Road to Ruin* (1978). Although the band would continue to record noteworthy songs and team with cult film director Roger Corman for 1979's *Rock and Roll High School*—a cinematic tribute to 1950's films such as *The Girl Can't Help It* (1956)—music critics increasingly saw the band as a shadow of its former self, and several line-up changes highlighted this artistic decline.

Impact Along with other New York City musical artists, such as Patti Smith and Blondie, the Ramones ushered in the "punk" era of music. For many people in the United States, as well as around the world, the Ramones were the first punk band, and their famously brief three-chord songs set the standard for the genre.

Subsequent Events In 1996, after twenty-years of making music, the remaining original members, Joey and Johnny, called it quits and disbanded. Six years later, the Ramones' lasting influence was recognized with their induction into the Rock and Roll Hall of Fame.

Further Reading

Bessman, Jim. *Ramones: An American Band.* New York: St. Martin's Press, 1993.

Ramone, Dee Dee, with Veronica Kofman. *Lobotomy: Surviving the Ramones.* 2d ed. New York: Thunder's Mouth Press, 2000.

Paul D. Gelpi, Jr.

See also   Music; Punk music.

■ Reagan, Ronald

Identification   Governor of California, 1966-1974
Born   February 6, 1911; Tampico, Illinois
Died   June 5, 2004; Los Angeles, California

While the American presidency lay ahead of him, Governor Reagan was already a political figure of national prominence in the 1970's. As governor of the most populous and third-largest American state, Reagan presided over an economy that, as he observed in his second inaugural address, would be the sixth-largest in the world if California was a separate nation.

The 1970's began for Ronald Reagan after a relatively unsuccessful first term as governor of California, Outgunned by Democratic majorities in both chambers of the state legislature, Reagan was unable to bring about the budget cuts and tax relief he had promised in his first term. In 1970, he responded to this impasse by reverting to the skills of his previous career as a Hollywood film star and took his case to the television cameras in the most media-conscious state of the union. It worked. In January, 1971, shortly after the start of his second term, Speaker of the California Assembly Bob Moretti, a liberal Democrat and Reagan's strongest opponent, met privately with him to talk out their conflicting views on welfare reform.

Welfare caseloads in California had quadrupled in the previous decade, and Reagan wanted to reverse that trend or at least slow the growth. The legislators, however, feared that "reform" meant loss of services to the truly needy. In their one-on-one meet-

ing, Reagan and Moretti achieved a first for the Reagan administration: an effective compromise. Reagan got his stricter eligibility requirements, antifraud assurances, and a community work requirement. His opponents got a work exemption for single mothers and guaranteed cost-of-living increases. The outcome—the California Welfare Reform Act—was a win-win situation for both parties, and by 1974, it had reduced welfare caseloads by 17 percent.

Reagan's continued struggle against state taxes was less successful. Despite campaigning for a second time on a small-government, tax-relief platform, Reagan left office in the mid-1970's with tax revenues more than double what they had been in 1970, from $1.1 to $2.6 billion. The irony of Reagan's attempts to cut taxes is that a 1978 grassroots initiative in which he played no part, Proposition 13, finally succeeded in giving relief from tax increases

California governor Ronald Reagan signs a bill restoring the death penalty in the state in 1973. (AP/Wide World Photos)

that his administration had produced, albeit against his will.

When his attempt to wrest the Republican presidential nomination from incumbent Gerald R. Ford failed in 1976, Reagan spent the rest of the 1970's preparing for another attempt in 1980.

Impact Ronald Reagan's second term as governor—from January, 1971, to January, 1975—allowed him to develop the conservative agenda he would take to the national level in his presidency: a call for smaller government, less taxes, and more private enterprise. To his chagrin, Reagan left California government and its taxes larger than when he took office.

Further Reading

Canon, Lou. *Governor Reagan: His Rise to Power.* New York: Public Affairs, 2003.

Hayward, Steven F. *The Age of Reagan, 1964-1980: The Fall of the Old Liberal Order.* Roseville, Calif.: Prima, 2001.

Smith, Hedrick, et al. *Reagan: The Man, the President.* New York: Macmillan, 1980.

John R. Holmes

See also Conservatism in U.S. politics; Elections in the United States, midterm; Elections in the United States, 1976; Ford, Gerald R.; Tax revolt; Welfare.

■ Real estate boom

Definition A rapid increase in commercial and residential building and prices

Forces that acted to increase demand for real estate met with forces acting to decrease the supply of real estate during the 1970's, creating a boom. Many demographic, regulatory, and economic causes were behind the precipitous rate of growth in real estate prices during this time.

Historically, owning one's own home has generally been considered an important part of the American Dream. During the 1970's, more homes were built, larger homes were built, and in turn, those homes were sold at prices that rose faster than the rate of inflation. Combined with an increase in the building of commercial spaces during this time, the real estate boom of the decade was a growth industry in an otherwise lackluster economic climate.

Between 1970 and 1980, the number of housing units in the United States grew by 29 percent—roughly twice the rate of the previous decade and the decade that followed. Fueling this rising demand for housing were the now-adult children of the baby boom, who were renting their first apartments and buying their first houses and condominiums. While the number of housing units was growing quickly, average household size was shrinking during this time as a result of divorce and smaller families. Despite this fact, the size of the average house was increasing, growing from an average of 950 square feet just after World War II to 1,400 square feet in 1970.

Inflation The presence of growing price inflation in the economy made real estate an attractive form of investment during the 1970's. Inflation, which had averaged 2-3 percent during the 1960's, had steadily grown to a rate of 5-12 percent during the decade—levels that had not been experienced during peacetime in nearly a century. Real estate was seen as an inflation-proof investment in part because land is a finite commodity and in part because the price of real estate was rising steadily.

During a decade in which the overall price level rose 90 percent, the median price of a new home had grown from $23,400 in 1970 to $64,600 in 1980—an increase of 176 percent. By comparison, new house prices had risen about 50 percent during the 1960's. Traditional investments in stocks and bonds were much less attractive during the 1970's, and the Dow Jones Industrial Average ended the decade only 31 points higher than it had been in 1970.

The Role of Regulation Against this backdrop of increased demand, real estate development costs were increasing during the 1970's. Some of the increased costs of building came from regulations prohibiting development in environmentally sensitive areas such as wetlands and floodplains. Land that might have been filled in and built upon in previous decades became off-limits for development. These new regulations limited the land on which houses and commercial developments could be built and resulted in higher prices for the remaining land.

Zoning regulations were tightened in many localities during the 1970's, which also resulted in higher real estate prices. Many municipalities introduced zoning regulations for the first time during the decade, in the process restricting the land available for commercial and residential construction. Towns and cities that had welcomed development during most of the postwar era were becoming concerned about the demands that further development would place on services such as water systems, police and fire protection, and schools. In an attempt to reduce the building of apartments and smaller, cheaper "starter homes," which paid lower property taxes than larger homes, many zoning authorities increased the minimum lot size for homes, placing further pressure on land prices.

The federal income tax system did not change appreciably during the real estate boom, but it too played a role in the increased demand for real estate. The purchase of a primary residence is not a tax-exempt purchase, but interest paid on the mortgage to purchase a residence is deductible for tax purposes. The same is true of commercial real estate. The highest personal income tax rate during the 1970's was 70 percent. Real estate owned for one year or longer qualified for treatment as a capital gain, which lowered the tax paid on the profit realized from the sale of the property to a maximum of 35 percent. When the benefits of interest deductibility for homeowners was added to the possibility of a potentially large capital gain, which would then be taxed at a lower rate than ordinary income, the benefits of owning real estate were particularly attractive to investors who were not enjoying similar benefits from traditional investments in the financial markets.

Impact Many incentives were in place to encourage investment in real estate during the 1970's. As a result of inflation and regulatory incentives, as well as disincentives, more capital was invested in real estate and less in the types of assets that could boost productivity and enhance future living standards for Americans.

Further Reading

"American Survey: Boom, Baby, Boom." *The Economist*, September 16, 1978, 52. Short article on the effects of urban sprawl and increasing prices in and around Washington, D.C.

Maloney, Laurence. "Houses in the '80's: Smaller, Fewer, Costlier." *U.S. News and World Report*, April 2, 1979, 54. A review of the causes of the real estate boom of the 1970's and its projected effects on the early 1980's.

"South Californian Bubble." *The Economist*, July 2, 1977, 44. A comprehensive review of the eco-

nomic factors behind the boom, paying particular attention to land restrictions and their role in rapidly increasing prices.

"Starting to Put Up Office Buildings Again." *Business Week*, February 13, 1978, 33. Provides a perspective on the real estate boom from the view of commercial real estate in Chicago.

Betsy A. Murphy

See also Architecture; Business and the economy in the United States; Demographics of the United States; Environmental movement; Environmental Protection Agency (EPA); Housing in the United States.

■ Recycling movement

Definition Removal of recoverable items from waste for reuse by cleaning, melting, or reprocessing into new products

Recycling programs began to attract national attention during the 1970's as a result of the environmental awareness initiated by the first Earth Day, the realization that Americans generated excessive and unnecessary waste, and the dawning comprehension that landfills were becoming filled to capacity.

Disposing of garbage has historically been a serious environmental issue, and public attention was finally focused on the problem in the United States during the 1960's and 1970's. Landfills were becoming filled to capacity, while locating new sites was becoming increasingly problematic. The environmental movement asked Americans to consider the impact of humans on nature and other animals. Encouraging consumers to recycle reusable materials became a way of addressing these concerns.

Programs and Their Benefits Recyclable materials include glass, plastic bottles, aluminum and steel cans, paper, cardboard, and lawn waste. The recycling movement discovered that successful programs had to combine community involvement with municipal support. Community members had to be committed to separating trash into appropriate categories, and the local government had to provide haulers with separate compartments for each material. It was found that recycling programs relying on homeowners to drop off recyclables typically had only minimal participation, while home-based programs had a considerable impact on the waste stream. At a recycling center, materials are compacted and sold to manufacturers to construct new products. A successful recycling program also requires a market for the reclaimed materials; in 1970, however, few U.S. paper mills were equipped to produce recycled paper from old newspapers.

Activists discovered that recycling not only reduces municipal solid waste but also is energy efficient and economical. Aluminum cans are 20 percent cheaper to recycle than to manufacture and require only 5 percent of the energy needed to produce a can from raw materials. Reusing old glass costs considerably less than forming it from new material. Recycling was also found to be less expensive than sending garbage to landfills, because landfills require transporting refuse over greater distances and each truck must pay a tipping fee based on the weight of the garbage. Substances to be recycled are typically transported fewer miles and generate income through selling of the reclaimed materials.

Composting was another form of recycling that first gained popularity in the 1970's. About 20 percent of municipal waste is organic kitchen and yard waste that can be shredded and arranged in piles for decomposition. The result is compost, which is useful for agriculture and landscaping.

Impact   The effects of the recycling movement have been clear: Recycling saves money, energy, raw materials, and land space; reduces pollution; and encourages individual awareness and responsibility for the refuse produced.

Subsequent Events   Since the 1970's, demand for recycled materials has been climbing, occasionally even passing the available supply, as a result of environment concerns, a shortage of landfill space, and increased demand for recycled products. By 2000, the United States was recovering about 30 percent of its waste stream, and several states had set goals of 50 percent. At that time, 50 percent of aluminum cans were being recycled (up from 15 percent in the early 1970's), as well as 61 percent of glass bottles and 40 percent of plastic soft drink containers. Unreused glass containers were being melted to produce new containers at a rate of 24 percent in 2000, while recycled plastic containers were converted into fiberfill stuffing for pillows, sleeping bags, carpets, and automobile seats. Although plastics account for 8 per-

cent of solid waste, third behind paper and yard clippings, only 6 percent were being recovered in 2000. However, 30 percent of paper waste (40 percent of the waste stream) was being recycled to paper products or insulation, and yard trimmings had achieved an impressive 45 percent recovery rate.

A variety of community programs to encourage recycling have emerged since the 1970's. Some communities require residents to sort their recyclable materials into color-coded containers for glass, metals, plastic, and paper products. Many municipalities forbid yard trimmings in the waste stream.

Further Reading

Anderson, Bruce N., ed. *Ecologue: The Environmental Catalogue and Consumer's Guide for a Safe Earth.* New York: Prentice Hall, 1990. A detailed catalog for making responsible environmental choices and helping solve the trash problem. Covers how to reduce the waste stream through careful selection of which products are purchased and how to maximize the recycling of refuse and worn-out property.

Cointreau, Sandra. *Recycling from Municipal Refuse.* Washington, D.C.: World Bank, 1984. Well-documented discussion of the means to minimize waste, create more durable goods, and recycle what cannot be retained.

De Graff, John, David Wann, and Thomas H. Naylor. *Affluenza: The All-Consuming Epidemic.* San Francisco: Berrett-Koehler, 2002. Explores the roots of the U.S. garbage disposal problem by identifying the underlying cause—the relentless pursuit of more material goods, more convenience, and resistance to the inconveniences imposed by recycling.

Gordon, Deborah. *Steering a New Course.* Cambridge, Mass.: Union of Concerned Scientists, 1991. Helps consumers have a less detrimental environmental impact through choices about which items are purchased, how they are used, and the means by which they can be recycled.

Narr, Jon. *Design for a Livable Planet: How You Can Help Clean Up the Environment.* New York: Perennial Library, 1990. Candidly details the causes and effects of environmental problems and offers practical solutions.

George R. Plitnik

See also   Earth Day; Environmental movement; Keep America Beautiful.

■ Red dye no. 2 ban

Definition   Restriction of a popular coloring used in food

Date   Enacted in 1976

Considered by many as an overreaction, the prohibition was caused and accelerated by public concern with harmful chemicals in food.

By 1970, red dye no. 2, a synthetic dye made from petroleum products, was the most common food coloring. Coal-tar dyes such as red dye no. 2 were more popular than natural food color from plants, animals, and minerals; effective in much smaller amounts, they were less expensive and left the food's flavor unchanged.

However, in the United States, coal-tar dyes, unlike natural dyes, were regulated by the federal Food and Drug Administration (FDA). Specific trouble for red dye no. 2 began in 1960, when amendments to the Federal Food, Drug, and Cosmetic Act of 1938 prohibited use of potentially cancer-causing chemicals in food, even if the amount was minuscule. This rule was popularly known as the Delaney anticancer clause.

In 1969, scientists at the Moscow Institute of Nutrition found increased tumors among rats that were fed red dye no. 2. Other tests showed no hazard, and the FDA's own studies were inconclusive. American scientists criticized the Soviet study's methodology. However, many among the American public became worried, and groups such as the consumer-advocate Health Research Group pushed to have the dye restricted. Eventually, the FDA concluded that while red dye no. 2 could not be proven harmful, neither could it be certified as safe. The United States banned red dye no. 2 as a food additive in 1976, though it continued to be allowed as a fabric dye. Canada did not ban it.

Public reaction to the prohibition was significant; for example, in order to avoid frightening consumers, the Mars candy company stopped making red M&M candies from 1976 to 1985, even though it had never used red dye no. 2. The primary replacement of red dye no. 2 was another coal-tar dye, red dye no. 40. Companies were motivated to further develop natural dyes, such as that from beet juice.

Impact   Critics viewed this event as an example of overreaction and the susceptibility of the American people to fear-based campaigns. In fact, the FDA did not rule out future approval of the dye, if petitioned. However, whether the specific chemical was harmful or not, the ban produced a greater public awareness and questioning of chemical additives to food, including preservatives. The movement toward natural foods, already begun in the mid-1970's, was aided by this sentiment. In general, the restriction on red dye no. 2 in the United States was part of a growing tendency to distrust chemicals and to carefully examine their effects both in food and in the overall environment.

Further Reading

Food and Drug Administration. "Color Additives Fact Sheet." http://www.cfsan.fda.gov/~dms/cos-221.html.

Junod, Suzanne White. "The Chemogastric Revolution and the Regulation of Food Chemicals." In *Chemical Sciences in the Modern World*, edited by Seymour Mauskopf. Philadelphia: University of Pennsylvania Press, 1993.

Bernadette Lynn Bosky

See also   Consumer Product Safety Act of 1972; Environmental movement; Food trends.

■ Reddy, Helen

Identification   Australian singer and lyricist

Born   October 25, 1941; Melbourne, Victoria, Australia

Reddy became best known for her Grammy-winning recording "I Am Woman," which was often described as an anthem for the 1970's feminist movement. She also was a prolific songwriter and performer, producing numerous albums during the decade.

Helen Reddy's style combined rhythm and blues, jazz, and easy rock. She recorded her own creations and those of such lyricists-composers as Billy Joel. Her most memorable hit was her single, "I Am Woman" in 1972; however, she first received accolades for a pop version of "I Don't Know How to Love Him," a single from the Broadway play *Jesus Christ Superstar* earlier that year. Shortly thereafter, she was signed by Capitol Records. Her singles "Delta Dawn" and "Angie Baby" became number-one hits in 1973 and 1974.

An examination of the lyrics of "I Am Woman" makes it clear why that particular song became such a favorite with feminists of the time. Phrases such as

"I am Woman, hear me roar, in numbers too big to ignore" and "No one's going to keep me down again" provided a battle cry for women seeking equal rights in many arenas. The assertion that "I am strong, I am invincible, I am woman" provided inspiration for women in all walks of life. Reddy received a Best Female Vocal Performance Grammy Award for this song, and in her acceptance speech, she said, "I want to thank God, for she makes everything possible."

Reddy also hosted a summer variety show on television in the mid-1970's and had her own late night variety show called *The Midnight Special.* She attempted filmmaking with *Pete's Dragon* (1977); however, her career as an actor did not materialize. She released a total of thirteen albums in the 1970's.

Impact Helen Reddy is arguably best remembered by the general public for the writing and recording of "I Am Woman" and its connection with the feminist movement. However, she developed a strong fan base, and many more remember the breadth of her musical style. "I Am Woman" was adopted by the United Nations as its theme for the International Year of the Woman.

Further Reading

Breithaupt, Don, and Jeff Breithaupt. *Precious and Few: Pop Music of the Early '70's.* New York: St. Martin's Press, 1996.

Scott, Barry. *We Had Joy, We Had Fun: The "Lost" Recording Artists of the Seventies.* London: Faber & Faber, 1994.

Mary C. Ware

See also Feminism; International Year of the Woman; Joel, Billy; Music; Singer-songwriters; Variety shows; Women's rights.

■ Redford, Robert

Identification American actor and producer
Born August 18, 1937; Santa Monica, California

Perhaps the most popular film star of the 1970's, Redford appeared in a wide variety of films, ranging from pure entertainments and romances to political thrillers.

A stage and television actor at the beginning of the 1960's, Robert Redford had become a major film

Helen Reddy. (AP/Wide World Photos)

star by the end of the decade through such films as *Butch Cassidy and the Sundance Kid* (1969). The blond, blue-eyed Redford not only was considered one of the most handsome stars of the time but was also a fine, underappreciated actor. In an era dominated by self-conscious, often mannered performers such as Robert De Niro, Dustin Hoffman, Jack Nicholson, and Al Pacino, Redford was a throwback to an earlier era, displaying little obvious technique and considerable star presence. Whether in action films or soap operas, Redford was loved by the camera perhaps more than any star of the decade.

Many of Redford's roles were in films aimed primarily to entertain. These roles included his thief character in *The Hot Rock* (1972), his frontiersman in *Jeremiah Johnson* (1972), his disillusioned screenwriter in *The Way We Were* (1973), his boyish con man in *The Sting* (1973)—which earned him his first Academy Award nomination—and his portrayal of a stunt pilot in *The Great Waldo Pepper* (1975).

Redford also became known for his strong political and social beliefs, and these concerns can be seen in several films. *The Candidate* (1972), for which he was executive producer, presents a relatively innocent lawyer talked into running for the United States Senate against an incumbent Republican. *Three Days of the Condor* (1975), which also starred

Faye Dunaway, presents the U.S. government killing its Central Intelligence Agency (CIA) agents to protect its oil interests. Cynicism clashes with idealism in *All the President's Men* (1976), which he also produced, as Redford portrays *Washington Post* reporter Bob Woodward during the Watergate investigation. Though a prominent spokesperson for environmental causes, Redford generally chose not to preach in his films, which touch only superficially on environmental issues.

Many of Redford's films examine various aspects of the American Dream, making him an ideal choice to play F. Scott Fitzgerald's romantic hero in *The Great Gatsby* (1974), but this ill-conceived project proved one of the decade's big disappointments. Redford ended the decade with *The Electric Horseman* (1979), his third film with Jane Fonda, the dominant actress of the era. Redford plays a former rodeo star who is reduced to wearing a neon cowboy outfit in a Las Vegas revue and who steals a valuable horse as a protest against their trivialization.

Impact   Robert Redford held wide-ranging appeal resulting from his good looks, his boyish charm, his penchant for playing idealist loners, and his choice of roles that reflected his social conscience. More than any star of the decade, he seemed to communicate directly to the audience without condescension.

Further Reading

Biskind, Peter. *Down and Dirty Pictures: Miramax, Sundance, and the Rise of Independent Film.* New York: Simon & Schuster, 2004.

Downing, David. *Robert Redford.* New York: St. Martin's, 1984.

Spada, James. *The Films of Robert Redford.* Secaucus, N.J.: Citadel, 1984.

Michael Adams

See also   Academy Awards; *All the President's Men*; Dunaway, Faye; Environmental movement; Film in the United States; Fonda, Jane; Hoffman, Dustin; Watergate; Woodward, Bob, and Carl Bernstein.

■ *Regents of the University of California v. Bakke*

Identification   U.S. Supreme Court decision
Date   Decided on June 28, 1978

In a closely divided decision, the Supreme Court upheld the consideration of race as a factor in university admissions

but otherwise limited the ability of governments to implement affirmative action programs.

By the last half of the twentieth century, the Supreme Court had established that laws intended to burden racial minorities were generally unconstitutional. The constitutionality of laws intended to benefit minorities, on the other hand, and commonly referred to as affirmative action programs, was a more divisive issue. Some courts and commentators insisted that the constitution required color-blindness—that all laws categorizing citizens of the basis of race were inherently suspect. Others argued with equal vehemence that the legacy of past racial discrimination in the United States could not be remedied without some consideration of race.

In *Bakke*, a closely divided Court established principles that would guide future affirmative action cases. Justice Lewis Powell fashioned a result that charted a middle path between the views of justices who were in general support of affirmative action policies and those largely hostile to these policies. In the first place, Powell's *Bakke* opinion held that governmental institutions could not adopt affirmative action programs as a way of undoing the harmful effects of past racial discrimination in American society. Such institutions—including public universities—could only attempt to remedy the effects of their own prior acts of racial discrimination. In practice, this part of the *Bakke* decision made it difficult for institutions outside of the deep South, where racial discrimination had been openly practiced by governments earlier in the twentieth century, to adopt programs to benefit racial minorities. However, a majority of the Court also approved another justification for affirmative action programs in the context of education. The Court held that colleges and universities, though they could not use anything so rigid as racial quotas in admission, could give some consideration to the race of student applicants as a way of obtaining a diverse student body.

Impact   The *Bakke* case established an uneasy middle position in what had become fierce public disputes about the legitimacy of affirmative action programs. It allowed a form of affirmative action to continue in college admissions but communicated a measure of suspicion about the constitutionality of other programs intended to benefit racial minorities. Over the following years, the Court became

Allan Bakke attends his first day of medical school at the University of California at Davis on September 25, 1978, after winning his reverse discrimination lawsuit. (AP/Wide World Photos)

even more wary of affirmative action programs in most contexts but continued to approve at least some consideration of race in university admissions into the twenty-first century.

Further Reading

Ball, Howard. *The "Bakke" Case: Race, Education, and Affirmative Action.* Lawrence: University Press of Kansas, 2000.

Curry, George E., ed. *The Affirmative Action Debate.* Reading, Mass.: Addison-Wesley, 1996.

Dreyfuss, Joel, and Charles Lawrence, III. *The "Bakke" Case: The Politics of Inequality.* New York: Harcourt Brace Jovanovich, 1979.

Schwartz, Bernard. *Behind "Bakke": Affirmative Action and the Supreme Court.* New York: New York University Press, 1988.

Timothy L. Hall

See also Affirmative action; Education in the United States; Racial discrimination; Supreme Court decisions.

■ Religion and spirituality in Canada

Definition   Organized and nonorganized expressions of spiritual belief and practice among Canadians

Far-reaching social and political changes in the 1960's encouraged secularization and a decline in church participation among mainstream religious groups in Canada. The decade also saw an increase in the visibility of non-Christian religions, especially Buddhism and Islam, as more immigrants arrived from non-Western areas, especially to Canadian cities. Evangelical Protestant groups such as the Pentecostals, however, showed growth rather than decline through the decade, as did new religious movements (NRMs).

Canada has been a strongly religious and Christian country from its outset, influenced heavily by Victorian thinking, but its religious anatomy has deviated markedly from that of the United States through history—that is, less denominationalism and more power in a few established churches with links to political elites.

According to the 1981 census, 90 percent of Canadians were Christians; 7.4 percent were atheists, agnostics, or had no religion; and the remainder were Jews, Muslims, Hindus, Buddhists, and Sikhs, in rank order. Before 1971, the proportion of atheists was less than 1 percent; by the end of the century, the proportion had increased to more than 16 percent. By 2001, the proportion of Christians had dropped to 72 percent, owing mainly to increases in Buddhism, Islam, Hinduism, and Sikhism.

During the 1970's, secularization made clear inroads into the mainstream religions, with losses most noticeable in the Roman Catholic, Anglican, United, Presbyterian, Lutheran, Baptist, and Orthodox faiths. Following the Quiet Revolution in the 1960's, the Catholic Church suffered precipitous decline among the French in Quebec Province so that churchgoing in Quebec eventually dropped to the lowest rate in Canada.

While Catholicism remained the largest single faith group in Canada, its face changed, with Catholics coming from Europe, Asia, and Latin America. The United Church, a fusion of Protestant groups dating from 1925, had trouble establishing a common religious identity from its diverse ecumenical elements. The Anglican Church declined as ties to the United Kingdom weakened. As immigration patterns changed after the mid-1960's, the mainstream religions attempted to redefine themselves and be more open to immigrants and indigenous peoples.

Indigenous peoples adhered to a variety of animistic spiritual traditions; many retained their native religions, while others were devout Christians or practiced a blend of Christianity and native spirituality.

The last decades of the twentieth century witnessed increases in NRMs, sometimes referred to as cults, such as paganists and Satanists; these groups, however, were not serious competition for the other faith groups.

Impact Although in decline, the Catholic, Anglican, and United Churches remained the essence of organized religion in Canada through the 1970's.

Further Reading

Curtis, J., and L. Tepperman, eds. *Understanding Canadian Society.* Toronto: McGraw-Hill Ryerson, 1988. Analyses of attitudes, values, and institutions.

Hewitt, W. E., ed. *The Sociology of Religion: A Canadian Focus.* Boston: Butterworth-Heinemann, 1993. Examines the role of religion in shaping Canadian identity, including its impact on nationalism and multiculturalism.

Stark, Rodney, ed. *Religious Movements: Genesis, Exodus, and Numbers.* New York: Paragon House, 1985. Emphasizes the recruitment and retention practices of nonmainstream groups, including some in Canada.

Ann M. Legreid

See also Buddhism; Christian Fundamentalism; Cults; Immigration to Canada; Minorities in Canada; Religion and spirituality in the United States; Scientology; Wiccan movement.

■ Religion and spirituality in the United States

Definition Organized and nonorganized expressions of spiritual belief and practice among Americans

Like many other aspects of American life, religion and spirituality changed at a rapid pace during the 1970's. Mainline religious denominations reevaluated their positions on women in the clergy and their engagement with popular culture. Alternative religious movements of varying worldviews and theological teachings caught the attention of the mainstream media.

In part because of the questions of civil rights that pervaded American social discourse throughout the 1960's and 1970's, many mainline religious denominations extended new rights and privileges to women and minority groups during these decades. Governing bodies of Lutheran, Reformed, Mennonite, and Episcopalian Churches all extended to women the right to preach during the 1970's. However, the changes widened the gulf between cultural conservatives and liberals within many large denominations. The former advocated for a strict interpretation of scriptural injunctions against the practice (for example, 1 Corinthians 14:34), while the latter argued that women's preaching had been sanctioned in the Hebrew scriptures (Joel 2:28) and was ordained by Jesus in his post-Resurrection instructions to the women who attended his tomb. In 1972, Sally Priesand became the first female rabbi, having been ordained at Hebrew Union College in the tradition of Reform Judaism.

Though the Roman Catholic Church emphatically rejected the women's ordination movements—Pope Paul VI issued his declaration against them in his *Inter Insigniores* in 1976—feminist Catholic theologians such as Mary Daly and Rosemary Radford Ruether began to explore what had come to be known as feminist or womanist theology. Daly's *The Church and the Second Sex* (1968) and *Gyn/Ecology: The Metaethics of Radical Feminism* (1978) and Ruether's edited work *Religion and Sexism: Images of Women in the Jewish and Christian Traditions* (1974) urged women's broader engagement not only in Christian social activism but also in challenging central Western assumptions about the Divine. Ruether also became active in liberation theology, a movement within Third World Christianity (primarily Catholicism) that integrates traditional Church teachings with Marxist views about struggle and revolution.

While many leaders in the women's movement worked toward inclusion with the larger churches, others rejected Judeo-Christian spirituality altogether, claiming that these traditions are inherently patriarchal and antiwoman. These attitudes were reflected in pagan, ecofeminist/Gaia, and Wicca movements that sought to reclaim or redefine women's spiritual practices.

In 1978, Mormon president and prophet Spencer W. Kimball reversed 150 years of church tradition by announcing that he had had a divine revelation advising him to extend church membership to African Americans. This change allowed the people carrying the "curse of Canaan" (Genesis 9:28) into the community of believers; male African Americans would thus be eligible for the Mormon priesthood.

Alternative Religious Movements   Two alternative movements with West Coast origins—the Jesus People and Jews for Jesus—represented an unusual combination of conservative theology and liberal expression. Theologically, the groups emphasized the authority of the Scriptures and the imminent return of Christ prophesied in the book of Revelation. However, they also often embraced the speech, dress, and music of hippies. Andrew Lloyd Webber's 1971 rock opera *Jesus Christ Superstar* exemplified this controversial but popular movement among younger Christians.

In addition to the changes that were occurring in the mainline denominations, the 1970's saw the development of new and unorthodox religious practices that some classified as "occult." Two sensational news stories in this category were the Tate-LaBianca murders and the suicides at Jonestown. The Tate-LaBianca murders—committed in 1969 but prosecuted in the early 1970's—were carried out by Charles Manson and a small group of followers who shared his apocalyptic worldview. One follower, Susan Atkins, received one of the stiffest sentences for her role in knifing the pregnant actor Sharon Tate. She converted to Christianity in prison and wrote about her experiences in the 1977 best-seller *Child of Satan, Child of God*. In 1978, Jim Jones, the charismatic leader of the People's Temple, convinced hundreds of his followers that the end of the world was near and led them to a mass suicide in the Jonestown colony that they had established in the South American nation of Guyana.

Impact   Religion and spirituality are not bound neatly within the context of a particular decade. Many of the events described here were influenced by patterns and trends from years and decades before 1970. The events, in turn, continued to shape spiritual and religious practices that extended beyond the decade. The ordination of women remained a controversial question in many large and small denominations, and many congregations split because of internal disagreements.

Subsequent Events   In 1999, Mary Daly lost her tenured position at Boston College because of her policy against allowing male students to attend a feminist ethics class. She increasingly distanced herself from the Catholic theology of her older works.

Further Reading

Jenkins, Philip. *Dream Catchers: How Mainstream America Discovered Native Spirituality.* New York: Oxford University Press, 2004. Ties the rise of the New Age movement in part to an appropriation of Native American culture and religion.

Lippy, Charles H. *Being Religious, American Style: A History of Popular Religiosity in the United States.* Westport, Conn.: Praeger, 1994. A comprehensive survey of religious figures, movements, and beliefs that have influenced American culture.

Noll, Mark A. *A History of Christianity in the United States and Canada.* Grand Rapids, Mich.: Eerdmans, 1992. Noll's work provides an outstanding introductory history of American and Canadian Christianity.

Jennifer Heller

See also   American Indian Religious Freedom Act of 1978; Buddhism; Castaneda, Carlos; Christian Fundamentalism; Cults; Episcopal Church ordination of women; Falwell, Jerry; *Jesus Christ Superstar*; Jesus People movement; Jewish Americans; Jews for Jesus; John Paul II; Johnson, Sonia; Jonestown and the People's Temple; *Late Great Planet Earth, The*; Manson Family; Moonies; Mormon Church lifting of priesthood ban for African Americans; New Age movement; Religion and spirituality in Canada; Robertson, Pat; Scientology; Wiccan movement.

■ Reynolds, Burt

Identification   American television and film actor
Born   February 11, 1936; Waycross, Georgia

Reynolds became one of the "megastars" of Hollywood during the 1970's, a designation earned with his sex appeal and overt masculinity.

Burt Reynolds's first passion was football. He played collegiate football while attending Florida State College and then played professionally for the Baltimore Colts. After an automobile accident suddenly ended his professional career, Reynolds moved to New York City to pursue an acting career. From 1962 to 1965, Reynolds's portrayal of blacksmith Quint Asper on the long-running Columbia Broadcasting System (CBS) network Western series *Gunsmoke* earned him widespread popularity with female audiences. From 1970 to 1971, Reynolds starred in the American Broadcasting Company (ABC) network detective series *Dan August*.

Although Reynolds had roles in numerous television films and motion pictures throughout the early 1970's, it was his starring role as Lewis Medlock in the film *Deliverance* (1972) that catapulted him to superstar status. Female audiences found Reynolds's sex appeal and raw masculinity riveting. That same year, the sexy actor posed nude for *Cosmopolitan* magazine. Not only did sales soar for the magazine, but the photographs also further solidified the actor's superstar status. Further fueling Reynolds's popularity was his very public private life. The actor was reportedly intimate with a long list of female celebrities that included Candice Bergen, Farrah Fawcett, Sally Field, Cybill Shepherd, and Dinah Shore. In

1977, Reynolds starred in the blockbuster motion picture *Smokey and the Bandit* with Field. Portraying the character of Bandit, the role showcased Reynolds's suave masculine image.

During the 1970's, Reynolds also found success as a film director. In 1976, he directed his first film, *Gator*, in which he also starred as the leading character, Gator McKlusky. In 1978, he directed and portrayed the character Wendell Sonny Lawson in the dark comedy *The End*, which did significantly well at the box office and led to Reynolds directing several more films.

Impact   A talented megastar of the 1970's, Burt Reynolds represented the male sex symbol of the era. His masculine good looks and charming personality, on and off the set, attracted both male and female fans. The characters that he portrayed in his action films not only entertained filmgoers but also defined what the American male image of the decade should be. The actor received nine People's Choice Awards, including several for favorite motion picture actor and favorite all-around male entertainer.

Further Reading

Reynolds, Burt. *My Life*. New York: Hyperion Press, 1994.

Smith, Lisa. *Burt Reynolds*. Palm Beach, Fla.: Magic Lights, 1994.

Streebeck, Nancy. *The Films of Burt Reynolds*. New Jersey: Citadel Press, 1982.

Bernadette Zbicki Heiney

See also   *Deliverance*; Field, Sally; Film in the United States; Television in the United States.

■ Rich, Adrienne

Identification   American feminist poet, theorist, and educator
Born   May 16, 1929; Baltimore, Maryland

Although Rich began to create her own style and voice prior to the 1970's, she was finally able to describe her self-transformation in a series of essays written during the decade, particularly her 1971 essay "When We Dead Awaken: Writing as Re-Vision" and in her retrospective collection On Lies, Secrets, and Silence: Select Prose, 1966-1978 *(1979).*

By the 1970's, Adrienne Rich had discovered a startlingly different voice of feminist outrage and began

Adrienne Rich. (Library of Congress)

to connect the political reality of herself and her world to literature. Her focus had shifted from the studied disillusion of formalism in her early award-winning collection of poetry *A Change of World* (1951) to ideas that directly confronted controversial issues such as lesbianism and sexual abuse. She worked from a theory that systematic male cruelty against women accompanies most failures of civilization, and a freer style infused her increasingly politicized poetry. Although her early experiments in this new voice were not well received, the apocalyptic *Diving into the Wreck* (1973) won the National Book Award. Rich's writing continued its unique discourse of visionary lesbianism in *The Dream of a Common Language* (1978), which was criticized by heterosexual feminists for its lesbian separatism. Rich revisited and revised her ideas constantly, later moving beyond themes of lesbianism and including explorations of her relationship with her own sons.

The 1970's concern with gender, politics, and race was Rich's crucible for her later work, and she produced books of poems approximately every two years and several collections of essays that further developed her engaged feminism. Moreover, in the 1970's, Rich began to date her books to emphasize that her poems reflected rapid changes in history. She noted that she tries to connect by continually expanding her pacifist lesbian perspective, linking cultural conventions about woman's physical body to issues of economics, homophobia, and race and, most of all, to the suppressed violence that she senses within female mental complicity.

Impact   The failure in the 1970's to anthologize Adrienne Rich's lesbian poems was held up as an example of heterosexist bias in feminist thought. Lesbian critics demanded that Rich's lesbian writings and those of other lesbians be included in anthologies. The canon did change, and Rich's unique vision eventually was recognized by awards such as the Bollingen Prize, the Lannan Lifetime Achievement Award, an Academy of American Poets Fellowship, the Wallace Stevens Award, the Ruth Lilly Poetry Prize, the Lenore Marshall Poetry Prize, and a MacArthur fellowship.

Further Reading

Yorke, Liz. *Adrienne Rich: Passion, Politics, and the Body.* London: Sage, 1997.

Zimmerman, Bonnie. "What Has Never Been: An Overview of Feminist Literary Criticism." In *Feminist Criticism: Essays on Women, Literature, and Theory,* edited by Elaine Showalter. New York: Pantheon, 1985.

Suzanne Araas Vesely

See also   Feminism; Homosexuality and gay rights; Jewish Americans; Literature in the United States; National Lesbian and Gay Rights March of 1979; Poetry; Sexual revolution; Women's rights.

■ Richler, Mordecai

Identification   Canadian novelist, screenwriter, and journalist

Born   January 27, 1931; Montreal, Quebec, Canada

Died   July 3, 2001; Montreal, Quebec, Canada

Richler, perhaps more than any other writer, brought attention to Canadian culture and the plight of Jews in the contemporary world.

Mordecai Richler was a third-generation Canadian Jew who grew up in a tightly enclosed ethnic society and at a young age became acutely aware of his mi-

Mordecai Richler. (Christopher Morris)

of *St. Urbain's Horseman* (1971), which many regard as his greatest artistic success. Here he returned to the neighborhood of his youth in a complex work that looks with ambivalence on his ethnic roots and what he regards as a frivolous national culture. The work was awarded the Governor General's Literary Prize for 1971, and in the following year, he returned to Montreal to live. In the 1970's, he wrote a children's book, *Jacob Two-Two Meets the Hooded Fang* (1975), and he published two collections of essays, *Shovelling Trouble* (1972) and *Notes on an Endangered Species and Others* (1974).

Impact   In spite of the critical success of his novels, Mordecai Richler was not well known until he collaborated with longtime friend, director Ted Kotcheff, to bring *The Apprenticeship of Duddy Kravitz* to the screen in 1974, which starred Richard Dreyfuss, Jack Warden, and Randy Quaid. Although relatively low-budget, the film attracted a mass audience and brought considerable attention to Richler as a novelist and screenwriter and proved to be one of the most successful and important films to emerge from Canada's burgeoning motion-picture community. It earned Richler an Academy Award nomination in 1975, and because of its moral ambivalence, it especially appealed to audiences attracted to films analyzing the moral malaise of post-Vietnam culture.

Further Reading

Iannone, Carol. "The Adventures of Mordecai Richler." *Commentary,* June, 1990, 51-54.

McNaught, Kenneth. "Mordecai Richler Was Here." *Journal of Canadian Studies* 26, no. 4 (1992): 141-144.

Robbeson, Angela. "Screening the Jury: Textual Strategy and Moral Response in Mordecai Richler's *St. Urbain's Horseman.*" *Critique* 42, no. 2 (2001): 205-218.

David W. Madden

See also   Dreyfuss, Richard; Film in Canada; Literature in Canada.

nority position in a mass culture. After two years at Sir George Williams University in Montreal, he dropped out and headed for Paris, where he resolved to become a writer. There he published a short story and made trips to other countries, most notably Spain, which inspired his first novel, *The Acrobats* (1954). Although he later lived in London, Richler would return to Canada literally a few times a year and imaginatively in nearly each of his works.

His fourth novel, *The Apprenticeship of Duddy Kravitz* (1959), although not initially a commercial success, established him as serious, controversial novelist. The work centers on a young man determined to pursue his desires and make a success of his life. In doing so, however, he becomes an amoral manipulator and ultimately a lost soul. Out of financial necessity, Richler began writing film and television scripts, work that he disdained but at which he excelled. Two more novels followed—*The Incomparable Atuk* (1963) and *Cocksure* (1968)—before the publication

■ Robbins, Harold

Identification   American writer
Born   May 21, 1916; New York, New York
Died   October 14, 1997; Palm Springs, California

Robbins's steamy sagas of sex, wealth, and intrigue dominated the best-seller lists throughout the 1960's and 1970's.

Harold Robbins began his writing career in 1948 with the publication of his first novel, *Never Love a Stranger.* The typical Robbins novel features a plucky young man or woman who is born into poverty but who manages to achieve wealth and success among the "jet set." The protagonist usually faces a deadly challenge to his or her position from a business rival or family member but is usually redeemed by the power of love.

By the 1970's, Robbins was well established as one of the United States' most successful writers, although his books were usually panned by critics as being formulaic, vulgar, and trite. *The Betsy* (1971) was an exposé of the automobile industry, whose characters bore more than a passing resemblance to the Ford family. *The Pirate* (1974) presented the saga of a ruthless Arab oil millionaire, while *The Lonely Lady* (1976) was a steamy Hollywood exposé. It was followed by *Dreams Die First* (1977), which appears to take its inspiration for the story of a successful pornographer from Hugh Hefner's career with *Playboy* magazine. *Memories of Another Day*, published in 1979, was the rags-to-riches story of a man who becomes a powerful labor leader.

A number of Robbins's novels were made into films that appeared during the 1970's. *Stiletto*, a 1960 novel about a Mafia assassin that starred Alex Cord and Patrick O'Neal, was released in late 1969. The same year brought *The Adventurers* to the screen, with Bekim Fehmiu, Candice Bergen, and Olivia de Havilland in starring roles. *The Betsy*, starring Laurence Olivier, Robert Duvall, and Tommy Lee Jones, was released in 1978.

Robbins also had an influence on 1970's television. The 1969-1970 season saw the premiere of *Harold Robbins's The Survivors*, which lasted for fifteen episodes. The series starred Rosanno Brazzi, Lana Turner, George Hamilton, and Jan Michael Vincent in a saga of power, greed, and sex involving the members of a powerful Wall Street banking family. In 1977, a two-part miniseries was made from Robbins's 1955 novel, *79 Park Avenue.* Leslie Ann Warren won an Emmy Award nomination for her starring role as a woman who, born poor and forced into prostitution as a young girl, rises to become the richest and most infamous madam in New York City.

Impact Although not critically acclaimed, Harold Robbins published more than twenty books and sold more than fifty million copies worldwide. He died of heart failure in 1997, but ghost-written novels continued to be published using his name and containing the usual Robbins trademark elements.

Further Reading
Lane, James B. "Violence and Sex in the Post-War Popular Urban Novel: With a Consideration of Harold Robbins's *A Stone for Danny Fisher* and Hubert Selby, Jr.'s *Last Exit to Brooklyn.*" *Journal of Popular Culture* 8 (1974): 295-308.

Parker, Ian. "Making Advances." *The New Yorker*, April 1, 1996, 72-80.

Robbins, Grace, and Frank Sanello. *Stranger than Fiction: My Wild Life with Harold Robbins.* Los Angeles: General Publishing Group, 1999.

J. Justin Gustainis

See also Film in the United States; Literature in the United States; Miniseries; Television in the United States.

■ Robertson, Pat

Identification American evangelist and television personality
Born March 22, 1930; Lexington, Virginia

By establishing the first Christian network and hosting a popular television program, Robertson brought Christian conservativism to a wide audience and planted the seeds of conservative Christian political activism.

During the 1970's, the Christian Broadcasting Network (CBN) entered its second decade of operation. Founded by Pat Robertson, a charismatic Christian, in 1960, the network was intended to provide Christian programming on radio and television networks. CBN's financial fortunes rested on the success of its annual fund-raising telethons and its *700 Club*, which began in 1963 as an appeal for seven hundred viewers to pledge ten dollars a month in support of the network. By the 1970's, because of successful fund-raising efforts, CBN's programming had become available on affiliates throughout the country, including stations broadcasting in major cities such as Los Angeles, San Francisco, and New York City. Moreover, Robertson reached an ever-widening audience through *700 Club*, which combined guest interviews and commentary about current events by Robertson with telephone calls from viewers for prayer and counseling.

By the middle of the decade, CBN had also taken

steps to enter the cable television market, offering programs on more than one thousand cable systems by 1975 and dedicating the CBN satellite earth station in 1977, allowing transmission of CBN programming to cable stations around the country. It had also begun to establish program affiliates in foreign countries. As the 1970's concluded, CBN relocated to a new international headquarters building in Virginia Beach, and Robertson expanded his influence into the arena of education by founding CBN University.

Impact   By the end of the 1970's, Pat Robertson had become one of the most prominent religious voices on television. He followed a long tradition of Christian evangelical attention to mass communication that dated back to the urban revivals of the nineteenth century. He also helped to steer charismatic Christian beliefs into the mainstream of American life and out of the backwaters of pentecostalism. Finally, his religiously tinged political conservatism found its voice during the 1970's and helped inspire Christian fundamentalists and evangelicals to engage more actively in American public life than they had throughout most of the twentieth century.

Subsequent Events   Toward the end of 1980's, Robertson wielded his prominence to found a conservative Christian political organization called the Christian Coalition and attempted to capture the Republican nomination for president of the United States.

Further Reading

Boston, Rob. *The Most Dangerous Man in America? Pat Robertson and the Rise of the Christian Coalition.* Amherst, N.Y.: Prometheus Books, 1996.

Donovan, John B. *Pat Robertson: The Authorized Biography.* New York: Macmillan, 1988.

Harrell, David Edwin. *Pat Robertson: A Personal, Religious, and Political Portrait.* San Francisco: Harper & Row, 1987.

Robertson, Pat, with Jamie Buckingham. *The Autobiography of Pat Robertson: Shout It from the Housetops!* Rev. ed. South Plainfield, N.J.: Bridge, 1995.

Timothy L. Hall

See also   Christian Fundamentalism; Conservatism in U.S. politics; Falwell, Jerry; Religion and spirituality in the United States; Television in the United States.

■ Rockefeller, Nelson

Identification   New York governor, 1959-1973; U.S. vice president, 1974-1977

Born   July 8, 1908; Bar Harbor, Maine

Died   January 26, 1979; New York, New York

Rockefeller gained prominence as the governor of New York, especially after the attention of the American public was focused on the 1971 Attica prison riot and Rockefeller's response to the violence.

Nelson Rockefeller was the grandson of John D. Rockefeller, the United States' first billionaire. He attended Dartmouth, and after he graduated in 1930, he went to work at Chase Bank, a family enterprise. Rockefeller was also attracted to government service; he was named coordinator of inter-American affairs in 1944 by President Franklin D. Roosevelt. Although other government posts followed, Rockefeller was frustrated by the lack of power in his appointments. Therefore, in 1958, he ran and won his first campaign for governor of New York, as he did in 1962, 1968, and 1972.

Vice President Nelson Rockefeller in 1975. (Burton Berinsky/ Landov)

As governor, Rockefeller was an activist: He constructed the state university system, hundreds of sewage treatment plants, and added more than fifty state parks. Rockefeller achieved a great deal as governor, yet his positive accomplishments must be balanced against his failures, especially the Attica prison riot and the New York Drug Law.

In September, 1971, inmates of Attica, New York's maximum security prison seized control of the jail and took twenty-nine guards as hostages. When negotiations failed, Rockefeller assented to the use of force, and the state police stormed the prison. Unfortunately, ten guards and twenty-nine inmates were killed. Initial reports, which blamed the prisoners for the guards' death, proved faulty after autopsies revealed that the guards were killed by the state police. Rockefeller never relented, obstinately insisting that the riot was part of an international terrorist conspiracy.

Rockefeller was equally stubborn where drug use was involved. In January, 1973, he offered a bill to the legislature providing that anyone who sold any amount of drugs receive a life sentence. The proposal was attacked by liberals, and even members of his own administration expressed reservations. However, the governor was adamant, and the measure, with amendments, passed the legislature and was signed by Rockefeller in May.

Vice Presidency   In December, 1973, Rockefeller, satisfied with what he had accomplished in his fifteen years in office, resigned. However, he was soon drawn back into government service when, in August, 1974, President Gerald R. Ford, elevated to the presidency when Richard M. Nixon resigned, offered the vice presidency to Rockefeller, who accepted. Hearings before the Senate and House Judiciary Committees follwed. Rockefeller was questioned on several issues, in particular his substantial money gifts to a score of public officials. In the end, his appointment was approved by Congress.

Ford assured Rockefeller that his would be a "working" vice presidency. Rockefeller, however, given his years of political experience, should not have been deceived. Indeed, he once told Kurt Waldheim, the United Nations secretary general, that "the vice presidency is not much of a job." True to form, he represented the president at the funerals of foreign leaders. Aside from such duties as chairing a study of the Central Intelligence Agency (CIA)

and commissions dealing with water quality, the right to privacy, and productivity, he attained little. Since Ford did not intend to keep him on the ticket in 1976, his political career was over.

Impact   Rockefeller's greatest impact, both negatively and positively, came in his role as governor. The Attica prison riot and the 1973 Drug Law must be weighed against the striking building projects he fostered, most impressive of which was the state university system, the world's largest such educational establishment.

Further Reading

Kramer, Michael, and Sam Roberts. *I Never Wanted to Be Vice President of Anything!* New York: Basic Books, 1976.

Moscow, Alvin. *The Rockefeller Inheritance.* Garden City, N.Y.: Doubleday, 1977.

Persico, Joseph E. *The Imperial Rockefeller: A Biography of Nelson A. Rockefeller.* Thorndike, Maine: Thorndike Press, 1982.

Richard Harmond

See also   Attica prison riot; Ford, Gerald R.

■ *Rocky*

Identification   Motion picture
Director   John D. Avildsen (1935-   )
Date   Released in 1976

Written by an unknown actor and produced on a limited budget, this film nevertheless became one of the most popular and critically acclaimed motion pictures of the 1970's.

The creator of the motion picture *Rocky* was Sylvester Stallone, a struggling actor and screenwriter whose only previous significant acting credit was a featured role in the 1974 film *The Lords of Flatbush*. Stallone, inspired by the 1975 performance of heavyweight boxer Chuck Wepner in a title match against heavily favored Muhammad Ali, reportedly completed the screenplay for *Rocky* in three days. His idea drew the interest of producers Robert Chartoff and Irving Winkler, who, after extensive negotiations, reluctantly agreed to cast Stallone in the title role.

Set in the slums of Philadelphia, *Rocky* is the story of an aging Philadelphia club boxer who is chosen virtually at random to challenge heavyweight champion Apollo Creed, a flamboyant character based on Ali who conceived the match with Rocky, to be held on the U.S. bicentennial, as a public relations stunt.

Aided by his grizzled manager, Mickey (played by Burgess Meredith), Rocky embarks upon a grueling, unorthodox training regimen that includes drinking raw eggs and punching sides of beef in a packing house.

In the weeks leading up to the match, Rocky undergoes a physical transformation symbolized by a triumphant training run up the steps of the Philadelphia Museum of Art and an emotional maturation represented by his relationship with girlfriend Adrian, played by Talia Shire. In the climactic fight with Creed, Rocky astonishes everyone by lasting the full fifteen rounds, losing in a split decision but gaining personal and professional redemption in the process.

Rocky was a modern interpretation of a dramatic theme popular throughout the history of American literature and film in which an obscure and disadvantaged individual achieves success through hard work, perseverance, and fortune. As in classic boxing films such as *Body and Soul* (1947) and *On the Waterfront* (1954), in *Rocky* the sport serves both as a metaphor for life and as a backdrop for the introduction of contemporary social themes. The film drew praise for both its realistic portrayal of the boxing world and its gritty treatment of urban life, which echoed other urban-themed films of the era such as *Midnight Cowboy* (1969), *Serpico* (1973), and *Taxi Driver* (1976).

Impact   Made in one month for less than one million dollars, *Rocky* achieved enormous financial and critical success, winning Academy Awards in 1977 for Best Picture, Best Director, and Best Editing. The film propelled the previously obscure Stallone to international stardom and a successful career as an actor, screenwriter, and boxing choreographer. Stallone subsequently wrote and starred in a series of sequels to *Rocky*, ending with *Rocky V* in 1990; although successful at the box office, these films failed to achieve the critical and dramatic impact of the original. The success of *Rocky* also inspired a subgenre of films featuring working-class hero charac-

Sylvester Stallone in a scene from the motion picture Rocky. (DPA/Landov)

ters, such as *Saturday Night Fever* (1977), *Urban Cowboy* (1980), and *Flashdance* (1983).

Further Reading

Daly, Marsha. *Sylvester Stallone: An Illustrated Life.* New York: St. Martin's Press, 1984.

Gross, Edward. *"Rocky" and the Films of Sylvester Stallone.* Las Vegas: Pioneer Books, 1990.

Stallone, Sylvester. *The Official "Rocky" Handbook.* New York: Grosset and Dunlap, 1977.

Michael H. Burchett

See also   Blockbusters; Boxing; Film in the United States; Sports.

■ *Rocky Horror Picture Show, The*

Identification   Cult film
Director   Jim Sharman (1945-   )
Date   Released in 1975

The Rocky Horror Picture Show combined allusions and plot elements from horror, science-fiction, and musical films of the 1950's with camp, rock music, and a theme of personal and sexual liberation. Audiences participated by dressing like the film's characters, dancing and performing in front of the screen, and using props and dialogue to interact with the film.

The Rocky Horror Picture Show starred British stage actor Tim Curry, up-and-coming American actors

Barry Bostwick and Susan Sarandon, and singer Meat Loaf. Produced in six weeks on a one-million-dollar budget, it was received poorly when released on a normal feature film schedule. On April 1, 1976, it entered the midnight circuit at the Waverly Theater in New York City. By summer, 1978, the film had grossed about four million dollars, and by 1979, there were two hundred prints in circulation, all grossing their full potential.

The plot involved an earnest, newly engaged couple, Brad and Janet (played by Bostwick and Sarandon), who, after being stranded as a result of car trouble, seek help at an old castle. They encounter Dr. Frank-N-Furter (Curry), a scientist from the planet Transsexual in the galaxy Transylvania, who has inhabited the castle and created a muscle-man monster, Rocky (Peter Hinwood). Besides marrying Rocky, he seduces both Brad and Janet.

The film's upbeat tone owes much to the musical genre on which it draws. Its optimism also stems from its catch line ("Don't dream it—be it," taken from Frederick's of Hollywood lingerie ads in period film magazines). Frank-N-Furter's androgyny (resembling rock star Mick Jagger), Meat Loaf's saxophone-laced rock songs, the pelvic thrust and hip swiveling of the "time warp" dance, and the costumes of fishnet hose, garter belts, bustiers, and high heels ensure that audience members have a good time and are freed from conventionality.

Perhaps the most notable way in which the film frees its audiences is the way in which it releases them from their conventional role as spectators. Five months into its run at the Waverly Theater, the audience began to "talk back" to the film. Soon people were chanting fifty dialogue inserts, many of them risqué. Viewers threw rice, toast, and toilet paper. Some shot water pistols and used flashlights or cigarette lighters. Amateur theater troupes, such as Midnight Insanity in Long Beach, California, formed to produce their own Rocky Horror show that paralleled the film during each midnight screening.

Impact   *The Rocky Horror Picture Show* became the unrivaled champion of cult films. Its success on the midnight circuit helped increase the market for other cult and limited-audience films. Interest persisted long past the 1970's. By the end of the twentieth century, it continued to be screened regularly at fifty theaters. The film received much scholarly attention, from sociological studies of its cult audi-

ences and their ritualistic behavior to analyses from Dionysian, performance, and carnival perspectives.

Further Reading
Dika, Vera. "*The Rocky Horror Picture Show.*" In *Recycled Culture in Contemporary Art and Film*. Boston: Cambridge University Press, 2003.

Henkin, Bill. *The Rocky Horror Picture Show Book*. New York: Hawthorn/Dutton, 1979.

Glenn Ellen Starr Stilling

See also   Film in the United States; Horror films; Science-fiction films.

■ *Roe v. Wade*

Identification   U.S. Supreme Court decision
Date   Decided on January 22, 1973

The Supreme Court held that states could not prohibit abortions in the first trimester and that a state's interest in future life had to be weighed against a woman's right to privacy. It was the first time the Court ruled that a woman had a right to an abortion.

Abortion was generally a taboo topic before the twentieth century, even though people throughout the centuries attempted to find herbal methods to end pregnancies. In the late nineteenth century, abortion was moved out of the private sphere and into the medical sphere, as doctors both wanted to control medicine and wished to stop midwives and others from selling remedies of questionable and sometimes dangerous natures. Abortion regulations were all on the state level, so those women living close to states that allowed abortions often went there for the procedure. A patchwork of laws existed.

In the early 1970's, the case of *Roe v. Wade* came in front of the U.S. Supreme Court. Norma McCorvey had wanted an abortion, but Texas law would not allow it. With the help of Sarah Weddington and Linda Coffee, McCorvey sued Henry Wade, the district attorney of Dallas County. In the case, she was referred to as "Jane Roe."

On January 22, 1973, the Court ruled 7-2 that states cannot universally ban abortion. In his majority decision, Justice Harry A. Blackmun pointed out the recent nature of most state laws banning abortion. Blackmun found that the only potentially viable state justification was protecting "prenatal life," and he stated that this justification must be weighed against the woman's right to privacy. He then noted that the right to privacy is not absolute but is fundamental, so that a "compelling state interest" was needed before it could be restricted.

Blackmun then turned to the difficult question of when life began, noting the widely differing views of various religious groups. The Court decided to come down on the side of having life begin at quickening (perceived fetal movement) but also ruled that states could not interfere at all before the end of the first trimester. From that point up to the point of viability, states could only issue regulations to make sure that abortions were safe, such as having abortions performed by licensed physicians. After viability, states were free to restrict abortions however they chose.

Impact *Roe v. Wade* provoked great controversy and inspired the creation of the pro-life movement. Even though it was limited by future rulings, the decision continued to grant women the right to control their own reproduction.

Further Reading

Hull, N. E. H., and Peter Charles Hoffer. *"Roe v. Wade": The Abortion Rights Controversy in American History*. Lawrence: University Press of Kansas, 2001.

McCorvey, Norma, and Andy Meisler. *I Am Roe: My Life, "Roe v. Wade," and Freedom of Choice*. New York: HarperCollins, 1994.

Solinger, Rickie, ed. *Abortion Wars: A Half Century of Struggle, 1950-2000*. Berkeley: University of California Press, 1998.

Scott A. Merriman

See also Abortion rights; Conservatism in U.S. politics; Medicine; Sexual revolution; Supreme Court decisions; Women's rights.

■ Roller skating

Definition Recreational activity

Americans combined the use of roller skates—with their newly invented plastic wheels—with disco music to make roller skating a wildly popular fad during the late 1970's.

Though invented some two hundred years before, roller skates did not enjoy their heyday in the United States until the 1970's. Until then, they were plagued with a variety of problems, ranging from the absence of toe stops (not present until the 1940's) and the use of metal wheels. In the early twentieth century, many roller skates were designed to fit over shoes, with skate keys used to adjust the size.

The 1970's brought two important improvements to the pastime of roller skating: plastic wheels and plastic-covered floors in skating rinks. The plastic wheels rolled more easily, did not jam as frequently, and could be used on most smooth surfaces, meaning people could roller-skate outdoors along sidewalks with much more ease than in the past. Sneaker skates also helped things, allowing skaters to tie their skates on their feet more securely and comfortably. Plastic-coated floors in roller arenas did not scuff as badly under heavy use as did their predecessors, and skaters could go much faster at the arena than they could down the sidewalk. These floors were also easier to maintain, allowing arenas to resmooth the surfaces regularly.

The 1970's were also the age of disco, and the combination of disco music and roller arenas led to an industry boom in the middle of the decade. Arenas added disco lighting, flashy colored lights, and disco balls to the music, and suddenly it was not just children who wanted to go to the roller arena on a Saturday night. While the younger set enjoyed skating birthday parties, modernized lighting and music attracted older teens and adults to late-night skates on a regular basis.

The plastic wheels that made roller skates so popular also created a new boom in the skateboard industry. Urethane wheels made the boards roll more smoothly, and by 1973, they had become extremely popular with a whole new generation of teens. While skateboards continued to grow in popularity as the 1970's waned, roller skates lost favor as the disco fad that had spurred the industry came to a close.

Impact When the disco fad began to fade, so too faded the roller craze in North America. However, inline skating became popular in the late 1980's, and pop music replaced disco as the roller arena staple.

Further Reading

Olney, Ross Robert. *Roller Skating!* New York: Lothrop, Lee and Shepard, 1979.

Shevelson, Joseph F. *Roller Skating*. New York: Harvey House, 1978.

Jessie Bishop Powell

See also Disco; Fads; Hobbies and recreation; Skateboards.